READER'S DIGEST

SCOUNDRELS & SCALAWAGS

51 Stories of the Most Fascinating Characters of Hoax and Fraud

The Reader's Digest Association, Pleasantville, New York
The Reader's Digest Association Ltd., Montreal, Canada

CONTENTS

iii

v

PHOTOGRAPH SECTION

(following page 320)

1 . . . Head and skull of fraudulent
Piltdown Man

2 . . . Alceo Dossena, noted imitator of
Renaissance art

3 . . . Dr. Ruth Drown, the quack
renowned for her radio machine

4 . . . Cardiff Giant boxed for shipment,
chart of his weight and dimensions

5 . . . Flamboyant Mrs. Cassie Chadwick,
would-be daughter of Andrew Carnegie

6 . . . James Landis, the man who robbed the U.S. Mint

7 . . . Famed violinist Fritz Kreisler, who fooled
the musical world

8 . . . Rebel captain Henrique Galvão and
the luxury liner he hijacked

9 . . . The Stone of Scone and the ruins of the Scots abbey
where it was recovered

10 . . . Charles Ponzi, the simple man who
bilked thousands of people

Henrique Galvão for 12 tense
days kept a ticking political time bomb
aboard a luxurious ship

INCREDIBLE CRUISE OF
THE "SANTA MARIA"

by Joseph P. Blank

"**S**trange, enchanting sights and sounds await you in intriguing ports of call," said the little folder that each passenger found in his cabin. But none of those aboard the 21,750-ton Portuguese luxury liner *Santa Maria* remotely dreamed *how* strange the sights and sounds awaiting them would be.

The *Santa Maria* was named after Columbus' flagship because she was the pride of the Portuguese merchant marine. She had taken off from Lisbon on Cruise No. 61 on January 9, 1961. Until 1 a.m. on January 22 the voyage was serene, relaxed and well ordered—just the way the brochures painted her South Atlantic and Caribbean cruise. She had called at Vigo, Spain, at Funchal in the Madeira Islands, then at Tenerife in the Canaries. After this, she made the long run across the Atlantic to La Guaira, Venezuela, where she picked up some new passengers. There followed a brief stop at the Dutch island of Curaçao, on January 21, for other passengers. Then the *Santa Maria* pulled anchor for the leg to Port Everglades, Florida.

On board now were 588 passengers, including 42 Americans, and a crew of 350. Among the passengers, however, were 24 men whose destination was not on the ship's itinerary. Followers of

General Humberto Delgado, leader of the opposition-in-exile to Portugal's premier, António Salazar, they planned to seize control of the vessel, to debark the passengers at a neutral port as quickly as possible and then to use the notoriety arising from the exploit to launch a revolt against the Salazar regime from the Portuguese colonies of Africa. The shipboard leader of the small band was Henrique Galvão, a thin, gaunt-faced Portuguese of 66 who had had a varied career as poet, translator of Shakespeare, army captain and colonial inspector for his government. He had been jailed in Portugal for his opposition to the regime, but had escaped in 1958 from a military hospital where he had been sent after feigning illness.

The plan for the capture of the *Santa Maria* had begun to form in Galvão's mind when he noted that on each of her trips to the Western Hemisphere the ship stopped at La Guaira, the port for Caracas, Venezuela, where he was then living. His chief accomplices, equal to him in authority, were Jorge de Souto Maior, an experienced seaman and an anti-Franco veteran of the Spanish Civil War, and another Spaniard, José Velo.

When the *Santa Maria* put into La Guaira on June 18, 1960, Galvão donned a broad-brimmed hat and dark glasses and boarded the vessel with other visitors. For two hours he studied the upper three decks, toured the bridge and even glanced around the master's cabin, where, at the time, the captain was entertaining friends. On the ship's subsequent calls Galvão's associates boarded her to find out if she carried arms or political police and to determine her supplies of fuel, food and water. On their request, the shipping line gave them a detailed plan of the ship. They also studied a big-scale model of the ship in the window of a Caracas travel agency.

Several deadlines for the venture passed because the group, composed of Portuguese and Spaniards, with a few Venezuelans and one Cuban, ran into money problems. They had to buy tickets at $200 each for the trip to Lisbon. Passage to Florida would have been cheaper, but the U.S. embassy in Caracas refused them visas. Finally, the plans were set for the trip that left La Guaira on Friday, January 20. Twenty-three men boarded the vessel there. Their larger arms—two machine guns and four rifles—were dismantled and packed in three suitcases marked with small white crosses, a warning to a bribed customs man who passed the bags without opening them. Galvão, who had flown on to Curaçao to avoid the risk of detection, joined them on Saturday.

At 11:55 Saturday night Third Officer João José Costa, Apprentice Navigator João António de Sousa and two sailors began their tour of duty on the bridge of the *Santa Maria*. De Sousa checked the vessel's position on the charts. She was about 150 miles northwest of Curaçao, headed for Jamaica Passage, some 500 miles away.

"Just before one o'clock," de Sousa recalls, "I noted in the log, 'Brilliant starlight. A string of cumulus clouds low over the northern horizon.' Just as I finished writing I heard one of the sailors shout, 'Costa, Costa! Come here! Look!' Then I heard two shots. I ran through the door to the bridge and saw Costa staggering in pain. He gasped: 'Go to the captain.'

"I ran to tell the radio operator, Carlos Garcia, in the wireless cabin about 45 feet aft of the bridge, to look after Costa while I roused the captain. When I opened the radio-room door, a man standing by the radio operator fired point-blank at me, hitting me in the left arm."

De Sousa bolted for the landing leading to the captain's side door below. Two more bullets slammed into his back, one puncturing two holes in his right lung, the other splintering two ribs before it lodged near his spinal column. Somehow he made the landing, stumbled and slid down the 20 steps, then crumpled at the side door of the captain's cabin. He didn't have the strength to bang on the door or shout. Blood spread around his body.

Captain Mario Maia slept on for another 15 minutes until a sailor knocked on his front door and excitedly reported that some passengers were shooting up the bridge and had wounded the two duty officers. Captain Maia hastily buttoned on a uniform.

"I assumed that a passenger had gone mad, or that there were disorders among passengers who had been drinking too much," he said later.

He ran out his front door and up the steps to the bridge. As his eyes reached the level of the bridge deck, he saw a man with a gun and Costa doubled over. He ducked, ran back to his cabin, locked the door and telephoned the engine room. After ordering the engines stopped, he made for the side door of his cabin. Through the glass panel he saw de Sousa lying motionless on the deck. He partially opened the door, saw a man aim a rifle at him, yanked the door closed, locked it and retreated into his room.

He telephoned the bridge and was answered by an unfamiliar voice, saying, "This is Captain Galvão, who, in the name of General Humberto Delgado, has taken over your ship by assault. You must not attempt any kind of resistance—it will be violently suppressed. Surrender will bring you benefits."

Nobody resisted. None of the crew or officers had arms, and all of them were numbed by the unbelievability of what was happening. Within 45 minutes the rebels had taken control of the bridge, the radio room, the engine room and the crew's and officers' quarters. The ship was theirs.

Costa and de Sousa were carried to the ship's hospital, where the doctor gave de Sousa immediate blood transfusions, probably saving his life. Chaplain Father Xavier Yrigoyen was awakened, and he administered last rites to both men. A short time later Costa, who only a few days earlier had received a cable telling him of the birth of a daughter, died.

Below, all but a few of the passengers slept on, oblivious to the shooting and shouting. Even on Sunday morning most of them awoke, dressed and strolled toward the dining room unaware that the *Santa Maria* had been transformed from a cruise ship into a political bomb that was supposed to explode into a revolution. But around nine o'clock the first- and second-class passengers were summoned by loudspeaker to the main lounge.

There Captain Maia made a speech in Portuguese, explaining

that command of the ship had been taken from him by force and that the crew was operating the vessel at gunpoint. Then Galvão and Maior delivered addresses about their fight for liberty, and another rebel told the group in English that none of the passengers would be harmed and that the ship would be at sea for five or six days before reaching an unspecified destination. The public-address system blared the same message to all parts of the vessel as it sped due east at 20 knots.

The announcements provoked a variety of responses among the passengers. "It didn't make sense to me," Mrs. Dorothy Thomas said. "Such a thing wasn't possible!" Eben Neal Baty, traveling with his wife, was not at all dismayed. "I felt rather thrilled," he reported. "I was glad we hadn't taken the other ship we'd been thinking about." Manuel Lourenço, returning to Portugal from Venezuela, was outraged. "This is a hell of a thing to happen to a man going home to retire after 30 years in a foreign country!"

Jane Smith, traveling with her husband, Delbert, and seven-year-old daughter, Deborah, decided with some other young women that they might as well take their usual morning swim in the pool. "But when we saw two men with machine guns standing on the deck above the pool, that took a little of the fun out of it," Mrs. Smith said.

As the *Santa Maria* proceeded eastward, no one not aboard the ship, except General Delgado and a few associates in Brazil, knew what had happened. At 7:30 a.m. on Monday, January 23, however, the two lighthouse keepers at Vigie Point on the placid West Indian island of St. Lucia spotted a big cruise ship looming out of the rain and haze. No such vessel was scheduled to arrive for another two weeks.

The lighthouse men trained their binoculars on the ship, but she was four miles away and they couldn't make out her name. They watched her pass across the harbor, sail northward, return to within a mile of the docks, drop a lifeboat, then move northward again. Galvão, apparently fearing that de Sousa might die aboard ship, had decided to unload him at St. Lucia.

14

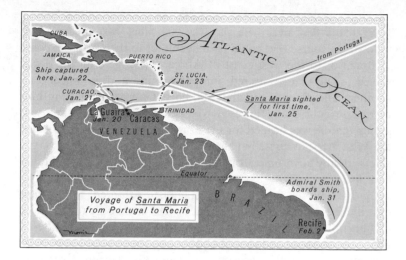

Map labels:
CUBA
JAMAICA
PUERTO RICO
Atlantic
from Portugal
Ship captured here, Jan. 22
ST. LUCIA, Jan. 23
CURACAO, Jan. 21
Ocean
La Guaira, Jan. 20 Caracas
TRINIDAD
Santa Maria sighted for first time, Jan. 25
VENEZUELA
Equator
BRAZIL
Admiral Smith boards ship, Jan. 31
Voyage of *Santa Maria* from Portugal to Recife
Recife, Feb. 2

Shortly after de Sousa—who subsequently recovered—was hospitalized, news of the hijacking flashed from St. Lucia to a startled world. Newspapers splashed headlines across front pages. Radio and television ran frequent bulletins. Reporters and photographers flew to Puerto Rico, St. Lucia, Venezuela and Brazil, not knowing where they should go—because the luxury liner *Santa Maria* had vanished.

The disappearance of the ship was attributed first to pure piracy. Great Britain dispatched the frigate H.M.S. *Rothesay* from St. Lucia to find the ship. Portugal alerted its navy. The United States sent out Navy search planes equipped with the most advanced radar equipment and ordered the destroyers *Wilson* and *Damato* at Puerto Rico to intercept the vessel under the well-defined terms of international law governing piracy and insurrection aboard ship. Merchant ships plying the Caribbean and South Atlantic were asked to keep a lookout for the vessel.

Finally, on Wednesday morning, the third day after the seizure, a Danish freighter reported sighting her. A few hours later a Navy plane flew over her; she was 900 miles east of Trinidad, following a course that could take her either to the northeast coast of Brazil or to the west coast of Africa. Passengers on the decks waved to the plane, cheered, jumped around and embraced one another. The plane commander radioed Galvão, requesting him to reverse course and proceed to Puerto Rico. Galvão refused, saying that he was headed for the Portuguese colony of Angola on the West African coast but that he was willing to confer aboard ship with any government officials other than those from Portugal and Spain.

By this time the tumult about piracy had subsided. In a stream of radio messages, Galvão said that he had acted only for the sake of "liberating" Portugal. The nations involved generally altered their original stand and viewed Galvão as a true revolutionary who was not out to obtain private gain from his venture. Everyone, however, was concerned about the safe debarkation of passengers.

The *Santa Maria* followed an irregular course, increasing the confusion among those aboard. "We never knew where we were or where we were going," said Arthur D. Patton, semiretired accountant from Boulder City, Nevada. "We never knew the correct time, either, because no one reported the passage through different time zones."

Despite the uncertainties and the fears, life with its personal problems and pleasures went on. During the first week seven-year-old Deborah Smith came down with the measles. A baby was born. A young Dutchman and a Spanish girl met, fell in love and promised to marry. A little Portuguese boy learned to walk. After watching the armed rebels for three days, Mrs. Smith and her friends decided to try the swimming pool again. Others went back to sunbathing, Ping-Pong, walking the deck, reading and playing cards. The ship's orchestra played for lunch, dinner and dancing.

Galvão, a man of considerable charm and courtliness, addressed the passengers in the first-class lounge, apologizing for causing them any inconvenience. When Mrs. John Dietz, of Gainesville,

Florida, complained that she could no longer play shuffleboard because the forward deck was off limits, Galvão answered, "Madam, you shall play shuffleboard." Next morning Mrs. Dietz was delighted to find a freshly painted shuffleboard court on the deck in front of her cabin.

Other passengers and the crew were not taking matters lightly, however. A Canadian, Laurence Williams, who expected the rebels' guns to begin firing again at any moment, made notes about his experiences and hid them between sheets of music. On several occasions he dropped bottles containing messages overboard. Professor Floyd Preston, of the University of Kansas, was irritated because the projected revolution would make him late for the beginning of the second semester at college.

On the lower decks, where more than 300 third-class passengers lived and ate, the failure of the air-conditioning system (it had gone out of operation at La Guaira) made the quarters stifling hot. Several pregnant women found the heat especially unbearable. Many of these passengers were Portuguese, and they were worried about getting involved in the politics of the hijacking.

The all-Portuguese crew grew progressively more depressed and demoralized. They had cause. What were Galvão's plans after he unloaded the passengers? Where would he take the ship? Would the Portuguese Navy shell it? Anxiety about their safety made the crew indifferent about cleaning decks and changing the linen in the staterooms. The operator of the beauty shop became so distraught that she canceled all appointments.

Rumors wildfired among the passengers. Once when the rebels uncovered the lifeboats, word spread that Galvão was going to put the passengers off at sea. "One of the big items of conversation was about the proper thing to wear in a lifeboat," Mrs. Joan Harberson, of Lincoln, Nebraska, said. "Some women wondered if it would be all right to wear their mink coats. The men worried about their cars in the hold, and all of us were concerned about our luggage and about souvenirs that we had picked up in Europe."

The captives waited constantly for some action or piece of news that would end their suspense. Even Galvão didn't know when or where the passengers could disembark, for his plans had been thrown awry by what he termed his humanitarian act of putting de Sousa ashore at St. Lucia. His original plan would have carried him well toward the coast of Africa before the ship was seen to be missing from her scheduled January 24 docking in Florida. When passengers asked him when the ship would land, he courteously answered, "As soon as possible. Perhaps tomorrow." "Tomorrow" became his standard refrain to all inquiries— whereupon passengers dubbed the ship the *Santa Mañana*.

Whatever their private opinions about Galvão and his cause, in public the passengers generally maintained strict neutrality and avoided political discussions. "As American citizens, we were just interested in getting off the ship as soon as possible," Mrs. Harberson said. "While Galvão and his men were polite and gentlemanly with us, we never forgot that they had killed one man and seriously wounded another. They had used their guns once. Depending on circumstances, they *could* use them again."

The rebels gradually eased their civil but distant attitude, and it was sometimes difficult to distinguish them from the passengers. Some splashed around the pool while their comrades stood guard. In the evenings, when a squad of rebels went off duty, they changed from their cotton khaki uniforms, black berets and armbands of red and green (the national colors of Portugal), and donned business suits. They sat in the lounge, "paid" for their drinks at the bar by stamping chits with "DRIL" (the initials of their organization) and danced with some of the passengers.

By the sixth day the passengers knew that the rebels hoped to debark them in some Brazilian port. "Galvão told me that Jânio da Silva Quadros, the incoming president of Brazil, was an old friend of his," said Mrs. Harberson, who communicated with him in Spanish, "and that it would be safe for the rebels to put into Brazil, unload the passengers and leave. I can tell you that the inauguration of Quadros became far more important to us Americans than the inauguration of President Kennedy. Not only did we count the days until January 31—we tried to figure out the hour of the inauguration ceremony."

Meanwhile, Galvão was dickering by radio with the U.S. Navy, which was growing increasingly anxious to see the passengers off the ship. After several exchanges the Navy suggested that Galvão meet Rear Admiral Allen Smith, Jr., aboard the *Santa Maria* 50 miles outside Recife, Brazil. "All right," Galvão radioed.

On the night of January 30 Galvão threw a farewell dinner, with a specially printed menu titled "The *Santa Maria* en Route to Liberty." The meal was elaborate: lobster, ham, steaks, roast beef, a variety of sauces and desserts. Galvão ordered free champagne for the third-class passengers. Several passengers asked for his autograph on their menus. After dinner a dance was held in the gaily decorated main lounge.

On January 31 Admiral Smith boarded the *Santa Maria* from a destroyer, and he and Galvão conferred. "We will enter Brazil tomorrow," Galvão said. "We have assurances of being able to continue from the present president of Brazil."

As a private citizen, Quadros had expressed sympathy for Galvão's cause. As president, however, he was pledged to the best interests of his nation and to its international relations. The solution: get the passengers safely off the ship, return the ship to her rightful owners and grant asylum to Galvão and his group.

The conversation between Galvão and Admiral Smith did not resolve the problem of safe debarkation. After the meeting, Admiral Smith addressed the passengers, urging them to be patient and assuring them that the Navy would not leave the vicinity. Most of the Americans, hoping for rescue, were disappointed.

World interest in the *Santa Maria* and its captives mounted as news items remained scanty and often conflicting. After the admiral retired to his destroyer, a small plane dipped near the ship and dropped a parachutist into the water. He bobbed to the surface, inflated a rubber boat and paddled to the side of the ship. Hauled aboard, he turned out to be a photographer for a French news agency. Another photographer tried to repeat the stunt, dropped wide of his target and, much to his disgust, was fished out of the water by a U.S. destroyer. Meanwhile, more than 100 reporters, photographers and TV and newsreel cameramen had gathered at Recife.

When Galvão brought the ship inside the three-mile limit on the morning of the 11th day—February 1—deteriorating physical and emotional conditions aboard were fast weakening his position. A delegation of Brazilian authorities refused to give him guarantees. Bring the ship in and unload the passengers, they told him, and then sit down and talk things over.

Galvão saw his plans collapsing. He couldn't take the ship out to sea without fuel. A turbine had broken down. The food supply was low. Water was critically short—an emergency largely caused by crewmen and officers opening the taps. Among the women in third class the heat and the poor food, along with the suspense, were causing hysterical breakdowns. The men, once docile, now were growling in resentment.

The temper of the crew had changed from fear to anger. When a group of them accosted several rebels near the first-class lounge and announced that all the crew intended to leave the ship at the same time as the passengers, there was a commotion. Galvão came running up. He was met by shouts of "Everybody leaves the ship! Everybody!"

"No!" Galvão screamed. "No! None of you will leave! Get back to your quarters!" His men drew their pistols. The crewmen made a reluctant retreat.

Early on the morning of February 2, third-class passengers, shoving their way into the first-class lounge, demanded that the ship be brought into port. In the melee that followed, a passenger was pushed through a glass door. The rebels drew their guns, but fortunately no one fired.

At 11:21 a.m. the ship raised anchor and stirred, and a passenger on the bow pulled up his fishing line. With pennants rippling, festoons of ribbons from shipboard parties flying and martial music blaring from the loudspeakers, the *Santa Maria* steamed into the port of Recife. During his last stroll among the passengers Galvão kissed Mrs. Dietz's hand in farewell.

The ship dropped anchor 500 yards from the docks, and tugs moved out to shuttle the passengers to shore. Brazilian marines climbed aboard, saluting smartly as they stepped on deck to take over the ship. Passengers hurriedly gathered what they could carry of their luggage, baby carriages, bicycles, camera cases and souvenir baskets, and made their way down the gangplank onto the waiting tugboats. Some cried in relief, some smiled; others wore expressions of indignation or concern.

For the passengers leaving the ship, for the crew impatiently waiting to leave, and for Henrique Galvão, standing proudly on the bridge, Cruise No. 61 of the *Santa Maria* was over.

The ship was turned back to her rightful owners, the Portuguese Line, and resumed her regular schedule. Galvão was granted political asylum by the Brazilian government. The next year he was tried *in absentia* in Portugal and given a 22-year sentence for treason, manslaughter and piracy. He lives quietly in Brazil.

◦◦◦

THE SECOND James Gordon Bennett, publisher of the New York *Herald*, was one who believed he could make the public do what he liked. So one night, in order to prove his power, he told his friends he would see to it that all the people of New York remained in their homes the following day.

The next morning the *Herald* came out with the terrifying news that all the wild animals had broken loose from the zoo and were prowling about the city. "Terrible Scenes of Mutilation" and "A Shocking Sabbath Carnival of Death" shrieked the headlines.

Hardly anyone dared to venture abroad; the schools were ordered closed, and New York for some hours was almost a dead city. Those who had to leave their houses went in terror of their lives. A dog's bark became a lion's roar, and a cat slinking along the wall became a leopard.

Bennett gave the public a huge fright. But as soon as the truth leaked out, calm was restored and life went on its usual way.

—Ralph D. Blumenfeld in Nash's

*Ponzi was a simple man with
a simple system—rob Peter to pay Paul*

PIED PIPER OF BOSTON

by Alan Hynd

Charles Ponzi, a 36-year-old clerk in the employ of J. P. Poole, a Boston import-and-export brokerage house, opened an envelope from Spain and made a fascinating discovery. The envelope contained a postal-reply coupon—something Ponzi had never even heard of. The coupon, which the writer had enclosed to cover the postage for a letter of reply, had been purchased in Madrid for about one cent in United States currency. Yet it was redeemable at any post office or bank in the United States for five cents. Charlie Ponzi pursed his lips and looked off into space. Here, he decided, was something worthy of serious investigation.

During the next few days of this hot June of 1919, Ponzi boned up on postal-reply coupons. Such coupons had for years been part of the international postal systems of most large countries. Gathering data on the prevailing monetary rates in various European countries, Charlie got busy with pencil and paper. His eyes must have glowed as he decided how a smart operator could go into the business of buying the coupons in countries where the currency was depressed, then cashing them in countries, such as the United States, where they would bring up to five times their purchase price. Ponzi could foresee the day when he would have dozens of agents wafted hither and yon by the changing winds of international financial fluctuation. He would make anywhere from 100 to 500 percent on a given investment in a batch of coupons.

The morning after he had completed his preliminary research, Ponzi, the soul of servility and punctuality during the two years he had been at Poole's, was an hour late for work. A toy-fox-faced man, standing five feet two and weighing only 110 pounds, wearing a shiny double-breasted blue serge suit that pinched his wasplike waist, Ponzi strode to his desk exuding a suddenly acquired belligerence. His boss, arms folded and tapping his foot, yelled, "You're late, Ponzi, an hour and three minutes late."

"What about it?" answered Ponzi with a sneer.

"I've a good mind to discharge you for such impertinence!"

"I'm quitting," Ponzi retorted. "I don't like it here anyway."

It was, as it turned out, a black day for Bostonians when Charles Ponzi quit his job with J. P. Poole, for he was soon to strike out for himself in a racket unique in all the annals of crime.

After quitting his job, Ponzi went home to a two-room flat he shared with his wife of two years in an Italian district in Boston's teeming North End. Mrs. Ponzi, the former Rose Guecco, the plump, thirtyish daughter of a wholesale fruit merchant, knew little about her husband. He had, a few years before, suddenly materialized out of thin air and, with some vague wartime cloak-and-dagger story to account for his immediate past, wooed, won and wed her over the apoplectic protests of her old man.

After marrying Rose, Charlie had conned her father into letting him manage the wholesale fruit business. Within nine months he wrecked the enterprise, driving it into bankruptcy. Then, at the age of 34, he went to work for J. P. Poole as a $14-a-week stock boy. When he threw up his job as a clerk with Poole, he had been making $16 a week.

"But what will we do now?" asked Rose as Charlie broke the news of his quitting. "The rent will be due next week."

He snapped his fingers. "*Poof* to next week."

23

Now that he had actually got down to the business of entering the postal-coupon game, Charlie discovered he had neglected to check one salient point. The sum total of postal-reply coupons used all over the world in any one year seldom exceeded $75,000. And there were certain rules and formalities to the postal-coupon business that might prove troublesome. A man attempting to make a living out of dealing in the coupons might eventually run into the law of diminishing returns.

Charlie, disillusioned but not discouraged, sent $5 to the man in Madrid, requesting the Spaniard to invest it in postal-reply coupons and forward them to him. When the coupons arrived, Charlie, flashing them, began to circulate among his friends in the North End. In a wise sort of way, Charlie asked his friends if they had ever heard of postal-reply coupons. None of them had. The general ignorance on the subject of postal-reply coupons was, Ponzi decided, refreshing.

One night in September—a hot night in Indian summer when the Italians in the North End were leaning out of the tenement windows for a breath of fresh air—a couple of hod-carrier friends stopped to chat with Charlie at his tenement stoop. "Gee," remarked one, having put in a tough day lugging wet concrete, "I sure wish I was rich."

"Me, too," said the other.

"How would both of you like to invest a little money with me— say $50?" asked Charlie. "In three months you would get all of $75 back."

"How?"

Ponzi smiled sagely. "Oh, it's a little secret I learned at that place I worked. I'm the only one who knows about it outside of Rockefeller and men like that."

"Any chance of gettin' stuck?"

Charlie laughed. "No more than if you lent your $50 to Morgan or Rockefeller."

Ponzi showed the postal-reply coupons to the hod carriers and got off a likely whopper about how he had contacts with agents who bought postal-reply coupons in various European countries dirt cheap and later converted the coupons for cash in New York for a killing. He might as well have been talking Greek to his two friends, but what he was saying sounded as authentic as a stock tip from J. P. Morgan.

Next night, the two men met Ponzi on the stoop and each handed him $50, practically their life's savings. Ponzi wrote out receipts for the money, promising, in each receipt, to repay the sum of $75 in 90 days.

Ponzi then conned a couple of other neighbors into investing in the nonexisting coupons—a couple of Peters who would be robbed to pay the two Pauls. Next he dug up somebody to pay *them*. Suddenly, Charlie had a monumental swindle going.

We might attempt to look into Ponzi's thought processes at this point. How did Charlie expect to get away with it? He was intelligent enough to know the simple rules of mathematics. He must have realized that his scheme had to keep growing bigger to cover him up, but that the bigger it grew the greater would be the risk of eventual detection.

The only explanation seems to be that Ponzi somehow had his feet firmly planted on a cloud. Then, too, he seems to have been strongly afflicted by egomania. He had a genuine thirst for power, as indicated by his statement to the press, when he was at the summit of his fraudulent scheme, that he thought he might run for mayor, that he imagined he might make a good movie star, and by his willingness to be compared with Columbus as the greatest Italian in history.

The word began to get around that Charlie, while working in the financial house, had discovered a remarkable secret that could make people rich. Charlie stuck a sign in the front window of his flat, reading:

Charles Ponzi
Foreign-Exchange
Investments

During the first week of December, when the skies were leaden and there was the feel of snow in the air, Ponzi's two original investors—the hod carriers—walked up to his flat after supper one evening and presented their receipts for $50. In a little while they bounced out of the tenement glowing.

"That man Ponzi!" one of them said to a neighbor. "He is a miracle man!" The hod carriers disclosed that Ponzi had been sitting there waiting for them, not only with their $50 but with 50 percent interest.

"Let me see the money," said the neighbor.

"*See* it! Why, we give it back to Ponzi. He's goin' to do the same thing all over again."

"You give him the profits, too?"

"Sure. We're goin' to make a *profit* on the profits."

A couple of days later, when the second pair of Pauls got theirs from the money the third group of Peters had turned over to Charlie, and reinvested the money with him, practically everybody in the block heard about it.

Ponzi's neighbors began to open tin cans in kitchen cupboards and turn up bed mattresses and hustle down the street to hand over their cash to Charlie. Ponzi was now settled behind a little oak desk acquired in a secondhand furniture store, writing out promissory notes guaranteeing the return of principal and 50 percent interest in 90 days. As each eager investor pressed his money on Charlie, he, with an impressive show of scorn for cash, tossed it in nearby paper bags.

During the second week of December, quite a few notes fell due, and little Charlie sat there at the oak desk, paying off. Some of his customers were grabbing the principal and the profits but others were forcing the money back on him. Every once in a while, though, especially when there were three or four new investors in the room, Charlie would refuse to accept money for reinvestment. "Take it," he would urge a client. "Christmas is coming on and you'll need this to buy presents."

The sight of Ponzi not only handing over the principal and the profit, but occasionally refusing to take the money back for re-investment, had a pronounced psychological effect on the new investors. They considered themselves fortunate to get in on the good thing, and went around crowing about their luck.

By mid-December, four months after he had severed his connections with Poole's, Charlie's snowball had gathered sufficient momentum for him to rent an office in downtown Boston. So, on December 20, we find him in a second-floor front room, about 20 feet square and with two windows in it, in a shabby, gray, five-story stone office building on School Street.

Charlie had a sign painter make him a couple of signs reading:

FOREIGN-EXCHANGE COMPANY
CHARLES PONZI, PRES.

He stuck one sign in a window facing School Street and the other in the vestibule on the ground floor, with an arrow pointing to a stairway leading to the second floor.

The very first day Ponzi opened up, several clients came to town from the North End, both to collect and to invest. Ponzi, sitting there at the desk, would reach for one of those 90-day notes, study it, glance up at the investor, flash a quick smile, then ask, "Do you wish to take the cash, or shall I reinvest it for you?"

The replies were about 50-50. When Ponzi was asked to pay off, he made a production of reaching into a drawer of the desk where bills had been tossed with an impressive abandon. "Don't forget to tell your friends about your good fortune," he would tell the lucky investor as he forked over the money. "There's plenty of this stuff"—he would pat the drawer where the money was—"to go around."

The first four days he was on School Street Charlie took in about $1200 and handed out about $750. On the afternoon before Christmas, he went around to Filene's department store and bought his wife a handsome wine-colored silk dressing gown. When he took it home and handed it to her, she was practically delirious with joy. "Oh, Charlie," she said, "it's wonderful."

Ponzi strutted around the room. "What has happened so far," he said to the admiring Rose, "is nothing. One of these days I'm going to buy you a mansion in one of those swell suburbs."

Charles Ponzi first opened his dark little eyes in the town of Parma in Northern Italy. His parents were farmers, who raised their own help. Charlie, quick-witted and impatient, could see no future plowing in a sunbaked field, the horizon shut off by the rear end of a beast of burden. In 1899, at 17, he sailed for New York. When he landed, he walked from the docks up Broadway, clutching his knapsack, craning his neck at the tall buildings. Two years after he first hit New York, Charlie, now speaking English with hardly a trace of an accent, turned up as a busboy in a New York restaurant.

A few years passed and Ponzi rose in the world. He became a waiter at Delmonico's. From all Charlie had been able to observe in his short time in this country, honesty may have been the best policy but it sure as hell wasn't paying off. The honest men were digging ditches, sweeping floors or breaking their backs in the mills, and the crooks were wallowing in wealth.

Charlie soon saw that the future in New York was bleak. Having heard that the people in Canada were a softer touch, he lit out for Montreal, where he was to make the misstep that would contribute very largely to his downfall in later years.

There were snow flurries in Boston when Ponzi opened for business in that second-floor office on School Street the day after New Year's 1920. Late in the afternoon, as he was writing out a $10 receipt for a North End Italian laborer, he got a hot flash. He looked up at the laborer, squinted his eyes and asked, "How would you like to stop digging ditches and go to work for me?"

"What I got to do?" the laborer wanted to know.

"Go around and get your friends to invest," said Ponzi, handing the son of toil a book of blank receipts. "I'll pay you 10 cents for every dollar you collect."

Charlie's deal with the laborer was one of those little acorns out of which great oaks grow. Within a week the laborer was not only rounding up investors for Charlie but was getting a friend to corral investors for *him*.

Ponzi was quick to realize that he had struck gold. So, every time he raked in money from a new investor he would toss out the same proposition as he had put to the laborer. Practically everybody went for it.

By the middle of February, some two months after Charlie had opened up in School Street, he was really off the ground. His agents had infiltrated the stevedore gangs on the Charlestown docks and were circulating among waiters, elevator boys, barbers and bartenders in speakeasies in downtown Boston and among the French-Canadians in Worcester and in Providence, Rhode Island, and even south to the Poles in Bridgeport, Connecticut.

By the middle of March, the flow of investors and the volume of mail from agents coming into that office on School Street became too much for Charlie to handle alone. So Rose left her mop and scrubbrush in the North End tenement and came into town to act as a sort of secretary.

Charlie installed a plywood partition, separating the front of his office from the rear. Then he plucked a couple of Italian friends from his home neighborhood—men who were as honest as they were stupid—and planted them as receiving tellers at the windows. The bulk of the suckers showed up on their lunch hours. Thus from noon until about two o'clock the line out in front of the gray building on School Street stretched around the corner into Washington Street. Charlie was sometimes taking in as much as $3000 a day—mostly in $1 and $5 bills.

Charlie kept his records in a small safe. A great man for avoiding complications, he simply marked down on a little white card the name and address of an investor, the amount invested and the date the principal and interest were due. Then, a couple of days before payoff time, Charlie's wife would send a postcard to the lucky client, advising that payment date was approaching.

By mid-April practically half of Boston was talking about Charlie. By now, there were six clerks busy behind the partition, raking in the money, tossing the stuff in wire baskets and writing out receipts.

Came the day when the office on School Street was no longer big enough to accommodate the customers. So Ponzi took over an abandoned saloon in Pi Alley, a narrow thoroughfare that ran off Washington Street near the Boston *Post* and the Boston *Globe*. When his clientele showed up at the School Street office and asked for their money, Charlie would send them around to the Pi Alley branch to get a check.

By this time Charlie had opened accounts in half a dozen Boston banks. But his biggest account was in that jug across the street from the *Post*. Sometimes, during the lunch hour, there were so many investors crowding into Pi Alley and into the Hanover Trust Company that traffic in Washington Street ground to an absolute standstill.

Loan sharks were doing a land-office business with suckers who were willing to pay them exorbitant interest rates to get money with which to make even more exorbitant profits with Ponzi.

Curiously enough, the press—every paper in Boston, and there were six of them—ignored Charlie as it would have ignored an elevator accident in a department store. Reporters on the *Post* and the *Globe*, going to and from work and out on assignments, had to fight their way through crowds of Ponzi investors, completely muffing the biggest story New England had known since Paul Revere.

One morning in June Ponzi told Rose to mind the store while he went out and did something. He returned late in the afternoon, looking like a tabby that had just swallowed a sparrow. Closing up shop, Ponzi hustled Rose into a waiting taxi. "To Lexington," he told the driver.

The place in Lexington was not so much as mansions went, but it was a dream for people like Charlie and Rose, who had always lived in tenements. It was a large, rambling brown house, in the Victorian tradition, set in the middle of sweeping lawns and fine shrubbery. "Oh, goodness, Charlie," said Rose, standing on the lawn and looking up at the house, "it's wonderful. But it'll keep me awful busy doing the housework."

"*Poof*," said Charlie. "We'll get servants."

After Charlie had shown Rose around the house, she asked him how much the place had cost. "Thirty thousand dollars," said Charlie. "I paid for it this morning—cash."

A minute later, Charlie was racing over the lawn to the waiting taxi. "Hey," he shouted to the driver. "Come help me carry my wife out and get her to a doctor."

"What's the matter with her?" asked the driver.

"She's fainted," said Charlie.

Rose of course recovered. A few nights later, when she was leaving the School Street office with Charlie, she stopped to admire a handsome big blue Locomobile limousine parked at the curb. "Twelve thousand dollars," said Charlie. "Custom-built. I paid cash for it this morning."

Rose looked at Charlie, saw he wasn't kidding and said she felt faint. Charlie snapped his fingers to a chauffeur who had been standing at attention clad in a uniform to match the car. "Open the door for the lady, Joe," Charlie said to the chauffeur, helping Rose into the car.

As the big blue Locomobile swung through the streets of Boston and then into the outskirts, Rose gradually recovered from her shock. "Hey, Charlie," she said, "he's not taking us home. He's goin' someplace else."

"We're on the way to Lexington," Charlie explained. "We're not going back to the North End anymore."

What Rose saw, when she stepped out of the blue limousine and entered a door opened by a liveried butler, was an interior decorator's nightmare. The house was a bad dream of costly Oriental rugs, antique furniture of various periods, billowing pea-green silk chair coverings and royal-blue and cardinal-red velvet draperies. Charlie took Rose by the arm and led her from room to room. When the tour was almost complete Rose asked, "What did all this cost, Charlie?"

"One hundred and six thousand dollars," Charlie replied. "Now don't you go fainting again, Rose."

One morning in the middle of June, six months after Ponzi had opened that office in School Street, there was a meeting of the board of directors of the Hanover Trust Company. Little Charlie, his hands folded over the top of his cane, was sitting outside of the directors' room as the directors filed in.

Two of the directors stopped for a moment to say hello to Ponzi; the others either gave him a refrigerated glare or ignored him altogether.

In about an hour the door of the directors' room opened, and a man sweating under a heavy black worsted suit beckoned to Charlie. "Mr. Ponzi," said the man, "the directors would be pleased to see you."

Charlie minced in, paused dramatically near the head of the directors' table and searched each face. Then he smiled and said, "Yes, gentlemen?"

One of the directors cleared his throat. "Mr. Ponzi," he said, "it would seem that you have purchased the controlling interest in this bank."

"It has long been my wish to control a bank, gentlemen," said Ponzi.

"What," asked the spokesman for the directors, "are your wishes, Mr. Ponzi?"

"I want," said Ponzi, smiling, "to be president."

The spokesman looked at the other directors. Then he said, "Gentlemen, I hereby propose Mr. Charles Ponzi for the presidency of this bank. All in favor will signify by raising their hands; all opposed need not raise their hands."

All the faces were frozen, in the best Boston tradition, but the right hand of every man went up. "The vote being unanimous," said the spokesman, "I hereby declare Mr. Ponzi our new president."

Upon assuming the presidency of the Hanover Trust Company, Charlie checked in first thing every morning, before the night watchman had gone off duty, and was the last man out at night. Between times he darted across the street to the office in Pi Alley and over to the main office on School Street.

One morning, not long after taking over the Hanover Trust, Charlie walked into the Poole brokerage house—the very place which he had left, practically by request, only 12 months before. Just inside the door, he searched the place with an unfriendly gaze. Finally, he spotted the man who had once been his boss. Charlie beckoned to him.

"Yes, what is it, Mr. Ponzi?" said Charlie's former boss, all oil and subservience.

"So," said Charlie, "you remember me."

"Indeed I do. You were one of our most valued employes."

"That wasn't what you thought that morning I came in late," Charlie said sharply. "Now, you can go to the cashier and get your pay."

"But I don't understand, Char—Mr. Ponzi."

Charlie tapped the floor with his cane. "I said go and get your pay. I purchased controlling interest in this company last night and you, my friend, are fired."

It was along about now that the key men in Boston's financial circles began to take serious notice of Ponzi. The big-time money changers began to grow apprehensive. One noontime seven Boston bankers met in a private dining room of the finest restaurant in Boston to discuss Ponzi.

"I can't see how this man Ponzi is doing what he is doing," said one banker. "It just runs counter to everything I've learned in 30 years in the banking business."

"What worries me," chimed in another money man, "is that so many of our depositors are drawing their savings out to give to Ponzi."

"Are any of these people putting the money back at the end of 90 days?"

"That's just it. Some of them are. They're getting 50 percent interest. I *wish* I knew how he was doing it." The speaker looked earnestly at the faces of the other men. "Gentlemen," he said, "I'll tell you one thing: if this man Ponzi continues he'll drain the resources of every bank in the city."

Ponzi was at his best when he presided over a directors' meeting at the bank. He was the toughest bank president in town when it came to passing on loans. Charlie had a fisheye for questionable collateral. The only time any of his associates in the boardroom ever heard him raise his voice was when he refused to okay a loan to some business because of the collateral offered. "Why," Charlie would say, "this collateral is *shaky*."

The most inquiring mind of all the Ponzi-watchers in Boston was that of Edward J. Dunn, the 41-year-old city editor of the Boston *Post*. Eddie Dunn, a hefty, soft-voiced man with gold-rimmed glasses, held forth in a swivel chair behind an old-fashioned rolltop desk in a second-floor cubbyhole that looked out across the street to the Hanover Trust Company.

Dunn had frequently seen Ponzi darting in and out of the bank, and now, in June, Eddie Dunn found himself waking up in the middle of the night, wondering about Ponzi. No man living knew more about what was going on in Boston's high and low places than Eddie Dunn. Dunn wondered why, if Ponzi's system were on the level, it had been overlooked by the proprietors of Boston's staid old countinghouses. So Eddie Dunn summoned one of his reporters. "Find out how it is *possible* that Ponzi is making all that money simply by dealing in postal-reply coupons," the city editor said.

Twenty-four hours later Eddie Dunn had his first facts. In an average year, there were less than $75,000 worth of the coupons printed. In the calendar year of 1919—the year when Ponzi had begun his extensive operations—there had been a total of $58,560 in coupons issued.

Dunn sat at his desk studying the figures. When he had digested them, he looked up at the reporter, squinted his eyes and said in a strained tone, "What *Mister* Ponzi claims to be doing just isn't possible."

Eddie Dunn had tipsters all over Boston who traded information for small payoffs. He called one of these in the Italian district of Boston's North End.

"Tell me something, Tony," he said. "Have you invested any money with Ponzi?"

"Not a cent, Mr. Dunn. Not a cent."

"Why, Tony?"

"I don't trust that man Ponzi."

"You don't say. And why don't you trust him, Tony? A lot of people down your way seem to."

"He's been in trouble somewhere."

"What kind of trouble?"

"Trouble with the law."

All Tony knew was rumor. He had heard, somewhere, sometime, that Charlie Ponzi had been in trouble with the law, someplace in Canada.

Dunn hung up, summoned several reporters. "I want you fellows to take a map of Canada," he said, "and divide it up among you. Cover every law-enforcement agency from Vancouver to Nova Scotia and find out if Charles Ponzi has ever been arrested. Use the phone. Use the telegraph. Use *any*thing. But get hold of everybody. Get 'em all."

A week went by. Dunn's boys drew nothing but blanks. He had them double-check and triple-check the police and prosecutors in such populous cities as Montreal, Toronto and Vancouver, where there were sizable Italian populations. But nobody knew anything about Charles Ponzi.

Yet something in Eddie Dunn's bones assured him that the tipster had been right when he said Charles Ponzi had once been in trouble in Canada.

Eddie Dunn now had permission of Richard Grozier, the *Post*'s acting publisher, to throw out a hint that the *Post* questioned the whole Ponzi operation.

The first headline in the *Post*, two columns on page one of the issue of Saturday, July 17, 1920, read:

DOUBLES THE MONEY
WITHIN THREE MONTHS

---

50 Percent Interest Paid in 90 Days
By Ponzi—Has Thousands of
Investors

Deals in International Coupons Taking
Advantage of Low Rates
Of Exchange

That first story didn't say very much, except that there was a financial wizard operating out of School Street and that the lines of investors were getting bigger every day. Then the *Post* ran a box showing how it was impossible that Ponzi's profits were accruing from dealings in postal-reply coupons.

If Eddie Dunn thought that series in the *Post* was going to put the paper in right with the populace he missed his guess. By midweek, after the fourth article hit the streets, crowds began to gather in Washington Street outside the *Post*. Men in yellow high-button shoes and women wearing babushkas stood there, in the midsummer heat, sweating and hurling imprecations up at the editorial rooms. Eddie Dunn, sitting there in his cubbyhole, would look down on the street scene and sigh.

One afternoon Dunn summoned a reporter, Jim Dempsey, and told him to interview Ponzi. Dempsey found the great man sitting at his desk in front of the money cages. "I should sue that paper of yours for what you've been printing about me," Ponzi said sorrowfully.

"If that's the way you feel, Mr. Ponzi," said Dempsey, "why

don't you come around and have a talk with our city editor? He'd like to meet you."

"That's a good idea," Ponzi said. "Come on. We'll walk around right now."

Dunn did not bat an eyelash as Dempsey appeared in front of his rolltop desk with Ponzi in the flesh. "I should sue you," Ponzi said to Dunn.

"That, Mr. Ponzi, is certainly your privilege." Dunn's voice was deceptively soft. The two men were standing face to face, not 18 inches apart. "Mr. Ponzi," Dunn said, his voice almost a whisper, "tell me about that trouble you were in up there in Canada."

Ponzi's face hardened and Dunn could see him stiffen under the summer suit. "Oh, that Montreal business," Ponzi said. "It amounted to nothing. Nothing at all."

"Tell me about it," said Dunn. Ponzi, caught off base, now quickly recovered. "It is a closed issue," he said. "Closed and unimportant."

That was all there was to the little talk. The two men just stood there glaring at each other. Then Ponzi relaxed, smiled, shook hands with Dunn and left.

The moment Ponzi was out of sight, Dunn summoned his star reporter—Herbert L. Baldwin. "Baldy," he said, "Ponzi has just admitted to me that he was once in trouble in Montreal. I want you to go up there and find out all about it."

On Friday, July 23, Ponzi, decked out in a new cream-colored suit and swinging a malacca walking stick, paid a call at the offices of Judge Dominick Leveroni, his counsel. "Judge," he said, "I want to do something about these stories that have been running in the *Post*."

The Judge thought things over. "I have an idea, Charlie," he said. "There's a publicity man here in Boston who might be just the man for you. Fellow by the name of McMasters. He's been handling some political campaigns." The Judge leaned back in his swivel chair. "Yes, the more I think of it the more I'm sure McMasters is the man for you."

William McMasters—a tall, slim man in his early forties—had been a *Post* reporter. He strode into the Judge's office within half an hour. Ponzi, sitting there with Judge Leveroni, jumped to his feet and pumped McMasters' hand.

Ponzi told McMasters he wanted, somehow, to counteract the stories in the *Post*. McMasters had been reading the stories and wondering if Ponzi was on the level. But now, as he searched the face of the Judge he found in it complete trust. "All right," said McMasters. "Let's see what I can do for you."

McMasters phoned the *Post* and was put through to Eddie Dunn. "Eddie," he said, "if you send one of your reporters over to Judge Leveroni's office you'll get an exclusive interview with Charles Ponzi."

"I'll have a man right over," said Dunn. "You say this is exclusive, Bill?"

"I'll guarantee it. I'm handling publicity for Mr. Ponzi."

Ponzi, calling all the turns and giving himself the best of it, gave out quite an interview to the *Post* reporter. He lambasted his critics, calling them green-eyed with jealousy because he had come upon a financial secret that was giving the little man a share of some of the gravy.

Eddie Dunn had given the reporter a loaded question. "How," the reporter asked Ponzi, "can you invest in postal-reply coupons all the money that you are obviously taking in, when there aren't enough postal-reply coupons in the world to match such sums?"

Ponzi, flicking the ashes off his cigarette, was glad the reporter had asked the question. "I can now divulge," he said, "that only a small percentage of the money I take in goes into postal-reply coupons. Just *where* I invest the bulk of the money must remain my secret." He leaned close to the scribe and looked him straight in the eye. "Do you think I am going to divulge my secret—the secret that is giving my investors such a handsome return on their investment—so that Morgan and Rockefeller and *those* men will get hold of it? I should say *not*."

But if Charlie was keeping one thing secret, he had something else to divulge. Figuring that the *Post* would hardly give him the best of it, he had thought up something by which to beat the *Post* at its own game. Charlie told the reporter that he was no longer going to give a 50 percent return on invested money in 90 days. "You're not!" said the reporter. McMasters, sitting there listening, gulped. "No," Charlie went on, smiling and walking around the room. "You can put this in your paper tomorrow morning: Ponzi is *now* going to pay 50 percent in *45* days! From now on, investors will be paid principal and interest in half the previous time."

"What about those 90-day notes?" McMasters broke in to ask.

"Beginning tomorrow morning," replied Charlie, "I shall honor all 90-day notes that are 45 days old."

The interview with Ponzi broke under a two-column headline on the front page of the *Post* on Saturday morning. At nine o'clock, when Ponzi's offices opened for business, the line of investors was four blocks long. Ponzi drew up in his limousine, got out, waved his straw hat to the crowd and pushed his way to his office. There he sat down at his desk. He took one look at the crush of people at the windows, practically all of them waving cash and begging the tellers to take it, then picked up the phone and called the police. "I need protection," he said. Six cops hustled right around.

As the morning wore on, the line down in School Street grew longer. By noon there were a dozen police trying to keep order. A second line, stemming from the payoff office in Pi Alley, had also snaked out into Washington Street. Charlie's clerks were wearing out pens writing checks to lucky investors.

Up in his School Street office, Ponzi sat at his desk, observing what was going on at the six windows. Every once in a while there would be a slight dispute between an investor and a clerk as to the age of one of Ponzi's notes. Ponzi would get up from his chair, examine the note and, finding it not quite 45 days old, but almost, he would smile at the investor, then turn to the clerk behind the wicket and say, "Pay this good man."

What made Ponzi possible was that he arrived in just the right place at just the right time with just the right dodge. He had popped up in conservative Boston in an era when there was no such thing as a Securities Exchange Commission and when the little man felt that he was not getting his share of the nation's growing wealth.

Charlie had something else in his favor, too—public opinion. Not a single one of tens of thousands of his investors uttered a word of complaint against him. While he was shearing the sheep, the newspapers and the law-enforcement authorities engaged in a conspiracy of silence, not daring to raise a hue and a cry. Politicians and editors, although trembling at the inevitability of a judgment day, considered it foolhardy to take a stand against a man who was a hero to the voters and to the readers. It was no trifling matter to step in and muss up a project that was paying 50 percent interest in six weeks to laborers, schoolteachers, butchers, office boys and old ladies in sewing circles.

Early one Sunday afternoon, McMasters went out to Ponzi's estate in Lexington and found the little wizard on the lawn. "Boy, am I happy!" Charlie told him. "Do you know how much money changed hands yesterday? More than $1 million. *That's* how much." Ponzi was rubbing his little hands together.

"I've arranged for a newsreel cameraman to come out today," McMasters told Ponzi.

"Wonderful," said Ponzi. "When will he be here?"

McMasters looked out into the street. "Any minute."

"I must go and change my clothes," said Ponzi. "I must look my best for my investors."

When the cameraman arrived, Charlie appeared in a freshly pressed summer suit, a red carnation in his lapel, and wearing a pair of two-tone shoes—black patent-leather bottoms and white-canvas uppers. He strutted and hammed for the cameraman for 20 minutes. When the shooting was over, the cameraman said, "Say, I'd like to get in on this 50 percent thing. I got $50 on me."

"You'll have $75 in 45 days," said Charlie, grabbing the money and scribbling out a receipt.

When the newsreel men left, Ponzi invited McMasters into his mansion. "I have a problem, Bill," he said. "I want to send for my mother in Italy. What's the best way to send her $1000 that she can quickly cash over there—traveler's checks?"

McMasters blinked; he thought Ponzi was kidding. But Ponzi was not kidding. He actually needed information as to exactly how to transfer passage money to his mother. This struck McMasters as peculiar. Here was a man, dealing in millions, and supposedly with connections in high international money circles, who did not know the ABC's of transferring $1000 from Boston to Italy.

"It's funny," said McMasters, "that you should be asking a guy like me a question like that—you with your connections."

Ponzi managed a tired smile. "I've got too many big things up here"—he tapped his forehead with his forefinger—"to worry about a small thing."

That Sunday night, McMasters was sitting with Ponzi in the great man's paneled library while Ponzi was going through a batch of accumulated mail. "Boy," Charlie said, "here's something!" He handed a letter to McMasters. It was from a shoe store offering Ponzi his choice of a pair of expensive shoes, free of charge. "I always did like nice shoes. I'm going around to that store first thing in the morning."

McMasters saw by the expression on Ponzi's face, somewhat to his surprise, that Ponzi was serious about accepting the offer of a free pair of shoes. This, like Ponzi's ignorance of the simple mechanics of a money transfer, simply did not add up. When Bill McMasters left Ponzi's estate that night he had begun to entertain serious doubts about the man.

First thing next morning McMasters walked in on Simon Swig, president of the Tremont Trust Company. Swig was known to have just about the sharpest eye in Boston for questionable collateral. "What do you think of Ponzi?" McMasters asked the banker.

"I think the man's a deadbeat."

"Exactly why, Mr. Swig?"

Swig said he had learned that Ponzi, who claimed to have foreign connections, actually had no connections abroad—a statement that McMasters, in view of Ponzi's ignorance about sending money to his mother, was quick to believe.

"Consider this, McMasters," Swig was saying. "Here is a man who makes 50 percent for his investors in 45 days—or claims to—and yet what does he do with his *own* money? Why, he has a third of a million dollars lying around here at $4\frac{1}{2}$ percent interest. He's doing the same thing with his money at other banks. If the man's on the level, why doesn't he invest his own money in that 50 percent stuff? Why *doesn't* he, McMasters?"

After he left Swig's office, McMasters telephoned to District Attorney Joseph C. Pelletier—a man he knew from his newspaper days. "Mr. Pelletier," he said, "I'm going to bring Charles Ponzi over to your office if I may. I'd like you to have a talk with him. Perhaps it would be in the public interest if you convinced him that he should not take any more of the people's money until you have some accountants go over his books."

"Why, Bill, you don't for a minute think there might be anything *wrong*, do you?"

"That's for your accountants to judge."

McMasters ambled into Ponzi's office at the Hanover Trust Company. "I've arranged for you to have a talk with the District Attorney," said McMasters.

Ponzi stiffened. "What for?"

"To counteract those stories in the *Post*."

"But those stories *have* been counteracted," said Ponzi. He pointed out the window to Washington Street. "Look at those lines there—one from School Street and one from Pi Alley."

"Yes," said McMasters, "I see the lines. But I've been tipped off that Pelletier would like to have a chat with you. We'd better keep the appointment."

Ponzi drummed his fingers on his desk and looked out the window. "All right," he said. "I've got nothing to hide."

Ponzi got up and left his office. When he came back, he was carrying his straw suitcase. "What's in there?" asked McMasters. Ponzi smiled. "You'll see," he said. "You'll see."

43

Pelletier got up and shook hands with Ponzi when Charlie walked into his office with McMasters. Ponzi, lugging that straw suitcase, put it down on the District Attorney's desk. "What's in there, Mr. Ponzi?" Pelletier asked. "A couple of million dollars," said Charlie, unlocking the suitcase and opening it. And there, sure enough, were stacks of bills. All of them, fresh off the presses, were goldbacks, as $100 bills were known in those days.

"I just wanted to show you," Ponzi said to the DA, "that I'm pretty liquid."

McMasters, standing there looking at that straw suitcase filled with money, now arrived at the unshakable conclusion that Charles Ponzi was one of the biggest crooks in the history of fraudulent misrepresentation.

Ponzi, one hand in his pocket, the other one free to wave around, started to pace up and down. "I love the little people, Mr. Pelletier," Charlie said, the words gushing out. "The little people should have some of the good things in life, Mr. Pelletier. Don't you think so?" Charlie was staring at the DA with a semireligious glint in his eyes. Pelletier cleared his throat, smiled and nodded.

McMasters figured it was time to break in. "I would suggest, Mr. Pelletier," McMasters said, "that Mr. Ponzi, as a gesture of good faith, temporarily abstain from taking in any more money—until one of your auditors goes over his books."

Out of the corner of his eye McMasters saw Ponzi stiffen. "Mr. Ponzi," McMasters went on, "is a highly ethical man. He has nothing to hide. He insists that he take in no more money—only pay out money to those clients whose notes are due—until he has been officially investigated."

"But I am perfectly happy," said Pelletier.

"I know," said McMasters, feeling like punching the DA in the nose for his gullibility, "but Mr. Ponzi here isn't happy." McMasters turned to Ponzi and said, "Are you, Mr. Ponzi?" Then, before giving Ponzi a chance to answer, McMasters caught Pelletier's eye and winked.

Now Pelletier seemed to catch on. "Fine," he said. "A great

suggestion, McMasters. You will agree, then, Mr. Ponzi, not to take in any more money until an auditor goes over your books."

"Yes, Mr. Ponzi will agree to that," said McMasters, knowing Ponzi could not very well disagree without arousing the DA's suspicions. "In fact, Mr. Ponzi will shake hands on it." Turning to Ponzi, McMasters said, "Won't you, Mr. Ponzi?"

"Yes," said Ponzi, having no other course.

Out on the street, after the meeting, Ponzi said to McMasters. "What did you do a thing like *that* for?"

"Oh, it was just a little scheme of mine to see that you take in more money than ever. Don't you see, Mr. Ponzi, that after the District Attorney announces that you are completely solvent you will draw more business than ever?"

Ponzi did not answer for a few seconds. "S-a-y," he said. "I think you're right!"

Before Ponzi realized it, he was sitting with McMasters in the office of United States Attorney Francis Gallagher. Gallagher, like Pelletier, was a highly cultivated man.

Ponzi, lugging that suitcase with the $2 million in it, gave Gallagher the same spiel he had given Pelletier. The result was the same. Gallagher did not understand much of what Ponzi was explaining (and no wonder), but when Ponzi was through talking the United States Attorney was simply enchanted.

"You're doing great, Mr. Ponzi," McMasters said to Charlie when they left Gallagher. "Boy, what an impression you're making on everyone!"

"You really think so?" asked Ponzi.

"Do I?" said McMasters, who was now outconning the con man. "Why, after you show your books to Pelletier's accountants, you'll be a cinch to clean up several million dollars and then run for mayor."

Ponzi smiled and lapsed into thought. "Bill," he said, "you know, I'd make a great mayor."

Late in the afternoon, McMasters made a third stop with his client—this time in the office of Attorney General J. Weston

Allen in the State House. Charlie was still carrying that suitcase. When he got in to see the Attorney General, Ponzi made more of a production of the audience than he had with either Pelletier or even Gallagher. After the interview, Allen grabbed Ponzi's hand, and the little swindler walked out of the office in a shimmering envelope of confidence.

On Monday, when District Attorney Pelletier called in the press and announced that Mr. Ponzi had agreed to accept no more money until accountants went over his books, Boston reacted as it probably would today if a hydrogen bomb were dropped on the outskirts. Heeding the newspaper extras, practically everybody who held Charlie's notes dropped what they were doing and rushed to School Street or into Pi Alley.

But Charlie was right on the job, right there to cope with the situation. And he was in a royal position to do so. Directing operations from his desk in the president's office of the Hanover Trust, he was dispatching armed guards with bags of bills across to Pi Alley and around to School Street every half hour or so. Once in a while he would leave his office in the bank and, giving the crowd the old hello, look in on the Pi Alley office, then get into the blue Locomobile, parked in front of the bank, and be driven around to School Street. He was the eye of the hurricane, calm as the furies swirled about him.

On Tuesday morning at eight o'clock, an hour before opening time, there was a line five blocks long at Ponzi's. Promptly at nine o'clock, the little man wheeled into School Street in his blue Locomobile. While the faces of some of the investors were dark, the morning was bright and so was Charlie. He asked for volunteers to help him carry six suitcases of money to the second floor. Several eager helpers crowded around the Locomobile, grabbed the bags containing the money and carried them upstairs. "You can see," Ponzi shouted to the crowd, "that Ponzi's words are as good as gold."

"Hurray for Ponzi!" shouted a hard-faced man up near the front. McMasters, hanging around, tilted his head as he looked at the fellow. "Yeah," shouted another character, "hurray for Ponzi! I don't want my money. Ponzi gives me more than the banks do. I'm leavin' my dough with Ponzi."

McMasters waited until Ponzi disappeared into the building, then approached the man who had said he was leaving his dough with Ponzi. "I'm representing Mr. Ponzi," McMasters said to the fellow. "Mr. Ponzi wants to know if you can come back tomorrow at the same price."

"Sure," said the man. "Same time?"

"Yes," said McMasters. "I've forgotten how much Mr. Ponzi is paying you."

"Ten bucks."

"Beat it, you bum," said McMasters.

McMasters found Ponzi at his desk, hands folded over his cane, beaming at everybody. "Did you hear that fellow down there who said he didn't want his money back?" McMasters asked Ponzi.

"Yes," said Ponzi, beaming brightly. "Wasn't that a splendid show of confidence?"

"He tells me you paid him $10 to do what he did."

Ponzi just blinked up at McMasters, and he was still blinking when he was saved by the bell. A commotion at one of the windows gave him an excuse to get up. At the window a clerk told Ponzi that a lady investor had raised her note to double its face value. Examining it, Charlie made a ticking sound with his tongue, then looked at the woman. "Madam," he said, "always remember: Honesty is the best policy."

It was along toward noon before a couple of auditors from District Attorney Pelletier's office showed up and asked Ponzi for his books. Charlie, glad to oblige, went to his little safe, twirled the dial and pulled out a couple of black books. Thumbing through the records, the auditors looked puzzled. "Are these all the records you keep?" one of them asked Charlie. Yes, that was all. Ponzi explained that it was not necessary for him to keep complicated books since his business was always in such a liquid state.

All of the notes that Ponzi gave out contained serial numbers.

The lower the number, the older the note was; the higher the number, the more recent the vintage. McMasters, deciding that Pelletier's accountants would not get very far, determined to do a little investigating on his own. "By this time," said McMasters later, "I felt that I would have to carry the whole burden of exposing Ponzi. The public officials were too stupid to see through him, and the press was half afraid of him."

McMasters got to work on Wednesday morning, the second day since the District Attorney, without knowing exactly why, had temporarily shut down on Ponzi. The crowds were still coming. But Ponzi, arriving every few hours with a new load of money and a broad smile, was still paying off.

McMasters, circulating among the crowd and posing as an investor, began to swap information with the more talkative suckers. Thus he got the numbers on the notes they held. He got 100 numbers within a few hours.

McMasters got more numbers on Thursday, when the mob was still being paid off, and still more on Friday, when Ponzi was continuing to shell out. What McMasters was after was enough serial numbers to work out a geometric ratio that would convince even somebody who did not understand mathematics that Ponzi was a crook who was simply robbing Peter to pay Paul.

Bill McMasters shut himself up at home early Friday night with the figures he had collected from the investors. He worked through the night. By dawn, he had come up with a geometric ratio confirming his suspicions about Ponzi's game.

It was shortly after noon on Saturday, July 31—exactly one week after Ponzi's own con man's story had come out in the *Post* and really got the ball rolling—that Bill McMasters approached Richard Grozier, the acting publisher of the *Post*.

"How would you like a story for Monday morning proving that Charles Ponzi is absolutely insolvent?" McMasters asked Grozier.

"Have you got the facts and figures to prove it?" Grozier wanted to know.

McMasters had.

McMasters briefed Grozier on the incongruities he had encountered out at Ponzi's estate the previous Sunday—Ponzi's ignorance of the mechanics of transferring money to his mother in Italy and his jumping at the offer of a free pair of shoes. Next McMasters showed Grozier some figures he had worked out—figures that McMasters felt indicated that if Ponzi were to meet every obligation outstanding, without paying the interest, he would be roughly $2 million in the red.

Grozier sat studying the figures for several minutes. His jaw was set and there was anger in his eyes. "I want you to do the story, Bill," Grozier said at length. "Can you turn it in to the city desk by the middle of tomorrow afternoon so that our lawyers can get a chance to go over it before we print it?" McMasters could. It was Grozier who brought up the matter of compensation. "Will $5000 be satisfactory?" he asked. McMasters nodded.

McMasters went home and shut himself in a room with a typewriter, some paper and a basketful of notes. He wrote and rewrote the story from early evening until dawn. Then he went to bed for a few hours, got up and polished the thing and delivered it to the *Post*. It was 2700 words in length, and Grozier was so pleased with it that he gave McMasters an extra $1000.

Ponzi got up shortly before seven o'clock on the morning of Monday, August 2. He stepped into a pair of fur-lined bedroom slippers, threw a blue silk dressing gown over his green silk pajamas and padded down to the front door to pick up his copy of the *Post*. Splashed all over the front page was the beginning of the McMasters story.

A slight drizzle began to fall, but Ponzi stood reading every word of the story. He was still there when Rose called, "Charlie, come on inside out of the rain. You want to catch a cold?"

Charlie, who had caught considerably more than a cold, got dressed, passed up breakfast, got into the Locomobile and was driven to the bank. It was shortly before 8:30 when he let himself in. "Nice morning except for that drizzle, Mr. Ponzi," said the night watchman. "Yes," said Charlie, "it's a nice morning."

Ponzi picked up the telephone and called McMasters at his home. "Bill," he said, "what on earth ever prompted you to write such a story?" Charlie, McMasters recalls, was speaking more in sorrow than anger.

"I have to tell the truth as I see it, Mr. Ponzi," said McMasters. "Too much is at stake here. Why, I understand schemes like yours are springing up all over the country."

There was one thing in Ponzi's favor—time. About $4 million in notes and interest would not be due for a month or more. We know, in retrospect, what Ponzi did. As president of the Hanover Trust Company, he had access to millions of dollars in cash. There was nobody to dispute his going into a big safe and taking practically anything he wanted to his office. He had already plastered the bank with his personal notes and had created a virtual flurry of paper between the Hanover Trust and the other banks in the city, so that nobody, Charlie included, really knew what the score was.

Shortly after the big vault was opened at nine o'clock that Monday morning, Charlie went in and took $2 million in $100 bills, leaving an IOU in place of the money. Putting the money into a suitcase, he instructed his chauffeur to drive him around to School Street just to see what was going on. The mob in School Street was something big and something fierce. It seemed that practically everybody in Boston had read that story in the *Post*. The suckers were really growing suspicious of Charlie now. So, ever a man with his finger on the public pulse, Charlie got out of School Street fast.

Charlie had his chauffeur drive him down to Saratoga Springs, in New York State. There, after checking into the United States Hotel as Charles Bianchi, he started to plunge at the gaming tables. He hoped to run that $2 million up to perhaps $10 million by betting not only at Saratoga but with bookies who would lay his money at racetracks all over the country. Thus, he could go back to Boston, pay off and still be in the clear. Of course nothing like that happened. Three days after he left, Ponzi was back in Boston, completely cleaned out of the $2 million.

But Charlie was still paying off his investors. The Peters whose

51

money he was using to pay the Pauls held notes that were not yet due. Charlie, as president of the Hanover Trust, decided that he would take another fling at gambling. But now the directors stepped in. They advised him not to drop any more IOU's in the safe. Charlie only blinked and nodded.

For several days, Ponzi just sat at the bank, or in his office at Poole's, twiddling his thumbs. He was living in a state of suspended animation. Boston was divided into two camps—those who thought Charlie was a deadbeat and those who thought he was wonderful.

After all, up to now not a man, woman or child who had handed his money over to Charlie had lost a cent. The worst that had happened to anybody—after Pelletier had issued that injunction against Charlie, and McMasters had come out with his blast—was that they had got their principal back without interest.

Meantime, in Canada, Herbert Baldwin was trudging through the twisted streets of Montreal's Little Italy from early morning till late at night. He flashed the Ponzi pictures on men holding up lampposts on the street corners, on housewives, on streetcar conductors and on the proprietors of small shops. Late one afternoon he happened into the offices of a man named Cordasco, a steamship agent on St. James Street. Cordasco, a taciturn little man, rubbed his chin as he looked at the pictures of Ponzi. "Yes," he said. "Yes and no."

The pictures rang a distant bell in the mind of the steamship agent. How distant? Oh, ten years or more maybe.

Baldwin, sure that he was now closing in, kept pressing Cordasco for just what was familiar and what was unfamiliar about the face. "Something about the mouth is not right," said Cordasco.

"Maybe you knew him when he had a mustache," Baldwin said.

Next morning, Baldwin was back at Cordasco's. "Take a look at these pictures now," he said. Baldy had been in the art department at the Montreal *Star* and had had an artist paint a mustache on the Ponzi pictures. Cordasco's eyes lighted up. "To be sure!" he said. "That's Bianchi."

"Who?"

"Charles Bianchi. And a clever devil he was, too!"

There had been, 13 years before, in 1907, a sharpshooter by the name of Zarrossi who had operated a loan company at the corner of St. James and Inspector streets. All the Italians in the neighborhood had implicit trust in Zarrossi. When any of them had a tale of woe they ran to Zarrossi with it, and Zarrossi straightened things out.

And then one day there appeared in Zarrossi's office a little, mustached fellow by the name of Charles Bianchi—a man about 25, mincing of step, bright of eye, glib of tongue. Presently changes began to take place in Zarrossi's. Zarrossi branched out. He began to accept money from the Montreal Italians to be sent to their relatives in Italy—with interest. His partner, Bianchi, was in charge of this branch of the business. "The Italians here got the interest," the steamship man was explaining to Baldwin, "and their relatives in Italy got the principal—or were supposed to."

Of course the relatives never got the principal. Letters began to cross the Atlantic, between Montreal and Italy, and soon the bubble burst. Zarrossi fled to Mexico, there eventually to lose himself in thin air. Bianchi was left holding the bag. And so, for being engaged in a scheme whereby he and Zarrossi kept money belonging to the suckers, Bianchi was sent to prison for three years. He was released in 1910, when he was 28.

Now, back at police headquarters, Herbert Baldwin officially established that Ponzi and Bianchi were one and the same. And so, on Wednesday, August 11, the *Post* broke the story.

Eddie Dunn, breathing hard at his desk in his cubbyhole at the *Post*, sent a man over to the bank to have a talk with Ponzi. Charlie, smoking a cigarette, just blinked at the reporter when the scribe told him what Baldwin had uncovered. "Let him who is without sin," said the little scoundrel, "cast the first stone."

Charlie had no sooner been revealed as Bianchi than another chapter of his life came to light—a chapter when he had told Rose he had been engaged in some cloak-and-dagger work. After being released from jail in Canada, Charlie, to make ends meet, had smuggled a couple of aliens across the border into the United States. Nailed for the caper, he had been given a three-year jolt in Atlanta. So now the *Post* broke *that* story.

It was all over for Ponzi now. Everybody—the city authorities, the county authorities, the state authorities and the government authorities—moved at once. Everything Charlie owned, including the house and furnishings in Lexington, was attached. He was locked out of the Hanover Trust Company and the doors at Poole's were barred against him. He was not allowed to set foot in his office on School Street or in the onetime restaurant in Pi Alley.

The cops watched Charlie to make sure he did not get away. It took the authorities nine days to make enough sense out of the shambles to learn exactly what Charlie had been up to. The best estimate was that Charlie had raked in about $15 million and paid back practically that much. There were about 5 million of his notes still outstanding. All of his assets were so heavily mortgaged that they were worthless as security.

One fine morning two hard-faced deputy United States marshals called at Ponzi's place in Lexington. Charlie personally answered the door. "You are under arrest for violating the postal statutes," said one of the marshals. The postal law is one of the most elastic on the books, covering a multitude of sins. Charlie, in notifying his investors that their money was due, had violated the law by notifying them by postal card to come in and collect money that had been obtained by fraudulent misrepresentation.

Charlie smiled sadly at the two deputies. "All right," he said, "I'll come with you without making trouble."

Things happened fast during the ensuing years. Charlie got five years from Uncle Sam and was sprung after doing three and a half. Then Massachusetts gave him a seven-to-nine sentence on a conviction for grand larceny.

Rose met Charlie at the prison gate when he was released in February 1934. Fourteen years had passed since Ponzi had taken Boston. His appearance had changed; he had put on quite a lot of weight. But several thousand investors still remembered him—

the investors who had missed the boat and lost their savings. They met Charlie and Rose when they pulled into South Station. The gendarmes had to be called out to whisk Charlie and Rose away to a little hotel.

Now Charlie's official past, which he considered a bucket of ashes, suddenly burst into flame. Uncle Sam decided that since Charlie had never taken out citizenship papers he was still an Italian citizen—and an undesirable one, at that. So Charlie was hustled into court and officially banished from the country. "I'll never forget you," he told Rose as he said good-bye to her.

It was a gray day in October 1934—just 35 years since he had first landed in New York from his native Italy—that Charles Ponzi, now 51, balding and suety around the middle, stepped out of a taxicab onto the dock of a New York pier in company with two sober-faced men. Handcuffed to one of the men, for his two companions were deputy United States marshals, Charlie minced toward the steerage gangplank of the *Vulcania*. Charles Ponzi had come full circle; he was going back to Italy.

In his white iron stateroom, which he was to share with three other passengers, Ponzi received the press. He sat on his bunk, his little legs dangling over the side, holding a cigarette in a holder. He cocked his head to one side and said, "Well gentlemen, I suppose you want to know if I have a statement to make."

The gentlemen of the press indeed wanted a statement.

"You can say," said Charlie, flipping some cigarette ashes on the iron floor, "that I'm going to start all over again in Italy."

"Doing what?" asked a man from the *Daily News*.

"That," said Ponzi, "is my secret. But you'll hear about it. Mark my words."

Arriving in Italy, Ponzi headed for Rome. He rented a furnished room on the Via Brescia, a thoroughfare of cheap new dwellings on the outskirts. There Signor Ponzi arose at dawn each morning. He was working on two books—one, his autobiography, which he was calling *The Rise of Charles Ponzi*, and the other, *Boston Merry-Go-Round*. This latter work was designed to rattle a few skeletons in Boston closets. Sitting at a table by a window that looked down on the street, Ponzi wrote for hours on end, using a pencil on a tablet of cheap yellow paper.

At first Rose was a faithful correspondent, telling him how things were in Boston and how she was making out in her job as a stenographer. But as the months wore on, Rose's letters became less frequent, and when she did write she had less to say.

There was, operating out of Rome while Ponzi was in residence, a man with whom he had much in common—Benito Mussolini. Mussolini, the same age as Ponzi, was at the height of his power, standing on balconies, his chin out, conning the peasants with promises of something for nothing. Ponzi used to join the crowds listening to Mussolini when the great man got up on his balcony in Rome. It seemed in the cards that these two boys should get together and, sure enough, they did.

It was in 1936, when Mussolini seized Ethiopia, that Ponzi saw his chance. He composed a letter to Mussolini in which he stated that he would be just the man to handle relations with the foreign press in Ethiopia if His Excellency thought he could be of value.

Three days later, a man in a Fascist uniform walked into Ponzi's little room. "You are to come with me, signor," said the visitor. "You have been summoned by His Excellency."

So there they were, the biggest fraud in Italy and the man who had been the biggest fraud in America, face to face. The two were together for almost 30 minutes. Mussolini seemed more interested in what Charlie had done in America than in sending him to Ethiopia. Charlie went back to his rooming house and waited. Days passed, and weeks, and no word from Mussolini. Ponzi wrote two letters to Mussolini, inquiring if he could be of any service. But he did not get an answer.

By now Ponzi was broke. He was not only broke but desperate. So he took to a form of blackmail. He sat down and got off a number of letters to some pretty well-heeled men in Boston, some of them high in politics, others of no prominence. Ponzi knew something about every one of the addressees—tidbits that he had picked up while engaged in the big caper in Boston. Each letter was quite clever. It stated that he, Ponzi, was writing an exposé of life in Boston, and it inquired as to details of a certain crooked or illicit episode—in which the recipient of the letter had been a participant. A flood of money came to Ponzi. Within the space of a couple of months, Charlie must have taken in about $5000—enough to supply his modest wants indefinitely in the Italy of those days.

There also came a letter from Rose, asking for a divorce. Ponzi never attempted to fight it, and the divorce went through on grounds that Ponzi had served more than five years in prison.

Ponzi, his vanity hit, took Rose's action pretty hard. He went around the wine shops in his neighborhood, getting drunk and babbling about how cruel life had been to him. Charles Ponzi became an alcoholic. He abandoned his writings and his transatlantic blackmail and drank wine from early morning till late at night. Then his cronies would carry him up to his cheap little room.

One day a Fascist soldier called at Charlie's room. "His Excellency commands you," the soldier told Charlie.

Mussolini sent Ponzi to Rio de Janeiro as the business manager for the Latin Airlines, a pet project of the dictator's. In Rio, Ponzi, at the age of 60, seemed to take on his old bounce. Bald, with tufts of gray at the temples, he lived in a flossy apartment, acquired a couple of mistresses and had a New York tailor send him suits.

Then Mussolini fell, and so did Charlie Ponzi. He began to drink heavily again. He suffered a stroke that left him partially paralyzed and blind in one eye. He was taken to a charity ward. There Charles Ponzi died in poverty.

〰️

A NICKEL tossed at a blind man's cup missed and rolled away. When the beggar retrieved it, the donor said, "I thought you were blind."

"Oh, I'm not the regular blind man," was the reply. "I'm just taking his place while he's at the movies."   —*Neal O'Hara, McNaught Syndicate*

He lived the lives of others—the monk,
the teacher, the military officer—better than his own

THE GREAT IMPOSTOR

by Robert Crichton

On the very cold morning of February 14, 1956, Detective Troopers Millard Nickerson and James Milligan of the Maine State Police boarded a Coast Guard cutter bound for North Haven Island out in Penobscot Bay. On North Haven they were fortunate in finding the island's only taxi.

"Got some good teachers up to school this year, I hear," Nickerson said to the driver, nudging his companion.

"Got a good crop," the driver said after a pause that was long, even by Maine standards. "Got this Martin Godgart. Come on the island out of the blue. Got all the kids in the Sea Scouts, teaches at the Baptist Sunday School and played Santa Claus to all the poor kids. We got plenty of those, you know."

The driver swung the car into the drive leading to the school, a large, somber, shingled affair. The detectives were upset to find that Godgart wasn't there. As they turned to go back to the taxi and plan what to do next, an old, mud-spattered Chevrolet spun into the school parking area. Before the car had come to a full stop, the door flew open and a massive, powerful-looking man with a crew cut climbed from behind the wheel and started up the slope

58

toward them, his arms swinging. His gait, combined with his bulk, gave him the appearance of a graceful bear.

"I have a feeling I can be of help to you two men," he said softly. "What took you so long to get here?"

Nickerson produced a paper, a warrant for Godgart's arrest. "You are Martin Godgart?" he asked, checking against a small notebook.

"In a manner of speaking, yes," the big man answered.

"Your real name is Ferdinand Waldo Demara, Jr., is that correct?"

"Sometimes it's hard to say what my name is."

"Alias Martin Godgart?" The man nodded yes.

"Alias Dr. Robert Linton French?" Another nod of yes.

"Alias Dr. Cecil Boyce Hamann?"

"You people have been doing your homework. Yes, at one time I was him too."

"Alias Ben W. Jones, assistant warden of the Huntsville Prison in Texas?"

"I'm not ashamed of that one."

"Alias Dr. Joseph Cyr, surgeon lieutenant in the Royal Canadian Navy?"

"One of my very best," the prisoner said. He saw that Nickerson was closing his notebook. "Go ahead, go ahead. You've missed one here and there."

"I think we've got enough to establish the case," Nickerson said with obvious irony. They started back toward the schoolhouse. Demara hung behind.

"I don't want to go back. I'm clean in there and I want to keep it that way, please."

The ride back to the harbor was stiffly silent. The big man stared morosely, tapping the window, then smacked the fist of one hand into the palm of the other. "Oh, God, I had so much work to do here," he said.

When they were several miles out to sea, Demara asked permission to go on deck and take a last look at the island. "Do you

know a play called *The Playboy of the Western World*?" he asked.
One of the detectives said he did.

"There's one of the saddest lines in all the world in there," Demara said. "I've lost my only haven in the western world."

Fred W. Demara, the great impostor, was tried in Augusta, Maine, for "cheating by false premises," found guilty and, as happened with almost every institution he had defrauded, in order to save themselves embarrassment, the North Haven School didn't choose to press charges. While Demara was in prison, a delegation of people came over to the mainland to plead in his behalf and ask him to return to North Haven with all forgiven and a fresh start promised. He refused. "I wouldn't want my children to be taught by a known impostor. It's all right if they don't know, of course."

Demara was put on probation in Maine, and then set free when he let it be known that he planned to leave the state. As almost always, Demara went home again.

Home for the great impostor was the dreary, textile-mill town of Lawrence, Massachusetts. The roots of his incredible career can be traced here to his childhood and family. Our hero was born Ferdinand Waldo Demara on December 12, 1921. Ever since the birth of his first child, Elaine, Ferdinand Waldo Demara, Sr., had been hungry for an heir. For several days the greats of Lawrence, what there were of them, streamed through the big Victorian Demara house on Jackson Street, clucking with admiration at the boy.

His early childhood was like that—all warmth and love and riches. But from his first year in school young Fred felt different and out of place. His family was the only one he knew that didn't work directly for the mills. His father and a partner owned a number of local motion-picture theaters. Many of the children in school were very poor and Fred's clothes never looked like their clothes. He was larger than anyone his age, and his hair was long and dark. His eyebrows also were dark and long as were his lashes, and his eyes were a startling, striking blue.

Fred was a lonely boy because the others left him alone, but he was the kind of boy who could entertain himself for endless hours at a time. He had two rules. He didn't like games of physical violence, and when he played he wanted to be leader or he didn't want to play. He was immensely strong. He was given to unexplained, wild rages in which he would hold his breath until he turned almost dark purple; and he was capable of smashing things. He frightened the others in school.

The rich, warm, all-embracing sweet solemnity of the Catholic Church and its rituals was a cloak which shielded Fred from outside shocks. He began spending a great deal of his time in the church sacristy. The pictures of him at the time show him to possess a fine, white, beatific quality. He was delicate for all his great size, and his enormous eyes, especially when seen against the black cloth of an acolyte's habit, were an impressive sight. Everyone had to admit that of all the boys in the school, the Demara boy was the one who most seemed to have a genuine vocation for the priesthood, and who showed the greatest promise.

Late one afternoon in autumn, Fred was coming across the lawn when he saw his sister Elaine standing on the porch.

"Mama and Papa are waiting for you," she said. There was something about the tone of her voice which caused him to feel frightened. Inside the house it was still and silent and Mrs. Larch, the housekeeper, had forgotten to turn on the lights. In his parents' dressing room, his mother sat next to the window, like Elaine downstairs, bathed in the sun's last rays. He could see that she had been crying.

"How can I tell you this?" his father asked.

"Just tell him the truth," his mother said. "He's a big boy now. He's 11 years old."

"Now try and follow this," his father said in a weak voice. "Nothing in this house belongs to us anymore. Someone is going to come and take it away."

"We're going to have to move away, son," his mother said. "You see, Daddy has lost all his money."

"But why do we have to move away?" the son suddenly blurted out. "This is our home. You don't need money to live in your home, because it's your home." He knew he was lying to himself but he wanted to say it and hoped someone would agree that he was right.

On Saturday morning the moving van came and a man from the bank told them what they could take and what they must leave. Young Fred sat in the front seat of their big touring Pierce-Arrow, watching the rain wash down the celluloid windows. The car followed the great clumsy van, down into town, past the hulks of the silent, empty mills, around through the rows of dormitories and then back out and up Andover Street to their new home, an old carriage house on the outskirts of Lawrence.

Instead of bringing young Fred closer to the other boys in school, his family's new-found poverty only separated him more. As a poor boy he was poor in a wrong way and the others knew it and resented it. Furthermore, the longer he stayed away from Jackson Street, the more he turned away from the Church.

That winter something happened that was to change the course of his life.

His father, who was deeply worried about his son's loss of religion, finally persuaded the boy to spend a weekend with a cousin of the family, a Father Desmarais (the Demara branch had Anglicized the spelling), pastor of a parish in the heavily French-Canadian city of Woonsocket, Rhode Island.

Fred took an immediate liking to Father Desmarais, a tolerant, gentle but firm man. In front of Father Desmarais it suddenly seemed ridiculous not to believe in God. One day they went for a drive and along the way they passed a monastery of Trappist monks, a branch of the Cistercians, called Our Lady of the Valley. "Of all the places in the world, this is where I would most like to be," Father Desmarais said. The boy did not forget it.

Several weeks after Fred's return home, his sister Elaine died. She had been shopping and had slipped on a patch of ice. When she came home she complained of a headache that aspirin wouldn't cure, but she went ahead making dinner. After a little while, she lay down to take a nap and she never got up.

A depression settled over the house that wasn't lifted for months, and the boy could hardly stand it. The things he had grown accustomed to suddenly looked shabby and dingy and sad. Just a little less than a month later, Fred started down the long slope to school, but he never got there. He sold his bicycle for $8 and took the train to Boston and Providence and finally a bus to Our Lady of the Valley monastery at Valley Falls, Rhode Island. He pulled the bell cord hanging by the gate.

"I was told you never turned anyone away. I have come to join you," Demara said.

As the Trappists warn, no religious order in America demands more of its adherents. No order has stricter fasts, more complete rules on silence or requires harder labor. The Cistercians of Strict Observance never touch meat or eggs or fish. Although they produce some of the world's finest cheeses, it is a rare and festive occasion when they are allowed to touch any. A glass of milk is a supreme luxury.

The Trappist arises at 2 a.m., at which time he begins his day with spiritual contemplation and worship of God. At 5:30, he receives a breakfast of hard bread and crackers and a hot drink, after which long physical labor begins. At 11:30, the main meal of the day is served. After an afternoon of hard physical work and mental study, a third scanty meal is served. But most important, all of this discipline is endured in absolute silence. The need to talk for many men becomes a far greater obsession than food or privacy or sleep.

Although Demara was eventually accorded the hooded robes and habit of the order and given the name Frater Mary Jerome, there was some skepticism among the other monks. He didn't seem to be as contemplative as he should have been, but appeared, in fact, to be having the time of his life.

Demara was put in charge of two big, half-trained mules. Typical of monastic humor at its best, one was named Lucifer and the other Luther, for both were bad actors. There are rare times when a contemplative is permitted to talk and one of them is when it is essential in carrying out duties. It is well known that you can't handle balky mules by sign language. The deep, sweet silence of the fields was continuously shattered by the roaring, joyous shouts of "Come on, Lucifer. Step lively there, boy. Gee, there, gee, boy," and other such vital talk.

After two years at Valley Falls, far longer than anyone ever expected the young man to last, the abbot and novice master had an earnest talk about their youngest novice and came to the agreement that, as fond of him as they were, he was simply not cut out for the silent life.

If there is one good thing about having no possessions in a monastery, it is that leaving poses no problem. Toward midnight, Demara went out across the quadrangle to the stable whose doors opened out into the back fields.

"Hey, boy, ho, boy." He led the beasts to the edge of the fields and there, with the stout handle of a cant hook, he whaled, as he puts it, "holy hell" out of the mules, then let out an earsplitting whoop the likes of which have probably never been heard inside a Cistercian monastery before or since.

In the spring of 1941 Demara went into a recruiting booth in Boston and enlisted in the U.S. Army.

Army life was not for him. He was ashamed of his ignorance about such things as sex. To hide his ignorance, he avoided all bull sessions dealing with such subjects, with the result that he got the reputation for being a "saint" which he deplored. When he was shipped out of Camp Devens for basic training at Keesler Air Force Base in Biloxi, Mississippi, he determined, with this fresh chance, to become a "real wise guy." It is to his credit as a character manipulator that he succeeded beyond even his expectations. It is his boast that he never actually pulled one full day of duty in the Army.

Demara decided to leave the Army—as a deserter. While thumbing a ride to St. Louis, he heard the news about Pearl Harbor and had a feeling he had to get home to Lawrence. He arrived there two days before Christmas and a week after the last military policeman had made a search of the house.

It was not a happy Christmas. His father, an ardent patriot, as is Demara, could not bring himself to speak to his son. "There's only one answer, son," his father finally said. "You've got to go back and face the music and take your medicine like a man. You'll get out from behind bars soon enough, believe me, and then you'll have a clean slate."

"All right, Dad," he said one morning, "I'm ready now. I'm going down to Boston and turn myself in."

With the freshness that characterizes much of his thinking, however, Demara, on the way down, decided that he could do himself and his country a lot more good by fulfilling his patriotic duties outside of jail. Under the name of Fred W. Demara he enlisted in the Navy.

War or no war, he hated the Navy. After eight miserable weeks in boot camp he was assigned to the U.S.S. *Ellis*, a destroyer operating on the North Atlantic run. He began a massive campaign to get himself accepted at Hospital School and his letters were so frequent, urgent and annoying that he actually succeeded. He liked medicine at once. In the school he studied hard and did well. After graduating from the basic course Demara applied for advanced training. His request was turned down flat. The reason given was that he did not have a proper or adequate educational background.

The rejection stunned him. He was sitting in a servicemen's club musing on his low estate when a sailor next to him left his seat. On it lay a booklet—a catalogue from Iowa State College of Agriculture and Mechanics at Ames, Iowa. Demara began flipping idly through it when it occurred to him that everyone in that booklet had what he needed. Some of the people had whole little clusters of academic honors stringing along behind their names like glittering jewels.

"I hadn't had much experience in life, but I knew that those little letters automatically gave those people prestige and positions of authority," Demara explains. "As a patriotic gesture, I felt I had better steal some academic credits."

The very first thing he figured was that he would need some official stationery. This he stole from Captain T. D. Canfield, who was in command of his base. Then, from the Iowa State College catalogue he picked the name of a man who possessed reasonable credentials and who also was on leave to the Navy. On the captain's stolen stationery he wrote to the college registrar requesting a transcript of the man's grades. For the captain's address he used that of a gas station where he had paid a dollar for the privilege of using it as a mail drop and pickup.

A set of transcripts arrived a few days later. Demara went to work doctoring his papers. He had tried erasing and using ink remover and found them to be useless. He typed his name and other relevant information on plain white paper and then cut them out in thin strips and pasted these on top of the real information. As an example: where it said "Place of birth—Waterloo, Iowa," Demara pasted over "Lawrence, Massachusetts." At the bottom of the document he pasted an official-looking seal bought in a dime store and under it he wrote: "Certified copy. Original records must be held." To this he added the signature of the Iowa State registrar which he had cut off the bottom of the answering letter accompanying the transcripts. He photostated the bundle of documents and then deposited it and covering letters with the board of Naval officers in Norfolk.

During the wait for his commission, he used the time to perfect his crude forgery techniques and to collect the credentials of a whole host of people. He sent away for various college catalogues and went to work with enthusiasm.

A choice project became one Dr. Robert Linton French, who was a graduate of the University of Michigan where he had also earned his master's degree, was a Ph.D. from Stanford and had been a research fellow at Yale. "Why did I choose French? For one thing, I liked the name. It is French and yet, oddly, unmistakably English and I felt it suited me. Besides, I have *always* been willing to bask in the glory of a Ph.D."

Also during this time Demara got leave and went home to Lawrence, where one afternoon he walked brazenly into the parish rectory office and picked up every kind of stationery and document he could. He got baptismal and confirmation certificates and wedding papers; and on these he imprinted the parish seal.

On his way back to Norfolk he stayed over in Boston, presented himself at Cardinal O'Connell's residence as Dr. Robert Linton French and filched several pages of the cardinal's red stationery, although he couldn't get a single envelope.

At Norfolk, an officer said at a first hearing: "After routine security check-outs I think we'll be happy to give you a commission. A splendid background."

Splendid, indeed, Demara thought. He had far overplayed his hand. He waited for the covering darkness of evening and then went out along the Navy docks. There, at the end of a pier, he left a set of Navy clothes and a hat with his name printed in it and a note which went: "I have made a fool of myself. This is the only way out. Forgive me. F. W. Demara."

Then he started out of Norfolk, thumbing westward by night, with a whole fresh life ahead. For Demara was dead. He was now Dr. Robert Linton French, doctor of psychology and decommissioned officer in the U.S. Navy, at anyone's service.

An old, unrequited love returned to burn in his bosom. Almost irresistibly Demara found his path leading back to Gethsemani, a Trappist monastery in Kentucky where he had once spent a week in contemplation.

Demara presented himself at the portal as Dr. Robert L. French, a man who had experienced the futility of war and who desired to become a contemplative. He was taken directly to the abbot, the Right Reverend Frederick Dunne, who was impressed by the convert's background and sincerity. Until "French" could be baptized he was confined to Visitors' Quarters, but when that was done he was allowed to enter the novitiate.

When the Trappists are at services each brother has in front of him a huge songbook in which, in elaborate script, is all of the Gregorian plainsong that makes up the Divine Office of the day. It takes some men years to learn the contents of their book. The sign of a rookie is his need for a light behind him. The old hands sit in darkness. After several weeks, Demara one evening reached up and switched off his light. The old monks, into whose eyes his light had shone, were thankful. They also were amazed that he could master the ritual so quickly.

The first corrosion in Demara's spiritual armor was created by hunger. The sight of a horse munching grass disturbed him and the sight of a finch eating pumpkin seeds filled him with envious rage. He began dreaming about food at night and, finally, filching it by day.

Late in his first autumn, Demara was assigned to work in the vineyards with another brother who turned out to have as little willpower as he. They recognized each other with that sure instinct by which one con man working in an area recognizes another. By the end of their first day, the two not only were talking breathlessly while mulching the roots of the vines, they were eating the grapes around them as well.

It was almost inevitable, since the grapes had to be eaten while crouching over, that some of the juice would dribble out and down onto the white habit of Frater Mary Jerome—that was Demara's Gethsemani name, as it had been at Our Lady of the Valley. A great purple stain spread out across the top of his monk's habit. It was Demara's red badge of discouragement, his scarlet letter for all to read. And no amount of washing could out the damn spot.

There were other matters. Demara was caught talking constantly. Finally his partner in debasement went before the Chapter of Faults and detailed his association with Frater Mary Jerome. Demara later said: "I could have murdered that saintly bum. He was cleansing his soul, but he was sending me down the road to ruin doing it."

After those revelations there was nothing to do but seize the initiative. He arranged a hearing with Abbot Dunne. The sum of his conversation was that his stay at Gethsemani had been immensely informative but he realized he could best serve the Church in a more active fashion.

"I am glad that you came to that conclusion, Doctor," the Abbot said, not without what sounded like a threat in his voice. Despite his apparent disapproval of the doctor's career with the Trappists, however, the Abbot did write a short, rather noncommittal note introducing Demara to whatever order he next might move on to.

Demara headed for Chicago where an order of intellectuals called the Clerics of St. Viator run a seminary and school. With only 11 cents in his pocket, he went directly out to the provincial house and had an interview with a priest whose name was Father Richard French, which Demara, still as Dr. French, took to be a happy coincidence. From the very beginning he was a success with the Viatorians; and in Father French he found a man he could admire.

His first serious challenge came when it was announced that, despite his degrees, he was being entered in De Paul University for a graduate crash course in theology. Father French handed Demara his list of studies and Demara felt a sudden sinking sensation in the region around his heart. The list read: Rational Psychology, Metaphysics, Cosmology, Epistemology, Ethics, Natural Theology. But he tried hard and he studied hard and he did as was expected of him. His grades were brilliant. In all six courses, the man who in real life had not quite managed the second year of high school scored a record of straight A's.

A question that puzzles people is how Demara, with such a very limited background, avoided exposure during arguments and debates. "The reason is simple," he says, "I always lost the debate."

If he made a statement and it was challenged, Demara would ask, "How do *you* think it should go?" As the man explained, Demara would nod his head wisely and, at times, even take notes. This was high flattery indeed.

Another reason for his excellent grades might have been that he made sure to cover every one of his papers with a note written on small, expensive, discreet stationery. At the top of the paper his name and academic titles were listed and in the upper left-hand corner, always inked out by Demara so that you could barely read it, was—"By Appointment Only." Professors getting papers from a practicing Ph.D. in psychology might naturally be hesitant about grading him down.

And then there was his "official" stamp, a seal such as notary publics use. At the top of the impression was his name, at the bottom his occupation of psychologist and in the middle his motto: ESSE QUAM VIDERE. That was the most splendid joke of all. It means, "To be, not to seem to be."

About his background, wherever he was later to go, Demara discovered a very vital thing for his future. "I call it Demara's law for passing, or the invisible past. I never mention *anything*. Wherever I have left, people are suddenly amazed to find they don't know one thing about me—where I was supposed to have come from or been—when the police ask for specifics."

At the end of the highly successful school year at De Paul and with the Clerics of St. Viator, Father French announced that it was time for Dr. French to begin his full novitiate training with an eye toward taking his sacred vows for the priesthood. This would take place at the now-defunct St. Viator's college in central Illinois.

"But Father, I thought I could take it here," Demara protested. He was afraid of another novitiate. Equally persuasive, however, was boredom, for which Demara suffers a low threshold of tolerance. From his first day at St. Viator's college he ran afoul of the novice master, and each day grew worse. Finally Demara went back to Chicago, where he had a sad and tearful parting with Father French.

In early autumn of 1945, while millions of GI's were returning home, Demara, alias Dr. French, sought an interview with a new, fast-growing Catholic college in Erie, Pennsylvania, named Gannon. They said they would be delighted to set up a department of psychology with Dr. French in charge. The interview was an unqualified success. Monsignor Joseph Wehrle, who had been fearful of meeting some stiff, pompous windbag, was pleasantly surprised to be faced with an exuberant, obviously willing and energetic young man. Demara felt similarly toward the Right Reverend Wehrle.

"Oh, one other little thing," he said smoothly. "About my title."

"Oh, yes," Wehrle said and sat down. Both men thought for several minutes. "Well, you can't be president because I'm president," Wehrle finally said. "How about Chairman of the Department of Psychology?"

A disappointed look crossed Demara's face and they thought again. It was a fine and delicate point. "Considering the vast, inevitable growth of Gannon," Demara said softly, "wouldn't Dean of the School of Philosophy be more in keeping?"

He saw the monsignor stiffen slightly. "All right, I'm sold," the Right Reverend Wehrle said, holding out his hand. "*Dean* of the *School* of Philosophy it is."

Dr. French plunged into work with an enthusiasm rarely seen around a college outside of the football squad. He was willing to take on just about anything. By midyear the dean was teaching courses in general psychology, industrial psychology and abnormal psychology.

Monsignor Wehrle was delighted with his "catch," but as the months rolled by, he began to sense that instead of herding a brilliant lamb into the fold he was holding a tiger by the tail. The major complaint, as always, was that Demara went ahead on all kinds of grandiose projects and asked permission later.

The school had taken on as instructor a priest with bad lung trouble who could not climb stairs. Because of this, Wehrle reluctantly asked Dr. French to give up his large room on the second floor and move upstairs into a smaller, darker room. Soon after, Wehrle, at work in his office, was surprised to see a group of men struggle past his door and upstairs with what appeared to be a rug. Soon after that he heard pounding noises and later another group

73

of men grunted by with a large crate. When the pounding continued into early evening he went up to investigate. The third floor had never looked like that.

The hall was carpeted and above French's door was a sign announcing his office. Inside, the room was carpeted prettily from wall to wall. On top of the rug was a great, gleaming, blond maple desk. Behind the desk was Demara.

"Delighted you could drop by," Demara said. "Now you can answer this: Should the desk stay where it is or should I put it by the window?"

Wehrle was taken aback by the luxurious modern furniture, but then he recalled the rumors of French's wealth and assumed that French was paying for the furnishings. "I would leave it where it is," he said cheerfully and went back downstairs. In the ensuing days, a typewriter, a couch, new drapes and an enormous cherry-wood bed were delivered. And finally, a large, gray, double-doored steel safe, much bigger than the one the college owned, arrived for French's office.

As far as Gannon and the new dean were concerned, Dr. French had arrived. But so had the bills—a stack of them, all made out to Gannon in Monsignor Wehrle's name. After a fierce showdown with Monsignor Wehrle, Demara moved off into the soft spring night, feeling as low and mean and miserable as he ever had before in his life.

The heat of summer made Demara's mind turn to the cool greens of the Pacific Northwest and he finally found the ideal place. It was St. Martin's Abbey and College, run by the Benedictines in Olympia, Washington, just outside of Seattle. He determined, for the first time in his life, to make a careful, plotted, scientific assault on St. Martin's. With little trouble, he joined the Benedictines, and now he determined to exercise two precepts he had learned. One was that in any organization there is always a lot of loose, unused power lying about which can be picked up without alienating anyone. The second was that if you want power and want to expand, never encroach on anyone else's domain;

open up new ones. "I call it 'expanding into the power vacuum,' "
Demara proudly explains.

At the beginning of the school year Demara struck hard into the
power vacuum. Without waiting for approval, he commandeered a
schoolroom, had it decorated and organized the St. Martin's
Student Psychological Center. The center offered a series of lectures by Dr. French on basic psychology and private psychological sessions for students needing help. He also expanded out
into public life. He noted that his fellow monks had little touch with
the outside, and he felt they needed a go-between with the town.

Few politicians could resist the cheerful monk. He became
especially close to Sheriff Frank Tamblyn, who was soon to be
running for reelection and saw in Demara a nice link with both
the Catholic and the egghead vote.

During this time, the abbot of St. Martin's, the Right Reverend
Raphael Heider, had gone East to attend an educational conference, and it was while he was there that he heard some disquieting
things about "Dr. French" and determined to put him under
close watch. When a monk reported to the Abbot that he had
watched Dr. French consume a full quart of whiskey without so
much as batting an eye, Abbot Heider sent out letters checking up
on Demara.

Demara was sitting in his cubicle, preparing a one-minute
recorded campaign speech for Sheriff Tamblyn (one was already
being played all over Thurston County), when a monk appeared
and said that the Abbot would like to see him. In the Abbot's
office he wasn't surprised to see Sheriff Tamblyn there, since the
two men had become close friends. The presence of the other two
strangers, however, did puzzle him.

"Good to see you, Frank," he said heartily. "Got the speech all
shipshape and ready to go."

"Good to see *you, Ferdinand,*" one of the strangers said.

There was no reaction evident on Demara's face. He simply
stood stunned and blank. He watched one of the men open and
close a wallet, and he realized that this was federal business—the

FBI. For some reason he had completely forgotten the military charges, perhaps because, of all the things against him, they were the worst.

"Desertion!" one of the men said.

"In time of war," the second added.

"The penalty is death," the first said sadly.

The charge *was* desertion in time of war, and the penalty *was* death.

"It was much too important to be left in the hands of lawyers," says Demara. "I felt I was familiar with all those little twists and veerings in my career that would only baffle a Navy lawyer. What I needed was a kind of honest liar. I was the exact man for the job of defense counsel."

He was given a copy of the judge advocate's file, a copy of the Navy Code and a booklet which proved to be a cram course in instant legal defense. After a week of study he found his plea: guilty with mitigating circumstances.

His plan was to throw himself on the mercy of the court and leave his soul in their, and God's, hands. He told them how, as a young lad just fresh out of a Trappist monastery, on an impulse of pure and idealistic patriotism, he joined the Navy. There, instead of finding the idealistic men he had hoped to meet, he fell into the company of hardened, salty, foul-talking seamen. With a trace of tears and a struggling hoarseness, he told how he had fraudulently tried to become an officer and a gentleman in the vain hope that he might avoid the sordid, corrupt and degrading role that was straining the limits of his soul. Failing at that, in the end he had run to the sheltering arms of Gethsemani, where he belonged.

Fred Demara was found guilty with mitigating circumstances. From a tough court-martial, he got a sentence of six years, one for each year of desertion. He served his term (cut down on review to 18 months because of good attitude and behavior) "standing on his head," as is said about an easy stretch. His rehabilitation was considered to be so effective that the Army, when it finally caught up with Demara at San Pedro, dropped charges. After a year and a half in jail, Demara was given his discharge. It was a dishonorable one.

As prodigal sons go, he got as good a reception in Lawrence, Massachusetts, as he could have expected. To his family he said, "I have paid my debt and now I am clear. But some of the places I was in and some of the things I did would have made you all very proud of me."

In September, Demara presented himself as a candidate for first-year law courses at the School of Law of Northeastern University as Dr. Cecil Boyce Hamann, a professor whose name and background he had learned about quite accidentally. But although his grades were good, he was driven to despair by the long hours of study.

One day, at the end of the summer of 1950, Demara left Northeastern and headed for Alfred, Maine, where he appeared unannounced at the Brothers of Christian Instruction. Would they be interested in a convert who was a Ph.D. from Purdue; a zoologist whose specialty was cancer research?

The brothers were overwhelmed. So overwhelmed, in fact, that Demara also announced that he would be delighted to join their humble order. Immediately he began putting into effect a plan to change the brothers' junior college into a full-fledged formal college. But before the plan got off the ground, he was informed that the time had come for him to report to the novice house— a farmhouse between St. Leonard and Grand Falls, New Brunswick—some 300 frosty miles north of Portland, Maine.

"It was a fantastic place. They had me, Dr. Hamann, out in the potato patches digging spuds at ten below zero!" Demara recalls.

The boredom that might have crushed him was made bearable by his contact with young, Canadian-born, Harvard-educated Dr. Joseph Cyr. Winter-locked in the almost snowbound village, the two men became friends, and Demara mined the young doctor for medical information. Near the end of his novitiate year, Demara told Cyr he might be of help in getting Cyr a license to practice in the States.

"You give me your records and credentials, and I can, Doctor," Demara said. Dr. Cyr went into the next room and began sorting through piles of papers.

"Put in everything," Demara called out. "Baptism, confirmation, high-school grades. Everything."

Cyr soon returned with a large packet of papers that weighed nearly a pound.

"I don't think you'll have reason to regret it," Demara said.

In the second week of March 1951, Demara headed for St. John, New Brunswick, with the aim of presenting himself for a commission as a doctor in the Royal Canadian Navy, using the name and documents of Dr. Cyr.

When Demara, alias Dr. Cyr, reported to the recruiting office, he was placed aboard a special Navy plane and flown to Ottawa and, on the very next afternoon, presented before the medical-officer selection board. He was asked a series of rather general questions which were directed toward finding out if he might just be thinking of using the RCN boys as practice patients to perfect his surgery or as potential proof of any theories. They found that Dr. Cyr had no strong or advanced theories about anything in medicine. He was returned to St. John, where he was entered into the Royal Canadian Navy and was commissioned a surgeon lieutenant. On March 19, Demara was formally assigned to duty in the RCN hospital in the Navy port of Halifax.

Demara's first duty was to take sick call each morning at the base. This can, of course, be a terribly important responsibility if a patient reports in with something like spinal meningitis. Demara did a smart thing. He went to his superior as an enlightened, intellectually curious, eager man with a problem.

"I've been asked by some people to work up a rule-of-thumb guide for the people in lumber camps. Could we get together a little guide that would pretty well cover most serious situations?" he queried.

To the lieutenant's superior, as Demara had hoped, this was a challenge and a pleasure. For two days he went through his books, culling and refining a basic code for the amateur diagnostician, and finally gave it to Demara, who made a copy of the code and followed it faithfully. This guided him correctly, as far as he knows, through most of his Navy career. And then he was sold on antibiotics. Whenever he saw a sore throat, heard a serious-sounding cough or saw someone who looked very ill, he rammed them full of penicillin and, after that, with whatever miracle drugs happened to be current and choice. If the patient persisted in staying sick, Fred would manage to maneuver him to any one of six or seven other doctors, using each one as sparingly as possible.

In May, however, Demara was shifted to duty on H.M.C.S. *Magnificent*, an aircraft carrier anchored in Halifax Bay. There was no other doctor aboard to question, only a rather stiff, stern command medical officer who would come around each evening. The CMO was not impressed with his new junior officer. Lieutenant Cyr, he wrote in a report, "lacked training in medicine and surgery, especially in diagnosis."

When Demara eventually heard of the CMO's uncomplimentary report he devised a marvelous system. Any patient about whom he wasn't certain or who seemed to offer complications, he hid. Without bothering to tell anyone higher than a boatswain's mate, he commandeered several seamen's rooms down in the bowels of the ship. On these he tacked up quarantine signs and into them he put his questionable patients. He worked on the theory that God was on the side of the big battalions and doctors who used quarts of penicillin.

"Swamp the enemy was my motto," he says. "Before I took the job I had done my research and one thing made me feel better; with or without medical care, outside of war and accidents and such things as lung cancer, no one—no strong man—actually dies anymore." Demara really seems to believe this.

One warm, surprising day in June, he meticulously dressed in his fresh, new officer whites and took the *Magnificent* launch into Halifax harbor. Sunshine washed the bricks of the harbor houses, and the park, when he passed, was bathed in the goldness of it.

The grass was green against the lemon drops of dandelions and banks of unfulfilled daffodils. On the grass, a Navy nurse sat. She was serene and beautiful, and Lieutenant Fred Demara fell in love with her at once.

He climbed over the low iron fence and began trotting toward her as if they had had a date of long standing, and only when he stood in front of her did he realize that she wasn't looking back at him and that he had nothing to say. He finally knelt down beside her and picked a dandelion.

"The most underrated flower in the world," he said, and he was delighted and thrilled when she seemed to smile in agreement.

She didn't answer but it didn't frighten him. There was no need to talk or answer and that was the way she handled it. Finally, she said, "Do you know what the name means?"

He thought for a moment and said, "It's from the French. *Dande de lion*, mane of the lion, because the flower looks like the mane of the lion."

"That's really very imaginative of you," she said, smiling. "It's *dent de lion*, tooth of the lion, because of the jagged leaves. But yours is much better."

That afternoon the citizens of Halifax were treated to the unusual sight of two Royal Navy officers dancing down the streets of town, hand in hand, singing at the top of their voices something about falling in love being wonderful. And it was.

There was a complication, however. Catherine (that was her name) was due to be discharged from the service and, as women in love are wont to feel, she wanted to be married—soon.

But who was in love with Catherine, anyway? Was it the Navy officer, handsome and clean in his whites, or was it really the dismal failure from the dismal Massachusetts mill town? For Demara there was, as much as he regretted it, only one solution—one he had used so often before that he turned to it instinctively without planning it. Escape. He went down to Naval headquarters and there he begged to be sent into action in Korea at once.

It was a glorious day in August when Surgeon Lieutenant Joseph

Cyr received his orders to report to CANAVHED (Naval Headquarters at Esquimalt, British Columbia) for assignment in Korean waters. Catherine rode all the way to Winnipeg with him before she had to leave and take a plane back to Halifax, and they were never closer or happier with each other.

At Vancouver, Demara took the ferry across the Strait of Georgia to Esquimalt, where he was told to report to His Majesty's Canadian Ship *Cayuga*—a destroyer—as medical officer. The lives of 211 seamen and 8 officers were in his hands. "May God help us all now," he whispered when the order was put in his hand.

No sooner had Demara stepped aboard the *Cayuga* than he was summoned to the captain's cabin.

"Lieutenant Cyr," the executive officer said, "this is your new captain, Commander Plomer."

Demara started to smile. The sight of the captain made him want to go into a dance. The commander's jaw was swollen to the size of a small melon. He obviously was the victim of several infected teeth.

"Glad haff you 'board," the commander mumbled. "Now pull these damn things. Thass order."

Demara peered into the officer's mouth for a moment. "I'll just zip down to my quarters and arrange my gear, sir. Have them out in a minute."

The moment he was in his cabin, he made a leap for his books. There was, amazingly enough to him, not a single word about teeth. The minute stretched out into an interminable quarter of an hour. Still, Demara leafed through pages, by now not really looking but merely doing something to stop from thinking.

He could hear people milling out in the passageway, grumbling and impatient, and he had to experiment and practice squirting Novocain from a syringe while his hands trembled. He loaded his largest hypodermic to the top, seized the biggest pair of forceps he could find, and started for the door.

"Oh Captain! my Captain! our fearful trip is done!"—before it ever began, Demara recalls thinking.

"What's the matter, anyway?" the exec demanded. "It's only a tooth, isn't it, Doc?"

"It's a lot more than that, I fear," Demara said sadly.

In Plomer's office he went directly to the captain, forced open his jaws and began to operate. "Whush that!" Plomer managed to gasp when his eye caught the syringe.

"Look, Commander. You run your ship, and I'll run my sick bay. Right?"

"Right," Plomer said.

Demara let loose the contents of the syringe and waited. "Feel anything?" he asked. He tapped around the swollen area and then he tapped all around the officer's head. There was apparently no feeling anywhere. The time was ripe. He took the forceps, found the obviously bad tooth and, wincing as he went, he pulled. It came so easily that he nearly fell backward into the cabin's wall. The second came as easily.

"Nicest job of tooth pulling I've ever had," Plomer cried the next day. "Glad to have you aboard, Cyr."

"Prouder than ever to be aboard, sir," Fred said.

Dr. Cyr's popularity as a messmate was instant and immense. "The reason for it was simple," he explains. "I wasn't afraid to lie for the men. They appreciated that no end. I am a superior sort of liar. I don't tell any truth at all, so then my story has a unity of parts, a structural integrity, and this way sounds more like the truth than truth itself."

In September the *Cayuga*, after refitting in Japan, sailed into Korean waters. They drifted down along the east coast of Korea, north of the 38th parallel, keeping a check on North Korean shore operations. For them it was a quiet, almost lazy war in which the worst casualty Demara had to treat was the burned hand of some seaman who forgot and picked up a red-hot shell casing.

But late one afternoon in September, on a rough and choppy day, the *Cayuga* pulled up close alongside a small Korean junk, and the men looked down at a pitiable sight. On the wet, matted floor of the junk, sprawled in filth and blood, lay a cargo of wounded Koreans. Some of them must have been in great agony but none of them showed a trace of it.

"Tell them," he heard Plomer say to the Korean liaison officer, "that the doctor's here. Tell them that they're going to be all right now, the doctor's here. You willing, Joe?" he asked Demara. "It's not required."

Demara climbed over the side and looked down again. The men in the junk—most of them boys—were smiling up at him. Their patience and courage in the face of pain and hopelessness still remain his strongest memory of Korea.

Three of the 19 soldiers were seriously hurt. All of them, unless they received competent surgery within the next day, would certainly die. Demara felt he had no choice. He cleaned and sutured and worked over the 16, and, as he did, some of his confidence came back. He could make incisions, he could clamp off bleeding, he could handle sutures. What did he fear?

He knew perfectly well what he feared—the internal structure of the human body which he had never seen before; the internal life of man, where one clumsy mistake, one shred of ignorance, could cause him, for all purposes, to become a murderer.

For several hours he worked in the small ship's sick bay, caught up in what he was doing, happy to find he was handling himself swiftly and professionally in front of the eyes of crew members. But never before had he felt, at the same instance, such an impostor and such a complete, lonely, isolated fraud. There was no place to run and no place to dodge and no assurance that he could find inside of himself the courage or whatever ingredient it would take to begin internal surgery on the three Koreans who lay on bunks drugged by heavy doses of morphine.

Demara went down to the mess, where he opened the rum locker. He dealt himself four ounces of raw Barbados rum and let it burn its way down into his stomach. He didn't know why it helped. He wasn't drunk or even relaxed, but the drinking was something akin to a ritual that gave him some new reason for daring to begin again.

"Commander Plomer," he said, "I'm going to risk it. The sick bay is too small for major surgery. I'm going to have to commandeer your cabin. Have four seamen get everything out that can be gotten out, have them scrub the place from top to bottom and then have them go over everything with rubbing alcohol or disinfectant. I'll be preparing the patients."

Father Ward and Hotchin, the medical assistant, would help, but that was scant solace. Neither of them had ever even assisted at an operation before. Demara went back to sick bay and began preparing for the surgery. Just as long as he kept active, the fluttery feeling in his stomach—which showed in his hands and in the twitching of a muscle over his right eye—did not bother him. Hotchin undressed, shaved and washed down each of the Koreans and kept them well doped with morphine. Demara sterilized his instruments, almost all of which he had never had a chance to use. Some of them he could never recall even holding. He balanced the scalpel in his hand.

"We're ready now, Doctor," a young seaman whispered over his shoulder and the shock of it nearly made him cry out.

"We'll take the worst one now," Demara said. He really did not want to know which one it was. Let the choice of the victim be up to fate or chance or ignorance.

"This is the worst one," Hotchin said. "Whatever hit him didn't come out. It's in there and it's trouble. He's hemorrhaging."

How did the boy know that? Demara wondered. The thought that he did suddenly made Demara feel much relieved. As he injected the tube which would carry the anesthetic, in this case an infusion of sodium pentathol, into the vein of the Korean, the soldier stirred and mumbled something which was heard by the Korean liaison officer.

"What did he say?" Demara asked.

"Well, he's only a peasant boy, you know."

"What is it?" Demara demanded.

"He said," the interpreter said to him shyly, " 'May God guide your hand.' "

"You can tell him that I just made the same prayer."

Then Demara lowered his cold scalpel onto the cold skin of the soldier, and began drawing the blade across his chest. He made a straight, horizontal line, following the course of the ribs. Where had he learned to do that? he wondered.

It was strange and marvelous and exhilarating. The knife moved easily, surely, in his hand. It was as if he were now playing out some part which had been predetermined. He knew exactly what he was doing and what he was going to do. "We've hit the bleeders," he mumbled to Ward. "He's going to bleed now. I'll need a sponge." He saw the first blood vessel he would have to tie off.

"I'll need a hemostat now. That clamp. That clamp there. Yes. That one, the clamp." He clamped the vessel and then tied it off, clumsily and slowly, but neatly, with catgut. "Rib spreaders," he said softly.

Demara had never seen rib spreaders used and had no idea how to use them, but when he found them among the surgical equipment he knew at once how to handle them. He exerted traction on the ribs and they spread and beneath them he could see the pericardial sac and the heart which was pounding furiously.

"Look at it," Demara said. The idea that he had exposed a living, beating heart and the man still lived thrilled him. "Look at it beat." The massive muscle, the pulsating blood pump rose and fell. "It makes one believe again in God," he said.

"God help me. *Blood!*" he suddenly called out. They had been neglecting to give the man blood and he had been bleeding badly. Hotchin set up a plasma transfusion.

Demara probed the pericardium and then he felt the object. It was metal and, by the shape of it, it was the lead nose of a bullet. At that moment, his objectivity seemed to leave him. He had been lucky and he had been a fake. He now realized suddenly that he didn't have one single idea, or intuition even, whether to leave the bullet where it was and rely upon nature eventually to heal the wound or to extract it and in all probability cause a hemorrhage that must kill the man.

The area near the bullet was still bleeding and that was bad. He took a syringe and put the needle in the blood and drew it out. When he had cleaned the area in this fashion he could see the tip of metal.

He looked at the darkness of the metal and the blood that once more was beginning to flow around it. Quite suddenly, he reached over for a forceps, luckily got a purchase on the metal and yanked. It resisted at first, but then quickly and easily slid out of the pericardium leaving, for a brief moment, a cavity and then more blood oozing in.

"Gelfoam," he cried. "Where is the Gelfoam?"

"In your hand, in your hand, in your hand," Father Ward cried. Gelfoam is a coagulant, and Demara flooded the wound with it. Then they waited for the sign of blood.

"If you have ever prayed very hard for anything before, Father, will you begin praying harder that this doesn't hemorrhage?"

"I've been praying, Doctor, like I've never prayed before. It's really been sort of a miracle, hasn't it?"

"You really don't know how much of a miracle it's been," Demara answered.

There was no blood. No hemorrhage. This human would live.

The rest was easy. His main worry was not to leave a clamp or sponge inside the soldier, so filled with Gelfoam was the wound. But Hotchin had had someone counting the instruments and they tallied. The going out was long and tiring because Demara was slow and crude with the sutures and his hands, unaccustomed to the strain, were tired. But two hours after he had begun, his first patient was taken away.

The next two patients were more rudimentary. One of the two had a bad shell-splinter wound in the groin area. The main problem was to clean the wound, to cut away sections of flesh, tie off a suspicious vessel and then sew up the area into reasonable shape and bandage it properly so that when it healed no muscle deformity would develop, causing the man to become a cripple.

What Demara felt to be the worst among the cases was actually the least bad. The wound was cleaner than it appeared, and the patient's chief complaint was that he couldn't puff properly on a cigarette. Demara says that he recognized this as a partial collapsing of the lung, possibly caused by a fragment of rib penetrating the lung wall. To alleviate that he took a long needle, and, using only a local anesthetic so that he could tell by the patient's reaction what effect he was making, he succeeded quite easily in creating a total collapse of the left lung.

During all of this, Demara never once noticed how much time was elapsing and he never once noticed the pitch and toss of the *Cayuga*. At last, they turned out the bank of emergency lights and he was dumfounded to see the faces of crew members pressed against every porthole. He was also amazed to see that it was light outside. He had gone through the night and it was early morning. He knew that it was obvious, but he could not resist making the Churchillian sign of victory, and the men cheered their doctor with a wild, spontaneous cheer.

With this and subsequent exploits, publicity reached the real Dr. Cyr in Canada. A Naval inquiry followed, in which it was discovered that Dr. Cyr was Dr. Hamann who was actually Dr. French who was really Fred W. Demara. While in the Navy as Cyr, however, under his own initiative, Demara managed to get a license to practice medicine in England and all the countries in the British Commonwealth. He also had a license pending in the United States.

On November 12, Demara appeared in full dress before a board of inquiry in Esquimalt. In the words of the Navy: "This inquiry was exceedingly short." It was possibly the shortest trial in history.

"Do you wish to make a statement about the allegation that you are not the man that you represented yourself to be?"

"Yes. I did enter the RCN under false pretenses and under a false name."

"What are your medical qualifications?"

"I'd rather let that go if I may, please. I am perfectly willing to be turned over to the civilian authorities for whatever action they may wish to take. I have hurt the Navy enough. I might add that I am a doctor."

"This being true, you are summarily discharged from the Navy."

In the afternoon mail, a letter arrived from Catherine: "Oh yes, you know how terribly hurt I was when I first found out about you, dear Joe. But then something strange happened to me. I woke up this morning, my Joe, and knew that nothing had changed. No matter what your name is, I am in love with *you*. Don't you see how simple it is? How simple and funny it is? I love you, not a name. I love you. . . ."

Instead of replying, Demara got drunk. Whenever the pain of reality and the memory of Catherine thrust itself on him, he pushed it out again by numbing his ability to remember or think. He was drunk in Seattle and Salt Lake City and in Chicago. He doesn't know how he got back to Lawrence but when he did, he was broke.

Without telling his family, he contacted a magazine and gave their writer a long interview. For this, he received $2500, of which he gave $2000 to his father and mother as a present. The resulting article was later to prove quite embarrassing.

Demara began rambling across the country, and it is axiomatic that when you are rambling—you sooner or later hit Texas. While thumbing through the Houston *Chronicle* one night, he happened upon the news that there were some openings for lowly positions in the Department of Corrections, a euphemism for the Texas prison system.

He applied for a job as a prison guard under the name of Ben W. Jones. For references, Demara supplied the names of a number of his previous aliases and manipulated the addresses so that the questionnaires were eventually forwarded to him in Houston. After he had filled out his own questionnaires, notarized them with his own seal and routed them back to the prison, it was no time at all before Demara was told that he could begin at once as lieutenant of the guard. After a week, he was transferred from active guard to recreation officer in charge of setting up a recreation program.

Captain Ben Jones organized letter-writing sessions for illiterates. He set up checker and domino tournaments and the winner's prize was a half day off from the fields. He tried unsuccessfully to set up a study period and finally he asked for, and got, a Ping-Pong table. A request was in for movies. To the watching director of the Department of Corrections, Mr. O. B. Ellis, it was a heartening enterprise.

"How would you like to come to the prison at Huntsville and work in maximum security?" Ellis asked. "It's the toughest of the tough."

The place was run exactly like a den of lions held at bay by a breathless combination of force, fear and wit. Into this den strode Daniel.

"I found," Demara recalls, "that almost all the time men will act about as good as you expect them to act. If you treat them like animals they'll act that way. Or like children. I saw that in the service. If you treat them with respect, then they try to act that way. I wanted to set up the idea that this prison was my house and they were my guests."

Very early the first serious incident happened. A boy who had crossed a guard in some fashion wouldn't come out of his cell. He stood in the rear of his cell and held a little spoon knife in front of him. Demara could see he was scared but that isn't always a solace. A scared man can be unreliable.

"Open the door," Demara ordered.

"Don't come in here, Cap'n. I got nothin' on you but I'll cut you." He looked almost sadly at Demara. "I got to cut you," he explained. The ancient code must be honored.

"No you won't, son. Not if I don't have a weapon," he spelled out. It was true that no one had ever tried that approach.

The boy tossed that one in his mind, still holding the knife ahead of him as if it were something alive that might jump and bite him. Demara bulked through the door.

"Now, before we talk about this, hand me that knife," he said.

"I can't *give* you the knife," the boy said. "That's going too far."

89

"Then I'll take the knife away. That fair?"

"Yes, sir. That's fair."

Demara suddenly reached out and got the boy's wrist with his powerful grip. He pushed the boy back to the wall and squeezed and knocked the wrist against it until the knife clattered to the floor and he kicked it out into the hall.

"Now we can talk, right?"

"Yes, sir. Now we can talk," the boy said. He was far happier about it than Demara.

Ben W. Jones, with Ellis' permission, began to establish new methods in maximum. Granted that the men were being punished, he argued, they had to have some way to work off their punishment and regain self-respect. He got movies for them and he began having schooling organized. He also established a schedule so the men could feel that the day had a ritual and a movement to it. B. W. Jones was establishing himself as one of the new liberal penologists who yet seemed to have his feet on the ground.

"I can't deny it and I don't see why I should," O. B. Ellis says. "B. W. or Demara or whatever it is you call him was one of the best prospects ever to serve in this prison system. His future was bright, if not almost unlimited. I can say this—if he could only appear again with some legitimate credentials, and somehow this past was wiped out, I'd be proud to hire the man again."

One afternoon, a young prisoner was lying on his bunk after lunch, leafing through a magazine.

"I'll be a three-horned, mean-eyed, long-lifed bastard," he shouted. "Oh, this is great, man. Great."

There was no question that the man billed in the article as "The Great Impostor" was their own Ben W. Jones.

A meeting was called at the home of Mr. Ellis and the top people in the prison attended. Demara was sent for, and when he strode in, Ellis held up the pages from the old magazine. "Is this you, Ben? Are you really Ferdinand Demara?"

"Why, no," he said, with an incredulous, quizzical look. He then proceeded to give one of the most smashing performances of his career, denying everything and accusing his accusers of taking a prisoner's word against his. "If there is still any among you who feel I am guilty of this accusation I'd like to ask him to rise and face me now," he concluded. "I will meet him at any time and in any fashion he chooses. My honor dictates that I can do no less. Everyone knows where I can be found."

At the door he slipped on his new five-gallon cattleman's hat which he had gotten that day in Houston. He hoped it gave him the hard, resolute look he admired in a man.

"Good night, Mr. Ellis. Good night to all of you gentlemen, and may God help you."

While the stunned audience debated what to do, back at his home on the prison farm, Demara went quickly to work. In 20 minutes he had loaded his car in a wild, slapdash fashion and headed for the main highway, with his lights off. "How many times I have died and how many times I have been orphaned," he has said.

Demara went home to Lawrence.

Contrary to what Demara had always believed—that he would get some mysterious premonition when there was serious trouble at home and he was needed—he had received not even a faint suggestion that while he was in Texas his father had died.

Ferdinand Demara now had a feeling that a major phase of his life had closed, and also that with the fiasco out of Texas he had lost his last chance to accomplish anything big or meaningful or even really decent.

"I had no way to repent. Wherever I turned, people forgave me, because they were too understanding or, worse, they just didn't care. Here I was, a martyr to a compulsion that was killing me, and there was no executioner at hand."

Under his own name, he got a job working in a children's home in western Massachusetts but that didn't last long. He was soon known and he left. He then signed on as Frank Kingston in a school for mentally retarded children in Brooklyn, New York.

Although he liked what he was doing, his old enemy, boredom, reappeared. Then, on the radio one afternoon. Demara heard about the predicament of North Haven School, destined to be teacherless out in the cold and cheerless waters off Maine. By judicious use of New York State Department of Education stationery, which he stole, and Brooklyn College papers, which he borrowed, Demara managed to acquire the completely adequate credentials of Martin Godgart.

The arrest of Demara on North Haven by Troopers Nickerson and Milligan has already been told. Some months after Demara's release, newspapers all over the country blossomed with stories about Ferdinand W. Demara, Jr. And afterward he appeared on television as the guest of Jack Paar.

Just a short time before this story was completed, I received a phone call from an unidentified place.

"I'm on the biggest caper of them all. Oh, I wish I could tell you," Demara's voice said on the other end. "I wanted you to know, anyway, that I'm doing *good* things."

"Good for you or for humanity?"

"Why, shame on you. For both of us, of course. Apart from Catherine I've never been more happy or excited."

Even as he said that I sensed I had lost contact with him.

"Apart from Catherine. . . ." I heard him repeat, but in that strange, withdrawn, lost way he can assume. There was a very long pause since neither of us knew what to say.

"I'm working on that difficult part of the story," I finally said, and at once wished that I hadn't.

"What part?" he growled. He knew.

"Where you tell me *why*," I said.

In a voice as cold and as dark as the night air outside my window he said, "Because I am a rotten man."

I was silent.

"All right," he said. "Tell them this, then. I have thought it out and I believe it's truth. It's rascality, pure rascality!"

He hung up and I stood there thinking, because it occurred to me that that is perhaps exactly what he is: the champion rascal of his age; one of the last sad playboys of the western world.

I was wrong. Later I learned that he had gone to Divinity college and graduated. Now he is an ordained minister of the Gospel, pastor of a church in the Pacific Northwest.

SUCH IS the state of political morality in Japan that few Japanese parliamentarians can summon up, even for the record, any show of indignation at a tasty bit of bribery or peculation. In the 1960's a notable exception to this rule was Shoji Tanaka, an irascible, 63-year-old member of the lower house of the Japanese Diet. As chairman of the Diet's Audit Committee— the government's fiscal watchdog—Tanaka loudly and fearlessly attacked bureaucrats and businessmen whom he suspected of wrongdoing. And his flamboyant behavior so cowed his colleagues in the Diet that it was said they feared Tanaka as much as they did the three traditional Japanese evils of fire, earthquake and thunder.

Suddenly, however, Tanaka's thunder fell silent. Dressed in a light summer kimono and slippers, the pudgy politician was picked up by detectives at Tokyo's Juntendo Hospital, where he was being treated for gout, gangrene and diabetes, and led away to prison. There he was booked on two charges of suspected fraud and one of suspected extortion. He allegedly extracted an estimated $695,000 from three prominent Tokyo businessmen.

A man with an enormous passion for possessions, Tanaka fathered 21 children by nine women and maintained seven separate residences in Tokyo. In addition, he owned a small hot-spring hotel and a sprawling ranch where he employed 100 people and bred thoroughbred horses. (One of Tanaka's dreams, in fact, was to win the English Derby; he invested some $1.4 million in something called the Ireland Tanaka Stud, which was headquartered in a lovely 17th-century castle 200 miles north of Dublin.) Police said Tanaka controlled no fewer than 16 businesses in Japan and was personally worth almost $3 million. Yet, he paid taxes only on his Diet salary of $8556 a year —and many of his companies failed to file tax returns at all.

To a foreigner, the most puzzling aspect of the Tanaka case is that anyone in Japan was surprised by it. A convicted extortionist before he was 30, Tanaka celebrated his first electoral victory in 1949 in a jail cell—where he had been sent for buying votes. This time, in prison, Tanaka announced that he was through with political life.   —*Newsweek*

A large part of the city was fired up by
the old man's marvelous project

SAWING-OFF
OF MANHATTAN ISLAND

by Herbert Asbury

One of the most extraordinary hoaxes ever perpetrated in New York originated almost 150 years ago in the fertile imagination of a little dried-up old man called Lozier, who had become a successful carpenter and contractor, then retired to enjoy life. For almost two months during the summer of 1824 Lozier's fantastic activities—which he carried on with the enthusiastic assistance of John DeVoe, a retired butcher better known as Uncle John—kept a considerable portion of New York in a frenzy of excitement.

In those early days, when the present American metropolis was a comparatively small city of 150,000 people, a favorite loafing place was the Centre Market at Grand and Centre Streets. A dozen long benches lined the Grand Street side of the market, and every afternoon from spring to winter they were filled with amateur statesmen, principally retired butchers and other small-business men, most of whom combined scant knowledge with excessive gullibility. Chief among them were Lozier and Uncle John DeVoe. Lozier did most of the talking at the daily forums in front of the market and was invariably able to produce a definite and apparently practicable remedy for every conceivable financial, political or economic ill. He was always listened to with enormous respect, for he was wealthy, possessed more education than his fellows and was a recognized traveler, having made several voyages to Europe as a ship's carpenter. There was no lack of subjects to talk about, for those were lively times. The first great wave of Irish immigration had begun to beat against American shores as a result of the potato famine of 1822; Brazil and Mexico had thrown off the shackles of Portugal and Spain; the first steamship had crossed the Atlantic only a few years before; President James Monroe had just promulgated the Monroe Doctrine; and Mrs. Monroe had almost precipitated a revolution in New York and Washington society by announcing that as the First Lady of the Land she would no longer return social calls. The gifted Lozier professed to know the inside stories of all these momentous events, and so convincing was he that there were many who believed that he was high in the confidence not only of the President but of foreign potentates as well.

Early in July 1824, Lozier was absent from his accustomed bench for several days, an unparalleled occurrence which aroused much comment. When he returned, he refused to join in the flow of conversation and even declined to settle arguments. He talked only to Uncle John DeVoe, but for the most part sat alone, brooding, obviously concerned with weighty matters. When his friends asked where he had been, and sought diligently to learn what mighty thoughts troubled his mind, he would at first divulge no information. At length, however, he admitted that he had been at City Hall in consultation with Mayor Stephen Allen. No one doubted the truth of this statement, which caused even more talk than had his absence. In those days the Mayor of New York was not so approachable as now, and a man who had been summoned by His Honor automatically became a person of considerable importance. For almost a week Lozier kept his friends and admirers on tenterhooks of curiosity. Finally, on a day when all the market benches were occupied and he was thus assured of an audience, he made a full and complete explanation.

It appeared that Lozier and Mayor Allen had had a long conversation about Manhattan Island and had reached the conclusion that it was much too heavy on the Battery end, because of the many large buildings. The situation was rapidly becoming dangerous. Already the island had begun to sag, as was plain from the fact that it was all downhill from City Hall, and there were numerous and alarming indications that it might break off and sink into the sea, with appalling losses of life and property. Lozier and the Mayor had decided, therefore, that the island must be sawed off at Kingsbridge, at the northern end, and turned around, so that the Kingsbridge end would be where the Battery end had been. The Battery end, of course, if it did not fall off in transit, would take the place of the Kingsbridge end. Once the turn had been made, the weaker end of the island would be anchored to the mainland, thus averting the danger of collapse.

When the conferences at City Hall began, it further appeared, Lozier and Mayor Allen were not in complete agreement as to the best method of accomplishing the mighty task. The Mayor thought that before Manhattan could be turned around it would be necessary to detach Long Island from its moorings and tow it out of the way, returning it later to its proper place. Lozier finally convinced him, however, that there was ample space in the harbor and the bay. It was at length decided, therefore, simply to saw Manhattan Island off, float it down past Governors and Ellis islands, turn it around, and then float it back to its new position. For political reasons Mayor Allen wished the job to appear as a private undertaking and had turned the whole project over to Lozier.

Such were the force of Lozier's personality, the power of his reputation and the credulity of his generation that practically none who heard him questioned the feasibility of the scheme. The few who were inclined to scoff were soon silenced, if not actually convinced, by his earnestness, and by the acclaim which had greeted the announcement of the project. Everyone realized at once that it was truly a gigantic plan, but they had Lozier's word for it that it could be accomplished. Moreover, as Lozier pointed out, the construction of the famous Erie Canal, which was then nearing completion, had once been called impossible even by competent engineers, and much derision had greeted the prediction that steamships would one day cross the ocean. If man could run a river through the very heart of a mountain and if he could cause a simple steam engine to propel a gigantic boat, why could he not saw off an island? Nobody knew the answer, and Lozier's story was swallowed hook, line and sinker.

Sawing Manhattan Island off soon became the principal subject of argument and conversation at Centre Market and elsewhere as news of the great project spread. Neither then nor later, however, did the newspapers of the period pay any attention to Lozier's activities. It is doubtful if the editors ever heard of him, for in those days the only way of transmitting local news was by word of mouth, or by letter, which was even more uncertain. Important happenings in one part of the city did not become generally known for weeks or months, and frequently not at all. And Grand Street then was as far uptown as the Bronx is today.

A few days after he had started the ball rolling, Lozier appeared at Centre Market with a huge ledger, in which he proposed to record the names of all applicants for jobs, pending an examination to determine their fitness. This and other clerical work which developed during the progress of the hoax was the special care of Uncle John DeVoe, who ceremoniously set down the names, ages and places of residence of all who applied. Work was none too plentiful that year, and laborers, many of them recently arrived Irishmen, answered Lozier's call in such numbers that the big ledger soon bore the names of some 300 men, all eager to begin the great work of sawing off Manhattan Island.

Lozier further aroused confidence in his scheme by notifying various butchers of his acquaintance to begin assembling the enormous herds of cattle, droves of hogs and flocks of chickens which would be necessary to feed his army of workmen. He estimated that he would require at once 500 head of cattle, an equal number of hogs and at least 3000 chickens. He was especially anxious to obtain as many fowl as possible, for he had prom-

97

ised that all who obtained jobs would have chicken dinners twice a week. There was great excitement among the butchers, the immediate effect of which was an increase in the prices of all sorts of meat. One enterprising butcher had 50 fat hogs awaiting slaughter, and to make certain of a sale to Lozier he drove them north and penned them near Kingsbridge, where he fed them for almost a month at considerable expense.

With his food supply assured, Lozier engaged a score of small contractors and carpenters to furnish lumber and to superintend, under his direction, the building of the great barracks which were to house the workmen during the sawing operations. A separate building, to be constructed of the best materials, was ordered for the convenience of the 20 or 30 women, wives of laborers, who had been employed to cook and wash for the entire crew. Several of these contractors let their enthusiasm get the better of their judgment and actually hauled a dozen loads of lumber to the northern end of the island and dumped them near Kingsbridge. They implored Lozier to let them begin building, but he said that actual construction must wait until he had engaged all the men he would need and had assembled all his materials. It was his intention, he announced, to muster his workmen at a central meeting place when everything was ready and march them in a body to Kingsbridge. He assured the contractors that by using a new method of building which he had devised, but which he declined to disclose in advance, they could easily erect the necessary buildings within a few hours.

The excitement was now at fever pitch, and Lozier added more heat by producing elaborate plans for the various appliances to be used in the project. First, there were the great saws to cut Manhattan Island loose from the mainland. Each was to be 100 feet long, with teeth three feet high. To manipulate one of these giant tools, 50 men would be required, and Lozier estimated that he would need at least a score. Then there were 24 huge oars, each 250 feet long; and 24 great cast-iron towers, or oarlocks, in which the oars were to be mounted, 12 on the Hudson River shore and 12 on the East River. A hundred men would bend their backs at each oar, and row Manhattan Island down the bay after the sawyers had finished their work, then sweep it around and row it back. Great chains and anchors were to be provided to keep the island from being carried out to sea in the event that a storm arose. Lozier gave the plans and specifications of these Gargantuan implements to a score of blacksmiths, carpenters and mechanics, who began estimates of costs and materials.

Lozier now turned his attention to the potential sawyers and rowers. He sent word for them to report at Centre Market for examination and announced that he would pay triple wages to those who performed the hazardous work of sawing off that part of the island which lay underwater. The longest-winded men would be awarded these dangerous but desirable jobs. Laborers swarmed to the market, and every day for a week Lozier sat enthroned on a bench while man after man stepped forward and held his breath. As each displayed his prowess, Uncle John DeVoe timed him and entered the result in his ledger.

Lozier kept delaying the commencement of actual work by professing dissatisfaction with the estimates on the oars and towers and by insisting that he had not hired nearly enough men to do the job properly. At last, however, Lozier was compelled to fix a date for the grand trek northward. He awarded the contracts for manufacturing the saws, oars and towers and instructed all connected with the great work to report at the Bowery and Spring Street, where they would be met by a fife-and-drum corps which he had thoughtfully engaged to lead the march to Kingsbridge.

The exact number who finally appeared at the rendezvous is unknown, of course, but there were probably between 500 and 1000 persons. Laborers were there by the score, many accompanied by their wives and children; the contractors and carpenters drove up in style, escorting wagons laden with lumber and tools; the butchers were on hand with cattle and hogs and carts loaded with crated chickens. Practically everyone who had ever heard of the project was there, in fact, excepting Lozier and Uncle John

DeVoe. When several hours had elapsed and they still had failed to appear, a volunteer delegation went to Centre Market in search of them. They found a message that both Lozier and Uncle John had left town on account of their health.

The crowd at the Bowery and Spring Street milled about uncertainly for another hour or two, while the hogs grunted, the cattle mooed, the chickens cackled, the children squalled and the fife-and-drum corps industriously dispensed martial music. At length, for the first time in weeks, if not in years, some of the more intelligent of Lozier's victims began to think, and the more they thought, the less likely it appeared that Manhattan Island would ever be sawed off. Gradually this conviction spread, and after a while the crowd began shamefacedly to disperse. A few of the more hot-headed went looking for Lozier, vowing that if they could not saw Manhattan off they could at least saw Lozier off, but they never found him. Lozier and Uncle John DeVoe had fled to Brook-

lyn as soon as Lozier had issued his final instructions, and had sought refuge in the home of a friend. There was much talk of having them arrested, but no one seemed willing to make a complaint to the authorities and so admit that he had been duped, and both Lozier and Uncle John went scot-free. However, it was several months before they again appeared at Centre Market, and when they did, Lozier found himself an oracle without a temple. The Centre Market statesmen had had enough.

A RESOURCEFUL packaging man was able to make a hair-growing preparation sell after it had previously had a sorry sales record. The solution: printing in red on the label, "Do not place this preparation on any part of the body where you do not wish hair to grow."

—*George B. Brown in Advertising & Selling*

101

Shrewd and brash, the regal lady
with the oddly piercing eyes needed no charm

MRS. CHADWICK
SHOWS HER METTLE

by Willis Thornton

When the varnished and shiny landau of Mrs. Leroy S. Chadwick rolled down Cleveland's Euclid Avenue, people turned and stared. Everybody knew of Mrs. Chadwick's entertainments, her jewels, her benefactions, her luxurious home. Within three years of her marriage to Dr. Chadwick, at Windsor, Ontario, she had become a celebrity. This much everybody knew. If they had known what many people in Eastwood, Ontario, could have told them, some would have been spared a great deal. Like many other Ontario girls, Mrs. Chadwick had gone off to a big American city to get ahead in the world. Surely no other had ever achieved more spectacular results.

When Mrs. Chadwick returned to visit Toronto, after making good in the United States, she purchased as gifts for her friends 56 diamond rings from Ryrie's, the fashionable jewelers of the day. Ryrie salesmen scurried at her bidding. One traveled 12,000 miles to bring her back a diamond worth $3000, and on the same shopping spree she spent $3000 at Renfrew's for the only seal dress ever made in Canada and a fur rug trimmed with fox tails.

The Chadwicks entertained with the lavishness expected of people of social position and wealth. One caller was overwhelmed.

"Two pieces of statuary," he recalled, "stood at either end of the fireplace with two vases, each six or seven feet high, before it. Persian and Oriental rugs, oil paintings, 'gingerbread' of all kinds—the rooms were crowded. I caught myself estimating the cost of the stuff in only one room—$20,000, I said to myself."

Other, more cultured, observers shied at artistic fumbles. Beneath a $30,000 John Constable painting hung a row of six pictures given away with the *Youth's Companion* magazine. Many cheap paintings, including several vulgar nudes, were hung in frames of pure gold. A great cathedral chair was made entirely of cut glass, ingeniously upholstered in sealskin.

Mrs. Chadwick's taste, however expensive, obviously ran to the bizarre. There was a "perpetual motion" clock under glass on an inlaid table and a golden bird which sang in a golden cage when one pressed a golden lever. There was a complete service of soup plates concealing music boxes which played when the liveried servants lifted them from the table. One silver service had 900 pieces; another was inset with rubies.

Mrs. Chadwick's jewels were dazzling. A rope of 240 pearls was known to have been appraised at $40,000; whole trays of crusted gewgaws were bought from local jewelers, whose jaws dropped at her imperious, "I'll take them all!"

Not least dazzled was Dr. Chadwick. One Christmas Eve his wife suggested they go to the theater and have supper at a downtown restaurant. When they returned home he found that Aladdin-like workmen had redecorated and refurnished their home during the brief absence, and this, with a $1100 fur coat, was Mrs. Chadwick's little Yuletide remembrance for her husband.

Stores fell over one another to merit Mrs. Chadwick's patronage. Once she bought eight grand pianos for friends. It was nothing for her to set out for Europe taking a dozen young friends, afterward presenting each with a lovely miniature portrait painted by a fashionable Parisian artist as a memento.

She liked to have young people around her, usually a bevy of beautiful ladies, possibly because she was rather homely herself.

103

Though Mrs. Chadwick was five feet five inches tall, she had a dumpy figure. Her dress and manner bordered on vulgarity and she was almost totally deaf. Yet she made up for it all with a regal magnificence that amused the few who were not stunned.

Cleveland saw less and less of Dr. Chadwick, who was occupied with his practice and the upbringing of a daughter by a former marriage. Quiet, solid and well-established, he stayed in the shadowy background.

Suddenly, on November 2, 1904, there dropped on the telegraph desks of Cleveland newspapers a brief dispatch from Boston. A Mrs. Leroy Chadwick of Cleveland was being sued for $190,000 on a personal note, which she had failed to pay when due, to one Herbert B. Newton of Boston.

The first reaction of Cleveland newsmen was that it could scarcely be Cassie Chadwick of Euclid Avenue. There must be some mistake. Only one editor, Harry N. Rickey, of the Cleveland *Press*, smelled something fishy and started digging.

On November 26, 1904, Rickey's *Press* appeared with what might be a daring scoop or a fiasco for the paper's owner, E. W. Scripps, and the *Press* itself (the progenitor of the present Scripps-Howard papers). Rickey published the remarkably parallel lives of an Elizabeth Bigley, a Mme. De Vere and Mrs. Cassie L. Chadwick. The implication was that the three were one.

"She is a striking personality," stated the *Press*, "striking because of brilliant, dark eyes, reserved and powerful; her gray hair combed high, patricianlike, and her mouth stern and inflexible." Scarcely the description of a siren, though the *Press* conceded that she "retained traces of early beauty."

The Elizabeth Bigley whose life the *Press* had dared to chronicle alongside that of Mrs. Chadwick had come from Eastwood, Ontario, where her father was the railroad section boss. It had become apparent early that Elizabeth was no ordinary girl. She had remarkable imitative powers and an expressive voice. She excelled at school entertainments. Once, in a barber shop, Elizabeth asked for a false mustache and, to buy it, tried to raise money on a gold watch. The barber called the police. At 21 she had cards printed with her name and the legend: "Heiress to $15,000." She progressed to buying $250 worth of dry goods with a note endorsed by a wealthy Brantford farmer, and an organ from another merchant on her own note. When this came due she gave a forged note in payment. She was arrested and tried at Woodstock for forgery. At the trial another merchant testified that she had once ordered a tremendous quantity of groceries, including several barrels of sugar, and tried to charge the order.

The court judged her vague attitude toward money to be abnormal and acquitted her on grounds of insanity. Elizabeth was one of those strange persons to whom the only reality is what is real to them. She insisted at one time that she had been born at sea; later, that she was born in England—anything but the plain facts. So, to find surroundings where her own realities might be less readily challenged, she crossed Lake Erie to Cleveland.

She changed her name to Lydia and soon married Wallace S. Springsteen. Within a few days he learned of the Woodstock affair and discovered also that Elizabeth (or Lydia) had once mortgaged her sister's furniture during that lady's absence. He divorced her, and she took the name Lydia D. Scott.

Soon there appeared in Toledo a Madame Lydia De Vere, later to be described in the papers there as a "clairvoyant," a "high-flyer" who was found to have many prominent men under her influence. But Mme. De Vere's powers were not sufficient to prevent her arrest for obtaining $10,000 by forgery. She had sheared one Joseph Lamb, whom she had persuaded to obtain cash for several of her worthless notes. Later he was to call her "one of the vilest, most dangerous women that modern history has ever known." She was sent to the Ohio Penitentiary for nine years; Lamb was acquitted on the ground that she had hypnotized him. At the penitentiary Elizabeth Bigley-Springsteen-Scott-De Vere sewed shirts until 1893 when Governor McKinley (later to be President) pardoned her.

Cleveland gasped at the implication that there could be any

possible connection between so checkered a career and that of Mrs. Chadwick. Nothing had yet come out in court; there was no charge against her but the mere civil suit on the note, which she brushed aside with the glacial comment, "The ugly charges against me are false, absolutely false."

Cleveland *Town Topics*, weekly organ of the well-to-do, applied the soft pedal. It deplored "the amount of petty detail ... concerning the Chadwick affair. ... When so scholarly a paper as the Cleveland *Leader* refers to Mrs. Chadwick ... as a Cleveland society figure, the absurdity is all the more palpable."

Many who had been entertained in her home, however, began to cast back and recall what little they knew about Mrs. Chadwick. All they remembered was that when Dr. Chadwick met her she had been living in Cleveland as Mrs. C. L. Hoover with her mother, sister and a small son, under circumstances which were more extravagant than exclusive.

National curiosity was piqued by a statement from the Boston lawyers of Herbert Newton (who had sued for $190,000) that "he [Newton] was not persuaded by feminine charms, but the inducement was, we might say, spectacular." Deputy Sheriff Thomas Porter, who had served the Boston papers at the Chadwick home, told reporters, "Every time Mrs. Chadwick looked at me I became dizzy." This was the *Press*'s cue to print a large and emphatic picture of the Chadwick eyes.

On November 28, the Citizens' National Bank of Oberlin, Ohio, near Cleveland, suddenly closed its doors. Its highly respected president, Charles T. Beckwith, had loaned Mrs. Chadwick $240,000, four times the entire capitalization of the small bank. She also had obtained $102,000 as personal loans from Beckwith and A. B. Spear, the bank's cashier. Writers on national banking were later to say that "for absolute imbecility of management [the incident] perhaps has no parallel in the history of national bank failures." Yet, an examiner had regarded the loan as well-secured the previous April. The *Press* printed a lurid story of Beckwith's having pleaded on his knees for payment that would

save his bank and reputation, and of his having fainted on being sternly refused.

The bank's story was grimly familiar to the department stores. Mrs. Chadwick had touched Beckwith for small loans at first, promptly repaid them; then larger and larger loans, repaid at first, but at last repudiated. Her huge unpaid bills at the stores had swelled in exactly the same way.

Daily revelations in the papers began to loosen tongues. There existed fabulous notes, it was said, in Mrs. Chadwick's favor, signed by no other than the financial titan Andrew Carnegie. In fact, Mrs. Chadwick had hinted to several men that she was Carnegie's illegitimate daughter.

This full report then came out: In 1902 Mrs. Chadwick had interested several well-known Cleveland lawyers in forming a giant trust company. To them she told this story—that she was a niece of Frederick Mason, life associate of Carnegie, and heiress through him of $5 to $7 million in Carnegie securities. Again hinting at blood ties between herself and the multimillionaire, she averred that Carnegie had been trustee for this estate and had increased it to $11 million. Now old and nearing retirement, he wished to be relieved of his responsibility.

Meeting the Cleveland lawyers in New York, Mrs. Chadwick drove with them to Carnegie's home. It was best they wait outside in the carriage, she suggested, lest Carnegie resent the presence of lawyers in matters so delicate. She entered the house and stayed inside for about 20 minutes.

When she returned to the carriage and the waiting lawyers, she jubilantly displayed two notes for nearly $1 million signed "Andrew Carnegie," and with them a package containing, she said, Caledonia Railway bonds.

The lawyers were evidently impressed, but after careful investigation they withdrew quietly from the scheme. Now, two years later, reporters got wind of the Carnegie implications and rushed to his offices. They received only a statement from a secretary that "Mr. Carnegie knows nothing about it."

Nonetheless, the tale persisted that Iri Reynolds, of the Wade Park Banking Company, Cleveland, was holding a formidable bundle of securities for Mrs. Chadwick.

On December 2, the *Press* printed a full chronology of the Chadwick life, from Elizabeth Bigley through Mrs. Springsteen, through a phase as Mrs. Scott, through the now well-known De Vere episode in Toledo, and that of Mrs. Hoover of Cleveland, down to the latest incarnation.

It was a thoroughly damning story and as Mrs. Chadwick left Cleveland for New York, the *Press* flatly asserted that the only person behind Mrs. Chadwick was Mrs. Chadwick herself, and that the great financial interest alleged to be backing her was comprised only of the aggregate of the suckers she had managed to dupe over the years.

The public began to be convinced at last, and even small creditors now flocked to recover something on the credit they had so eagerly extended. Besides a formidable array of stores in the Cleveland area, a New York milliner contributed an attachment for $1000 and a claim for $250 for bric-a-brac recently arrived from Brussels.

At this point a determined U.S. district attorney stepped into the picture. John J. Sullivan found and made public the note which had been held by the Oberlin bank as collateral for its loan. It read:

January 7th, 1904
One year after date I promise to pay to the order of C. L. Chadwick Two Hundred and Fifty Thousand Dollars at my office New York City. Interest 5%.

ANDREW CARNEGIE

It was an obvious forgery similar to the notes she had two years before brought out of the Carnegie home to show the Cleveland lawyers waiting in her carriage.

Mrs. Chadwick had carried the previously prepared notes and

the package of bonds with her when she entered Carnegie's house. She had somehow contrived to remain inside the house, perhaps feigning sudden illness, long enough to give the impression of having had an interview.

Faced with a swindle so colossal as to imperil all local banking, Cleveland bankers hurriedly got together a public statement to reassure restless depositors. There was only $17,000 of Chadwick paper in Cleveland banks, they assured the public, all at the Wade Park bank.

Small banks in Elyria, another nearby town, were found to be involved. And now it was learned that in Pittsburgh the same thing had taken place. There, too, the magic Carnegie name provided an open sesame to several bank vaults.

Mrs. Chadwick, oscillating between New York's Holland House and the New Breslin Hotel, fought to the last. She dashed furiously about in a carriage, making ostentatious stops at buildings where great financial interests had their offices, then dodging out some back exit to avoid reporters. But the rope was growing shorter and shorter.

On December 8 she was arrested while ill in bed at the New Breslin Hotel on charges of aiding and abetting a national bank official in misappropriation of funds. She was imprisoned in New York City's Tombs.

The next day her package of securities on deposit at Cleveland's Wade Park bank was opened by authorities. Even the most cursory inspection showed them to be worthless stocks in corporations that were defunct.

The manner in which she had deluded Iri Reynolds was ingenious. One day she appeared at the bank with a package of securities, and after hinting at her relationship with Carnegie and the absolute need for secrecy, she sealed the envelope in his presence and left it "only for safekeeping." She gave Reynolds a list of what the envelope supposedly contained. As the securities were not to be negotiated, there was no particular reason for Reynolds to check the contents.

When she had returned home, Mrs. Chadwick telephoned Reynolds in evident agitation. She had no copy of the itemized list, she had found. Would Reynolds be so good as to furnish her with a copy? He would and he did, unfortunately for him, on the bank's letterhead and over his own signature, still without having checked the envelope's contents.

This paper, once in Mrs. Chadwick's hands, was an impressive item to show to other bankers and prospective lenders. They could scarcely fail to be impressed by a paper indicating that Mrs. Chadwick had more than $5 million in the hands of the Wade Park bank, even if the securities listed were not being directly offered as collateral.

But at last, when the fabulous envelope was opened, the truth was out.

Mrs. Chadwick was indicted on December 13 and was brought to Cleveland the following day to face trial. A huge crowd greeted her at the station shouting, "Where's the money?" and "Where's Papa Andy?"

The Toronto *Mail* and *Empire* sent to Cleveland its famous sob sister Kit (Kathleen Blake), the best-known woman reporter of her day. Kit obtained an exclusive interview with Mrs. Chadwick, whom she called "the cleverest, the sharpest, the boldest financier of the last century or this."

She described Mrs. Chadwick in prison, right down to the broad gold signet ring on her finger and the quilted jacket of black silk she wore. Her hand was "the littlest, the whitest of hands," Kit wrote; "her mouth is stern and might be cruel." As Mrs. Chadwick looked at her, "the most searching, the quickest glance I ever got thrilled my being."

Poor Charles Beckwith, of the bankrupt Citizens' National Bank in Oberlin, utterly and pathetically broken, died before the case ever came to trial. He called Mrs. Chadwick "the most deep-dyed fraud in the world."

When the trial opened there were still many who insisted that Mrs. Chadwick would pay all her debts and emerge with several spare million. A 15-year-old son by a former marriage appeared and loyally stood by his mother.

But the whole affair was quickly laid bare. Andrew Carnegie was present in person, twinkling with amusement. A grim-faced jury wasted no time in arriving at a verdict of guilty, and the judge sentenced Mrs. Chadwick to ten years in the Ohio State Penitentiary.

Taken back to jail, Mrs. Chadwick cried out, "I'm not guilty, I tell you. Let me go! Oh my God, let me go!" Two nurses stood by her while she went into 15 minutes of hysterics on a sofa. Then she was led to her cell.

Dr. Chadwick, apparently as innocent as he was deluded, left Cleveland. Later he earned $100 a week giving concerts to the curious on the $9000 pipe organ his wife had once bought for their home.

Mrs. Chadwick was sent to the penitentiary in Columbus to resume the trade of shirtmaker at which she had already served her apprenticeship. While there, she showed little bitterness, but appeared to take the gambler's attitude that you mustn't squawk when you lose.

She died behind bars on October 10, 1907, and was buried in her home town, Eastwood.

No one will ever know exactly how much money Mrs. Chadwick persuaded people to give her. Surely it was not less than $1,500,000. Claims in bankruptcy totaled $818,300, but much of the loss to banks and individuals was silently made good by red-faced bankers who preferred the monetary loss to public knowledge of their foolishness.

She also had repudiated the fiction that a feminine swindler must be a beauty. She built her career on more effective and enduring principles, which might be summed up as follows:

First, a 47-year-old woman without physical charm can do much socially with lavishness and by surrounding herself with pretty and amiable young women.

Second, if one lives as though one has money and unlimited

credit, one can buy almost anything and persuade people to go to almost unlimited lengths to curry favor.

And third, bankers tend to lend money gladly and freely to those whom they believe to have plenty of it already.

Such lessons the daughter of an Ontario railway section boss taught the world of society and finance.

~~~

FOR MANY years Miss Marion Tucker occupied an impressive residence in the sedate 60's on New York's Fifth Avenue. One summer, when she was getting ready to close the house, a distinguished-looking Frenchman called. He introduced himself as a representative of the company which insured Miss Marion's extensive art collection.

"We're interested in how you protect your art treasures against thieves while the house is shut," he said.

As you have probably guessed, the Frenchman was a crook. Working in cahoots with a minor official of the insurance company, he would inspect a house, examine the locks, doors and burglar alarms, and even get the owner to point out what was most worth stealing. Miss Marion took him on a tour of inspection, and when it was over the young man suggested that before she left she make certain that deliveries of milk and newspapers were stopped. "Such articles," he said, "piling up on the front doorstep, are an invitation to any thief who happens to pass by. I'd also advise you not to pull the window shades down. Drawn blinds are responsible for a considerable percentage of all burglaries."

The afternoon after Miss Marion left town, the Frenchman broke into her house, pulled down the shades and wrapped half a dozen of her finest *objets d'art* in a neat bundle. As he let himself out the front door, he stepped into the arms of a couple of cops.

"I'll go quietly," he assured them. "I abhor disturbances. But would you be good enough to tell me how on earth you knew that I was in there?"

One of the policemen pointed to the lowered blinds. On each one, printed in bold white letters against the dark-green background, were the words, "Burglar Inside."   *—From Billy Rose's column, "Pitching Horseshoes"*

A SAN FRANCISCO bank cashier cashed six phony checks for the same forger within a two-week period. When police and the bank's manager asked the girl why she had suspected nothing and kept accepting the checks, she explained, "Because he looked familiar."   *—Douglas Scott*

The extraordinary tale of a bank that
didn't know what was going on beneath the surface

HOW TO BLAST A BANK

by Evan McLeod Wylie

At noontime on Valentine's Day in 1961 a pretty teller at the People's National Bank of Washington, in Seattle, started to take a drink from a water fountain, then changed her mind. "The fountain's full of plaster dust and paint chips again," she told the group at the lunch table a few minutes later. "What's going on around here anyway?"

All during that week the bank's employes had noticed a gentle but persistent rain of plaster dust that seemed to be sprinkling down from hairline cracks in the ceiling. The bank is close to Boeing Field, and huge jet planes roar overhead at frequent intervals. Some of the employes attributed the cracks and the plaster dust to the planes. "They're shaking this building apart," one said. But, instead of being shaken apart, the bank was actually being blown open.

Reaching its climax that week was one of the most preposterous bank robberies of 1961 or any other year. The job took more than four months to accomplish, but it netted its lone amateur burglar more than $45,000 and, long before he had spent the money, a term in jail.

It was in October 1960 that James Brennan Weart, Jr., a tall, clean-cut, well-mannered, 25-year-old commercial flier, grounded by a slump in his business and hard-pressed for cash, came up with the notion of robbing a bank. Many men in dire financial straits have toyed with this idea and put it aside, but Weart seems to have had no second thoughts. He immediately got into his blue Renault and drove around Seattle to case the possibilities.

Soon he was reconnoitering a branch of the People's National Bank of Washington. The bank is surrounded by residential buildings and small industries. Busy in the daytime, the area is deserted after dark. Directly behind the bank is a driveway that serves the drive-in window; behind that is an embankment and a vacant lot. Weart decided to go into the bank the hard way.

Although his previous earth-moving experience was nil, he began to dig a tunnel into the weed-strewn embankment. This would go under the driveway and, he hoped, into the bank. He dug steadily until he had burrowed about eight feet; then the tunnel caved in. But Weart was not discouraged. Early the next day he was on the telephone, ordering timber from a lumberyard. After dark he was back on the job, redigging his tunnel and shoring up the shaft with the ardor of a gold prospector who feels sure he has hit a rich vein.

Weart became one of the hardest-working ditchdiggers in town. Night after night, while Seattle slept, he labored industriously. In the hours before dawn he hauled out the dirt on a board, camouflaged the tunnel entrance with brush and scraps of lumber, and went home to a hard-earned rest.

Weeks passed, and still Seattle police and the People's National remained unaware of Weart's molelike assault. During the day, above the tunnel, tellers dispensed cash to drive-in customers; and by night as well as day police patrols made their appointed rounds, passing within a few feet of the tunnel entrance. Nobody noticed the blue Renault which was frequently parked in the neighborhood at night.

By Halloween, Weart had burrowed 18 feet beneath the driveway and commenced slanting his shaft upward, expecting to

strike the floor of the bank. Instead, he broke through into a crawl space, about four feet high, beneath the bank. Its function was to provide access to plumbing and electrical installations.

Exploring his grotto with a flashlight, Weart discovered a ladder leading up to a steel plate. He pried up the plate and found himself staring into the bank's furnace room, directly adjacent to the vault. Wary of burglar alarms, Weart did not venture further. He withdrew his head and replaced the manhole lid, noting that the cement foundation beneath the bank vault was at least 18 inches thick.

In the crawl space Weart was able to sit snug and dry, and plan his attack on the vault overhead without fear of interruption. After chipping away with a chisel at the concrete, he concluded he

needed heavier tools or perhaps even a dynamite blast. Passing up the dynamite for the moment, he inquired at a tool-rental shop and was assured that a power hammer and star drills could penetrate thick concrete. That night he stole the equipment from the tool shop.

There remained the small matter of obtaining electricity for the power hammer. But by this time Weart was completely at home around the bank. He simply plugged his electric cord into a convenient wall outlet in the furnace room. From then on, the People's National was supplying the electric current for its own burglary.

The first time Weart set about breaching the foundation, the stolen power hammer gave off such a hair-raising clatter that he dropped it and fled, certain that police sirens would be converging from all directions. But not a soul showed up to ask what was going on. Nevertheless, the nerves of the pilot-turned-burglar were so shaken by the experience that he shut down his tunnel works temporarily and flew east to visit relatives.

By the time he returned he had decided not to risk the racket of the power hammer night after night. The safer approach after all was to blast a hole right into the bank vault. So he telephoned a powder company and asked about the use of dynamite in blasting rock. He was directed to a town about 60 miles south of the city, where he purchased $25 worth of nitroglycerin. He set up his private munitions dump not far from the bank, and then went to the public library to bone up on blasting techniques.

In mid-February Weart started drilling holes in the foundation for his dynamite charges. This made clouds of dust in his cavern, so the resourceful burglar borrowed a garden hose from an adjoining utility room and sprinkled the dust with water in a nice, tidy fashion.

Deciding the time had come to shoot the works, he spread the dynamite liberally around his drill holes. The booming explosion shook the People's National from stem to stern but took out only about five inches of concrete. It was again enough, however, to scare the daylights out of Weart, and he fled, feeling certain that the next day somebody in the bank would notice that strange things were happening. True, tellers, bookkeepers and vice-presidents began to complain about dust and plaster cracks turning up mysteriously in the walls and ceilings. A search for the cause was organized, but the search party went *up* instead of *down*.

Mounting to the second floor, the group finally decided that a large paper cutter, whose thumps could be heard throughout the bank, was to blame, and there was also the theory that the vibrations of the jets overhead might be causing the damage. But no action was taken. At close of business on Friday, February 17, the massive steel door of the vault was swung shut and its timers set for Monday morning. No qualms were felt over the fact that the vault contained approximately $150,000.

118

About 11 p.m. Weart ventured back beneath the bank, drilled more holes into the base of the vault, stuffed them with dynamite and scrambled out of the tunnel. At 1:40 a.m. the nitroglycerin let go with a detonation that nearly lifted the People's National off its foundations. Weart, sure that the concussion must have set off every alarm in the bank, whizzed away in his Renault. The muffled boom had indeed reached residents in the neighborhood. A block away two women engrossed in a late TV movie decided it had "something to do with those sonic booms airplanes make."

On Saturday afternoon Weart drove cautiously past the bank; he was prepared to see it tilted lopsidedly, but there was no sign of excitement. Within the bank, however, a janitor was complaining to a teller who had come to catch up on some paper work. The floor of the utility room was deep in fresh plaster dust; mops and brooms had been knocked helter-skelter. Were repairmen working around the bank when he wasn't there? What was going on? The teller could offer no explanation. The mystified janitor cleaned up and left. So, at the end of the afternoon, did the teller.

Just before midnight Weart was back in his tunnel. Squirming through the explosion's debris, he gazed rapturously at a hole in the vault floor big enough for him to crawl through. By a fantastic stroke of luck the hole had been blown dead-center in the vault without triggering any alarms.

Clambering up, Weart began prying drawers open with a screwdriver. For the rest of the night he made trip after trip through the tunnel, loading the Renault with bank notes and heavy bags of coin. At dawn he drove away with more than $45,000 and buried most of it in his woodland munitions dump. Sunday night, he returned to the scene of the crime to destroy any evidence that might connect him with the robbery, then made his way out of the tunnel for the last time.

At 8:45 Monday morning, the People's National discovered it had been divested of a goodly portion of its liquid assets. Amazed by the painstaking tunneling and blasting, police immediately assumed that professionals were involved and began dragneting the city for known burglars. The FBI moved in with mine detectors and other electronic equipment. State police combed the area.

If ever there was a time for a successful robber to lie low, this was it. But Weart saw things differently. He opened a savings account in a rival bank, made payments on his house and, using some of the stolen cash, put down $1000 for a station wagon.

As must have occurred to nearly everybody in Seattle, except Weart, the FBI and police were keeping close tabs on all large cash transactions. Serial numbers on the stolen bills that the amateur safecracker handed over for the station wagon were found to match those from the burgled vault. Early the next morning FBI agents were deployed around Weart's home. He surrendered peaceably, and not long afterward he was sentenced to 20 years in prison.

The young man who bungled the almost-perfect crime put himself out of circulation for a good deal longer than the money he stole in his subterranean treasure hunt.

<hr />

SHORTLY BEFORE 1 p.m. on September 1, 1935, a man in prison clothing crawled out onto a third-floor ledge of the Federal House of Detention on West 11th Street in New York's Greenwich Village. Agile as a mountain goat, in spite of his enormous belly, he teetered on his precarious perch and began to polish a window industriously with a large white cloth. He immediately caught the attention of passersby and loungers in front of a saloon across the street, because, despite the narrow ledge, he wore no safety belt.

Suddenly he reached under his shirt, and, as his potbelly deflated like a pricked balloon, he pulled out a coil of white rope. The free end, weighted with a ball of tinfoil, snaked down the side of the prison wall to the ground. With the other end apparently anchored to something inside the window, the prisoner slid briskly down the rope. Landing cat-footed on the sidewalk, he whirled, grinned at the openmouthed spectators and disappeared around the corner. Not until they read the papers the next day did these people learn they had been privileged to witness a virtuoso performance by Count Victor Lustig, one of the greatest confidence men, escape artists and counterfeiters of this or any other century.

—*Donovan Fitzpatrick, in True, The Man's Magazine*

*For two years, only this man
beheld the Smile of Mystery—was it for
this that he stole the* Mona Lisa?

POINT OF HONOR

by Milton Esterow

In London, King George V congratulated Prime Minister Herbert Henry Asquith on the settling of the nationwide railway strike. In Washington, President William Howard Taft signed a resolution admitting New Mexico and Arizona into the Union. And in Paris, the *Mona Lisa* was stolen from the Louvre.

Paris newspapers reported the theft under the headline "UN-IMAGINABLE." It was front-page news all over the world, on this Monday, August 21, 1911.

Fantastic solutions to the crime were reported. The masterpiece had been stolen by a dreamer who had fallen in love with the painted head; it had been taken by a French newspaper in an attempt to prove the original painting had already been stolen; the theft had been engineered by an American collector who would have an exact copy made and return the copy to the Louvre, keeping the original for his private collection. It was "authoritatively" announced that the painting had not been stolen, that the theft was a hoax to show how easy it was to rob the Louvre.

The newspaper *Paris-Journal* and the magazine *L'Illustration* offered large rewards. *Le Matin* appealed to any clairvoyant who could coax a clue from "the beyond." There were daily stories about mysterious strangers with rectangular packages at railway stations and piers, and reports said that the picture had been taken to Russia, Italy, Germany and seven other countries. The police organizations of the world joined in the search.

The first description of the theft was made in *Le Temps* on Tuesday, August 22. Half an hour after it appeared, Georges Benedite, curator of Egyptian antiquities and second in command at the Louvre, made a statement to reporters:

> *La Gioconda* is gone. So far we have not the slightest clue as to the perpetrator of the crime. The picture was last seen in its usual place yesterday morning at seven o'clock when two of the cleaners stopped before it and exchanged remarks about the enigmatic smile of the painting. Yesterday was cleaning day and the museum was closed to the public. Thus no one noticed the absence of the picture. This morning the guard of the Salon Carré, where the painting hung, noticed its disappearance and attributed it to the negligence of the official photographer, who often takes it up to his own studio and returns it the next morning before the gates are opened to the public. Toward midday, however, the man became uneasy and informed the superintendent, who rushed to my office and told me nobody knew what had become of the picture. I called Lepine [Louis Lepine, prefect of the Paris police], who ordered the closing of the museum and sent an army of detectives who, after searching an hour, discovered the heavy frame of the picture standing alone on a staircase leading to one of the cloakrooms. The frame bore no marks of violence. The thief or thieves evidently took plenty of time for the operation of dismounting the picture and discarded the frame as too bulky. How he or they came or left is a mystery.

One of the first persons questioned by Monsieur Lepine, a

small man with a white beard who habitually wore a white bowler hat and an old-fashioned morning coat, was the head of the museum's maintenance department. He said that at 6:30 on Monday morning, August 21, he had entered the Louvre as usual to continue some repairs that had been started in the Grand Gallery, adjacent to the Salon Carré, where Napoleon married Marie Louise of Austria in 1810 and which contained some of the Louvre's proudest possessions—works by Leonardo, Titian, Raphael, Veronese, van Eyck, Rubens, Rembrandt, Holbein, Velázquez. With two of his workmen he had passed through the Salon Carré at 7:20 a.m. and had paused with them for a moment before the *Mona Lisa*, saying, "This is the most valuable picture in the world. They say it is worth a million and a half." Then they continued on to the Grand Gallery.

At 8:35 a.m. they passed again through the Salon Carré, and the maintenance man noticed that the picture was no longer there. He said to his colleagues, "Ho, ho. They have taken it away for fear we would steal it." All three had a good laugh and went back to work.

On Tuesday at 7:20 a.m. Brigadier Poupardin of the Louvre guards, in passing through the Salon Carré, noticed that the *Mona Lisa* was not in its place. He thought that it was in the photo studio. At 9 a.m. a man named Louis Beroud arrived. He was painting a scene of the Salon Carré, including the wall on which the *Mona Lisa* was hung. He set up his easel, spotted Poupardin and asked him what had happened to the Leonardo. "It is being photographed," was the reply. At 10 a.m. Poupardin passed by again, and Beroud asked him to stop at the photo studio and send back the painting. Poupardin returned within minutes. "The picture is not there and they know nothing about it," he said excitedly. He thereupon notified Benedite, who immediately called in the police.

Reports about suspects came from all over Europe. The Cherbourg police, on Sunday, August 27, notified the Paris police that on Wednesday two men, one of them small and dark, carrying two framed canvases separated by a wooden panel, sailed aboard the *Kaiser Wilhelm II* for New York. The New York police were alerted, but nothing came of it. Clue after clue failed. Gradually, France and the art lovers of the world sadly came to the conclusion that the glorious painting would never be seen again.

Then, almost two and a half years later, around the first of December 1913, well-known art dealer Alfredo Geri, a round, jovial man, began reading a pile of letters in his office in Florence, Italy. The mail had been heavy for the last few days because Geri had advertised in French, Italian and German newspapers for the purchase of art objects for a forthcoming exhibition.

One letter, written with directness and simplicity, was different from the others. The writer said he was an Italian. He had been suddenly seized with the desire to restore to his country at least one of the many treasures which, especially in the Napoleonic era, had been stolen from Italy. He had taken the *Mona Lisa*, and it was currently in his possession. He would not ask a price for it but he was a poor man. The letter was signed "Leonard" and gave as a return address a street in Paris.

Geri's first reaction was that the letter was from a practical joker or a madman. He laughed and showed it to one of his friends. The man must be crazy. Geri was about to throw it in the wastebasket when the thought struck him, what if it is genuine? What if it were really true? It was now more than two years since the disappearance of the *Mona Lisa*. Could the thief, after finding it impossible to sell, have decided to give himself away? The next morning Geri went to his friend Giovanni Poggi, director of the famous Uffizi Gallery in Florence, and showed him the letter. Poggi was skeptical, too. But the two men decided to answer it. Geri wrote in reply that he was enchanted by Leonard's sense of patriotism, that he did not consider the question of price an obstacle because he would better any offer that Leonard might have received elsewhere. He wrote that he had spoken to Giovanni Poggi, the director of the Uffizi, and that Poggi's desire was for the *Mona Lisa* to smile once again in the city where she had smiled 400 years earlier. But he would have to make sure the work was genuine, and this he could only do by examining it. Would Leonard bring it to Italy? Leonard replied almost immediately. On December 6, Geri received a letter stating that Leonard would meet him in Florence on the following Wednesday. The subsequent events were recalled by Geri:

That Wednesday, in the afternoon, a young man, thin, with a small black mustache, modestly dressed, appeared at my office and said he was the possessor of *La Gioconda* and invited me to accompany him to his hotel to see the picture. He answered all my questions with much assurance and told me he wanted 500,000 lire [$95,000] for his picture. I said I was prepared to pay this sum and invited him to return the next day at three o'clock. At three the next day, Poggi was at my house. At ten past three the man was not yet there. Had the business fallen through? We became impatient. Finally, at 3:15, Leonard arrived. I introduced Leonard to Poggi. They shook hands enthusiastically, Leonard saying how glad he was to be able to shake the hand of the man to whom was entrusted the artistic patrimony of Florence. The three of us left together. Poggi and I were nervous and also anxious. Leonard, by contrast, seemed indifferent. We arrived in the little room that he occupied on the third floor of the Hotel Tripoli-Italia. He locked the door and drew out from under his bed a trunk of white wood that was full of wretched objects: broken shoes, a mangled hat, a pair of pliers, plastering tools, a smock, some paintbrushes and even a mandolin. He threw them onto the floor in the middle of the room. Then, from under a false bottom in the box, he took out an object wrapped in red silk. We placed it on the bed and to our astonished eyes the divine *Gioconda* appeared, intact and marvelously preserved. We took it to the window to compare it with a photograph we had brought with us. Poggi

examined it and there was no doubt that the painting was authentic. The Louvre's catalogue number and stamp on the back of it matched with the photograph.

Poggi and Geri, moved by the recovery of the *Mona Lisa*, shook Leonard's hand effusively. Realizing that it was necessary to get the painting to a safe place, they reassured him that they would respect and defend his right to a generous reward. Poggi said he would like to take the picture to the Uffizi where he could verify its authenticity. Leonard accepted and placed the picture under his arm, still wrapped in the red silk.

At the Uffizi, Poggi double-locked his office door and took out a number of other photographs of the *Mona Lisa* that had been made at the Louvre. The more he checked, the more his certainty mounted. Everything conformed—specific cracks; certain smudges on the back of the right hand; marks on the index finger of the right hand; abrasions around the mouth; marks on the right side on the back of the poplar panel; a network of cracks over the painting's surface. There was no more doubt. The *Mona Lisa* had been found.

Leonard went back to his hotel. Soon he had visitors—the Florence chief of police accompanied by detectives. Leonard had registered under the name of Vincenzo Leonardo. He was packing the white box, but he let himself be arrested quietly. He said that his real name was Vincenzo Peruggia, that he had been born in Dumenza, Italy, that he was a house painter, that he had worked for a contractor at the Louvre and that his motive for the theft was the glory of Italy and vengeance for the depredations of Napoleon. An amazing motive, but quite possibly a strong one, although the *Mona Lisa* had not been stolen by Napoleon. There was still great resentment throughout Italy at the losses the country had suffered because of Napoleon, and many citizens were willing to blame him for almost anything.

The Minister of Public Instruction announced, "The *Mona Lisa* will be delivered to the French ambassador with a solemnity worthy of Leonardo da Vinci and a spirit of happiness worthy of Mona Lisa's smile. Although the masterpiece is dear to all Italians as one of the best productions of the genius of their race, we will willingly return it to its foster country, which has regretted its loss so bitterly, as a pledge of friendship and brotherhood between the two great Latin nations." Meanwhile, Italy asked France for permission to exhibit the *Mona Lisa* in several Italian cities before its return, and France gladly consented.

Peruggia now began to give conflicting stories, and doubt developed that patriotism was the sole motive. Once he possessed it, he said, he gradually fell in love with the mysterious face. "I shall never forget the evening after I had carried the picture home. I locked myself in my room in Paris and took the picture from a drawer. I stood bewitched before *La Gioconda*. I fell a victim to her smile and feasted my eyes on my treasure every evening, discovering each time new beauty and perversity in her. I fell in love with her."

Why, then, did he try to sell the *Mona Lisa*? "I was anxious to insure a comfortable old age for my parents. Besides that, I felt I must take myself away from the influence of that haunting smile. I sometimes wondered in those two years whether or not I had not better burn the picture, fearing I should go mad." But the police were convinced that Peruggia was playing a role and they sought to prove he stole the picture only for love of money.

The arrest of Peruggia was a humiliation to the French police. After the theft, several fingerprints had been found on the glass that had covered the painting. One of the prints, that of a left thumb, was perfect. Since Peruggia had been previously arrested in 1908 and 1909, the police had two sets of fingerprints. The thumbprint on the glass was later compared with these sets of prints and was found to correspond perfectly. Why, then, could they not have traced Peruggia? Alphonse Bertillon, the criminologist who gave the world its first successful means of classifying and identifying criminals, offered an explanation. There were in his department 750,000 criminal records. These were catalogued and classified under different body measurements, arranged in various categories of fingerprints. Only the print of the right thumb, however, was used for classification purposes, and the only clear mark found on the glass was that of the left thumb. In the absence of the thief's name or his right thumbmark, the left print was untraceable.

The French police had other reasons to be embarrassed. Detectives had actually questioned Vincenzo Peruggia early in the investigation. Soon after the theft, an assistant conservator at the Louvre said that he was convinced that the picture must have been stolen by one of the men employed in the framing of paintings, since the manner in which the *Mona Lisa* had been removed indicated an expert's hand. A list of 257 persons was furnished to the investigators, including the name of Vincenzo Peruggia. His room was said to have been searched. But apparently his frankness disarmed suspicion, and he escaped the formality of being fingerprinted at that time. How, France wanted to know, could he have escaped the formality that had been imposed on such men above suspicion as the curator of paintings and Theophile Homolle, the former director of national museums?

Ironically, the Louvre itself had inadvertently laid the foundation for the theft by the precautions it took to keep the *Mona Lisa* from being damaged. In October 1910, ten months before the painting vanished, the Louvre had decided to have all masterpieces put under glass. Peruggia, working for the company that had contracted the job, was one of four men assigned to the task. Since it was a complicated operation, it had to be done four times before everyone was satisfied. In this way, Peruggia had had sufficient time to see exactly how the *Mona Lisa* was hung. The job was completed in January 1911, and Peruggia went to work for another firm, but he remained friendly with his old working companions and continued to visit the museum.

Many times, Peruggia told the police, while working at the Louvre, he had stopped before the *Mona Lisa* and was outraged by the thought that the great painting was on foreign soil. When his job at the museum ended, he vowed that he would return, take it and present it to Italy. "I had only to choose an opportune moment," he said, "and a mere twist would put the picture in my hands. The idea took possession of me, and I decided to take the step. One morning I joined the decorators at the Louvre, exchanged a few words with them and quietly stole away. I was wearing the same long white workmen's blouse as they and attracted no attention. I entered the deserted salon in which the picture was hung. In a moment I had taken it from the wall. I carried it to the staircase, took off the frame and slipped the painting under my blouse. It was all done in a few seconds."

He swore that he had no accomplices, that nobody knew of his plan before its execution and that nobody knew he had the painting. When he crossed the French frontier on the way to see Geri, he had so readily opened his box for the customs people that they neglected to search it. Apparently they believed it contained only a few rags and his tools. He did not intend to sell the picture to Italy, he said, but he thought he should have adequate compensation for the great service he had rendered his country.

After his arrest, the police searched the room that Peruggia had occupied in Paris and that for more than two years had been the home of the *Mona Lisa*. As a result, they became even more convinced that Peruggia was lying. They found a diary in which, under a date in 1910, was a list of art collectors and dealers in the United States, Germany and Italy. Among the Americans on the list were John D. Rockefeller, J. P. Morgan and Andrew Carnegie. Among the Italians listed was Alfredo Geri. It thus seemed apparent that, ten months before the theft, Peruggia was thinking less of vengeance than of money.

Now, Italy was ready to exhibit the *Mona Lisa*. In Florence, on December 14, 1913, a riot broke out at the first public exhibition at the Uffizi Gallery. Huge crowds had gathered outside the gallery, and the police were frequently pushed aside by the excited Florentines. *La Gioconda* was back where it was born. Carried by two guards from the Uffizi's Hall of Gems and escorted by Giovanni Poggi and Corrado Ricci, the director of the Department of Fine Arts, in a gilded 16th-century walnut frame, the *Mona Lisa* was placed on an easel behind a balustrade between portraits by Raphael and Titian.

The early arrivals crossed themselves as the painting was carried past them, and *carabinieri* pleaded with the visitors to remain calm. No group in the long procession was allowed more than three minutes to look, and at closing 30,000 had seen her. Ricci was asked if he were sure the painting was genuine. He replied, "I only wish the French experts would consider it a copy. Then it would remain in Italy."

Minutes away from the Uffizi Gallery, the Florence jail housed Peruggia, who had suddenly become a celebrity. The chief of police turned down huge sums for permission to take photos of him, to buy his mandolin, his old paintbrushes, his rags, his unpaid bills and all the other items seized by the police in his room.

This was only the beginning. Rome and Milan were next on the itinerary. In Paris, Henri Marcel, who had recently been appointed director of the Louvre, had left for Italy with other experts and government officials to take possession of the painting. When they arrived in Florence, they found immense crowds continuing to view the *Mona Lisa*—people from all over Italy and from other countries, too. The painting finally left for Rome in a rosewood box on December 20. The entire route was guarded in the same way it would be for a train carrying royal personages. King Victor Emmanuel went to the Ministry of Fine Arts with cabinet ministers, members of the diplomatic corps and their families to see the painting. It was officially handed over to the French ambassador with befitting ceremony, then went on public display at the French embassy and the Borghese Gallery. Extra police had to be called out to handle the crowds.

A special escort of Italian police accompanied the painting on the train to the frontier. An order to the Italian customs officials permitted it to pass the border duty free. The return to Paris, on the afternoon of December 31, was not spectacular. In fact, while

Paris was making preparations for the welcome, the theory about the painting's not being the original was dusted off again. The painting was taken to the School of Fine Arts in Paris, where officials of the Louvre opened an envelope in which had been sealed after the theft a list of all the masterpiece's identifying and secret marks. After an examination lasting three quarters of an hour, the *Mona Lisa* was proclaimed the original.

Vincenzo Peruggia had been incarcerated on the same day he was arrested, December 11, 1913. He was quiet and calm, as if he had to experience an annoying but necessary formality. But as the days and months passed, Peruggia protested to his lawyer again and again that he had stolen the painting for patriotic reasons and could not understand why he had been sent to prison. He began receiving gifts in his cell. Every morning an unknown admirer sent him milk and coffee, and at noon a little lunch— a bottle of wine, soup, salami or some other meat, cheese—and cigarettes. Another admirer sent him supper. And there were also gifts of money. Many were anonymous. Some bore the signatures of the donors. One Italian sent him 12,000 lire ($2400) over a period of several months. If visitors mentioned the *Mona Lisa* Peruggia became excited and talked volubly about the painting. When his lawyer reported that it was back in the Louvre, Peruggia shook his head from side to side and said, "It's obvious they have understood nothing."

His initial tranquillity did not last. At first he had faith in the "justice of Florence." Then he began to brood and had frequent crying spells. The numerous postponements of the trial further depressed him. When he was told he would be examined by a psychiatrist, he went into a rage. "Do you want me to be thought insane?" he shouted. "I'm not crazy."

But he quickly became friendly with the psychiatrist and submitted to all questions. Eventually, however, his unknown benefactors stopped sending him food and money, and, by May 1914, he had to live like the other prisoners.

On June 4, 1914, Vincenzo Peruggia went on trial before a

tribunal in Florence on charges of stealing the *Mona Lisa*. In Italy then, a trial was held even if there was a confession of guilt. At 9 a.m. he was brought into the crowded courtroom, dressed in a gray suit and wearing a black tie. He glanced at the reporters and the spectators while the police removed his handcuffs. He appeared quite calm as he took the witness stand to relate how he had stolen the painting.

When asked why he committed the theft, he replied:

"I know that the Italian paintings which are in the Louvre have been stolen."

"Where did you find that out?"

"From books and photographs."

"Why did you choose *La Gioconda*? Couldn't you have taken other paintings?"

"Certainly. I could have taken a Raphael or a Correggio. But I preferred Leonardo's masterpiece, which I wished to occupy a place of honor in Italy, just as it had occupied one in the Louvre."

"After the theft, why did you write to your family that you had finally obtained your fortune?"

"Romantic words, your honor."

"I repeat. You said that for some time you had dreamed of taking that painting."

"Not before I went to work at the Louvre."

"Hadn't you been at the Louvre at other times?"

"Yes, but I did not know *La Gioconda* had been stolen from Italy. I found out only after reading some books."

The judge pointed out that the police had established that Peruggia went to London to try to sell the painting.

"This is a misunderstanding," Peruggia replied. "I never said that. I went to Dieppe by train. I met and made friends with some people who, like me, were going to the seashore. We decided to take a sea voyage and we boarded a ship to London. In London we went to a hotel near Victoria Station. In Trafalgar Square I asked a postcard vendor the name of an antique dealer. When I went to the shop I asked the dealer for advice on how to return the *Mona Lisa* to Italy. The dealer did not take me seriously. He said I surely must be speaking of a copy, and I left. Had I wished to sell the painting I would not have gone to the trouble I did. I took the painting for Italy and I wanted it returned to Italy. I waited to come to Italy until the tumult from the newspapers had quieted down."

"How did you get the idea to propose the sale to the art dealer Geri?" asked the judge.

"While I was reading a newspaper, my eye caught his name, and so I thought of turning to him to make a gift of *La Gioconda* to Italy."

"Gift? But when you first met him you proposed getting from the Italian government payment of 500,000 lire."

"But who says this? Geri? It was he who suggested that 500,-000 could be gotten from the government and that we would share the money."

"Why did you offer the painting to a dealer rather than to the director of the Uffizi Gallery?"

"I didn't think."

"Did you expect a reward from the Italian government?"

"Certainly. I heard talk of millions and I expected that Italy would present me with something which, for a modest family such as mine, would have been a fortune."

The prosecutor, in summing up, said immediately that Peruggia should be held completely responsible for the theft, declaring that he committed the crime with premeditation and with astuteness. Peruggia's past, he said, was not entirely pure, since he already had had two convictions in France. He insisted that Peruggia stole the painting for no other reason than money, and demanded a prison term of three years.

Peruggia listened with lowered head to the summation, deeply absorbed. He was extremely pale when the prosecutor sat down but regained his color when one of his attorneys, Giovanni Carena, summed up. At the age of 12, Peruggia had had to emigrate to earn a living, Carena said. He sought to minimize the importance of the two previous arrests and pointed out that Peruggia's French co-workers and bosses had played practical jokes on him, had teased him cruelly so that he rebelled against life in a foreign land. They had called him "macaroni eater," a term used derisively by the French for the Italians, had stolen his tools and had put salt and pepper in his wine. The attorney read letters Peruggia had written to his parents to show that the defendant was not a coarse, selfish man. This, he said, was not a professional thief. He had worked hard and sent money to his parents, and the words in his letters were those of a truly affectionate son, of a gentle man. The attorney excused Peruggia for not having known that the *Mona Lisa* had been acquired legally by Francis I, not stolen by Napoleon. The theft itself, he said, was a simple act, requiring no special criminal knowledge or talent. The counselor insisted that money was not the motive. Concluding, he asked the judge to return the unfortunate Peruggia to his family. At this, the spectators burst into applause.

The tribunal returned in about an hour. The judge said that they had taken into consideration extenuating circumstances and, instead of acquiescing to the prosecutor's demand for three years' imprisonment, he gave a sentence of a year and 15 days. Amid murmurs in the courtroom, Peruggia was handcuffed and led to jail. Perhaps it was inevitable that one newspaper reported that Peruggia listened to his sentence with an expression resembling Mona Lisa's enigmatic smile. And as he walked out of the courtroom, someone asked him what he was thinking. Peruggia shook his head and said, "But . . . it could have been worse."

Peruggia did not have to spend the entire term in prison. On July 29, 1914, his attorneys appealed the sentence, and the court reduced the term to seven months. Since Peruggia had been in jail for that time, he was ordered released immediately.

Peruggia listened without any signs of satisfaction. He was worried by the fact that he was penniless and he pulled out the empty pockets of his trousers. Leaving the courtroom a free man, he told his attorneys that he did not know where he would go.

135

Then, smiling, he said, "I will return to the hotel where they arrested me—the Tripoli-Italia Hotel."

"It is now the Gioconda Hotel," said Ferdinando Targetti, his other attorney. "They changed the name after you were arrested and they have a picture of the *Gioconda* painted on the walls at the entrance."

Eventually, Peruggia went back to his hometown, Dumenza. After serving in the Italian army during World War I, he traveled to Paris. He returned to Dumenza in 1921 to marry one of his cousins and, with his bride, moved back to Paris, where he opened a paint-and-varnish store. He died several years later, still disdainful of the Italian government, which he believed responsible for wrongfully sentencing him. But he was not without admirers. In Dumenza, said the parish priest, there was love and esteem for Vincenzo Peruggia.

⁕

A WEALTHY American art collector came across a newly discovered old master in Italy and secretly bought it. Knowing that the Italian government would not allow a picture of this value to be taken out of the country, he thought up an ingenious way of smuggling it out. He hired a run-of-the-mill Italian painter to paint a modern landscape over the old master, knowing that this could be removed when the canvas arrived in New York. The plan worked successfully, and the collector took the painting to a well-known restorer to have the superimposed painting removed. A week later he received the following wire from the restorer:

"Have removed landscape, also old master, and am now down to portrait of Mussolini. When do you want me to stop?"   —*Alexander Barmine*

AT NOON on a spring day in Paris some years ago, an old motor truck broke down in the center of the Place de l'Opéra, requiring the driver to spend a half hour under it to make the repair. After apologizing for the trouble he had caused the policemen who had been directing the traffic around him, the truckman drove away—to collect several thousand dollars from friends who had bet that he could not lie on his back for 30 minutes at the busiest hour in the middle of the busiest street in Paris. He was Horace DeVere Cole, England's celebrated practical joker.   —*Collier's*

*It was the largest cash robbery
in history—$7 million in small bills*

BRITAIN'S GREAT TRAIN ROBBERY

by Pete Hamill

Every evening through the British summer of 1964, the routine on the ground floor of Block B in Winson Green Prison had been the same. Charles Wilson, in Cell 12, would remove his blue uniform, fold it neatly and place it outside the door. Then the door would be locked by a guard who would thereafter peer in every 15 minutes, for Wilson was a maximum-security prisoner. Meanwhile, Charles Wilson would stretch his 32-year-old, six-foot frame on the bunk, run his hands through his curly brown hair and stare at the ceiling, as if engaged in some gorgeous daydream.

More than most men in Winson Green, Charles Wilson had reason for wishing he were not there. For Wilson was one of 12 men serving an aggregate of 291 years for their parts in the $7 million Great Train Robbery, the biggest cash robbery of all time. Only $942,250 had been recovered, and Wilson knew where the rest of the money was hidden.

Wilson's routine was broken in the early hours of August 12, 1964. That night he reduced his 30-year sentence by 29 years and eight months. Shortly after 3 a.m. three men scaled the prison's 20-foot walls with ladders and, with duplicates of two master keys, made their way into Wilson's corridor and cell. When Wilson's

137

guard appeared on schedule they smashed him into unconsciousness. They provided the prisoner with civilian clothes and left the way they had entered—with Charles Wilson.

Eleven months later another of the gang made his break for freedom. Ronald Biggs, also serving a 30-year maximum-security sentence, broke from the exercise yard of Wandsworth Prison in a slick daylight escape. Biggs and three others scaled the 20-foot prison wall and plummeted onto a makeshift canvas rig in a furniture van on the other side. They then sped away in three automobiles. Police launched a massive and thorough search, but Biggs had disappeared completely.

The Great Train Robbery, already a British legend, fascinated Englishmen even more now that the gang had added two such daring jailbreaks. Today, more than four years after the train was relieved of £2,500,000, picture and story in periodicals and newspapers tell of the jailbreaks and of what happened at that lonely rail crossing.

Just before 3 a.m. on August 8, 1963, the stillness of the countryside of Buckinghamshire and Bedfordshire was broken by the sound of the Glasgow-to-London mail train making its nightly run. At the controls of diesel engine D326 were engineer Jack Mills, 57, who had been making this uneventful run for 12 years, and his fireman, 26-year-old David Whitby. Strung out behind them were 13 cars that made up a post office on wheels. In the last ten cars 71 postal clerks sorted ordinary mail. In the second of the two coaches directly behind the diesel five postal workers sat with a very special cargo—128 mail sacks stuffed with neatly wrapped £1 (then worth $2.80) and £5 notes on the way to London from banks all over the north country.

As Mills approached Sears Crossing, he saw an amber warning light and began to apply the brakes. At the crossing itself, there was a red light, and Mills slowed to a stop. It was 3:03 a.m. Whitby swung down from the engine to walk a few feet to a trackside emergency telephone. When he lifted the telephone, it hung loose in his hands. The wires had been cut. Looking around, he saw a man in a knitted khaki mountaineering hood peering at him from between the second and third coaches.

"What's up, mate?" Whitby said, and walked over. The man grabbed him and pushed him down the railroad embankment.

"There were two men at the bottom," Whitby reported later. "One pushed me to the ground and the other showed me a cosh [club] and said, 'If you shout, I'll kill you.' When he finally took his hands off my mouth I said, 'All right, mate. I'm on your side.' He answered, 'Thanks.' "

Meanwhile, Mills had been waiting in the cab. He had little reason to feel alarm: the rolling post office had never been robbed in more than a century of operation. Then he heard someone coming up the steps to the cab. "I turned around," he said afterward, "and saw a masked man holding an iron bar. He raised it to hit me and I thought, 'Well, I'm not giving up without a fight.' But I was struck from behind. The next thing I remember I was on my knees and they were hitting me."

The cab was now full of men in blue suits. One of them tried to start the train, cursed, tried again, failed and shouted, "Get the driver!" Mills, lying face down on the floor, his head exploding, blood running down his face, was wrenched erect. One of the hooded men wiped the blood from the engineer's eyes, then ordered him to drive ahead about three quarters of a mile to Bridego Bridge, an overpass with a country lane beneath. Meanwhile, other members of the gang had uncoupled the second and third cars from the rest of the train. When Mills started the engine, the mail clerks in the last ten cars simply sat there sorting mail.

At Bridego Bridge all but one of the masked men in the cab dropped to the ground. Two smashed a window of the second coach and climbed in. A third shattered a door with an axe, and eight to ten men followed him. They forced the postal workers to lie face down and began to knock the locks off the wooden cupboards containing the money.

In the diesel a man handcuffed Mills and Whitby and ordered them from the cab. For a moment they caught a glimpse of the entire scene: perhaps 20 masked men, all silent, working in military fashion, tossing the bags of money along a line to Bridego Bridge, where they were dropped into waiting vehicles. "They were like a ruddy bunch of commandos," Mills said later.

Mills remembered that one of the masked men seemed to be supervising the operation. He kept studying his wristwatch. Obviously, he knew that a scheduled freight train was due soon and after 15 minutes of unloading he raised his hand and said, "That's our lot." The bandits bounded down the embankment, there was a roar of automobile engines and the men were gone. It was 3:45, and the greatest cash robbery in history had been accomplished. The bandits carried off two tons of easily passed notes. The robbery was a perfection of planning, logistics and, particularly, of timing.

As police reconstruct the case, it probably all began in the summer of 1962. The first step was to raise enough money to finance the project. This was accomplished at London Airport in November 1962. Four men impeccably arrayed in the uniform of London's financial district—bowler hats, black coats, gray-striped trousers, complete with slim briefcases and rolled umbrellas— came strolling in and drifted to an elevator behind a security guard and two pay clerks with the airline payroll. From the elevator came three hooded thieves. They scuffled briefly and escaped with $175,-000. Not a penny was ever recovered. And only one of the men involved went to prison. Two others were tried for the robbery and were acquitted.

One of those found innocent was tall, 33-year-old Douglas Gordon Goody. He looked like a blond Marlon Brando, with hair combed forward, and pursed lips drawn in an ironic smile. His taste in clothes ran to Savile Row; in automobiles, to gleaming dark-green Jaguars. He owned three hairdressers' shops and seven convictions dating back to a robbery case in 1947. His last conviction was in 1956, when he received a three-year sentence for larceny. Police described him as a man with a good mind who could have done well in a legitimate business but who decided to become a superior criminal.

Scotland Yard believes that the Great Train Robbery was probably planned all through the winter of 1962–1963, and that Goody was involved from the beginning. His closest friends shared a regard for large sums of money and professional respect for one another. One was Charles Wilson, with a record of four convictions, who had been acquitted with Goody on the London Airport job. Another was Bruce Reynolds, a 31-year-old antique dealer with a police record.

These men acted as a board of directors, and they brought in five confederates. After choosing the stretch of track near Sears Crossing and Bridego Bridge for the robbery site, the gang scouted the territory for miles in all directions. The regularity of the mail train was checked. The signals and emergency telephone were observed, and an expert electrician, another ex-con, was added to the group. Some of the gang strolled into Euston Station in London and quietly watched railroad men uncoupling cars. To be sure that they had the procedure down pat, they filmed the action with a movie camera.

The tangled side roads and lanes in Buckinghamshire could confound any ordinary driver, especially if he had to drive without headlights. So the gang brought in a professional racing driver. For a hideout, they purchased Leatherslade Farm, a house on five acres, well-hidden half a mile up a dirt road, and 20 miles from the robbery scene.

During the following month small groups of men traveled to the farm at night, laying in provisions for what was to be a two-week stay. A shortwave radio was hooked up; playing cards and magazines were provided. A three-ton army truck and two Land-Rovers were purchased, and runs took place between Sears Crossing and Bridego Bridge to time the journey.

Everything was now set, and the date was chosen—August 6. The men drilled through their assignments once again, the tension built, and suddenly the phone rang. According to police, the call was from Glasgow. The voice on the phone said, "Not tonight. There are only 40 bags."

The next night the call came again. This time, the train was worth taking. They took it.

Soon after the robbery, the gang split up. Some, including most of the leaders, returned to London or other cities until the heat should cool. Others remained at the farm, with instructions to stay as long as two weeks, to burn the mail bags and bury the ashes and to wipe the farm clean of fingerprints, before leaving.

Everything was working according to plan, but the gang had not planned on Lieutenant Colonel Douglas Stewart. On the Sunday after the robbery, the colonel sat alone at his home on his 450-acre farm 18 miles from Leatherslade. "I decided to visit friends over at Oakley for tea," he said later. It was Colonel Stewart's habit to do his visiting in his Piper Cub, and he went out and climbed into his plane. "During my journey, I realized I hadn't told my friends that I was coming, so on the village outskirts I began circling to let them know I'd be dropping in."

The route he took brought him over Leatherslade Farm. The gang members at the farm thought it was a police plane and panicked. They decided to leave immediately, and, instead of wiping the farm clean of fingerprints, they left good prints everywhere —damaging evidence, since almost all of the gang had police records.

There was really no need for haste. The police had been working from the robbery site outward, and Leatherslade was near the search perimeter. But a herdsman named John Maris called the police at Aylesbury on Monday morning. "You should look at a place called Leatherslade Farm," Maris said. "There's something odd going on. Odd men about. Windows blacked out. And there's a big lorry in the yard."

When Maris called, the police were receiving a great many similar calls a day. Leatherslade was added to the list, but by Tuesday morning it still had not been checked. Maris called again. This time two police were dispatched to Leatherslade Farm, and by lunchtime a party of top brass were on their way. They approached the farm cautiously on foot through the tangled underbrush, but the house stood closed and silent. In the shed were two Land-Rovers and a truck. Inside, on the kitchen window, the bathtub rail, a can of beer and elsewhere, were fingerprints. In the cellar they found dozens of mailbags stuffed with post-office wrappers.

While police combed the farm, Scotland Yard's Flying Squad began sweeping through the gaudy nightspots of London's West End—Douglas Gordon Goody's world. "The odd thing," said one member of the squad, "was that, even with the pressure on, most of those blokes went to the same places as they did before the robbery." For a while Goody continued to show up in his usual haunts; the police had nothing on him at the time. But when other members of the gang were picked up, he suddenly disappeared.

At Leicester, an officer noticed a man wearing sharply cut London clothes and pegged him for the missing Bruce Reynolds. Ironically, it was Goody, and the police took him to the station. There detectives found in his pocket a small address book. In its pages were the names of some of those already arrested, and Goody knew it.

When Goody was brought to trial on January 20, 1964, in Aylesbury, seven miles west of the robbery site, police still had not found one member of the "Board of Directors," Reynolds. Board member Charles Wilson, whose palmprint had been found on a window at the farm, and ten other members of the gang faced the court with Goody. All but one pleaded not guilty. The jury heard 255 witnesses in a trial that lasted 51 days. The seven major figures in the robbery received sentences of 30 years. Four others got 20 to 25 years. Two of the men on trial then already were free by 1967. They were John Denby Wheater, who had been jailed for three years, and Leonard Field, whose five-year sentence was reduced. Wheater, a solicitor, and Field, a merchant seaman, had been involved in purchasing Leatherslade Farm.

All through the trial Goody wore his ironic smile. While being sentenced to 30 years behind bars, he stood ramrod straight, not batting an eyelash, and when he turned to go off with the guard, he shot one last fleeting smile behind him, looking out past the audience in the direction of the door. Somewhere, out past the door, either buried in plastic bags, or stashed in false walls, or hidden in cellars, or locked in attics, somewhere out there, there was still $6 million. Until that money was found, Goody knew, the police could never say that they had completely solved the case.

Although the bulk of the money remained missing, two other members of the gang were rounded up in 1966. James White, the organization's transport manager, was arrested in the small Kentish resort of Littlestone-on-the-Sea and sentenced to 18 years in prison. In the two and a half years since the robbery most of his £100,000 share of the loot, he said, had been taken by blackmailers.

Soon afterward Ronald "Buster" Edwards, a 34-year-old former club owner, surrendered in South London and was given a 15-year sentence. He told police he had found the strain of being hunted too great. And in January 1968, Wilson was recaptured in a small town near Montreal, Canada. With his wife and children he was living the life of a typical suburban squire in a $40,000 house with two cars in the garage.

ONE MONDAY morning a salesman at Harry Winston, Inc., New York jewelers, was taking a tray of rings from the safe for display when he noticed an item that, to his trained eye, looked like a jalopy alongside a Cadillac. An executive confirmed the salesman's judgment. After all, a 3.69-carat marquise diamond hardly is a worthy stand-in for a 5.30-carat marquise diamond. The replacement ring carried a Tiffany marking, so Winston's called Tiffany's.

A Tiffany salesman remembered showing a fashionably dressed woman a tray containing a 3.69-carat diamond. She had left without buying. Now Tiffany's noticed a cheaper ring in *its* tray, and the story fell into place. The woman had dumped a $7500 ring in a Tiffany tray, plucked out a $19,800 ring and took it to Winston's, where she dropped it into a tray as a substitute for a similar $38,500 ring.

It was enough to set one to thinking. Was that all of the story? Where had the lady started—in Woolworth's filching a glass chip? And what did she end up with—a diamond as large as the Koh-i-noor?

—*Ralph Hancock, The Compleat Swindler (Macmillan)*

*The lowly government worker planned
a robbery that even the greatest masters of
larceny would never attempt*

OPERATION U.S. MINT

by William S. Fairfield

The Bureau of Engraving and Printing, an ancient brick building where the government prints its paper currency, is as heavily guarded as Fort Knox, so discouraging to the criminal eye that even America's most clever thieves have always looked elsewhere for their plunder. Over a 30-year span, from 1923 to 1953, the Bureau could boast that of all the billions of dollars it had printed, an average of less than $100 a year was missing, from all causes, including misplacement and clerical errors as well as petty theft.

On December 30, 1953, however, this proud record was placed in dire jeopardy, and a lowly, unassuming Bureau employe named James Landis was solely responsible. His plan was so carefully conceived and so deftly executed that the theft, involving a total of $160,000, was not noticed until January 4. And except for an accidental discovery made by a fellow worker on that date, the discrepancy might have remained hidden for several months. After such a delay, authorities are frank to admit, it would have been almost impossible to track down the culprit.

Landis, a dark-skinned man with mournful eyes and a scraggly, drooping mustache that lent his face an air of perpetual dis-

146

appointment, had been employed by the Bureau for ten years. His superiors had never felt any doubts as to his honesty. His record in World War II was excellent; he received the Purple Heart, Bronze Star and Good Conduct medals, rose to the rank of sergeant and was medically discharged after being twice wounded. His neighbors in suburban Chapel Oaks, Maryland, where Landis lived with his wife and two young sons, considered him a devoted family man.

When he was finally picked up by the Secret Service, Landis, nattily clad in a $150 cashmere overcoat, confessed that the idea for the theft had come to him purely by chance. Several years earlier, according to his story, he had managed a local sandlot baseball team. To advertise the team's games, he had printed a number of small handbills which he distributed to fellow employes and to neighbors. When the team disbanded, he found himself with a large stack of blank white paper cut to handbill size. Later, he noticed that these blank sheets were the same size as dollar bills; and he discovered that by inserting a sheaf of them between real bills he could surprise friends with a "flash roll."

In August of 1953, more than four months before the theft at the Bureau of Engraving and Printing, Landis stumbled upon a more profitable if less innocent use for the blank handbills. If they could look genuine when stuffed between dollar bills, he realized they would look even more genuine when packaged exactly as the government packaged its currency.

Landis' job with the Bureau was a menial one, but because one of his main duties was to carry currency between the vaults and the packing machines, he had learned how real currency was handled. The newly minted $20 bills, he knew, were assembled in stacks of 4000 with wooden blocks at each end. A machine then placed these so-called bricks under great pressure while two steel bands were welded around them lengthwise. From the banding machine, the bricks were taken to another machine where they were wrapped in heavy brown paper. A Treasury seal was glued to one end of the final package, and a label, including the serial numbers of the bills, the date and the initials of the packer, was glued to the other end. The packages, each worth $80,000, were put in vaults to await shipment to a Federal Reserve Bank.

As Landis was aware, Bureau inspectors occasionally broke into these packages to recheck them. The bills were promptly returned to the packing machines along with the labels—revised to note the date of the check and the initials of the inspector. But a wooden end-block, an unbroken steel band or a whole Treasury seal was occasionally overlooked in the rubbish—overlooked, that is, until James Landis saw the value of such odds and ends.

Slowly he began carrying scraps home in his pockets—a wooden block here, a piece of wrapping paper there. By day, he studied the composition of the genuine bricks he was handling. By night, while his wife was busy with the children, he practiced duplicating these bricks. Two months later, in October, he was satisfied with his homework. The label was still missing from one end of each of his two packages, but this was according to plan: Landis had no way of knowing in advance which bricks would be lying around loose the day of the theft or what serial numbers would be stamped on their labels, and thus he would have to use the real labels if his dummy bricks were to be substituted without inviting immediate detection.

In mid-October, just when everything seemed set, the Bureau suddenly changed the grade of its wrapping paper. Landis waited patiently until he could filch suitable samples of the new paper, and then, on December 30, he was again ready.

The key to the success of Landis' plan would lie in his ability to use the homemade bricks to take the place of the stolen currency. Merely getting a brick or two past the guards was not enough, for the discrepancy would almost certainly be noticed within 48 hours, the serial numbers of the missing bills would be broadcast throughout the nation and the thief would find himself in custody almost as soon as he tried to cash the first "hot" bill.

Landis arrived at the Bureau that morning in time to join the peak flow of workers reporting for the 7:30 shift, and under his arm was a paper bag containing the two counterfeit bricks. He knew regulations required that he check this bag at the parcel booth, to be picked up on his way out that evening. But he hoped that the door guards, in the midst of the holiday season, might be somewhat lax. He was not disappointed.

A guard did glance at him as he entered, and Landis obediently walked toward the parcel booth, quite willing to check his bag and try another day if the guard's eyes followed him. When the guard turned to inspect other arriving employes, however, Landis slipped down the hall and took an elevator to the men's room on the third floor.

The wastebasket in this room was lined with a burlap bag to ease the job of trash removal, and Landis had selected the bottom of the basket, underneath the burlap, as a temporary haven for his handiwork. The choice was not an idle one, for later in his plan, if all went well, he would have use for still other facilities provided by this men's room, including hot water, a radiator and a cubicle with a lock on it.

After stowing his dummy bricks in the bottom of the wastebasket, Landis went to the locker room on the first floor, hastily changed into his work clothes and reported for duty in the packing room next door. He helped clear out the vaults so that others could work inside them, and then was assigned to carry bricks, in serial sequence, from the banding machine to the wrapping machine.

At 7:50 he had loaded the platform leading into the wrapping machine. From long experience, he knew it would be 20 minutes before the reloading.

Bending over, Landis picked up a slightly torn sheet of wrapping paper, as if to throw it in a wastebasket. But his path carried him past the wrapping machine to where a stack of recently packaged $20 bricks rested against the wall. With his back to the room, Landis picked up two of the bricks, with the same motion folding them into the sheet of wrapping paper. A second later he was out the door.

Painstaking exploration of the Bureau had led Landis to decide on a seldom-used storeroom as the safest hiding place for his contraband. This presented certain problems since he was now on the first floor of A-wing, the storeroom was on the fifth floor of D-wing, and the only passage between the two wings was in the basement. But his pace to the basement and then across to D-wing was slow; and his manner in the elevator to the fifth floor of that wing was calm. On several earlier occasions, he had timed a dry run of this step in well under 20 minutes.

In the dusty storeroom, amid broken platforms and dilapidated office furniture, Landis unwrapped the two bricks, first carefully tearing off the package ends bearing the labels and stuffing these in his pockets. He next pulled out a pair of pliers he had borrowed from the packing room, placed each unwrapped brick firmly between his feet so that its contents would not explode when the pressure was released, and twisted the steel bands until they broke. With a sound much like the shuffling of a deck of cards, $160,000 in crisp, new $20 bills spilled across the floor. Landis brought out two additional paper bags he had carried to work neatly folded in his pocket, stuffed the money into these bags and pushed the bags out of sight under a low platform. Then, with no show of haste, he retraced his steps to the first floor of A-wing. He entered the packing room at 8:05, in plenty of time to reload the wrapping machine.

The next step of Landis' plan required at least 15 minutes, and he would not have that much free time until his rest period arrived at 10:40. Finally, after two and a half agonizing hours, he was relieved.

Landis quickly returned to the men's room on the third floor. Under hot water, he separated the genuine labels from the brown wrapping paper and placed them between the radiator flanges to dry. Five minutes later, he retrieved his dummy bricks from the bottom of the wastebasket and stepped quickly into a toilet booth, locking the door. With a small bottle of glue he had taken from the packing room, he fastened the labels to the bricks, at last

completing the imitations started at home so many weeks before.

Only one flaw remained: since the real bricks downstairs were constantly being moved about, Landis was not sure he could deposit his counterfeits exactly where the stolen bricks should now be resting, more than three hours after their removal. His only choice was to stamp new dates below the original packaging dates, as if the two bricks had just been checked and rewrapped. When he had done this, using a rotary stamp also borrowed from the packing room, and when he had added a fictitious set of initials, he was one careful step nearer success.

At 10:55, he reentered the packing room on the first floor, the bricks tucked under his arm in the same paper bag that had carried them to work that morning. Five seconds later, the bag was in the wastebasket and the bricks were innocently stacked with their genuine counterparts against the wall.

Landis waded through the rest of the morning, through his lunch hour and through his afternoon duties, hardly able to conceal his elation; everything had gone perfectly so far. Then, at 3:10, he embarked on the final leg of his voyage.

He left the packing room, changed into street clothes in the locker room next door and then, with an extra pair of work pants over his arm, went down to the basement, crossed to D-wing and took the elevator to the fifth-floor storeroom.

Landis found the two bags of currency undisturbed beneath the platform, but he also discovered that a slight hitch had developed: neither of the bags was large enough to hold the entire $160,000 and at the same time leave enough room on top for his work pants. He therefore stuffed as much money as he could—$128,000 —into the larger bag, placed his work pants on top of this maximum load and returned the second bag, containing the remaining $32,000, to its hiding place.

For the fourth and last time that day, Landis crossed the long basement corridor of the Bureau. He climbed the stairs to the first floor of A-wing, ducked through the locker room and headed for the doorway to freedom.

The guards were instructed to check closely on employes leaving with packages, and the man now on duty immediately noticed the paper bag under Landis' arm. He questioned its contents with a frown. Landis pulled out one leg of the work pants, but he kept on walking. The guard nodded, turned away, and Landis was out the door. Seconds later, he had lost himself in the swarm of home-bound government employes.

With his expert imitation packages snugly resting in the Bureau, Landis could operate on the well-founded theory that the theft might not be discovered for a long time. According to their labels, as revised by Landis in the men's room, the dummy bricks had already been checked, and there was little chance they would be checked a second time. Instead, they would be stored in the Bureau vaults for as long as two months. They would then be shipped to one of the 12 Federal Reserve Banks, where they would again be placed in storage for a month or two. Finally, they would be shipped to a local bank where, after an additional delay, they would at last be opened.

Only at this point would it be discovered that the bricks contained blank white paper, and perhaps as much as six months would have elapsed in the meantime. Landis could spend every day of these six months busily disposing of the new $20 bills, the fact that they were "hot" known only to himself.

Discovery of the crime at this late date would place the Secret Service, charged with tracking down the theft of government currency, in an extremely difficult position, especially if Landis destroyed all the hot money remaining in his possession as soon as the crime hit the newspapers. The federal agents would be saddled with a cold, six-month-old trail, and even the actual scene of the theft would be a mystery. It might have occurred at the Bureau of Engraving and Printing itself, but then again it could have happened at the Federal Reserve Bank or at the local bank— or, for that matter, on either of the occasions when the money was in transit.

On the evening of December 30, these thoughts ran happily

through the mind of James Landis as he made his way to the home of a friend named Charles Nelson. Landis had previously asked Nelson to get a steel box with a good lock on it, hinting that he had a "big score coming up." But when Landis spilled $128,000 onto his bed that evening, Nelson went out of his mind. "I didn't know what to do," he later told Secret Service agents. "I just jumped up and down, up and down."

Landis himself was more businesslike. Although the theft itself had been a one-man operation, he explained quickly, he would need help disposing of the loot. Even allowing for the greatest possible time lag before the theft was discovered, 36 or so bills would have to be cashed each day in order to spend the entire $128,000 within six months. Obviously, one or two men could not cash that many new twenties a day without arousing suspicion, so additional recruits were necessary.

Eventually, others were brought into the scheme, including William Giles, Roger Patterson and Edith Irene Chase, the last two being Landis' cousins. According to the plan outlined by Landis, the hot $20 bills would be used to make small purchases, and the "good" money left over would be deposited in a second box, to be split up later. If each of the six conspirators held up to his end of the operation, passing an average of just six bills a day, the $128,000 would be exhausted within the allotted six months. The recruits were only too glad to assure their coöperation, and Landis went to bed that night confident that he had covered every angle.

Less than four days later, however, the entire operation came crashing down about his head. Even to the practiced eye of a Bureau inspector, Landis' imitation bricks were perfect, but they were something short of that to the touch. For although he had packed his homemade bricks as tightly as possible before slipping on the steel bands, Landis could not hope to match the pressure applied by the banding machine at the Bureau. The real bricks weighed eight pounds, but the imitations were one pound and five ounces less.

On the morning of January 4, 1954, while Landis remained home pleading sickness, a fellow employe at the Bureau of Engraving and Printing was returning a load of packaged $20 bricks to one of the vaults, picking them up two at a time and placing them in a bin above his head. If this man had selected both of Landis' bricks at the same time, the deficiency might have passed unnoticed. But as fate would have it, one of his hands fell on a genuine brick, the other on one of the counterfeits. He lifted them, frowned at the difference in weight and reported his discovery to a superior. Within an hour, Secret Service agents were at work, following a trail that was still white-hot.

Meanwhile, Landis' accomplices were rapidly demonstrating that their benefactor had one huge blind spot: a complete lack of ability to judge his fellow human beings. Charles Nelson, who was supervising the spending operation, later told federal agents that the four other recruits were all holding back a sizable share of the "good" money they had obtained, and when agents asked Nelson what he saw in the deal for himself, he replied, "Why, I'll tell ya, when those thieves got through stealing from each other, I was gonna take it all."

Roger Patterson further rewarded Landis' trust by telephoning him one evening to ask if he could use some of the loot to pay a personal debt. Landis generously suggested that he take "a couple bills." Within an hour Patterson had joined a crap game, slapping at least $6000 in newly minted twenties on the floor and announcing that no one was going to break him that night.

The very morning the theft was discovered, Patterson, Nelson and Edith Chase were in Prince Georges County, Maryland, embarked on a spending spree that left a score of flabbergasted merchants in its wake. They bought half pints of whiskey at every liquor store they passed, each time paying with a fresh $20 bill. And apparently they decided to partake of their merchandise, for two hours later Nelson was seen lighting a cigar with a new $20 bill.

This was too much. Merchants called the Prince Georges

County police; and the police, suspecting that the money was counterfeit, called the Secret Service. The report of the theft at the Bureau had reached the Secret Service less than five hours earlier, so the agents wasted little time in getting out to Prince Georges County. When they found that both Roger Patterson and Edith Chase were involved in the spending orgy, they quickly focused their suspicions on a Bureau employe and cousin of the pair, named James Landis.

Eventually, all of the culprits were rounded up and all confessed. Landis led authorities to the $32,000 still concealed in the fifth-floor storeroom at the Bureau; and in initial raids on various homes and hiding places, agents confiscated $95,000 of the remaining $128,000 in missing twenties. They also collected almost $6000 in ones, fives and tens—obviously the change from bills already passed—and from this figure they were able to estimate that the Landis crew had been cashing a total of almost 100 bills a day, or three times the necessary quota.

Landis pleaded guilty, and in June 1954 he received a sentence of three to nine years in prison. Each of his accomplices received lesser sentences, ranging down to 20 months, except for Edith Chase who was placed on probation.

⚬⚬⚬

WHEN Rutherford County, North Carolina, Sheriff Damon Huskey went to California to pick up a prisoner, he tried to board a plane at a local airport for the return trip, only to be told that the airline didn't allow prisoners on its planes—it was passenger-pacifier policy. So Sheriff Huskey and his man rode a train to Arizona. By that time the sheriff had had it, but at another airport the answer was the same—no prisoners allowed.

The sheriff gave that one a good think, walked his man off a few paces, removed the handcuffs, mumbled a few words and came back to try again.

"You cannot take this prisoner aboard," the clerk insisted.

"He's not 'zackly a prisoner," drawled the sheriff. "I just deputized him."

Smooth flight.   —*Kays Gary in Charlotte, North Carolina, Observer*

*Daniel Dunglas Home brought spirits
to Earth, enthralled wealthy aristocrats—and never
gave any of his secrets away*

KING OF THE SPOOK WORKERS

by William Lindsay Gresham

The place is London. The town
house of a noble lord. A clear, crisp winter evening about a
century ago.

The curtain of our true melodrama rises to reveal a Victorian
drawing room jammed with sofas, massive oak tables, spindly
tables of mahogany, armchairs, footstools, bric-a-brac. A mixed
gathering, gentlemen in tailcoats and white stocks, ladies in the
enormous hoopskirts of the era, billowing with petticoats of stiff
crinoline. Buzz of excited conversation held in check by a note
of reverence and awe. The doorbell jangles, and then the butler
announces, "Mr. Daniel Dunglas Home."

He stands, smiling wanly, upon the threshold. The host hurries
forward, takes his arm and presents him to the company. He kisses
the ladies' hands with a stateliness already a bit old-fashioned,
and when he comes to you and grips your hand between his two
cold, moist palms you shudder in spite of yourself. He is a gaunt,
cadaverous man, an inch or two under six feet. His voice is hollow,
low-pitched, with a faint trace of a Scottish burr. You are prepared to dislike him at once.

He is about to pass on when he pauses, shades his eyes with his hand and says softly, "Three years ago you had a splendid idea which might have developed into something profitable. But the conditions were not right for its inception. Now ... you have met a person—a lady, in all likelihood—who will help you to achieve what is nearest to your heart." The china-blue eyes seem to search into your very soul. "Isn't that right?"

A swift review of your past finds just such a situation. You nod, puzzled. Home smiles, giving out warmth like a fireplace on a cold night, and places his hand gently on your shoulder.

"I thought so. Awfully good to have you. God bless you."

He passes along. Your hostility has vanished. It is simply impossible to dislike the fellow, in spite of the rumors circulating about him—charlatan, cheap humbug—and hints of "secret vices." Home comes, sees and conquers.

After a tray of wine has gone the rounds, the host invites you into a small sitting room. Here he becomes simply one of the group. The king of the evening is Home, the greatest spirit medium who ever lived. A lively fire is popping on the hearth and Home places a wire screen before it. Then he takes you gently by the hand and says, "Our new friend ... over there at the table."

You squeeze into your place between a long oak table and the wall. A lady is placed on each side of you; between the billowy oceans of taffeta you feel hemmed in and a little trapped. One by one the medium assigns the places. The company of eight is seated along one edge of the table and at each end, leaving the other side empty. Home draws up his chair.

"I feel that conditions are excellent this evening," he murmurs dreamily. "Excellent. My lord, will you lead us in prayer?"

The old earl, in a muffled and somewhat embarrassed tone, prays, "for open hearts, charity, courage and greater knowledge of God's will for all present." Subdued amens follow.

Rap! Rap! Rap! Rap! Rap!

The sounds seem to come from the table on which everyone has placed his hands, palms down, little fingers touching those of his neighbors. Home sighs, closes his eyes and says softly, "They wish the alphabet. Will you, sir, start to repeat it, letter by letter?"

This means you. You begin. "A—— B—— C——"

At L there is a loud rap. You start again, to be stopped at E. Then again at S.

Home speaks. "The message is clear. *Less light.* Is that it?" *Rap! Rap! Rap!*

Languidly he rises and blows out the flame of a candelabrum on the mantelpiece. This leaves the room illuminated only by the bright flicker of the fire. More raps, and then the table tilts and gyrates; the hands of the sitters seemingly try to hold it down but to no avail. Home leans back in his chair, his eyes closed. From his lips comes the voice of a child.

"Good evening, everyone. This is Danny Cox. Your lordship . . . please, m'lord. . . ."

The old earl leans forward intently. "Yes, my dear boy?"

"Please tell Mama and Papa not to mourn for me so. Tell them not to be sad. There's a little dog here, very much like our Toby at home. . . ."

The messages come, the voices change. At last Home sighs and opens his eyes. "Did anything of interest occur?"

The tension broken, the sitters all babble at once. Home rises, stretches his gaunt shoulders. Then he resumes his chair and asks, "May we have the accordion?"

The host quietly gets up and brings it. The medium takes it, a small instrument, in his left hand—by the end which has two bass keys. His other hand is seen lying motionless on the tabletop. As he holds the accordion by one end, its bellows quiver and elongate. A faint melody comes from it:

> Ye banks and braes of bonnie Doon,
> How can ye bloom sae fresh and fair . . .

You strain your eyes in the gloom to see what is moving the accordion, but it seems to be fingered by an invisible hand. The firelight glints on it as it continues to play.

Home holds it across the table to the lady on your right. She seizes it by the bass end and again, with no motion of her hand or fingers, it goes on playing softly. Then it is twitched from her grasp, floats and skitters across to the medium and then off and under the table, this time moaning in discord.

Home speaks gently. "Hear the discordant notes? That means that someone here is not in harmony with the others."

This strikes at you, for you have been wondering: *How does he make the thing play without touching the keys?*

Beneath the table the instrument bumps along, coming to rest under the chair of the host. The girl on your left tenses and whispers, "Something is *moving* under the tablecloth."

Home's hands are outstretched before him on the velvet covering. He moans softly. The cloth at his right is pushed up; you can see it dimly against the firelight. Then, sliding over the edge of the table, comes a slender white hand that glows faintly. It feels its way down the table, seems to pick up a pencil and write on a tablet. The pencil drops, a page is torn off and folded and a note is tossed down before you. Later it proves to be a greeting from your grandmother in the spirit world.

The hand now approaches the medium, gently feels its way up his shoulder and caresses his hair. When it passes across his face, you see that the wrist terminates in a faintly luminous cloud. At last it vanishes below the table again.

Home smiles, rises and goes to the fire. He kneels down, removes the screen, stirs among the coals with the poker, picks out a blazing coal between thumb and forefinger and carries it to the host. Standing above him, the medium asks resonantly, "Have you faith?"

The old man frowns.

Home turns away. "I'm afraid not enough, my lord."

A lady stretches out her hand, her eyes, in the firelight, flowing with fanatical devotion to the medium. Gently he lays the red coal in her palm and asks, "Do you feel anything?"

"It's . . . it's *warm*. Not painfully."

"Faith. Faith. How great is faith," the medium says in a sort of chant. He picks up the coal, now black, and returns it to the grate, takes the shovel and extinguishes the fire somewhat with ashes. The room is now dark, save for the pale oblongs of starlight which are the windows.

His voice comes from the darkness beside the curtains. "I . . . I am rising. They are bearing me up gently . . . gently as a mother lifts her babe from its cradle. I am rising . . . up . . . up. . . ."

The girl beside you now grips your hand tightly. "Look. Look! He is being *floated* across the window."

Sure enough, against the night sky you see the form of the medium, seven or eight feet from the floor, lying horizontally in the air; it floats across the window and then slowly returns.

His voice comes again, faintly. "Now I am descending, gently, gently as a snowflake. . . ."

He steps forward out of the darkness to the last glowing embers of the fire, warms his hands, crosses the carpet to the gas jet, turns it on and lights it by pointing to it with his forefinger.

Home, now collapsed in a chair, is deathly white. The host rings and sends for a bottle of porter for their honored guest.

That is what you would have seen, had you lived in London during the 1860's, had you moved in high society and had you been fortunate enough to be admitted to a séance by the king of the spirit mediums, Daniel Dunglas Home. He played his role from start to finish. His life, or the facts of it, are commonplace and an open book. He lived with the privacy of a goldfish all his days, and he died at the age of 53, full of honors and decked out with diamonds—jewels he had been given by the crowned heads of Europe.

He is regarded as the greatest enigma of psychical research— a medium who was never exposed and discredited and who never took cash for his séances, one whose phenomena remain "inexplicable" to this day.

In the 1850's the Western world was on the verge of a religious

upheaval. Darwin and his champions had blown a wide breach in the bulwark of fundamentalism, and the time was ripe for a reevaluation of creeds and dogmas. The old-fashioned hell-fire preachers, after scaring a portion of every generation into St. Vitus' dance or atheism, were becoming more subdued.

It was time for religious fervor of a different kind, and one of the most popular new directions was spiritualism—a widespread, fanatical belief in messages purported to come from the dead, transmitted by certain gifted individuals called mediums. Sometimes these messages came from the mouth of the medium, who was in a state of trance. But as often, the signals from the other world were conveyed by means of raps on tables and woodwork. It is significant that the spirits never thought of this means of making themselves known until the invention of the Morse telegraph in 1844.

Born on March 20, 1833, in the hamlet of Currie, Scotland, not far from Edinburgh, Home was christened Daniel Dunglas Hume. His father, a workingman given to strong drink, sired numerous children. Little Dan was given to a childless aunt to raise, and when Dan was nine, she emigrated to the United States, settling in what is now Norwich, Connecticut.

He was sickly from the start and spent much of his childhood in bed, dosed with home remedies for "his chest." He fought tuberculosis all his life. Few men ever had a more dismal start and from so meager an inheritance built so glittering a life.

A pampered invalid child, unable to play with other children, Dan specialized in all of the nonathletic arts—reciting the heart-throb narrative poems of the day, singing sentimental ballads and accompanying himself on the piano. If his early personality disgusted the more robust of his neighbors, middle-aged women doted on him.

Then, when he was in his teens, came the mania for spirit rappings. On his mother's side—the McNeills—he was descended from Highlanders possessed of the "second sight," and Dan soon began entertaining his aunt and her friends with accounts of angelic visions and heavenly dreams in which he saw his dead relatives living blissfully in the hereafter, imploring the living not to grieve over them. Then Daniel began to produce raps. Relations with his aunt, Mrs. McNeill Cook, became strained the more Dan leaned toward spiritualism. Mrs. Cook, a devout member of the Church of Scotland, would have no doings with such impious things.

One morning in 1850—Dan was 17—he came into the kitchen where his aunt was preparing breakfast and suddenly a torrent of raps began to resound from the floor, the woodwork and the table itself. Mrs. Cook screamed, "So ye've brought the devil into my hoose, hae ye?" She picked up a kitchen chair and shied it at Daniel's head.

He ducked without much difficulty and left the cottage in silent dignity. Mrs. Cook threw his Sunday suit out the window after him, and Daniel retreated to a previously prepared position—the house of some kindly, credulous neighbors who were fascinated by the new fad of spirit rappings.

Dan now claimed that his father was really an illegitimate son of the Earl of Home, and he began to spell his name with an *o* although he always pronounced it "whom." This gave him the added glamour of noble birth—even with a bar sinister. In the evening, when the supper dishes had been cleared away and the family sat about the dining-room table, hands pressed against its surface, waiting for the spirits, they were not disappointed. The table began to rock and roll.

Much of an acrobatic table's behavior depends on the unconscious pushing and pulling of the sitters, helped out by the medium, of course. Dan discovered the postern gate in the human mind by which one can enter unobserved—suggestion.

"Look, look—the table is trying to tip up at my end! Don't you feel it? I can't hold it down. . . . Do you feel it dipping under your hands?" His shock of auburn hair bent intently over the polished surface, his long, waxen hands spread before him, his intense, pale face taut, Daniel conjured spirits from the vasty deep. "Wait!

Over Miss Cynthia's head . . . a spirit light. A spark . . . no, now it's like a pale-green cloud. . . . Don't you see it?"

They saw it. They felt ghostly touches on their shoulders and hair, heard strange whispers (ventriloquism is an ideal art for an invalid boy to master).

The more séances Dan held, the more remarkable grew the phenomena. If you place your fingers on a polished tabletop, press hard and then let one finger slip a fraction of an inch, you will be rewarded by a distinct rap. Similarly, if you brace the heel of your shoe against one of the legs of your chair and slip it the same way you'll get another rap. But that is only the kindergarten stage of the art. Tie a bolt or a small fishing sinker on a black silk thread, let it down a crack in the woodwork or a hole in the wall and you can produce raps that sound—in a silent house at night— like the blows of a sledgehammer.

Dan decided then and there never to take money for exercising his gifts of mediumship, and he stuck to it all his life. He was intelligent enough to realize that if he took no money there was no legal fraud, and he counted on his powers as a charm artist always to have a roof over his head.

Dan mastered the speech of cultured people as he was later to master several European languages. He soaked up elegant manners like a blotter. When he wanted something he subtly let his friends know it, and when they got it for him it always seemed to be their idea. His gratitude was explicit, delivered with the intense, burning sincerity of the talented confidence worker. Going from one family to another, learning his trade of professional mystery man and charmer, Dan made the acquaintance of many of the most prominent spiritualists in the northeastern United States.

Finally, when the chill of a New York winter laid him low with a serious chest complaint, his doctor, an ardent spiritualist, told the youth that only the climate of Europe could save his life. In 1855 he sailed for England, his passage paid by a Mr. and Mrs. Jarves of Boston, wealthy cosmopolites, art collectors and spiritualists. He knew not a soul in Europe, but he had a little black book of addresses and the first of these was a Mr. Cox, who ran a hotel in London. Mr. Cox was a spiritualist, and Dan and he became lifelong friends. Dan paid no board at the hotel; or rather, he paid in raps, table tipping and "messages."

Dan by this time had discovered another trick of the trade: You can tell a person of the marvels which have happened to other people, and he will soon take some of them and retell them as his own adventures, without realizing that he is decorating the truth. Much of the myth of Home can be explained by this simple manipulation of minds.

One of the most persistent legends about Home, which got a powerful assist from his own memoirs, was that he always performed "in the full light." Of course he did not. By "full light," his Victorian chroniclers meant the flicker of a double gas jet, sometimes helped out by a brace of candles. And in such a light most of the business went on under the table. Dan—or the spirits, rapping on the table—would call for "less light" and it was logical; only in the dark can you see the luminous forms, faces and hands.

Once in England and safely ensconced at Cox's spiritualist hotel, Home found the *haut monde* of believers awaiting him with open arms—the Baroness de Ruthyn, the Marchioness of Hastings, Lady Combermere, Sir Charles Isham. He dined out every evening on the strength of what he could make the dining-room table do after dinner. He kept to his original principle of never accepting cash, but he let it be known that he liked beautiful things, such as diamonds, which are a medium's best friend.

Invitations came so thick and fast that Dan could afford to play hard to get. This boosted his stock. It became impossible to have a "sitting" with Mr. Home unless one could secure an introduction into his circle from someone whose social position was all but unassailable.

It is no discredit to such men as William Cullen Bryant, famous American poet and editor of the staid New York *Evening Post*; the great English novelist William Makepeace Thackeray; or, later, the eminent chemist Sir William Crookes, that they were mystified by the things they saw happening at Home's séances. They were men of great intelligence, but they simply were not trained observers of mediumistic tricks.

Once in a great while there were bitter articles in the press, such as the time Miss Celia Logan, a lady journalist who moved in high circles, saw Home place something quietly on the mantelpiece. The host saw it too and slipped it in his pocket. Afterward it proved to be a vial of olive oil in which bits of phosphorus had been dissolved. During the evening Home had produced glowing spirit hands. Such unfavorable press notices had no effect on Dan's staunch supporters. A lifted eyebrow and a word on the lengths to which some skeptics would go in order to discredit him and the glorious truth of survival which he, by means of his spirit controls, was bringing to the world—this was more than enough.

Since Dan always played it safe, never openly took money and paid his way with mystery and fascination, his marks never "rumbled" and his "gaffs" never beefed. He gave them nothing to beef about. And while he frequently performed before doubters, they were always gentlemen, and Dan was the guest of honor of mutual friends. To have grabbed a spirit hand would have been an insult to the host.

There was one time, though, when Dan had a very close call indeed. This involved Britain's most romantic couple—the poet Robert Browning and his wife, Elizabeth Barrett. Elizabeth was an ardent spiritualist, Robert a thunderous nonbeliever. It was the only subject on which they ever seriously disagreed. At the one séance with Home which the Brownings attended, the medium brought forth a ghostly face resembling, in the dim light, a baby's head; he claimed that it was a son of Robert Browning's who had died in infancy. Here Dan Home's pipelines of gossip failed him. The Brownings had, in truth, lost a baby—Elizabeth had had a miscarriage—but there were no infant deaths in their marriage, and the inference was that Robert had had a son out of wedlock. In a towering rage the poet seized the ghostly face and later claimed that he had found it to be "the rascal's bare foot."

Despite the incident and after scoring a tremendous success in Britain, Dan left for the milder climate of Italy and the colony of English and Americans who wintered there. Then, in Rome, on the tenth of February 1856, Home's "power" strangely left him. The spirits informed him that it would return in one year to the day, but now he was without it. There has been much speculation about this odd circumstance. One explanation has never been advanced and it is this: Dan may have had a genuine religious conversion. In any event, he became a Roman Catholic.

Traveling to Paris, he found himself broke and friendless, except for his confessor, the famous Father Xavier de Ravignan, a Jesuit scholar to whom Dan had been referred by the Pope. Without his miracles—viewed as black magic by the Church— Home was just a "vulgar American." His fashionable friends faded away; he had no wonders to amuse them now. People who knew him by sight would see him sitting for hours in a church, his pale, haggard face twisted by some inner torment. Then, true to the spirits' promise, his "power" returned—to the day.

And with it came a messenger from Louis Napoleon, Emperor of the French, demanding a séance. In vain did Father Ravignan entreat Home to fight against the powers of darkness. Daniel explained that he had no control over the mysterious presences; he was merely the medium through which they manifested themselves to the living. The good father offered to exorcise the demons, but Dan bade him a sad farewell. Dan could turn on real tears at the drop of a friendship. The Tuileries and all the pomp and glitter of the French court were waiting for him. He put on his good suit, took his courage in both hands and presented himself to the Emperor and his beautiful, stormy Empress Eugénie.

Our only account of what happened that night is from Dan's own memoirs and, according to him, he did everything but raise a fresh corpse. Whatever happened, Louis Napoleon and Eugénie were duly impressed, and Dan came through with flying colors and more jewelry. Soon he had the nobility in the hollow of his bony hand. He came back to the United States just long enough to collect his little sister, Christine, and take her back to France. The Empress wanted to have the child educated at a convent school at her expense.

Dan's life was brightened at this point by romance. He met a Russian girl of good family, a 17-year-old beauty called Sacha, and they announced their engagement. Alexandre Dumas, creator of the *Count of Monte Cristo*, a jovial, 300-pound mountain of a man who never stopped talking about his own greatness, delighted in Dan Home, who was a magnificent listener. Dumas gleefully agreed to go along to Russia as Dan's best man. The bride, formally known as Alexandrina de Kroll, was the daughter of General Count de Kroll of the Imperial Russian Army.

Dan was a miracle man in very truth now, for the girl's family— Czar Nicholas had been her godfather—offered no objection to her marriage to a penniless adventurer of humble origin who was obviously in wretched health. It seemed as though Dan had found his proper place at last. The following year a son, Grischa, was born to the happy couple. But in those days no one knew that tuberculosis is contagious. Little Sacha began to lose weight. Her eyes grew too large and bright. Soon Daniel was accepting invitations alone while Sacha stayed home in bed. After four years, she died, believing to the end in the genuineness of her husband's psychic gift.

Home was sincerely stricken by her death. Also it was a double tragedy, for a venomous cousin of Sacha's started suit to regain her estate. Dan was broke in England, with a small son to support. Kindly spiritualists offered to care for the child, but Dan needed cash. He tried lecturing, giving dramatic readings, acting. Finally he got an advance on his memoirs and this tided him over for a while. A friend of his helped him write the book. At last a group of sympathetic spiritualists founded a Spiritual Athenaeum in London, made Dan its full-time secretary on a small salary and gave him rooms over the office and hall.

But misfortune was lying in wait. Mrs. Jane Lyon was 75, a widow, and she believed in spirits. She wanted to get in touch with her dead husband, Charles. Charles arrived on schedule, speaking in the trance voice of Dan Home, and expressed his great love for the medium, advising Jane to give Dan some £40,000 in cash and securities. The old woman, much taken with Home, insisted on adopting him as her son, and he began to sign himself Daniel Home Lyon. Hurriedly liquidating some of his windfall, he sent a good sum to his aunt in Connecticut to buy a house; if times got bad enough he now had a place to duck into. Then the axe fell. Dan's spirit controls had overlooked an important precaution. They did not counsel Mrs. Lyon against consulting another medium. The second medium's production of dear Charles warned Mrs. Lyon that Dan was a fraud and to get her money back. She asked Dan for it and he refused. His mission was a sacred one and the money was sorely needed to spread the revelation of immortality. Mrs. Lyon took him to court.

The press held high holiday with "Daniel in the Lyon's den," but at the trial Dan was reserved and polished, all too plausible. He defended himself ably. Mrs. Lyon showed herself to be a lying, coarse, social-climber type who drew scathing comments from the judge. But the court ordered Dan to return the money. He was penniless once more.

And again friends rallied. One of these was the young Lord Adare, later the Earl of Dunraven, an Irish sportsman and big-game hunter. He was a popular youngster, and Dan set about fascinating him so deliberately that he was later accused of homosexuality, although there is not the slightest evidence of it. Dan had merely turned on the charm.

In Adare, Dan found a perfect foil, for the young Viscount was an excellent hypnotic subject. On late visits Dan often slept on the spare bed in Adare's room. A highly suggestible person usually talks in his sleep, and at such times a skilled operator can switch normal sleep into hypnotic sleep and give posthypnotic suggestions. These can well take the form of hallucinations: "When I tap three times tomorrow night you will see clearly the spirit of Adah Mencken hovering over my head. . . ."

Adah Mencken was an American actress, the toast of the fast set in London and Paris. She had recently died, but kept appearing in spirit to Adare after he had gone to bed, praising the talents of Dan Home. A critic said, "I don't know anything about spiritualism, but that part about appearing after the chap had gone to bed —that was Adah to the life."

Into his magic circle Dan now drew the old Earl of Dunraven, Adare's father; a dashing young officer, the Master of Lindsay— later the Earl of Crawford; and his cousin, Captain Charlie Wynne. Eventually, Adare published a book on his experiences in spiritualism with D. D. Home, and the miracles recounted therein did much to build Dan's legend.

The greatest marvel in the book is an account of a supposed levitation performed by Home, wherein he went into an adjoining room on the third story of the house, threw up a window and was "levitated" along the wall outside, appearing at the window of the séance room, raising it and stepping through to the floor. There have been more arguments pro and con and more fantastic explanations advanced for this "levitation" than for anything else Dan Home ever did. Yet on stripping to the facts, there is an explanation so simple it is incredible that grown men in their right minds could be taken in by it. Dan had only to go into the next room, make plenty of noise raising the window, then pussyfoot down the hall and back into the séance room, sneak over to the window, slide behind the heavy draperies, raise the sash, slip out, hold on for a moment and then noisily step into the séance room again, claiming to have been levitated out of one room and into the other. For both rooms were pitch-dark.

An expert like Dan could give a powerful buildup to such events: the aura of mystery which always clung to him, the blue-eyed innocence of his gaze, the dreamy charm of his personality, the great bulk of legend and the wonders told of him by the fashionable world, the simple religious faith which he exuded, the eloquence of the prayers with which he began a séance, the spiritual timbre of his voice raised in an old hymn—all this was potent stuff when aimed at three hard-drinking young fellows who came from a social milieu in which "cleverness" was distrusted while courage and devotion to duty were the ideal. The miracles recounted by these three men set the elite world once more at the feet of the Scots-American wizard.

Although he had been a great favorite at the French court, when the disastrous Franco-Prussian War broke out, Dan showed up at the headquarters of the German Army as an accredited correspondent for the San Francisco *Chronicle*. Adare, also a correspondent, had obtained the job for him. Dan's dispatches were sentimental "think pieces," flowery "color stories" and rewrites of handouts, full of "usually reliable sources." Between battles, in the billets of the German officers, he made the tables tip and float. And on several occasions, with Adare, he gave a hand with the wounded under fire. Cold courage, after all, was Dan Home's stock-in-trade.

The ruin of Louis Napoleon by the war reduced the number of Dan's patrons and cut off a source of jewelry and fur coats. He began trying bolder and bolder effects. Dan was an eager listener when the tricks of other mediums were recounted to him. When he heard of a new wonder-worker who produced some striking piece of spirit business, the same effect often found its way into Dan's séances some time later.

A boon to "spook workers" of this period was the invention of the "patent pocket fishing rod." This was a collapsible device of telescoping steel sections, which could be carried in a pocket or saddlebag, when it was no larger than a lead pencil, but could be extended to five or six feet. One of these, painted dull black, came in very handy for causing distant chairs to leap and glide, making glowing hands float over the heads of sitters and even brush their cheeks. On one occasion Adare spotted it without knowing what he was seeing. He wrote: "Going to the window, he folded the curtains around him, leaving only his head clear. We all saw a very curious appearance form itself about his head; it looked at first like a lace handkerchief, held out by a stick or support of some sort; soon, however, it became more distinct and appeared to be a shadowy human form enveloped in drapery; it was about two feet in length."

On sifting the mass of material about Home's doings, one is struck by the similarity of all his séances. After his bag of tricks was perfected, he seldom changed the act.

Dan begins with the raps in the "full light" of candles. Next the table tips, slides and cavorts. Often the large tables of his séances were observed to rise straight up in the air for a foot or more. The standard equipment for this is a heavy leather belt worn under the medium's vest with a hook in front of it. A confederate is similarly equipped, and at a signal they hook the table from opposite sides and heave it up.

Dan never had anyone to help him. His sitters were constantly changing. He worked alone. Somehow he used a device by which he could raise a heavy table by leverage. A hinged steel bar which could open out at an obtuse angle could be carried under the coat, one part in the sleeve and one hanging close to the body. Covered with velvet, this would not be observed and Dan could snake it out and under the table during the hymn singing. Opening it out, with one end braced under the center post of the table, he could, by stepping on a stirrup attached to the other end, lever up the table, balancing it by the pressure of the sitters' hands against the tabletop.

Believers down the years have often pointed out that whereas other mediums insisted on sitting in a cabinet to work their wonders, Daniel Dunglas Home operated while seated at the table —or near it—in the light. A dummy hand, probably made of flesh-colored leather, could be placed on the table in the dim light, or hooked on his vest, leaving his real right hand, with a black mitten or glove to conceal it, free to do its work.

Dan's fire-resistant tricks are in the program of many a carnival fire king but it is doubtful that Dan used their methods. He probably had a bit of asbestos cloth with which he handled the live coals and on which he placed them when he conducted his faith trial by setting a coal in the hand of a firm believer. It would work in a room almost completely dark.

Adare and Lindsay testified that they had several times observed Home's body grow at least a foot longer. But a similar illusion has been presented in modern times by a magician billed as "the man who grows." It is clever showmanship and muscle control.

There remains only the levitation, observed by the sitters against the faint light of the window. And here we have an explanation right under the voluminous skirts of the female sitters—that stiff material called crinoline which made their hoopskirts fluff out like haystacks. A life-size silhouette of Dan, cut from black crinoline, could be carried under the coat and at the proper time unrolled, creased down the middle and passed before the window on one end of his telescopic reaching rod.

There were mediums by the score in Europe and America, doing the same stunts. Of them, only Dan Home was never exposed. Of all that shady host of rappers, players of accordions in the dark and producers of glowing faces, only Dan has the distinction of a biographical note in the *Encyclopaedia Britannica*.

At last romance again smiled on Daniel. This time the lady's name was Julia de Gloumeline. She, too, was a Russian of good family, but she was not an impressionable child like poor Sacha. Julia was a sophisticated, cosmopolitan young woman. She fell deeply in love with Home, and the wedding took place in October 1871. Shortly afterward, the long litigation with Sacha's relatives was decided in Home's favor. Miracle man? He had battled the Russian nobility in a Russian court and won! Now Sacha's estate gave him a comfortable income of his own, his diamonds were safe from the unsentimental clutches of pawnbrokers, and in Julia he had a doting wife, a gracious hostess and a staunch believer in his spiritual powers. After Home's death she wrote a glowing biography of him with love in every line. Dan had pulled off another miracle by keeping a secret from an intelligent wife over the years. Of all his fabulous feats this one seems the greatest.

Dan began to give fewer and fewer séances; the phenomena

grew more and more trivial. He was just not exerting himself. And why should he? Finally he withdrew tactfully from his old friends, the extreme believers in spiritualism, and developed a new set among the idlers of the fashionable resorts. A celebrity himself, he associated only with other celebrities and socialites. Mark Twain knew and liked him.

Dan now wrote his book *Lights and Shadows of Spiritualism*, telling people how to trap fraudulent mediums who used mechanical rappers, reaching rods and luminous gauze. In his declining years he was a familiar figure at spas and health resorts, his gaunt frame more cadaverous than ever, leaning heavily on his cane, his fingers and shirt front ablaze with diamonds, rubies and emeralds. Finally, on June 21, 1886, his frayed lungs gave up. He was buried in the Greek Orthodox cemetery of St. Germain-en-Laye at Auteuil, France.

In his day he had "performed" before such noble sitters as the Emperor and Empress of France, Queen Sophia of the Netherlands, King Maximilian of Bavaria, Czar Alexander II of Russia (a close friend), the King and Queen of Württemberg, the Crown Prince of Prussia—the list reads like an *Almanach de Gotha*. Thousands of séances and never once caught faking.

Wise as a serpent, gentle as a dove, Dan Home gazed with passionate, utter sincerity into the wondering eyes of a victim. He may have been the highest-paid amateur in the history of show business.

〰️

IN A SPEECH on honesty, Mark Twain said that, as a boy, he saw a cart of melons which sorely tempted him: "I sneaked up to the cart and stole a melon. I went into the alley to devour it, but I no sooner set my teeth into it than I paused, a strange feeling came over me. I came to a quick conclusion. Firmly I walked up to that cart, replaced that melon—and took a ripe one."
—*Edison Voice Writing*

The two sourdoughs told a story of a
great jewel mine in the sky—and proved it

A CASE OF SALTED GEMS

by Harold Mehling

On an October afternoon in 1956, two South African scientists were ambling through the Mweza Hills of Southern Rhodesia. They were searching for a mineral that performs some mundane task in the hardening of iron and copper. As they happened onto a clearing the size of a suburban development backyard, the scientists decided to evade the punishing African sun under a stunted tree. There they became wealthy, for they stumbled on emeralds— so many of the bright green stones that they scooped them up in their hands. Experts have described the gems as the most beautifully colored the world has ever seen, and the scientists, at last report, were rejecting offers of $2 million for a one-fourth interest in their discovery.

The most engaging aspect of the story is that it is true. Nobody swindled anybody. Nobody planted emeralds in the African soil so he could reap a fortune from enchanted investors. Nobody was dishonest and nothing was crooked.

The same sort of discovery occurred a number of years ago in the Wild West of the United States, with one compelling exception. This discovery *was* a swindle, and enchanted investors did get taken in. People *were* dishonest, and everything *was* crooked.

In the early days of February 1872, San Franciscans excitedly received news of the greatest find since the gold discoveries of '49. Somewhere in the West, someone had stumbled onto an entire mountain of diamonds. Imagine, a whole mountain! No one knew just where, but they knew the story had to be true.

The bearers of this astonishing news looked exactly as they should. John Slack and Philip Arnold were their names, and they were grizzled sourdoughs with proper mats of beard and the dust of the hill trails on their jeans. Slack, a short, quiet fellow, did not leave a distinct impression; when a question arose, he let Arnold handle it. Arnold was a long, articulate stringbean with a face full of honest excitement. He was known to have served with Morgan's Raiders during the Civil War and, regardless of sentiments, a soldier was a straight shooter.

The picturesque pair did not ride into town shouting their discovery up Market Street, of course. They arrived on a Union Pacific train on the first or second day of the month, Arnold carrying a canvas sack and Slack, beside him, dangling a Winchester in the crook of his right arm. After checking into a hotel they went out for a drink, carrying the sack and standing it upright on the floor between them at the bar.

By the middle of February half the barkeeps in San Francisco were conjecturing on the contents of the bag and wondering why it received such close attention. Their interest was also piqued when the sourdoughs conducted all conversation in a whisper. One tavern owner said they seemed frightened, as if they had something too hot to handle, too good to let go.

Either way, the sack was at least heavy, and so Arnold and Slack carried it into the Bank of California and asked to have it deposited in a vault. No sooner had they received a receipt and departed than the inquisitive cashier was in a back room inspecting the contents. He found precious stones—a bagful of rough, uncut diamonds, emeralds, sapphires and rubies. That was too hot for *him* to handle, so he took his discovery to the bank's president, William C. Ralston.

Bill Ralston was one of San Francisco's big men. He was an investment banker with a freewheeling urge to take a chance. Rarely losing on a venture, he had put together a fortune that elevated him to ranking position among the city's elite. When he peered into the canvas, rubbed the gems in his hands and heard about the whiskered men, he decided that a big deal was lurking. But being a sharply honed man, he called in an assayer to inspect the stones on a confidential basis. The expert said they were worth about $125,000 and must have been taken out of the ground fairly recently.

Ralston decided that the approach to Arnold, the Civil War veteran, should be made through channels of military camaraderie. So he confided his discovery to an occasional investment partner, George D. Roberts, who had come out of the war as a Union Army general. Roberts immediately suspected that Arnold was the man who had investigated some mining properties for him only two years earlier. At their first meeting the General was delighted; it was the same Arnold.

Roberts seated the sourdoughs around several bottles of good liquor, and soon he and Arnold were reliving adventures from Sumter to Appomattox.

Although they had fought on opposite sides, new friendships were stronger than old animosities, they agreed. And so they got down, eventually, to the amazing gem discovery, which caused Arnold to fall back into whispers.

"I thought it would blind us," he said. "We came onto the field and the glittering in the sun was so strong we blinked. Everywhere we turned we saw the stones. Slack here went wild. He dug away with a boot heel and scratched them right out of the ground."

The General's eyes stared glassily. He could almost see the gem field himself. "You fellows are in for a fortune," he said, "if you can just get those stones out of there." He poured another drink and let them ponder his remark.

Arnold and Slack stared uneasily at each other. Then Arnold unburdened himself. "General," he said, "that's what has us

179

stirred up. We've got hold of this thing but we don't know what to do with it. If we start hauling the stones out in sacks, someone'll trace the field. The only way to do it is to tie up the land and bring rigs in to mine it out. But we can't get money for that without selling what we brought out and that would raise suspicion. Now, we don't know who's got that kind of money and some kind of real honesty."

The General nodded sympathetically. It was a dilemma he could understand. He talked for 15 minutes about the sad state of mankind's morals, how things had come to where one human being could not trust another. Then he brightened.

"Tell you men what I'll do," he said. "I don't have that kind of money myself, but I'm close to men who do. I can take the problem to them and see if they won't agree to finance a company that would obtain legal title to the field and mine the stones. Naturally, you would be partners in the company. Now, how does that sound?"

Slack seemed just a bit suspicious of the General, but it was clear that Arnold was running the show. He agreed and Slack subsided. But that was as far as the General got. Try as he would, he could not get the two sourdoughs to tell him where they had made their great discovery.

By the following morning several pressures were working through San Francisco. The cashier who had received the sourdoughs' sack began to speak publicly about his discovery, and Arnold and Slack found themselves a magnet for the curious and acquisitive. They stopped denying their find, but refused to discuss its location, even vaguely. One evening, however, Arnold, apparently after a drink too many, hinted that the field was west of Omaha and south of Laramie. Despite the fact that this narrowed the field to about half the West, a rumor whistled through town that the cornucopia was in the northeast corner of Arizona. Within a week, fully 1000 men had departed in search of remarkable riches.

Another pressure came from banker Bill Ralston. General

Roberts, feeling that he had cut himself in by laying the ground-work, handed the problem of Arnold's and Slack's silence back to Ralston, who had the most persuasive tongue south of the Columbia River. Soon the banker was telling the sourdoughs, in terms they could almost feel, what exploitation of the gem field would mean to them. He spoke of mansions, wine cellars, servants, carriages, women and position in the community of the rich.

Arnold's hands trembled with excitement as Ralston orated. When he could no longer contain himself he burst out with, "You've got a deal, Mr. Ralston."

"Call me Bill, boys," Ralston said.

Bill got the pair to agree to lead two of his associates into the field for a thorough inspection. Arnold insisted on only one condition: Ralston's representatives must be blindfolded until they reached the field.

Two weeks later, when the party returned to San Francisco, the banker's associates were dazed. They didn't know where they'd been, but they had seen more jewels than they could count and had brought back a bag of them. "Not because we thought anyone would doubt us," they told Ralston, "but because we wanted to be sure ourselves that we hadn't been dreaming."

With Ralston's acquiescence, the news leaked out. It spread through the city as fast as the earthquake of 30-odd years later. People accepted the reports without doubt, for the gem find was simply another proof of what they fervently believed: the West, and San Francisco in particular, was fated to become the richest, most powerful area in the burgeoning United States. Without going so far as to use the exact phrase, civic leaders talked of the city's manifest destiny.

Twenty-five bold citizens gave banker Ralston $80,000 apiece to get in on the ground floor of the new San Francisco and New York Mining and Commercial Company. Then Baron Ferdinand Rothschild of London and Paris came in and so did a couple of New Yorkers named Horace Greeley and Charles Tiffany. Greeley had left the New York *Tribune* but was still a formidable name,

and Tiffany was the founder of the well-known jewelry firm on Fifth Avenue in Manhattan.

With over $2 million in capital at his disposal, Bill Ralston continued to combine caution with a keen sense of public relations. He told Arnold and Slack he wanted to submit their bag of gems to Tiffany, the most noted American authority on precious stones. The sourdoughs quickly agreed, setting the scene for a publicity-laden meeting at Tiffany's offices in New York. Present, in addition to the sourdoughs and the luminaries mentioned, was Abe Lincoln's unsuccessful Presidential opponent, General George B. McClellan, one of the directors of the firm.

When everyone was seated and the reporters had been briefed, Ralston and his friends approached a round table at which Tiffany sat. Arnold carried a sack of gems which were spilled into a large heap before Tiffany, and the audience gasped. The jeweler fingered a few and rubbed them. He held them up to the light and finally subjected them to searching inspection through a jeweler's glass.

"These are precious stones of enormous value," he said.

"How much value?" Bill Ralston asked.

"I will have to submit them to my lapidaries for an exact appraisal," Tiffany replied. The fact was that the jeweler was not very experienced in uncut gems.

For 48 hours the newspapers kept the story boiling, and then came the verdict. When cut, the gems would be worth $150,000. Ralston, who had brought only a tenth of the stones from his vaults, hurried down to Washington to conduct some further business. He looked up Senator Ben Butler and hired him as a legal consultant. Butler, a Westerner whom the Senate looked to in matters of mining and minerals, agreed that he would be invaluable in getting Congress to legalize the firm's claim to the gem field.

It might seem that Bill Ralston had subjected the sourdoughs' veracity to the ultimate test. But no. An insatiable pursuer of peace of mind, he suggested that, as a last condition, the field be examined by a consulting engineer whose reputation was without a blemish. When Arnold and Slack again agreed, Ralston retained Henry Janin, an engineer so conservative in appraisals that he was said to have approved 500 mines in which clients later prospered, none in which they lost money. Janin received his price: $2500, all his expenses and the right to buy shares in the firm at a low price.

Again Arnold and Slack interrupted the gracious life they were enjoying in San Francisco, on a cash advance of $100,000 made by Ralston, and conducted a blindfolded expedition to their Shangri-la. But this time Arnold laid the groundwork for his exit by first protesting bitterly that he and Slack were being put to immense trouble. When they returned to San Francisco, Janin added his expert opinion to the others that had confirmed the find. Soon Ralston was turning down offers of as much as $200,-000, plus 20 percent royalties, for one-acre claims near the still undisclosed site. One hundred thousand shares of stock in the mining company were issued and distributed among the original investors. This was too good a thing to let the grubby public share.

Ralston found that Arnold's patience had been too sorely tried, and Slack's emotions slavishly followed suit. Arnold said that while the big-money men had set themselves up to earn a fortune, he and Slack had been continually stalled. He wanted out, and would settle for $550,000. Ralston happily paid it in cash and said a fond farewell to the sourdoughs, who stated that Arizona was the location of the gem field and immediately left town— Slack to disappear forever and Arnold to return to his birthplace in northern Kentucky, where he was triumphantly received as a true and successful son of the South.

Knowing nothing of these startling developments, Clarence King, a young geologist, arrived in San Francisco in September 1872, after having spent the better part of five years studying the mineral lands of the West. King was a product of Yale and, at 30, a scientist respected for both theoretical and practical knowledge. One of his most recent tasks had been to survey the 40th parallel for the government, and as a result he received the gem-field news with surprise. He had reported that the geological makeup of Nevada, Utah, Colorado and Wyoming showed little possibility of precious stone formations. He felt the same about Arizona.

King found Janin, whom he knew, and got the story. The engineer, high with excitement, said he and Arnold had traveled 36 hours on the Union Pacific before debarking in western Wyoming.

"Then he blindfolded me," Janin related, "and put me on a horse. We rode for two days with the sun in our faces a lot of the time. When we got there and Arnold took my blindfold off, I saw the most beautiful view I've ever come across. We were high, I figure about 7000 feet, and standing on a tableland that was mostly desert, but right near us was a conical mountain with a flat top. That was the field. In ten minutes I dug out maybe $10,-000 worth of stones. They were everywhere, in gulches, between rocks and in shallow holes. Clarence, you ought to get in on this yourself. I know you said there wouldn't be diamonds around the 40th parallel, but swallow your pride and take a look yourself. Anybody can make a mistake, Clarence."

King would swallow neither his pride nor Janin's story. Instead, he reviewed the method by which the engineer had been taken to the gem field. Arizona was out of the question, he decided, because two days' ride from Wyoming would only get a man halfway. Then he recalled that Janin had said the sun was in his face "a lot of the time." To the suspicious King, that sounded as if the engineer had been sandbagged. He had been led back and forth over the same general area for a couple of days. So King went back over his Rocky Mountain field notes and found a description that matched Janin's. He was not precise in his recollection of the mountain, but he knew it was somewhere in eastern Utah, in the foothills of the Uinta Mountains, just south of the Wyoming line.

Taking the Central Pacific line into Wyoming, he located an old prospector who had cared for his packhorses during geological expeditions. Together they scoured the Uinta foothills country until they reached a lofty elevation. There they found the conical mountain. It was no more than 25 miles south of the Central Pacific tracks. King grinned as he recalled that when Janin told Arnold he thought he heard a train whistle, the Kentuckian said, "You're suffering from gem fever, man! That was an Indian yell."

While King bedded down for the night, his helper, intrigued by the story of the gems, began scratching in the sandy soil. Ten minutes later he brought King a large, rough diamond. He had found it in a hole that, on inspection, looked as if it had been made by a miner's steel tool. Then, as King was dropping off to sleep, the old prospector whooped.

"Mr. King," he shouted, "this is the greatest gem field in the world. It even produces cut diamonds!"

He held a stone whose face had felt the knife of a lapidary.

In the morning King went to work. He found sapphires, rubies and emeralds, a disparate collection that nature could not possibly produce in one area. He found them stuck between rocks that showed toolmarks under a magnifying glass; rocks without scratches yielded no stones. He even found a diamond in the crook of a tree branch. The field ran over a quarter-mile area and ended as abruptly as it started. It had obviously been salted, loaded with stones that nature had manufactured in various parts of the world.

King and the prospector rode out to the railroad station, where the geologist wired Ralston that he had been duped. The banker refused to believe it until he established King's identity. Then he wired back that he and Janin were coming out to Wyoming and wanted King to lead them into the land of the deflated bauble. King obliged, and the end of the saga came quickly.

The San Francisco and New York Mining and Commercial Company retreated into obscurity, and embarrassed explanations were issued to a bewildered public. Ralston and General Roberts had been taken in by greed fed on rumor; Janin, having been called in only after eminent figures had endorsed the field, was also ready to believe anything.

The deluded San Franciscans finally pieced together the story of how they had been fleeced. Arnold and Slack had gone to

Europe in 1871 and visited several Amsterdam diamond merchants. All they ever showed interest in were low-grade diamonds, stones that had been rejected because of flaws or poor coloration. The merchants called the two men "the dumb Americans." Then they suddenly departed for London, where they stimulated additional disrespect for American intelligence. Altogether, they spent almost $50,000 for the biggest mess of low quality, rough diamonds and other gems ever collected by anybody. As a bonus of inadvertence, they also got the polished diamond which Clarence King's helper came onto after they had salted the Uinta foothill.

Banker Ralston knew that since Kentucky was still not gently disposed toward outlanders and particularly outlanders who called a Southerner a swindler, he would never get $650,000 worth of satisfaction out of Arnold on his home ground.

But one investor, whose bitterness was proportionate to the amount of greed that had led him to buy out other investors, traveled down to Kentucky and found Arnold in Elizabethtown, operating as a highly respected banker. He initiated such a pester of legal actions that Arnold finally bought immunity from prosecution by returning $150,000. The rest he used to finance his bank's expansion, an action so vexing to the owner of the other bank in town that he strolled up to Arnold one day and shot him dead.

The West was still without native-born diamonds, but it was not lacking in excitement. Two years after the exposure of the great fraud, Bill Ralston's Bank of California failed under the weight of his wild speculations. Ralston, short by $5 million, was found floating in San Francisco Bay. The ghost who stalks abandoned old mines—even nonexistent gem fields—had claimed its final victim.

◦~∞~◦

IN FORT WORTH, Texas, burglars lifted $2186 in cash and a 600-pound steel safe from the Helpy-Selfy Grocery and Market. —*Time*

Pretended gallantry and valor
can be as real as they look

SHATOUNI THE MAGNIFICENT

by Rouben Mamoulian

This little story shows how sometimes the Theater can leave the footlights to intrude into life, cross swords with reality and come out triumphantly victorious. The hero of such a story is one Vahan Shatouni.

When I first knew him I was a kid going to high school in Tiflis, in the Caucasus Mountains near the Russo-Turkish border, and he was a promising young actor on the Armenian stage. He stood over six feet, with wide shoulders, no hips and a walk that combined the grace of a tiger with the high spirits of a stallion. Strikingly handsome, he had huge dark eyes full of smoldering fire, the curved proud nose of an eagle and bold black eyebrows that met at a dashing angle. He was the doom of every young girl and every woman—and the envy of every man.

In those days Shatouni's lofty ambition was to play two parts: one was the melancholy Dane; the other, the character lead in a popular drama called *Ouriel Akosta*. This last part he finally did play, under most peculiar circumstances. Whether he ever played Hamlet I don't know, but at the time I knew him he was assigned the part of Laertes—and he made the most of it.

To Shatouni, even more than to the average actor, entrances and exits were of utmost importance. Needless to say, with his figure and legs he looked staggering in tights. So his stormy entrance in the fourth act—where Laertes appears, sword in hand, to challenge the king—was not unlike an earthquake in its effect. Shatouni would stop for a moment in the open doorway and then leap over the threshold onto the stage like a fighting Nijinsky. There was always a satisfying gasp from the audience.

Whenever he went on tour Shatouni would send me postcards telling of his triumphs from city to city. I still cherish one. It is a portrait of Napoleon, and the message reads simply, *"Veni, vidi, vici."* An incurable romantic, he had a great gift for telling exciting stories. They were all about himself: his adventures, his acting triumphs, his escapades with women. No one believed a word, but everybody listened anyway, fascinated.

When World War I started, Shatouni enlisted at once in the cavalry. It was an undeniable fact that he looked tremendous in uniform. The sight of Shatouni striding down the street, his spurs clanking, his high-top boots shining like two black suns, his silver filigree Caucasian sword cutting a dashing curve at his side, was pure theater. Then he left Tiflis—for the front, he said. Others, who knew, said he left for the city of Yerevan, assigned to a staff job. In any case, after a few months, Shatouni decided that it was time for the second-act climax.

He received two weeks' leave and came back to Tiflis. Before alighting from the train he put his left arm in a black silk sling—and thus made his appearance. To anxious questions he replied that he had been wounded in battle, and told how hundreds of Turks had paid dearly for that wound. No two people heard the same story; yet all agreed that if anyone ever looked the brave hero, Shatouni did.

Came the Revolution of 1917—and eventually Shatouni's great third act, which proved to be a performance of actual unmitigated heroism. With the Revolution, all the officials of the old regime were booted out of their mighty offices, some into the streets and some into kingdom-come. The Commandant of the City of Yerevan was one of them, and Shatouni was elected to take his place.

The people of the city adored him. Several times a day and often at night, he drove through the streets of the town just to show the people that he was keeping an ever-watchful eye on their welfare. He used a smart open touring car. (He never sat in it but invariably stood up, the better to observe his domain, and also the better to be observed.) In front of his car six cavalry soldiers in Caucasian dress rode their spirited horses at full gallop, and six more followed. As he went by, in a blaze of sound and glory, people on the streets instinctively shouted, "Hurrah!" and some even applauded.

Partly because official business bored Shatouni, and partly because he thought it romantic, he decided to have a "heart condition." He never *said* he had it, but implied it through mysterious references to the brevity of life and the immortality of the soul, and at times by an eloquent clutching at his chest with his hand, bending double and asking in a soft, gentle voice for a glass of water. He would take a few sips, then, half closing his long curved lashes, say quietly and firmly, "It is nothing, nothing at all!" It gave him an added aura of somberly romantic grandeur. When overly bored by an interview he would have such an "attack," then leave the office.

While Shatouni was perfecting his role as Commandant, events were preparing a climax for his career. Shortly after the 1917 Revolution the Russian army, with sagging war spirit, began to leave the fighting fronts almost en masse. Long trainloads of armed soldiers (they refused to surrender their rifles) were soon passing through Yerevan on their way from the Russo-Turkish front back to Russia proper. These soldiers had suffered much during the Czar's regime, and they nursed a bitter hatred for their officers. Now they had accounts to settle.

One morning a train pulled into Yerevan from the front. It was a train of freight cars and one passenger car with 65 officers aboard. Shortly after it, another train arrived, this one filled with hundreds of soldiers. Within seconds the first train was completely surrounded by a solid mass of armed and angry men who insisted that the officers come out and submit themselves to an immediate tribunal. This request meant only one thing: the officers on the train would all be shot!

With the possibility of a massacre hanging thickly in the air, the stationmaster telephoned the local military headquarters. An old lieutenant general arrived, accompanied by his aide-de-camp. With difficulty, and one must say courage, they squeezed through the mob. The brave general faced a wall of shiny rifles and hostile eyes. He cleared his throat and began to speak: "I order you . . . I *ask* you to disperse . . . go into your coaches." A soldier's voice interrupted harshly, "Beat it, old man!" Another cried, "We'll try you with the rest of them!" In one more moment they would have torn the old warrior to pieces, but he knew when to retreat.

In the meantime, the stationmaster had been telephoning everybody for help. In vain. Then he had an inspiration: "The Commandant! Shatouni the Magnificent!" A quick telephone call; an explanation. Then, just as the old general left, the soldiers heard what sounded like distant thunder—hooves, horses' hooves. And, while they watched, the glorious cortege came into view. Twelve horsemen were in front this time, twelve in the rear; in the middle was an open touring car, wherein stood the Commandant.

With one eagle's glance, Shatouni took in the whole situation. Before the car had come to a full stop, he was out of it, striding swiftly down the platform, proud, handsome and alone. The soldiers watched open-mouthed as he strode past them, his silver spurs tinkling sharply. In three tigerish bounds, the Commandant reached the top of a pile of packing cases and stood there, backlighted by the setting sun. Then, stretching out both arms toward the crowd of uniforms, he shouted, "Soldiers, come to me!" Whether it was curiosity that pulled them, or the supreme, complete authority of that voice, slowly the armed multitude started forward. They hesitated, then came on again until they had reached the packing cases—a sea of shining bayonets and puzzled faces staring up at the young Zeus standing like a statue on a pedestal.

Shatouni looked around, meeting each pair of eyes squarely

with his own. Then, when the pause was ripe: "Brothers in arms, lend me your ears! I am the Commandant of the City of Yerevan, elected by the Revolutionary Will of the People! I am Shatouni!"

He stopped. There was a great silence. The name meant utterly nothing to any of them.

And now Shatouni did the unexpected. Moved by some inspiration which must have come to him direct from heaven, as it had no connection with sense or reason, he tore his uniform open with both hands, baring his chest, golden buttons scattering on the cement platform, and embarked on the soliloquy from *Ouriel Akosta*, the drama he had always longed to play. It starts: "Throw stones into my chest! Unleash your fury!" and goes on for three fiery pages. It had not the remotest bearing on the situation at hand, but how Shatouni read it! And how he acted it! The few townspeople who witnessed the scene said later that it was the greatest performance they had ever seen.

The soldiers stood breathless, completely engrossed—so engrossed they were oblivious to the fact that the train containing the 65 officers was slowly pulling out of the station. Not so Shatouni. Out of the corner of his dark eyes he watched its progress. And when he finished the last sentence of the soliloquy, the train was a mere puff of smoke on the horizon.

The whole crowd broke into a thunder of applause. And now ...

Now, suddenly, the Commandant clutched at his heart and bent double. A dead silence fell at once. A soft voice said, "A glass of water, please!" Several soldiers dashed away and came back with many glasses of water. Others supported the Commandant with their strong arms. Shatouni took a few sips, then said gently, "It is nothing, nothing at all." He was helped into his car; this time he sat, leaning back on the cushions. In a few seconds his cortege was gone, the sound of many hooves dying away like distant thunder.

When the soldiers recovered their emotional balance, they turned back to the problem at hand. But, instead of the train containing the 65 officers, the mob saw only empty tracks glistening in the sunset.

HE STOLE A BILLION

by Allen Churchill

On an afternoon 42 years ago, a world-famous financier strode into the office of the president of a Brussels bank. Tossing a bundle of currency down on the desk, he said, "Four hundred million francs. Let me have a receipt."

Flattered at a visit from such an important man, the president immediately obliged. Days passed before it was discovered that the package contained only 5 million francs. Then the financier apologized, saying it had been a mistake. But he had what he wanted—a receipt for 400 million francs on a reputable bank. Already he was using it to raise more hundred millions on credit.

The man who performed this bold bit of financial legerdemain was Ivar Kreuger, whose career added a new dimension to the suave, top-hatted swindler of fact and fiction.

For 20 years he was able to live in luxury, rub elbows with kings, prime ministers and presidents, enjoy worldwide fame as the multimillionaire "Match King," with a reputation as pure as the snows of Sweden, where he was born. And all the time he was using the tricks of the swindler, forger and confidence man on a scale never before attempted. When he died it was discovered that he had plundered more millions than any man who ever lived.

194

Slight, dark, medium-tall, he had a puffy, immobile face, pursed lips and a pale skin that always seemed moist. People were impressed by his persuasiveness, his calm and the quiet confidence he radiated. He was a bachelor who seemed to cross oceans as often as the average man crosses streets. He liked to travel incognito, and his expensive apartments in Stockholm, New York, Paris, London and Berlin were always fully staffed, in readiness for his sudden and dramatic appearances.

He also knew how to win the public. As an individual, he did not resemble John D. Rockefeller, who had to be advised to pass out dimes in order to capture the public fancy. Kreuger devised his own idiosyncrasy, and the public ate it up: Whenever he was asked for a match, the Match King never seemed to have one.

He was supposed to be a wit. That reputation was based on the one bon mot he ever made. When a customs inspector asked him what matches his companies made, he replied, "It would be simpler to tell you the ones I don't make."

He manufactured his own legends. During his lifetime it was widely believed that Kreuger's boyhood nickname in Kalmar, Sweden—where he was born on March 2, 1880—had been "The Quiet One." After his death it came out that he had really been called "The Sneak."

He earned that title by thinking up schemes that trimmed the edges of honesty. Hating school, he persuaded the smartest boys to combine in a secret group. Each studied only his best subject, then pooled his knowledge. The canny Ivar studied nothing. He listened to them all.

Yet he demonstrated early that he could study if he had to. At age nine he sat in a class which was given a half hour to commit the Lord's Prayer to memory. After only a few minutes little Ivar's hand shot up. He rose and began, *"Fader Var . . . ,"* continuing perfectly to the end. Then, instead of sitting down in triumph, he announced, "I can also recite it backward." Without waiting for permission, he started spouting, *"Armen evighet . . . ,"* back to the prayer's beginning.

Such accomplishment, with its inevitable accompanying sense of superiority, was galling to some. In the school yard, later, an older boy walked up to young Kreuger and slapped him hard across the mouth. The shock was enough to shatter even Ivar's composure. "Why did you do that?" he gasped. "Because you never *do* anything," the older boy snapped, and walked away.

Eventually, young Ivar was able to rationalize such reaction. He would say in later years, "People can never understand superiority. They always try to destroy it."

Kreuger graduated at 19 from the Royal Technical University in Stockholm and began roaming the world as a journeyman engineer and draftsman. At the age of 20 he came to this country and had a chance to observe Rockefeller and other titans of the time who were at work merging hundreds of small businesses into huge monopolies.

Ten years of wandering taught Kreuger much about engineering too, and back in Sweden in 1910 he went into business with Paul Toll, a Stockholm architect. Kreuger and Toll prospered, but the work bored Kreuger, and one day he moodily informed Toll that business offered no sure road to success.

"It does if you make something people really need," the practical Toll answered.

Kreuger suddenly brightened. His family owned three small match factories in Kalmar. *They* were making something people needed. He had never considered it before, but now Kreuger decided to enter the family business.

On the surface it appeared to be a happy decision all around. Kreuger's engineering knowledge helped him improve machinery and make superior matches. His American experiences led him to take an industry exhausted by internal competition and transform it into a prosperous trust. Then he looked abroad. In every country he bought up small match factories and merged them. From 1914 to 1918 the European countries were embroiled in battle, but Kreuger, a neutral Swede, was free to consolidate his trusts. As soon as the war ended, Kreuger began roaming impoverished

Europe, his pockets bulging with profits from the prosperous Swedish Match Company.

He was aided by history, which had produced an upside-down financial world. Governments had no money, but people did, for the speculations leading to 1929 had already begun. If profits were on paper, no one seemed to mind. Kreuger had money—the paper profits of Swedish Match, plus the vast credits those profits commanded. The sudden power that money gave him brought dreams to Ivar Kreuger, dreams of a worldwide match monopoly. And that seems to have been the point at which he developed his acute megalomania, almost on the scale of a Napoleon.

"It is the utilization of money for power that the financier aims at," said Ivar Kreuger. It sounds like a line from a third-rate movie, but Kreuger spoke from the heart. Power, attained by any means, became the obsession of his life.

He began to lend money to governments—at a price. The price was the match monopoly in each country, and even when the industry was state-controlled, as in France, the shrewd Kreuger had an answer. "Give me the monopoly on match sticks," he said.

In the years following 1920, governments fell over themselves to borrow from the Match King. In all, he loaned over $350 million, in return for long-term monopolies. His loan of $125 million to Germany is said to have saved that country from financial disaster. In ten years his control of matches spread glacierlike over the world. In the United States he owned Lion Match and 10 percent of Diamond. Only two countries, Russia and Japan, resisted him. On the day he died, every third person alive who lit a match, lit one of Kreuger's.

The surface Kreuger ends there, and the real man takes over. While he lived, this man hid in deep shadows, for the real Kreuger was a criminal. As early as 1915 he was cutting corners to attain the power he lusted for, in a manner reminiscent of the boyhood "Sneak." He began to falsify the profits of companies under his control, attracting investors into Swedish Match and frightening competitors into selling.

There was no stopping him. Using Swedish Match as a means of commanding credit, he turned Kreuger and Toll into a giant holding company, and soon he was expanding beyond all legitimate limits. To hide this he began to create a bewildering number of Kreuger and Toll subsidiaries.

The nicest feature about these companies was their ability to show neat, convincing profits year after year. Sometimes Kreuger would project the earnings a year ahead on the balance sheet, to the consternation of some stockholders. "But how can our company make up a balance sheet for the future this way?" they would ask.

With his superior smile, Kreuger would answer, "The public wants to see its shares rise and it wants to get as much interest as possible on its money. In order to do this, we must perhaps anticipate the profits of coming years, and this anticipation will always be as good for the company as for the shareholders." Then he would give an overwhelming array of facts and figures to prove that profits would rise, and his listeners would think, "He certainly knows what he is talking about."

The more he got away with, the more serious some of his depredations became. One of the biggest of his subsidiaries supposedly was the Garanta Company, with listed assets of $25 million. Actually, the mighty Garanta was an Amsterdam garret. Its sole employe was a bearded old man who faithfully entered in the books exactly what Kreuger told him to enter there.

On the balance sheet of Kreuger and Toll there stood for years a loan of $60 million to the Spanish government. The final reckoning showed that there had never been such a loan.

In 1930 Kreuger shut himself in his palatial Stockholm office and himself forged the signature of Mussolini's Minister of Finance to fake bonds that had been printed in Sweden. When he finished he had accomplished one of the great forgeries of all time —$148 million in Italian government bonds. Kreuger used these to raise more money to keep his empire going for nearly two years, but he was afraid of them. Telling Kreuger and Toll associates about the bonds, he would put finger to lips. "In return for a loan

to Italy," he said. "The money is to rebuild the Italian fleet. If France hears of it there will be war."

Still, there were times when members of his staff, thoroughly confused by some financial hocus-pocus, dared to ask, "But, Ivar, how can you do that?" He would rise very slowly to his feet. "Are you suggesting," he would hiss, "that I am falsifying the books?"

Kreuger's colossal frauds are approached only by what he got away with in his private life. As with all swindlers, his most valuable asset was his reputation. To this end he created a domain in Stockholm worthy of the King. He built a 125-room edifice on a dignified residential street just off the Royal Gardens, which he called "The Match Palace." In it were his executive offices, staff offices, a boardroom and a match museum. His own suite was paneled with the finest mahogany inlaid with walnut. Across one entire wall hung a Gobelin tapestry. At his elbow were three telephones, one with an extra-sensitive mouthpiece and earpiece which enabled him to talk and listen while pacing the floor. Another phone was connected to a button near his foot which he could press to make it ring. With this contraption he was able to hold spurious conversations with the crowned heads and dictators of Europe to impress people, or have himself excused from unimportant visitors with faked private calls.

There was another office even more important—a tiny, hidden cubicle he called "The Silence Room." This satisfied his desire for the utmost secrecy in his dealings. He often quoted the Swedish proverb, "Great things happen in silence." When asked the three rules of success he invariably replied, "Silence—more silence—and still more silence." In every one of his offices and homes around the world he had these small rooms to which he could retire to perform in total silence the prodigies of concentration of which he was capable.

To the world he showed the facade of a man of complete integrity, so dedicated to finance that he had no time to relax or enjoy the company of women. Yet the real Kreuger was a voluptuary in the manner of Roman emperors. "Women are for rich men," he said, and he proved it to his own satisfaction by buying them just as he bought match factories.

He had official mistresses in each of the big cities where he kept apartments, but that was not enough. Often he roamed the streets looking for prostitutes, taking them to hideaways he maintained for the purpose. He subsidized a Stockholm theater so that he could have his pick of chorus girls. He traveled with a pocketful of diamond rings for casual encounters.

He was able to keep his varied love life secret because he paid women for their silence. It was not unusual for him to give a girl $25,000 at the end of an affair. Women protected him for another reason. In him was the strong mystic streak that often appears in criminals who are Casanovas. When traveling, he insisted that the girls he left behind communicate with him by mental telepathy; he claimed he could receive their messages. This and other qualities made him genuinely attractive to women. Though some did black-mail him, the majority kept his secret because they remained under the Match King's spell.

Kreuger has been described by one of his mistresses, whom he first saw as a beautiful girl of 20 and promptly made his favorite mistress. In articles published after his death she relates how they met at a Stockholm party. "He did not ask me to go to the theater with him the next night," she recalls. "He *told* me to go. It impressed me."

She remained his mistress for many years and watched hundreds of women come and go in Kreuger's life. "But even when I had proof of his duplicity," she wrote, "he was able to persuade me to forgive him."

People were disposed to speak of the man's preternatural calm in all things, but nothing shows the extent of the Match King's aplomb better than his dealings with Wall Street as the end approached. He had taken millions out of the United States by floating Kreuger stocks and similar deals. One such operation was so complex, however, that even the Wall Streeters sitting on his own American board of directors did not understand it, and they sent an emissary, one of the nation's biggest financiers, to Sweden for amplification. As with most of Kreuger's deals, there were falsifications Kreuger did not want the emissary to know about. While the visitor sat across from his desk, Kreuger's dummy telephone pealed out constantly. He would say to his visitor, his hand over the transmitter, "Mussolini." Then, "Greetings, Benito. How are you and what can I do for you?" There would follow long conversations about the Italian match monopoly. Similar calls would come in from Raymond Poincaré, Stanley Baldwin and even— the amazed financier reported to his colleagues—Stalin.

Kreuger took the American to his estate at Angsholmen for the weekend and received similar calls, this time from his executives, whom he had instructed before the event. "I am playing a joke on my American friend," he told them.

Finally the Wall Streeter asked for information about the stock deal. "I'm glad you brought that up," Kreuger said disarmingly, "but of course today is Sunday, and my accountants even now are working overtime to assemble all the details. So until they finish, why not just ask me? I have a remarkable memory, you know."

The Wall Street investigator asked about some figures he had with him which Kreuger had supplied three years before. Kreuger explained them, in the process rattling off the long columns to the last dollar. "They were the same ones," the financier reported back, "that had been written down."

Satisfied, the American emissary left for the United States without waiting for the report from the accountants.

From the moment of the Wall Street crash Kreuger was doomed. Depression dried up credit all over the world, and Kreuger's empire existed on credit. He had obtained billions on credit and had only millions to pay them back. Still, he kept on borrowing, and even in 1931 he was able to pull off an enormous coup. By overpaying the United States government $1.5 million in taxes, he made his companies appear prosperous in spite of world depression. On the basis of this he obtained a loan of $10 million from American bankers.

In February 1932, he came back for more. His first stop was Washington, where he spent half an hour giving an optimistic report on world conditions to President Hoover. Then he returned to New York—and reality.

Several months before, he had sold the Ericsson Telephone Company of Sweden to International Telephone and Telegraph. Incredibly, this was the first time outside accountants had ever examined the books of a Kreuger and Toll subsidiary. They quickly found book assets of $7 million which did not exist.

In New York, Sosthenes Behn, president of ITT, demanded the money. Kreuger tried his celebrated persuasion, but Behn stood his ground.

In the midst of one session the strain of years rose up in Kreuger and his steel nerves snapped. Head in hands, he moaned, "I'm losing my mind, I can't remember, I can't think."

Representatives of Lee Higginson, his American bankers, rushed him to his penthouse at 791 Park Avenue, and in the days that followed he seemed to age 20 years. Like other megalomaniacs whose collapses are on record, his speech thickened and his walk became jerky.

Nevertheless, he still made efforts to save himself. By transatlantic phone he ordered his staff to raise money by any means. There seemed little chance of success until Kreuger and Toll directors appealed to the Swedish Prime Minister. Reluctantly he ordered the Swedish Credit Bank, to which Kreuger already owed $50 million, to advance $2 million more. In return the government demanded that Kreuger return immediately and open the Kreuger and Toll books.

Kreuger rallied. With the old persuasiveness, he talked Behn into accepting the $2 million on account. Then he boarded the *Île de France*, determined to head off the Swedish investigation.

But in Paris another blow fell. At his office, he learned that the Swedish Prime Minister had examined the Kreuger and Toll books.

"He wants to know about the Italian bonds," Kreuger was told.

On the way to his apartment, Kreuger bought a revolver. When he got there, he sent cables to friends in Stockholm and New York. They carried one word: SELL.

How he spent the evening no one knows. In the morning one of his aides arrived to take him to a meeting of bankers at the Hôtel du Rhin. "You go ahead," Kreuger said to him. "I'll be along in a few minutes."

He went to his bedroom and stretched out on the unmade bed. Taking the revolver, he pointed it at his chest. With the luck that had characterized so many of his earthly actions, he put the bullet into the exact center of his heart.

In destroying himself he also destroyed what he most admired, for the shot that killed him ended the era of the Grand Illusion. He had perpetrated great frauds on the public, but he had just as easily swindled the great financiers of the day, whose period in history it had been.

How much did Kreuger swindle? Final claims on his estate totaled more than $1 billion, and that might be said to be the amount. Some $98 million of this represented losses to American banks and investors. In an effort to get some of this back, the Irving Trust Company worked 13 years finishing the most involved bankruptcy in history.

<hr />

IT WAS the Hollywood premiere of *The Broadway Melody* at Grauman's Chinese Theater. Thousands were straining against police lines to watch the celebrities when the fabulous Wilson Mizner, accompanied by a beautiful damsel, pulled in to the curb in a woebegone, dilapidated jalopy. He alighted casually, assisted the lady to the sidewalk and proceeded toward the lobby with a shocked usher at his heels.

"Do you," asked the usher, "want your—er, car—parked, sir?"

"Don't bother," Mizner replied haughtily. "Keep it."

The broken-down contraption stalled traffic and made a shambles out of the opening, until the furious Grauman finally located Mizner inside the theater and had him arrested for disorderly conduct.

—*Dorothy Kilgallen,* © *King Features Syndicate*

HOW I MADE A CRIME WAVE

by Lincoln Steffens

Every now and then there occurs the phenomenon called a crime wave. New York has such waves periodically; other cities have them; and they sweep over the public and nearly drown the lawyers, judges, preachers and other citizens.

I made a crime wave once: I was a reporter on the New York *Evening Post*. Jacob A. Riis helped; he was a reporter on the *Evening Sun*. But it was my creation, that wave. I feel, therefore, that I know something the wise men do not know about crime waves, and so get a certain sense of happy superiority out of reading editorials and speeches on my specialty. It was this way:

The basement of the old police headquarters was a cool place in summer, and detectives, prisoners and we reporters used to sit together down there and gossip or play cards. Good stories of the underworld were told—true stories. One day in this way I heard a particularly good story about two New York burglars who, by posing as caretakers of a certain house, got the policeman on that beat to help them load some valuable furniture from the sidewalk, where they had carried it, into a wagon. The policeman had even put the parlor clock in by himself. Because the victim of that robbery was a well-known broker, I wrote a news story about it, though I did not give away the source of my information. Since only the *Post* had the story, the morning newspapers printed the "beat," and Riis was asked by his editor why he did not have it. In the course of his irritated reply he said that he could get all he wanted of that sort of stuff.

"All right, get it, then."

That afternoon Riis reported a burglary which I knew nothing about, and it was my turn to be called down. My editor wanted to know why I was beaten.

I called my assistant and told him we must get some crimes. We spent the day buttonholing detectives. I sat an hour in the basement in vain. Nothing but old stories. My assistant saved the day by learning of the robbery of a Fifth Avenue club. That was a beat on Riis, but Riis had two robberies that were beats on me. By that time the other evening papers were having some thefts of their own. Soon they were beating me. I was sorry I had started it. I picked up some crimes, but Riis had two or three a day, and the combine had at least one a day. The morning papers not only rewrote ours, they had crimes of their own, which they grouped to show that there was a crime wave.

It was indeed one of the worst crime waves I ever witnessed, and the explanations were embarrassing to the Reform Police Board which my paper and my friends were supporting in their difficult reform work. The outbreak of crimes all over the city so alarmed Theodore Roosevelt, president of the Police Board, that he was almost persuaded the opposition was right. He called a secret meeting of the board and was making one of his picturesque harangues, when Police Commissioner Parker interrupted him.

"Mr. President, you can stop this crime wave whenever you want to. Call off your friends Riis and Steffens. They started it— and they're sick of it. They'll be glad to quit if you'll ask them to."

Parker explained that when the crime wave was running high he inquired into it, not as the editorial writers did: he asked for the police records of crimes and arrests. These showed no increase at all; on the contrary, the total crimes showed a diminution and the arrests an increase. It was only the newspaper reports of crimes that had increased. The poker-playing reporters were tired of it because it was hard work, but they had to keep it up as long as Riis and I kept it up. And, in their opinion, we got our dope from some inside office detective, who was squealing.

T. R. adjourned the meeting, sent for Riis and me—and *bang:* "What's this I hear? You two getting us into trouble?"

Riis told him about it: how I got him called down by printing a beat, and he had to get even. And did. "I beat the tar out of you," he boasted to me, his pride reviving. "And I can go right on doing it. I can get half a dozen crimes a day if I must, or a dozen.

"But," he turned to T. R., "I don't want to. So I'll tell you where my leak is and you can close it up."

And Riis, the honest, told us how the reports of all robberies were sent by the precincts to the heads of inspection districts and were then compiled in a completed list, which was filed in a certain pigeonhole in the outer office of the chief inspector. He had observed this one day long ago.

"I never did pry into that pigeonhole till you"—he turned on me—"got so smart. Mr. President, that file should be kept in the inside office."

Thus the crime wave was ended. T. R. took pleasure in telling Parker that he had deleted not only the wave, but the source of the wave, which was in Parker's department. He would not say what it was. Parker had to resolve that mystery by learning from the chief of detectives that the president had ordered the daily crime file installed in the inner office.

⁂

WHILE PASSING a lonely corner on a dark night, a pedestrian was stopped by a voice coming out of the shadows. "Would the gentleman be so kind as to help a poor, hungry fellow who is out of a job?" it asked, then added: "Besides this revolver, I haven't a thing in the world."

—*University of Washington Columns*

*Why had this wartime hero cast
his lot with the enemy?*

RISE AND FALL
OF A SOVIET AGENT

by Edward R. F. Sheehan

He was a shy man and he spoke with a stutter. He was handsome, in a melancholy way, and he had charm to burn. Men liked him. Women wanted to mother him. His name was Harold Adrian Russell Philby, but everybody called him "Kim"—a nickname that evoked his Kiplingesque boyhood in India.

Kim Philby was a correspondent for two English weeklies, *The Observer* and *The Economist*, when I first met him in 1958, in Beirut, shortly after I had assumed my duties as U.S. press attaché in Lebanon. I used to enjoy watching him at cocktail parties. Entering a room crammed with chattering diplomats, foreign correspondents and Arab intellectuals, he would step hesitantly, tentatively, looking like a letter delivered to the wrong address. But after consuming a respectable quantity of whiskey, he might turn to the attractive wife of a diplomat, embrace her with roguish ferocity and give her bottom an affectionate tweak.

"If I did that," an American diplomat might remark, "I'd never get invited again."

Kim always got invited again. And of course Kim and Eleanor, his American wife, were invited to the convivial dinner party that Hugh Glencairn Balfour-Paul, first secretary of the British embassy in Beirut, gave on the evening of January 23, 1963. Eleanor arrived alone, however, explaining that her husband had telephoned to say he would be along a little later.

As the evening progressed, she became visibly concerned over Kim's failure to show up. Kim had seemed preoccupied in recent weeks. His moods had alternated between sullenness and almost hysterical gaiety, and he had been drinking more than usual. That night she had "a dreadful feeling"—she said later—"that something had happened to him."

The morning after the dinner party, Eleanor called a close friend, a U.S. businessman with high government connections in Beirut. "You've got to help me find Kim," she said. The businessman immediately telephoned Colonel Tewfik Jalbout, chief of the Lebanese secret police. Jalbout mounted an intensive search of all hospitals and jails and scrutinized the departure records of Lebanon's air and surface exits. Not a trace. Philby had vanished.

Next day, less than 48 hours after the Balfour-Paul dinner party, Eleanor called off the search. She had, she said, gone to the Normandy Hotel—her mailing address—and found a farewell letter from Kim. He was off on a news assignment and "a quick tour of the Middle East." Everything, she insisted, was all right.

Was it? Eleanor had already confided to friends that Kim's toothbrush, razor and other personal effects were untouched. He had taken with him only the clothes on his back. Furthermore, Colonel Jalbout had established that Philby had not left Lebanon by any legal route, as he would on a normal reporting assignment.

Rumors began to build. Philby was in Cairo. Philby had been kidnaped by British Intelligence. Philby had killed himself. The most persistent rumor was that Philby had fled to the Soviet Union and that a major new security scandal was in the making. For Philby was no ordinary foreign correspondent. He had been a high official in British Intelligence, and in 1955 a member of Parliament had publicly accused him of being the "third man" in the famous Burgess-Maclean case—the man who, by tipping off Guy Burgess and Donald Maclean, had enabled the two diplomats to flee behind the Iron Curtain before they could be arrested for spying for the Soviets.

By early March, Eleanor Philby was receiving a series of messages from Kim—often in his handwriting—ostensibly sent from various Middle Eastern cities and promising that they would soon be reunited. Then, in April, a message gave Eleanor a specific "operational plan."

1. She should purchase for herself and the two young Philby children a BOAC ticket to London for a certain date.

2. Next she should go inconspicuously to the Beirut office of the Czech airline, where a ticket would be waiting for her.

3. The Czech plane was to leave Beirut at approximately the same time as the BOAC aircraft. She should ignore the BOAC departure announcement and join the passengers for the Czech flight.

4. To contact Kim "in case of emergency," she was to place a certain flowerpot in her kitchen window, and a "trusted intermediary" would communicate with her at once.

Eleanor, now possessing the first tangible indication that her husband might be behind the Iron Curtain, refused to go ahead with the scheme. But, driven by love, she decided to send his emergency signal. She placed the flowerpot in the kitchen window.

Less than an hour later her doorbell rang, and a thickset young man with thinning blond hair asked, in a heavy Slavic accent, "You wanted to see me, Mrs. Philby?" He was an official of the Soviet embassy.

From that moment, we may assume, Eleanor Philby was forced to face the likelihood that her husband was in the Soviet Union. How had it happened? How had Kim Philby, the recipient of a decoration from King George VI for his wartime services, come to cast his lot with the enemies of his country? The answers, as assembled from the most authoritative sources, abound in paradox.

Kim Philby was born in 1912, in Ambala, India, the only son of Harry St. John Bridger Philby, at that time a civil servant in the government of India and destined to become, second only to

211

T. E. Lawrence, the most famous Arabist of this century. After serving as interior minister of Mesopotamia (now Iraq) and chief British representative in Transjordan (now Jordan), the elder Philby went on to become a powerful adviser to King ibn-Saud and an explorer of the immense Empty Quarter of Arabia.

But if St. John Philby was an intrepid pioneer, he was also an imperious egoist. Kim's lifelong stutter can plausibly be attributed to fear of his father. Superimposed on this childhood awe was the memory of his father's violent opinions—his contempt for the methods of British bureaucracy, his rampages against British policy in the Middle East. From all of this emerges a significant clue to Kim's subsequent behavior: He inherited his father's bitterness toward the British Establishment. Also, he determined that, somehow, his own life would come to equal in distinction the saga of his father.

Kim began by attending his father's college—Trinity, at Cambridge. There he was caught up in the social upheaval of the 1930's. It was the dreadful decade of unemployment, hunger marches and, among intellectuals, a considerable depth of feeling against the Establishment. Antipatriotism was not only tolerated, it was fashionable; Marxism was not only respectable, membership in the Communist Party was considered a badge of valor.

Intelligence sources believe that Kim was recruited into the Communist Party while at Trinity—and told to keep quiet about it. Two of Kim's contemporaries at Cambridge were Donald Maclean and Guy Burgess, both convinced Marxists; Kim became an eager disciple of Burgess. Burgess, already a historian of considerable promise, was also a drunk and an obsessed homosexual. Still, he exerted an uncanny influence on practically everyone who came in contact with him, and he was probably the one who persuaded Philby to join the Party.

Philby graduated from Cambridge in 1933, traveled on the Continent, became a journalist and got married. His first wife, Liza, was a high-spirited Polish girl. In Paris at the start of the Spanish Civil War in 1936, the couple turned their apartment into a recruiting office for the Republican forces. Western intelligence officers believe that it was during his first marriage that Philby was drawn into the Communist espionage network and that he spied for the Republicans while covering the Franco side for *The Times* of London. Later, he and Liza were divorced. After World War II, she reportedly disappeared behind the Iron Curtain with her second husband.

Philby wanted to fight in World War II, but his stutter precluded an officer's commission. Through friends he was appointed to a high post in M.I.6—the branch of British Intelligence that conducts espionage and counterespionage overseas. Before entering this service, Philby made what was accepted as a clean breast of his earlier Communist connections. His particular task in M.I.6 was to mastermind British double agents, to penetrate enemy intelligence and—ironically—to feed false information to the Soviets. He soon established a reputation for brilliance in his work and became head of the entire counterespionage operation.

The British government now believes that Philby passed secret information to the Russians throughout the war. Since one of his official duties was maintaining liaison with Soviet Intelligence, however, his open and frequent contacts with them were above suspicion, and at the end of the war he received the Order of the British Empire. Also, by V-E Day he was installed, with his second wife, in an elegant house on Carlyle Square and was living beyond his official income.

A number of knowledgeable people were now predicting that in due course Philby would become *chief* of British Intelligence. In 1949 he was sent to Washington as first secretary of the British embassy in charge of liaison with the U.S. government on security matters. Here his contacts with the State Department, the Defense Department and the CIA were frequent and close. Some U.S. officials suspect that Philby passed American secrets to the Russians during this period. Other officials consider this unlikely, since the Soviets might not have wanted to take premature advantage of a man they hoped would reach the top position in M.I.6.

In August 1950, Guy Burgess reentered Kim Philby's life. Burgess came to Washington as second secretary of the British embassy. Philby gave him quarters in his home. Then, in April 1951, Burgess learned that the FBI suspected both him and Donald Maclean of spying for the Soviet Union. He left the United States in haste, and within a few weeks both he and Maclean fled from Britain to Russia.

British Intelligence subjected Philby to intensive questioning about his role in the affair. He admitted that he had passed on to Burgess the gist of an FBI report entrusted to him through his liaison with the U.S. government. When Burgess happened to come into his office just after he had read the report, he said, he had blurted out, "Can you imagine the bloody nonsense the FBI is peddling now? They're claiming you're a Soviet spy!"

Philby claimed that Burgess joined him in incredulous laughter. But when Philby returned home later, Burgess had cleared out. Philby stated that he then realized Burgess might indeed be an enemy agent and that he immediately reported his friend's disappearance—and his own indiscretion—to the British ambassador.

Why did Philby endanger his whole position in British Intelligence by admitting that he had warned Burgess? He had no choice: He had been the only official in the embassy to read the FBI report. He gambled that his explanation would be believed—and he was partly right. British embassy colleagues in Washington rallied around Philby, justifying themselves on the ground that any English gentleman would have done what he did for an old school chum. They made allowances for Philby's background and believed its complexities were beyond American comprehension.

The FBI and CIA were furious. "Get rid of Philby, or we break off liaison on secret matters," General Walter Bedell Smith, then head of the CIA, demanded. This was a threat the British could not afford to take lightly. In June 1951 they called Philby home and fired him. For a year afterward he lived with his second wife and five children in near penury.

Many British officials felt that Philby had suffered a shocking injustice. But the inner circles of British Intelligence now believed otherwise. In their investigations they began to entertain grave misgivings about Philby's relations with the Soviets during the war. And they realized that the circumstances surrounding his indiscretion to Burgess were too curious to be filed and forgotten.

They began to concoct a devious scheme to make the most of his case. To uncover the spy apparatus of which Philby might be a part, they would put him back in action by getting him to a place where the Soviets were active and where he could be of potential use to them. Why not in the Arab world? There Philby would enjoy all the prestige of his father, plus adequate freedom of movement.

How did M.I.6 stage-manage this risky intrigue? The plan took years to gestate; a premature move might have aroused Philby's suspicion. There were other problems: In 1955 Marcus Lipton, a Labor member of Parliament, rose in the Commons and accused Philby of being the "third man." Harold Macmillan, then Foreign Secretary, replied, "While in government services Mr. Philby carried out his duties ably and conscientiously. I have no reason to conclude that he at any time betrayed the interests of his country."

Macmillan knew that Philby was under grave suspicion, but he exonerated him in Parliament at the specific request of British Intelligence—and at the price of great subsequent damage to his own prestige. He cleared the statement with the leaders of the Labor opposition beforehand, however, and explained at least some of the reasons behind it. A few days later Lipton withdrew his charges, and M.I.6 was free to proceed with its plan.

The following spring, a member of the Foreign Office, who made it clear that his approach was official, asked the editor of *The Observer* if he had a place for Philby. He said the Foreign Office felt it was unfair that in spite of full clearance of Philby's name he was finding it impossible to practice his profession. *The Observer* agreed with this point of view and asked *The Economist* to share his services in the Middle East. In September 1956, in the middle of the Suez crisis, Philby embarked for Beirut.

During Philby's first year in Beirut he had a large accumulation of debts to pay off, plus the expense of supporting the family he had left in England. The combined *Observer-Economist* job paid him relatively little money. He lived in such modest circumstances that no one could discover where he actually spent the night. He collected his mail at the Normandy Hotel, but if anyone wanted to run him down at odd hours, all one could learn was that "he lives up there somewhere," as the Normandy barman would say, pointing to the labyrinthine streets behind the hotel.

Shortly after his arrival, a British official confided to certain British and American private citizens in Lebanon that Philby might have Communist connections and that any information bearing on this suspicion would be appreciated. This "quiet surveillance" produced nothing.

As a correspondent representing two highly respected journals, Philby had plenty of opportunity to inquire into semiconfidential British and American matters. But when he made his occasional embassy calls he displayed no particular curiosity and never nibbled at the pieces of bait that were discreetly dangled in front of him.

During this period a new romance entered Philby's life. His second wife, who had been forced to find work as a domestic servant, died in England in 1957, and relatives assumed care of the five children. In Beirut, Philby met Eleanor Brewer, wife of Sam Pope Brewer, Middle East correspondent for the New York *Times*. In 1958 Brewer and his wife were divorced, and, in January 1959, Kim and Eleanor were married.

The Philbys moved into a pleasant apartment. And suddenly Kim seemed to have much more money than in the past. His two youngest children arrived from England. Shortly, Kim and Eleanor began to exchange invitations with the diplomats and intellectuals in Beirut. I met Kim often at these parties. A British official had informed me of the suspicions against him, but I found nothing to confirm them. His articles in *The Economist* and *The Observer*, far from betraying extremism, frequently expressed his fear of

Communist influence in Iraq and Soviet penetration into Arabia.

By early autumn of 1962, virtually everyone concerned with the Philby case had decided that he was not an active Soviet spy. Then an incident occurred which brought the case back to life: Philby approached a prominent Arab politician, cultivated his friendship and finally stuttered out the suggestion that the gentleman might be of value to Her Majesty's government "in certain ways." He was clearly making an intelligence proposition. The Arab led Philby on and got a definite offer of money out of him. It so happened that the Arab was *already* working for British Intelligence.

When the politician reported the conversation to his "case officer," M.I.6 concluded that Philby might well be recruiting agents for the Soviet espionage network, while pretending to the recruits that they would be working for the British. British Intelligence decided to place Philby under day-and-night surveillance. Since M.I.6 was watching many others in the area at the time, however, and since its surveillance staff was small, a representative approached Colonel Jalbout.

The Lebanese secret police chief's surveillance of Philby soon produced extraordinary results. Philby was discovered turning up for secret meetings with a number of suspicious personalities. And on two successive nights a police agent observed Philby emerge onto the open terrace of his apartment, glance at his watch and begin waving a dark object in the air. Philby's apartment building was situated on a hill, and his terrace could be seen from literally thousands of windows in Beirut. Nevertheless, after a sweeping search, the Lebanese apprehended an Armenian who admitted receiving Philby's messages—they were sent in "black light"—and passing them on to another intermediary.

Unhappily, the Armenian, while he could repeat the cryptic content of Philby's messages, had no idea what they meant. Nor could they be deciphered by the Lebanese secret police or British Intelligence. The Lebanese imprisoned the Armenian, thereby severing Philby's line of communication. After nearly a month of getting no response to his messages, Philby violated the cardinal rule of espionage: He "broke security" and communicated directly with his superiors.

Late one night he hailed a taxi and drove to the traffic-choked nightclub quarter of Beirut. He hopped out, walked briskly to a one-way street running in the opposite direction, hailed another cab and proceeded to a public telephone in a different section of the city. There was a brief conversation, followed by additional taxi rides and highly professional attempts to thwart surveillance. His shadows finally pursued him to the shabby Furnesh-Shebbak quarter of Beirut. There Philby emerged from his taxi and mounted to a darkened apartment above an Armenian candy shop. A few minutes later he was joined by an official of the Soviet embassy—the same man who later appeared at Mrs. Philby's doorstep in response to her flowerpot signal.

The details of the meeting above the Armenian candy shop remain unknown. But late in 1962 the British decided to confront Philby with some of the suspicions against him. Two high-ranking security officers flew in from London and questioned him. Although his answers apparently were incriminating, they could not arrest him on alien soil. Moreover, they could not assume that the Lebanese would extradite him: Disloyalty to Great Britain is not a crime in Lebanon. Nevertheless, Philby must have realized that the game was up.

The alternatives open to him were hardly cheerful: he could commit suicide—or he could run. On the evening of the Balfour-Paul dinner party, he ran. Some weeks later, Colonel Jalbout tracked down a witness who had observed a man answering Philby's description boarding the Russian ship *Dolmatovo*. The vessel left Beirut on January 24, before dawn. Destination: Odessa.

When Eleanor Philby finally became convinced that her husband had defected to Russia, she decided to seek British help. In May, the British and Lebanese authorities arranged her secret departure from Beirut with the two young Philby children. Eleanor deposited the children in England with relatives of Kim. Later, apparently on the verge of a breakdown, she went into seclusion.

On July 1, fearing that the Soviets were about to unveil Philby at a press conference in Moscow, the British government publicly disclosed that Philby had, in truth, been the "third man" in the Burgess-Maclean affair and that he had worked for the Soviets "before 1946." On July 30, *Izvestia* finally announced that the Soviet Union had granted political asylum to Philby. In September, Eleanor Philby, faithful to the last, boarded a plane in London and flew to her husband in Moscow.

Was the Philby case an intelligence success or failure for the British? It appears to have been a mixture of both. M.I.6's vigilance definitely identified Philby as a Soviet agent—but then he got away. We may never know whether British Intelligence succeeded in realizing its primary hope—that Philby would expose key members of the Soviet espionage network in the Middle East. If it did, the British government cannot boast about it. You do not broadcast to the enemy how much you have uncovered of his secret operations.

What exactly was Philby doing for the Soviets? There was no doubt he had access to valuable information. He visited Western homes and embassies where the Soviets were rarely invited and, by acquiring an odd cocktail-party fact here, an odd dinner-party fact there, he must have learned a great deal. And he may well have *made up* a great deal, some Western officials believe. He appears to have created for the Soviets a special intelligence apparatus populated by a mixture of real and nonexistent agents, which he pretended was feeding him "inside" information. As a spy, he would have been under tremendous pressure to produce—and when he could not, he apparently invented.

Soon after Kim's defection, the Soviets placed him on a health farm for a period, and it is believed that their subsequent "debriefings" included the use of truth drugs. In 1967 it was reported that he was working for a Russian publishing house. He had divorced Eleanor and was married for the fourth time—this time to the former wife of Donald Maclean. In an interview, he said he was comfortable in Moscow and missed little of English life.

One wonders. Shortly before he defected to Russia, Philby had been having nightmares. One night, as Eleanor revealed to friends later on, she woke to find him sitting up in bed, his eyes shut, trying to stutter out a cry for help. That was the first time she had ever heard him stutter in his sleep. On another occasion, she subsequently disclosed, she had gone into the bathroom and found Kim standing over the sink, staring into the mirror, sobbing.

One considers this scene, and one wonders.

⌒⌒⌒

"**JUST BEFORE** closing time one day," said Charles MacArthur, recalling the times when he was a reporter on the Chicago *Tribune*, "an Indian potentate, gorgeously turbaned and bejeweled, came into City Hall with a paper to be witnessed and recorded. It seemed there was an Indian heiress who must be married to an American by midnight in order to inherit a fortune in Bombay. The Chicago *Herald-Examiner* ran only a short account of this; but to us on the *Trib* it looked like a clue to a highly romantic story.

"Next day we reporters ransacked the town until we found the fortunate American. He was a bum in a flophouse. Some lawyers, he admitted, had come with a beautiful dark girl and he had married her. He showed us the $5000 that had been given him for signing a paper promising he would never see her again or make any claims on her.

"The *Trib* came out with its 'exclusive' story of the mysterious heiress from Bombay, with photographs. The same morning, on the front page of the *Herald-Examiner* appeared a box announcing an exciting new fiction serial by Arthur Somers Roche. The blurb thanked the *Trib* for falling for this press-agent stunt and giving such wonderful publicity to the *Herald-Examiner*'s serial.

"The $5000, as it turned out, had been *Herald-Examiner* money, and the 'bum' the disguised son of one of the paper's executives."

—*J. P. McEvoy, in Cosmopolitan*

A MAN called up the New York office of the FBI and reported that he had stolen a suitcase in Grand Central Station. "It's full of blueprints and other stuff that looks like secret military information," he said. "I've checked it in one of the public lockers and I'm mailing you the key.

"I'm a thief. But I'm a loyal American thief."

—*George Dixon,* © *King Features Syndicate*

*With painstaking thoroughness, he forged
the documents to create an empire*

FABULOUS BARON OF ARIZONA

by Clarence Budington Kelland

On May 9, 1881, there appeared in Phoenix, Arizona, a distinguished-looking gentleman, with fine eyes and a patrician nose, named James Addison Reavis, who asserted that under the Spanish titles of Baron de Arizonaca and Caballero de los Colorados he owned every ranch, every homestead, every inch of city real estate in a vast surrounding area of 10.8 million acres. The tract, said to be worth $300 million, embraced the populous city of Phoenix and many smaller towns, and included the fabulous Silver King mine, millions of dollars' worth of copper, gold and silver ore, and the right of way of the Southern Pacific Railway. With considerable pomp Reavis posted public notices that everybody occupying this land under any sort of title must make suitable financial arrangements with him or be ousted as a trespasser.

Thus blossomed the most intricate and firmly based imposture in all the history of chicanery. For years the claim was to cloud every title, hamper every business transaction involving real estate, make dubious the ownership of every ounce of ore mined in this huge area. Reavis' tortuous road of forgery and fraud was to reach its apex when he and his Baroness were received at court in Madrid, where their twin sons were said to have been playmates of little

King Alfonso. Its lowest point was reached in a penitentiary cell in Santa Fe, New Mexico.

While he was a Confederate soldier, Reavis made a discovery which was to be the foundation of his amazing career: He wrote a pass giving himself a few days' leave, and his forgery of the captain's signature was honored without question. He repeated the performance again and again and, doubtless for a small consideration, wrote similar passes for friends. Reavis was well aware that this talent would pay dividends if efficiently and cautiously used. If he could forge one signature, he could forge any signature—or an entire document. So in his spare time he devoted himself to the mastery of his art.

Following his discharge from the army, Reavis worked for a time in St. Louis and then turned up in the ancient town of Santa Fe, where there was a bureau for investigating Spanish land claims. It had been the custom of Spanish kings to reward their favorite *caballeros* with vast grants of land; and under the Treaty of Guadalupe Hidalgo and the subsequent Gadsden Purchase, we Americans guaranteed to recognize and protect Spanish titles to land within the borders of our newly acquired territories.

Reavis got himself a job in the record room in Santa Fe, where he was up to his ears in ancient Spanish documents enriched by the penmanship of padres of old and embellished by enormous and impressive seals. Here he worked day and night to master the Spanish language—not merely as it existed around 1867 but as it had been written 150 years before. He whittled out quill pens in order to copy yellowing parchments, rejecting and copying again, until he thought he had achieved perfection.

Reavis suffered under one major disadvantage, if he was to appear as claimant to a Spanish grant: He was a Missourian, of known family and antecedents. So, as foundation for his fraud, he invented Miguel de Peralta, distant kinsman of King Ferdinand of Spain, Gentleman of the King's Bedchamber, Grandee of Spain, Knight of the Military Order of Carlos III, Knight of the Insignia of the Royal College of Our Lady of Guadalupe. Miguel's father was José Gaston Gomez de Silva y Montux de Oca de la Cerda y de Caullo de Peralta de los Falces de la Vega, which was quite a mouthful of ancestor. And his mother's name was almost equally impressive—Doña Francesca Ana María Garcia de la Cordóba y Muñiz de Perez.

Now Reavis had to endow these Peraltas with historical existence, and he must provide Miguel with legal heirs to succeed to the ownership of the Peralta Grant. And the life story of each descendant must be capable of legal and documentary proof to be adduced in court. It seemed an impossible task, yet Reavis accomplished it. No records remain of how he financed himself on the tour of forgery that carried him through Mexico to Portugal and Spain during the 1870's. But apparently he could always lay his hands upon the necessary money.

It is difficult enough to forge a check so that it will pass the eagle eye of the bank teller; it is a stupendous task to forge a historical document so that it will be convincing to scholars; it savors of black magic to produce such a document and then place it among the official archives of a nation. Not only did Reavis manage to elude the guardians of old Spanish records, but he was able to seclude himself with certain parchments long enough to erase the original words with chemicals and insert other words with which to bolster his case.

At last, spotted all over the Spanish world of Europe and America, were documents providing a legal, historical account of a man and a family who never existed outside the inventive head of James Addison Reavis.

Next Reavis had to establish some chain of title between the Peralta family and himself. At this time he became acquainted with one George Willing, a nomad pioneer. Reavis' story was that Willing, for $1000 cash, bought from one Miguel Peralta, a poverty-stricken Mexican, the whole of the enormous Peralta Grant. This Miguel Peralta was, according to the forged deeds and transfers, descendant and heir of King Ferdinand's Gentleman of the King's Bedchamber. Willing then resold the grant to Reavis for a consideration, said to be $30,000. So James Addison Reavis finally had legal color of title to his barony in Arizona.

Upon the very night that Reavis recorded his deed, Willing conveniently died in the roaring frontier town of Prescott. Organized law was negligible there, and the quiet death of an inconspicuous citizen aroused no inquiry. Unofficial records, however, inform us that George Willing died of poison.

Reavis was early on the ground after that death. He searched Willing's attic and discovered in a gunny sack under the eaves certified documents bolstering the Peralta claim, including a letter from General Antonio López Santa Anna to Willing. According to this remarkable letter, the President of Mexico had, for an unknown and impecunious American, ransacked Mexican records and procured certified copies of important papers.

Armed with all the impressive documents in the case, Reavis now filed with Royal A. Johnson, surveyor general for the government, a petition to be declared owner of the vast Peralta barony. Boldly he posted his public notices in Phoenix warning all "trespassers" to settle up, whereupon the populace started buzzing like frightened bees, mobs gathered, committees were formed for common protection against the usurper.

The Southern Pacific Railroad Company, the Silver King mine and Wells, Fargo and Company, sweating with anxiety, called in their legal counsel for frantic consultations, at which Reavis obligingly presented his forged documents. The best legal minds of the nation scrutinized them, then gave their opinion that the Reavis-Peralta claim was unassailable! Lawyers advised their clients to settle, as cheaply as Reavis would let them.

The Southern Pacific Railroad actually paid him $50,000, and the Silver King mine paid an installment of $25,000. With the government in Washington Reavis was negotiating a settlement in the amount of $25 million—to make good the titles under which the government had granted homesteads to pioneers.

Now, with ample money for lavish living and luxurious travel, Reavis seemed to have the world by the tail. But he still had misgivings. The chain leading from the papers to himself was not strong enough to content him.

So he set out in quest of a girl: She must be approximately 14 years old, a Spanish or Mexican waif, and must know practically nothing of her origin. At last he found her—a little servant who drudged for her board on an eastern Arizona ranch owned by one John Slaughter. Since infancy, she had passed from hand to hand, being taken in by people who pitied her or who could get enough work out of her to pay for her keep. Reavis appeared at the Slaughter ranch in the guise of rescuer and friend. He told of his years of search for the true heir of the Peraltas, and as usual he fabricated an intricate story of lineage, journeys and abandonment to prove that this little Carmelita was the great-granddaughter of a Gentleman of the Bedchamber. Forged documents and perjured affidavits proved every step of the journey, each essential event.

The little servant girl began to live a marvelous dream. Reavis took her to California, declaring her to be his ward, and fitted her out with clothes befitting her rank. Then he turned her over to the good sisters of a convent school and instructed them to endow her with all the accomplishments of the most exalted lady.

When Carmelita was old enough, Reavis made her his wife, and took upon himself the high-sounding title of Don James Addison de Peralta-Reavis, Baron of Arizona. When twin sons were born to them, he asserted a secondary and stronger claim to the Peralta Grant on behalf of his wife, the direct heir, and his twin sons, who continued the name.

Now came a period of ostentatious pomp and luxury. Reavis formed lumber companies, mining companies, irrigation projects in his barony. The Mohave mines, included in the tract, were producing $482,000 worth of silver by 1887. The Silver King mine was declaring annual dividends of $200,000. Many of Reavis' frightened tenants paid him $50 to $500 for quitclaim deeds to their ranches, homes and farms. His income, it is said, amounted to some $300,000 a year.

However, the frightened, bewildered inhabitants of the barony found a champion. Tom Weedin, editor and proprietor of the newspaper in Florence, Arizona, belabored Reavis and his spurious pretensions and urged the people to fight for their rights. The Phoenix *Gazette* also urged that "some man who has a patent to his land commence suit to quiet title."

There was more talk, and threats of action, but nothing was done. Meanwhile, the Baron went his amazing way, traveling the earth with his Baroness and twin sons. In one year he is said to have spent $60,000 in travel alone. He owned a mansion in St. Louis, a sumptuous house in Washington, a home in Madrid and an extravagantly beautiful palace in Mexico. Awed subjects of the barony saw him drive in a carriage behind six white horses. They saw his little sons dressed as Spanish princes in red velvet, the Baroness richly garbed after the fashion of a Spanish lady of high estate. Their every public appearance was a parade.

It was not until 1890 that Royal Johnson, the surveyor general, reported the findings of his investigation into Reavis' petition. It was an adverse report, excellently reasoned, and it pointed out certain historical discrepancies and broadly suggested forgery. Its conclusion was that the claim of Reavis was spurious and should be disallowed. This judgment seems not to have discouraged Reavis, who continued diligently to exploit the resources of his barony. Nor do the legal authorities seem to have done anything about it until, in 1891, the U.S. Court of Private Land Grant Claims was established with plenary powers and the largest territorial jurisdiction of any tribunal in the world. It was an ambulatory court, sitting wherever it found facts to investigate.

Agents of the court trailed Reavis through California and Mexico to the monasteries of Spain, which were the repositories of documents in his chain of title. Chemical and photographic examination demonstrated that in certain documents the first and last page or two were genuine, but the intervening pages were forgeries, written upon parchment. The original had been written with iron ink, while the substitutions were written in dogwood ink. Chemicals were utilized to remove the dogwood ink, and others to

restore the iron. In the document appointing Peralta Baron de Arizonaca and Caballero de los Colorados, quite another name and title were uncovered. Mallet Prevost, agent for the court, also investigated Carmelita. It developed that her birth was duly recorded in the records of the Mission of San Salvador near San Bernardino, California.

It was established that Reavis had removed from the register pages containing births entered on certain convenient dates. He had procured paper as nearly like the original as possible, and on it had copied truly the list of such births, but had added the name of Carmelita.

But the padres methodically indexed their records day by day in a separate volume. Reavis was ignorant of this separate index and had not tampered with it. It contained no mention of Carmelita. So it was demonstrated that the Baroness was actually a foundling, nameless and without lineage.

By the time Reavis' claim came to be adjudicated by the Land Grant Court, sitting in Santa Fe in January 1895, he had spent his last penny in preparing his case and in luxurious living. He had not a cent to pay for counsel. The great names who had been his gulls or his confederates had taken to the tall timber. Reavis sat alone and friendless in the courtroom, save for the sad-eyed and bewildered woman who had lived a fairy story as his wife. On question from the presiding judge, merciful attorneys for the government declared that, in their opinion, Carmelita was a dupe who had believed Reavis' tale of her ancestry, and that she was innocent of any part in the conspiracy.

Reavis was convicted and sentenced to six years in the penitentiary at Santa Fe. Some years later, the Baroness, then living in poverty in Denver, sued for divorce. And with the record of that divorce proceeding she disappears from visible history. As to the twins, no effort has been made to identify them, for reasons of decency and humanity.

Reavis served his term, emerged a wraith of his old, distinguished self. In those last shadowy days, the impostor spent his waking hours in the Phoenix library reading newspaper stories about himself and the days of his grandeur.

The Baron of Arizona—one of the most daring, adroit and ambitious criminals of all time—died without his death being more than casually noticed. A pitiful, broken old man, he vanished, ghostlike, from the scene, to take his place among the great impostors of history.

⌒〰⌒

ON FRIDAY, June 12, 1924, near Rondout, Illinois, train No. 57 of the Chicago, Milwaukee and St. Paul Railroad was rushing through the starlit night when a rifle was thrust against the neck of the fireman and a revolver in the back of the engineer. The train ground to a halt. From a parked automobile four men with gas masks made for the mail car where 18 clerks were sorting the registered mail. A robber's bullet shattered the glass of an upper window and a gas bomb whizzed through the broken pane. Choking and sobbing, the mail clerks clambered out. The thieves tossed 64 bags of treasure into the automobile and sped away with their loot—$3 million.

A formidable battery of detective brains was assembled to solve this expert crime. The generalissimo was William Fahy, shrewdest of government criminal investigators. On the second night, one of the detectives got a telephone call from a stooge in the underworld. When the detective hung up the receiver he was in a daze.

What was he to do? The tip he had received was incredible—but, like a good detective, he decided to follow it through. He led a woman of the underworld into the office of Rush D. Simmons, Chief of Postal Inspectors.

The woman's husband had been sent to prison for a postal theft of which, she swore, he was innocent. She flirted with the detective who had arrested him; now the sleuth was in love with her, and this moment was the apex of her revenge—because she had wormed out of him the fact that he was head of the gang which had staged the Rondout train robbery.

"Name him!" snapped Chief Simmons.

"Postal Inspector William Fahy!"

The tip was true—it was actually the ace of federal sleuths who had planned the train robbery. He was sent to prison for a long term.

—Anthony Abbot, in True, The Man's Magazine

229

The thief found that the Lord couldn't
be pawned with the rest of the loot

THE MAN WHO STOLE GOD

by Fred Dickenson

In a shabby rooming house just off Tenth Avenue in New York City, a lanky, red-headed youth stood under the dim electric light in a basement bedroom. His name was, or could have been, Jim Lacey. From a dresser drawer he took a chisel, pocketed it, then left his room and mingled with the Saturday-night strollers on Tenth Avenue.

Lacey halted at 57th Street, then turned east. He kept to the outer edge of the sidewalk, peering casually into the cars parked along the curb. No one so much as looked at him. He had, in fact, trained himself deliberately in the art of being inconspicuous. For Lacey was a thief.

He had walked several blocks, alert for a good opportunity, when a sedan nosed into a vacant space several yards ahead of him. As the driver got out and locked the doors, Lacey observed him carefully. The man had longish dark hair and a thin, black mustache. He looked prosperous. Pocketing his car key, he hurried away.

Lacey's alert eyes took in one important fact that the car's owner had missed: the ventilator window on the curb side was open a quarter of an inch. Lacey looked in the car, then leaned back against it, his right hand behind him. The chisel found the slit beside the ventilator; Lacey pressed, and the window snapped open. He reached in, boldly opened the car door. He took out two suitcases and unhurriedly walked away.

Meanwhile, at Steinway Hall on 57th Street, the car's owner was making last-minute plans for an important trip to Buffalo. He was Alfonso D'Artega, well-known composer and conductor. Often he had led orchestras at Carnegie Hall and on national radio shows. Several of his lighter compositions were popular. The next Tuesday evening, just three days away, he was to conduct the Buffalo Symphony Orchestra in its home town in a "pops" concert. He had worked for days preparing the arrangements and scores. Tomorrow he planned to drive to Buffalo for a Monday rehearsal.

Finishing his business at Steinway Hall, D'Artega returned to his car. He cried out when he discovered that his suitcases had been stolen, for in them were not only the clothing for his trip but also his carefully prepared scores for all the instruments in the Buffalo orchestra. He ran to a telephone. Detectives answered his call promptly.

"My scores!" D'Artega said to them. "I must have them! You must find them!"

The detectives dusted the glass for fingerprints and asked questions.

D'Artega listed the clothing that had been taken and then said, "The thief can have the clothing—it's the *scores* I must have back! There is no time to prepare new arrangements before my concert!"

"What kind of music is it?" a detective asked.

"Orchestrations, special arrangements. Victor Herbert, Cole Porter, Jerome Kern and some of my religious compositions."

"Religious?"

"Yes. One is a hymn, 'Everyone Must Have a Friend,' and another is music I wrote for the *Ave Maria*."

When the detectives left, D'Artega drove to the Church of St. Francis of Assisi on West 31st Street. As a lay member of the Third Order of St. Francis he often assisted at Mass in that church.

231

He made his way through the quiet dimness to the Shrine of St. Anthony. There he prayed for two hours, pleading for the saint's help with his problems.

Meanwhile, in his dingy room, Jim Lacey was emptying the suitcases. The clothes would bring a nice batch of cash. But this music junk! Lacey picked up a few sheets, glanced at them and threw them down disgustedly. Then he repacked the clothing and took it to a nearby pawnbroker—one who asked no questions and who would, even late at night, unlock his side door for a regular customer. When he left the pawnbroker he had seven pawn tickets and $140 in his pocket.

Back in his room, Lacey got out two grocery bags and was stuffing the music into them when he saw familiar words: *Ave Maria*. He held the sheet, remembering. When he was a kid, back in Chicago, he used to sing in school. In his imagination he could hear a choir singing it, an organ playing. He put the sheet down and picked up another. He read the words:

> Everyone must have a friend
> To tell his troubles to;
> And I found mine, O dearest Lord,
> My truest friend is you!*

Lacey picked up a concert program. On it was a man's picture, the man who owned the car he'd robbed. There was his name: Alfonso D'Artega, Conductor.

Lacey dropped the hymn and "*Ave Maria*" into a drawer, then stuffed the rest of the music into the bags and took them with him out into the night. He was back in half an hour. He lay a long time in the dark, thinking and remembering.

The next morning, Sunday, as Mrs. Hetty Braine, the widow of a pianist and composer, left her basement apartment on West 77th Street, she was stopped by the superintendent, Mrs. Lillian

---

*By Cecile Donnelly and Alfonso D'Artega, © 1951, 1954 by MCA Music, a division of MCA, Inc.

Green. "Look at all this music somebody threw out," Mrs. Green said, holding up some scores and pointing to the two sacks beside the ashcans. She knew the widow's son Robert was also a pianist. "Maybe your boy can use it," she suggested.

"Thanks, I'll tell him," Mrs. Braine said. But she had not yet had an opportunity to do so when she tuned in to the 11 a.m. news on radio station WQXR, which specializes in good music. Its news editor, knowing that music lovers are its constant listeners, broadcast the story of D'Artega's stolen scores.

Mrs. Braine and her son at once retrieved the scores and notified the police. D'Artega arrived not long after, to thank the widow. While he talked with her, his professional eye noted the signs of a musical household. Mrs. Braine explained that her late husband had been a composer. "Here's his best work, a composition called 'S.O.S.,'" she said, handing D'Artega the score.

D'Artega studied it, then said, "I like it! I'll play it in Buffalo. You and your son will go with me as my guests." So, a few nights later, the composer's widow stood with tears on her cheeks, listening to the Buffalo audience's enthusiastic applause.

Meanwhile, Lacey read a newspaper item which mentioned D'Artega's midnight trip to the church to ask St. Anthony to intercede. Lacey took the scores from his dresser drawer and read the words again.

A few weeks later D'Artega received a letter containing the pawn tickets. The letter said, "I am sorry about breaking into your car and putting you to all this trouble. But with the bad sometimes comes good, and in my case it is that I quit this kind of business that night. I now have a job and live as I should." The writer, who signed himself "J. L.," said that the religious songs had started him going to church again. "I have gone three times, and when I get nerve enough I'll go to confession. I'm glad all this happened because I really feel different now, and I'm trusting you have forgiven me."

D'Artega redeemed his pawned clothes and asked the police to call off the search. He thought that ended the matter.

Nearly three years later, however, on May 27, 1954, D'Artega conducted "S.O.S." at Carnegie Hall, again with Braine's widow and son present. He was unaware of a red-headed young man in the audience listening with rapt attention. He was unaware, too, that the same youth sometimes watched him in church. Then one Sunday morning a few months later an usher touched D'Artega's arm and pointed to a young man kneeling at St. Anthony's shrine. "He says he wants to speak to you."

D'Artega knelt beside the stranger. The young man whispered, "There's something I have to tell you. Can we go somewhere for a cup of coffee?"

In a nearby restaurant Jim Lacey counted out $140 and gave it to the astonished musician. "Sorry this took so long," he said. "I had to save it up before I spoke to you. I've often seen you in church. I finally went to confession. Your suitcases were the last things I ever stole. I'm ready now for my punishment. You can call the police."

"I'll never notify the police," said D'Artega. "Let us go back together to St. Anthony."

He left the young man at the church. Since then he has seen him frequently. And letters signed "J. L." come regularly. They have told of Lacey's marriage, his promotions, the birth of a son, the redemption of a man who found God in a stolen suitcase.

⌬

"PEOPLE can't fool a burglar by leaving lights in the first floor hallway or living room of their homes when they go away for the evening," a professional burglar once told me. "There are several ways we can check this—ringing the doorbell and asking for a handout, calling on the telephone and so forth. The best place to leave a light to prevent burglary is in an upstairs bathroom and adjoining bedroom, with the blinds so arranged that the light shows just a little at the sides. It's easy to spot a bathroom in almost any house, and when there's a light there—well, we'd rather not take a chance, that's all."

—*Perry Van Horne*

He was socially impeccable, president of the
New York Stock Exchange and the charming
swindler of friends, family and clientele

THE TWO FACES
OF RICHARD WHITNEY

by Harold Mehling

W hen Richard Whitney fell off his pedestal, he shattered
the teacups of the Four Hundred. America's wealthiest families
were astounded, for he went from the gray stone of Wall Street up
the Hudson River to the red brick of Sing Sing. That was an un-
pardonable offense, as J. P. Morgan immediately made clear.

"Do you know Richard Whitney?" the banker was asked.

"I knew him," Morgan replied, and without further word everyone understood that Whitney had been excommunicated from the
temple of high finance.

Richard Whitney was an all-American boy, patrician division.
His forebears arrived with the Pilgrims and he arrived when he
was included in the Social Register. He sat in exclusive schools,
then sat in exclusive clubs. He began at the top in business and
ultimately became the leader of that community of wealth, the
New York Stock Exchange. Among his possessions were a country estate, a town house, eight automobiles, 47 suits, 12 walking
sticks and four pink coats for fox hunting. On his day of judgment,
he had to teach lowbrow accountants the proper nomenclature for
champagne bottle sizes.

"Gentlemen," he pointed out, "they're not two-quart and four-quart bottles. They're magnums and jeroboams." Ignorance of the social graces appalled him.

In addition to being almost a religious disciple of rugged individualism, Whitney was a crusading foe of shady stockbrokers. His denunciations, delivered in after-dinner speeches and radio addresses, provided solid assurance to investors. If the law was sometimes the stock swindlers' hellfire, Richard Whitney was their brimstone.

Yet there were, indeed, two faces of Richard Whitney, for he led a double existence that deceived even those who were closest to him. He swindled during a dozen of his 20 years of prominence in Wall Street. He valued family, caste and privilege, but he stole from his father-in-law, from his yacht club, from his customers and from his friends. He dealt in enormous financial propositions, but his business judgment was incredibly poor. His pride was devastating, though when he finally stood morally naked before the world in March 1938, he delivered himself to his captors with staggering detachment. It was as if he and the prosecutors and the lawyers and the judges and the prison guards were all talking about somebody else.

As a character in fiction, Whitney would defy belief. He almost does as fact.

Few men could have been better cast for the role Whitney assumed on a morning of lingering chill in May 1930. At the age of 41, he became the youngest president the Stock Exchange had ever known. The son of a Boston banker—unrelated to the more famous Whitney clan—he had been captain of the baseball and football teams at Groton and manager of the school play. His financial bent was recognized when he was made treasurer of the prep school's summer camp. He was no campus clod at Harvard, either, becoming treasurer of Hasty Pudding and pulling a strong oar in the shell that beat Yale in 1909.

Psychiatrists have since revealed certain of Whitney's characteristics that show the kind of student he was. He had an utterly factual mind—the kind that a quarter of a century later enabled him to recall the full name of every Harvard classmate. He was no rounded scholar. Philosophical concepts bored him and abstractions repelled him; he paid attention to practical problems, such as campus activities and popularity. This probably explains why Dick Whitney made more of a splash at Harvard than had his brother George, who preceded him there and then led the way to Wall Street. George was bookwormish, Dick was raccoon.

For all that, George was to be the Whitney strength, Dick the family trial. By 1916 George was preparing to become a partner in J. P. Morgan and Company. That year, Dick married Gertrude Sheldon Sands, widow of a son of Mrs. William K. Vanderbilt, and decided to buy a seat on the New York Stock Exchange. He did not want to borrow so quickly from father-in-law George Sheldon, president of the Union League Club and treasurer of the Republican National Committee, so he tapped an uncle for the price of the seat and established himself as a bond broker.

Whitney quickly generated respect, if not idolatry. Aggressive, assured, he drove with authority toward the Exchange's inner circle. He had a sharp tongue, a short manner and no time for nonsense, which included almost anything not connected with business. Some associates thought him unduly grim, but most were content that he gave so much time to organizational affairs. He soon became a member of the Exchange's governing committee, a post he held until the day of his expulsion. He sat with the committee on business conduct (that is, misconduct) and eventually became its chairman. In 1928 he was elected vice-president of the most powerful securities exchange in the world.

That was the progress registered by one Richard Whitney. Another Richard Whitney, carrying on in the same body, was meanwhile having a devil of a time keeping his own house as tidy as he did the Big Board's. This, despite his acknowledged position as the Morgan broker. He handled approximately 30 percent of the bond orders placed by J. P. Morgan and Company, where brother George spent his days. This fraternal arrangement netted Dick Whitney $50,000 a year in commissions.

The problem was that Dick had been infected by a speculative bug that constantly diverted his attention from the ploddingly gainful bond business. Early in the exuberant 1920's, for instance, he was attracted by a Florida company that wanted to transform humus into a commercial fertilizer. He began investing an average of $200,000 a year. Then he saw possibilities in a firm organized to mine and sell mineral colloids. He did not have enough liquid cash for such investments, so brother George made him a series of loans that came to $575,000 for these two flings alone.

George could afford it; whether he worried about payment is unknown. It is also difficult to know if he wondered about Richard's judgment, or merely thought it not cricket to pry. As he explained later, "If my brother was to borrow, it was better that he should borrow from me."

But Richard's investment ventures failed to justify hopes, and his neglected bond business was suddenly in deep crisis. Some men fold up under extreme pressure, while others drive to Himalayas of resourcefulness. Whitney was resourceful. Scouring his office vault for stray assets, he came onto $105,000 in stocks belonging to the account of his father-in-law; Sheldon had died, and Whitney was an administrator of his estate. He hurried over to the Corn Exchange Bank and put up the trust securities as collateral for a loan. It was to be a temporary device, to alleviate his crisis, and it is probable that his narrowly focused mind did not associate his action with criminal conduct.

In any event, Richard Whitney broke the honesty habit, consciously or not. If he was slightly nervous at the next meeting of the committee on business conduct, at least it was not because his firm was in peril. In fact, he felt secure enough to relocate Richard Whitney and Company in 15 rooms of a building on Broad Street, where his private office overlooked the Stock Exchange.

When some costly stock speculations created a new peril only two years later, the Sheldon securities were still in hock. Such things have a way of happening, as any practiced embezzler could have told Whitney. To meet the new crisis, he mortgaged his upper

East Side town house for $110,000, thus taking the first step on a treadmill of interest payments that would eventually exhaust him. Like a poor man visiting a loan shark with desperate regularity, the boy from Groton and Harvard became a moneylender's dream.

Those were the contrasting achievements of the two Richard Whitneys—the vice-president of the New York Stock Exchange and the bumbling businessman—as America turned into 1929, the climactic year of the era of wonderful nonsense.

Investors had been watching the financial bubble expand, hearing that stock prices were still lower than true values, buying such issues as RCA—which rose from $85 a share to $420 in 12 months without ever having paid a dividend. Exhilaration was so intense that sporadic spring and summer turndowns worried few people. But, familiarly enough, the situation became alarmingly clear by October, when the market sagged under hammering blows of selling. Down in Wall Street, the big bankers conferred, and J. P. Morgan decreed that the market had to be supported. A social expression of heredity was at work: Twenty-two years earlier, in the financial panic of 1907, Morgan's father had organized the support of several failing banks.

So it was that in mid-October, the duality of Richard Whitney's life was accented once more. On the one hand, caught up in the possibilities of the frenzied price rise, he had borrowed more money from brother George with which to buy another seat on the Exchange, and he had increased his personal investments heavily. On the other hand, the president of the Exchange, Edward H. H. Simmons, was off in Europe, and Whitney found himself the market's instrument of authority in the whirl of panic.

On October 24, Black Thursday of 1929, with investors' margin accounts expiring under the heaviest price slide in securities history, Whitney enacted the role that would make him famous and set his future course even more decisively. At 1:30 p.m. he interrupted the near hysteria that gripped the Exchange floor by appearing from the members' lobby and walking slowly toward Trading Post No. 2, where transactions in the stock of United

States Steel were handled. As more and more brokers noticed him a buzz arose; by the time he reached the circular trading post, a thousand pairs of eyes abandoned the high, illuminated tickers and fixed on his commanding frame. No one had to explain the significance of his rare appearance on the floor. The Morgan broker had arrived. In his hand was a slip of paper. The bankers were making their move. Whitney was their emissary.

"Two hundred five for Steel!" he called. Then he placed orders with the steel-stock specialist for 10,000 shares at that price—a commitment of over $2 million. Since $205 was the price of the last previous sale in Steel, it was obvious that the bankers had decided to shore up the market. But more, Whitney then toured to several other trading posts and, with studied lack of haste, placed $25 million more in orders for 15 to 20 other stocks, in 10,000-share blocks.

The gesture was temporarily effective. For the first time in days the selling wave abated. The ticker, tardily announcing the demise of fortunes that had vanished hours earlier, began catching up. Prices firmed and, as a matter of fact, Whitney's demand for 10,000 shares of Steel at $205 was met by only 200 shares. Who knew but that at this moment the price direction might be about ready to reverse?

But history, economics or whatever dynamic had already sealed the fate of the stock market, continued the irreversible pressure. The market went on to crash, the experts gulped and the Great Depression settled on the land. Whitney lost $2 million in the collapse, or so he said, and friends later advanced this misfortune as his motivation for embezzling. But a great many other men lost money in the crash too, other men who were not already living two lives.

Out of the wreckage of October and November emerged a hero, a man who had selflessly abandoned his own affairs to work with the bankers and try to save the market. In May 1930 the brokers crackled with appreciation and elected Richard Whitney president of the Stock Exchange. They also presented him with a touching souvenir—Trading Post No. 2, the polished wooden post at which he had tried so resolutely to redirect the course of history. He installed it in the lobby of his Broad Street offices, where it became a Wall Street memento.

The other Richard Whitney, the beggar on horseback, was deeper into George's wallet by then, having borrowed more money with which to reorganize his firm into a partnership. It was a strange partnership; despite the addition of four new members, Richard Whitney and Company was a one-man firm. A discerning Morgan man referred to Whitney's colleagues as "office boys" and suggested that stronger partners be brought in to curb the bond broker's speculative imagination. But Whitney preferred his office boys. He never called a partners' meeting and no partners were consulted when he committed the firm to huge loans. He ignored them in the same way he ignored as much of the world as he could.

But he could not ignore his sinking fortunes. By now, he was paying fantastic interest on his multifarious loans—and the compensating returns were meager. Humus was not making out and neither were the mineral colloids. So, no sooner did he become president of the Exchange than his new firm was in trouble. Again the man demonstrated his resourcefulness. He had been elected treasurer of the New York Yacht Club and had thus come into possession of over $100,000 worth of securities. In May, June and July of 1930, he used the Yacht Club's bonds in an ungentlemanly way. With them, he floated 13 separate loans, using one to pay off another as quickly as they could be arranged, and thus he saved himself from drowning.

A year later his position was still critical and again one Richard Whitney was able to save the other. Having become a director of the Corn Exchange Bank, he appreciated the difficulty fellow directors would have in turning him down, and asked for a loan of $300,000. He offered no collateral and they requested none. He got the money, as he was fond of saying, on his face. It may be that the bankers subscribed to the homily of the elder J. P. Morgan, who resolutely held that a man's character was worth more than his collateral.

But one Corn Exchange director, a Morgan partner named Francis Bartow, was unhappy over the transaction. He did not consider Whitney's action improper, he said, but felt that others might misunderstand it. Appearances must have counted heavily with Bartow, because he reported his apprehension to George Whitney. Shortly afterward, the loan was quietly picked up by the House of Morgan—thus keeping it in the family closet. The Morgan partners naturally placed utmost confidence in character, and they too asked Whitney for no collateral.

Under the circumstances, the president of the Stock Exchange was reasonably free from harassment for the next couple of years, finding it necessary to appropriate his father-in-law's securities only once more. He was living well on his country estate, a 495-acre gentleman's farm at Far Hills, New Jersey, where he was a member of the township committee, a leader of the so-called New York Colony and master of the foxhounds at the Essex Hunt. The monthly payroll for his farm, where he employed a superintendent, herdsmen, grooms, a jockey, a gardener and teamsters, came to $1500.

If times make the man, this period made Whitney. He became the acknowledged spokesman for the policies and practices of the New York Stock Exchange. He was its Depression president, as Franklin Roosevelt, a contrasting product of Groton and Harvard, was the nation's Depression President.

Whitney despised the New Deal, and the New Deal despised the private-club nature of the Stock Exchange. He railed at the braintrusters, warning them to keep their governmental regulators away from the securities market. He made speeches, testified before Congressional committees and otherwise confirmed his leadership of the Old Guard among the men of the market. Some of the younger crowd felt that the reform mood of the nation called for compromise, but they got Whitney's sharp tongue for their trouble.

The New Deal surged forward under Roosevelt's huge Congressional majority and one day, as Whitney sat in the Senate gallery, final approval was given a bill creating the Securities and Exchange Commission. To him, an SEC was socialistic, and he returned to New York with his blue blood high in adrenalin.

That was in 1934, and the men named Richard Whitney must have found a way to get 26 hours out of a day. While spokesman Whitney was spending his evenings on podiums, businessman Whitney had been paying out almost $250,000 in interest on his multiple loans. He owed George almost $2 million and was in so deep that when he borrowed $110,000 from a friend for 30 days (without collateral), the loan ran 43 months before he paid up at the insistence of the friend's partner.

Despite his already dangerous position, Whitney started down an even riskier path. When repeal of prohibition was just around the corner, he had become attracted to the Distilled Liquors Corporation, a firm organized to produce applejack. A lot has been said for and against diversification of holdings, but the case of "Applejack" Richard Whitney at least provides dramatic proof of the danger of putting all your borrowed dollars into one liquor bottle.

When Distilled Liquors floated its first stock issue, Whitney bought 15,000 shares at $15. That cost him $225,000, most of which he borrowed. Then he watched DLC's price rise until it hit $45. Some men might have taken their profit of almost a half million dollars and run. Not Whitney. Since his need for funds was Gargantuan, he pledged the stock as collateral for still more bank loans.

The securities, however, were destined for disaster. They sold well but the applejack didn't. Partly on Whitney's advice, the company expanded production and enlarged its sales organization. When that failed to help, it added a line of rye whiskey, which didn't go either. The firm was losing money at the rate of $55,000 a year and, as this news inevitably reached Wall Street, where the pulse of a corporation is taken through its balance sheet, the stock's price slipped. Nothing could have injured Whitney's position more. If DLC's price fell, so would its value as loan collateral; next would come the dreaded bank call for repayment or additional collateral.

So Whitney was forced to compound his debts and to hasten his own exposure. In an effort to keep DLC's price pegged at a level that would protect it as collateral, he began buying heavily. He bought until he owned 75,000 shares. The price continued to drop and, frantically, he bought more. He used clients' securities, the Sheldon estate, the New York Yacht Club bonds, his wife's jewelry and whatever else he could grasp and hold on to long enough to hock. All of it went into collateral for bank loans that would either buy more DLC stock or repay other bank loans that had already been used to buy the stock. Personal, unsecured loans from other brokers added to the Niagara of debt and interest. It was an incredible juggling operation, a nerve-racking procedure that was not only illegal but a sure path, barring a miracle, to insolvency and jail.

If this occurred to Richard Whitney the businessman, it was not obvious in the actions of Richard Whitney the president of the New York Stock Exchange. He warned the man in the street to beware of stock swindlers and told a national radio audience that investors should deal only with "financial houses of established responsibility, houses whose operations are controlled not only by law, but by their own pride in fair dealing."

By May 1935, when he gave up the Stock Exchange presidency, Whitney had lost over $400,000 in speculations other than the Distilled Liquors venture. And DLC was still sliding, even though he had aggregated more than 100,000 shares. Desperately, he pledged $250,000 worth of life insurance policies as collateral for fresh loans.

The climax, a tortuous, yearlong affair, began developing in the spring of 1937 when Whitney visited his brother George and told him of a fresh difficulty. It had familiar overtones. He had received permission from three friends to pledge their securities for bank

246

loans, but now the friends wanted their securities back and he was in no position to oblige them. So George put up $1,225,000 to make this possible, and Richard paid up the loans and got the stock back. He was supposed to return it to his vaults, since his firm held the three brokerage accounts in question; instead, he took the securities to another bank and pledged them all over again. His bank loans now totaled more than $5 million, but that figure had only a limited meaning, since some loans merely paid off others in a bewildering race against due dates.

The pace of Whitney's demise was quickened, unknowingly, by the New York Stock Exchange itself. Among the official positions he held after leaving the presidency of the Big Board was one as a trustee of the Gratuity Fund, a trust for which members were taxed and which was used to benefit their widows and orphans. The Fund consisted of $2 million in bonds and cash, and Richard Whitney and Company handled its investment transactions under the direction of the trustees.

Early in 1937 the trustees voted that two blocks of bonds should be sold and a $175,000 block purchased. The bonds were sent over to Whitney's office and the deal was made. Instead of returning the $175,000 in new bonds and a cash remainder, however, he kept them. Then bonds worth $225,000 more found their way into Whitney vaults by the same method. By October he held $900,000 in bonds and $221,000 in cash belonging to the Fund.

While he had devotedly attended every meeting of the Gratuity Fund trustees, for some reason he was unable to attend a session that took place on Monday, November 22. Near the close of that meeting, George W. Lutes, a clerk for the trustees, remarked casually that Whitney had not returned the securities and cash. He also said he had reminded the broker of this fact five times in six months. Later, Lutes and an investigator for the Securities and Exchange Commission engaged in this exchange:

Q: As the months rolled by, Mr. Lutes, didn't you talk to him a little more vigorously about those bonds?

247

A: Absolutely not, because Mr. Whitney was a more or less sharp person, and I could not go up to him and say, "Here, Mr. Whitney, you send those bonds over to us," or anything of that sort, because Mr. Whitney was my superior. I was under him as an employe of the Exchange and I am only a clerk of the committee.

Q: Were you concerned about your job, Mr. Lutes?

A: Certainly.

When Lutes made his revelation at the November 22 meeting, Edward Simmons, the trustees' chairman, accused the $43.50-a-week clerk of inefficiency. Simmons finally turned his attention to the higher-priced malefactor. He put in a call to Whitney's office and was assured that the securities and cash would be returned forthwith.

The following morning, Tuesday, Whitney dropped in on Simmons and agreed that the holdings should really be in a bank vault. He said his office would try to deliver them that day, but that he was shorthanded at the moment. Simmons, who knew that that was one of the reasons Whitney had given Lutes for his earlier failures to return the assets, insisted he have them by three o'clock that afternoon. Whitney said he would do his best.

But his best would not be good enough, for a certainty. He had already put up two thirds of the $900,000 in securities as collateral for loans. Moreover, he had only $74,000 in cash to cover the Fund's $221,000. The shortage was formidable.

Whitney ran his only course. Mortification before brother George was preferable to public exposure, so he hurried to George and told all. George was properly aghast. Exactly what was said between them remains a mystery, but George, who did not have a large amount of cash on hand, went to another Morgan partner, Thomas W. Lamont, and, despite differences in later recollections, told him at least enough to borrow $1,082,000.

When Whitney called on Simmons at the 3 p.m. deadline, he said the securities would be returned the next day and added,

248

for reassurance, that he had "talked with George." Simmons, now concerned over the significance of Whitney's inability to hand over the securities and cash at once, called George Whitney himself and received Morgan-type assurances. On Wednesday the sum was returned and—officially, at least—the matter was closed. The record of a subsequent meeting of the Gratuity Fund trustees states that "all securities of the trustees held by Richard Whitney and Company have been received and placed in the vault, and the cash balance of the trustees held by Richard Whitney and Company has been turned over to the trustees and placed in the bank." The widows and orphans were safe.

Privately, however, the matter was wide open. On Thursday, Thanksgiving Day, two meetings were held at George Whitney's home. At a morning session the Whitney brothers conferred with Edward Simmons. At an afternoon session only the brothers were present. When Richard left that evening, it was with the firm understanding that his company would liquidate. George had suffered enough.

Conceivably, he might have carried Dick till doomsday with loans that had taken on the character of outright gifts, but the revelations of the morning session, when he and Simmons had pried deeply into Dick's affairs, were too much. The pattern was clear; Whitney had been appropriating money wherever he could. The only way to avoid a public debacle was to get him out of Wall Street in an "orderly" way.

If the way could have been made orderly, the world might never have known about the other face of Richard Whitney. Like the bank teller who returns from the racetrack with his winnings and erases the faint pencil notations of his temporary embezzlement, Whitney's depredations might have gone forever undetected. But he had rarely won and was still losing heavily. His Distilled Liquors stock was down from 45 to 11 and he was out $1 million there. He had mortgaged his New Jersey estate for $250,000, which added to interest payments that were already grotesque. Frantically, he tried to borrow from everyone who crossed his erratic path and often succeeded, despite the fact that gossip was beginning to get about.

His exposure, like many great discoveries, came about accidentally. The catalyst was a change of policy by the Stock Exchange's governors. For some time they had required financial reports only from brokers who carried the public's margin accounts. Whitney, a broker's broker, having little to do with public investors, had been exempt from filling out a questionnaire that would have revealed his condition. But late in 1937 it was decided that all brokerage houses should report.

Coincidentally, Whitney approached Bernard E. Smith, the legendary short seller, and asked for $250,000. Instead of offering collateral, he again used the expression "on my face." Smith, who had rarely received a tip of the hat from Whitney, told him he did not like his face and reported the incident to Charles R. Gay, the Exchange president. Then another broker picked up a rumor that Greyhound Bus stock was involved in distress selling and that Whitney was the seller. Since distress selling meant an order to sell regardless of the market price, it connoted severe financial trouble, and the broker dutifully reported the rumor to the chairman of the committee on business conduct. As it turned out later, the rumor was false; there were no distress sales of Greyhound stock. But the wheels began grinding. The business conduct committee, being at least tacitly aware of the Gratuity Fund incident, decided to send Whitney a financial questionnaire without delay.

The caged broker now fairly flew between banks and individuals. He pledged $800,000 more in customers' securities in order to raise cash and buy another 40,000 shares of Distilled Liquors stock, hoping to send its price up and recoup everything. It stayed down; in fact, during January and February he was DLC's sole purchaser. To disguise his heavy involvement with one security, he put thousands of shares in his partners' names and, since they had never developed the habit of questioning his conduct, they said nothing.

After a week's delay, Whitney delivered his questionnaire. Despite all the deceit it contained, he could not make it show sufficient operating capital under Stock Exchange rules. An audit of his books was immediately ordered, and by March 1 the auditor reported evidence of extensive misappropriations. On that day, Whitney went to W. Averell Harriman, later a renowned diplomat, then a partner in Brown Brothers, Harriman and Company, and asked for $100,000. Whitney said he had no collateral at the moment but would deliver securities in a few days. He got the money but Harriman did not get the collateral. If that loan seems extraordinary, consider that in the four months between November 1937 and March 1938 Whitney floated no less than 111 loans totaling $27 million. He was in a revolving door that threatened at each turn to trap him.

On Saturday, March 5, Whitney spent a remarkable two hours with President Gay of the Stock Exchange while the members of the committee on business conduct were preparing charges against him. He neither begged nor pleaded, but was businesslike and, above all, practical. Pointing out that the Exchange would receive adverse publicity if he were exposed, he offered to relinquish his membership and leave the Street. Gay said no. Whitney remained emotionless, continuing the negotiations as if he were a lawyer for someone else in trouble. Then he left, knowing he was finished, and waited calmly for the formal blow to fall.

The last effort to save him, or to save the Whitney name, was made on Sunday. Francis Bartow, the Morgan partner, spent that afternoon discussing the affair with other Morgan men, not including George Whitney, who was in Florida because of ill health. On Sunday evening, Bartow drove out to the Long Island home of John W. Davis, the Morgan attorney who had been the Democratic Presidential candidate in 1924. Davis flatly prohibited giving financial help on grounds that, with Whitney facing criminal action, the Morgan firm's motives might be misconstrued. Bartow phoned George Whitney in Florida, but told him there was no point in his returning; nothing could be done to save Dick.

On Monday morning, Bartow returned to Long Island, this

time to make a final appeal to J. P. Morgan himself. But Morgan stood with Davis.

On Tuesday, March 8, after the clang of the opening bell, President Gay appeared on the elevated rostrum at one end of the Stock Exchange floor. The brokers turned to him and heard the terrible news: Richard Whitney and Company had been suspended for insolvency.

That was politeness in the extreme, on a par with the Exchange's news release that spoke of Whitney's "conduct apparently contrary to just and equitable principles of trade."

District Attorney Thomas E. Dewey quickly obtained a New York County indictment charging Whitney with having embezzled $105,000 from the estate of his father-in-law. Richard's total deficit was $5,600,000, of which brother George Whitney was on the short end by $2,897,000.

Arrested, Whitney stood in court, hands clasped behind a fitted overcoat with velvet collar, and was arraigned. Then he was taken to a police station on the lower East Side for booking. A group of Bowery derelicts was herded into a back room for the occasion and Whitney was brought before a desk sergeant who was clearly nonplussed by the tall, gray, dignified figure before him. Awkwardly, he asked if the prisoner had been searched.

An officer stammered, "Not yet." Whitney smiled and opened his coat. "Have you got any knives?" a policeman asked.

"No," he replied.

The desk sergeant stood up, reached over and extended a hand. "Mr. Whitney," he said, "I'm sorry to see you in this trouble and I wish you the best of luck."

Whitney shook the hand and said, "Thank you."

The sergeant started to sit down, then stopped. "The Whitneys have always had a good name," he said. Then, perhaps on the suspicion that he had offended, he sat down hard.

"Thank you again," Whitney said. He was mugged, fingerprinted and released on $10,000 bail.

A few days later, when the state indicted him, too—for misusing $120,000 in bonds of the New York Yacht Club—a judge held court open until 5 p.m., so the prisoner would not have to spend a night in jail before arraignment. "I'm sorry for your trouble," he told Whitney.

A week later the broker was expelled from the Stock Exchange. Then he pleaded guilty to the combined indictments and received a five-to-ten-year prison sentence. He was handcuffed to a rapist and sent up to Warden Lewis E. Lawes at Sing Sing, where a problem of deportment developed. Convicts tipped their caps, stepped aside as he passed and addressed him as Mr. Whitney. A guard called out, "All men who came in Saturday, Monday or Tuesday, and Mr. Whitney, please step out of the cells." But the novelty soon passed, and normalcy prevailed once more.

The real problems, the social ripples that started with Whitney's arrest, spread rapidly across the nation. There was resentment that a gigantic swindler had been indicted for only two of his numerous larcenies and that he could be paroled in less than three and a half years. The depth of this feeling was illustrated by a St. Louis judge who was sentencing a young man for stealing $2 from a filling station. "Some people think there's one law for the rich and another for the poor," the judge said. "We'll correct that right now."

Taking pencil and paper, he made elaborate computations and then announced his decision. "Richard Whitney got five years for stealing $225,000," he said. "That would be $45,000 a year, $120 a day, $5 an hour. You stole $2. That would be 24 minutes and that is your sentence."

The philosophy behind the judge's maverick behavior might have been lost on the prisoner, but it was not lost on others. The New York Stock Exchange became a target for considerable criticism. The Securities and Exchange Commission climaxed its investigation of the case by accusing Stock Exchange officials of having known for months of Whitney's actions and of shielding him with their code of silence. The commissioners pointed out that he had borrowed over $6 million from 16 persons connected with the Big Board, that he had been turned down by 21 others and that such wholesale borrowing was an obvious signal of deep-seated trouble. "Thus," the SEC concluded, "Richard Whitney, as a member of the Stock Exchange fraternity, was able for years to hide his misdeeds behind that code of silence."

Exchange officials, represented by attorney Dean Acheson, steadfastly denied moral guilt and rode out the storm—a storm that was intensified by J. P. Morgan's admission that he would not have informed the authorities of Whitney's actions under any conditions.

Despite this attitude, the private club was indeed changing under the pressure of the times. For the first time in its history, the Exchange appointed a nonbroker as president and added three "public representatives" to its Board of Governors. But eight months after Whitney went to jail, the governors voted 27 to 1 against reviewing the conduct of their members in the Whitney case. Robert M. Hutchins, then president of the University of Chicago and the public-member minority of one, resigned with a public protest.

As for Whitney, he scrubbed cell walls, clerked, played a creditable first base on the Sing Sing ball team and was paroled, in 1941, after serving three years and four months. George Whitney, who had meanwhile become president of J. P. Morgan and Company, picked him up at the prison gates and saw him off to Massachusetts, where he managed a dairy farm and later rose from apprentice in an explosives plant to become executive assistant to a vice-president.

Today, in the handsomely appointed rooms of the New York Stock Exchange's Board of Governors, you can see large oil paintings of its past presidents—all but Whitney. The official explanation of this omission is lack of space. While that may sound like a public relations contortion, the Exchange's rationale does have undeniable logic. Surely two portraits of Richard Whitney would be unthinkable, and one would tell only half the story of a man who lived a double life.

This romantic swashbuckler
rallied to his country's
cause at a critical time

JEAN LAFITTE—PIRATE PATRIOT

by Donald Culross Peattie

FIVE HUNDRED DOLLARS REWARD

To be paid to any person delivering the said John Lafitte to the sheriff that the said John Lafitte may be brought to justice. Given under my hand at New Orleans on the 24th day of November 1813.   By the Governor:

(Signed) *William C. C. Claiborne*

The said Jean Lafitte, as he read this proclamation with a mocking smile, must have been recognized by hundreds of New Orleans citizens. Yet no one laid hands on him, for this handsome young pirate was a popular figure in the gay Creole capital.

Three days later, so the story goes, Claiborne stared hard at the spot where his notice had been posted and grew turkey-red. There, slapped over his bid for Lafitte's arrest, was Lafitte's counter-offer: $1500—three times as much—for the capture of the said William Claiborne and his delivery to Grande Isle, the pirate's hideout. How New Orleans laughed at this impudent sally!

Grande Isle guarded the mouth of Barataria Bay, some 50 miles southwest of New Orleans. Here the pirates brought their captured ships—Spanish, British, a few American. Lafitte maintained that his men were not pirates but "privateers," sailing under letters of marque from the Republic of Cartagena (later part of Colombia), which was fighting for her independence from Spain; and he claimed that his men attacked only Spanish ships. It was impulsiveness, perhaps, that caused mistakes in identity.

From Grande Isle it was easy to whisk the smuggled goods into New Orleans, and Jean Lafitte had established a luxury shop on fashionable Royal Street. With his younger brother, Pierre, he had organized this black market, and it had been accepted lightheartedly by many of the city's Gallic population. In the ten years since the Louisiana Purchase the residents had scarcely begun to think as Americans. They felt little loyalty to faraway Washington, and to avoid the unpopular U.S. tariff they gladly dealt with the Lafittes, asking no questions about how they had come by their silks and velvets, wines and brandies, silver plate and jewels.

Lafitte's background is obscure. Born in France in 1782, he ran away to sea at 15 and a few years later appeared in the Caribbean as a privateersman—a lucrative profession at the time, since Spain, France and England were often at one another's throats and a privateersman could sail with "letters" from any of them and prey on the commerce of the others.

In the Barataria region Jean Lafitte was the unchallenged ruler of 500 to 1000 outlaws. Here at headquarters he directed the sea activities of his lieutenants while he himself handled the business end of the operations. He banked the money, hired lawyers and met customers. He lived in elegance in the midst of Barataria's swamps and loved to astonish visitors by setting a table that sparkled with fine wines and old silver. Once he captured revenue officers sent out to seize him, and sent them away loaded with gifts.

But times were changing, even for this high-living, lawless band. America was at war—the War of 1812—and it was going badly. By September 1814, the British blockade of our eastern ports became a stranglehold. No port was more vital than New Orleans, a thriving city of 30,000 and key to the whole Mississippi Valley.

However, the British had not yet appeared there, and to New Orleans' citizens the war seemed remote and none of their affair.

In this hour of crisis, while British troops were collecting for the attack on New Orleans, His Britannic Majesty's ship *Sophia* anchored off Grande Isle, and Captain Lockyer, with Captain McWilliams of the British Army, came ashore with a tempting offer for the pirate leader: If Lafitte would join forces with the English in a descent upon New Orleans, the King would reward him handsomely and give him a Royal commission as captain to boot, while his men would be granted lands in the territory of Louisiana. If Lafitte refused, the *Sophia*'s guns would blow the Baratarians out of their stronghold.

The British agreed to give him two weeks to make up his mind and returned to the *Sophia*. Jean promptly forwarded to Claiborne papers warning of the British plan of attack. He offered to help the American cause in return for amnesty to the Baratarians and restoration of their American citizenship in good standing. Then, day after day, he awaited Claiborne's answer.

At last it came—a fleet of U.S. gunboats that dashed into the bay, captured the prizes anchored there, seized much of Lafitte's goods, fired his town and drove his men into the inner recesses of the swamp. The United States, said Claiborne, would make no compact with outlaws. And Major General Andrew Jackson, hastening from Mobile to take charge of the defense of New Orleans, told Claiborne he had been right to punish those "hellish banditti." "The undersigned calls not upon pirates and robbers to join him in the glorious cause," Jackson wrote grandiloquently.

But when the General arrived in the Creole city he was appalled to find only a few hundred regulars at his disposal, with little ammunition and less artillery. By now the town was in a panic, banks were closed, business suspended. The population of Louisiana had belatedly realized that Sir Edward Pakenham, with 9000 well-trained veterans, was about to seize their beloved city.

Citizens of all ranks flocked to the Stars and Stripes; the many free Negroes offered their fighting services; Choctaw Indians,

burning to take Redcoat scalps, came in from their swamps. In the nick of time some 2000 Tennessee and Kentucky sharpshooters, in their coonskin caps, arrived after a long, forced march over mountains and through swamps. But Jackson still lacked ammunition, cannoneers and ships to guard the water flanks of the city.

The outlook was black when, one December day, a commanding figure appeared in the General's doorway. The man was six feet tall, attired in a green uniform and a feathered hat. His expression was sardonically friendly, with that droop of one eyelid, half calculating, half humorous, that was habitual. It was Jean Lafitte, with a price on his head, come to put himself in the power of the man who had called him a "hellish bandit."

"I place at your disposal," he announced, "all my men, my ships and my ammunition." Not a word did he say about reimbursement or amnesty. He offered his all for the American cause.

Under his jutting epaulets "Old Hickory" squared his high shoulders and made an instant decision. "We accept your offer," he answered. "It is timely, and the United States is grateful." And New Orleans widened its eyes to see the pirates swagger through the city and march out, with the rest of the motley American Army, to meet the British on the fateful January 8, 1815.

Pakenham expected an easy victory, since he outnumbered the defenders nearly two to one. He ordered a frontal attack against the Americans, crouching behind their ramparts of cotton bales. But the bales absorbed the British fire, and the deadly marksmanship of the frontiersmen and pirates mowed down the advancing waves of red. Lafitte's men had brought their own ships' cannon, and they blew up gun after gun of the British. Three times the British attacked with reckless bravery; three times they reeled back with heavy losses.

"The General," wrote Jackson in his official report, "cannot avoid giving his warm approbation of the manner in which these gentlemen [Lafitte and his crew] conducted themselves and of the gallantry with which they defended the country."

On January 23 a great Victory Ball was held. The Creoles paced a minuet, and General Jackson stepped a reel to the tune of "Possum up a Gum Tree." That night Jean Lafitte was in his glory. He danced with the finest Creole ladies and hobnobbed with Claiborne, who treated him as an old school friend.

Early in March President James Madison sent a full and grateful pardon for all the Baratarians. And here Romance would gladly end the story, with Jean sheathing his sword and settling down in the gay capital as a respected citizen.

But such a life was not for Jean Lafitte. Within a few months his ships were again on the prowl and honest merchants were losing their goods, honest citizens their lives. Finally England, Spain and America united to throttle the pirates, until the Baratarians were forced to flee their beloved bayous.

When New Orleans next heard of Jean Lafitte, he had established a new colony, named Campeche, on Galveston Island. Several thousand daring men and gay ladies flocked to join him, and for a while they prospered. But it became increasingly harder to find ships to loot, for the Spanish were now convoying their merchant fleets with warships. In defiance of Lafitte's orders, the pirates began attacking American shipping. In vain Lafitte hanged one of the worst offenders, delivered four others to American justice. He had lost control over his men.

In 1821 the U.S. brig *Enterprise* appeared at Galveston, and Lieutenant Kearney went ashore to tell Lafitte that he must evacuate his island immediately, by order of the U.S. government. Lafitte agreed. Perhaps the man who had never trembled at Spain or England sensed the rising power of the United States. Perhaps, as he said, he would not take arms against this country. Whatever the reason, he divided the loot among the members of the colony and sailed away with a few faithful friends.

No one is sure what became of Jean Lafitte, the gentleman rogue and pirate patriot. He disappeared from the American scene as mysteriously as he arrived. But in a museum in New Orleans there remains the old sword, still twinkling wickedly, which Jean Lafitte drew in the defense of his country.

*The brothers Fortunato seized
the chance to sell fruit from the busiest
information booth in the country*

GRAND CENTRAL'S $100,000 DEAL

by Alan Hynd

The winds of misfortune blew on two highly successful fruit dealers—brothers Tony and Nick Fortunato—one spring day of 1929. A brisk, mustached stranger dropped into their store in midtown New York and handed Tony, the older of the two brothers, a card reading:

T. Remington Grenfell
Vice-President
GRAND CENTRAL
HOLDING CORPORATION

"You are," Mr. Grenfell explained to the Fortunato brothers, "the lucky ones." What he meant was that Tony and Nick had been selected by the holding corporation, after a lengthy investigation of the city's top fruit dealers, to run the information booth in Grand Central Terminal on lease when it was converted into a fruit stand.

The change from information to fruit (plain and fancy and candy, too) was being made, Mr. Grenfell explained, because far too many travelers, seeing the big circular booth out in the middle

of the busy terminal, were impelled to ask unnecessary questions. Essential information was to be given out at the ticket windows after April 1, the date the change was to go into effect.

Though Tony and Nick had prospered since arriving in New York from their native Italy about a quarter of a century before, they were still singularly naïve. They were quick to see, however, that the information booth was a perfect spot for a fruit stand and highly flattered that they had been selected. They asked Grenfell what the rental would be.

"The money is secondary to us at Grand Central," explained Mr. Grenfell. "We're asking only $100,000 a year—in advance."

Hefty as it was, the figure didn't faze Tony and Nick. For one thing, they had the money. For another, almost $2000 a week rent, though a stiff sum, was not unreasonable for the information booth, which was to operate around the clock. The traffic passing the booth, particularly during the daylight hours, would be heavy. The real profit would come from the expensive baskets of fruits and boxes of candy and nuts, dates and figs, rather than from the apples and oranges.

Now, as a semiclincher, Grenfell dropped the word that if, after six months, the booth did not show a profit of at least $1000 a week, Tony and Nick could cancel their contract and get half the rental back.

Next, Grenfell, who had not stopped talking since his arrival, opened a handsome briefcase and brought out a blueprint that detailed precisely how the fruit stand was to be constructed, fanning out all around the circular booth. There were so many restrictions—how high the display steps were to be, how many there were to be and how far out from the booth they were to extend—that the whole plan could hardly have appeared more genuine to the Fortunatos.

When Grenfell eventually stopped to catch his breath, Tony and Nick said they wanted to think it over.

Grenfell looked hard at the brothers, blinked and cleared his throat. "I'm afraid," he said, "there won't be time for that. After all, we at Grand Central are not asking you for anything. We're offering this opportunity to you."

Now the con man, applying the clincher, dropped a name—the name of a bitter rival of the Fortunato brothers in the realm of apples, oranges and bananas. If Tony and Nick did not see fit to grasp their opportunity forthwith, their rival was waiting.

That did it.

Hustling Tony and Nick into a chauffeur-driven limousine, Mr. Grenfell led the brothers to a tall building that was connected to Grand Central Terminal and then to the door of a suite of offices that bore the legend:

Wilson A. Blodgett
President
GRAND CENTRAL
HOLDING CORPORATION

Just inside the door, Mr. Blodgett's attractive blonde secretary sat at a small desk. Blodgett was in a second room, behind a frosted-glass door, but the three arrivals could hear him putting the finishing touches on a telephone conversation. "Very well," he said, and now Blodgett dropped the name of Tony and Nick's rival, "the deal's closed. Have your certified check for $100,000 in my hands by noon tomorrow and the booth is yours."

Ushered into Blodgett's office with Grenfell, Tony and Nick were introduced to the president and learned that there had been a mix-up. It seemed that Blodgett, a man with many things on his mind, had somehow got the erroneous impression that Tony and Nick had been unable to produce a certified check for $100,000.

"But these two gentlemen can produce such a certified check, W. A.," said Grenfell. Turning to Tony and Nick, Grenfell asked, "Can't you, gentlemen?"

"Sure," the brothers replied in unison.

Blodgett, who seemed to be a man of painful integrity, mulled things over. "I guess," he said to Grenfell, "the only fair thing the railroad can do now is to let the first one here with the check have the booth."

The next morning, not long after their bank opened, the Fortunato brothers arrived at the office of the Grand Central Holding Corporation with a certified check. Grenfell was there, sitting at Blodgett's side, and his stenographer went out and came back with a notary public. There was a flurry of papers and signature-writing. Then, the deal wrapped up, everybody shook hands and went his separate way.

Thirteen days later—Monday morning, April Fool's Day, a few minutes before nine o'clock, when the one-year contract was to go into effect—Tony and Nick appeared in Grand Central with a small army of carpenters. The lumber for the display steps was in two trucks on Lexington Avenue.

The magic hour of nine came, but four men in the booth dispensing information showed no signs of leaving. Tony and Nick waited only a few minutes. Tony approached one of the men in the booth.

"It's after nine o'clock," said Tony. "You and the others here are supposed to be out of this booth."

When the man looked puzzled, Tony flashed the contract. When the man read it, he looked even more puzzled. When the three other men in the booth read the contract and shrugged, the first man handed it back to Tony and said, "This must be a joke of some kind."

"Joke!" roared Tony. "Me and my brother here have leased this booth for $100,000."

By now the lumber was being carted in and dumped around the booth, making it difficult for travelers to get close enough to ask questions. A railroad policeman appeared, studied the sawing and hammering that had begun and then, after asking some questions, inspected the contract. After exchanging glances with the men in the booth, the policeman hustled off to get some action.

It was more than an hour before his report filtered through the complicated administrative levels of the New York Central Railroad—to reach the office of the vice-president with the power to deal with the problem. The work was on in earnest by the time a little man with piping on his vest came on the scene.

"There is," he explained to Tony and Nick after viewing the action and studying the contract, "no such thing as the Grand Central Holding Corporation."

When Tony and Nick took him to the suite where they had turned the certified check over to Mr. Blodgett, the suite was, of course, deserted. Now the vice-president tried, without success, to explain that they had been the victims of a confidence game. The Fortunato brothers were not convinced. They were sure the railroad was involved in the swindle. They had to be forcibly ejected from the terminal.

Tony and Nick went to their bank to discover the bank where their certified check made out to the Grand Central Holding Corporation had been deposited. An officer named a bank in the Grand Central area. Zooming into the second bank, Tony and Nick did not get the quick coöperation they were looking for. An officer they talked to was not at all willing to impart information about a depositor to a couple of wild-eyed characters barging in off the street. So Tony and Nick went to the police.

Toward noon the brothers reappeared in the second bank in company with a policeman who specialized in confidence work. He quickly got the surface facts about Messrs Grenfell and Blodgett and the Grand Central Holding Corporation.

The two con men had first appeared in the bank about a month before, to open a checking account. Banks did not peer into the backgrounds of new depositors in those days, so Grenfell and Blodgett, passing off the Grand Central Holding Corporation as a brokerage outfit, had opened a joint checking account. They avoided the need to supply references for themselves by charming a bank officer, who opened an account for them with their cash deposit of $100,000.

When Blodgett had deposited the Fortunatos' certified check and made no attempt to draw on it, the people in the bank thought that the Grand Central Holding Corporation had got off to a nice start. It was not until the big check had been deposited for about a week that Blodgett and Grenfell began making withdrawals—$10,000, $15,000, $25,000 at a time. By Saturday, March 30, the last banking day before the roof fell in, Grenfell and Blodgett had been carrying a balance of little more than $1000.

The New York police did not seem to have any photographs of either Grenfell or Blodgett, obviously assumed names, in their rogues' gallery. Weeks passed. Somebody suggested to Tony and Nick that they take their problem to Raymond Schindler, the private detective who specialized in identifying con men, running them down and, in assorted ways, making life so miserable for them that they sometimes returned part of the take just to get rid of Schindler.

Schindler took the case. But nobody who had laid eyes on Grenfell and Blodgett—Tony or Nick, the bank people or the man who had leased the office to them—was able to give Schindler a morsel of useful information. After about a year, he was forced to tell the bilked brothers that he could not help them.

The more time passed, the more Tony and Nick became convinced that the railroad had somehow been involved in the swindle. That blind spot was to remain with the Fortunato brothers to the end of their days. For several years, catching or leaving suburban trains in Grand Central, Schindler would hear that one or both of the Fortunatos had been in. They would stand around the booth that had cost them $100,000—Tony or Nick or both of them—shaking their fists and hurling imprecations at the poor men who were doing nothing but trying to make a living giving out information.

IN THE BRONX, New York, a gunman burglarized a dentist's office, reassured the dentist: "Shut your mouth. This won't hurt a bit."   —*Time*

Rarely are self-sacrifice and
deception the same tactic

MASTER OF THE DOUBLE CROSS

by William C. White

This is really General Yablonsky's story. He was the old man who sat nightly in a corner of that little Russian café on Nollendorfplatz in Berlin. The rows of medals that blotted his blouse would attract your attention. The General was a typical Russian émigré, poverty-stricken, alive only in his roots which were all buried in the past.

Sometimes, when there had been vodka without stint, he would tell the story of Captain Tanama. "One man alone is responsible for the Russian Revolution and for all the following filth of the Bolsheviki," he would say, leading up to that story. "One man, a Japanese, Captain Tanama. There would be a czar in Holy Russia today had it not been for this scoundrel. You see, the Japanese defeated us in 1905, and that defeat produced the revolutionary movement in Russia. And the Japanese would not have won, had it not been for that traitor Tanama. You have never heard of this infamous man?"

I had not heard.

This is the story which the old General, once of the Czar's Intelligence Service, then told:

Captain Tanama first came to St. Petersburg as military attaché to the Japanese embassy in 1901. He was of some special breed, I guess, not like most of his people but nearly six feet tall. His face was the color of bronze and ugly, like some Tibetan devil mask. Ugly, yes, but he looked striking in uniform, and women seemed to be attracted to him.

In those days I was a captain, serving as assistant to the chief of the Military Intelligence Division. Naturally, we were interested in Tanama. He was a foreign military attaché, which is a polite way of saying "spy." He came from one of the oldest families in his country, and his father was one of the Mikado's closest advisers. Thorough breeding and long residence abroad had given Tanama a proud grace and polish that marked him in any gathering.

As a matter of fact, we were more than usually interested in him. We knew that it was only a matter of time before we would have to fight the Japanese in the Far East. Furthermore, we were receiving information from our own agents in Tokyo that the Japanese War Office was continually securing our military secrets. Tanama could tell us where the leak was, that was sure.

He had a way of making friends, with officers, actresses, officials —it made no difference. It is not a far step from making friends to using friends. Tanama had a lot of money and was an inveterate gambler. He always lost and always with a smile, and he paid losses of the size which makes smiling difficult. A couple of my fellow officers bought diamonds for their mistresses with winnings from the Japanese captain.

For a year we put him under the closest observation, but with no results. We watched every Russian officer with whom he was friendly but we found nothing suspicious. Tanama was mixed up with a number of girls around town, but these were only the usual sort of liaisons. We knew, because the girls were on our payroll. Yet every report from our agents in Tokyo told us that the leak still existed and was, if anything, growing larger.

There was one thing that we could do—drive Tanama out of the country in the hope that his successor would be neither so clever nor so ingratiatingly charming nor so efficient. We planned to threaten Tanama with disgrace, hoping that he would either leave or commit suicide. It made no difference to us, so long as we got rid of him.

It was easy to "frame" him. He was most friendly with an actress, Ilyinskaya. We went to her and told her what we wanted, but we had to use threats to get her to promise to help us. I think she really loved that scoundrel! But she finally promised.

One evening she went to Captain Tanama and said that it was necessary for him to marry her, at once. He refused, like a polished gentleman of course, pointing out that when a Japanese officer marries a non-Japanese, he must leave his country's service. Besides, he added, somewhat as an afterthought, he had a wife in Japan. He offered Ilyinskaya money, but she would not touch it. It was either marriage—or publicity. "You can think about it until tomorrow night," she told him. "I will come to you then for an answer."

The next day my telephone rang. It was the Captain, asking to see me alone immediately, "most urgently."

I went to his apartment. I must say that he was frank, for he began, in straightforward fashion, "Do you know of this Ilyinskaya affair?"

Unable to return his frankness, I said that I did not. He explained briefly the situation and said, "You realize what choice is left for me if she carries out her threat? Don't think me cowardly. I am not afraid of disgrace or even suicide. But my family is a very proud and ancient one, and my father, on the Emperor's Privy Council, is a very old man. I should hate to have him know of my disgrace, at the very end of his life. He would think it his duty to follow me in a disgraceful death. And my uncle. You do not know us Japanese."

Then, abruptly, he stared me in the face and asked, "*Monsieur le capitaine*, you can help me if you wish. What are your terms?"

I was rejoicing within that we had won as simply as that. But I answered with pretended hesitation, "I am not sure that I can help you. In any case you would have to leave Russia."

"Certainly. And what else?"

I was too confused by the connotation of that question to think clearly, but I managed to say, "I must speak to my superior officers about that."

I returned to my office and told my associates of the conversation and of the terms. They laughed loudly at the idea of a Japanese officer, and one of high caste at that, offering to aid the intelligence service of a potential enemy in order to escape from a mix-up with an ordinary actress. "He puts a low value on our intelligence," Major Oblomov, my superior, said. "Japan must want very badly to furnish us with false information. But it would be a shame not to play with him. We might ask him to supply us with copies of plans for troop movements around Port Arthur and in southern Manchuria. It would be interesting to know just what the Japanese War College would prepare for us. We could be sure that in reality they would carry out the opposite."

That was an appealing idea, and, after discussing it, we decided to play Tanama's game. He left St. Petersburg on the following day. It was late summer in 1902 and we were busy with our own preparations for the war that appeared inevitable. We forgot Tanama until one day in December 1902, when a package came to us by diplomatic pouch from our military attaché in Tokyo. It contained plans, to the minutest detail, for Japanese action around Port Arthur, showing where troops would be landed, how they would be distributed and what the objectives of any drive there would be.

We examined the plans carefully. There were several novelties in proposed tactics which surprised us. Everything had been done with the most meticulous care. "The Japanese are thorough, even in such imitation works of art as these," said Major Oblomov.

"Perhaps they are genuine," one officer suggested.

"Nonsense. Of course they would do a trick like this with the greatest air of authenticity." This was the common opinion. The plans were put in the archives and forgotten.

Six months later, in the summer of 1903, another set of plans arrived in just the same way. The same detail, the same meticulousness. These were plans for action on the south Manchurian peninsula in general, focusing on Mukden. The care with which the plans had been prepared increased the number of skeptics in our department. Two or three officers now said that, in the possibility that the plans might be genuine, we should study them carefully and revise our counterplans accordingly. But such work would have called for a complete revision of our own defense tactics and these plans too were finally set aside in our archives.

Late in December of the same year a third set of plans arrived, for action along the Yalu River. There was no chance for any of the usual discussion this time. A day or so after the arrival of this third package came startling information from Tokyo, information almost unbelievable but fully corroborated by our military attaché there: Tanama had been caught stealing plans from the War Office and had been executed as a spy.

We were inclined to scoff at this at first as another Japanese trick. But every source of information that we had, supported it as a fact. And whatever doubts may have remained were erased a few days later by a story carried by the press of the world saying that his father, Prince Tanama, of the Privy Council, had committed suicide on hearing of the disgraceful death of his son.

And in our archives we had three sets of Japanese plans!

We went over them with all speed. Day and night we worked to correct our own tactics, to take advantage of these mobilization orders. Then the war broke out, in February 1904, the war that was to result eventually in the Revolution of 1905 and the later Revolution of 1917.

In April we fell back on the Chiuliencheng position on the Yalu River. The battle there, on April 30, 1904, is one of the important battles of the world. There for the first time in modern history an army of Orientals defeated an army of the white race.

We had the plans of the Japanese there. But wherever we stationed one regiment to offset them, there were two Japanese regiments waiting. Wherever we had one artillery battery there were two of the Japanese. And the battle ended with our army in flight, with our rear guard completely destroyed because its left flank took the wrong direction in retreating. Why did we take the wrong direction? I knew then, and Captain Tanama's ghost, if he really had been shot, knew.

But it was too late to revise our general tactics. They had been built on the basis of Tanama's plans. We were defeated at Nashan, at Mukden, at Port Arthur. History tells you that we lost the war because the Trans-Siberian Railroad could not bring us men and supplies fast enough. Nonsense! We had enough men, more than the Japanese. But in the wrong place, every time.

I was at the front, and in December 1904 I heard the rest of the story from a captured Japanese officer. I asked him about Tanama.

"He is a great national hero," the prisoner said. "The Emperor has given him and his family the Order of the Rising Sun."

"Then he was not really executed?"

"Oh, yes, he was executed as a spy and disgraced. But a few months ago there was published the true story, how he had eagerly chosen the privilege of disgrace and of being executed, so that he could completely deceive you Russians. It was a great honor."

"And his father?"

"He committed suicide, of course. That was likewise a great honor."

So we lost the Russo-Japanese War. But what can you do with a people who will face a firing squad or commit suicide in order to double-cross you?

⟨✦⟩

ECONOMISTS about a year ago detected a sign that better times were in store for Indonesia—forged currency was beginning to appear again in Jakarta. In recent years, the Indonesian rupiah has been so inflated (10,000 to the dollar on the black market) that forgery wasn't considered worth the trouble.   —*The Insider's Newsletter*

*Frederick Emerson Peters was
an unusual con man—his haunts were
not the hot spots but the libraries*

A CROOK EVERYONE LIKED

by Beverly Smith, Jr.

One Saturday morning, a telephone operator at the Hotel Taft in New Haven, Connecticut, repeatedly rang Room 510. No answer. The small, elderly, professorial-looking gentleman in 510, who had registered as Dr. B. A. Morris of Bala Cynwyd, Pennsylvania, had left a call for 9 a.m. Finally a bellboy was sent up to knock on the door. When there was still no answer, an assistant manager, opening the door with a passkey, found "Dr. Morris" unconscious on the bed. Apparently he had suffered a stroke. He was taken to Saint Raphael's Hospital, where he died the next afternoon without regaining consciousness.

Thus ended, two months short of his 74th birthday, in 1959, the career of a learned, engaging, ingenious and talented man who had applied his gifts to establishing one of the longest police records in American history. As a confidence man, impersonator and bad-check artist, he had amiably swindled a modest living since the dawn of the 20th century.

Sympathetic hotel officials, not suspecting the illegal eminence of their guest, tried to notify his family. Their phone calls revealed that the Bala Cynwyd address was fictitious. Puzzled, they examined the good doctor's scanty personal effects. Here was

275

further mystery, including uncashed checks made out to Dr. J. A. Logan, a used airline ticket in the name of Dr. Morton and shirts with the laundry mark "CAR." There were also a gold wristwatch, a stopwatch, $38.09 in cash and four unused Scandinavian Railways tickets from Oslo to Bergen, Norway, made out to "Dr. Logan and party." Now the New Haven police took over. They, too, were baffled by the varied names and addresses of the stricken man. They mailed his fingerprints to the FBI in Washington.

The FBI does not become excited easily. But on the evening when the prints from New Haven reached the FBI Identification Division, it is fair to say there was a sensation—hurried phone calls and exclamations of wonder not untinged by regret.

And why not? With the death of Frederick Emerson Peters—for the fingerprints were his—it seemed that an institution, an entire era of crime, had passed away. Here was a malefactor who had been bouncing rubber checks in 1902, when J. Edgar Hoover was a seven-year-old boy bouncing rubber balls. The old Bureau of Investigation, predecessor of the FBI, first arrested Fred Peters in 1915; he was by then a seasoned alumnus of reformatories, jails and state prisons. In 1920, before the modern FBI was formed, President Woodrow Wilson commuted his time in Atlanta Penitentiary from ten to five years. Since then, quickly resuming his mild depredations, Peters had built an FBI file as tall as he was.

Here I had better explain the word "mild." Other con men and check passers known to the FBI are after big, fast money. When they get it they spend it on high living. Not so Mr. Peters. His bite was gentle, his tastes scholarly and simple. His main pleasure was in the impersonation of prominent or learned people and in the opportunities this gave him for what he called "intelligent conversation." He was willing to devote hours or days of artistic buildup to realize a profit of from $5 to $30 on a bouncing check. He did not want or need much money.

Consider his last illegal ramble, which lasted from December of 1958 until his death in July 1959. After leaving Washington, D.C., where he had "gone straight"—or almost—for four months, he

276

called at the Baltimore shop of an engraver of fine silver, introducing himself as R. A. Coleman, of the American Peace Society. He explained that the society, founded in 1828 and headed by Major General Ulysses S. Grant III (Ret.), wished to purchase a silver chalice and paten for presentation to the National Cathedral in Washington.

"Mr. Coleman" took much time and care in selecting the chalice and prescribing the lettering. On the underside of the paten he wished engraved a portrait of St. Matthew. The engraver figured that the total cost would come to $225. "Mr. Coleman" looked thoughtful. "Peace," he murmured. "How much extra would it cost to engrave the chalice with the symbol of peace—a dove?" he asked. That would be $15 more, bringing the cost to $240.

"Good," said the visitor, tendering an American Peace Society check for $250, made out to R. A. Coleman and purportedly signed by U. S. Grant III, president. "Mr. Coleman" accepted the $10 change, chatted further about the art of engraving and embossing silver and departed. Fortunately for the jeweler the check bounced before he had well started his laborious engraving task. Soon afterward, FBI men called. They displayed photos of various check passers. From among them the store owner promptly picked Frederick Emerson Peters.

Shortly afterward, when I talked with the owner, he bore Peters no ill will. "You know," he said, "I was so sold on the old boy that I would have handed over $100 if he had asked for it. He didn't want to take me for even as much as $25—so he thought up the peace dove to make the bill $240. I'm keeping the chalice as a souvenir to show my customers."

In May of 1959, Peters, wearing a lapel pin of the St. Andrew's Society, entered a shop—specializing in Scottish imports—on Fifth Avenue in New York. "Have you any MacGregor tartan material?" he asked. Before the owner of the shop could answer, he had pointed out a bolt of the MacGregor on the shelf. He was Dr. J. J. Morton, of the University of Kansas, he explained; his daughter wanted the material to make a suit. While they discussed how many yards would be needed, "Dr. Morton" talked so learnedly of the Scottish clans that the shop owner did not even ask for identification in accepting a check for $75 and giving him $28 in change. The check was marked "Lecture." As he endorsed it with one of the almost illegible scribbles he used for this purpose, he looked up with a smile.

"I'm just a physician," he said, "and who but a pharmacist can read a doctor's scrawl?"

Soon afterward he dropped in at a Rockefeller Center shop specializing in Oriental antiquities. Again he was J. J. Morton, but this time he was professor of history at Yale. He was interested in Egyptian scarabs and had, he confessed, a rather worthy little collection of his own. As he studied the shop's selection he talked knowledgeably of the customs and castes of India. Finally he selected a 3500-year-old scarab—$50—and then added to it, "for my wife," a silver cuff bracelet and other gifts totaling $27.41.

No, the professor would not take his purchases with him—he seldom did, preferring not to be cluttered with possessions. "Just send them to my home, 1162 Norfolk Street [fictitious], in Cleveland." He offered a check for $100, made out to J. J. Morton, with the notation, "Seminar Fee." Without hesitation he was given the $22.59 in change.

Note that in paying for the tartans and the scarab, Peters had taken in change a little sharper bite than usual. As if to readjust his average, he went to a specialty shop on Park Avenue. There he spent hours in selecting presents worth $97.63, to be sent to "my daughter Patricia at Sweet Briar." He tendered a check for $100 made out to "Dr. Alexander Duncan," and contentedly departed with the change—$2.37 for a morning of artistic conversation and impersonation.

These are a few random samples of Peters' work. They give but a glimpse of his astounding versatility. As a surgeon he knew precisely what equipment he wanted—and why—for his new operating room. As a bibliophile he was familiar with rare first editions and unusual typography. As an Orientalist he was pre-

pared to discuss the religions and dynasties of ancient China. "The Versailles Conference of 1919? It so happens I was there—with our Naval delegation, you know." And he was ready with supporting anecdotes and authentic detail of that historic confab—not a flaw in his story unless you knew that he was securely imprisoned in Atlanta from 1915 to 1920.

Peters' wide array of knowledge seems incredible until you consider his background. He came from a respectable family in Ohio. He was a brilliant student in high school, a fast reader with a quick mind and retentive memory. In 1902, at 17, his formal education was cut short by bad checks and a term in the reformatory. Whence, then, all the knowledge?

The college graduate has four years of academic study, the professional man from seven to ten years. To Peters ten years of study seemed mere kindergarten stuff. He studied intensively for 30 years. Where? In the libraries of various state and federal prisons. If the prison lacked a library, Peters created one. For example, while he was in the federal pen at McNeil Island—1924–1931—Peters assembled and indexed a library of 15,000 well-chosen volumes. How he did this, without spending a cent of his own or the taxpayers' money, I will explain later.

My point here is that a good student, with access to a sound library, can absorb a vast amount of information without the help of professors, frat pins or college yells. Prisoner Peters, a natural scholar, found his cell ideal for concentration and reflection. He once pointed out to me that much of the learning of the Middle Ages originated in the cell—the monastic cell. In prison Peters was also free from the bonds of curriculum. He could read as he pleased in medicine, law, architecture, history, fiction, memoirs, psychology, comparative religion, poetry, English literature. I don't say his knowledge was deep in these fields, but it was wide enough for him to talk shop with the experts. He was an expert himself in the use of reference books. If there were gaps in the knowledge needed for a new impersonation, he headed for the public library. After a couple of days there among the encyclopedias, *Who's Who in America*, the *Readers' Guide*, *Current Biography* and the latest learned journals, he was ready to discuss the fine points in his newly chosen field.

"Of course, I don't know all the answers," he once told me, "but I know the right questions. Those alone are often the key to a stimulating discussion."

I first met Peters in the spring of 1958, when he was still in the federal reformatory at Lorton, Virginia.

When we were introduced, I was not favorably impressed. A short, stocky, balding man with a limp, and wearing ill-fitting prison denims, he looked like any other aging convict. Now, as he talked, this sordid image faded. It was replaced, as he spoke discerningly of his favorite American and English authors, with the picture of a genial old professor of literature. I was enthralled, and the warden pushed aside his desk work to listen.

He went on to lament the passing of the "lusty, creative critics" such as James Huneker and H. L. Mencken, and I mentioned that my first magazine article had been bought by Mr. Mencken for the old *Mercury* in 1925.

"That's a coincidence," said Peters. "In 1925 I was working at the *Mercury*, in the office on Fifth Avenue."

"Editorial work?" I asked, not without suspicion. Peters quickly disarmed me. "I used to call myself an editorial assistant but, to tell you the truth,"—he chuckled at the recollection—"a better title would have been 'bartender.' I took care of the liquor and mixed the drinks for Mencken and George Jean Nathan and their visiting friends and authors—Red Lewis, Joe Hergesheimer, Theodore Dreiser and the rest; scofflaws all, Mr. Mencken used to call them."

So help me, I believed him. His air was so casual, his detail so plausible, his self-deprecation so winning that it hardly occurred to me to doubt—until I got back to my office. Then I checked his record. During 1923 and early 1924 he was skipping busily from coast to coast, bouncing small checks under scores of imposing identities. In July of 1924 he was arrested in California and sent to

281

McNeil Island for seven years. I do not question, however, that he had sometime visited the offices of the old *Mercury* and was a reader of that magazine.

I made further inquiries about Peters at Lorton Reformatory, where his excellent conduct was shortly to win him parole after six and a half years of a maximum nine-year sentence. All the reports were favorable. He had the rare distinction of getting along well with both the officials and his fellow inmates. He had the further distinction of drawing $69 a month in Social Security, earned as a master printer during a few years of rectitude in the 1940's. He used this, his own lawful money, to contribute modestly to a number of charities; to purchase good books, magazines and records which he shared with his fellows; and to order an occasional box of fine Havanas from New York—good cigars were one of the few luxuries he allowed himself. He also taught classes in English and business management and was active in church work within the prison.

Several penologists who knew Peters, and whom I asked about his chances of going straight after his release, were of divided opinions. One said, "I believe he'll make it. After all, he's 73 now. He's still lame in his left arm and leg from that stroke he had five years ago. He has Social Security. There are prominent citizens and churchmen eager to help him. Why should he drop his comfort and security and dodge around the country again, a fugitive, picking up the kind of chicken feed he takes in change for his bum checks?" Another authority, who had known Peters for 35 years, was skeptical. "He has carried impersonation to a high art and he loves it. He can't give it up for long. If he lives, he'll go back to it."

After his release from Lorton on August 11, 1958, Peters occasionally dropped by my Washington office for a chat. He said he had a job as a night clerk in a small hotel (true)—lots of time for reading. Through the courtesy of Bishop Beverley D. Tucker of Ohio (true) he had met Canon Robert George of the National Cathedral (true) and was a regular communicant at his 9:30 services (true). He reported that he hoped to get work at the cathedral either in public relations or in soliciting contributions. Here he added with a quick smile, "Of course, no money would pass through my hands."

On a later occasion he told me he was negotiating with the American Bankers Association to write a booklet warning against fake drivers' licenses, credit cards and other phony identification, and explaining how easily they could be stolen or fabricated. I never found out whether this was true or false.

Toward the end of November 1958, he dropped by again. He was doing some research work with the American Peace Society, he said, and had dined the other evening at the Cosmos Club with the society's directors, including General U. S. Grant III. This was true, but Peters did not mention that he had introduced himself to the society as a retired professor from Western Reserve University in Cleveland, engaged in writing a biography of Charles Franklin Thwing, formerly president of that university and former vice-president of the Peace Society. I assumed that the society, like others trying to help Peters, knew of his background.

I asked him about recent books he had read. He responded with less than his usual animation. As I walked with him to the elevator, his limp was quite noticeable. He seemed vaguely depressed. "You're making wonderful progress, Mr. Peters," I said.

"Everybody's most kind," he murmured absentmindedly. Then, as he stepped into the elevator, he managed a smile and waved his right hand. "*Adios,*" he said.

During the next two months I did not hear from him. Then came a phone call from a friend at the FBI. "Our old pal Peters is on the loose again," he said.

"No!" I said.

"Yes! Since a week before Christmas. Dropping his bad little checks in a dozen states."

"Think you'll catch him?" I asked.

"It's not easy. The old rascal charms his victims so and hits them so light—lots of them don't even make a complaint. That chills the trail. But with the circulars, the pictures, the descriptions and that obvious limp—we'll catch him, all right." Five months later, however, death caught him first.

Peters, an only child, was born in West Salem, Ohio, on September 26, 1885. He later moved with his family to Cleveland, where he went to the Central High School. His father became an auditor with the Willard Storage Battery Company. The elder Peters was a respected citizen, numbering among his friends Newton D. Baker, city solicitor of Cleveland, 1902–1912, and later Secretary of War under President Wilson. Peters often expressed affection for his father, but said his mother "didn't understand me." Who, after all, ever did?

Because young Peters' misdeeds began before the general use of fingerprinting, and because his fondness for fictitious names began in his teens, it is hard to pinpoint his early offenses precisely. According to his own account, he ran away from home when he was 17 following a quarrel with his parents over their refusal to let him go to a high-school dance. He went to Cincinnati, got a job as a clerk under an assumed name and promptly began supplementing his income with bum checks under other assumed names. Soon caught, he was sent to the state reformatory, still under an assumed name.

Many months later his father, learning of the son's plight, enlisted the aid of his friend Newton Baker. The city solicitor sympathized with the young first offender and sponsored his parole.

Newton Baker thus became the first of those prominent citizens who, over the next 55 years, were to put faith in Peters' reform. Peters went on to serve other sentences in Pennsylvania, Kansas and California (San Quentin). But he did not appeal to Baker again until 1920, when he had served five years of an apparently unbeatable ten-year rap. Only Presidential intervention could spring him. This time Secretary Baker, more wary, asked Attorney General Mitchell Palmer, then in Georgia, to talk with Peters. The hard-boiled Palmer was so moved by the brilliant prisoner's story that he joined with Secretary Baker in presenting the sad

284

case to ailing President Wilson, who signed the commutation papers in May 1920.

Soon afterward Peters again hit the check-passing trail, posing as Franklin D. Roosevelt, Gifford Pinchot II and Theodore Roosevelt, Jr. The fact that he bore no physical resemblance to such people never bothered Peters—his talk did the trick. As "Samuel de Grasse, chief electrician for the Mary Pickford Productions," he passed out thousands of dollars' worth of checks for movie lighting equipment—but his total take on these large deals, over a period of weeks, was only $50.

In 1924 the authorities arrested Peters in San Francisco. He obligingly confessed to all his misdeeds and was sentenced to ten years at McNeil Island. For a while he was not happy there. He went to warden Finch Archer, who had taken a liking to him, and explained that the prison library had only 500 dog-eared volumes, "most of them trash."

Warden Archer explained that the prison, under the Coolidge economy, had no money for more books.

"Suppose I can build a library free?" said Peters.

"Go to it," said the warden.

Peters wrote to the leading publishers in the United States. He did not write form letters. For each publisher he had discriminating praise for the proudest products of his presses. Then to business—this great prison had no library worthy of the name; hundreds of the worthier prisoners thirsted for the knowledge which would enable them to be useful citizens once they had paid their debt to society; only the great publishers of America could slake this thirst.

The publishers responded nobly, not only with shopworn and returned books but with some of their best. Mrs. Mabel Walker Willebrandt, dynamic Assistant Attorney General of the United States, visited the prison. Hard as flint toward prohibition violators, she softened at once when Peters told her of his efforts to bring light and truth to his benighted fellows. She enlisted in his crusade. Among the many influential friends she approached was

Mary Roberts Rinehart. That kind and vigorous lady, beloved of publishers, scolded them into sending more and better books to the good Mr. Peters.

The harvest, as I have said earlier, was some 15,000 excellent volumes—fiction, biography, science, textbooks, technical works and the rest. All of these Peters indexed and put into good library form. Mrs. William Montgomery Smith, former administrative assistant to Mrs. Willebrandt, told me the estimate of 15,000 was "conservative."

Among those who helped with the library were Daniel B. Updike and John Bianchi of the Merrymount Press. Experts also in fine typography, they encouraged Peters to set up a press at McNeil. They gave him type fonts and helpful criticism. Peters, with his *Island Lantern Press*, won awards for the best prison magazine in the country. His persuasive letters drew distinguished contributors, including Clarence Darrow, leading criminal lawyer of the day.

Doubtless one can find selfish motives for such achievements. They helped convince President Hoover's Attorney General, William D. Mitchell, that Peters had "found himself" at last, and thus paved the way for Peters' parole in 1931, after seven years of his ten-year term. It was 1937 before he was caught again and sent back for five more years of postgraduate studies in Lewisburg, Leavenworth and Atlanta.

On the other hand, these ventures involved an immense amount of hard work which Peters carried out with zest. By the library alone he conferred benefits on his fellows which not so many of us self-satisfied, respectable citizens can match. On a balance these, and the wry entertainment he provided for his innumerable victims, may offset in part what he used to call "mine often infirmities"—his misuse of his good gifts, his betrayal of the hopes of kind persons who tried to help him, his persistent petty peculations of a lifetime.

Could marriage have reformed him? Apparently not. According to his own varying accounts, he was married once, twice or three times. Each marriage was quickly overtaken by galloping incompatibility, followed by divorce.

Soon after Peters' death I was talking to a police detective who had known him, and who had missed many a meal and many a good night's sleep in trying to track him down.

"Poor Peters," I said.

"Poor Peters nothing," said my friend. "He's up at those pearly gates right now, trying to con old St. Peter into believing that he—Peters—is one of his collateral descendants. And if St. Peter can see through him, he's a lot smarter than most of us humans."

A more charitably Christian view was expressed by the Reverend H. Coleman Lamb, then director of the New Haven Council of Churches, following Peters' burial. Since the deceased man had only a few dollars in cash, and no relatives came forward to claim his body, his modest funeral was paid for by the City Welfare Department. Present were only the undertakers, a reporter, Albert Callan of the New Haven *Journal-Courier,* and two small boys who had wandered in from the street.

The next day—Sunday—the Reverend Mr. Lamb read a seven-minute service over the grave, marked only by a metal disk with the number 858.

"Every human soul is sacred," he said. "Who are we to judge? . . . We trust that somehow good will be the final fruit of ill."

A FEW years ago a man operating a soft-drink stand was called before a magistrate for selling adulterated syrups and was instructed to tell the truth about the ingredients. Later, when an agent checked up on the man, he was found to be complying with the law and his business was better than it had ever been. In front of the stand was a new sign reading: "All of our soft drinks are guaranteed to be highly adulterated."

—*Better Business Bureau of Long Beach, California*

Editor's note: One of the great archaeological discoveries of the era after the Civil War was the Cardiff Giant—or so many believed. *Fortunately for all reasonable men of the day, the erudite Andrew D. White, educator and diplomat, cofounder of Cornell University, was a witness to the event. Here, in his own words, is the story condensed from the fascinating chapter of his autobiography, published in 1905.*

CARDIFF GIANT

by Andrew D. White

In the autumn of 1869, New York's peaceful Onondaga Valley was in commotion from one end to the other. Strange reports echoed from farm to farm. It was noised abroad that a great stone statue or petrified giant had been dug up near the little hamlet of Cardiff, almost at the southern end of the valley. Soon, despite the fact that the crops were not yet gathered in and the elections not yet over, men and women and children were hurrying from Syracuse and from the farmhouses along the valley to the scene of the great discovery.

I had been absent in a distant state for some weeks, and on my return to Syracuse met one of the most substantial citizens, a highly respected deacon in the Presbyterian Church, formerly a county judge. I asked him, in a jocose way, about the new object of interest, fully expecting that he would join me in a laugh over the whole matter. To my surprise, he became at once very solemn.

He said, "I assure you that this is no laughing matter; it is a very serious thing, indeed. There is no question that an amazing discovery has been made, and I advise you to go down and see what you think of it."

Next morning, my brother and I, driving a light buggy pulled by a fast trotter, were speeding through the valley to the scene of the discovery; and as we went we saw more and more, on every side, evidences of enormous popular interest. The roads were crowded with buggies, carriages and even omnibuses from the city, and with lumber wagons from the farms—all laden with passengers. In about two hours we arrived at the Newell farm and found a gathering which at first sight seemed like a county fair. In the midst was a tent, and a crowd was pressing for admission. Entering, we saw a large pit or grave and, at the bottom, perhaps five feet below the surface, an enormous figure, apparently of Onondaga gray limestone. It was a stone giant, with massive features, the whole body nude, the limbs contracted as if in agony. It had a color as if it had lain long in the earth, and over its surface were minute punctures, like pores. A special appearance of great age was given it by deep grooves and channels in its underside, apparently worn by the water which flowed in streams through the earth and along the rock on which the figure rested. Lying in its grave, with the subdued light from the roof of the tent falling upon it and with the limbs contorted as if in a death struggle, it produced a most weird effect. An air of great solemnity pervaded the place. Visitors hardly spoke above a whisper.

Coming out, I asked some questions and was told that the farmer who lived there had discovered the figure when digging a well. Being asked my opinion, I answered that the whole matter was undoubtedly a hoax; that there was no reason why the farmer should dig a well in the spot where the figure was found; that it was convenient neither to the house nor to the barn; that there was already a good spring and a stream of water running conveniently to both; that, as to the figure itself, it certainly could not have been carved by any prehistoric race, since no part of it showed the characteristics of any such early work; that, rude as it was, it betrayed the qualities of a modern performance of a low order.

Nor could it be a fossilized human being; in this all scientific observers of any note agreed. There was ample evidence, to one who had seen much sculpture, that it was carved, and that the man who carved it, though by no means possessed of genius or talent, had seen casts, engravings or photographs of noted sculptures. The figure, in size, in massiveness, in the drawing up of the limbs and in its roughened surface, vaguely reminded one of Michelangelo's *Night* and *Morning*. Of course, the difference between this crude figure and those great Medicean statues was infinite; and yet it seemed to me that the man who had carved this figure must have received a hint from them.

It was also clear that the figure was intended to be considered neither as an idol nor as a monumental statue. There was no pedestal of any sort on which it could stand, and the disposition of the limbs and their contortions were not such as any sculptor would dream of in a figure to be set up for adoration. That it was meant to be taken as a fossilized giant was indicated by the fact that it was made as nearly like a human being as the limited powers of the stone-carver permitted and by the minute imitations of pores covering it.

Therefore, in spite of all scientific reasons to the contrary, the work was very generally accepted as a petrified human being of colossal size, and became known as the "Cardiff Giant."

One thing seemed to argue strongly in favor of its antiquity, and I felt bound to confess that it puzzled me. This was the fact that the surface water flowing beneath it in its grave seemed to have deeply grooved and channeled it on the underside. Now, the Onondaga gray limestone is hard and substantial, and on that very account used in the locks upon the canals; for the running of surface water to wear such channels in it would require centuries.

Against the opinion that the figure was a hoax various arguments were used. It was insisted, first, that the farmer had not the ability to devise such a fraud; second, that he had not the means to execute it; third, that his family had lived there steadily for many years, and were ready to declare under oath that they had never seen it and had known nothing of it until it was accidentally discovered; fourth, that the neighbors had never seen or heard of it; fifth, that it was preposterous to suppose that such a mass of stone could have been brought to and buried in the place without someone finding it out; sixth, that the grooves and channels worn in it by the surface water proved its vast antiquity.

To these considerations others were soon added. Especially interesting was it to observe the evolution of myth and legend. Within a week after the discovery, full-blown statements appeared to the effect that the neighboring Indians had abundant traditions of giants who formerly roamed over the hills of Onondaga. Finally, the circumstantial story was evolved that an Onondaga squaw had declared, "in an impressive manner," that the statue "is undoubtedly the petrified body of a gigantic Indian prophet who flourished many centuries ago and foretold the coming of the palefaces and who, just before his own death, said to those about him that their descendants would see him again."

To this were added the reflections of many good people who found it an edifying confirmation of the Biblical text, "There were giants in those days." There was, indeed, an undercurrent of skepticism among the harder heads in the valley, but the prevailing opinion in the region was increasingly in favor of the idea that the object was a fossilized human being—a giant of "those days."

Such was the rush to see the figure that the admission receipts were very large, and soon men from the neighboring region proposed to purchase the figure and exhibit it through the country. A leading spirit in this "syndicate" deserves mention. He was a horse dealer in a large way and banker in a small way from a village in the next county—a man keen and shrewd, but merciful and kindly, who had fought his way up from abject poverty, and whose fundamental principle, as he asserted it, was "Do unto others as they would like to do unto you, and—*do it fust.*" A joint-stock concern was formed with considerable capital, and an eminent showman, one "Colonel" Wood, was employed to exploit the wonder.

A week after my first visit I again went to the place, by invitation. In the crowd on that day were many men of light and leading from neighboring towns—among them some who made pretensions to scientific knowledge. The figure, lying in its grave, deeply impressed all; and as a party of us came away, a doctor of divinity, pastor of one of the largest churches in Syracuse, said with awe, "Is it not strange that any human being, after seeing this wonderfully preserved figure, can deny the evidence of his senses and refuse to believe what is so evidently the fact, that we have here a fossilized human being, perhaps one of the ancient giants mentioned in Scripture?"

Another visitor, a bright-looking lady, was heard to declare, "Nothing in the world can ever make me believe that he was not once a living being. Why, you can see the veins in his legs."

A prominent clergyman declared with ex cathedra emphasis: "This is not a thing contrived of man, but is the face of one who lived on the earth, the very image and child of God." And a writer in one of the most important daily papers of the region dwelt on the "majestic simplicity and grandeur of the figure," and added, "It is not unsafe to affirm that 99 out of every 100 persons who have seen this wonder have become immediately and instantly impressed with the idea that they were in the presence of an object not made by mortal hands. . . . No piece of sculpture ever produced the awe inspired by this blackened form. . . . I venture to affirm that no living sculptor can be produced who will say that the figure was conceived and executed by any human being."

The current of belief ran more and more strongly, and soon embraced a large number of really thoughtful people. A short time after my first visit came a deputation of regents of the State University from Albany, including Dr. James Hall, the state geologist, perhaps the most eminent American paleontologist of that period.

On their arrival at Syracuse in the evening, I met them at their hotel and discussed with them the subject which so interested us all, urging them to be cautious and stating that a mistake might prove very injurious to the reputation of the regents and to the proper standing of scientific men and methods in the state; for if the matter should turn out to be a fraud, and such eminent authorities should be found to have committed themselves to it, there would be a guffaw from one end of the country to the other at the expense of the men entrusted by the state with its scientific and educational interests. To this the gentlemen assented, and next day they went to Cardiff. They came; they saw; and they narrowly escaped being conquered. Luckily they did not give their sanction to the idea that the statue was a petrifaction, but Professor Hall was induced to say: "To all appearance, the statue lay upon the gravel when the deposition of the fine silt or soil began, upon the surface of which the forests have grown for succeeding generations. Altogether it is the most remarkable object brought to light in this country, and, although not dating back to the Stone Age, is nevertheless deserving of the attention of archaeologists."

At no period of my life have I ever been more discouraged as regards the possibility of making right reason prevail among men.

There seemed no possibility even of *suspending* the judgment of the great majority who saw the statue. As a rule, they insisted on believing it a "petrified giant," and those who did not, dwelt on its perfections as an ancient statue. As a matter of fact, the work was wretchedly defective in proportion and features. In every way it showed itself the work simply of an inferior stone-carver.

Dr. Boynton, a local lecturer on scientific subjects, gave it the highest praise as a work of art and attributed it to early Jesuit missionaries who had come into that region about 200 years before. Another gentleman, who united the character of a deservedly beloved pastor and an inspiring popular lecturer on various scientific topics, developed this Boynton theory. He attributed the statue to "a trained sculptor ... who had noble original powers; for none but such could have formed and wrought out the conception of that stately head, with its calm

293

smile so full of mingled sweetness and strength." This writer then ventured the query, "Was it not, as Dr. Boynton suggests, someone from that French colony, someone with a righteous soul, sighing over the lost civilization of Europe, weary of swamp and forest and fort, who, finding this block by the side of the stream, solaced the weary days of exile with pouring out his thought upon the stone?" Although the most eminent sculptor in the state had utterly refused to pronounce the figure anything beyond a poor piece of carving, these strains of admiration and adoration continued to multiply.

There was evidently a "joy in believing" in the marvel, and this was increased by the peculiarly American superstition that the correctness of a belief is decided by the number of people who can be induced to adopt it. The current of credulity seemed irresistible.

Shortly afterward, the statue was raised from its grave, taken to Syracuse and to various other cities, especially to the city of New York, and in each place exhibited as a show.

As already stated, there was but one thing in the figure as I had seen it which puzzled me, and that was the grooving of the underside, apparently caused by currents of water, which, as the statue appeared to be of our Onondaga gray limestone, would require very many years. But one day one of the cool-headed skeptics of the valley, an old schoolmate of mine, came to me, and with an air of great solemnity took from his pocket an object which he carefully unrolled from its wrappings, and said, "There is a piece of the giant. Careful guard has been kept from the first in order to prevent people touching it; but I have managed to get a piece of it, and here it is."

I took it in my hand, and the matter was made clear in an instant. The stone was not our hard Onondaga gray limestone, but soft, easily marked with the fingernail, and, on testing it with an acid, I found it, not hard carbonate of lime, but a soft, friable sulfate of lime—a form of gypsum, which must have been brought from some other part of the country.

A healthful skepticism now began to assert its rights. Professor

Othniel C. Marsh of Yale appeared upon the scene. Fortunately, he was not only one of the most eminent of living paleontologists, but, unlike most who had given an opinion, he really knew something of sculpture, for he had been familiar with the best galleries of the Old World. He examined the statue and said, "It is of very recent origin and a most decided humbug. . . . Very short exposure of the statue would suffice to obliterate all trace of toolmarks, and also to roughen the polished surfaces, but these are still quite perfect, and hence the giant must have been very recently buried. . . . I am surprised that any scientific observers should not have at once detected the unmistakable evidence against its antiquity."

Various suspicious circumstances presently became known. It was found that Farmer Newell had just remitted to a man named Hull, at some place in the West, several thousand dollars, the result of admission fees to the booth containing the figure, and that nothing had come in return. Thinking men in the neighborhood reasoned that as Newell had never been in condition to owe any human being such an amount of money and had received nothing in return for it, his correspondent had, not unlikely, something to do with the statue.

These suspicions were soon confirmed. The neighboring farmers, who in their quiet way kept their eyes open, noted a tall, lanky individual who frequently visited the place and seemed to exercise complete control over Farmer Newell. Soon it was learned that this stranger was the man Hull—Newell's brother-in-law. One day, two or three farmers from a distance, visiting the place for the first time and seeing Hull, said, "Why, that is the man who brought the big box down the valley." On being asked what they meant, they said that one evening in a tavern on the valley turnpike some miles south of Cardiff, they had noticed under the tavern shed a wagon bearing an enormous box; and when they met Hull in the barroom and asked about it, he said that it was some tobacco-cutting machinery which he was bringing to Syracuse. Other farmers, who had seen the box and talked with Hull at different places on the road between Binghamton and Cardiff, made similar statements. It was then ascertained that no such box had passed the tollgates between Cardiff and Syracuse, and proofs of the swindle began to mature.

But skepticism was not well received. Vested interests had accrued; a considerable number of people, most of them very good people, had taken stock in the new enterprise, and anything which discredited it was unwelcome to them.

It was not at all that these excellent people wished to countenance an imposture, but it had become so entwined with their beliefs and their interests that at last they came to abhor any doubts regarding it. A pamphlet, *The American Goliath*, was issued in behalf of the wonder. On the title page it claimed to give the "History of the Discovery, and the Opinions of Scientific Men Thereon." The tone of the book was moderate, but its tendency was evident. Only letters and newspaper articles exciting curiosity or favoring the genuineness of the statue were admitted; adverse testimony, like that of Professor Marsh, was carefully excluded.

Before long the matter entered into a comical phase. P. T. Barnum, King of Showmen, attempted to purchase the "giant," but in vain. He then had a copy made so nearly resembling the original that no one, save possibly an expert, could distinguish between them. This new statue was also exhibited as the "Cardiff Giant," and thenceforward the credit of the discovery waned.

Catastrophe now approached rapidly, and soon affidavits from men of the highest character in Iowa and Illinois established the following facts:

The figure was made at Fort Dodge, in Iowa, of a great block of gypsum found there. This block was transported by wagon to the nearest railway station, Boone; on the way the wagon broke down and, as no other could be found strong enough to bear the whole weight, a portion of the block was cut off. Thus diminished, it was taken to Chicago, where a German stone-carver gave it final shape; as it had been shortened, he was obliged to draw up the lower limbs, thus giving it a strikingly contracted and agonized appearance. The underside of the figure was grooved and channeled in order that it should appear to be wasted by age; it was then dotted or pitted over with minute pores by means of a leaden mallet faced with steel needles and was stained with some preparation which gave it an appearance of great age. It was then shipped to a place near Binghamton, New York, and finally brought to Cardiff and there buried.

Furthermore, Hull, in order to secure his brother-in-law Farmer Newell as his confederate in burying the statue, had sworn him to secrecy; and, in order that the family might testify that they had never heard or seen anything of the statue until it had been unearthed, he had sent them away on a little excursion covering the time when it was brought and buried. All these facts were established by affidavits from men of high character in Iowa and Illinois, by the sworn testimony of various Onondaga farmers and men of business, and, finally, by the admissions and even boasts of Hull himself.

Against this tide of truth the good people who had pinned their faith to the statue—those who had vested interests in it and those who had rashly given solemn opinions in favor of it—struggled for a time desperately. A writer in the Syracuse *Journal* expressed a sort of regretful wonder and shame that "the public are asked to overthrow the sworn testimony of sustained witnesses corroborated by the highest scientific authority"—the only sworn witness being Farmer Newell, whose testimony was not at all conclusive, and the highest scientific authority being an eminent local dentist who, early in his life, had given popular chemical lectures, and who had now invested money in the enterprise.

The same writer referred also with awe to "the men of sense, property and character who own the giant and receive whatever revenue arises from its exhibition"; and the argument culminated in the oracular declaration that "the operations of water as testified and interpreted by science cannot create falsehood."

But all this pathetic eloquence was in vain. Hull, the inventor of the statue, having realized more money from it than he expected, and being sharp enough to see that its day was done, was evidently bursting with the desire to avert scorn from himself by bringing the laugh upon others, and especially upon certain clergymen, whom he greatly disliked. He now acknowledged that the whole thing was a swindle, and gave details of the way in which he came to embark in it.

He avowed that the idea was suggested to him by a discussion with a Methodist revivalist in Iowa. Being himself a skeptic in religious matters, he had flung at his antagonist "those remarkable stories in the Bible about giants." When he observed how readily the revivalist and those with him took up the cudgels for the giants, it occurred to him that, since so many people found pleasure in believing such things, he would have a statue carved out of stone which he had found in Iowa and pass it off on them as a petrified giant. In a later conversation he said that one thing which decided him was that the stone had in it dark-colored bluish streaks which resembled in appearance the veins of the human body. The evolution of the whole affair thus became clear, simple and natural.

So elated was Hull at his success that he shortly set about devising another "petrified man" which would defy the world. It was of clay baked in a furnace, contained human bones and was provided with "a tail and legs of the ape type." This he caused to be buried and discovered in Colorado. This time he claimed to have the aid of one of his former foes—the great Barnum; and all went well until his old enemy, Professor Marsh of Yale, appeared and blasted the whole enterprise by a few minutes of scientific observation and commonsense discourse.

In 1898 Hull, at the age of 76 years, apparently in his last illness and anxious for the glory in history which comes from successful achievement, again gave to the press a full account of his part in the affair. He confirmed what he had previously stated, showing how he planned it, executed it and realized a goodly sum for it; how Barnum wished to purchase it from him; and how, above all, he had his joke at the expense of those who, though they had managed to overcome him in argument, had finally been rendered ridiculous in the sight of the whole country.

The innocent victim's role
in this venture cost him $300,000

THE BARON AND HIS URANIUM KILLING

by Toni Howard

"The Baron," said Aimé Gaillard, looking over the blue Mediterranean at Nice, "was my pearl. I found him. And a man's got to crack a lot of oysters to find a pearl like that!"

During the summer Gaillard ran beach concessions at Nice; off season he engaged in various off-the-record "transactions." His lustrous pearl was the young, wealthy Baron Scipion du Roure de Beaujeu, who, in the spring of 1950, approached Gaillard.

The Baron, worried about the state of Europe, wanted to clear out to America before the Communists took over; but first he wanted to make a financial killing. Being himself concerned with turning an easy franc, Gaillard understood the Baron perfectly. And, by chance, he had just what the Baron was looking for.

It so happened that Gaillard had a friend, Inspector Jacques Alberto of the French Border Police, who was at that very moment engaged in a delicate operation of getting some uranium out of Germany, from under the very noses of the Russians, and into Spain to sell to the Franco government, "the last anti-Communist bastion in Europe." Anyone who got in on the operation could not only perform a great service to Western civilization, but could easily double—or even triple—his investment. Gaillard wasn't sure Alberto would let the Baron in on this highly confidential operation, but they could see.

Inspector Alberto, a clean-looking fellow of about 35 who wore the Croix de guerre and the Medal of the Resistance, explained the situation in more detail to the Baron and his attractive wife. The operation was backed by the Deuxième Bureau, France's secret police, but, since parliament had not voted sufficient credits to carry the operation off, the police were looking for a private citizen to put up 10 million francs—roughly $28,000 at the time— to pay for the first consignment. If the Baron would put up the money and get the uranium into Spain, the Spanish would pay him 17 million francs—a profit of around $20,000.

There was one hitch, however. Since Soviet agents suspected what was going on, the operation had to be performed in the strictest secrecy, and, of course, the Baron would have to go to Paris and be investigated by the chief of the operation, a Lieutenant Colonel Berthier.

Colonel Jean Berthier of the Counterintelligence Service, a handsome, swarthy man in impeccable uniform, looked every inch a colonel. He questioned the Baron sharply on his political ideas. As to financial solvency, the 26-year-old Baron said that he was rich; also, his wife, Eleonore Patenôtre, was the daughter of a former French finance minister. At last Colonel Berthier agreed to let him handle the first consignment of uranium for Spain.

The next day the Baron turned over 10 million francs to Berthier. And that night Inspector Alberto, Gaillard and the Colonel struggled up in the tiny elevator of the Baron's Paris apartment house with the first case of the precious metal. From the outside it resembled a big army footlocker. Inside was an immense lead cask sealed with steel tape and marked: "Danger! Do not open!" The case measured nearly a cubic yard and weighed about 135 pounds.

When the Colonel turned it over to the Baron's custody, he spoke again of the dangers of the mission and the need for secrecy. Then he handed the Baron an envelope marked "Top Secret," and stamped military orders for the Baron and Baroness to get into Spain.

They hid the uranium in their car and set out across France, keeping in almost constant telephone communication with the Colonel. All went well until they reached Angoulême, where the Colonel told them that there would be a slight delay, as he was beginning to doubt Gaillard's loyalty. In Bayonne they were met by Inspector Alberto and the Colonel in an army staff car, with soldier escort. The Colonel's face was grave. Gaillard, the Colonel explained, had tipped off the Russians. They would have to be ultracareful now. The Colonel himself would rush back to Paris and send word when the coast was clear to proceed.

For three more days the Baron and Baroness waited nervously. On the fourth day came a wire: "TOO DANGEROUS. COME BACK." In whispered conference with Alberto, they decided it was too risky to drive back to Paris with the uranium—better to cut across France to the Baron's villa at Cap d'Antibes on the Mediterranean.

They arrived there at three in the morning after a worried dash over poor roads. They put the uranium in a locked closet. Fearful of harmful radiations, the Baron wore a specially designed asbestos vest constantly, even in bed. Still, the uranium seemed to be affecting their nervous systems, so one night they buried it in the garden. And then one day Inspector Alberto brought word that Soviet agents had picked up the radiations with an electroscope. In haste, he mounted a military guard around the Baron's property. The Baron breathed a little easier.

But not for long. The Colonel summoned them to Paris and explained how narrowly they had missed falling into the hands of Communists. Then he advised that, since transporting uranium to Spain now presented such dangers, they should get several more cases of the stuff and take it all over at the same time. Could the Du Roures finance, say, another 50 million francs' worth?

They didn't have another 50 million they could lay their hands on, but the Baroness did have a magnificent diamond necklace valued at 55 million. Would that do as collateral?

The next week the Colonel motored to the Baron's villa with another four cases of uranium, plus an enormous flask of heavy water. He said that, since they had been able to borrow only 30 million francs on the necklace, he would appreciate it if the Baron could make up the remaining 20 million. The Baron, a little cramped for francs, furnished dollars and gold from his bank account in Switzerland. The Colonel took the money and disappeared—into Spain, the inspector said, to arrange for the delivery.

During the next six months nothing happened. This made the Baron restive. He had a lot of money tied up in the Atomic Age and he wanted to collect his profit.

The Colonel finally turned up again. But he said they still must wait awhile. Then one night a mysterious Arab came to call on the Baron. After a series of polite evasions, the Arab divulged that he was a Soviet agent, authorized to offer 360 million francs for the uranium. Although flabbergasted at the price—more than $1 million!—the Baron loyally tossed the Arab out. Then he telephoned Colonel Berthier in Nice. The Colonel questioned the Baron minutely. What did this Arab look like? Height, coloring, distinguishing marks or scars? He assured the Baron that he and Alberto would "have" the Arab before nightfall.

Late that night Alberto and the Colonel called at the villa and grimly drove the Baron to a deserted beach. There, behind a clump of rushes, they asked him to identify a blood-splattered corpse. The Baron looked closely. "It's the Arab," he whispered.

"Exactly," said the Colonel. "We do not mince matters."

They then drove the Baron home, leaving the poor Arab to get rid of his bloody, bullet-torn jacket and hoof it back to Nice.

The Baron now felt sure that anything he threw into the enterprise up to 360 million francs was covered by the real value of the uranium he was sitting on.

Later that year, when the Colonel asked him for 30 million francs—only about $85,000—to help Counterintelligence track down the Russian agents who had stolen the plans of the supersecret French jet, the *Mystère*, how could he refuse? Especially when the Colonel promised him something he had wanted all his life—the little red ribbon in the buttonhole that meant so much to friends, enemies and headwaiters—the Legion of Honor. Excitedly, the Baron filled out the necessary papers for the award and handed them to the Colonel, along with $85,000.

Soon the Baron got restive again. Alberto, like the Colonel, took to going off on long trips, leaving the Du Roures with no word of what was going on.

By now 18 months had gone by with no sign of a payoff. It suddenly occurred to the Baron that Alberto and Berthier could have stolen the uranium and planned to use him as a fence. He and the Baroness decided to confront Colonel Berthier. They dug up the uranium, put it in the car and left for Paris.

The Colonel was all sympathy. He was getting impatient himself, he said. He did not say that the Baron was now so broke that even he, the Colonel, wasn't interested anymore. All the Colonel could do was stall for time. He told the Baron that, because of his good work in the cause, the "chief" had asked to see him.

Enter the general. His name was General Combaluzier—an unusual name, but as familiar to Parisians as Otis is to New Yorkers, since it stares at them from the nameplate on nearly every elevator, which is where the General picked it up. The minute the Baron met General Combaluzier, he forgot his worries. The General, in civvies, wore the rosette of the Legion of Honor. He had dignity, military bearing. He exuded confidence.

He assured the Baron that, by the first of the year, the affair would be liquidated, and the Baron would have his profits. And the Baron's nomination to the Legion of Honor was being pushed by the Secret Service itself. It would be announced on January 1. Meanwhile, big people in high places were watching the Baron for a possible diplomatic post. Waiting for the first of the year was difficult. By now the Baron had emptied his bank accounts in Paris and Switzerland. He had even given his radio and camera to Colonel Berthier for counterespionage use.

On New Year's Day, in his Paris apartment, Du Roure scanned

the *Journal Officiel* for the list of those awarded the Legion of Honor. No Du Roure. With this final disillusionment, he called his lawyer.

Thus ended the Great Uranium Pipe Dream. The police came with a special truck to take the footlockers to the government Atomic Control Center at Châtillon. There they were tested with Geiger counters. No reaction. Using the greatest caution, experts opened them. They found sand, mixed with a judicious amount of heavy water from the Mediterranean and with a stable isotope of rusty lead pipe. For this the Baron had handed over about a third of a million dollars.

Colonel Berthier turned out to be a wily tough named Carlicchi, who had done six months in 1947 for theft. General Combaluzier was a jailbird named Gagliardone who had done five years' hard labor for fencing stolen goods. Alberto—that was his actual name—was a former Nice cop who had been dropped from the service for "irregularities." Gaillard was just what he said he was —a beach concessionaire with an interest in good "transactions."

At the trial Gaillard, as witness for the prosecution, and the three others, as defendants, stuck together on their testimony. The diamond necklace had been fragmentized among four or five jewelers of the Riviera whose names and faces all four had conveniently forgotten. The money had been spent. None of it was recoverable. Alberto was sentenced to five years, Carlicchi to four, and Combaluzier-Gagliardone to three.

A month after the trial I saw Aimé Gaillard at Nice. "Listen," he said, "that Baron ought never to have squawked. For a couple of years there he lived a real spy thriller. Maybe it did cost him a little dough. But how many people can actually live an *histoire* like that?"

⁂

BECAUSE safecracking and housebreaking had become too heavy work for him, an 85-year-old man, arrested recently in New York, was earning a living by renting out his kit of burglar tools.　　　—©*King Features Syndicate*

*For more than 50 years
this fantastic clan has duped
householders all over the country*

THOSE TERRIBLE WILLIAMSONS

by John Kobler

Among the craftiest professional swindlers at large in America today is a teeming, heavily interbred tribe of nomads known to law-enforcement agencies as the "Terrible Williamsons." Of Scottish origin, established here for more than half a century and sporadically enriched by fresh migrations of relatives, they ply a countrywide, door-to-door trade in bogus goods and services. In the course of a year, traveling two or three families together in trucks, trailers and glossy late-model cars, they may invade every state, including Alaska. The Better Business Bureaus estimate their annual haul at nearly $1 million.

Their spending reflects this prosperity. Besides expensive cars, they own race horses, pedigreed dogs and gilt-edged securities. When prosecuted, they retain the sharpest legal brains available. If arrested, they usually jump bail, and have forfeited thousands of dollars rather than submit to courtroom examination. Such disbursements they regard as normal operating expenses. In their ceaseless roamings they stay at deluxe motels and trailer camps. Combining business with pleasure, they follow the sun to Florida and Texas in winter; in summer they travel to the Canadian border.

Many of them look and talk alike, with burrs thick as taffy. Marriages between first cousins are common, marriages outside the tribe almost unheard of. The name Williamson predominates, but many of the kinsmen bear other fine old Celtic handles. The vice-president of the National Better Business Bureau once attempted to construct a genealogy from police records. He clarified the relationships of 38 Williamsons, 18 Stewarts, 11 McMillans, 6 McDonalds, 4 Greggs and 7 Johnstons, but the bloodlines then became so entangled that he abandoned the project.

The Williamsons began operating on this side of the Atlantic, after generations as bunco artists abroad, during the first Cleveland administration. The first to arrive was Robert Logan Williamson. He resided for a while during the 1890's in Brooklyn, took a Scottish _émigré_ wife, who bore him numerous progeny, and embarked upon the itinerant life. Kindred McDonalds, McMillans _et al_, fired, probably, by letters Robert wrote home recounting the easy pickings in the land of opportunity, began emigrating too. By 1914 the prolific tribe was a fixture of the American underworld. Since then, neither frequent arrests nor the vigilance of Better Business Bureaus, the Federal Trade Commission and state and local police has noticeably curtailed their depredations.

The Terrible Williamsons stick to merchandising swindles, with occasional digressions into con games, thievery and assault. They peddle, at seemingly bargain prices, "Oriental" rugs from New York's Seventh Avenue, "antique Irish" lace that never saw Ireland, "British woolens" containing mostly acetate or rayon, or rabbit skins dyed to resemble baby seal. Sometimes they display fabrics of good quality; then with sleight-of-hand substitute fakes. An Oklahoma City tailor told the local BBB that he had turned down almost 200 customers who wanted suits cut from woolens for which they had paid the Williamsons $15 a yard. "It retailed at maybe $1.59," he said, "and wasn't worth tailoring."

They are fine actors, masters of dialect and the plausible build-up; their characterizations include a British merchant mariner just off the boat with smuggled prayer rugs from Istanbul, a

Canadian fur trapper who has eluded the border patrol, an orphaned colleen forced to sell her tuberculous, dying mother's handiwork. With such farragoes they have duped many lawyers, doctors, teachers, businessmen who pride themselves on their shrewdness and sophistication.

Purchasers of the Williamsons' textiles, however, fare better than those who succumb to another swindle. The younger males of the clan prowl the back country in trucks full of paints and spray drums, looking for peeling houses or barns. Flashing business cards, ten-year certificates of guarantee and cans of nationally known paint, they offer a fast, cut-rate job. They then stretch a few dollars' worth of the paint with so much crankcase oil that with the first rainfall it washes off, leaving the house and grounds below in a hideous and highly flammable mess.

A profitable Williamson swindle is the installation of lightning rods. Impersonating electrical engineers, complete with fraudulent university diplomas, endorsements from insurance companies and factory guarantees of free maintenance, they try to frighten their prey by showing them photographs of gutted houses. They promise that customers will automatically get a 50 percent reduction in their fire-insurance premiums. The rigging they fasten to the roof (for $200 to $300) consists of rope or wood painted to look like metal. Other schemes include "sealing" cracks in roofs and driveways with crankcase oil, and cleaning septic tanks for outrageous prices.

How have they endured so long? Mainly because, though their profits are enormous, their operations generally involve mere misdemeanors, such as peddling without a license or misrepresentation. Moreover, victims often hesitate to stand up in court and admit they have been swindled. Nor are the authorities themselves always aggressive. In a good many towns with overcrowded jails and jammed court calendars they are content to chase the nomads away and let some other community worry about them.

One of the BBB's richest sources of information about the Terrible Williamsons has been a series of letters from an unknown correspondent, a man who claims to be a Williamson himself and who deplores the crimes of his kin and aims to put an end to them. At times he has apprised local BBB's that the Williamsons were nigh. Hard on the heels of his disclosure to the Pittsburgh bureau one summer when more than 50 Williamsons were scouting the suburbs with paint sprays, woolens and laces, complaints flooded in from duped bargain hunters. Three Williamsons were arrested and fined; the majority escaped.

The BBB informant cites some impressive financial statistics. "Lightning-rod materials worth $40," he calculates, "will bring in $600 to $700 profit to the Williamsons. Two of them fleeced $28,000 in Iowa and Minnesota, all profit." Another branch of the family, he attests, once netted $60,000 paint-spraying their way through Michigan.

Rivalry over the division of territory and loot sometimes leads to intrafamily clashes in which shooting and stabbing are not uncommon. One such tribal bloodletting occurred after some 40 Williamsons and McMillans had a brawl in an Atlanta, Georgia, trailer park and parted sworn enemies. Tooling through Springfield, Pennsylvania, months later, the Williamsons halted for lunch at Zimmermann's Tourist Camp. As they piled out of their cars they ran into the McMillans, and the air turned blue with curses. As other tourists scurried for cover, John McMillan reportedly pumped revolver bullets into two Williamsons. McMillan was arrested, but so evasive and contradictory was the testimony of the warring families that the jury deliberated for 26 hours. In the end, it acquitted him.

As an ethnic group the interbred Williamsons are distinctive. The men tend to be thickset, of medium height, virile and personable; the women high-spirited and bold of eye, exerting their sex appeal to obfuscate their male victims.

A bonny 21-year-old clan girl, displaying swatches of genuine famous-name imported woolens, solicited orders for custom-made suits, part payment in advance, the customer to be measured later by her brother ("Brither's the tailor o' the family"). One year in

311

Kansas City she approached seven college boys, baiting her hook with a promise to date them after working hours. The smitten students handed over $200. It was the last they heard of her or her tailoring brother.

Most Williamsons lack formal education, never having tarried in any community long enough to attend school. The arts of dupery, however, they learn young from their elders. Even toddlers play a role in the nomads' activities, accompanying their parents to create pathos.

"Poor wee chap," the mother will sigh, hugging the babe to her bosom as she entices her victim to buy some phony heirloom. "He hasn't had a right proper bite to eat for days."

Cincinnati has been the clan's headquarters for many years, probably because of its central location. For a good many of the Williamsons, Cincinnati's Spring Grove Cemetery is the final resting place. Each family maintains its own plot there and strives to outshine the others in mortuary magnificence. At the funeral of a George Williamson, a cemetery attendant counted in the cortege 125 cars, all fancy-priced late models. The florists' bills exceeded $5000.

"They're very jealous of each other, very competitive," says a Cincinnati investigator who has long studied their ways. "They can't compete in their homes because they have no homes. So they compete in the lavishness of their funeral celebrations." Though the mourners may have brawled with the deceased for years and years, they shed copious tears. Three or four of the women regularly swoon.

Unfailingly, every May, the bulk of the clan returns to Cincinnati to honor their dead, to baptize children born on the road and to hold a convention—a custom which impels the local BBB to circulate warning bulletins. Most of the celebrants, however, refrain from swindles while in Cincinnati, although a few zealots in whom love of craft runs particularly strong cannot resist mispainting a house or two or peddling a bolt of shoddy.

Some Cincinnati merchants find it hard not to welcome the

Williamsons' annual remigration because, in addition to commemoration and palaver, it is a time of replenishment for the clan. Denying themselves no luxury, they scatter money lavishly, and the shop that satisfies one of them is likely to be patronized by the others.

Without haggling or hesitation the Williamsons plunk down the full price in cash for whatever they desire. Once 35 of them bought new cars from the same agency, all in the $5000 range.

The Williamsons keep moving. One year their caravans were known to have touched at more than 40 points as widely scattered around the country as Orting, Washington, Goshen, Indiana, and Spartanburg, South Carolina.

Can nothing stop them? The BBB is not sanguine. "As long as people allow themselves to be swayed by greed," warned George Young of the Cincinnati bureau, "as long as they delude themselves that goods or services can be bought at less than a fair price, the Terrible Williamsons will flourish."

ᑤᗯᑕ

A PERENNIAL swindle thriving on businessmen's vanity is the "puff sheet" racket. In editing a puff sheet, the promoter watches newspapers and business reports from all over the country. When the "editor" finds an item stating that a businessman has been promoted, an announcement of the formation of a partnership or any item of a business nature, he rewrites it, packing it full of laudatory phrases. This version he reads to the subject over the telephone, representing himself as the editor of a "business journal" bearing a title that sounds important and closely resembles that of a reputable business journal. The fake editor asks for an okay and suggestions on the article which, he says, "is going into the issue we are now closing." This is usually more flattery than the victim's vanity can stand, and he readily complies with the "editor's" request that he purchase 50 to 100 copies at 35 cents each. He later finds that the "business journal" with the impressive title has no subscribers, no regular publication date, no rating in publishers' data books and no revenue except that derived from the sale of copies to flattered dupes like himself. The profits of puffeteering are very large, since the publication itself is a skimpy, inexpensive pamphlet. —*E. Jerome Ellison and Frank W. Brock*

*These gentlemen crooks set out
on an impossible task—to storm the impregnable
bastion of British finance*

FOUR AGAINST
THE BANK OF ENGLAND

by Ann Huxley Kings

Punctually at 10 a.m., as the first customers filed into the bank, Colonel Peregrine Madgewick Francis, the manager, closed his door against this muted traffic and began the daily ritual of opening his mail. The letters stacked neatly before him on the massive rolltop desk were addressed:

> The Bank of England
> Western Branch
> Burlington Gardens
> Mayfair
> LONDON

Among them was a registered packet from Birmingham. It bore the postmark of the previous day—February 27, 1873—and the Colonel recognized the familiar handwriting of one of his valued customers. Slitting it open, he found a covering note asking him to discount the enclosed bills of exchange to the credit of the customer's personal account.* The note concluded:

---

*A bill of exchange is a written order that requires the person to whom it is addressed to pay at a fixed date a certain sum of money.

314

I take this opportunity of thanking you for the trouble you have taken in my behalf. Accept, dear Sir, the assurance of my esteem, while I remain yours faithfully,

FREDERICK ALBERT WARREN

There were 24 bills of exchange in the packet, totaling over £26,000—which would presumably be collected in due course from the acceptor of the bills. Although the amount involved was unusually large, the transaction was otherwise routine; Colonel Francis had often put through similar bills of exchange for Mr. Warren. He rang for the discount clerk and handed him the bills for routing to Threadneedle Street, the head office of the Bank of England. A few minutes later the discount clerk returned and tapped discreetly. "I think I should draw your attention to these, sir." He handed Colonel Francis two bills of exchange for £1000 each. "The dates of issue seem to be missing."

"Quite right," Colonel Francis agreed after examining the bills. "There does appear to be an oversight here."

The acceptors of the bills were B. W. Blydenstein and Company of 20½ Great St. Helens, a banking house of impeccable reputation. Francis was not unduly disturbed by the irregularity. He instructed the clerk to send the two bills back to Blydenstein's for correction during the bank messenger's normal rounds that afternoon. Despite this leisurely means of communication, there was a reply before the end of the day. The note, signed "William Henry Trumpler, Member," was marked "Urgent and Confidential." Blydenstein's had no record of the enclosed bills of exchange. Mr. Trumpler could only assume they were forgeries.

This dread word threw Francis into a state of extreme agitation. He rang for Mr. Warren's file, seized his hat and hurried out to find a hansom cab. It took well over 30 minutes to reach Threadneedle Street, where he at once sought out Frank May, deputy chief cashier of the Bank of England.

The interview which ensued, and the investigation it set off, was to make that day—February 28, 1873—the blackest Friday

315

the Bank of England has ever known. For it was soon established that "Frederick Albert Warren" had methodically fleeced the world's most august financial institution of £100,000. In today's purchasing power this represents more than $3,250,000.

It was incredible. The Bank of England had been duped by one of its own customers. In 180 years, it had never before suffered such humiliation (nor has it since). And the final insult was that the perpetrator of the disaster was a foreigner—an American from New York.

Today, 95 years after the event, the Bank of England still smarts from this affront to its infallibility. At the time, the anguish and resentment of the bank officers were matched only by their horror. From governor to the most junior clerk, they were asking themselves: "How on earth did it happen?"

The plausible young American who called himself Frederick Albert Warren was not a veteran confidence man. He was only 27 years old and had no police record, although he had certainly engaged in crime. His real name was Austin Byron Bidwell, and he was the son of a South Brooklyn grocer.

His first job had been with a firm of sugar brokers. American business was expanding with intoxicating speed in those post-Civil War years, and the boomtown atmosphere in New York was infectious. Young Austin responded to this get-rich-quick climate with vaulting ambition—he wanted to get ahead fast. His duties around the sugar exchange brought him in contact with some of the sharpest operators on Wall Street, and he took due note of their methods.

When he moved to another brokerage house at the then very good salary of $10 a week, Austin met an equally impatient young man named Ed Weeds, who soon proposed that they start a business of their own. With the backing of Weeds's wealthy father, the new firm was incorporated as E. Weeds and Company. The next years were golden ones on Wall Street, and with stocks booming and new ventures mushrooming, the fledgling brokers had commissions in plenty and enjoyed a large income.

But Ed Weeds and Austin Bidwell were both gay blades, far more interested in the activities of the night than of the day. They frequented the theater, sought out the company of chorus girls, gave lavish wine suppers at Delmonico's and gambled heavily at the roulette tables. In short, the two young partners neglected their business in a reckless pursuit of pleasure, and there was never enough money, whatever their earnings. Eventually they lost their entire capital. Ed Weeds at once deserted the partnership and sailed for Europe.

At this dismaying juncture, hard-pressed Austin Bidwell received a tempting offer from the underworld (whose denizens, never far from the gaming tables and other night haunts of dissolute young men, gauged his despair exactly). The approach was made one night after he had lost at roulette and was drowning his sorrows at the bar. Would he be willing to dispose of a large cache of stolen bonds in Europe? Payment would be handsome, and his stockbroking experience ideally fitted him for the task.

It was undisguised crime, and it would require exquisite finesse and cast-iron nerve; but it was also a way out of his difficulties. Almost with relief Austin agreed to do it. He went to Europe and carried through the job with a flourish, returning to America some months later. His commission was $13,000, and from that moment on he never engaged in legitimate work again.

In crime, as in everything else, he remained surpassingly ambitious, aiming only for the top; and in 1872, at the age of 26, he was active in London, coolly pitting his talents against the Bank of England. By now Austin Bidwell had become a most impressive figure. He was a handsome man nearly six feet tall, with a shock of hair falling across a high forehead. Somewhat dandyish, he had developed a quietly arrogant bearing, sported large diamond rings, wore sideburns and a small mustache. He had obliterated all traces of his humble beginnings, and in dress, conversation and charm of manner was a match for the most socially acceptable young men in London. But of all his qualities Austin's most valuable was his ability to inspire confidence.

He was not a lone operator. In his role as Frederick Albert Warren, Austin Bidwell was simply acting as front man for his brother George. George Bidwell was the brains behind the coup, the organizer who directed it. Seven years older than Austin, he had piled up a modest fortune swindling wholesale houses out of goods by using fictitious credit references. Ranging the whole eastern seaboard, he had finally run into trouble in Virginia and been given a two-year prison sentence. Four months later, on Christmas Day, 1871, George and four other prisoners escaped.

Returning to New York, he looked up Austin, and the two brothers decided to try their luck in England. America, they reasoned, was no longer hospitable to either of them; at the moment they were both well supplied with funds; and both had boundless confidence in their ability to amass great riches by using their wits. Although their plans were vague, they took with them Austin's close friend George Macdonnell, who was an expert and meticulous forger.

The three adventurers arrived in England early in April 1872. They were all young—Macdonnell being only 27, Austin 26, George Bidwell 33—but between them they had a working capital of $40,000. Using assumed names, they took modest lodgings in Haggerstone, a suburb of North London, and like any other tourists spent their first few days sightseeing.

Returning from a steamboat trip up the Thames one evening, they disembarked at Blackfriars Pier in high spirits. As they walked through the deserted City sector in search of a place for dinner, they passed the Bank of England in Threadneedle Street. Austin gestured toward the massive, porticoed building with a mocking smile. "I'll bet we could hit that place for a million as easy as rolling off a log," he said. "They'd never miss the money."

George merely snorted. The Bank of England was impregnable. Everyone knew that.

Next day the three went by stagecoach to visit Windsor Castle. Joining a party of sightseers, they filed slowly through the royal apartments, listening to the guide's droning patter. Macdonnell,

whose flowing beard made him look conspicuously like the Prince of Wales, excited sidelong glances, though he himself remained unimpressed by the scene. Finally, amid the splendors of the Throne Room, he drew George and Austin aside.

"All we need is $100,000 apiece," he murmured to the startled Bidwell brothers. "Then we could all go back home to the States very happy."

Waiting until the tourist group had moved well beyond earshot, he added, "The bank's got plenty to spare, and the whole organization is probably riddled with dry rot. I vote we try it." George Bidwell was scornful. By temperament he was methodical and rather sober-minded, and he sometimes found the recklessness and conceit of Austin's friend difficult to bear. Now the sheer arrogance of his proposal appeared insufferable.

"Let's hear no more such talk, Mac," he snapped, and strode off to rejoin the tourist party.

But Austin's brash suggestion, now seconded by Macdonnell, was already beginning to have its effect. Later that evening the three Americans were seated comfortably around the fire at the Crown, an old coaching inn. The two younger men, both tall, handsome and easy-mannered, were discussing their future social plans while George Bidwell, thick-shouldered, short, his chin sunk deep against his chest, gazed moodily into the embers. Suddenly he stirred and leaned across toward the others.

"Listen quietly now," he commanded, effectively stopping their chatter. "The only way we could possibly pull off such a coup is from the inside, as valued customers. So the first thing we must arrange is for Austin to open an account at the bank. While we reconnoiter, such an account must be conducted with absolute correctness and with considerable cash sums passing constantly through it to promote confidence." He paused. "Meanwhile, we can look for the flaw in the system."

Mac and Austin listened openmouthed, eyeing each other in amazement. Finally Austin clapped his brother admiringly on the shoulder. "I honestly believe you think we can do it," he said.

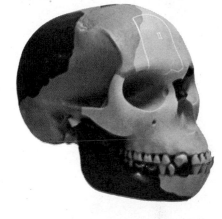

1. Head and skull models of Piltdown Man, one of the most successful hoaxes in scientific history. An amateur dabbler in archaeology named Charles Dawson devised a scheme whereby fragments of bone and teeth were discovered near his home in Sussex, England. He had doctored the fragments so that scientists believed they were 500,000 years old. (See "Unmasking of the Piltdown Man," page 434.)

2. Alceo Dossena was a little-known Italian stonemason who dreamed of th Renaissance and the artistic glory of that time. Living in his fantasy worl he turned out sculpture similar to that of Pisano, Michelangelo and other gre artists. Unscrupulous dealers sold his work as genuine old masters, but Dosser himself was innocent of fraud. (See "A Renaissance Man," page 350.)

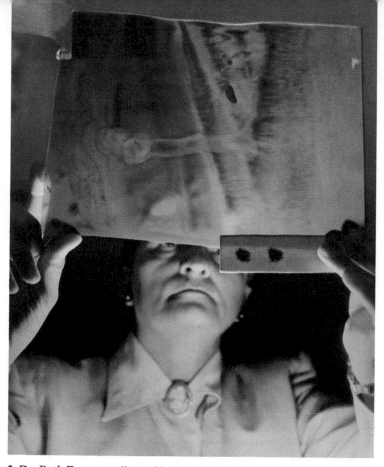

3. Dr. Ruth Drown studies an X ray taken from one of her radio machines. These diagnostic machines, claimed Dr. Drown, could treat patients from afar. Here she is holding an X ray she said was taken in New York of a subject in Wisconsin. On this occasion she had placed a blood sample from the patient into her machine. The resulting plate, she said, showed that the subject was suffering from an abscessed tooth. (See "The Unreal World of Dr. Drown," page 413.)

4. The Cardiff Giant, shown here boxed for shipment, was discovered in 1869 on a farm in New York's Onondaga Valley. The huge stone figure (dimensions, *right,* as posted at one exhibit) was said to be a petrified man from prehistoric times. Admission was charged for viewing the statue, and it became a popular showpiece of the day. The whole enterprise, of course, was a hoax of the first magnitude. (See "Cardiff Giant," page 288.)

5. The formidable expression on the face of Mrs. Cassie Chadwick was an unusual one for her. Despite her plain looks, she was as charming a female swindler as ever bilked a banker. (See "Mrs. Chadwick Shows Her Mettle," page 102.)

6. James Landis (*center*, with his wife) walked out of the U.S. Mint with $128,000 in new $20 bills after a carefully planned robbery. (See "Operation U.S. Mint," page 146.)

7. Famed violinist Fritz Kreisler fooled the musical world with compositions he wrote himself under the names of early composers. (See "Fritz Kreisler's 'Discoveries,'" page 449.)

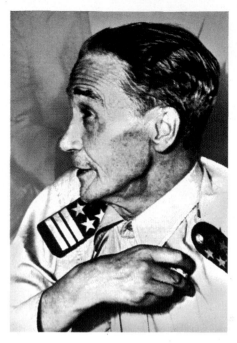

8. Captain Henrique Galvão (*right*) is shown after hijacking the Portuguese luxury liner *Santa Maria* (*below*). Captain Galvão and his followers, rebels against the Portuguese government, posed as passengers, then took over the ship at sea. After 12 days, and an intensive search by the world's navies, the captain finally put in at Recife, Brazil. (See "Incredible Cruise of the *Santa Maria*," page 9.)

9. Policeman with Scotland's famed Stone of Scone (*right*) and the abbey ruins (*above*) from which it was recovered. A group of young patriots had stolen the Stone, symbol of Scottish freedom, from Westminster Abbey and spirited it back to their homeland. (See "No Stone Unturned," page 609.)

10. By a simple method of robbing Peter to pay Paul, Charles Ponzi (*right*) stole millions from Bostonians, most of them tenement-dwelling poor. He promised his victims 50 percent interest on their investment after 90 days. Ponzi took in so much money he had no trouble paying off—until the District Attorney started investigating. (See "Pied Piper of Boston," page 22.)

11. Dutch artist Hans van Meegeren (*below*) working on his canvas of the Christ Child in the Temple of the Elders. Van Meegeren painted this picture at the request of Netherlands authorities to prove that he could imitate the style and method of famed 17th-century Dutch master Jan Vermeer. (See "A Man Who Fooled Göring," page 534.)

12. Under the name F. Donald Coster, Italian immigrant Philip Musica (*left* and *below,* hand over face) built a $150 million drug business, most of it on paper. Musica's empire came tumbling down when a business associate grew curious about inflated inventories. (See "The Great False Front," page 456.)

13. Prince Grigori Potemkin (*left*) and his mistress, Catherine the Great of Russia (*right*), for a while literally lived in a dream world. After the Prince became governor of the Crimea, he told Catherine of his wonderful work in the area—his new roads, factories and vineyards. With an elaborate entourage from her court, she came to visit and indeed found what seemed to be a land of plenty—dancing subjects, gaily painted villages and bountiful farmland. What Catherine did not know was that Potemkin had staged the whole spectacle. He had forced the peasants to dress up and caper happily, carpenters to build houses with false fronts, and he even had farmers herd their cows over long distances to graze before the Empress. (See "Catherine in Wonderland," page 470.)

14. John Romulus Brinkley made millions of dollars performing a goat-gland operation that was supposed to renew the sexual vigor of older men. Later he branched out into advertising patent medicines over his own powerful radio station. A combination of the American Medical Association, a Kansas newspaper and various government agencies finally caused his downfall. (See " 'Goat-Gland' Brinkley," page 560.)

16. Richard Whitney leaves prison after being paroled. He had served three years and four months of a five- to ten-year sentence. Before and during the time he was president of the New York Stock Exchange, he embezzled hundreds of thousands of dollars from clients and friends. (See "The Two Faces of Richard Whitney," page 236.)

17. Harold "Kim" Philby (*right*) is one of the world's most notorious traitors. A wartime hero, he rose to a high place in British Intelligence. But he later defected to the Soviets, admitting that he had been a spy for them against his country. (See "Rise and Fall of a Soviet Agent," page 208.)

◀ **15.** Four members of Britain's train robbery gang (*left to right*): Bruce Reynolds, Charles Wilson, Ronald Edwards and James White. The robbery in 1963 was the largest cash haul — $7 million — in history. (See "Britain's Great Train Robbery," page 137.)

18. Ferdinand Demara puffs on a cigarette after pleading guilty to obtaining a teacher's license under false pretenses. During his incredible career Demara posed as a teacher, a monk, a prison warden and a doctor. Commissioned a surgeon in the Canadian Navy, he performed major operations successfully on Korean War wounded. (See "The Great Impostor," page 58.)

19. Oscar Hartzell (*right*) promised millions of dollars to contributors to his Sir Francis Drake Association. The money was to help him in his battle against the British Crown, which supposedly was withholding the Drake estate from its rightful heirs. (See "The Drake Fable," page 477.)

20. One of the high points of the career of Willie "The Actor" Sutton (*right*) was his escape from Holmesburg Prison at Philadelphia (*above*). At the time he was serving a 25- to 50-year sentence for one of his many bank robberies. He was recaptured after being recognized on a New York subway by a young clothing salesman. (See "My Story," page 542.)

21. The mighty Bank of England was impregnable until it was robbed in 1873 by four young Americans with an ingenious scheme. They got away with £100,000—about $3,250,000 in today's purchasing power—before the bank uncovered the plot. (See "Four Against the Bank of England," page 314.)

22. Ivar Kreuger, Sweden's "Match King" (*right*) was a master of financial legerdemain. For years he lived in luxury, hobnobbed with kings and prime ministers. Yet all the while he was a swindler, forger and confidence man on a grand scale. He stole more money than any other one man in history. (See "He Stole a Billion," page 194.)

The Western Branch in Burlington Gardens, Mayfair, George decided, might prove generally less formidable than the institution in Threadneedle Street. But even here it would be impossible to open an account without suitable references, so Austin had to find someone who would vouch for him. After inconspicuously watching the comings and goings of the bank's customers for a few days, he narrowed the choice of potential Samaritans to three local tradesmen—an optician, an East Indian importer and a tailor. Dressing impeccably and in quiet taste except for an oversize Stetson—the accepted trademark of a rich American visitor—he set out to investigate these unsuspecting candidates.

Entering the optician's shop first, Austin asked to see a number of items, finally selecting an expensive opera glass. He ordered it inscribed "To Lady Mary, from Her Friend," offered a £100 note in payment and said he would return for the purchase the following day. Meanwhile, he had been sizing up the optician, and some sixth sense told him, "No, not this man."

He went next to the East India house and picked out a costly white-silk shawl and a fine camel-hair traveling rug. Again he casually offered a £100 note in payment, covertly studying the proprietor. But again instinct said, "No."

Last, Austin visited Edward Hamilton Green, master tailor and army clothier, of 35 Savile Row, and here, in this prosperous and ultrarespectable little man, he felt at once that he had found the right sponsor. At first, however, he ignored both Mr. Green and his eager assistant and simply looked over their heads at the many cloth bolts that lined the walls. Then, puffing at a large cigar, he began a slow march around the shop, barking orders to the assistant. "One suit from this, one from that, a topcoat from that, a suit from this. . . ." Altogether he listed seven suits and two topcoats. "Now show me some dressing gowns," he concluded.

In an instant Mr. Green himself had reached for the most expensive dressing gown in his stock. Stroking it lovingly, he said, "This is our most beautiful robe, sir. It is 20 guineas."

"I'll take it," said Austin.

321

As the tailor measured his new client, Austin talked pleasantly of his recent arrival in England and of his pleasure in visiting Windsor Castle and other historic places. Mr. Green warmed to the charming young American (who was obviously so rich), then discreetly asked for references so that he might open an account for him. He proffered his customer's signature book to Austin.

The American took the book and entered "Frederick Albert Warren, Golden Cross Hotel, London."

"I'll pay cash for everything, Mr. Green," he said. "There is no need to open an account as I'm not a resident." On leaving the shop, Austin took a cab to the Golden Cross and registered a room in his new name, in case the tailor inquired for him there.

During the next fortnight Austin returned for two fittings, each time improving his acquaintance with Green, and on the second occasion adding to the tailor's incredulous delight by ordering more clothes. Then on a Saturday morning he rolled up to the shop in a brougham loaded with luggage, topped off with an expensive new leather traveling trunk appropriately monogrammed "F.A.W." Leaping down lightly, Austin strode into the tailor's.

"Would you be so good as to have my clothes packed in that, Mr. Green?" he said, indicating the new trunk. "And send it to 21 Enfield Road, Haggerstone. I'm off to spend a few days in Ireland with Lord Clancarty."

"Yes, of course, sir. At once, sir," Green replied, sending his assistant scurrying out to the cab.

"And I'd like to settle my account now, if you please," Austin went on, tendering a brand-new £500 note in payment of the £150 owed. When Green gave him the change he stuffed it unconcernedly into his pocket, shook the tailor's hand warmly and walked out. But at the door he paused and asked if he could request a favor. "I have rather more money on me than I care to take on this visit," he said. "Could you look after a small amount of cash for me until I return?"

"I certainly can, sir. I'd be only too delighted to assist." But when Austin offered him a wad of notes amounting to well over

322

£1000 the tailor blanched. "Oh, no, sir. I'm afraid I could not take responsibility for so large an amount. You really should put it back into your bank."

Here at last was the moment that Austin had planned for, and at once he sprang the trap. "But I have no account here, Mr. Green. I am a visitor to your country."

The ruse worked like a charm. "I'm sure we can attend to that in a matter of moments, sir. I'd be delighted to introduce you to my bank. It's only just along the street."

The rest was routine. Green introduced Austin most warmly to Mr. Fenwick, the submanager (since it was Saturday, the manager was absent), who promptly went through the minimum formalities for the opening of an account. Austin wrote out "Frederick Albert Warren" for the usual specimen signature, described himself as an "agent" visiting Europe for business reasons and duly deposited £1000 in pound notes, £3 in mixed coin and a draft on the Continental Bank for £197—making a total of £1200.

He then naïvely asked whether Green would have to accompany him when he next wished to deposit a considerable sum—which might well be in a few days' time. It depended on the arrival of proceeds from a business transaction.

"Not at all, sir," explained Fenwick. "You now have your own account with us, and can make your own remittances and withdrawals just as you wish." And he handed "Mr. Warren" a checkbook containing 50 checks.

That evening, Frederick Albert Warren, Captain Bradshaw (George Bidwell) and Mr. Mapleson (Macdonnell) drank to their success at a celebration dinner in the smart new Grosvenor Hotel, Victoria, where they then decided to move from Haggerstone, deeming it a more fitting address for gentlemen of substance.

The next move, George Bidwell felt, was to establish the new American depositor as an enterprising businessman used to handling large sums. Accordingly, "Mr. Warren" began to move funds in and out of his account very actively, so that the tellers soon knew him, and neither his name nor his person excited the least curiosity. Although the trio's combined capital was used in these manipulations, George shortly decided that it was not enough. They needed to improve the impression of Mr. Warren's wealth, and to this end began a series of swift forays abroad.

The technique was simple. George Bidwell went to Liverpool and, as a visiting American businessman about to undertake a trip to the Continent, purchased a letter of credit for £300 from the Bank of South and North Wales and also obtained a letter of introduction from the manager to go with it. Macdonnell, using his skill as a forger, then made copies of the letter of credit, varying the amounts called for and issuing them in three fictitious names. He also made copies of the manager's letter of introduction and addressed them to several continental banking houses.

Thus armed, Mac and Austin went to Berlin and Dresden, and George to Bordeaux, Marseilles and Lyons. They took care that each transaction was small enough for the unsuspecting bankers to honor their credentials on sight, but it was still a most hazardous way of making money. George breathed a sigh of relief when they were all safely back in London—the richer by £8000.

It was still not enough, George thought; they had to raise even more funds. But this time they would give themselves a greater margin of safety by operating in South America. In Europe, if any skeptical banker doubted their credentials, he had only to telegraph the alleged issuing bank for confirmation, and the game would be up. From Brazil, the only way to communicate with England was by letter, and it would take 40 days to receive an answer to any query. They would go down to Rio de Janeiro, George decided.

Again the indispensable factor in this operation was George Macdonnell. He was an extraordinarily gifted young man, fluent in five languages, a brilliant conversationalist and a man of great personal magnetism. Unlike the Bidwell brothers, he had enjoyed a highly privileged upbringing. Scion of a wealthy Boston family, he had been privately tutored until he entered Harvard. The headstrong boy left college after his second year, squandered the

$10,000 his father put up to establish him as a stockbroker in New York and then drifted into crime.

At 22 he earned a two-year sentence in Sing Sing for passing a forged check. But after he met George Engels, a superforger known as "the terror of Wall Street" because of his faultless duplications, his technique vastly improved. He became an ardent pupil of the master, and the sheer artistic challenge forgery posed had held his imagination ever since. Most things came easily to Macdonnell, and his great charm and ability to talk himself into or out of any situation tended to make him act first and think afterward—a trait which made George Bidwell perpetually nervous.

On the Rio exploit, however, Mac discharged his duties to perfection. Speaking faultless Portuguese, he presented his own forged letters (drawn this time on the London and Westminster Bank, and introducing "Mr. George Morris") requesting that Maua and Company, Brazil's foremost banking house, should honor his drafts for cash. This they did for their distinguished visitor in the sum of £10,000 on June 18, the first day after his arrival in Rio on the liner *Lusitania*.

Nearly $100,000 richer from their combined European and South American harvests, the ebullient trio were back in London by mid-August—spoiling for a handhold on their main quarry, the Old Lady of Threadneedle Street.

From now on George insisted on the most stringent precautions. The three of them were never to live in the same hotel, and all were to move frequently, each time using a new alias. During daylight hours they were to meet only at a café in a narrow alley off Finsbury Circus. It was inconspicuous and isolated—George had cased the city's coffeehouses street by street to find it. A small back room offered privacy. This grubby hideaway became their "office" during the ensuing months.

But much of their time was spent on the Continent visiting the various cities from which they assiduously kept Mr. Warren's account active. This now had an average balance of some $67,000, and if any bank official examined the account he was certain to be confused by the complexity and wide range of the transactions. Checks and drafts drawn on a dozen different banks in Paris, Vienna, Frankfurt, Amsterdam, Hamburg and Rotterdam were remitted to the account, then withdrawn again, so that there was a continuous cycle of apparent business deals. Bank officials had no reason to suspect that it was the same money going round and round, but nonetheless, George felt it was high time that Mr. Warren paid his respects to the manager of the Western Branch; and on September 3 Austin undertook this mission.

Colonel Peregrine Madgewick Francis had been manager of the branch for only three months, and it was typical of Austin's luck that he still relied greatly on the advice of the submanager, Fenwick, who introduced Warren with evident enthusiasm. Warren explained the developing nature of his business and said he was now principally engaged in introducing the newly invented American Pullman Palace railcars to the Continent in time for the Great Exhibition in Vienna the following year.

"I am looking for manufacturing facilities in this country, and at the same time studying the railway systems of the Continent," he explained to the interested Colonel. "Since each of these luxury cars costs £4000 to build, I shall be dealing in largish sums of money before the year's end, financing contractors and the like." Warren paused. "It may even be necessary to request credit facilities from time to time," he continued. "I hope that will be in order, sir."

Without a moment's hesitation, Colonel Francis said this could be satisfactorily arranged.

"Meanwhile," concluded Warren with nice timing, "I would like to deposit these Portuguese bonds for your safekeeping. They amount only to some £8000, but I think it unwise to have them lying about." The bonds were genuine, and, as Austin intended, they purchased a sizable slice of the Colonel's trust.

With mounting urgency all three now began examining every detail of European business procedures, alert for any possible weakness. Finally it was Macdonnell who, toward the end of

October, found the chink in the armor. From London he cabled to George in Frankfurt: "HAVE MADE GREAT DISCOVERY COME IM-MEDIATELY MAC."

George returned without delay and, for once breaking his own rule, breakfasted with Mac and Austin at the Victoria Hotel. As they lingered over the hearty meal, Mac excitedly explained his discovery. In Rotterdam he had purchased a bill of exchange dated for settlement the usual three months ahead. It was drawn on the London and Westminster Bank by Baring Brothers, an impeccable London mercantile finance house. When he presented the bill at the London and Westminster Bank, they discounted it at once and paid him in cash without sending it back to Baring's for authentication and initialing.

Mac was dumfounded. In America such bills of exchange were always sent back to the issuing house for initialing before being honored. Yet here in London, the money center of the world, there was no such precautionary routine. Between the date of first issue of a bill of exchange and its maturing three months later, there was no checking by the bank. The whole procedure was based on the satisfactory reputation of the customer who presented the bill for discounting.

It was almost too good to be true, but careful investigation confirmed that the procedure was standard. It meant that forged bills of exchange might be deposited in Mr. Warren's account, and, if they were accepted by the Bank of England, the money would be paid out, and there would be a clear three months before the fraud was discovered.

The three Americans were elated. This was the loophole they had been searching for.

If their ambitious plans against the Bank of England were to succeed, they would need another bank account into which their Bank of England funds could be siphoned. On December 2, at George's bidding, Austin deposited £1300 in the Continental Bank on Lombard Street, opening an account under the name of "Charles Johnson Horton," an American businessman. This precaution would make it unnecessary for anyone to make withdrawals in person at the Western Branch.

He also felt they needed another man—one whose sole job would be to handle deposits, withdrawals and other transactions so that it would be difficult to trace the money. Such a person would be "employed" as Horton's confidential clerk, enjoying full latitude of action on his boss's behalf. This would enable Horton—*i.e.*, Austin—to be elsewhere when the coup was pulled.

Edwin Noyes, an old friend of Austin's from Hartford, Connecticut, was selected for this chore. A small-time check forger, Noyes had recently been released from the New Jersey State Prison after serving a seven-year sentence. He would doubtless be at loose ends, and on November 8 Austin wrote him:

MY DEAR NOYES:

You will be surprised to hear from me from London, but I have been here with George and a friend of ours for a year, and have made a lot of money from several speculations we have embarked in. In fact we have been so successful that we have determined to make you a present of $1000, which find enclosed.

We may be able to give you a chance to make a few thousand if you would care to venture across the ocean. Perhaps we can make use of you. If so, I will send you a cable. Be cautious and preserve absolute secrecy when you leave home as to your destination. Hoping you are quite well,

I remain your old friend,

AUSTIN

To the considerable amusement of Austin and Mac, George had for months displayed an almost compulsive habit. Wherever he went he methodically shopped the stationery stores, laying in an enormous stock of different papers, various colored inks, types of sealing wax, pens, nibs, rubber stamps and other supplies which might prove useful in forging documents. Now that he knew what they were to forge, he began to pick up blank bill-of-exchange forms (obtainable at any large stationer's), and during his travels he acquired bill-of-exchange forms printed in French, German, Dutch, Italian, Russian, Turkish and Arabic.

But much that appears on a bill of exchange—printed letter-heads, endorsement stamps, company seals and so on—is virtually impossible to reproduce by hand. So George would have to ar-range for a little private printing. From the city directory he listed 40 printing firms near Paternoster Row and visited each in turn. He was looking for good craftsmen with uninquiring minds who would make various metal, rubber and wooden printing blocks—and even lithographic plates—reproduced from parts of genuine bills. Macdonnell, he hoped, could then use bits and pieces of these mosaics in the meticulous building up of each forged document. He was delighted when he discovered James Dalton, a deaf-mute engraver whose work was of top quality.

But was the Bank of England prepared to accept bills of ex-change from Warren in routine transactions? On November 29, at George's prompting, Austin undertook to find out. Purchasing two first-class bills of exchange, each for £500, with the respected London firm of Suse and Sibeth marked as acceptors, Austin proffered them to Colonel Francis.

"During financial negotiations in connection with the Pullman-car contracts," he said, "I shall be handling many bills comparable to these, Colonel. Before dealing in paper of this sort I would ap-preciate an assurance that you will be prepared to discount them in the usual way."

Colonel Francis said the head office in Threadneedle Street would have to pass on the bills. "But if you care to return later this afternoon, Mr. Warren," he added helpfully, "I shall doubtless have the necessary confirmation for you."

The bills were duly discounted that afternoon—which meant that Warren was now, in fact, accepted as a discount customer. This privilege was normally accorded solely at the head office, and only to individuals known personally by one or another of the bank's directors. By coming in through the side door, and comporting himself with his usual brand of apparent naïveté and openness, Austin had once again achieved the impossible.

Elated with his brother's success, George cabled Noyes on Monday, December 2: "COME WEDNESDAY STEAMER ATLANTIC WITHOUT FAIL." This allowed the unfortunate Edwin Noyes a scant two days in which to arrange the trip; but George had the blood scent now, and was chafing to close in on the quarry.

When the White Star liner *Atlantic* docked at Liverpool on December 17, Edwin Noyes was on it. George and Austin met the boat train in London and whisked him to the Grosvenor Hotel. Noyes, aged 29, was a quiet little man whose decent, clean-cut features bespoke a modest respectability. He was at first much alarmed when George, in outlining his proposed duties, disclosed that they would be going up against the Bank of England. But a promised 5 percent of the proceeds—if he would follow instructions implicitly—eventually won his agreement.

"I will do it," he said resignedly. "I need money badly, and the Bank of England after all will not miss it."

One of George's first moves was to take Noyes to a tailor in Hanover Square and order a complete wardrobe of somber hue and rather poor quality; he then bought Noyes a derby hat in the Strand and an umbrella which he was told to carry furled—all measures to make him indistinguishable from other city clerks.

To establish Noyes as a complete stranger to Mr. Horton, George had him insert an advertisement in the *Daily Telegraph*:

A gentleman of active business habits seeks a situation of trust or partnership. Address particulars to: Edwin Noyes, Durrant's Hotel, Manchester Square.

The announcement ran for six days, and Noyes received between 50 and 60 replies. One of them was from a Mr. C. J. Horton.

A few days later Austin, in the role of Horton, called to see Noyes at Durrant's Hotel and interviewed him within hearing of the hotel staff. "I am looking for a confidential clerk," he said. Noyes outlined his past experience in a quiet, rather nervous voice, and finally, after some discussion, Horton rose to leave. "I am quite satisfied with your qualifications, Mr. Noyes," he said. "If you care to accompany me to my solicitor, we will have a formal agreement drawn up."

In the dingy office of David Howell, solicitor, of 105 Cheapside, the contract "between Charles Johnson Horton, of London Bridge Hotel, Manufacturer, and Edwin Noyes, of Durrant's Hotel, Merchant's Clerk," was drawn up and signed. Noyes agreed to serve as clerk and manager at a salary of £150 a year, and to deposit a sum of £300 as security "for the due performance of his duties and honesty, such sum to be returned without interest on his leaving." George's instructions were that Noyes should carry this agreement and a copy of the *Daily Telegraph* advertisement with him at all times. They would serve to establish his innocence should the need arise.

As Horton, Austin then introduced his new clerk at the Continental Bank, explaining that in future Noyes would be acting for him in every way. "I wish you to treat Mr. Noyes just as though you were dealing with me," he said.

Two days before Christmas, Austin switched to the role of Mr. Warren, visited the Western Branch, and extended the compliments of the season to Colonel Francis. He then informed the manager that he would be away from London for some weeks early in the new year. "I am going up to Birmingham to locate a site for the Pullman-car factory," he explained, "and I shall stay on until the building of it is in satisfactory progress."

Mr. Warren went on to say that, as he did not know where he would be staying from time to time, it would be better for any letters to be addressed to him in care of the General Post Office, Birmingham, where the bank could always be sure of reaching him. And finally, he said, he would henceforth be remitting bills of exchange, not in person as before, but through the post from Birmingham by registered mail.

Colonel Francis accepted these new depositions as a matter of course—and thus freed Austin so that later, when the spate of forged bills was channeled through the bank, he could be out of the country. George had devised the arrangement as a means of protecting Austin. George himself would act as F. A. Warren in Birmingham, as he could well do since his only contact with the bank would be by correspondence—from an untraceable source. Five days later, on December 28, George went up to Birmingham to test the elaborate machinery he had set up. Forging Austin's handwriting, he posted a registered letter to the Colonel:

> SIR,
> Enclosed I hand you bills for discount as per accompanying memorandum. Will you please place the bills to my account and oblige.
>
> Yours faithfully,
> F. A. WARREN

There were ten bills of exchange enclosed, all genuine, drawn on the foremost financial houses in Europe. They totaled £4307 4s 6d, and they were immediately discounted at the Western Branch without question. The machinery was working perfectly.

Before they were passed on to the bank, Mac had made exact copies of the bills, except for the actual amounts. These forgeries were put aside for future use.

At this 11th hour George suddenly decided to abandon the project. Perhaps his conscience troubled him. He and Austin had been reared in almost abject poverty, but their parents had been completely honest and of stern religious convictions. George was married, and the fact that, like the other two, he was now living with a mistress in London may have increased his burden of guilt. In any case, when he received a letter from his wife beseeching him to return home, he experienced a fit of remorse, bought a ticket for New York and announced that he was sailing the next day. "I want my share," he said. "I'm going back to Chicago."

His companions, dumfounded, used every argument to dissuade him; but not until they made it clear that they intended to go ahead anyway did he finally relent. He was certain that without him the others would rush headlong to disaster. "All right, then, I'll stay in," he conceded reluctantly, "but only on one condition. I want a final gilt-edged proof for Colonel Francis of Frederick Albert Warren's financial standing."

He insisted that Austin go to Paris and buy a bill on the House of Rothschild, drawn directly to the order of "F. A. Warren." This would indicate that Warren was known personally to Baron Alphonse de Rothschild, head of the Paris branch of the greatest banking house in Europe, and would provide an immediate passport to the utmost financial respect.

"You must be mad," said Austin angrily. "There is no way I could possibly do that."

"Nevertheless, you must try," said George curtly.

On January 12, Austin caught the night boat train to Paris, engaging a "coupé," or small private compartment. He was morose and, for once, confident only of failure. At 2:30 a.m. he was awakened by a grinding crash, the floor suddenly lifted at a startling angle, and he was hurled violently across the compartment.

The engine had plowed off the rails, and several of the following cars overturned, Austin's among them. Austin was jammed in the wreck and could not get his leg free. Eventually he was found, pried loose, and carried on a stretcher into Marquise Station, where he was wrapped in blankets and given first aid. As he lay there with other injured passengers, cursing his luck and his brother even more, his gaze took in the notices on the walls. Each one was prefaced: CHEMIN DE FER DU NORD.

Suddenly he remembered that the president of the Chemin de Fer du Nord was none other than Baron Rothschild himself. The Baron, a responsible and conscientious man, would certainly not wish his passengers to be involved in wrecks. As he lay there shivering and nursing his pain, Austin reflected that there must be some way of turning the situation to good account.

Arriving in Paris at dusk, Austin spent a fitful night at the Grand Hotel. At ten the next morning, limping badly and leaning on a cane, his ashen face swollen and bandaged, he hobbled across the paved courtyard of Maison Rothschild, Rue Lafitte, and through a door marked "English Department." His pathetic condition at once aroused the sympathy of the staff, and when he explained that he had been in the train crash their solicitude knew no bounds. "If there is anything we can do to help, sir. . . ." ventured Mr. Gatley, the department manager.

Austin pointed out that he was in no condition to carry out his business in Paris and that he intended to return to London without delay. "I therefore wish to transfer certain funds back again and it would assist me if you would draw a three-month bill in my name on your London house for £4500," he said.

The request was unusual, Mr. Gatley said, but if Mr. Warren cared to call back later that afternoon. . . .

On his return, Mr. Warren was introduced to the great Rothschild himself, who expressed his sympathy and asked for first-hand details of the accident. Austin played his cards to perfection, explaining some of his own Pullman-railcar negotiations, and when he finally said good-bye to the rotund and awesome Baron, he had obtained Rothschild's signature on the bill he required.

The bill of exchange was drawn on cheap blue paper, and when Austin discovered blank bill forms in this same blue paper at the nearest stationer's, he purchased several for Mac's future attention. With the aid of a fortuitous train wreck, it had taken him less than 48 hours to complete George's impossible mission.

On Friday, January 17, he went to see Colonel Francis at the Western Branch. "I'm afraid I've had a bad fall hunting in Warwickshire," he said, to explain his banged-up condition. "I'm just down for a few days from Birmingham, where I've been offered three sites for factories. So I thought I'd take this opportunity to call on you."

The Colonel expressed appropriate regret at his accident. "From now on, my money transactions will be larger than ever, Colonel,"

Austin went on, "but my bills will all be of the usual standing, I can assure you. Like this one." And he casually passed over the Rothschild paper made out to "F. A. Warren."

"Excellent, Mr. Warren," said the Colonel, beaming as he eyed the magic signature. "We will do all we can to facilitate your transactions."

Austin never went back to the Western Branch again. His part of the job was done, and he left for France the next day.

On January 21 George made the first test run of Mac's forgeries. After warning Mac and Noyes to be ready for instant flight in case anything went wrong, he posted from Birmingham three bills for amounts totaling £4250, with this note:

> DEAR SIR,
> I hand you herewith, as per enclosed, bills for discount, the proceeds of which please place to my credit. I remain, dear Sir, yours very truly,
>
> F. A. WARREN

George received the Colonel's reply in 48 hours.

> DEAR SIR,
> Your favor of the 21st, enclosing £4250 in bills for discount, is received, and proceeds of same passed to your credit as requested. Hoping you are recovering from the effects of the fall from your horse, I remain, dear Sir, yours faithfully,
>
> P. M. FRANCIS

George was elated. The tone of the letter implied a perfect trusting relationship between manager and customer. He returned to London immediately to supervise collection of the money.

This was Noyes's task and it was a delicate one. Austin had left behind a book of blank checks on the Western Branch of the Bank of England, signed F. A. Warren, and these Noyes used to transfer funds into C. J. Horton's account at the Continental Bank. But Austin had left him blank checks on this bank too, signed C. J. Horton, and with these Noyes began to make cash withdrawals. The amounts of cash involved were so large as to be an embarrassment, and to make them less traceable Noyes resorted to all kinds of expedients—changing notes into gold sovereigns at the Issue Department of the Bank of England in Threadneedle Street, then changing the gold back into notes and finally putting the money into U.S. bonds and foreign currency.

Everything had gone according to plan, and George went again to Birmingham on January 24, this time increasing the number of bills to eight, totaling £9850. Two of them were on cheap blue paper—with Rothschild's as the acceptors. All were discounted at the Western Branch without question.

In the first five days the Americans had cleared £14,000, and Noyes had to beg George to hold off for a few days while he converted the funds from one currency to another. Noyes was most apprehensive about the situation, for he now had every available suitcase in his lodgings at 5 Charlotte Street filled with gold or bank notes, and even had £5000 worth of U.S. bonds stuffed under his mattress. To help clear the decks, George sent Mac to Paris with several thousand pounds, which Austin used to purchase more U.S. bonds on the Continent.

George waited until February 3 before posting the next batch of bills, which totaled £11,072. Of the original 24 forged bills Mac had prepared, there were now only two left, and Mac had to go to work again. To avoid detection, he had to keep moving, and George found him two ground-floor rooms at 17 St. James's Place, a small private hotel run by Miss Agnes Belinda Green. Here, in an improvised workshop, with the gas burners turned full up and supplemented by candles to increase the light, and with the blinds pulled down lest some passerby be overcurious, Mac bent over his inks and plates and papers hour upon hour.

By the completion of the third posting from Birmingham the coup had netted some £25,000 (in terms of today's purchasing power, equivalent to more than $800,000). At this point an unexpected complication arose. From Paris, Austin calmly wrote George that he was getting married. He had met an 18-year-old society beauty, Jane Devereux, at a function in London some months earlier and had fallen in love with her, but George had forbidden him to get married lest he endanger the coup. Now that things were going so well, Austin felt—correctly, as it turned out—that George might be more indulgent.

On February 7 George and Mac crossed on the night packet from Dover, met Austin at midnight on the pierhead at Calais, congratulated him warmly and handed him a wedding present. It was a shiny new black bag containing £11,072 in notes and bonds—the entire previous week's takings. Then they returned to England, and Austin was married the following afternoon.

Back in England the trio resumed their now familiar routine, Mac busy forging, George posting letters in Birmingham on February 8, 12, 20 and 24 for ever-increasing amounts (the last comprising 16 bills worth £19,253) and Noyes siphoning off the money. Correspondence between Warren and Colonel Francis contained an almost intimate note of affability:

BIRMINGHAM, FEB. 20

MY DEAR SIR,

I am happy to inform you that my doctor reports me as doing finely, with the prospect, should no drawback occur, of resuming my active life again in a few days. . . . I remain, dear Sir, yours obliged,

F. A. WARREN

In fact, the active life contemplated by George was preparation for their getaway. He wanted to be out of the country by the beginning of the first week in March, leaving a safe three weeks before certain discovery on March 25, when the first forged bills fell due for payment by their acceptors. In exchange for 70 pieces of worthless paper the Americans now had £78,400 safely stashed away—all seven consignments from Birmingham having been accepted without query. The Bank of England was still sleeping soundly—and now was the time to tiptoe away.

On February 26, after Noyes had collected all the money from their final coup, George prepared to go out of business. He, Mac and Noyes had a jovial lunch by way of celebration, then repaired to Mac's lodgings in St. James's Place and locked themselves in. Mac stoked up the coal fire in the bedroom, opened the locked box containing all the paraphernalia of his forgeries, and the three of them began to commit all evidence to the flames. George's carefully collected stocks of paper, printers' proofs, discarded forgeries, all were tossed into the devouring fire—all, that is, except the finest specimens, which Mac ceremoniously kept aside for one final conflagration. Thumbing lovingly through them for the last time, he murmured, "These are perfect works of art. It seems a pity to destroy them."

George riffled through the bills, studying them pensively. They *were* astonishingly convincing. "Are they good enough to send in, Mac?" he asked.

"With a few minor details filled in, yes," replied Macdonnell.

"Well, let's do it then," George said. "Just one more time."

They selected 24 in all, the largest batch so far, and after Mac had filled in such details as he found missing, George once again went through the familiar routine of writing to Colonel Francis in F. A. Warren's hand. Next day, Thursday, throwing caution to the winds, all three of them went to Birmingham to post this final packet of bills. The proceeds from them would add £26,265 to their haul.

But, as we have seen, Mac overlooked one vitally essential detail in failing to date two £1000 bills of exchange. Colonel Francis at first assumed the omission was a minor clerical error, and discounted all the other bills without question. Late that Friday afternoon, however, when Blydenstein's, the alleged acceptor, returned the undated bills, calling them outright forgeries, the machinery for uncovering the fraud was set into motion.

Colonel Francis rushed over to Threadneedle Street to consult Mr. May, the deputy chief cashier, whose practiced eye immediately noticed irregularities in Warren's file. There was no permanent address. There were no references. There was no introduction by a director. There was only an unusually large number of disbursements made to a Mr. Horton and passed through the Continental Bank, on Lombard Street. It was too late in the afternoon to make any inquiries at the Continental Bank, but May felt sure his discoveries in the morning would not be savory.

Noyes was among the first customers when the Continental Bank opened its doors on Saturday morning, March 1. This was his last visit, to clear out the Horton account, and he asked for both English and foreign money. He was requested to call back for the foreign currency later in the morning. When he returned, Noyes was first identified by officials as Horton's clerk, then unceremoniously arrested.

Waiting to meet him in a coffeehouse in Exchange Alley, George and Mac began to wonder what was keeping Noyes, and eventually went in search of him. They did not have to go far. Hearing a great commotion from the direction of Lombard Street, they hurried to investigate and, elbowing through the surging crowd, found Noyes at the center of it—in custody. As he was dragged past them, Noyes looked desperately toward his friends, though he gave no sign of recognition. George and Mac joined the throng long enough to catch the words "forgeries" . . . "thousands and thousands, they say" . . . "the Bank of England" . . . "how could it happen?" and then they eased off down a side street.

"My God, George, what do we do now?" Mac whispered.

"Do?" replied George. "We do nothing. Ed can clear himself with his alibi, and there's nothing to lead the police to us."

But for once George Bidwell had underestimated the Bank of England. However much it might cost, they would stop at nothing in their attempt to find the forgers. Already the full strength of Scotland Yard was being mobilized.

Within two hours a WANTED notice was being widely circulated,

340

offering a £500 reward for the apprehension of "F. A. Warren, alias C. J. Horton." The wanted man was described by the staff of the Western Branch as: "About 40 years of age, five feet nine or ten inches in height, thin, dark, sallow, with dark hair and eyes, speaking with a strong American accent and dressed fairly well in a frock coat and loose brown overcoat."

The discrepancy of more than ten years in Austin's reputed age was perhaps a tribute to his posed maturity, though the rest of the details did him scant justice; but the forgeries raised such a public outcry that almost any description would have served the purpose, since just about every American in London was now being viewed with suspicion.

By Monday night, through questioning of Green, the Savile Row tailor, and inquiries at the Americans' original address at 21 Enfield Road, Haggerstone (where Austin's new suits had been delivered), detectives had discovered that at least two men besides Noyes were possibly implicated in the plot. And on Tuesday, March 4, this supposition was confirmed when Francis Herold, manager of the St. James's Place hotel, reported his suspicions about the habits of a certain American, Captain Macdonnell, who was frequently visited by another mysterious American. Detectives hurried to the address and found that Macdonnell had hastily departed a few hours earlier. But, searching the ashes of his fireplace, they discovered a crumpled ball of blotting paper bearing such decipherable phrases as: "Accepted payable at" ... "The Bank of Belgium and Holland" ... "Ten Thousand" ... and other words and signatures which clearly established connection with the forgeries. A reward of £500 was immediately offered for the capture of George Macdonnell.

When Mac bolted from the St. James's Place hotel, he fled to the Pimlico lodgings of his girl friend, Daisy Grey, a barmaid at the Turkish Divan. He apparently planned to take her with him to America, for he bought two tickets for the *Peruvian*, which was sailing for New York on March 6, and sent Daisy on ahead to wait for him at Liverpool.

Meanwhile, he shipped off a trunk that he had labeled:

MAJOR GEO. MATTHEWS, c/o ATLANTIC EXPRESS CO.,
57 BROADWAY, NEW YORK
Contents: *Wearing apparel actually in use*
TO BE KEPT IN BOND UNTIL CALLED FOR
Sender: *Charles Lossing, Tunbridge Wells, Kent,* ENGLAND

Between the layers of soiled clothes was neatly folded some
$225,000 worth of U.S. bonds.

Mac tried to keep his appointment with his mistress, but when he
reached Liverpool he suddenly became aware that he was being
followed. Swiftly doubling back, he caught a train to Southampton
and boarded a cross-Channel steamer to Le Havre, where he
sailed on the *Thuringia* for New York.

This temporary escape availed him nothing. For Daisy, finding
herself jilted, returned to London and was hauled in for questioning when she was found looking for Mac at 17 St. James's Place.
The outraged girl was not slow in telling the police all she knew.

During the coup, Austin and George between them had used
nearly 40 different aliases, but Mac usually scorned such melo-
dramatic subterfuges, and this typical arrogance was now his
undoing. When Scotland Yard checked the passenger lists of de-
parting liners and found a George Macdonnell on the *Thuringia*,
they cabled the New York police, asking them to detain him. He
was arrested at New York, before he even stepped ashore.

Austin Bidwell was also now using his own name. He had been
married under it and was honeymooning with his new bride in
Havana. As usual, he could not resist using his great talent for
making a favorable impression; the Bidwells entertained ex-
travagantly and were conspicuously popular in the island capital's
smart set. Thus, when Scotland Yard sent a routine circular to
British embassies and consulates in many countries, asking them
to watch for Austin Bidwell—Daisy Grey's revelations and other
information having by now pinpointed his true identity—the

British consul in Havana recognized the name. Austin was arrested at an elaborate dinner party at which he was the host.

Thus, within three weeks after the discovery of the forgeries, three of the four perpetrators had been accounted for. Only George Bidwell remained, and to track him down Scotland Yard now assigned 75 detectives for the biggest manhunt in its history.

When the forgeries were first discovered, George felt no concern for his own safety. He believed they had concealed their tracks so well that there was no danger that he, Mac or Austin would be implicated. With his mistress, Nellie Vernon, he went to St. Leonards-on-Sea for a long weekend, during which he sent £300 to David Howell, the Cheapside solicitor who had drawn up Noyes's contract with Horton, asking that Howell undertake Noyes's defense. Otherwise, he spent his days unhurriedly "thinking things over"—and so lost the chance to get away at a time when he might still have left England unchallenged.

On Tuesday, March 4, George returned to London and, after vainly trying to get in touch with Mac (who was already in flight), decided to take off himself. He converted bonds and gold into the universal currency of diamonds at various jewelers on the Strand, and arranged to take Nellie back to America with him, perhaps as a means of silencing her, since she knew his actual identity (though not his connection with the bank fraud).

This precaution merely put the police on his trail. George planned to sail from Ireland, and on Thursday, March 6, asked Nellie to meet him at Euston Station, where they would board the night mail train for Dublin, via Holyhead. Nellie had been entrusted with most of George's luggage, and in the station its sheer quantity attracted attention. The police picked up Nellie and found £2717 in gold in the bags. Under questioning the girl broke down, and from her Scotland Yard learned for the first time of George Bidwell's existence.

George, now clean-shaven as an elementary precaution, on failing to find Nellie at their Euston Station rendezvous, decided to go ahead to Holyhead, and managed to board the train without incident. He crossed by the night ferry to Dublin, where he arrived on March 7, intending to wait for Nellie to join him. But when he found his name in the Dublin papers, together with an uncannily accurate description of himself and an offer of a reward for his apprehension, he guessed that Nellie had been arrested. Now, at last, he knew that he was a marked man, on the run.

George's objective was to sail for New York from Cork, on the Cunard ship *Cuba*. He had no difficulty leaving Dublin by train, but coming out of Cork station he was stopped by a police officer. "Have you ever been in this town before, sir?" the officer asked politely.

"Yes, officer, many times," George replied in a brusque manner, and without allowing time for further questions he strode off into the town.

Realizing immediately that he had not the slightest chance of getting aboard ship—or of returning safely to the station—he holed up in the Temperance Hotel, signing the register as "Charles Burton." Next morning he bought an ulster cape and a plaid cap and hired a jaunting cart to drive him to a small country station a dozen miles up the line, which he hoped would not be watched. But even there, at Fermoy, a man was standing beside the ticket office, so George took no chances and purchased a ticket to Lismore, a town at the opposite end of the line to Dublin.

But wherever he went there was a grave risk of arrest. The local papers were full of the search, and it was particularly dangerous for a foreigner to be on the run in the thinly populated Irish countryside. George realized that he must get back to Dublin at all costs. He finally reached there one morning at two, roused the night porter at the Cathedral Hotel and secured a room for the night. Next morning, by the simple expedient of buying a silk top hat from a secondhand clothes dealer, and a valise in place of his London-style leather bag, he was able to pass as a Frenchman.

He had now decided to go to Scotland as the only possibly safe move, and he first had to get from Dublin to Belfast to catch the boat across to Glasgow. At the Dublin station ticket office he purposely made himself conspicuous by asking for a ticket in execrable broken English, a ruse which got him past the scrutiny of two detectives checking the passengers.

Reaching Belfast at 9 p.m. on March 10, he at once went aboard the Glasgow steamer—two hours before it was due to leave— and bought a ticket from the ship's purser. "*Bon soir, monsieur. Un billet à Glasgow, s'il vous plaît,*" he said. He went into the adjacent washroom to clean up after his long journey. He had just finished when he heard a clatter of feet on the saloon stairway.

"Purser, a cab just brought a man from the Dublin train. Where is he?" demanded an authoritative voice.

"Oh, you mean the Frenchman," replied the purser. "He's over there in the washroom."

Hearing this interchange, George hurriedly put on his silk hat and, with mincing foppishness, stood in front of the mirror flicking dust off his lapels, smoothing his eyebrows and adjusting the tilt of his hat to perfection. Taking a good look at this bizarre spectacle, the two detectives shrugged and left. George, much shaken by his narrow escape, went immediately to his cabin and did not emerge again until the ship docked in Glasgow next morning. Meanwhile, in a frenzy of action, the Belfast police had actually arrested one man on board, and 12 others in various parts of the town.

George left Glasgow at once for Edinburgh, still in the guise of a Frenchman. He took a room at 22 Cumberland Street in the name of "Monsieur Couton." And from there he wrote to Mac, at his old address in New York, that he would "make a dive for home in one or two weeks longer." Meantime he could relax a bit. In the water jump between Ireland and Scotland the police had for the moment lost the scent.

The hue and cry was nevertheless deafening. The Bank of England had spared no expense in the chase, and hordes of private detectives were assisting the police all over the Continent as well as in the British Isles. The Pinkertons had been engaged in America. "The police are looking wildly about them, apparently without the remotest notion which way to turn," the London *City Press* commented on March 15 (when neither Mac nor Austin had yet been apprehended). "They are ready to take anybody into custody, on the very faintest suspicion, or on no suspicion at all."

Numerous false arrests resulted, including the detainment of three suspects in Liège, Belgium, and a rag merchant in Cork, Ireland, who was found to have £500 on his person. The rag merchant turned out not to be George Bidwell—his name was Jonas Wolfe—but he was wanted on a forgery charge anyway.

In Edinburgh, George settled into a cautious daily routine. He ventured little from his room, explaining to his landlady that he was convalescing from a bout of sickness. His one routine daily outing was to a bookshop in Dundas Street, where he always purchased the London and Edinburgh papers. This hunger for news ultimately betrayed him, for the bookseller became intrigued by "Monsieur Couton," and after some days it suddenly struck him that his new customer somewhat resembled George Bidwell, the wanted forger.

The bookseller mentioned this casually to another customer, a clerk in the employ of Gibson, Craig, Dalziel and Brodies, the Edinburgh agents of the Bank of England. The clerk passed it on to his superiors, who decided to put a private detective to watch Couton—"just in case."

As one of his typical precautions, George suddenly switched his patronage to a bookshop in Broughton Street. The operative, apparently well below Sherlock Holmes in mental capacity, continued to observe the Dundas Street shop unavailingly for two weeks; only then did it occur to him to ask the bookseller if he knew George's address—which he did.

On Wednesday, April 2, in the early afternoon, the detective and a uniformed constable from the Edinburgh police watched George come down the steps of 22 Cumberland Place. He walked up the street to a pillar box, posted a letter, then turned and saw he was being followed. Quickening his pace, he tried vainly to elude his pursuers. Then he began to run, the two detectives hot

on his heels. Nimbly scaling a series of garden walls, he dived through the back door of a house, came out the front, rushed through Royal Crescent and was finally overpowered when he could run no farther.

George protested vehemently that he was a Frenchman, but a diligent search of his room by police disclosed (in addition to a quantity of diamonds) several letters addressed to "George Bidwell." The two officers then knew they had at last captured the most wanted man in Europe.

At the trial, which was held at the Central Criminal Court, Old Bailey, more than 100 witnesses from Europe and America testified against the four accused. It took 23 days of preliminary hearings, and 9 days at the full trial, for the whole story to be told.

George, Austin and Macdonnell all tried to minimize Noyes's complicity, and each of them tried to place full blame on himself for the plot. But in only 20 minutes the jury reached a verdict of "guilty" for all four of them.

"Within living memory there has been no such case," said the London *Times*. And within living memory there had been no harsher sentence than the one passed on their crime: "It is not the least atrocious part of your crime," said Mr. Justice Archibald, "that you have given a severe blow to that confidence which has been so long maintained in this country. You must be met with a terrible retribution, and I feel no hesitation as to the sentence it is my duty to pass—that each of you be kept in penal servitude for life."

The Bank of England could have been awarded no more savage vengeance.

And to achieve its revenge, the bank had spent the enormous sum of £43,420 on reward money, private detectives and the tracking down and transporting of witnesses. But they had recovered £73,420 of the stolen money, and to some extent their wounded pride was healed.

Mac, George, Austin and Noyes could also have one cause for pride.

The three confidence men had forced the Bank of England to overhaul its security regulations on bills-of-exchange procedure (which was changed in some undisclosed but presumably adequate manner); and this feat alone, during the long years in Dartmoor Prison, must have made each of them smile just a little.

SINCE EVERYTHING else seems to have happened there, it was only a question of time before a Walter Mitty, too, showed up in Katanga in the Congo. This time, the James Thurber character stood six feet in his stocking feet, weighed 210 pounds and was 38 years old. He had long blond hair, two medical diplomas and the name of Colonel-Doctor Victor Lionehearte-Reichardson.

He had been hired by Katanga's recruiting agents in Paris, and arrived in what was then Elisabethville carrying a British black-leather diplomatic dispatch box. It contained a book on basic anatomy pilfered from London's Lambeth Public Library, and his credentials: a medical diploma from the University of California and a special degree in tropical medicine from the University of Wisconsin. That he spoke neither French nor Swahili seemed to matter little to the Katangans, who packed him off immediately to a hospital in remote Baudouinville.

Soon the bush telegraph spread the good news: The white doctors were back. Natives began pouring into the modern and splendidly equipped hospital, which had been locked up since the Belgian staff fled.

A visiting journalist found it a bit odd when Lionehearte-Reichardson asked *his* opinion whether watered-down penicillin would be effective against advanced leprosy. He became alarmed when the "doctor" made notes of his suggestions on how to amputate a gangrenous arm. Checks with the universities of California and Wisconsin revealed they had never enrolled anyone named Lionehearte-Reichardson.

The Katangan authorities promptly brought Lionehearte-Reichardson back to Elisabethville from the bush to explain. He was stripped of his white medical gown and given a new uniform: the blue-and-white-striped shorts and shirt of a Katangan prisoner. Asked how he managed to run a hospital, he explained: "I gave the patients plenty of morphine and penicillin, and avoided abdominal operations. I acted the part so much that I really and truly believed I was a great doctor." —*Newsweek*

Alceo Dossena was no villain;
he was just born six centuries too late

A RENAISSANCE MAN

by Myron Brenton

In 1920 an obscure Italian stonecutter named Alceo Dossena sat in his tiny studio in Rome, his thoughts centuries away from his workaday job of making cornices for new buildings. With every stroke of his hammer and chisel, he slid deeper into a world of fantasy. He saw himself as Leonardo da Vinci. Then Michelangelo —then as other great Renaissance sculptors whose work he knew and loved.

One day Dossena could stand it no longer. Pushing aside for all time his detested cornices, he turned to a chunk of marble and began carving, unaware that his fantasies had launched him on a career which would eventually bring him worldwide notoriety.

For eight years, the little stonemason lived his dreams of glory, creating dozens of brilliant sculptures. One bleak November day in 1928, an earthquake rocked the art world; in New York, Cleveland, Boston, Rome, Berlin and Munich, museum authorities learned that some of their most prized sculptures were fakes— magnificent pieces produced in all innocence by the cornice maker.

For years Dossena had studied the works of the old masters. One artist in particular fascinated him: Simone Martini, a 14th-century painter. Martini had never worked in stone, but Dossena,

studying the powerful canvases, felt that Martini *should* have been a sculptor. He could shut his eyes and actually see what Martini, six centuries before, might have done in marble.

By poking around abandoned quarries and rummaging through unguarded ruins, Dossena gradually accumulated a stockpile of the richly veined marble used by the Renaissance sculptors. Then, skillfully imitating Martini's style in painting, he carved a beautiful Madonna and Child.

Next, Dossena turned to other Renaissance artists he admired, producing stunning works in their special manners. Then he reached further back in time—using marble dating to the time of Athens which he had unearthed in nearby Greek ruins—to create fine statuary that might have come from the Golden Age of Greece.

The studio of the stonecutter began to resemble a museum. In every corner stood seemingly genuine 15th-century tomb pieces, 14th-century marble fonts and Grecian goddesses. Dossena made no attempt to sell his work until an antique dealer named Alfredo Fasoli came to look at the stonemason's Renaissance statues. Carefully concealing his excitement, Fasoli told Dossena, "There's not much demand for copies such as these, but perhaps I can get rid of some for you at bargain prices."

Unknown to Dossena, the art dealer had another plan in mind. He took one of the stonecutter's sculptures to a colleague named Pallesi, who had excellent connections in the international art market. Both men could count their future profits as they gazed on the statue's seemingly authentic chips, cracks and discolorations. Outwardly, at least, it looked centuries old.

The statue was offered to a museum in Rome. "We doubt the authenticity of this," the dealers told museum officials, then settled back to await developments. A team of art experts examined the sculpture, and to the jubilation of Fasoli and Pallesi reported that it was indeed genuine! The museum paid a tidy sum for what it considered an artistic find. Dossena, however, was told that the statue had been sold as a cheap copy and humbly accepted the few bank notes that Fasoli handed him. And when the unscrupulous art dealers offered him a contract for exclusive rights to his work, he signed gratefully, somewhat bewildered at the interest in him.

Subsequently, more of Dossena's statues were offered as genuine Renaissance sculpture, and museums and private collectors throughout Europe snapped them up. Informed that his works were being sold inexpensively as imitations, Dossena never questioned the small sums Fasoli gave him. Instead he kept hammering out one bogus masterpiece after another.

Dossena's imitation Renaissance and Greek art fooled an imposing array of museums. New York City's Metropolitan Museum of Art bought a statue of a Greek maiden supposedly dating back to 500 B.C. The Cleveland Museum purchased a wooden Madonna and Child attributed to Giovanni Pisano, a 14th-century sculptor whose wood pieces had never been discovered. And Boston's Museum of Fine Arts was stuck with a sarcophagus supposedly made by Renaissance sculptor Mino da Fiésole. When the hoax was exposed, a Boston Museum spokesman said: "If that sarcophagus was a forgery, it is worth preserving. It is beautiful, no matter who did it."

As recently as 1958, some art experts insisted that *Diana With Fawn*, a statue in the St. Louis Museum, had originated in Dossena's studio. But the museum issued a 51-page report defending its statue as original and kept it on display.

How is it possible that so many art experts, using the finest scientific equipment, were either fooled or put on the defensive by Dossena's work? For one thing, Dossena conceived his works on a grander scale than any forger before him. He reportedly invented a secret chemical that penetrated stone and gave it an earth-stained appearance, thus duplicating the effects of natural erosion. For another, many museums failed to investigate the pieces fully. But one overriding reason is that his counterfeit works of art passed the closest inspection because Alceo Dossena was a genius.

As they went about peddling Dossena's work, Fasoli and his colleague tried to be circumspect. Whenever a museum became suspicious about one of the statues, it received an immediate refund. Nevertheless, in 1928 the dealers made two mistakes. They tried to cheat Dossena on his contract, and they tried to sell counterfeit statues to the Frick Collection of New York.

Though attracted by supposedly rare pieces, the Frick authorities cautiously decided to send their own experts to Italy before completing the purchase. The American visitors arrived at a most inopportune time: Another visitor to Dossena's studio had recently informed the sculptor that his works were being represented as actual Renaissance pieces in a Berlin museum. Appalled that his work had been misused and enraged that others had amassed a fortune by making him a party to deceit, Dossena sued.

Fasoli and Pallesi tried to keep the Frick representatives from hearing the news, but it soon made headlines on both sides of the Atlantic. Authorities estimated that Fasoli, Pallesi and certain anonymous international art firms had pocketed over $2 million from the sale of Dossena's phony art. One piece alone had netted $150,000. The Italian government conducted an investigation that cleared 53-year-old Dossena of all blame and forced the dealers to make at least partial restitution to the victimized buyers.

After the furor Dossena continued to work in the Renaissance style he loved. He died seven years later, but his story has an ironic sequel.

On March 9, 1933, in the grand ballroom of New York's Hotel Plaza, National Art Galleries, Inc., auctioned off 39 pieces of Alceo Dossena's remarkable work. The largest single sale netted a mere $675. The entire group of statues was sold for only $9125. With each purchase, the buyer was handed a handsome certificate issued by the Italian government. It solemnly stated that what the buyer had just purchased was guaranteed to be a "genuine fake."

A **CHICAGO** man admitted in court that he stole 75 checks, worth $600, from mailboxes, but asserted he always sent $5 from every stolen check he cashed to the chaplain of the federal penitentiary at Terre Haute, Indiana, "for the betterment of prison conditions." —*Copley News Service*

Even Henry Ford
seemed to believe the old man
could make cars run on a magic formula

MAN WITH GREEN MAGIC

by Harold Mehling

Louis Enricht was a man who never promised the ordinary. He specialized in pledging the miraculous, and in presenting each miracle as more stupendous than the previous. His career was unusual in that he swindled boldly from 1890 on, but remained obscure until 1916, when he was 70 years old. It was then that he offered the world his most fabulous discovery. He said he had found a substitute for gasoline that could be manufactured for a penny a gallon.

Since gasoline was selling at 30 times that price and was scarce because of the war raging in Europe, Enricht became a sensation overnight. He found himself a subject of controversy between warring governments, an object of investment to Henry Ford and an inspiration to crackpots the world over.

But after Enricht had become considerably wealthier as a result, he was—like many swindlers—only a source of extreme embarrassment to those who had coveted him and his "secret."

On the afternoon of April 11, 1916, Enricht faced a score of skeptical reporters who stood and sat on his small, trim lawn in rustic Farmingdale, Long Island. Some of the newsmen exchanged quips about the old man's bushy, gray mustache, which flowed

355

from above his lip down past his mouth, as they waited for what they expected would develop into a humorous feature story about a harmless crank.

Then Enricht silenced them with his announcement: "I have learned to do what chemists have been dreaming of for years. I can transform water into gasoline by the addition of a chemical that has been compounded under a secret formula!"

The reporters chuckled in disbelief, but the towering, white-haired man glowered down on them and said he would demonstrate the power of his discovery. He took a small vial, turned to an automobile in his driveway and thrust a long stick into its gas tank. He pulled it out dry. He tapped the tank and it rang hollow. The reporters pressed forward and peered through the tank's filler opening to convince themselves it had no false bottom or sides.

Enricht picked up a white china pitcher, filled it from a garden hose and offered it to a reporter, who tasted it and said, "Pure water, nothing else." Then Enricht poured in a green-tinted fluid. He stirred the mixture and dumped it into the gasoline tank. The engine was cranked and it caught and raced furiously.

The reporters buzzed among themselves, no longer laughing. Enricht watched cheerfully as two of them climbed into the car and drove it around the village of Farmingdale. They returned enthusiastic, whereupon the old man kissed his petite, silver-haired wife, Anna, who had come out to watch, and strolled back into his home.

The reporters rushed off to tell the world how they had witnessed a mixture of water and a penny-a-gallon chemical of some sort operate an automobile.

Enricht realized that his sensational announcement would inevitably be greeted with some skepticism, and that his first task would be to deal with the skeptics—one of whom appeared almost immediately. He was William E. Haskell, publisher of the Chicago *Herald*. Haskell had bought his first motor car back in 1895, and felt he was an automotive authority. He arrived in Farmingdale,

eager but reserved, on the Sunday after Enricht's first demonstration. "I am frank to confess," he said, "that I approach the proposition with caution."

Haskell found Enricht no less cautious—or rather, just as prepared. "So many agents from big oil companies have been here disguised as newspapermen," the self-styled inventor said, "that I must be careful to know who I'm dealing with." He explained that one oil firm was his enemy because the firm had snubbed him 25 years earlier when he had offered it a secret that would have saved it thousands of dollars a year. He had asked for $20,000, but the company had tried to get his secret for $1500. That was all but banditry, he said, and he hadn't sold.

Haskell was more than a little impressed, but he grew suspicious again when he touched a drop of Enricht's green fluid to his lips. He smacked and asked darkly, "What's that bitter almond taste?"

"Prussic acid," Enricht replied. "I put it in to disguise another odor that would come up strong and identify the formula's more important ingredients."

The inventor explained morosely that his discovery had brought him a dilemma. He would probably have to sell for a song because chemical analysis of the formula's ingredients would be easy. The ingredients, he said, were "so cheap and common that no one could possibly corner the market on them. This means that anyone can manufacture the substitute. It's the secret that is complex —not the manufacture after the parts are known. This green fluid is a white elephant."

Enricht's long, lined face was bleak as he demonstrated the formula for Haskell, who had first satisfied himself that the car had no hidden fuel supply and that its gas tank had no false bottom of any kind.

"A couple of turns at the crank and the engine started, racing fiercely with an open throttle," Haskell reported. "It ran even and true. I got in the car and drove it all around Farmingdale, and never had a bit of trouble. It was a most remarkable demonstration indeed."

That evening the publisher departed for Chicago to write that he had just sat in on "the beginning of an industrial revolution."

"If anyone had tried to convince me of what I witnessed myself," he added, "I could not have believed him."

The gasoline substitute was big news, as Enricht had correctly figured it would be. With essential gasoline supplies low because of the war in Europe, chemical engineers were spending a good deal of their time lecturing on the urgent need to find a cheap and plentiful substitute.

And that, said Louis Enricht, a man who understood the art of timing, was exactly what he had found. One pound of his green magic mixed with water, he said, would produce 667 pounds of fuel. His telephone rang incessantly, and every day mailmen delivered 200 offers of financial assistance in putting the remarkable discovery on the market. Enricht, biding his time, put all the letters into a carton and stored the carton in his attic.

Two days after the demonstration for publisher Haskell, the reporters returned, hungry for more news, and Enricht did not send them away unsatisfied. He cannily let slip what he called a "principal secret of my formula." He said his chemical was not combustible in itself, but that it had a passionate affinity for the oxygen in water. This affinity caused the oxygen to separate from the hydrogen. When the hydrogen atoms were released, they combined in a violent manner with the next nearest oxygen atoms, those in the air. This resounding, shotgun-type marriage produced an explosion, which created the power. It was as simple and as enchanting as that.

But not everyone was enchanted. Dr. Thomas B. Freas, associate professor of chemistry at Columbia University, took sharp and public exception. "No chemical can be added to water that will make it combustible," he declared. "Water may be broken up by electrolysis, but the energy required will be exactly equal to that produced on burning. That is, nothing would be gained. Absolutely nothing."

Sniffing a controversy, newsmen dashed this heresy out to

Farmingdale. "The professor says your idea is impractical," one of them told Enricht.

His nimble mind was more than equal to such skepticism. "That's nothing," he replied easily. "They always say that when an important discovery is made."

But then an even more forceful dissent was heard. Dr. C. F. Chandler, a founder of the Columbia University School of Mines and a scientist of international standing, said: "The proposition is absolutely impossible. It's trying to get something out of nothing." Dr. Chandler said several substances—metallic sodium, for one—would release hydrogen from water most effectively. "But to get enough hydrogen to equal the energy in one gallon of gasoline would take $57\frac{1}{2}$ pounds of sodium," he added. "At 25 cents a pound, such energy would cost $14.37."

Enricht laughed grimly. "It's fortunate I'm not using metallic sodium, isn't it?" he stated.

With public curiosity at the spillway, Ferdinand Jehle, laboratory engineer of the Automobile Club of America, then asked Enricht to submit a sample to test, pledging that no attempt would be made to discover the formula's constituents. "We want to find out if it's of value," Jehle said, "or to be plain, if it's fake."

"Call it a fake if you like," Enricht retorted. "It makes no difference to me." But while he was talking, he was thinking, and the result was a decision to call up a diversion. He invited the reporters to talk to a gentleman whose word could not be questioned. That gentleman was Benjamin Franklin Yoakum, a financier, board member of several railways and onetime president of the St. Louis and San Francisco Railroad. Yoakum lived on Fifth Avenue in New York and was a member of the proper clubs, but he was also a summer neighbor of Enricht's, owning a large estate just outside Farmingdale. All this made him a scientific authority, too, naturally.

"I have known Louis Enricht a long time," Yoakum said. "I have confidence in his invention. I have used it in my own motor car." He added that his interest in Enricht was not financial; he simply wanted to see cheaper motive power developed.

360

The skeptics held their fire and a clamor arose for a public demonstration. Everyone wanted to see the green liquid marvel. Enricht, feeling the need for another diversion, refused to give any further demonstrations.

"I could not demonstrate it if I wanted to," he said, "for I am about out of material. I went into New York to buy some, but found it would not be safe. I was being followed. At a restaurant, a man watched from out in the street. And when I went to a chemist, he came there, too." Enricht said he had bought five tubes of petroleum jelly and returned home.

Into this shadowy atmosphere now slipped a strange man who had made industrial history once and longed to do it again. He was Henry Ford, whose publicity man flew up from Washington and drove out to Farmingdale.

The Ford press agent, Theodore Delavigne, handed Enricht a telegram he had received from the motor tycoon: "Put Mr. Enricht aboard the Wolverine Express and, rain or shine, deliver him f.o.b. at my office in Detroit."

Enricht was courteous, but declined the rail ticket. He said he was afraid to carry his secret formula with him and afraid to leave it home, even though he had reduced it to code.

The following Monday, just 13 days after the first revelation of the discovery, the New York *Times* itself headlined the extent of Ford's interest:

FORD SEES ENRICHT
ABOUT MOTOR FUEL

Inventor Talks for an Hour, and
Ford Will Come Again and See
Cent-a-Gallon Mixture Work

How could Henry Ford get involved with Louis Enricht? How, for that matter, could he not? The 52-year-old tycoon was as ornery and unpredictable as he was gifted. It was utterly in character that this remarkable inventor should hurry to Long Island himself to see and touch and hear Enricht. After a meeting in the Brown Hotel in Farmingdale, Gaston Plantiff, Ford's New York sales manager, announced: "He thought it was worth following up; that is about all that can be said." That is all that should have been said, but Plantiff could not resist going on. "Mr. Ford is careful in his moves, going forward a step at a time," he said, unconscious of the fact that everything in Ford's life belied such a remark. "You see, Mr. Ford is something of a chemist himself and he no doubt could ask Mr. Enricht a number of questions. The answers must not have been unsatisfactory or the matter would have been dropped."

It was not. The next day the motor magnate declared he would buy Enricht's formula outright if it passed tests. "I wrote Mr. Enricht today," Ford said. "We will have a test in a week or so and I'll be there. I don't know what to think of it, but we've had men working along that line for some time."

Enricht himself would say nothing of his relations with Ford. He smiled coyly and hummed a pleasant little tune as he went for neighborhood walks. The world, its appetite stimulated by the newspapers, hungered for more miracles.

Not that people were without news of other remarkable events in this field. One of the fascinating features of Enricht's initial announcement is that, in the period that followed, an astonishing number of similar gasoline-from-practically-nothing schemes received wide publicity. A Detroit laboratory was producing a fuel that had been "reatomized" so none of it could reach auto engine cylinders in liquid form; a saving of 50 percent was promised. A Trenton, New Jersey, inventor demonstrated "gasafoam," which was produced by agitating various oils and would sell for ten cents a gallon. In Sandusky, Ohio, Harrison G. Shoupe, a pioneer auto man, announced that he had discovered a way of making gasoline out of water, à la Enricht. A wealthy Chicagoan promptly agreed to pay him $10,000 plus $500 a month for life, and arrived with a chemist to begin exploiting the process. When Shoupe could not produce water-gasoline by his process, the chemist investigated and found two hidden pipes, one connected to a can of standard gasoline.

All this was like contagion, but it was also quite in the pattern. When a swindler comes up with a "revolutionary scientific discovery," several others—swindlers and merely crackpots— immediately claim the bounder has stolen their life's work. But very few considered Enricht a swindler—that is, until April 27, 1916, less than a month after his opening performance. It was then that folksy Farmingdale picked up its morning newspapers and read that their suddenly famous neighbor was more than an aged refugee from the severe winters of the Midwest.

Enricht, it was revealed, was a German who had emigrated to this country in his early 20's. He had no particular skills but he did have a stern manner that bespoke honesty and straightforwardness. He had not had even a smattering of scientific training and worked mostly as a salesman. All through the years in the New World, he longed to have wife Anna look up to him as a man of accomplishment, and at the age of 44, he succeeded. Deciding that a railroad line from Canyon City, Colorado, to Cripple Creek was desperately needed, he collected funds to build it. That was in 1890. When, in 1903, no track had yet been laid, bankruptcy separated the investors from their investments and Enricht was arrested. But no one could make the charge stick, and Enricht was released.

Seven years later, in Chicago, he gave Anna more to admire when he began selling 45,000 acres of the vast Cumberland Plateau in Kentucky and Tennessee. He operated with what he described as deeds handed down in Colonial days by Patrick Henry. Enricht was indicted for using the mails to defraud, fined $500 and warned to be careful how he used U.S. postage in the future. Anna did not understand such matters; she did know, though, that something important was always going on around her husband, Louis.

The presumably chastened fellow went to New York and dabbled in the stock market, but in 1912 he again entered bankruptcy. Looking around for another outlet for his boundless imagination and energy, he somehow interested a number of wealthy Englishmen in a formula for making artificial stone. This time, he meticulously kept his transactions out of the mails. The Englishmen gave him a considerable amount of money when he claimed he could make stone out of sand, ashes or sawdust, that he could turn a swamp into a concrete bridge in six hours and that he had a railroad tie transformed from sawdust. But when he delivered the formula, the Englishmen strongly intimated that they had been fleeced. Enricht was so hurt he quietly left the city and settled in Farmingdale.

Those were the revelations the newspapers printed, and they made it unmistakably clear that the quiet villager was, in reality, an inexhaustible ragbag of swindlery.

But was that really clear? Not, apparently, to Henry Ford, for as dusk of that day fell on Long Island, the Model T genius reappeared. Ford drove up and closeted himself with the charlatan in a garage. At midnight, after Enricht had asked for forgiveness for the big-boned skeletons in his past, Ford departed with a promise to send a new car for experimental use. He did, and added another expression of his cavernous inability to accept the obvious —$1000 in cash.

The townsfolk of Farmingdale should have been slower than Ford to forgive, for many of them, it emerged, had been patronizing a curious Enricht sideline. Their neighbor had been selling them bottles of "radium water" and a tonic that was supposed to make their hens more prolific egg layers. Now the villagers began reassessing the virtues of these nonsensical products, but they were diverted by an electrifying series of events.

This time the old man's salvation came from the huge Maxim Munitions Corporation of New Jersey, manufacturers of ammunition and bayonets. Ignoring the wrinkles and dents in Enricht's character, the firm announced it had arranged for exclusive rights to manufacture his gasoline substitute. Maxim said it would buy land in Farmingdale on which to build a laboratory and factory. It applied for a patent and cheerfully promised that motorists would not be the only ones to benefit; farmers would get cheap power for wood sawing and threshing. "Experiments prove that Enricht's invention, perfected in some minor details, will be revolutionary in character," the company said.

If anyone thought Maxim's action seemed incredible in light of the exposure of the old man's past, he would have been overwhelmed by reports of the high finances involved. "It was said that Enricht received $1 million in cash and 100,000 shares of Maxim stock" ($10.50 a share), said *Patent News*, the inventor's journal. *Patent News* called him "Dr." Enricht. With so much money involved, how could the "doctor" be thought dishonest?

Henry Ford, shocked at Enricht's duplicity, opened a futile campaign to retain rights to the invention. Ford's agent was asked if the Ford Company would discontinue its tests. "No," he said, "we are going ahead as before. I was talking with Mr. Enricht today and he said there was absolutely no truth in the statement that Maxim Munitions had acquired the rights to the mixture."

The next round went to Maxim, whose treasurer said, "I do not think Mr. Enricht was correctly understood. We certainly have the contract."

Thus, men who were considered wise old business heads endowed Enricht with a new mantle of respectability. The staid New York *Times*, which had supplied its share of scoffing, commented in an editorial:

> It looks at least a little as if the wise ones had been somewhat hasty in saying offhand what can and can't be done, and it may be that—not for the first time—they are to be proven wrong by an inventor whose pretensions they had loftily ridiculed.

Henry Ford, now furious, sued to recover his automobile. Then, probably on strong advice, he suddenly dropped from the scene to run (unsuccessfully) for the United States Senate and dream of becoming President. So ownership of Enricht's formula seemed settled—except that nothing remained settled for long in this bizarre story.

Maxim Munitions, in the kind of action that drives newspapermen to drink, pulled in its horns after the price of its stock had doubled and denied it had made any deal with Enricht. Hudson Maxim, the firm's consulting engineer, said in a letter to the *Times*, "Why, I haven't even met Enricht."

Although the statement sounded definite enough, it was heavily discounted in light of the signs of wealth that suddenly sprouted all over Enricht's Farmingdale property. There the old man had begun work on a laboratory and ordered architect's plans for a new home. He said he would build a large factory of his own, too.

An artist at making diversion as mighty as the sword, he also decided to reveal that he had found a substitute for babbitt metal, the antimony-tin-copper-lead alloy used in motor bearings. His alloy, he said, would have an even stronger antifriction quality than that which Isaac Babbitt had devised, and it would be 75 percent cheaper. As reporters scribbled furiously, Enricht dropped in the additional revelation that he was experimenting with a revolutionary new method of extracting nitrogen from the air for use in explosives and fertilizers. The old man was never at a loss for inventions.

Now, however, no one laughed out loud. Those who took exception to his freewheeling mental processes kept their own counsel. But since there were few developments to keep the Enricht story humming, he gradually slipped out of the newspaper columns. The supposition was that he was perfecting his gasoline discovery. Then the United States entered World War I and eight months later, the day after Thanksgiving, 1917, his name bounced back onto the front pages.

Railroad financier Benjamin Yoakum made the big news this time. He revealed that the Maxim firm's little-heeded disclaimer *had* been true. Maxim had not acquired rights to Enricht's formula. The man who had supplied the inventor with his new wealth was Yoakum himself. He had closed a deal on April 12, 1917, six days after the United States had entered the war. He and Enricht now controlled a firm known as the National Motor Power Company, which was to produce auto fuel from the famous Enricht formula.

But that was only a prelude to a shocking charge that Yoakum made public. In Nassau County Supreme Court, he contended that Enricht was refusing to make his formula available to our government. Furthermore, Yoakum charged, Enricht had dickered with "spies and representatives of the German government" to sell the formula for a million and a half dollars. Thus was joined a second great battle of futility.

The difficulties began, Yoakum explained, when a British Army technical officer made exhaustive tests of Enricht's method, went back to England with a favorable report and returned with authority to buy.

"When the company called on Enricht to go ahead with the work," Yoakum declared, "he confessed he had withheld an essential ingredient from the formula he had given us. He handed us a signed statement in which he asserted he would not go on with the project during the war. So we started an investigation."

Yoakum had put private detectives on Enricht's trail. They reported that he had met secretly with Captain Franz von Papen, who had been the military attaché of the German embassy in Washington until he was expelled by the U.S. State Department (and went on to become one of Hitler's aides). Enricht's meeting took place, the detectives said, while the submarine *Deutschland* was tied up in Baltimore Harbor from July 1 to August 3, 1916.

Naturally, Yoakum was upset. "We have grave fears," he said, "that Enricht has already disclosed his secret to the German government, and that the seeming plentifulness of gasoline in that country is due to the fact that they are manufacturing Enricht's liquid on a large scale." Accordingly, Yoakum asked U.S.

Attorney General Thomas W. Gregory to seize the inventor's papers and plant. Gregory could not act without proof, so now Yoakum wanted the courts to intervene.

And so they did. An injunction restrained Enricht from disposing of his formula and the Nassau County sheriff threw guards around the Farmingdale laboratory. Enricht, who could have been expected to grow nervous under the gravity of such charges, showed instead that he had the situation more in hand than his adversaries. "Absurd," he said quietly, and then offered one of his complex, many-tributaried explanations. He conceded he had met Von Papen, but said they had discussed his "new system of making artificial stone." Von Papen, he said, offered him $10,000. "I laughed at him." To close the matter, Enricht inserted a couple of typical confusions: "I am a patriot. If the government wants my process for extracting nitrogen from the air, it can have it." He also revealed that inflation had increased his costs, and that his penny-a-gallon substitute might have to be sold for as much as four cents.

Yoakum, trying desperately to be heard above this comic-opera noise, stuck with the matter at hand and won a court order to search Enricht's safe-deposit box in the First National Bank of Farmingdale. Nothing was found but 20 Liberty bonds. Enricht said he had burned the formula.

Yoakum was defeated. Since no one had ever held the highly publicized formula but Enricht, no case could be made; there was only hearsay evidence. The railroader took his loss, described by the administrator of his estate as substantial, and went on to invest in a scheme to extract more gasoline from crude oil with a special furnace. Like Enricht, the furnace burned him financially.

As for the United States government, which was presumably deprived of a secret weapon, it chose to let the affair fade away and to muddle through the war without Enricht's formula.

That might have been the end of the green-magic gasoline swindle, but it was by no means the end of swindler Louis Enricht's capers. With monumental casualness he retreated into a $20,000 home, which in those days was a good bit of home, and planned new enterprises.

Now 72 years old, Enricht proved he was incorrigible. He closed 1920 by seeking a patent on yet another wondrous invention—a process for making gasoline of peat. "I can get 460 gallons out of one ton of common peat," he asserted. Patent Office technicians turned him down on grounds that his scheme was contrary to all known laws of chemistry, but such timidity failed to discourage the indomitable fellow. He went right on making gasoline out of peat, or in any event saying he was, through a stock firm known as the Enricht Peat Gasoline Corporation. Fresh investors, believe it or not, rushed in where chemists feared to tread, and brought over $40,000 with them. Enricht proceeded to build what he called a gasoline manufacturing plant, five miles south of Farmingdale.

This venture inevitably led to the creaky old man's indictment a year later for grand larceny. Specifically, he was charged with using investors' checks for personal purposes, but that did not keep him from bailing himself out with a $2000 check made out to the firm. He explained that he would give the company some stock in return. In October 1922, when he came to trial in Nassau County's rambling, high-domed Old Courthouse, Justice Lewis J. Smith became entranced with the scientific aspects of the case and asked him if he could really make gasoline out of peat.

"Certainly," the unquenchable one replied. "I will demonstrate the machine in court."

The following afternoon he arrived with a machine and a load of peat. A fascinated crowd gawked as he worked from two to five o'clock in the afternoon setting up the contraption. When it was assembled, he dropped several handfuls of peat in, added a few pails of water, ignited a blowtorch and waved it at a bailiff, then lit the peat. Court attendants worked a suction pump and a compressor until they were exhausted, but no gasoline flowed. Enricht explained that the compressor was leaking and said he would renew his demonstration the next afternoon.

Justice Smith, patient but only human, said no. Then a Patent

Office official threw cold water on the peat theory, and another witness testified that the only gasoline Enricht's machine produced came from an underground tank and a hose. The jury found him guilty of larceny.

Justice Smith, who could have imposed a lengthy sentence, gave the doddering old fellow five to nine years unless he repaid the investors. Enricht said he would, by selling the 20,000 acres of land he owned in Georgia. Four months later he was back, having failed to repay a cent. On February 28, 1923, Justice Smith re-sentenced him to three to seven years and committed him to Sing Sing the same day.

In recent years, a court clerk, who was 21 at the time, recalled Enricht as a pathetic frame of a man standing for the last time before the bench. His trademark mustache had grown so long it was part of his beard. His eyes were cloudy and he seemed not to comprehend all that was taking place.

A year and 18 days later, Governor Alfred E. Smith was moved to commute Enricht's sentence to time served. In April 1924, at the age of 78, Sing Sing prisoner No. 74699 was paroled to return to Farmingdale a broken man, stripped of his arcane pretenses. But Louis Enricht, when he died shortly afterward, took one secret to his grave. No one has ever proved how he hoodwinked the reporters and publisher Haskell back in April 1916.

One explanation, however, seems logical to the point of certainty. It was offered by Thomas Alva Edison's chief engineer, Dr. Miller Reese Hutchinson, who told of a similar "invention" in which water was mixed with acetone, a volatile, inflammable liquid then used in smokeless gunpowder. The scientist duplicated this mixture, took it to the Brooklyn Navy Yard and ran an engine with the stuff.

"But isn't that a substitute for gasoline after all?" Dr. Hutchinson was asked by a reporter.

"Why, yes," he said, "but you should have seen the cylinders when our experiment was over. The engine was corroded out of commission. You see, the water was merely a vehicle to get the explosive into the cylinders. It was as if a man took the ashes from his furnace and saturated them with oil. They would burn, but then the ashes would be left as before and unless you put in some more oil, you could not get another fire out of them."

If that disposes of Enricht's chemical legerdemain, it does not destroy the fact that he was a talented man with an exceptionally selective mind. Starting out as he did with no scientific education, Louis Enricht learned how to absorb exactly what technical data he would need and to repel all information that would only clutter his mind.

The narrowness of this kind of knowledge made it impossible for Enricht to debate the validity of his so-called formulas with genuine scientists, but he understood that this kind of discussion would rarely be necessary. Instead, he counted on the public to accept his likely tale as reality.

And people did.

⟨∽∾⟩

AN OILMAN in Texas, needing funds to drill a well, advertised for 1000 investors with $100 each. He guaranteed unconditionally that they would get back their original investment in ten years, and if the well "came in" they would, of course, share in the profits. Within a few days the oilman had received the $100,000 through the mails. Postal authorities watched the transaction with dubious eyes and quietly began to investigate.

They found no basis for complaint. Upon receipt of the money the oilman sent each of the investors a $100 Savings Bond which would mature in ten years. Having spent $75,000 for the bonds, he had $25,000 in cash with which to operate, and the well was drilled.   —*Edward Verdier*

TRAVELING a deserted road in Montana, a salesman ran out of gas 40 miles from the nearest gas station. He was dismayed until he noticed the phone lines along the road, and remembered an AT&T ad which stated that, if a break occurred anywhere in their wires, troubleshooters were rushed out instantly to make repairs. The salesman drew his revolver, shot two wires apart and sat down to wait. A repair truck arrived within an hour. The salesman got his gas.

He was a fine highwayman, but
he kept falling off his horse

HORSE PLAY

by Eugene B. Block

Ff Dick Fellows were to come
before a court today, a judge would order him to undergo intensive psychiatric observation. Complex, ego or just plain foolhardi-
ness—whatever it may have been—gave him a strange assurance
that he was a competent horseman despite recurring proof to the
contrary. Ignoring one unfortunate equine experience after another, he persisted in trying to be a mounted road agent. Horses
seemed to recognize Dick and apparently found satisfaction in
throwing him, either on his way to hold up stages or fleeing the
clutches of the law. They showed their disdain for him even when
he tried to steal them. Ironically, too, he purportedly came from
a horsey Kentucky family.

There is little known of Dick Fellows' early life. He was not born
Dick Fellows, though he preferred to be known by that name. At
times he called himself Richard Perkins; at others he used his true
name, George Bret Lytle, especially when he posed as a professor
of languages. Legend credits him with having been a Harvard
graduate, but there is no evidence that he ever attended that university or, for that matter, any other. Nor is there proof that he

ever was a linguist, and some insist he had only a superficial knowledge of Spanish. Others attest to his unusual familiarity with classic literature. What he may have lacked in education he made up for in manner, appearance and, above all, a glib tongue. He was short but well proportioned and muscular; his features were good, though partly obscured by a thick, black beard sometimes described as curly. He had a rare sense of humor and, according to one writer, he could not take a purse without jesting.

Fellows was an "extraordinary character" in the opinion of James B. Hume, the chief detective of Wells, Fargo, who once paid Dick this questionable tribute in a published interview with a writer for the San Francisco *Examiner*:

> For daring he is the equal of any outlaw with whom I have ever had dealings. His nerve, morally and physically, is superb. His resource in hours of peril is apparently inexhaustible and his ability, natural and acquired, would have made him as great in any honest profession he might have chosen as it has in that to which he devoted his energy, his talent and his wit.

Dick Fellows' first stage robbery occurred late in 1869. He waylaid a stagecoach outside of Santa Barbara and fled with considerable plunder. But he was quickly captured, found guilty and sentenced to San Quentin on January 31, 1870. He was then 24 years of age.

Inside the walls his glib tongue served him well. He had no difficulty in convincing the experienced officials of his academic training, and they soon assigned him to the prison library, a job that prisoners regard as "gravy."

Before long he was lecturing to the felons, discussing world history, literature and other subjects. He even organized a Bible class, in which he often deviated from reading Scripture to moralize on ethics and human virtues. So ardently did he plead the cause of honesty and upright living that prison authorities came to look upon him as an example of effective rehabilitation, and Governor Newton Booth pardoned him on April 4, 1874. He had served about half of his sentence.

At the gates of San Quentin, Dick met newspapermen and told them that he was through with crime. He may have meant it, but his good intentions—if he ever had them—soon were shattered.

A year had passed when Detective Hume, with a keen nose for discharged stage robbers, learned that Fellows had been seen about the town of Caliente below the Tehachapi Mountains. It was a busy period at Caliente, for the Southern Pacific was cutting through the rocky slopes to extend its line from San Francisco south past Caliente. Passengers and freight in the interim were being transferred to stages for the long, hot ride to Los Angeles.

Hume might not have been so concerned over the report on Fellows had it not been that the railroad was preparing to send an extraordinarily large shipment of gold coin over this route. A Los Angeles bank had been in difficulty, and the express company had been called on to transfer $240,000 from San Francisco to the southern California city to relieve the situation.

It was the detective's job to see that the money was transported safely. Because of the heavy construction work under way at Caliente, large numbers of laborers had been brought into the town, and there were questionable characters among them, even some former convicts. Dick Fellows' presence gave Hume cause for added worry.

On December 3, Wells, Fargo directed Hume to meet the train which would arrive at Caliente at seven o'clock of the following morning, guard the transfer of the fortune to a waiting stage and ride with it to its destination. Detective Hume was at the station when the train arrived.

On board was S. D. Barstow of Wells, Fargo and Chief of Police Jerome Meyers of Stockton. They had sat together in the baggage car with the treasure and intended to accompany Hume on the second part of the trip.

The gold coin, in three boxes, was transferred to the inside of the stage, with the two officers, both well armed, sitting close by, while Hume took a place on the driver's seat. With two shotguns and two rifles at his side, he felt ready for any trouble. Actually, he was somewhat uneasy because he had observed Dick Fellows and a stranger watching closely as the gold was being moved, but he doubted that the two or anyone else about the town knew what was in the heavy cases.

Dick had heard rumors of a contemplated gold shipment of unusual proportion but knew little else. However, as he recognized Hume and saw his attention fixed on men carrying heavy chests, he readily surmised what was going on, and he conceived a plot. He and his companion would gallop ahead of the stage and intercept it on a secluded stretch of roadway. There was only one minor difficulty. He had no horse, though his friend owned a fast and trusted animal.

Dick hurried to a nearby stable to rent a mount and join his partner at a designated spot outside of town. He had no difficulty in accomplishing his purpose, although he was then unaware that horses were to be his nemesis. This was his initial experience in a Western saddle.

He rode proudly out of Caliente—but not for long. In less than two miles, his horse suddenly reared without apparent provocation. Rolling in the dust, the stunned rider looked up in time to see the animal galloping back toward town.

A short time elapsed before Dick regained his senses, realized his predicament and felt a stinging blow to his pride. His companion, waiting at the rendezvous, would conclude that he had turned back through fear. They might never meet again, and there would be no opportunity for explanations.

Fellows walked back to Caliente, meanwhile forming a new plan. He knew that a stage coming the other way—from Los Angeles—was due in Caliente that evening. If he waylaid it alone, certainly he could prove his courage, and his pride would be fully vindicated—to himself at least.

But first Fellows had to find another horse. His experience of a few hours earlier was no deterrent.

He saw a saddled horse hitched to a post in front of a nearby store, quickly untethered the animal, mounted it and started off. This time all was going well. He had not traveled far on the dusty road when he observed the approaching northbound stage.

Taking a position by the roadside, he waited until the stage drew near. Then, darting out, he drew his gun and shouted the usual command to "throw down the box."

The order from Fellows was promptly obeyed by the driver, and Dick, not wanting to strain his luck by robbing passengers, motioned him to proceed.

As soon as the stage was on its way, Dick, flushed with a feeling of success, jumped from the saddle to ransack the treasure chest. He was chagrined, however, when he realized that he had brought nothing with which to open the locked box.

The highwayman figured he must not be seen on the highway with his prize. He decided to lift the chest onto the saddle, get on his mount and ride with the box to some secluded spot where he could try leisurely to smash it with rocks or, if necessary, bury it until he could return with tools.

He had raised the heavy box and was trying, in a bungling sort of way, to slide it onto the saddle when he inadvertently jabbed a corner into the horse's ribs. The animal reared and started off, and the strongbox dropped to the ground. Again Dick was a victim of equine revolt.

Dick looked about, observed that railroad workers had been boring for tunnels close by, and the high mounds of earth and rock would provide safe hiding until morning. Lifting the bulky express box to his shoulders, he started off over dark and unfamiliar paths. But he had traveled only a short distance when he plunged headlong over a precipice, landing 18 feet below in an excavation approaching a tunnel.

When he regained consciousness, he was in agony. He took stock of his injuries and discovered that his left leg was broken

above the ankle. The box had landed on his foot, mangling it badly. Fellows, however, was not one to give up. He resolved to make a successful getaway with his plunder.

His first step was to turn over on his hands and knees and push the box ahead at arm's length until he had reached the mouth of the excavation. Sitting up, he looked about and saw that far below were the banks of Tehachapi Creek, lined with the tents of Chinese laborers. Dragging himself still farther and shoving the box ahead, he reached a thicket only a few feet from the creek bed. He was now near exhaustion and in severe pain. The cool water relieved his thirst, and he crawled to a nearby tent where he found an axe. Now, finally, he opened the express box and counted from it $1800 in gold coin.

After stuffing his pockets, he concealed the box and the remainder of the money. His bowie knife was still in his belt, and with it he cut forked willows which he was able to use for crutches. With these, he made his way to another part of the camp and bought food with his stolen coin.

He remained secluded until early evening when he hobbled to a nearby road and headed for a farmhouse in the distance. What he wanted most was another horse, and by now he was ready to press his luck still further.

Fellows sighted a mare staked out in a field, and before long he was once more a mounted man, though he little realized that his ill fortune was destined to continue.

In the morning the horse's owner, a farmer named Fountain, discovered his loss and notified the sheriff, setting in motion a chain of events which proved again that Dick Fellows and horses were not meant for each other.

When Detective Hume, in Los Angeles, received word of the stage holdup, he started back for Caliente, accompanied by Chief Meyers. They had successfully fulfilled their mission in getting the heavy load of gold safely to the southern bank. Hume and the police chief rode to the scene of the holdup and began searching the area for evidence. What followed was a rare occurrence, one that undoubtedly would come only in a case involving Dick Fellows and a horse.

The officers were scrutinizing the countryside when they saw a young boy riding toward them, his gaze fixed closely on the ground. "Looking for something?" Hume inquired.

"I am, sir," the youth replied, introducing himself as Tom Fountain. "A man stole one of our horses off my father's farm last night."

"And what do you expect to find looking at the ground?" the detective asked curiously. "Hoofprints, perhaps?"

"That's just it," the lad exclaimed. "This horse should be easy to find. You see, she lost a shoe a few days ago, and my father shod her with a mule shoe until he had time to go to the blacksmith's. I just thought maybe I could find some prints—a horseshoe and a mule shoe together, you know, are something you don't run into every day."

The detective told young Fountain to resume his search and report to him if he met with any luck. As for Hume and Meyers, they were deeply absorbed in the hunt for a mounted stage robber and far too busy at this time to be concerned with Tom Fountain's troubles.

After several days, Tom found the hoofprints for which he had been looking. Hastening to Bakersfield, he notified the sheriff and Hume, and all rode back to the place where the tracks had been discovered. They were not long in capturing Dick Fellows, who was found hiding in a barn. The mare with the mule shoe on one hoof was grazing close by.

Dick was searched and, though more than $1000 was taken from his pockets, he denied all knowledge of the stage robbery, admitting only that he had stolen the horse. After a few days, however, Dick confessed. He even described the spot where he had hidden the box containing the balance of his booty, but a search for it was futile.

Some time elapsed before Dick's broken leg and injured foot had healed sufficiently to permit his appearance in court. He pleaded guilty but again brought his persuasive powers into play. His touching appeal for clemency, in which he emphasized the futility of crime, so moved the judge that Dick escaped with a sentence of only eight years at San Quentin. The date of his sentencing was June 8, 1876.

Because there had been rumors that friends might try to rescue him, a guard was posted in front of the Bakersfield jail on the night before his scheduled transfer to the state penitentiary. No one appeared, but in the morning the jailer opened the door of Dick's cell and found it empty, with a large hole in the wall.

His freedom was brief. Still using crutches, he had hobbled to a barn several miles away where he remained for two days while posses, spurred by a reward of $500, searched the countryside. When hunger finally forced him into the open, he stole a horse and was quickly thrown—as might be expected.

On the following day he reached a ranch house where a farmer's sympathetic wife offered to serve him dinner. Dick ate heartily, thanked his hostess profusely and started off. Some hours later her husband returned and was told of the "nice gentleman" who had received their hospitality.

The farmer at once recognized his wife's description of the stranger and knew that she had harbored Fellows. With two neighbors, he hurried to Bakersfield where they found Dick on a street and turned him over to the sheriff.

Back in San Quentin, his fertile mind began searching anew for a scheme that might result in a shortened term. Meanwhile, he again was teaching ethics and morals to the convicts. Good behavior shortened his sentence, and after another five years in San Quentin he was free once more. It was now May 1881.

Dick went directly to Santa Cruz, a popular resort town on the Pacific, and a few days later the local newspaper carried an advertisement announcing that Professor George Bret Lytle had settled there and was ready to teach Spanish to anyone desiring his services.

After a few weeks the advertisement no longer appeared, but

there were front-page headlines reporting the holdup of a stage. A hundred miles from Santa Cruz, a daring bandit, operating alone, had escaped with the express box, which, incidentally, contained only a letter written in Chinese.

Detective Hume heard of the robbery and, after carefully checking a description of the road agent, he concluded that Dick Fellows was back at his old tricks. With one of his most trusted men, Captain Charles Aull, Hume traveled through the area, enlisting the help of local authorities and distributing posters bearing detailed descriptions of the wanted man. Despite their efforts, stage holdups by the same lone bandit continued for months, and in each case it was obvious that Dick was responsible. More men were assigned to the search and at times they were close behind him. Then, a ranch foreman in the little town of Mayfield chanced to see a stranger of Dick's description sleeping in his barn. He summoned a local officer, one Constable Burke, who soon caught the fugitive and had him in handcuffs.

Burke notified Hume of the capture and, following instructions, boarded a train with his prisoner for San Jose, the county seat, where Dick would be held pending decision as to where he would be tried. On the way Dick was thinking fast. He began by complimenting Burke on his astuteness as an officer, telling him that the capture would lead to fast promotion and the approbation of his constituents. The constable, a guileless man, took the flattery at face value; so much so that when they left the train at the San Jose depot, the constable readily accepted Dick's suggestion that they go into a nearby saloon for a farewell drink. It would be his last for many years, Dick said sorrowfully.

The bandit toasted his captor and assured him that he had no hard feelings. As the pair was about to leave, Fellows caught Burke off his guard and struck him a felling blow on the head with his handcuffed wrists. A moment later the prisoner was out of sight.

Thoroughly humiliated, Burke sent word to Hume, who had been waiting at the jail, and a countrywide search soon was under way. Days later Dick narrowly escaped capture when he was found by a Dr. Dunckol in a stable. The glib robber, who by now had freed himself of handcuffs, convinced the physician that he was merely trying to sleep off a hangover. Not until hours later did the doctor realize that he had been duped and reported the incident to the local authorities.

On the following day Chief of Police Haskell of San Jose learned that a man resembling Dick Fellows had been seen near Los Gatos. Hastening to that town with one of his officers, Haskell was informed that a stranger, obviously Dick, had visited a small inn there and had departed only a short time before. That same night Haskell and his aide sighted a lonely cabin on a hillside. While the officer stood by with leveled shotgun, Haskell threw open the door and found Dick sitting leisurely at a table enjoying a meal prepared by an unsuspecting rancher.

Fellows was quickly handcuffed and led away to the San Jose jail where his captors took no chances. This time the prisoner was held under heavy guard for several days until his removal to Santa Barbara for trial. Dick was sentenced to life imprisonment in Folsom Penitentiary, and he lost no time confiding to his guards that he was resigned to his punishment, that he realized at last the futility of trying to evade the law.

His jailers again relaxed their watchfulness, as Dick had anticipated. On the morning of April 2, 1882, only a day before he was to go to the penitentiary, a turnkey stepped into his cell with a breakfast tray. Dick knocked the officer to the floor and fled with his gun. Moments later Dick again came face to face with his nemesis—the horse.

The animal was nibbling grass in a lot close to the jail. Dick did not stop to ponder his previous experiences but leaped on the back of the unsaddled animal. And once more his strange incompatibility with horseflesh became apparent. Dick had ridden only a short distance when his mount suddenly collapsed, rolling over the ground in a fit. What Dick did not know was that the animal had been chewing locoweed and had been staked out by its owner to recover.

Stunned by his fall, the ill-fated robber was still trying to get to his feet when officers from the jail were upon him and his brief span of liberty was over.

That same day he was on his way to the state prison, but not before dashing off a letter to the editor of the Santa Barbara *Press* which has been preserved in the voluminous records kept by Detective Hume:

To the Editor
Santa Barbara Press
Dear Sir:

I have just noticed your article of this date in reference to my recent attempt to escape and also your editorial in regard to my fast career entitled "It Don't Pay." After thanking you for your kindly notice, I have to say that both are in the main correct and I most heartily concur in what you have to say in the last-named article and would only add that the same may be said of any unlawful calling no matter what the provocation.

My unfortunate experience has thrown me into this society of thousands of lawbreakers from every clime and all walks of life and, in every instance, the result is the same and it is the same sad story. It don't pay in any sense. I have learned that the boat will leave in a few minutes and I bid you and the people of Santa Barbara good-bye.

Dick Fellows

Thirty-three years had passed since the writing of this letter when a gray-haired man, somewhat stooped, walked into the office of the sheriff in Santa Barbara. It was 1915, the year that California was playing host to the world, for the Panama-Pacific International Exposition was under way in San Francisco.

"Is Judge Smith still alive?" the visitor inquired. "I was once a friend of his."

"And your name?" the sheriff inquired.

The other man smiled. "I was once known in this county as Dick Fellows."

The two shook hands warmly, and the sheriff asked his caller if he was employed.

"I am," said Dick Fellows proudly. "I'm in charge of the Kentucky state exhibit at the Panama-Pacific Exposition."

⌒⚬⌒

A LITTLE GIRL wandered into a bank vault in Galena, Illinois, about closing time. The vault door was shut, the time lock went on—and reporters were rushed down to cover the story.

Time locks in those days could be picked from the outside, and Walter Howey, managing editor of the Chicago *Herald-Examiner*, knew it. He called the warden of the penitentiary at Joliet and asked, "Do you have any good safecrackers?"

The warden answered with a good deal of professional pride, "Certainly, the very best."

Howey identified himself, then went on, "I want you to rush four of your best ones to Galena. There's a little girl locked up in a bank vault. She'll be suffocated by morning."

"You'll have to get permission from the Governor."

"You'll do as I say or I'll have the Governor throw you out on your tail," answered Howey sweetly. Then he phoned the president of the railroad, hired a private car, had it loaded with Joliet's best Jimmy Valentines and with his own star reporters and photographers, and sent it roaring into Galena.

When Howey's safecrackers opened the vault there was no little girl in it. She was found at a friend's house. Any other editor would have been ruined, but not Howey. He played up the story on his front page: how the Governor released the safecrackers; how these hardened criminals wept like babies as they worked feverishly to liberate the child; and when the little girl was not there, how they fell down on their knees and gave thanks. Across the page was Howey's big black headline: HUMANITY IS A WONDERFUL THING. His coup was a sensation.   —*J. P. McEvoy, in Cosmopolitan*

WHEN A masked man entered the Western National Bank in Casper, Wyoming, and demanded money, the bank's newest cashier had a ready answer. "Don't bother me," she replied. "I'm just a beginner."   —*UPI*

*The Soviet Boss was only too happy to take
the treasure for "safekeeping"*

HOW STALIN
RELIEVED SPAIN OF $600 MILLION

by Alexander Orlov

There was still a glimmer of light that evening when I drove out of Cartagena, a seaport on the southeastern coast of Spain. Beside me in the car, unable to hide his nervousness, sat a high official of the Spanish Treasury. Behind us rolled a column of 20 five-ton trucks. Our destination lay in the hills four or five miles to the north: a Spanish naval munitions dump. But we were after something more important than shells and gunpowder.

By the time our convoy came to a halt, night had fallen. Not until we alighted did I notice the series of heavy doors, braced with iron bars, set into the hillside and guarded by military men. A guard drew the massive bolts and swung open a double door.

We peered into a spacious cave, dimly lit by several electric bulbs. Inside, awaiting our orders, stood 60 Spanish sailors. And stacked high against the walls were thousands of identical wooden boxes. The crates held gold ingots and coins—hundreds of millions of dollars' worth! Here was the treasure of an ancient nation, accumulated through the centuries. This was what I had come for. My job was to get it to Moscow.

This event at the cave took place in 1936, in the early months of the Spanish Civil War. I had been organizing "Operation Gold" in minute detail for ten days. Certain Republican leaders, fearing that their national gold reserves might fall into the hands of Generalissimo Francisco Franco's attacking Nationalists, had decided to entrust the treasure for "safekeeping" to Joseph Stalin. Though authorized (with doubtful legality) by these Republican leaders, the transaction may represent the biggest single act of plunder in history.

The transfer to Soviet Russia of the bulk of the Spanish gold reserves—at least $600 million of it, I estimated—has been the subject of rumor and surmise for three decades. Of the handful of men who were involved in the inception of the enterprise, only two are still alive—one Spaniard and me.

I had arrived in Madrid on September 16, 1936, about two months after the outbreak of the Spanish Civil War, to head a large Soviet mission of intelligence and military experts. As a general in the Intelligence Service (NKVD), I was chief Soviet adviser to the Republican government on intelligence, counter-intelligence and guerrilla warfare, a post I was to hold for nearly two years. Like all the Russians in Spain, I was passionately devoted to the Republican cause.

We set up shop on the top floor of the Soviet embassy in Madrid, with powerful radio equipment at our disposal. I had been there less than a month when my code clerk came into my office with the code book under his arm and a radiogram in his hands. "Just in from Moscow," he said, "and here are the first lines: 'Absolutely secret. This must be decoded by Schwed personally.'"

Schwed was my code name. I deciphered the rest of the message. After an introductory note from Nikolai Yezhov, head of the NKVD, it read: "Arrange with Prime Minister Largo Caballero for shipment of the gold reserves of Spain to the Soviet Union. Use a Soviet steamer. Maintain utmost secrecy. If the Spaniards demand a receipt, refuse—I repeat, refuse. Say that a formal receipt will be issued in Moscow by the State Bank. I hold you personally responsible for the operation. (Signed) Ivan Vasilyevich." The signature was the rarely used code name for Joseph Stalin himself.

Could it really be that Largo Caballero and his colleagues—honest, patriotic Spaniards—would consent to put their country's gold in Stalin's hands? Could they suppose that the Kremlin, which held "bourgeois" morality and law in contempt, would ever relinquish such wealth? My inquiries showed that the answer was yes. In fact, the idea of "protecting" the gold reserves from Nationalist capture by sending them to Russia had originated with the harried Republican leaders themselves!

The Nationalists were tightening a noose around Madrid, and the city's fall seemed imminent. Transfer of the gold and silver from the Bank of Spain vaults was ordered in a secret decree of September 13, signed by President Manuel Azaña and Finance Minister Dr. Juan Negrín. This decree empowered the Finance Minister to transport the precious metal from Madrid "to the place which in his opinion offers the best security." It provided that "in due time" the transfer would be regularized by submission to members of the Cortes (the parliament of Spain). This, however, was never done.

Whatever the legality of the decree, it surely did not contemplate shipment of the treasure outside the country. But as the military situation deteriorated, Negrín, in desperation, stretched his authority. With the knowledge of only the President and the Prime Minister, he sounded out our Soviet trade attaché about storing the gold in Russia. The envoy cabled Moscow, and Stalin leaped at the opportunity.

Two days after receiving Stalin's orders, I conferred with Negrín at our embassy. A physiology professor and a newcomer to government, the Finance Minister seemed the very prototype of the intellectual—opposed to Communism in theory, yet vaguely sympathetic to the "great experiment" in Russia. This political naïveté helps explain his impulse to export the gold to that country. Besides, with Hitler and Mussolini supporting the Nationalists, and the democracies standing aloof, Russia was an ally, the one great power helping the Spanish Republicans.

"Where are the gold reserves now?" I asked.

"At Cartagena," Negrín replied, "in one of the old caves used by the navy to store munitions."

Stalin luck again, I thought excitedly. My problem was immensely simplified by the fact that the cargo was already in Cartagena. That capacious harbor was where Soviet ships were unloading arms and supplies. So not only the ships but also trustworthy Soviet manpower were within easy reach.

One more Spanish official had to be taken into confidence: Indalecio Prieto, Minister of the Navy and Air Force. We would need his warships to escort the shipment across the Mediterranean to Odessa on the Black Sea. When consulted, he agreed to give the necessary orders.

Speed was imperative. Even a rumor would expose our ships to interception by either Italy or Germany. More important, the temper of the Spanish people was such that, if it leaked out that so much of the nation's treasure was being sent abroad—and to Communist Russia!—the whole operation, and the operators, would be killed.

On Negrín's instructions, a high Treasury official gave me details about the gold and its storage. There were about 10,000 boxes, measuring 12 by 19 by 7 inches. Each contained 145 pounds of gold—altogether some 725 tons.

Next day I drove to Cartagena. Our naval attaché there was my old friend Nikolai Kuznetzov (who during World War II became the Soviet Minister of the Navy). I instructed him to commandeer all Soviet vessels reaching Cartagena, to unload them with the utmost speed and to place them under my authority. One Soviet freighter was in port; others were expected. We also conferred with the Spanish commander of the navy base. He put 60 sailors at my disposal. I then turned to the problem of transporting the gold from the cave to the piers. A Soviet tank brigade had disembarked in Cartagena two weeks earlier and was now stationed in

Archena, 40 miles away. It was commanded by Colonel S. Krivoshein, known to the Spanish as Melé. Krivoshein assigned to me 20 of his army trucks and as many of his best tank drivers.

Finally all was in readiness. My trucks were parked at the railway station in Cartagena, each with a Soviet tankman at the wheel dressed in a Spanish army uniform. The 60 Spanish sailors had been sent to the cave an hour or two in advance. The crews of four Soviet ships, down to cooks and mess boys, were alerted to expect several nights of loading important cargo. And so on October 22, in the expiring twilight, I drove to the munitions dump, the cavalcade of trucks behind me.

The Spanish sailors, all from the submarine fleet, were young men of slight build. It took two of them to carry each crate and hoist it onto a truck. To facilitate the count, I limited each truck to 50 boxes, dispatching ten trucks to the harbor when they were

loaded. By the time they returned, about two hours later, the other ten trucks were ready to depart with another 500 boxes. My car, with myself or another NKVD man and one of the Spanish Treasury men in it, led each convoy.

When the loading was smoothly under way, I finally put to the Treasury official standing beside me the question I had carefully avoided until then: "How much of the gold are we supposed to ship?" So haphazardly had the operation been prepared at the Spanish end that he answered, "Oh, more than half, I suppose." It would be, I said mentally, a lot more.

The loading and transport went on for three nights, from 7 p.m. until morning. Those nights were moonless and pitch-dark. The town was rigidly blacked out, and we could not use headlights. Sometimes a driver lost sight of the truck ahead of him and part of the column got detached. I had several big scares on this account, for the Russian tankmen, though in Spanish uniforms, spoke not a word of Spanish. What if they were detained by a military patrol and taken for German spies? Civil war justice could be quick and rash. What if the trucks were searched? The news that foreigners were making off with truckloads of gold would touch off political violence. Another hazard was the possibility of German bombing. The adjoining caves were filled with explosives; a direct hit could spell the end for all of us. Or our ships in the harbor might be sunk.

I averaged no more than four hours' sleep a day. Locked into the cave between loadings, the sailors slept, too, sprawled on the floor. We gave them sandwiches, coffee, cold drinks and peanuts. To while away the time, many of them played cards. Ironically, they played for stakes of copper coins and, in some cases, peanuts —surrounded by millions in gold!

Luck was with us until the third and final night. At about 4 a.m. German bombers zoomed over the low range of hills. From the cave, we could hear the thump of bombs hitting the piers. I learned from returning drivers that the Germans had hit a Spanish freighter tied up close to our ships. I decided to wind up the operation and send my ships out of the bay as fast as possible. When the last truck was dispatched that night, I asked the supervising Treasury official for his final figure. "I make it 7800 boxes," he replied, "about three quarters of the gold reserves."

At 10 a.m. on October 25 the last box was put aboard the last ship. An uncomfortable but inevitable moment was upon me—I was asked for a receipt! Avoiding the Treasury man's bloodshot and pathetic eyes, I tried to sound casual. "A receipt? But, *compañero*, I am not authorized to give one. Don't worry, my friend, it will be issued by the State Bank of the Soviet Union when everything is checked and weighed."

The man gasped, thunderstruck. He could scarcely muster coherent words. He didn't understand. . . . It might mean his life in these times. . . . Should he call Madrid?

I decidedly did not want him to spread alarm by telephoning.

Instead, I suggested that he send a Treasury representative on each of the four ships as official chaperon of the gold. In the light of cold logic this concession meant nothing. But the distraught man grasped at it, and two hours later the ships sailed. I was able to report to Moscow that the precious cargo was heading for Odessa.

Later, from intelligence officials coming and going between Russia and Spain, I was able to piece together the Soviet end of the gold operation.

A large number of high NKVD officers from Moscow and Kiev had converged on Odessa. There for a number of nights they served as stevedores, unloading the gold and carrying the boxes to a special train. A large area from the docks to the railroad tracks had been cordoned off by special troops. When the train left for Moscow, hundreds of armed officers accompanied the shipment, as if crossing enemy territory.

The night after the cargo reached Moscow, Stalin threw a lavish party for the top NKVD brass to celebrate the coup. The whole Politburo was present. The dictator was in high spirits. What an achievement for a man who had begun his political career by organizing bank robberies for the cause! NKVD Chief Yezhov quoted to a friend of mine Stalin's gleeful words: "They will never see their gold again, just as they do not see their own ears!"

In the 21 months between "Operation Gold" and my defection from the Soviet regime, I was in constant touch with the Spanish Republican leaders, but the affair remained an unspoken and painful secret between us. I was certain that their action had begun to look to them like a monumental blunder. The only time the subject was mentioned was in the course of a talk with Negrín, who was by then Prime Minister. "Remember those four Treasury men who were put on your ships?" he asked. "They are still in Russia, and it's now over a year. I wonder why the poor fellows are not allowed to go home."

The four unfortunates, I discovered long afterward, were permitted to depart only at the end of the Spanish war.

Franco must have learned about the missing gold as soon as he took Madrid. But not a word was said about it by his government for almost 18 years. The Spanish currency, already weak, would have surely collapsed if it had become known that the national coffers were nearly empty. The official silence was broken in December 1956, after the death of Dr. Juan Negrín. From among his private papers, the Spanish Foreign Office asserted, it had finally retrieved an official receipt for gold deposited in the Soviet Union. A few months later, a typically ironic article in the official Soviet paper *Pravda* admitted that some 500 tons of gold had indeed been received in 1936 and a receipt issued by the Soviet government. The gold, it went on, was to guarantee payment for Soviet planes, arms and other goods delivered to the Spanish Republic. Not only had it all been spent, but a balance of $50 million was owed to Soviet Russia!

There the matter still rests.

THE UPSWEPT bristles of Major Michael Woodfall's military mustache alone were enough to command the respect of the stoniest of Mayfair's headwaiters. Then there were his Savile Row suits, his DSO, his Military Cross and the verve with which he followed the hounds.

Junoesque Barbara Sweiland, among other attractive women, found the Major's gallantry well-nigh irresistible. Signed on as his private secretary, Barbara spent many a happy hour in the Major's company, dropping in at supper clubs at night, driving through the countryside by day. Inevitably, he proposed, and they visited a London jeweler to purchase wedding gifts, £6800 worth, for which the Major paid immediately by check. The following day the check bounced, and Miss Sweiland was left alone and forlorn.

The police tracked Major Michael Woodfall, better known to them as Champagne Charlie, to a fashionable Irish country house where he was staying as a weekend guest, and once more wearily turned him over to London's Old Bailey for trial. In a lifetime of high living, 35-year-old Charlie had suavely separated hundreds of impressionable Britons, mostly women, from thousands of pounds. Born to middle-class respectability, he had spent a third of his life in jail and only nine months in the army. His sole decoration was a dishonorable discharge.

—*Time*

At the time it was a nightmare;
afterward, a fantastic dream

VOYAGE OF THE INNOCENT PIRATES

by Evan McLeod Wylie

The lean, hard-muscled figure with the mustache and the dazzling smile held his two companions in the Chicago bar spellbound. He talked casually of years of voyaging to East African ports, of jungle safaris, of trading in contraband. "If a man has the guts," he remarked with a faraway look in his eye, "he can make a fortune."

His companions, John Fernandez and Marty Rosen, salesmen for an awning company, were bowled over. Fernandez, 37, was garrulous and friendly. Rosen, 40, was small and round. Both led casual lives. Neither had domestic ties. Now, in June of 1957, as they listened to this adventurer who said his name was Joseph Schmitz, he seemed "the most fascinating guy we were ever going to meet."

Schmitz held a master mariner's license, he said, and was planning a cruise to Africa. All along the Dark Continent's coastline, from Zanzibar to the Limpopo River, were countless jungle coves and isolated native villages. With a small schooner one might rendezvous with Portuguese and Arab traders who handled contraband gems.

These illicit jewels could be carried north to Cairo or Casablanca and sold at staggering profits. Schmitz had been corresponding with New York yacht brokers about a 52-foot boat named the *Tashabog* that fitted his specifications.

Fernandez and Rosen were beside themselves with excitement. "When are you leaving?" they asked Schmitz.

The adventurer shrugged. "Not until next year. It will take me that long to save the money to buy my schooner."

"Next *year!*" cried Rosen. "Let's go now! We'll put in with you, as partners."

Schmitz appeared to deliberate for a long time. Then suddenly he stuck out his hand with a flourish. "It's a deal," he said. "We'll sail in August."

Neither Fernandez nor Rosen had ever been in anything bigger than a canoe, but Schmitz reassured them. Steering a yacht, he said, was just like driving a car. Rosen and Fernandez applied for passports and descended on sporting-goods stores to buy yachting caps and jungle equipment, including elephant guns. At Schmitz's suggestion they kept their plans secret, and early in August they drove to New York in Schmitz's car. (The two salesmen had sold theirs to help finance the expedition.) There Rosen and Fernandez got their first good look at a real yacht. It seemed "damned small" to them, but the *Tashabog* would have delighted any yachtsman. The stoutly constructed schooner had three suits of sails and an auxiliary engine. Below deck was a spacious saloon furnished with beige carpets and easy chairs.

While Fernandez and Rosen waited anxiously on deck, Schmitz retired to the saloon with the owner, a New York advertising executive. A few minutes later Schmitz announced that he and the owner had reached an "agreement."

It was not until months later that the two salesmen learned that the contract called only for a ten-day charter on Long Island Sound. The *Tashabog*'s sails were in no way fit for ocean voyaging, the owner had warned. Under no circumstances should she be taken out on the high seas.

The following day the *Tashabog* slipped down the East River on a strong ebb tide. That night, in a sheltered anchorage, the yacht's name and registration numbers were painted out. In the early hours of August 14—in a season when hurricanes begin to build up in the South Atlantic—Schmitz and his hapless assistants set sail for Africa.

New York's skyline had scarcely slid below the horizon before Rosen and Fernandez, stumbling about the *Tashabog*'s rolling deck, handling lines and setting sails, found that Schmitz's earlier assurances about yachtsmanship were not based on fact. "To turn one of these schooners around," Fernandez said later, "is a big operation—everybody jerking on the ropes and the captain making with the yacht lingo and all the time a big boom flying around that is liable to whack your head off."

Fernandez and Rosen finally went below to nurse barked shins and blistered palms and refresh themselves with beer before stowing away the baggage and foodstuffs. Before long they became aware of an eerie whining in the rigging. Suddenly the floor of the saloon rose like an elevator and then plummeted downward with a corkscrew motion that sent both men sprawling. An explosion above served notice that a sail had blown out, and immediately everything about them was rolling, banging and crashing. Scrambling on deck, they beheld Schmitz fighting the wheel in a screeching squall.

As the squall developed into a full-fledged storm, the *Tashabog* staggered through waves so mountainous that Schmitz, ordering his crew to stay below, lashed himself to the wheel. One particularly high wave rolled the schooner nearly on her beam ends, whereupon a huge cake of ice, lugged aboard for sunset beer parties, burst like a bomb from the refrigerator and, with nine dozen smashed eggs, melted into a huge omelet of tomatoes, potatoes and cornflakes.

For three days of howling winds and torrential rain, Schmitz remained at the wheel. Fernandez and Rosen took turns creeping out to spoon-feed him from a can of beans. On one such occasion Rosen yelled in his ear that water was bubbling up in the cabin.

Schmitz told them to man the pumps. Unable to start the engine, they began the back-breaking job of pumping by hand. First to go overboard, it was later discovered, was 100 gallons of gasoline. Thanks to fractured fuel lines, this had all leaked into the bilge.

At last the storm died. Schmitz, as enthusiastic as ever despite his ordeal, directed a massive cleanup campaign. Groceries were retrieved and stored. The saloon's carpets were removed, dried and stowed away. The galley was scrubbed until every pot gleamed.

As the days progressed, Rosen and Fernandez gradually learned to hoist canvas without becoming hopelessly entangled. But almost every morning began with a squall which reduced the sails to tatters. The rest of the day was spent patching them together.

Back in New York, the *Tashabog*'s owner, at first only mildly provoked when the yacht did not return on schedule, was soon alarmed enough to notify the Coast Guard. Planes and cutters searched every inlet along the Atlantic coast; finally agents of the U.S. Customs, the Bureau of Narcotics and even the FBI joined in the hunt, but the *Tashabog* was far beyond their reach.

Schmitz, cheerfully consuming sauerkraut for breakfast and dried prunes and peanut butter for lunch, seemed to be having the time of his life. But his companions, unable to get used to such a diet and exhausted by their struggles with the wind-whipped canvas (52-foot schooners normally carry a crew of four or five at sea), were growing weaker and weaker.

Too small to be much help with the heavy sails, Rosen was occasionally allowed to steer. The wake he left was often erratic. One night Schmitz appeared unexpectedly on deck and discovered that either by accident or blind homing instinct Rosen had let the *Tashabog* swing about 180°, so that its bow pointed directly back— toward downtown Chicago. Thereafter Rosen was given duties that kept him below most of the time. He spent so much time sitting around the saloon in wet sneakers, dealing himself losing hands of solitaire, that his ankles and toes began to swell.

Fernandez also suffered from an odd ailment which caused his voice to sound unusually high. He now believes this condition was

brought on by pure terror; he never could get used to the "waves as big as apartment houses coming at you."

Presently a new phenomenon appeared: flat calms. Days passed as the *Tashabog* remained motionless under a broiling sun. "You'd go up on deck," Rosen recalls, "and see the same bean can bobbing right along with you in the same spot it had been when you tossed it overboard two days ago. I found this very demoralizing."

It was easy to see that the end, whatever it might be, was in sight. Drinking water was fast dwindling. The Spam was running out. Water was rising in the bilges, and Fernandez, down 50 pounds, and Rosen, down 30, were becoming too weak to pump it out.

One morning Schmitz assembled the crew and pointed to a certificate he had tacked on the wall. It was a master mariner's license—and Fernandez and Rosen were stupefied to find it was made out to one Chester N. Larson. From now on, they were told, they were to address their leader as Captain Larson. The next day Larson announced that according to his calculations they were within 80 miles, or less than a day's sail, of Madeira. But his crew barely had time to digest this before the *Tashabog* was plunging through the most terrifying storm of the voyage, 1957's Hurricane Carrie, which, only a few hundred miles away, sank the huge four-masted German bark *Pamir*, with a loss of 80 lives.

It was about this time that Rosen began a piteous document dealing with "The Last Days on Earth of Marty Rosen." Excerpts:

Constantly wet. Working 18 hours a day. If I ever come out of this alive, I'll never set foot on a boat again.

Bad storm again! God has never heard three bums pray as loud as we did last night!

Rolling from side to side. Winds 70–90 miles per hour. Going nowhere. Fernandez says let the damn ship sink and get it over with. Larson says no, he will make it or go down with the ship.

Another day, another hurricane. This is the worst mistake two men ever made.

Somehow or other they got through the storm. Finally the tattered, battered yacht lay becalmed in a heavy mist.

In his bunk one morning, semiconscious and expecting the bilge waters to envelop him at any moment, Fernandez heard Larson arguing with Rosen. "I tell you they're right here," the skipper insisted. "My calculations show we ought to see them any minute."

Wondering dimly who "they" were, Fernandez tottered up on deck, prepared, he recalls, to see anything from Congo pygmies to a ferryboat full of Irishmen. Instead, up out of the mists loomed the peaks of a large green island. The *Tashabog*, blown far south of Madeira, had reached the Canaries, 100 miles off the African mainland. The date was October 2; they had been at sea 50 days.

Larson, ordering shaves for all hands, broke out new yachting caps, hastened below to put the carpets back in the saloon and unfurled flags for the triumphant entrance into Santa Cruz harbor. "Five minutes after we dropped anchor," Fernandez recalls, "he was over on somebody else's boat yapping about yachts as if he'd just come back from a Sunday-afternoon spin around the bay."

Larson adapted himself enthusiastically to life in the islands, but he was soon preparing eagerly to get on with the voyage. Rosen rebelled. He told Fernandez that the time had come to make a crucial decision. Even if they did reach Africa, which he doubted, the prospect had lost its luster. The thing to do was to pull out and use whatever funds might be left for passage back to the United States. Fernandez reluctantly agreed. Adventure or no adventure, they told Larson, they had had it.

Larson, affable as ever, declared he was genuinely sorry to hear of their decision, but he would not stand in their way. Much as he would like to give them back some cash, he said, the expedition's treasury was even more depleted than they thought. In fact, he would like to borrow five bucks.

Taken aback by this, the two salesmen deferred their final decision. Then one morning they were presented with a truly ghastly proposal. In the harbor was a tiny ketch bound for California. Its crew, two American aircraft engineers, offered them a ride to the

West Indies. The prospect of starting another ocean crossing in a craft a fraction the size of the *Tashabog* was horrifying, but it was the only solution. They boarded the ketch. As she cleared the harbor, a sudden squall blew out the spinnaker, and Fernandez and Rosen settled down to the familiar routine of pitching decks, and gales springing up from all points of the compass.

Thirty days later, weather-beaten and wasted, they arrived at Barbados. Wobbling ashore, they were delighted to receive a packet of letters forwarded from the Canary Islands. But when they opened the first envelope they were shocked to read, "Why did you steal that yacht? The FBI is looking for you."

Joseph Schmitz, the FBI had learned, was indeed a master mariner named Chester N. Larson. The stories he had told about his seafaring career and his African adventures were substantially correct. But what he had neglected to tell Fernandez and Rosen was that he was on probation from a 20-year suspended sentence imposed by the state of Washington for forging checks. Fernandez and Rosen used their last dollars to fly back to Chicago, where they learned that the FBI was interested only in Larson.

Larson, however, was an elusive quarry. It was nearly a month before the law caught up with him. Brought back to New York for trial, Larson impressed both the prosecuting attorney and the judge. Although he was convicted of theft of the yacht, he had evidently lost none of his charm. The judge canceled the $10,000 fine and sentenced him to only a year and a day, adding, "I think he is a very brave man."

In Chicago, where they became salesmen once again (though not for the awning company), Fernandez and Rosen bore Larson no malice. "He was the greatest," said Fernandez.

And Fernandez never forgot that Larson got him into the supreme romantic adventure of his life. Perched on a stool in the same bar where he first heard Larson's tantalizing plans, he would think back wistfully to those occasional starlit evenings at sea when the skipper gazed up into the heavens and pointed out a constellation which Fernandez named "O'Brien's Belt Buckle."

As holdups go, this
one had creeping paralysis

A VERY, VERY LATE BANK ROBBERY

by Ted Hall

When the Great Bank Robbery was finally over, everyone in Mendham, New Jersey, breathed a deep sigh of relief. Mendham (population 3000) is not used to much excitement, and getting ready for the robbery had kept things stirred up for a year and a half. The butcher store across the street from the bank had been thrown into confusion by false alarms. Eddie Fagan, the school custodian, who lives within sight of the bank, had got good and tired of sitting in the window every Friday night with his carbine in his lap (the bank stays open late Fridays). One of the robbers kept dropping in on the grocery store and the grocer began to worry that maybe *he* was going to be held up. Police Chief Earl Moore had been so busy following the two robbers while they were casing the bank that he had little time for anything else. It really was too much, and everyone was glad when it was over.

Mendham is a pleasant country town, well removed from any main road. It is the kind of place where everybody knows everybody else—and newcomers are noticed the first time they appear and studied closely the second time. So when a pair of strangers showed up one day in March of 1960, parked in front of the Morris County Savings Bank and studied it with obvious appetite, Police

Chief Moore, who was shoveling snow a little way down the street, could not help paying attention.

It happens that in Mendham the bank is not far from the police station, which is located—along with the borough tax office, the local civil-defense organization and the room where the Borough Council and the ladies' garden club meet—in an old white brick Colonial hostelry on Main Street called Phoenix House. So it is not an ideal bank for stickups. When Chief Moore wanted a better look at the two strangers all he had to do was shovel in their direction. As he approached they hastily drove away. He finished shoveling the walk, then went indoors and recorded the incident on a card which he dropped into an unmarked manila folder.

The next day was full of developments. To begin with, Chief Moore got a telephone tip that someone was planning to rob the Mendham bank. The chief typed out this information on a new card and dropped it into the folder. Then he labeled it, "Planned Robbery of Mendham Bank."

Later that day when he was standing on Main Street, a car drew up right in front of him and the two visitors of the previous day asked him for directions to an auto-body repair shop. The chief, startled, told them he had never heard of the place. As they drove off, Moore stepped back into the station and dropped a new card into the folder.

Half an hour later the chief strolled past the Mendham Soda Shop, a few stores down from the bank, and saw one of the men there. He noted that the man had a mustache and a moon-shaped scar above his right eye.

"After that I kept seeing that car, or some other one with the same men in it," says the chief. "It was always where they could see the bank."

Fascinated, Moore sent out tracers on the license numbers and made inquiries among other police departments. In nearby Madison he hit pay dirt. A man there had boasted within earshot of a police officer that the bank at Mendham would be easy to knock off if you first lured the cops away from the center of town.

404

Moore dropped more cards into his folder. By now information was starting to pour in. These were surely the world's gabbiest bank robbers. It seemed that they planned to use a red 1950 Ford sedan for the job. They were going to switch to an old Nash for the getaway; the Nash would be parked on Ironia Road, west of town. The number of men involved appeared to fluctuate, but the ringleaders were two Madisonians named William Redic, an odd-jobs man with a moon-shaped scar over his eye, and Robert Grogan, a Madison candy-store proprietor.

After Moore had amassed all this data there was a lull. For a while the would-be bank robbers stopped showing up in Mendham. The chief was a little unnerved by this—what had gone wrong? Had they found a better bank? But he made good use of the lull. For the first time he passed word around Mendham that a bank robbery would be in the offing. "I kind of confided in the bank manager, the postmaster, storekeepers along Main Street and other interested parties," the chief says. Naturally, there were no *un*interested parties; soon most of Mendham knew.

And then in December of 1960, after a hiatus of nine months, a car pulled up in front of the bank and, much to Chief Moore's satisfaction, William Redic stepped out and entered the bank for the first time.

The Mendham branch of the Morris County Savings Bank is enough to throw any orthodox bank robber off his stride. Instead of being located in the kind of severe brick or stone building that a bank robber feels most at home in, the Mendham bank is in a pleasant 140-year-old shuttered frame house furnished with antique pine and cherry tables. The walls are hung with oil paintings.

This decor seems to have thrown Redic into confusion. At any rate, he acted extremely nervous. That made bank manager Herbert Miller nervous too. Miller, a six-foot, 28-year-old former Morristown High School football and basketball star, did not ordinarily get upset easily. But he recognized Redic immediately and saw that he was jittery—and if there is one thing bankers do not like it is nervous bank robbers.

Yet their meeting went well. Redic said he had come to discuss getting a mortgage and they talked about this for a while. Toward the end of the visit Miller was called away to the phone and Redic wandered around the bank's homelike lobby getting a good look at things.

Miller's call was from Murph Rae, who works in the butcher shop across the street. Murph reported that he had just seen one of the bank robbers enter the bank but that the other one was sitting in a car outside. "It doesn't look so good," Murph said. But just as he was hanging up, he saw Redic walk sedately out of the bank and get into the car, which quickly drove off.

During his visit to the bank Redic had asked Miller about night banking hours. Miller told Redic that the bank stayed open until 8 p.m. on Fridays. As soon as Redic left, Miller did two things. He arranged to have the main office of the bank in Morristown phone in periodically during banking hours just to make sure everything was all right. And he suggested to Chief Moore that perhaps some special precaution was indicated for Friday nights.

Accordingly, the following Friday found Chief Moore staked out in the darkened butcher shop along with Mendham's other policeman, Officer James Cillo. School custodian Eddie Fagan, a special officer on the force, took up his window watch with a loaded carbine. Five minutes before closing time, the two bank robbers drove up in front of the bank and the watchers tensed. Then, inexplicably, the robbers drove off, and the police officers went home disgruntled.

From that night on, the bank robbers stepped up the frequency of their visits to Mendham. Soon they were coming into town almost every day, usually heralded by helpful citizens. "The bank robbers are here again," the callers would say. There was some discussion about whether the police should not intervene right then and there, but Moore was against it. "After all," he said reasonably, "you just can't walk up and say, 'Hey, you waiting to rob the bank?' You just can't do that."

Months passed.

Then one day in September 1961, William Redic swung his car through the municipal parking lot and pulled up by the bank's drive-in window, in plain sight of Phoenix House. He made it that far, then got so excited he became almost incoherent. "I want ten cents' worth of dimes," he blurted.

Miller, at the window, stared in astonishment.

"I mean a dollar's worth," said Redic hastily.

Redic got his dimes and drove off with half the people in town watching him. He parked in front of a grocery store owned by Bill Fagan, Eddie's brother, and went in. Chief Moore watched from a discreet distance. Bill Fagan, loading groceries into a customer's car, dropped them and hastened into the store after Redic. But Redic had merely bought cigarettes and was on his way out. "Hiyah," Redic said. "Hiyah," said Fagan.

A week later Redic showed up at Fagan's grocery store again and asked Mrs. Fagan for a job repairing disabled shopping carts. The Fagans didn't give Redic the job, but they began to worry. Had the bank robbers decided to switch to grocery robbing? Chief Moore said he doubted it.

It was apparent from the stepped-up pace that the big moment was approaching. Mendham got ready. Murph Rae in the butcher shop was set to pass the word the minute the robbers showed up. Mrs. Ann Neill, the lone woman employe of the bank, had instructions to head for the ladies' room and lock herself in the minute the robbery started. The bank in Morristown was making regular telephone checks, ready to flash the alarm. Officer Cillo, attired in white coveralls, began painting the rectory of St. Joseph's Roman Catholic Church, next door to the bank, with his gun hidden in the rain gutter. Officer Frank Geraghty of the Mendham Township police (the township is the governmental unit of which the Borough of Mendham is a part, and it has its own police force) was brought in to help keep watch. Chief Moore concealed himself in a basement window of Phoenix House.

One day a girl from the tax collector's office upstairs hurried down to the chief in the basement and reported that he was wanted

on the phone urgently. The caller was Captain Benjamin Waer of the Morris County Police Radio. Mrs. Neal Uptegrove of Mendham had just been warned by an anonymous phone caller to get her children out of school because a bomb was to go off in 50 minutes. Was this the diversion everyone had been expecting?

Diversion or not, both of the town's schools were warned to start evacuating their students. Officer Geraghty ostentatiously drove off to oversee the procedure and Chief Moore slipped over to the bank. Murph Rae took up his sentry post in front of the butcher's; Mrs. Neill edged toward the bank's ladies' room; the main office in Morristown stepped up the frequency of its calls; and Officer Cillo began painting his way closer to the rain gutter.

Nothing happened. Chief Moore watched the bank robbers heading out of town. He questioned Mrs. Uptegrove later and learned that the caller had been a man, apparently in a pay booth, and that she had heard the tinkle of glassware in the background. Later, a waitress in the Mendham Soda Shop told Chief Moore that just about the time of the phone call a man with a moon-shaped scar over his eye was using the phone booth.

Chief Moore went back to the police station and wrote out a new card for his "Planned Robbery of Mendham Bank" folder. But what did it mean? Was it a rehearsal? He ordered the state of readiness maintained.

The next day it happened.

Officer Cillo had got in several hours of painting on St. Joseph's rectory when the bank robbers' car drove up and parked in front of the church. Across the street in the butcher shop Murph Rae recognized the car and tried to telephone Chief Moore, but the line was busy—two visiting cops were on the phone checking out a local resident they were investigating. The butcher handed a bag of bones to customer Mary Cacchio as a cover, and asked her to deliver it to headquarters and tell the chief the robbers were back.

Meanwhile, bank manager Miller, who had brought his lunch to work that day because his wife needed the car, went out to throw his sandwich wrappings into the incinerator behind the bank and saw the robbers cruising slowly around the block. They passed the bank three times and then stopped at the end of the walk, 30 feet from the front door of the bank. The bank manager hurried inside, checked the phone arrangement with Morristown, warned Ann Neill to head for the ladies' room and turned to greet the bank robbers, Redic and Grogan.

"I want to open an account," Redic said. He took the application card Miller handed him and went to one of the tables near the front door. Grogan engaged Miller in conversation. He said he had a headache and Miller advised him to go to Robinson's Drug Shop and get some aspirin. Then the only honest customer in the bank departed. Grogan produced a .38 caliber automatic, pointed it at the bank manager and told him it was a stickup.

"I'm desperate, I'm desperate," said Grogan, a close student of television crime shows. "I have cancer and don't care what happens. Make no false moves and nobody'll get hurt!"

"Yeah! Yeah!" Redic yelled anxiously. He asked for a bag for the money Miller was piling on the counter. The bank manager then produced a nice new bag marked "Federal Reserve," which seemed to please Redic. He began to stuff the money into it.

The telephone rang. Grogan motioned for the bank manager to answer it, but Redic did not see his partner's motion. When Miller answered, Redic punched him in the face. It was the main bank in Morristown calling, and they got the idea right away.

The bank robbers, with $10,679 stuffed in that new Federal Reserve bag, proceeded to herd the manager and Jerre Budd, a substitute teller, into a small supply room. Redic set about tying them up, but the rope kept slipping. Seeing that Redic's temper was getting worse, Miller and Budd finally obliged by holding the rope in place so it would look as if they were bound.

Outside the bank the police—who knew the robbery was on—were frantic. In front of Phoenix House a crowd of women had arrived for a meeting of the Mendham Garden Club and completely blocked the view and path of the police. At last Chief Moore and Officer Geraghty, who had been staked out in Phoenix

House, squirmed their way through the ladies and took up positions on the sidewalk covering the front door of the bank. The two visiting policemen, drafted for the occasion, likewise took battle stations, and Officer Cillo grabbed his gun out of the rain gutter and moved in quickly from his side of the bank.

The bank robbers stepped out onto the sidewalk. Chief Moore met them, pointing his carbine, and said, "Git 'em up!"

Neither robber complied. Instead, Redic hurried frantically toward the getaway car, explaining loudly that he didn't have anything to do with all this—he had just stopped in to cash a check. Grogan ducked back into the bank. Moore called for him to come out, and Grogan did. "Git 'em up!" the chief repeated. Grogan put up his hands and dropped the $10,679.

The bank robbers were handcuffed and marched across the street, up the front steps of Phoenix House, through the room where the Mendham Garden Club was assembling and into police headquarters. Mrs. James L. McFadden, in charge of refreshments for the garden club meeting, arrived with bottles of cider to find Phoenix House swarming with police and other people. The 35 ladies fretfully switched their meeting to Mrs. McFadden's home.

The Great Bank Robbery at Mendham was over. The butcher went back to his butchering; Redic and Grogan were convicted; the police chief went back to helping schoolchildren across the street and enforcing Main Street's 25 miles-per-hour speed limit; Officer Cillo thankfully removed the ladder from St. Joseph's rectory; and Herbert Miller, the bank manager, explained to interested citizens that it wasn't so bad getting punched in the face, but he never again wanted to go through another wait like that as long as he lived.

⁓⧓⁓

RETURNING from a vacation, a writer of detective stories found his apartment rifled by burglars. On his desk was a note, written on his own typewriter: "Figure this one out in your spare time, brother."   —*Parade*

412

She always kept faith in the magic machine

THE UNREAL WORLD
OF DR. DROWN

by Walter Wagner

Radio was still a novelty in the 1920's, and the medium that was soon to produce Amos 'n' Andy, Kate Smith, Fibber McGee and Molly, Jack Benny and Franklin Roosevelt's "fireside chats" also produced, in December 1929, Dr. Ruth Drown. Capitalizing on the public's interest in the new medium as well as its ignorance of radio technology, Dr. Drown, a slight, unsmiling, grim-visaged osteopath, by her own reckoning treated more than 35,000 patients. Investors estimate her fees, conservatively, at over $500,000.

Unlike the usual medical pretender, who cynically bleeds money from patients in exchange for what he knows is worthless treatment, the humorless Dr. Drown was a fanatic believer in her own preposterous theories. Stormy, contentious, self-mesmerized, she clawed like a tigress for 35 dogged years at the world of organized medicine and the law.

In 1952, acting as her own counsel, she filed a $5-million damage suit against the American Medical Association and other groups, charging violation of various antitrust laws. An AMA lawyer, after observing her in court, wrote: "She is a woman of very severe appearance, obviously with fixed convictions, a firm belief in her

413

imaginary facts and a crusader's determination. She was accompanied by a very well dressed, attractive lady of middle age who gave every appearance of being a disciple, and she might well be Mrs. Drown's 'banker.'

"I suspect that Mrs. Drown is going to keep at it indefinitely and no one in the world will convince her that she is completely in error and that the 'facts' which she believes to be true are wholly the product of her imagination. The presiding judge attempted to give her a kind lecture and, in a very nice way, to persuade her to seek legal advice. From the expression on Mrs. Drown's face while the judge was talking to her, I feel sure she wasn't listening to a word he said."

Prior to her emergence as a healer in 1929, Mrs. Drown was an obscure employe in the addressing department of a utilities company in Southern California. There she stumbled on the idea of radio and its possibilities as an "aid to physicians in the diagnosis of disease." Radio had struck the public fancy and obviously was here to stay. To round out the marriage of crystal set to medicine, she sought further medical background, attending the School of Osteopathy at Kirksville, Missouri, for one year, but not bothering to graduate.

On her return to Los Angeles, she studied at the Los Angeles Chiropractic College, became a member of the American Naturopathic Association and a licensed chiropractor, a background sufficient to qualify her as a "doctor." Over the next few years the hardworking little lady developed a formidable complex of pseudoscientific apparatus, and such companion facilities as a "research laboratory," a manufacturing plant and a "college" to teach her methods.

Organized as Drown Laboratories, Inc., her system covered all the medical bases—invention of the equipment, its production, its sale to other healers, the tuition-based school, establishment of a mother clinic for diagnosis and treatment, as well as branch clinics elsewhere in California. Already hypnotized by what she had wrought, she applied to the American Medical Association in

1934 for "a fair investigation" of her basic machine, the Homo-Vibra Ray:

Should you find this instrument to be scientific, as we know it to be, and it meets with your approval . . . we would deem it a great privilege to give to the good of the cause a certain percent royalty over a set period of time on each instrument sold, feeling that this money would be utilized for the purpose of assisting humanity, even as we feel our instrument is for that purpose.

The AMA's reply was not encouraging:

Neither in your letter nor in your advertising matter is there any scientific support for the claims made for your Homo-Vibra Ray device. Nor do you give information regarding its physical contents or the electrical "hookup." In other words, the device seems to be surrounded with the secrecy common to all nostrums.

Dr. Drown huffily ignored the AMA and continued her self-styled mission of assisting humanity. She prospered. By 1936 she had sold more than 150 machines to Los Angeles chiropractors, osteopaths, naturopaths and some doctors of medicine.

Soon she had branches in Beverly Hills, San Luis Obispo and Santa Maria. By 1940 the use of her machines had spread to major American cities, England and western Europe.

She manufactured the machines in various sizes, from a small $250 model sold to patients for home treatment, to a large laboratory type for which she charged other quacks almost $5000.

In 1941 she founded her School of Radio Therapy and sent letters to physicians announcing the "one Known Method at present that will acquaint the doctor with his patient from all angles, and help him keep his patients instead of losing them for lack of equipment, and the complete knowledge to use it."

In urging the course for doctors, she said: "The people of the general public are fast becoming educated to the fact that there is some way whereby they may have their physical conditions analyzed, diagnosed and treated from a purely scientific method. They are demanding that method and it behooves every doctor, whatever the school of healing art he has graduated from, to keep up with the times, and supply the need himself and not have to send his patient to someone else and thereby lose that patient's confidence."

Price of the course was $200. But "if the doctor passes his examination" the tuition would be applied to the purchase of a Drown machine. "Your business," she assured prospective student doctors, "should never be below $500 per month and can run as high as you desire." Patients and students flocked to Dr. Drown and her "purely scientific method." The *Drown Atlas*, a book of instructions for purchasers of the machine, added some remarkable medical insight concerning the efficacy of shower versus tub baths.

> Any patient who is weak and depleted should never take shower baths and stand in the water over the drain, because the patient's magnetism is washed down with the water through the drain, leaving him depleted.
>
> Also a weak patient after having had a tub bath should leave the tub and have someone else drain the water and clean the tub. . . . Too many people sit in the tub and drain the water while finishing the bath and their own magnetism is drained through the drainpipes to the ground, leaving the patient with that much less reserve.

It was the Homo-Vibra Ray, her mighty medical machine, that was the cornerstone of Dr. Drown's burgeoning medical empire and her foremost contribution to the art of healing. The black box that she had invented, said Dr. Drown, not only had the unique capacity to diagnose and treat disease, but it all could be done by remote control!

Once a sample of the patient's blood was on file in her office, only a forest fire burning somewhere between machine and patient could interrupt the healing power of the Homo-Vibra Ray. In addition, the machine was capable—also by remote control—of *photographing* the tissues and bones of a patient through mysterious "vibrations." It was also able to stop hemorrhaging in patients, and because of this boon Dr. Drown advocated that a portable model of her instrument be made compulsory first-aid equipment in every American automobile.

One visitor reported on the remote-control healing pitch she was given at the Drown premises. She had become aware of the Drown technique through a circular she received that advertised the laboratory's "radio findings for differential blood count, urinalysis, blood pressure, temperature, endocrine gland function, diseases of the body and mind."

"I have an aunt living in the East," the visitor had explained to one of Dr. Drown's assistants. "She's not feeling very well. I want her to take the train out to Los Angeles but I don't know if she's strong enough."

"If your aunt can't make the trip, we can treat her by radio. All we need is an original diagnosis."

"You mean from another doctor?"

"No, a sample of her blood, taken from the ear. We treat hundreds of people all over the country by radio. We'll send you a blotter and you have your aunt send in a blood sample on the blotter and we'll diagnose and treat her case." The visitor refused the treatment for her aunt, but most of those who came to the clinic soon became converts.

Over the years, Dr. Drown, who received her personal patients only by referral, perfected her mechanical charade. It was quite a show. Once inside her sanctum sanctorum, the patient was seated with feet on two silver foot pads. Huddled in white uniform, Dr. Drown sat before the machine, furiously working a system of nine dials with indicators that registered from 0 to 100. With one cotton-covered finger, she rubbed a pad in a corner of the machine until noises or "vibrations" were heard (likened by one patient to the sound of a finger scraping on a balloon). The vibrations bounced the indicators, and Dr. Drown gave her "readings" to a somber assistant, also in white uniform, who jotted them down on the patient's chart. The readings were then miraculously transformed into a diagnosis of the patient's ills.

Treatment was invariably recommended at prices starting at $25 per month. If a patient did not want to bother making the trip to the clinic, a machine could be purchased for long-distance healing at home. When Dr. Drown's hocus-pocus machine finally was examined by AMA investigators, they concluded it was a piece of gadgetry with a simple electrical circuit that activated the dials much like a battery tester. An engineer said that with the connection of a speaker to the instrument it became a radio set comparable in operation and workmanship to many radios selling for less than $15. Oliver Field, director of the AMA's Bureau of Investigation, proved the point by rigging a speaker to a Drown machine and using it as an office radio. The reception, he reported, wasn't bad.

Among the less sophisticated, however, use of the Homo-Vibra Ray was spreading, particularly in Chicago, where a nest of quacks was busily treating patients and selling the machines. Posing as a patient at the office of a quack with a Homo-Vibra Ray, a Chicago *Tribune* reporter was informed that the machine could tell "if there's a short in any part of your body. It is much like static on your radio."

The Drown disciple added: "It's just like tuning in Kansas City, New York, Los Angeles or even Mexico City. There are certain intricate combinations. Turn a couple of knobs one way, and you get Station H-E-A-R-T. Turn them another for programs coming over L-U-N-G-S or K-I-D-N-E-Y-S and so on."

The reporter, prior to visiting the quack, had undergone a thorough physical examination and was found to be in excellent physical health. She was diagnosed by Dr. Drown's man as suffering from feverish infection, malaria, undulant fever, afternoon

temperatures, weak glands in the neck, bad ears, rheumatism, weak bladder, infected pancreas, infected lung (left lobe; right lobe O.K.), an infected liver, the possibility of diabetes, gas on the stomach and constipation.

The reporter's story ridiculed the Drown treatment, but even newspaper exposure of such blatant quackery did not shake the belief of Chicago devotees, many of whom had considerable influence. Among the believers was a society matron whose husband was a member of the citizens' board of the University of Chicago. Through her husband, she managed to persuade the august university that Dr. Drown was entitled to a thorough investigation of her claims.

The official announcement from the university was couched in diplomatic language: "On the face of it, the Drown claims appear to be totally unworthy of serious consideration by anyone, least of all a university. However, certain friends who are members of lay boards that have been of great assistance to the university have urged that the Drown claims be investigated so that they may be repudiated if found unworthy or adapted to the benefit of mankind if they should prove to be worthy."

Robert Maynard Hutchins, then chancellor, added that he "considered it a public responsibility" for the university to conduct the inquiry. Five distinguished doctors and scientists were duly assigned to proceed with the investigation. In Los Angeles, meantime, Dr. Drown had finally run afoul of the law. She was charged by the government with a violation of interstate commerce and misbranding in the sale of one of her machines. But the government agreed to delay prosecution until the outcome of the Chicago tests was known.

Dr. Drown breezed into the Windy City for the crucial confrontation. She took up residence at the enormous Stevens Hotel. In her entourage was Mrs. Tyrone Power, the mother of the movie star and another devoted follower. Dr. Drown claimed she had once "tuned in" her machine to the screen idol after he was involved in an automobile accident 3000 miles away. On another occasion she beamed her radio-vision device from London and obtained a picture of a man's stomach as he was undergoing surgery in a New England hospital.

At 4 p.m. on December 30, 1949, Dr. Drown, dripping confidence, walked into the boardroom of the University of Chicago. Her attorney and an attorney for the university set the ground rules for testing her claims that her equipment could photograph tissues and bones by remote control, could diagnose disease and control bleeding. The university agreed that blood specimens of ten patients and ten dogs would be furnished to Dr. Drown, and she was also to be furnished film for the purpose of demonstrating her technique in "soft tissue" photography.

The tests began the next day in the university's darkroom. A sample of blood and an X ray of a patient with a fracture in the neck of the left femur were supplied to Dr. Drown. The university doctors asked her to make a radio photograph that would show the present stage of healing in the patient's hip. Using her own compass to line up her instrument so that it pointed in an east-west tangent, Dr. Drown inserted a piece of filter paper containing the blood sample into a slot at the rear of her machine.

The morning was spent taking six "photographs." None of them satisfied even Dr. Drown. "It's strange," she said, "that I can get such good results at home and such poor results here."

The group broke for lunch at the Quadrangle Club, then reconvened in the boardroom. As the doctors watched with barely concealed amazement, Dr. Drown proceeded with her diagnostic readings of the blood samples of three patients. The final test was made on January 3, 1950, in the animal surgery rooms of the university. The arteries of two dogs were opened, and Dr. Drown's two little machines for controlling the bleeding were set up in the next room.

Science had met head-on with quackery. The official results of the tests were announced by the university a short time later. They were an unmitigated disaster for Dr. Drown. Her photographs, the doctors said, "are simple fog patterns produced by exposure of the film to white light before it has been fixed adequately. The so-called radio photographs are mere artifacts and totally without clinical value."

Her machine diagnoses of the three patients by means of the blood samples were way wide of the mark. Patient number one, she claimed, had cancer of the left breast, was blind in one eye, had defective ovaries and trouble with heart, liver, gall bladder, kidneys, lungs, stomach, spinal nerves, intestines and ears. In actuality, the patient suffered only from tuberculosis. Patient number two, in reality afflicted with hypertension, was assigned a whole series of ailments. Dr. Drown also talked of the patient's "uterus," which was particularly remarkable since the patient was a male. Dr. Drown's diagnosis for the third patient, a perfectly healthy young man with normal blood pressure, was "an ischiorectal abscess, serious trouble with the prostate, probably carcinoma with spread to urethra, pelvic bones, and with loss or at any rate nonfunction of the left testicle." His blood pressure she reported as 166/78, and his prognosis was "very poor."

So erroneous were her diagnoses that the university doctors did not bother submitting the blood samples of the seven other patients. Their report said: "The machine is a sort of Ouija board. It is our belief that her alleged successes rest solely on the noncritical attitude of her followers. Her technique is to find so much trouble in so many organs that usually she can say 'I told you so' when she registers an occasional lucky positive guess. In these particular tests, even this luck deserted her."

In the test of the two dogs, the results were pathetic. "Mrs. Drown stood in the doorway watching the animals bleed," the report said, describing the hemorrhage control experiment as a fiasco. "In the opinion of all observers, including herself, Mrs. Drown failed completely to control or modify hemorrhage," the report noted.

The dogs were destroyed. The wife of the university official who had originally pressed for a hearing for Dr. Drown and had observed the tests on the dogs had bolted from the surgery room in horror as her idol stood by helplessly while the dogs bled to death. "She was thoroughly convinced of the fallacy of all of Mrs. Drown's ideas," the university doctors concluded.

On the heels of the Chicago experiments, the AMA branded Dr. Drown "a fake and a fraud." Still undeterred, she puffed back to Los Angeles, ready to face the government's charges. The case against her had grown out of the purchase of a Homo-Vibra Ray by Wilson Ellis, a businessman from Evanston, Illinois. He had bought one of Dr. Drown's machines in October 1948, after his wife discovered a lump in her breast.

Ellis had phoned Dr. Drown in Los Angeles and was referred by her to a doctor in Chicago who used her equipment. Mrs. Ellis began visiting the local practitioner, but complained of being tired by the long and frequent trips.

"You don't need to come here," Dr. Drown's acolyte assured her. "Just stay at home and we can treat you by radio wave. That's what's wonderful about the Drown machine; it's just as effective when the patient is miles away as it is when he or she is here."

On a business trip to Los Angeles, Mr. Ellis stopped by the Drown Laboratories and bought a machine for $412. He returned home with it, and his wife used the instrument to treat the lump in her breast. Dr. Drown had assured Mr. Ellis his wife's illness was not cancer, but was caused by a fungus that had spread through her digestive system into the liver.

The Evanston man had come forth with his story when his wife's condition failed to improve and he read of the possibility of the Drown quackery. In court, Dr. Drown, despite the disastrous results of the Chicago tests still fresh in her memory, defended her device and contended that the sale of the machine to Ellis was purely an intrastate transaction.

The government put six expert witnesses on the stand, who again proceeded to destroy Dr. Drown's pretensions as a healer. An eminent physician ridiculed her gimmick and said, "These things would be laughable if they were not so dangerous."

A member of the State Board of Chiropractic Examiners said

that the Board had examined Dr. Drown's machine and concluded "that the machine did not have any therapeutic value."

Dr. Moses A. Greenfield, radiologist and head of the radiation physics division at UCLA Medical Center, testified that the machine was worthless and that it had "an electrical potential no greater than a flashlight battery." Another expert described the machine as simply an "inefficient battery tester" which wiggled its needles better when used with a glass of water instead of with a human patient.

Dr. Drown was decidedly getting the worst of it. Then the trial was suddenly sparked by the appearance of a voluntary, unsubpoenaed witness—who came forth on behalf of the healer. The witness was another of Dr. Drown's highly placed followers, Mrs. Eleanor B. Allen, the prestigious president of the Los Angeles City Board of Education.

Mrs. Allen testified that she was a firm, longtime believer in Dr. Drown's radio therapy. She had two of the Drown machines in her home. She and her husband had known Dr. Drown for 18 or 19 years, and they both had implicit, provable faith in her methods. Mrs. Allen said that the Drown device had once treated her for a severe cold that could have led to pneumonia when she was in Atlantic City, New Jersey, and the machine was in Los Angeles. On another occasion, the board of education president said, the machine had cured a rash that had appeared on the hands of her son.

Under cross-examination, Assistant U.S. Attorney Tobias G. Klinger posed a hypothetical question to Mrs. Allen: "Assume you were riding in an automobile in Moscow and Dr. Drown and her device were in Hollywood. You had an accident and received a broken leg, a fractured skull and were hemorrhaging. By telephone, Dr. Drown was informed you had been in an accident—nothing more.

"Using your blood sample on file, Dr. Drown would tune in the machine, which would diagnose your condition. Then she would tune in the treatment device. It is, then, your contention that this would cure your broken leg and fractured skull and stop your hemorrhage?"

"Yes, yes," Mrs. Allen answered. "The way you state it, Mr. Klinger, sounds like black magic, but it isn't. It's science."

She was also asked if she would seek a surgeon instead of the machine if she required surgery. Mrs. Allen said that use of the machine would preclude any need for surgery. She was asked why, if the machine is so effective, her husband had been ill for five years.

Mrs. Allen replied that the machine had kept him alive.

The testimony shocked Los Angeles officials. The grand jury, fearful that Mrs. Allen, because of her position, might advocate adoption of the machine for treating the city's schoolchildren, prepared to launch a full-scale inquiry. But it never came off. Mrs. Allen stuck to her testimony, and resigned from the board of education.

Dr. L. S. Goerke, Director of the Bureau of Medical Services for the Los Angeles City Health Department, announced the publication of a special bulletin to counteract Mrs. Allen's advocacy of the Drown machine.

"Confusion caused in the public mind by endorsement of such gadgets by the president of the board of education should be clarified and corrected by factual information," he said. "In 1951, in the world's most literate country, we have magic for the cure of disease."

There was no confusion, however, in the minds of the jurors. They convicted Dr. Drown on the misdemeanor charge. She was fined $1000. Outraged, she then personally drew up her complaint for a $5-million damage suit, naming as the chief defendant the U.S. Pharmacopoeial Convention, an organization chartered by the U.S. Congress, ten other medical groups (including the AMA), plus 154 medical corporations.

In her suit she asked for the dissolution, no less, of the AMA, the California Medical Society, the medical departments of the U.S. Army and Navy, the U.S. Public Health Service, the U.S. Departments of Agriculture and Commerce and the medical colleges of Pittsburgh and Johns Hopkins universities. She said the defendants had combined to "engineer" her prosecution. This was done, she said, in order to create a monopoly by the defendants and was in violation of the antitrust laws. In due course, her complaint, one of America's more remarkable legal actions, was thrown out.

Dr. Drown went back to twirling her dials. Despite the exposure by the University of Chicago and the misdemeanor conviction, she persevered for the next 13 years, free to pursue her healing and minister to hundreds of patients a year.

Two patients, both attractive young housewives, turned up for treatment at her clinic in 1963. Mrs. Jackie Metcalf complained of stomach trouble. She was also worried about the health of her three children. Her Drown diagnosis disclosed that she suffered from aluminum poisoning of the stomach and gall bladder, malfunction of the right ovary and left kidney. She was advised to throw away all her kitchen utensils and return for treatment. After submitting blood samples of her children, she was told they had chicken pox and mumps.

Mrs. Concetta Jorgensen complained that she had been diagnosed by another doctor as a cancer victim. On the Drown machine, however, no cancer or tuberculosis showed up. But the machine did find cysts and her salt-sugar ratio out of balance, caused by malfunction of the liver and thymus gland. She was charged $50 for the diagnosis and was offered treatments at either $50 a month on a month-to-month basis or $35 a month on a six-month contract.

Mrs. Metcalf and Mrs. Jorgensen were acting as agents for the Los Angeles District Attorney's office and the California Bureau of Food and Drug Inspection.

The two women agents told Deputy District Attorney John W. Miner and Grant S. Leake, supervising inspector of the state bureau, that they had also been shown photographs of astronauts and dogs in orbiting space capsules at the Drown clinic. These were represented as having been obtained by "chance" when Dr. Drown's photographic machines picked up energy waves from the cosmos. Also Dr. Drown had boasted that she had 100 inpatients and 200 outpatients a month, plus about 80 patients a month at her San Luis Obispo office.

Both Mrs. Metcalf and Mrs. Jorgensen had been examined by doctors and pronounced in good health before visiting the Drown premises. Mrs. Metcalf's children were not suffering from chicken pox or mumps. The blood samples of her "children" were actually from a turkey, a sheep and a hog. Armed with the evidence, court warrants were drawn and Dr. Drown's health mill was raided. Some 80 of her machines were confiscated. One investigator said, "Rube Goldberg would be proud of these."

Dr. Drown was charged with two counts of grand theft and two of attempted grand theft. Still peppery, she declared confidently, "The advertising will be wonderful for me. When I get back to my office I'll have more patients than ever."

This time, however, it was not to be. The district attorney checkmated Dr. Drown's attempt to have her machines returned.

Her trial was scheduled for early in April 1965. Miner was confident of victory. Dr. Drown was confident of vindication. But three weeks before the trial, Dr. Drown suddenly died of a heart ailment. Investigators learned she had had her first stroke 14 months earlier and had secretly been under the care of a legitimate specialist.

In the end, the queen of the quacks had been a physician unable to heal herself.

───※───

A WOMAN appeared in a Minnesota tax office with a return on which there was a deduction of $500 for bad debts. When that item was questioned, she replied haughtily that they were bills she owed to people about town, and that she knew they were worthless because she had not paid any of them in the last two years and did not intend to pay any of them.

—Farrar's News Features

The man and the method
behind this plot are still a threat

THE "MIRACLE INK" SWINDLE

by Conrad Christiano and John Van Buren

One day in 1955 a tall, nattily dressed man strolled into a Buffalo, New York, bank, wrote a check for $10 and had it certified. Less than 48 hours later a stocky, humbly clad man cashed the same check in a Rochester, New York, bank for $17,790!

Behind this incredible transaction lies one of the most fantastic forgery plots in U.S. history. And behind the plot lies a "miracle ink," the exact formula of which is still not known. Furthermore, though some of the conspirators have been convicted, the threats raised by the insidious scheme continue to exist—for its mastermind is still at large.

It was on March 2, 1955, that the smart-looking man walked into the Buffalo bank, a branch of the Marine Trust Company of western New York. Identifying himself as Sam Mancuso, he drew four $10 checks against a three-week-old account. He wrote the checks with his own fountain pen and requested that each be certified. Asked why he wanted certification of such small checks, he explained: "I'm just starting business here as an importer. I can get my merchandise sooner if my checks are certified."*

---

*Certification is a guarantee that the money indicated on a check is in the bank. Customarily, a certified check is honored immediately wherever presented.

The request sounded reasonable, and the checks were duly stamped. "Sam Mancuso" then walked out of the bank—and has never been apprehended. Police are sure the name was fictitious.

The scene shifts now to Rochester, 70 miles east of Buffalo, where the four checks turned up a few hours later in the hands of a mystery man. This man, whom we shall call Mr. X, was the master-mind of the fraud.

Mr. X called on Benjamin Chartoff, a husky 57-year-old sal-vage dealer, and asked where he could get a checkwriter—a ma-chine which punches the desired sum on a check in indelible ink. Chartoff drove Mr. X to a produce firm where he borrowed such a machine. Then he drove Mr. X to the latter's home. Alone in his house, Mr. X went to work. From present knowledge, we can surmise what he did. Using a damp cotton swab, he traced over the writing on the four checks. The ink disappeared. All that remained were four blank checks clearly marked with certifications.

This was not a case of a simple disappearing ink. It must have taken months of tedious experimenting to produce the ink that Sam Mancuso had used. Most checks are printed on a safety paper devised to protect against "doctoring." This paper is sensi-tive to ink eradicators and erasers, and any tampering with its surface, through a chemical reaction, either interferes with its en-grained pattern or brings out the hidden warning word VOID re-peated all over the paper. But somehow Mr. X discovered two things: first, that cobalt nitrate, with certain ingredients added, will flow smoothly, dry quickly and look like ink; second, that the resulting compound will dissolve readily in water.

After removing all the "miracle ink," Mr. X laid two of the certified checks before him. How much should he fill them in for? Mr. X was realistic; he wanted to go high, but not too high. He finally punched $17,790 across one with the checkwriter, then wrote in Benjamin Chartoff's name as payee, using standard ink. On the second check he punched in $10,253; this he made out to Albert Scarlata, another Rochester salesman. Both checks were signed "Harry Rosenberg."

On March 4—a Friday, and the bank's busiest day—Chartoff and Mr. X went to the Genesee Valley Union Trust Company in downtown Rochester, during the noon rush hour. Mr. X hovered in the background as Chartoff presented the $17,790 check to a bank officer, saying: "I would like to pay off my $2500 loan and $56.67 interest." No questions were asked—the check was certified and Chartoff was known at the bank. He also allayed suspicion by not asking for the balance in cash. He took his "change" in two bank drafts for $9000 and $6233.33.

After leaving the bank, Chartoff gave Mr. X the $6233.33 draft as his "take." Then the two strolled over to the Lincoln Rochester Trust Company, a few blocks away. Again Chartoff asked to pay off an obligation, this time for $2119.84. He offered the legitimate $9000 draft from Genesee Valley, took his change in a draft for $3880.16 and $3000 cash.

The two men then drove to Scarlata's. Scarlata was uneasy. "I'm scared to go through with this deal," he said. Chartoff reassured him: "I cashed mine. It was easy."

So Scarlata went with the two men to the Genesee Valley bank—less than an hour after Chartoff had been there before. This time Mr. X and Chartoff waited in the car while Scarlata, explaining that he wanted to pay off a $2500 loan plus $57.10 in interest, presented the $10,253 certified check. "I want the balance in two drafts," he told the banker. "I'm going to New York on business."

He received two drafts, for $4000 and $3695.90, then rejoined his friends. They drove at once to the Lincoln Rochester bank, where Scarlata, like Chartoff, tendered his $4000 draft, saying he would like to settle a loan which, plus interest, came to $188.37. He asked for the balance in large bills.

Up to this point the elaborate scheme, which included taking out the loans in advance, had worked to perfection. But that very fact was the undoing of the plot. Flushed with his initial success and in a hurry to get his hands on more easy cash, Scarlata rushed to a nearby branch office of Genesee Valley. Presenting the $3695.90 draft, he told a teller: "I'd like cash. I'm leaving for New

York City and, with the weekend coming up, I'm afraid I might have difficulty cashing this."

The teller referred Scarlata to a bank officer. "We'll have the money for you in a few seconds," the officer said, disappearing behind the tellers' cages. He returned shortly—with a police officer.

Scarlata's role in the venture was over. While he, Chartoff and Mr. X were making their rounds, Norman Steinmiller, an alert note teller at the Genesee Valley's main office, became suspicious when the two fraudulent checks reached his desk. He took them to Assistant Vice-President James J. Cullen. "Isn't it strange," he asked, "that these large certified checks, both signed by Harry Rosenberg, came in here less than an hour apart?"

Cullen took the matter right to the top—to Board Chairman John W. Jardine, who ordered an immediate call to the Buffalo bank on which the checks were drawn. The latter reported no record of checks certified for a Harry Rosenberg.

Now Genesee Valley began calling its branches and all other banks in the city, spreading the alarm to be on the lookout for Chartoff, Scarlata and Rosenberg. By coincidence, just as one branch vice-president received the alarm, he could reply, "Scarlata's here now." The caller said: "Get a policeman and hold him!"

Then Scarlata made his second mistake. When questioned, he immediately embarked on a fantastic story of how he came by the $10,253 check. Up to this point, the worst possible fate he faced, had he refused to answer any questions, was a civil action. But the more he talked, the more he implicated himself. "I buy and sell wholesale lots of perfume, men's wallets, ladies' handbags," Scarlata told the investigators, headed by Assistant District Attorney John A. Mastrella. "I get my merchandise from New York and keep it at my mother's house."

The tall tale continued, with prodding, for four hours. Scarlata said that Harry Rosenberg, whom he described as "not too thin or husky," had come from Buffalo to buy some merchandise, and had paid him with the certified check.

During the next few days Mastrella and his aides worked to

find holes in Scarlata's story. Unable to locate Chartoff, who had taken off for New York, they focused on the method employed in faking the checks. Mastrella, a captain in Army intelligence during World War II, noticed that both checks bore identical checkwriter imperfections. He also knew that in order to prove that Chartoff and Scarlata were involved in the swindle, he had to link them with the checkwriter.

Infrared photography now showed that the ink writing was *over* the certifications, proving that the checks were written *after* being certified. Also, the photographs showed a loss of material in the engrained pattern of the checks. There were whitish blotches, invisible to the naked eye, where the "miracle ink" had been previously removed. Next, detectives scanned microfilms of canceled checks at Rochester banks, looking for the check-writer's telltale imperfections. They finally turned some up— written by the produce dealer who owned the checkwriter. With this evidence, authorities swooped down on the dealer, only to learn that the checkwriter had been "borrowed" by Chartoff without the dealer's permission. But Mastrella now had information linking Chartoff and Scarlata to the checkwriter.

Now Mastrella questioned a former business partner of Chartoff. This man suggested investigating a certain Rochester manufacturing plant—but refused to say why. Detectives found that the firm used large amounts of cobalt nitrate. Mastrella immediately called the city chemist, John A. Temmermann.

"Is it possible that cobalt nitrate could be used in some kind of disappearing ink?" he asked. "Can you find out by Monday?" He explained that Scarlata's attorney had obtained a writ of habeas corpus which required the D.A.'s office to show cause by Monday —72 hours away—why Scarlata should not be released.

Temmermann went to work. He tried 50 different "recipes" before obtaining a solution which would flow and dry like ink and would not damage check paper when removed. Monday morning he called Mastrella: "I think I've got it. It's not 100 percent perfect, but it's pretty close."

Meanwhile, Chartoff imprudently returned to Rochester and found a welcoming committee of detectives. Taken into custody, he, like Scarlata, swung into the tall tale about Harry Rosenberg. "I'm in the salvage business," he said, "and I sold some old motors and pumps to Rosenberg. He gave me a $17,790 certified check to cover the stuff." Later, Chartoff admitted that Harry Rosenberg was a fictitious character created by Mr. X.

And what about the ink? Chartoff admitted he knew a chemist at the plant which used cobalt nitrate, but denied that the chemical came from there. Principals in the case still insist that the chemist named by Chartoff was not involved—but, oddly enough, he disappeared as soon as the case broke.

Investigators never learned how Mr. X discovered the possibilities of an ink formula based on cobalt nitrate. Mr. X apparently did not reveal its secret to other members of the ring.

Both Scarlata and Chartoff drew suspended sentences of five to ten years. But the man who concocted the scheme, Mr. X, today walks free, with two unused certified checks and the legitimate $6233.33 "payoff" draft given him by Chartoff. Mastrella said there is no evidence that the draft has ever been cashed. Most important, Mr. X carries in his brain the "miracle ink" formula, which scientists still have not duplicated exactly.

What is to prevent Mr. X, or some other "Mr. X," from pulling similar swindles with the miracle ink? At first glance, it would seem that repeat performances could be stopped simply by making all check paper sensitive to water, just as it is to ink eradicators and erasers. But this idea has drawbacks, for legitimate checks often get wet in the mails, or in rain or snow. Another suggestion has been for banks to use checkwriters on all certified checks. But frauds have been successfully perpetrated on checkwriter drafts in the past.

The best answer at present, banking and investigative officials believe, is extreme care in cashing checks. A 50-cent telephone call to Buffalo would have kept the Genesee Valley Union Trust Company from dishing out $28,043.

Upon diligent scrutiny, the celebrated "missing link" began to develop flaws

UNMASKING OF THE PILTDOWN MAN

by Alden P. Armagnac

For more than 40 years Piltdown Man was a member in more or less good standing of the society of "earliest humans," rubbing mandibles with such distinguished, if lowbrow, company as Neanderthal Man and Peking Man. The startling discovery that he was an out-and-out humbug abruptly terminated his membership in December 1953.

It was early in 1912 that an amateur fossil hunter, Charles Dawson, brought the first of the Piltdown finds to the British Museum. He said he had found them in a gravel pit near Piltdown Common, Sussex, in the south of England. Dr. Arthur Smith Woodward, eminent paleontologist at the Museum, took part in later diggings. All told, more than 20 fragments were found.

Outstanding among these bits of bone, teeth and flint was a piece of jaw, plainly the jaw of an ape in all but one sensational respect—the surfaces of the two intact molar teeth were flat. Only a human jaw, with its free-swinging motion, could have worn them down to that flattop shape. Thus the owner of the jaw appeared to be a "missing link" in human evolution. Fragments of the brain case of a prehistoric human skull, found nearby, seemingly identified him.

Remains of prehistoric animals found in the same gravel pit placed Piltdown Man in the early Ice Age, half a million years ago. This made him the earliest known human. In honor of the amateur discoverer, Woodward gave Piltdown the scientific name *Eoanthropus dawsoni*—Dawson's Dawn Man.

For decades the reconstructed Piltdown skull, with its incongruously high forehead and simian jaw, was a storm center of scientific controversy. But Piltdown began really to hit the skids in 1950 when Dr. Kenneth Oakley, a British Museum geologist, applied a chemical dating test. The longer bones lie buried, the more fluorine they absorb from groundwater. Dr. Oakley's measurement of the fluorine content convinced him that the remains were only 50,000 years old instead of a half million.

(Dr. Oakley's estimate for the age of the Piltdown Man's cranial fragments was correct, but he was wrong in innocently assuming the jaw to be equally old.)

Oakley's discovery made Piltdown Man more of a riddle than ever. A half-million-year-old missing link had been conceivable. But a missing link as recent as 50,000 years ago was an utterly incredible throwback.

So went the table talk one summer evening in 1953, when Dr. J. S. Weiner, then an Oxford University anthropologist, dined with Oakley in London. Home in Oxford that night, Weiner revolved in his mind everything that made Piltdown such an impossible misfit.

Above all, he remembered those "human" teeth in an apelike jaw, worn flat as if by a file. . . . A thought struck him like a blow: *Could* they have been deliberately filed flat? He recalled Sherlock Holmes's words: "When you have eliminated the impossible, whatever remains, however improbable, must be the truth."

With the help of a colleague, Professor Wilfred Le Gros Clark, Weiner secured a chimpanzee's molar tooth, filed and stained it, and had a good likeness of a Piltdown molar. Next stop was the British Museum, where Weiner and Clark enlisted Oakley's aid. Out of a locked, fireproof steel safe came the hallowed Piltdown fragments for the most searching anatomical, chemical and physical examination they had ever received. Instruments such as the X-ray spectrograph and Geiger counter came into play. An improved chemical dating test measured the bones' loss of nitrogen against the passing of time.

Weiner was right. The jaw had come from a modern ape, probably an orangutan. Cunningly the faker had "fossilized" it by staining it a mahogany color with an iron salt and bichromate. An oil paint, probably red sienna, had stained the chewing surfaces of the teeth. Meanwhile, telltale scratches on the molars showed beyond doubt that the teeth had been artificially filed. And they were unnaturally sharp-edged, just as a file would leave them. In plaster casts of the Piltdown jaw studied the world over these details were lost, but they were only too clear in the original Dawson specimen.

In 1953 the three investigators announced that the jaw and teeth were bogus. At this time they still assumed that some prankster had planted them in the diggings, near genuine relics, to confuse the excavators. But when the three later came to testing the other Piltdown trophies, every important piece proved a forgery. Piltdown Man was a fraud from start to finish!

The hoax must have been an inside job—by someone, said Weiner, who "can hardly fail to be among those whose names we know." Weiner set out to reconstruct every possible detail. He traveled around the countryside to talk with witnesses who had been contemporaries of Dawson, and with relatives and friends of others no longer living. He pored through yellowed journals of the time and read all the scientific reports of the discoveries.

To Weiner, the resulting mass of evidence clearly exonerated every figure in the Piltdown case but one: Charles Dawson, the original "discoverer." And while Weiner did not, for lack of "positive and final proof," flatly accuse him, the circumstantial evidence pointed to Dawson as the author of the hoax.

A successful lawyer, married, living in the little "county town" of Lewes in a part of England rich in fossils, Charles Dawson had

pursued his hobby of hunting them with notable success. He had sent Woodward many unusual specimens, including fossils of a dinosaur and a prehistoric mammal of a species new to science, which Woodward named after him.

By Dawson's own account, he was walking along a country road near Piltdown Common when he noticed that the road had been mended with brown flints unusual to the district. He found that they came from a small pit nearby, where gravel was dug for road repairs. Finding two men at work there, he asked them to keep a lookout for bones or other fossils. On another visit one of the men handed Dawson a thick fragment of human skull. Later, Dawson claimed, he found a larger piece himself. He journeyed to London then, and showed Woodward what he had "found": skull fragments, fossil animal teeth, prehistoric flint tools.

Woodward's eyes popped. He didn't know, of course, that all the principal items were faked, or that the animal remains, whose extreme antiquity supported a similar date for the human ones, had come from elsewhere. Actually, as investigations revealed, a fossil rhino tooth came not from Piltdown, but from East Anglia. A fossil elephant tooth must have traveled from as far away as Tunisia. Any established fossil collector like Dawson would have had little difficulty in assembling these specimens, by trading or in shops catering to collectors. As for the cranial fragments, human skulls 50,000 years old are not exactly common, but Dawson was known to have possessed some unusual skulls.

The unsuspecting Woodward joined Dawson in excavating at the gravel pit—with a success, if he'd only known it, too good to be true. One summer evening a pick struck the ground, and the faked jaw flew out. First public announcement of the "discoveries" followed in December 1912.

Miraculous luck continued to favor the diggers. The last spectacular discovery was a "second" Piltdown Man, found, according to Dawson, in a field two miles from the first site, in 1915. Like Piltdown I, Piltdown II was later found to have been artificially stained with iron and bichromate.

During this period no one publicly questioned Dawson's honesty. But some of his fellow amateurs in his home town expressed the opinion among themselves that Dawson was "salting the mine."

And a visitor who entered Dawson's office without knocking found him in the midst of some experiment, with bones immersed in crucibles of colored and pungent liquids. Dawson explained with apparent embarrassment that he was staining fossils to find out how natural staining occurred.

The Piltdown "discoveries" ended with Dawson's death in 1916, at the age of 52 and at the height of his fame. Always hopeful, Woodward kept on digging at Piltdown for many years, but never found anything more.

Nevertheless, a "new" Piltdown find did turn up. It was located by Weiner himself, and furnished what may be the most direct evidence of the hoaxer's identity.

Harry Morris, a bank clerk and flint collector of Lewes, had somehow obtained from Dawson a "Piltdown" flint tool that never reached the British Museum—and had discovered for himself that it was spurious.

Morris had died, and left his flint collection, including the "Piltdown" flint and notes about it, to A. P. Pollard, a Lewes surveyor, who told Weiner about it.

Where was the flint now? Pollard had traded the cabinetful of flints to Frederick Wood of Ditchling for a collection of birds' eggs. Wood had died, but Mrs. Wood might still have the missing cabinet. Weiner hastened to Ditchling and found the cabinet, holding 12 drawers of neatly labeled specimens. The 12th and last drawer yielded the Piltdown flint. It bore an inscription in Morris' handwriting: "Stained by C. Dawson with intent to defraud (all).—H. M."

An accompanying note of Morris' repeated the accusation, indignantly adding: ". . . and exchanged by D. for my most valued specimen!" A second note declared that hydrochloric acid would remove the brown color, leaving one of the relatively common white flints found on the Chalk Downs of Lewes. Morris was right about that, Weiner found.

The "Morris flint," inscription and all, now reposes in the British Natural History Museum.

The fantastic Piltdown case seemed closed, except for the puzzle of the hoaxer's motive. He gained nothing in money; the specimens were presented to the British Museum.

Was fame Charles Dawson's object? Was the deception an intended joke of his that went too far? Whatever prompted the impostor lay beyond reach of chemical and physical tests—and perhaps must remain always a mystery.

A WOMAN we know who spent some time in Egypt was telling us of a bazaar she visited in one of the side streets of Cairo. As a special attraction, the proprietor was exhibiting at one end of the room "The Skull of Cleopatra." Beside it was a smaller skull, and this one piqued our friend's curiosity. She asked the proprietor whose skull that was.

"That is Cleopatra's too," he explained kindly, "*as a child.*"
—*Caskie Stinnett in Speaking of Holiday*

AN ASTUTE gentleman in Cairo, meeting an Arab just in from the desert, offered to sell the man a city streetcar for £200. The credulous Arab—whose pockets were filled with Egyptian pounds—looked at the crowded streetcars and quickly concluded the deal. By the time the desert yokel attempted to eject the conductor and collect fares for himself, the clever entrepreneur had vanished.

But when publicity in the Cairo papers made the Arab sucker a public figure, the Egyptian rascal really showed his genius. Somehow he made peace with the Arab and expounded a new scheme. He had a tent in the Arab section where he would exhibit the sucker, charging admission, and they would split the profits.

Business was excellent, and the Arab finally got weary of being gaped at; so he hired a stand-in who would undertake the arduous job of allowing the natives to look at him. It was then that the police swooped down and closed the exhibition on the ground that fraud was being practiced.
—*Quentin Reynolds, The Curtain Rises (Random House)*

In Joe Sherman's case, the
job never really found the man

HOT PROSPECT

Condensed from *Time*

Fired from his job as a sales-
man for an electronics company, Joe Sherman could not find
another. At 54, his age counted against him. His real education
was skimpy. So Sherman put a new and imaginary personality on
paper. He subtracted 15 years from his age, added a *cum laude*
degree from the University of Pittsburgh, work on a Ph.D. at the
University of Florida and a broad array of engineering experience.
Then he mailed his résumé to a wide range of electronics firms all
over the country.

Aerospace and electronics companies were desperate for skilled
technicians, and soon Joe Sherman was flooded with responses
from personnel managers. In accordance with practice in this
competitive field, all were eager to pay for his expenses if he would
just appear for a personal interview. Joe judiciously accepted
offers, pocketed the money for his air fare and took off cross-
country from his Pasadena, California, home in his battered
automobile.

Sherman never accepted a job, and he never intended to, but
in a hectic two years he collected some $15,000 from 40 companies.
Foresightedly, he asked that the firms he talked with abide by "the

code of the companies" and contact none of his "previous employers" until interviews were complete. Using alias after alias, he was not once asked for identification. Some firms actually offered jobs. So confident did Sherman become that he threatened to sue one firm that was tardy with his expense payment.

Finally, after Sherman had collected expenses from Radio Corporation of America for separate interviews at different plants, RCA got suspicious and notified postal inspectors. Later an engineering placement service sent one of Sherman's résumés to Radiation Incorporated of Melbourne, Florida, a firm that Sherman had listed as a "former employer." Radiation officials checked with the federal postal authorities, and Sherman's jig was up. Arrested in Orlando, Sherman pleaded guilty to three counts of using the mails to defraud and was sentenced to 20 months in jail. Sighed Sherman when it was all over: "It was horrible on the health. Driving 100,000 miles a year is more than anybody can stand."

<hr />

ONE OF the assistant editors on a national magazine wore a new hat to the office one day. While he was in conference with his boss, a writer on the staff inspected the hat, then went down to the store it came from and bought an exact duplicate, complete even to the monogrammed initials on the sweatband. There was only one difference—it was three sizes larger than the original. Back at the office, he switched the hats.

At the end of the day, when the editor put on his hat, it fell over his ears. Thoroughly mystified, he took it off and examined it. There were his initials—it must be his hat.

The next day, he was again wearing the hat, which now seemed to fit pretty well. As soon as he went out of the room, the writer inspected the hat. He found the sweatband was stuffed with tissue paper; so he took the paper out, stuffed it in the original hat and put that on the rack. At the end of the day, when the editor put on his hat, it just sat on the top of his head. Again he looked inside—and immediately went off to Bellevue Hospital for an examination.   —*Robert Markewich*

*He wasn't a cheat—he just
liked to use credit instead of cash*

UNCLE E. P. AND
HIS SUNSHINE SCHEMES

by Stephen Leacock

When I was six my father settled on an Ontario farm.
There we lived in an isolation the like of which is almost unknown
today. We were some 35 miles from a railway. There were no newspapers. Nobody came and went, for there was nowhere to come
and go.

Into this isolation broke my dynamic uncle, Edward Philip
Leacock, my father's younger brother. E. P., as everyone called
him, had just come from a year's travel around the Mediterranean.
He was about 28 but, bronzed and self-confident, with a square
beard like a Plantagenet king, he seemed a more than adult man.
His talk was of Algiers, of the African slave market, of the Golden
Horn and the pyramids. To us who had been living in the wilder-
ness for two years it sounded like the *Arabian Nights*. When we
asked, "Uncle Edward, do you know the Prince of Wales?" he
answered, "Quite intimately"—with no further explanation. It
was an impressive trick he had.

In that year, 1878, there was a general election in Canada. E. P.
was soon in it up to the neck. He picked up the history and politics
of Upper Canada in a day, and in a week knew everybody in the
countryside. In politics E. P. was on the conservative, aristocratic

side, but he was also hail-fellow-well-met with the humblest. A democrat can't condescend, because he's down already; when a conservative stoops, he conquers. E. P. spoke at every meeting. His strong point, however, was personal contact in barroom treats, which gave full scope to his marvelous talent for flattering and make-believe.

"Why, let me see," he would say to some tattered country specimen beside him, glass in hand, "surely if your name is Framley you must be a relation of my dear old friend, General Sir Charles Framley of the Horse Artillery?"

"Mebbe," the flattered specimen would answer, "I ain't kept track very good of my folks in the old country."

"Dear me! I must tell Sir Charles that I've seen you."

Thus in a fortnight E. P. had conferred honors and distinctions on half the township of Georgina. They lived in a recaptured atmosphere of generals, admirals and earls. How else could they vote than Conservative!

The election was a walkover. E. P. might have stayed to reap the fruits, but Ontario was too small a horizon for him. Manitoba was then just opening up, and nothing would satisfy E. P. but that he and my father should go west. So we had a sale of our farm, with refreshments for all comers, our lean cattle and broken machines fetching less than the price of the whiskey. Off to Manitoba went E. P. and my father, leaving us children behind to attend school.

They hit Winnipeg on the rise of the boom and E. P. rode the crest of the wave. There is a magic appeal in the rush and movement of a boomtown—a Carson City of the 1860's, a Winnipeg of the 1880's. Life is all in the present, all here and now, no past and no outside—just a clatter of hammers and saws, rounds of drinks and rolls of money. Every man seems a remarkable fellow; individuality shines and character blossoms like a rose.

E. P. was in everything and knew everybody, conferring titles and honors up and down Portage Avenue. In six months he had a great fortune, on paper; took a trip east and brought back a charming wife from Toronto; built a large house beside the Red River, filled it with pictures of people he said were his ancestors, and carried on in it a roaring hospitality that never stopped.

He was president of a bank (that never opened); head of a brewery (for brewing the Red River); and secretary-treasurer of the Winnipeg, Hudson Bay and Arctic Ocean Railway that had a charter authorizing it to build a road to the Arctic Ocean (when it got ready). They had no track, but they printed stationery and passes, and in return E. P. received passes over all North America.

He was elected to the Manitoba legislature; they would have made him premier but for the existence of the grand old man of the province, John Norquay. At that, in a short time Norquay ate out of E. P.'s hand. To aristocracy E. P. added a touch of prestige by always being apparently about to be called away—imperially. If someone said, "Will you be in Winnipeg all winter, Mr. Leacock?" he answered, "It will depend a good deal on what happens in West Africa." Just that; West Africa beat them.

Then the Manitoba boom crashed. Simple people like my father were wiped out in a day. Not so E. P. Doubtless he was left utterly bankrupt, but it made no difference. He used credit instead of cash; he still had his imaginary bank and his railway to the Arctic Ocean. Anyone asking about a bill was told that E. P.'s movements were uncertain and would depend a good deal on what happened in Johannesburg. That held them another six months.

I used to see him when he made his periodic trips east—on passes—to impress his creditors in the west. He floated on hotel credit, loans and unpaid bills. A banker was his natural victim. E. P.'s method was simple. As he entered the banker's private office he would exclaim, "I say! Do you fish? Surely that's a greenheart casting rod on the wall?" (E. P. knew the names of everything.) In a few minutes the banker, flushed and pleased, was exhibiting the rod and showing trout flies. When E. P. went out he carried $100 with him. There was no security.

He dealt similarly with credit at livery stables and shops. He bought with lavish generosity, never asking a price. He never suggested payment except as an afterthought, just as he was going out. "By the way, please let me have the bill promptly. I may be going away," and, in an aside to me, "Sir Henry Loch has cabled from West Africa." They never saw him again.

When ready to leave a hotel, E. P. would call for his bill at the desk and break out into enthusiasm at the reasonableness of it. "Compare that," he would say in his aside to me, "with the Hotel Crillon in Paris! Remind me to mention to Sir John how admirably we've been treated; he's coming here next week." Sir John was our prime minister. The hotelkeeper hadn't known he was coming—and he wasn't. Then came the final touch. "Now let me see . . . $76 . . ." Here E. P. fixed his eye firmly on the hotelman. "You give me $24 and then I can remember to send an even hundred." The man's hand trembled. But he gave it.

This does not mean that E. P. was dishonest. To him his bills were merely "deferred," like the British debt to the United States. He never made, never even contemplated, a crooked deal in his life. All his grand schemes were as open as sunlight, and as empty.

E. P. knew how to fashion his talk to his audience. I once introduced him to a group of my college friends, to whom academic degrees meant a great deal. Casually E. P. turned to me and said, "Oh, by the way, you'll be glad to know that I've just received my honorary degree from the Vatican—finally!"

Of course it could not last. Gradually faith weakens, credit crumbles, creditors grow hard and friends turn faces away. Little by little, E. P. sank down. Now a widower, he was a shuffling, half-shabby figure who would have been pathetic except for his indomitable self-belief. Times grew ever tougher and at length even the simple credit of the barrooms broke under him. My brother Jim told me of E. P. being put out of a Winnipeg bar by an angry bartender. E. P. had brought in four men, raised his hand haughtily and said, "Drinks for Mr. Leacock and friends." The bartender broke into oaths. E. P. hooked a friend by the arm. "Come away," he said. "I'm afraid the poor fellow's crazy."

Presently free travel came to an end. The railways found out

446

at last that there was not any Arctic Ocean Railway. Just once more E. P. managed to come east. I met him in Toronto—a trifle shabby but wearing a plug hat with a crape band around it. "Poor Sir John," he said, "I felt I simply must come down for his funeral." Then I remembered that the Prime Minister was dead, and realized that kindly sentiment had meant free transportation.

That was the last I ever saw of E. P. Finally someone paid his fare back to England. He received from some family trust an income of £2 a week, and on that sum he lived, with such dignity as might be, in a remote village in Worcestershire. He told the people of the village—so I learned later—that his stay was uncertain: It would depend a good deal on what happened in China. But nothing happened in China. There he stayed for years and there he might have finished, but for a strange chance, a sort of poetic justice, that gave him an evening in the sunset.

In the part of England where our family belonged, there was an ancient religious brotherhood with a centuries-old monastery and dilapidated estates. E. P. descended on them, since the brothers seemed an easy mark. In the course of his pious retreat he took a look into the brothers' finances and his quick intelligence discovered a longstanding claim against the government, very large and valid beyond doubt. In no time E. P. was at Westminster. British officials were easier to handle than Ontario hotelkeepers.

The brothers got a lot of money. In gratitude they invited E. P. to be their permanent manager. The years went easily by among gardens, orchards and fishponds as old as the Crusades.

When I was lecturing in London in 1921 he wrote to me. "Do come down; I am too elderly to travel, but I will send a chauffeur with a car and two lay brothers to bring you here." Just like E. P., the "lay brothers" touch. But I could not go. He ended his days at the monastery, no cable calling him to West Africa.

If there is a paradise I am sure the unbeatable quality of his spirit will get him in. He will say at the gate, "Peter? Surely you must be a relation of Lord Peter of Tichfield?" But if he fails, then, as the Spaniards say, "May the earth lie light upon him."

When the great violinist chose music
for his concerts, he did it in his own way

FRITZ KREISLER'S "DISCOVERIES"

by Louis Biancolli

Some years ago, while serving as annotator of the New York Philharmonic Symphony, I was obliged to write a program note about a Concerto in C major by Fritz Kreisler, the great violinist who died in 1962. Now, when this same concerto was first published in Mainz, Germany, in 1912, Antonio Vivaldi was billed as the composer, with Kreisler credited only as arranger and editor. The 1912 score, however, did carry a telltale inscription—in German, French and English—which included the following: "This concerto is freely treated from old manuscripts and constitutes an original work.... When the concerto is played in public Fritz Kreisler's name must be mentioned in the program."

Several previous "arrangements" by Kreisler from "classical manuscripts" carried similar statements. Even with so many clues lying around, it was not till February 1935, on his 60th birthday, that Kreisler's secret finally leaked out. It was then discovered that all but one of the pieces "edited" by Kreisler and ascribed to Vivaldi, Pugnani, Couperin, Francoeur, Porpora and Padre Martini were Kreisleriana, pure and simple. The music world promptly split into two camps—those charging Kreisler with having played cheat, as opposed to those applauding the supreme mastery involved in carrying off the hoax and successfully concealing it for so many years. To get the full story I went to the best authority on the subject—Fritz Kreisler himself.

"I was at the beginning of my career when it all started," Mr. Kreisler said. "For a while I wasn't sure what I wanted to be. I had studied medicine and art. I also wanted to be an army officer and had entered training. But the violin was really my first love. I had begun to study it when I was four. I entered the Vienna Conservatory when I was seven and finished at ten with first prize. Then came the Paris Conservatory and the French gold medal at 12. At 14 I was already touring America."

"What made you undecided about continuing as a violinist?"

"My father was a medical doctor, and at the time I thought of becoming one, too. He himself had wanted to be a violinist, but his parents wouldn't let him. Being a violinist then was like going around in the streets with a hurdy-gurdy, unless, of course, you were a Wilhelmj, a Sarasate or a Joachim. Well, in spite of the risks, I decided to remain a violinist."

"I suppose by 'risks' you mean more than the dangers of bucking competition with the spectacular personalities of that time."

"Well, there was the problem of programs. . . . The violinist's recital repertoire was then very small."

"I don't follow you," I interrupted. "How about all the standard violin concertos?"

"Anybody playing a violin concerto with piano accompaniment at that time would have been laughed off the stage."

"How about Bach's unaccompanied sonatas?"

"They were not very popular."

"Beethoven and Schubert?"

"There were some sonatas by Schubert, but Beethoven's sonatas were out of the question. You had to be big to do them and you needed a big pianist to collaborate with you, a combination, let us say, equal to Horowitz and Elman, or Rubinstein and Heifetz."

"Couldn't you hire an orchestra to play the concerto accompaniments?" I asked.

451

"You could scarcely do that, if you were poor and unknown. The result was that if you were a concert beginner, you never played a concerto. And if you were poor and unknown, no great pianist would appear with you. Therefore, no Beethoven sonatas."

"I begin to see why medicine and a military career seemed more attractive to you than music."

"So what did you do if you began to give concerts?" Mr. Kreisler went on. "You fiddled around with Bach's 'Chaconne' or the 'Devil's Trill' of Tartini or sonatas by Corelli, Veracini and Geminiani. The rest of the program was made up of smaller pieces, like Ernst's 'Elegie,' Raff's 'Cavatina,' Wieniawski's 'Mazurka' and 'Polonaise' and Vieuxtemps' 'Ballade.' They were all good pieces as far as they went, but I wanted to play other things. And there just weren't any."

"How about arrangements of compositions originally written for voice or piano, which is such a growing practice today?" I asked the maestro.

"That wasn't done then," replied Mr. Kreisler. "The great exception was Chopin's E-flat major Nocturne, which was called 'The Virgin's Prayer' in the violin version."

"That left you with repertoire enough for about one concert-size program, complete with encores."

"That was why I resolved to create a repertoire of my own." Mr. Kreisler leaned forward, his brow furrowed. . . . "I then began to write music under other composers' names. I took the names of little-known composers like Pugnani and Louis Couperin, the grandfather of François Couperin.

"Not a single composition of Couperin's was known. Maybe in faraway libraries there were pieces by him, on yellow, illegible manuscripts. You had to rummage around to find them. So with Padre Martini. Naturally, Vivaldi was a bit different. Bach had made arrangements and transcriptions and even borrowed ideas from him. So had others. And his music was scattered around everywhere."

"Was it ever your idea to imitate the style of these composers?"

"Not for one moment. I could have done a better job of copying their style if I had intended it. That wasn't my plan at all. I just wanted some pieces for myself . . . and I wrote them. I was 18 then and I wanted to be a violinist, not a composer. I wanted to give recitals and I couldn't put several pieces on the program and sign them all 'Kreisler.' It would have looked arrogant.

"So I took those old forgotten names. First I brought out a piece by Pugnani. There is extant only one little piece by Pugnani."

"Was there anything in the composition to give you away?"

"A child could have seen Pugnani never wrote it. There was a semicadenza in the middle of it completely out of style with Pugnani's period. I played it and it was a huge success."

"What did you answer when people began to ask you where you had found these little pieces?"

"I was stumped. I didn't want to be known as a composer. Finally I said: 'I found them in libraries and monasteries while visiting Rome, Florence, Venice and Paris. They were in dusty old manuscripts. I copied them.' "

"Didn't they ask you to name the libraries and monasteries?"

"Oh, yes, but I told them to go around and find out for themselves. I assured them there was plenty of material to choose from."

"Were you the only violinist to play these pieces of yours?"

"For a couple of years I was. Then a colleague of mine asked, 'Can I have that Pugnani piece to play?' I made a copy and let him have it. Others began asking for copies. I asked nothing except mention in the program that the piece was brought out from manuscript and edited by Fritz Kreisler, with bowing and fingering."

"How about the critics?"

"They were calling them 'little masterpieces,' worthy of Bach and so forth."

"You must have been really stumped when the publishers approached you."

"I told Schott, the publisher in Mainz, the whole truth. The pieces were all mine, I said, but I didn't want my name appearing on them. Schott agreed."

"Were you paid very much for them?"

"He bought the whole set of 25 pieces at $10 each, bringing me exactly $250. That was all the revenue I ever derived from them in Europe. Later I sold them to Carl Fischer's in America and earned some money on them."

"Did Schott profit from the deal?"

"Did he! Hundreds of thousands of copies were sold."

"You must have had lots of fun reading what the critics had to say about these 'old and forgotten' composers."

"I remember one German reviewer in particular. He once wrote as follows about me: 'We heard Fritz Kreisler again last night. He played beautifully, but naturally his temperament lacks the strength and maturity to reach the heights of the Pugnani music.' "

"You didn't write him a little love note telling him the truth?"

"No, but one day I did tell Eugène Ysaÿe, the great violinist, that the pieces were all mine."

"What was his reaction?"

"He smiled and said, 'You pig, so you wrote all these things? Then why do you let these fellows run around playing your music without giving you proper credit? I would have given them hell if I were you.' "

"I'd like to hear more about the music critics, being one myself. I feel that there but for the grace of God, write I."

"Let me tell you the most beautiful instance of all. Once I wrote a few special pieces for a Viennese recital. I called them 'Posthumous Waltzes' by Joseph Lanner. The following day Leopold Schmidt, the critic of the *Berliner Tageblatt*, accused me of tactlessness. He raved about the Lanner waltzes. They were worthy of Schubert, he said. How dared I bracket my own little salon piece, 'Caprice Viennois,' with such gems?

"I wrote to Dr. Schmidt. I said I was pained, but I felt compelled, for once, to say that he was 'not devoid of tactlessness' himself. I was terribly sorry, but if the Lanner pieces were 'worthy of Schubert,' then I was Schubert, because I had written them! The letter was reprinted everywhere.

454

"Now don't you suppose critics and musicians who saw that letter would have said to themselves: 'If this is so, then the same thing must be true of the Francoeur, Couperin, Vivaldi and Pugnani pieces'? All they had to do was look at the pieces themselves and read the inscription, which almost gave the whole thing away."

"Did no one ever ask you point-blank whether you had composed those pieces yourself?"

"Not until my 60th birthday. I was in Vienna. Yehudi Menuhin was playing at the Brooklyn Academy of Music. Olin Downes, the critic of the New York *Times*, was on the program as lecturer and commentator. Mr. Menuhin was paying me a tribute by including several of my pieces. Mr. Downes wanted material for his talk. He came to see my publisher Fischer.

"Fischer hemmed and hawed. He told him he wasn't 100 percent sure himself. Mr. Downes immediately smelled a story. He cabled me in Vienna for the information.

"That was really the very first time I was ever asked directly. I did not want to lie. So I cabled back, 'I COMPOSED THEM ALL MYSELF,' and gave my reason: I had needed program material and thought it unwise to use my own name. The story appeared in the New York *Times*. That started the avalanche."

Mr. Kreisler picked up a copy of his Concerto in C and signaled me to come over and inspect it with him. He conceded that the themes of the first and third movements might be rightly termed "Vivaldian" in style. Then he pointed to the sudden harmonic changes in the second movement. These, he said, were strictly Schubertian and Berliozian.

"It should have been obvious to anyone studying the score carefully that the rest is Kreisler," he remarked.

"You may be right," I said, "but on behalf of my fellow critics and musicians I like to feel that even Antonio Vivaldi might have been fooled."

"Or Fritz Kreisler himself," he replied, smiling. "That is, if someone else had discovered the concerto among 'classic manuscripts' in a monastery."

455

A big business and a big fake
went, for a while, hand in hand

THE GREAT FALSE FRONT

by Craig Thompson

He was a testy little man who wore shoes with heels that added an inch to his stature and spats that matched his pants. He had a broad, flat, owl's face with black eyes that roved restlessly behind his glasses, and a brain so cunning that it enabled him to be, at the same time, the president of an $86-million corporation and one of the master swindlers of the century.

In his 61 years he used many identities, but the one he made most infamous was the one he furnished the unsuspecting editors of *Who's Who in America,* for their 1938–1939 edition. It ran:

COSTER, Frank Donald, corpn. official; b. Washington, D.C., May 12, 1884; s. Frank Donald and Marie (Girard) C.; Ph.D. U. of Heidelberg 1909, M.D. 1911; m. Carol Jenkins Schiefflin, Jamaica, L.I., May 1, 1921; practicing physician, N.Y.C., 1912–14; pres. Girard & Co. Inc. (successor Girard Chemical Co.), 1914–26; pres. McKesson & Robbins, Ltd.; dir. Bridgeport City Trust Co., Fairfield (Conn.) Trust Co.; Methodist. Clubs: N.Y. Yacht, Bankers, Lotos, Advertising (N.Y.), University, Black Rock Yacht (Bridgeport), Brooklawn Country.

Seldom have so many lies been told in so short a space. The man's name was Philip Musica, not Coster; he was born in Naples, Italy, not Washington; in 1877, not 1884. His wife's name had been Carol Jenkins Hubbard, not Schiefflin, and they were married in 1926, not 1921. Elmira Reformatory and the Tombs prison, not Heidelberg, had been his universities, and he had never been closer to the practice of medicine than as a conveyor of alcohol for the bootleg trade. He was neither a Methodist nor a member of most of the clubs he listed.

But he most assuredly was a director of the two banks he named and the president of McKesson and Robbins, an old-line drug house which, in 1937, transacted nearly $150 million of business. When he acquired control of McKesson and Robbins, it was a small manufacturing firm. He expanded it into a giant, and though he plundered it rapaciously and embroiled it in one of the most resounding scandals in commercial history, he could not destroy it. McKesson and Robbins is today sounder, richer, more flourishing and respected than it ever was.

Philip Musica was six years old when Papa Antonio and Mamma Maria spent most of their savings for steerage tickets and moved from the slums of Naples to the equally redolent slums of New York's lower East Side. There Maria gave birth to a daughter, Louise; then Grace, Arthur, George and finally Robert, 23 years younger than Philip.

At about the time he attained his majority, Philip persuaded his father to put up his meager savings for a joint venture into the import business. They called it A. Musica and Son, and specialized in Italian foodstuffs such as cheese, pasta and sausages.

When the Musicas received a shipment of goods, Philip would have false invoices and bills of lading made out to show only a fraction of the true weight. Then a customs inspector would be bribed to substitute the originals of these for the true records supplied to the customs service by the shipper. When this had been done, the Musicas could take copies to the warehouse or the pier and claim their merchandise by paying duty on only a part of its actual value. It amounted to duty-free entry of about half their imports and permitted them to undersell competitors without any sacrifice of profits.

In a few years the Musica business climbed from nothing to a gross yearly turnover of $500,000. The family moved from the slums into a spacious house in Brooklyn, with landscaped grounds, horses, stables and a carriage house. In 1909, however, the scheme was uncovered, and Antonio and Philip were indicted.

Now 32, Musica was a dapper little man with a certain social polish. This came from expensive clothes, a reserved manner, a quiet voice and some punctilio. When he dramatically entered a plea of guilty, taking the blame for everything and exonerating Antonio of all guilt—even though the evidence included 26 false invoices with Antonio's signature on each—he got credit for possessing nobility of spirit as well. Antonio was freed; Philip was fined $5000 and sentenced to a year in Elmira Reformatory, then used for federal prisoners. But such was the impression he made that President William Howard Taft was persuaded to pardon him when only five months and 15 days of the term had run. Musica returned to the import business and a bigger fraud.

His next scheme was more complex and more quickly detected. He set up a business in human hair—in wide demand because of the high coiffures women wore at the time—and using the commercial paper that accompanied his shipments, he stole $600,000 from 22 banks. For this he spent three years in jail. And so, from one piece of criminality to another, he moved into his middle 40's. Then national prohibition opened a new field for him.

The first step toward the creation of F. Donald Coster was taken in Brooklyn, with the formation of the Adelphi Pharmaceutical Manufacturing Corporation. Calling himself Frank Costa, Musica set up the Adelphi with $8000 borrowed from his mother.

As a manufacturer of drugs, Costa obtained a federal permit for 5000 gallons of alcohol a month, which he used to make hair tonics, dandruff removers and furniture polishes. To remove the scents, soap, oils, waxes and coloring matter, all a customer had to

GIRARD CHEMICAL CO.

Girard and Company

W W Smith & Co

MANNING & CO.

P. PIERSON & COMPANY

459

do was run an Adelphi product through an ordinary still. Then the alcohol could be cut with water, color and flavoring added to it, and one gallon of "dandrofuge" made into nearly two of "fine old Scotch whisky, just off the boat."

The trouble was that Costa could not get along with one of his partners, Joseph Brandino. In the quarrels that arose, Brandino alternately threatened to beat him to a pulp or tear him into pieces. Costa became so terrified that he tipped the Treasury Department's Alcohol Tax Unit to the true nature of Adelphi's business, and the permit was revoked. "It's too bad, Joe," said Costa, "but that's the end of it."

Only it wasn't. Some years later, noting the meteoric rise of F. Donald Coster, Brandino blackmailed him for $3000 on threat of exposure. Coster paid, and kept on paying until at the time of his death the cumulative count of Brandino's hush money came to more than $100,000—an average of about $10,000 a year.

Coster next emerged in Mount Vernon, New York, in 1923. There he rented a small, two-story brick structure for another "dandrofuge" factory he called Girard and Company. Purportedly, the enterprise belonged to an elderly chemist named P. Horace Girard. To give the federal investigators a checkpoint on Girard, Maria Musica, a widow now, and her younger daughter Grace assumed the name and moved to Westbury, Long Island, where they lived in a house listed as P. Horace Girard's home. For the rest of her days Maria Musica remained Maria Girard. Arthur Musica now became George Vernard, agent for a fictitious firm called W. W. Smith and Company. George Musica became George Dietrich and Coster's right hand. Robert, now 23, also took the name Dietrich and worked close to George.

After ten years of going their separate ways, Girard and Company reunited the multi-aliased Musicas in a common enterprise. All, that is, but Louise, who got married and moved out of the family orbit.

Coster's new enterprise would have died in infancy had anyone investigated Smith and Company, Girard's biggest customer. The only evidence of its existence was a one-room Brooklyn office occupied by George Vernard and a typist. Much of the alcohol that flowed into the Girard factory flowed out again to commercial warehouses designated on Smith and Company orders. Bootleggers' trucks then picked it up, paying Vernard in cash, while he, in turn, paid Girard by check. At the same time, Vernard made out and filed in his office sheaves of phony papers which indicated that the stuff had been shipped to buyers all over the world. Coster was betting that no investigator would unravel this complex trail. He was right for 15 years, and during that time nearly $8 million passed through George Vernard's bank account.

By December 1924, Girard and Company had come along nicely enough to give Coster big ideas. His first move was to invite the impeccable Price, Waterhouse and Company, one of the most highly respected accounting firms in the country, to conduct an audit of his books.

When the auditor came to Mount Vernon, Coster and Dietrich watched him with hawklike concentration. What they learned was that, as a matter of established practice, an auditor did not check a company's inventory, but accepted whatever tally of stocks on hand the company officers offered. As for the audit, it showed Girard and Company to be a tidy little business with assets of $279,000, gross sales of $252,000 and net profits of $33,300. Coster took it to his Mount Vernon bank and asked for a $100,000 loan. Unable to advance the sum, the bank introduced him to a Wall Street man named Julian Thompson.

Of all the people touched by Coster's schemes, Thompson comes closest to being the tragic figure. He was a sensitive romantic, who wore pince-nez with his crew cut, and divided his talents between business and the arts. A competent playwright, one of his plays, *The Warrior's Husband*, raised Katharine Hepburn to stardom. The meeting took place in Coster's office. Upon the walls hung two masterpieces of printing-press forgery—phony diplomas attesting the fictitious Heidelberg doctorates. Coster talked skillfully of drug manufacture and only fleetingly of hair tonic. Thompson became a Coster booster. "You're too small for Wall Street now," he told Coster, "but maybe I can help."

To that end, he arranged a meeting with officials of the Bridgeport City Trust Company. With his slightly old-fashioned clothes, his earnest, punctilious manner and his Price, Waterhouse audit, Coster captured the Bridgeport bankers. Not only did they lend him $80,000 of the bank's money but added $27,500 of their own to buy 275 shares in his company. Girard and Company moved to Bridgeport, upped its alcohol withdrawals to 15,000 gallons a month and turned in a banner year in 1925. Sales jumped to $1,100,000, profits to $250,000, and the bank loan was repaid. Word spread that F. Donald Coster was a wizard.

He was, too, in his fashion. During that 1925 year-end audit a Price, Waterhouse accountant noted that Smith and Company owed Girard $22,500, and was moved to ask George Dietrich (Musica) just what this Smith and Company was. For reply, Dietrich pulled out a report by Dun and Company, one of the predecessor firms of Dun & Bradstreet, that characterized Smith as a globe-girdling trading concern, itemized properties it owned from Montreal to Bombay as worth about $7 million and gave it top credit rating. The report was a forgery, but it was so expertly done that the auditors unhesitatingly accepted it as genuine.

Coster, meanwhile, began focusing on McKesson and Robbins. Established in 1833, this firm had grown old without growing big. But it had one thing Coster needed—a good name. Negotiations were begun, a price agreed upon, a stock issue floated, and eventually Coster handed over a check for $1,100,000 in exchange for a corporate identity which raised him above suspicion. By the end of 1927, with the details of consolidation completed, the annual audit showed him in control of a $4,100,000 manufacturing company, drawing 25,000 gallons of alcohol per month and earning $600,000 a year net profit.

What Coster did has since caused sweeping changes to be made in auditing practices and added millions of dollars to the costs of operating America's business, but at the time it was not the custom for an auditor to go into the warehouses and stockrooms and count the bales and bottles on hand. Coster made the most of this fact.

The swindle was based upon a fictitious trade in crude drugs, each transaction of which was carried through a chain of many steps. The responsibility for hoodwinking the auditors fell to George Dietrich, whose office was next to Coster's and whose devotion to his job was such that on one occasion he went into a hospital at the close of one business day, had his tonsils removed and was back at nine o'clock the next morning. During 11 years Dietrich looked at all the incoming mail. He had to, because he could never risk letting someone else see it first.

In a typical transaction Dietrich would make out a McKesson and Robbins order to P. Pierson and Company, Montreal—one of five nonexistent Canadian warehouses he used—to purchase for the McKesson and Robbins account a quantity of, say, oil of lemon. Next he would clip to the carbon of the order an invoice on a printed P. Pierson form showing that the purchase had been made. Then a receiving ticket would be made out, to show that the goods were stored at the Pierson warehouse. After the bill had been duly entered on the inventory book as an account payable, a letter would be written to Manning and Company, Montreal—a fictitious bank—authorizing it to pay Pierson. There then would be added to the file a printed Manning and Company form certifying that Pierson had been paid. This completed the phony purchase, except that, on the books, McKesson and Robbins now owed the nonexistent Manning and Company thousands of dollars for nonexistent goods in a nonexistent warehouse.

The next step was to sell the stuff. To start the new phony-paper chain Dietrich would notify W. W. Smith and Company that McKesson and Robbins had, in Pierson's warehouse, a quantity of oil of lemon. There then would appear on Dietrich's desk an exquisitely printed Smith and Company form saying that the oil had been sold. In the same way and with the same detail that he had built up a sheaf of papers to record the purchase, Dietrich created another file to record its disposal, ending with a Manning statement showing payment by the purchaser. Supposing the fictitious sale price of the nonexistent goods to be $100,000, Dietrich would send a check on a real McKesson and Robbins bank account to Smith for $750, representing a sales commission of ¾ of 1 percent. This George Vernard converted into cash, which came back to Coster.

The printer who made the phony forms was never found. But the blanks were kept in Vernard's office and all typed by one girl, who used seven different typewriters. When asked if she ever felt strange, working on all those different letterheads with a separate machine for each, she replied, "Oh, no. I thought they were holding companies or something."

To complete the setup, Vernard maintained an office at the Montreal address of Manning and Company, where another girl kept one of the loneliest vigils on record. Perhaps twice a year she received two or three letters from Price, Waterhouse asking for a verification of the McKesson and Robbins balance on hand and a list of the company's stocks in the five warehouses. Such letters were mailed to Vernard, who sent back a packet of fat envelopes, all addressed to Price, Waterhouse in New York. These she stamped and dropped in the mail—and thus the swindle went on through the years. It was so good that the auditors, all honorable men, called Dietrich's crude-drugs division "the best-run department in the business."

Having developed his scheme, Coster saw that the only way it could ever be made to pay big money was to make McKesson and Robbins a big company. It would be manifestly absurd, and a sure source of suspicion, for a little company to carry on its books big sums tied up in crude drugs stored in foreign warehouses. Coster's lifetime drive had been toward bigness, and he had now created a situation in which being big was his only way out.

In 1928 most of the drugs used in the United States were sold through locally owned and operated wholesale houses. It was Coster's idea, which he broached to Julian Thompson, to weld these into a nationwide chain under the McKesson and Robbins banner. "Now," said Thompson enthusiastically, "you are big enough for Wall Street."

With promises of financial aid from two investment houses, Coster undertook to gather in the wholesalers. Wheedling, bragging, cajoling, pleading, even at times showing them McKesson and Robbins' fictitious inventory of nonexistent crude drugs to prove how solid a firm it was, he put the merger through. In return for some cash—provided by the public through purchases of McKesson and Robbins preferred stock—and large chunks of common stock, the wholesalers transferred ownership to McKesson and Robbins.

Coster was so successful that by the middle of 1929 he stood astride an $80-million Goliath, composed of 49 of the most respected jobbing houses in the country, a $5-million manufacturing division turning out 238 different products, and a crude-drug division which dealt strictly in fraud. To these, after repeal, was added a liquor division, which, almost overnight, became the largest liquor-distributing agency in the country.

As president of the new giant—third-largest drug house in the world—Coster fixed his salary at a modest $40,000 a year. "I'm not interested in making money," he explained to the 80 new vice-presidents who surrounded him, "I live for this company."

His mode of life bore witness to the lie. Back in 1926 he had gone one afternoon to a little church in Jamaica, Long Island, and there married the divorced sister of his onetime partner, Leonard Jenkins. Though many of his new associates stood quite high in the social world, the Costers made no efforts to use them for social climbing. They did not entertain much, and seldom went to nightclubs or any other public gathering places. Installed in an 18-room, stucco-and-tile house in Fairfield, Connecticut, which Coster bought for her, Mrs. Coster raised chow dogs.

Coster's only extravagance was a 134-foot, secondhand yacht, which, to honor his wife, he called the *Carolita*. The vessel was old and had previously been used by Marconi, the wireless man, and John Hays Hammond, Jr., the inventor, as a floating laboratory.

It could not be said that many of Coster's directors genuinely liked him, but, considering the way he lived and the long hours he spent at his desk, they did believe he told the truth when he said he lived for the company alone. As an executive he was irascible, sometimes arrogant and a tireless memo-writer. In the factory, his chemists had to throw out most of his ideas for new products, for, despite the Heidelberg diploma on his office wall, Coster knew next to nothing about medicine. In the merchandising field, his ideas were similarly bad, and almost as frequently thrown out. Some that were tried proved to be costly errors.

Nonetheless, Coster's directors came to believe that he was indispensable. Largely, this was based on his crude-drug operations. Year after year, no matter how badly things went in other departments, the crude-drug division always turned a profit. True, the profits kept on being plowed back into more crude drugs, but all those assets on the balance sheet looked mighty comforting. "Coster," they told one another, "is the greatest authority on crude drugs alive."

This was the facade, the external picture. Behind it Coster lived in a nightmare world of worry, vigilance and frenzied manipulation. His greatest crisis, next to his last one, came only a few months after he finished putting the merger together. Buying on margin, Coster had plunged far beyond his depth in the greatest bull market in history. When it finally broke, in October 1929, he was faced with total ruin just as his greatest adventure was getting under way. To save himself, he cranked his swindling machinery into high gear and in one three-day period he stole $634,000.

The irony was that his thefts saved his company. For, to steal so much so fast, Coster had to increase by many millions the company's inventory of nonexistent crude drugs. Since these appeared on the balance sheets as company assets, McKesson and Robbins seemed in sound condition. While self-appointed committees of stock or bond holders, guided by eagle-eyed operators out to make a killing, threw hundreds of companies into bankruptcy or receivership, no one lifted an eyebrow at McKesson and Robbins.

The business recession of 1937, and not the Great Depression, doomed Coster. Fearful that the United States economy had hit another bottomless skid, McKesson and Robbins' directors ordered a general conversion of stocks on hand into cash. Coster was told to turn at least $2 million of his crude-drug stockpile into dollars. But Coster, who had no drugs to sell, could do so only by pouring $2 million in cash into the company treasury and dropping an equal amount of nonexistent items from its inventories. This he could not or would not do.

Julian Thompson now became Coster's nemesis. Back in 1929, Thompson had left Wall Street to become McKesson and Robbins' controller and treasurer. It was his duty to see that the orders of the board were carried out. When months had passed and there had been no sign of reduction of the crude-drugs stockpile, Thompson demanded to know why.

"I told those fellows to cut down," Coster replied. "I'll just have to give them hell."

Still more months passed while Coster figured a way out. He cut his thefts to a whisper and proposed borrowing $3 million, purportedly for various company improvements, but more likely to get funds by which he could liquidate part of his phony stockpile. Before the company could borrow, however, Thompson had to swear that every item on the balance sheet was, to his knowledge and belief, a true statement.

As a result of a chance discovery, he had begun to wonder if that was so. The discovery was simply that, although the company had $21 million worth of drugs in five Canadian warehouses, there was not a penny's worth of insurance on any of it. Approaching Coster with this, he was airily dismissed.

"Oh," said Coster, "W. W. Smith takes care of that."

For the first time, Thompson cast his mind back over all he knew about W. W. Smith and came up shaken. He had seen the Dun report, but he decided to find out. Learning that it was a forgery, Thompson went to Montreal, then to call on George Vernard and finally back to Coster.

With the truth at last on the table between them, Coster leaned back and said, "What is it that you want, Mr. Thompson?" It was then, after 15 years of association, that Thompson at last saw Coster for what he was.

But it was Coster who had the steel in his makeup. "You," he told Thompson accusingly, "are deliberately trying to wreck this company. If you do not sign that certificate [for the $3-million loan], I shall throw the company into receivership."

McKesson and Robbins was Thompson's creation too. But he did not sign. . . .

The following morning Thompson went before a committee of the New York Stock Exchange and told what he knew. McKesson and Robbins was suspended from the big board. By late afternoon half a dozen investigations had been opened. In ten days Philip Musica had been completely unmasked.

In his Fairfield home, on the morning of December 16, 1938, Musica stood before a mirror with a pistol in his right hand. The calves of his legs touched a bathtub behind him, the rim of which was just below his knees. The sound of a shot echoed through the house, and the force of the bullet in his head slammed Musica back and down into the tub, where his blood ran vividly onto the white porcelain and down the drain. Even in suicide, he wanted to be a tidy man.

For a time, the survival of McKesson and Robbins as a going business was a touch-and-go matter. But Musica had limited his thievery strictly to the crude-drug manipulation, and the core of the company was sound. More than that, the company had become so important a part of the drug industry's distribution system that other manufacturing firms supported every effort to keep it alive. With the company placed in capable, energetic hands, it not only survived but grew steadily stronger.

The amount that Musica stole from McKesson and Robbins was eventually fixed at $2,900,000—the other $5 million that went through Vernard's bank account probably represented bootlegging operations—and only $51,000 (the value of the yacht and a piece of real estate) was ever recovered. The search for the missing money went on for years, and the searchers finally were convinced that much, if not most, of what Musica stole he paid over as blackmail to people who knew him when.

Philip Musica's widow refused to acknowledge the past and the truth that made him kill himself. She had his body laid away in an ornate Long Island mausoleum and caused the marble slab that covered it to be carved with this enduring alias: "F. Donald Coster, 1884–1938."

THE JEWEL swindler who acquires a really fine diamond or several fine diamonds can stay in business for life. A typical professional in this field is Henry Windsor. He usually works in places where a respectable-seeming foreigner might not be out of place, for he dresses the part and affects an accent. When he taps a prospect, he is furtive. Surreptitiously he pulls out a small packet of diamonds and shows them to the mark. "Smuggled in today from Johannesburg," he whispers. "Five thousand dollars for the lot."

If the mark is skeptical, Henry puts the packet in his hands and tells him to go to any jeweler and get the diamonds appraised. Few suckers can resist this bait. They take the diamonds to any convenient jeweler, while Henry trustingly waits outside. The jeweler, if he knows his diamonds, will appraise them at $8000 and may even offer to pay that for them. The wise mark will figure they are worth at least $10,000, so when he returns to Henry, he starts to dicker. If they are smuggled diamonds, he figures he can get them for half the price offered. Henry puts on his insulted act and, with an air of hauteur, returns the packet to his pocket.

The mark won't let him go. A little more haggling and the packet changes hands for $4500. Or, rather, a similar packet changes hands, but it contains only paste duplicates of Henry's real stock-in-trade. How many paste copies he peddles in a year might be determined by an order he gave a Manhattan manufacturer: "Five hundred each of five different sizes," corresponding to the five different diamonds in his first-show packet. In that quantity, copies are cheap. Our "smuggling foreigner," who was born in Little Rock, Arkansas, averages about 2000 percent profit on each deal.

—*Ralph Hancock, The Compleat Swindler (The Macmillan Company)*

*This lover created a fairyland world—an
awesome fake—for his Empress*

CATHERINE IN WONDERLAND

by Gina Kaus

Catherine the Great, Empress of Russia, never lost the capacity to fall in love. But even those later, bizarre amours which scandalized Europe were really nothing compared to her indestructible attachment to one man: Grigori Potemkin. Something more than physical passion gave distinction to this affair. The love of these two, whose common bond was ambition, realized itself in a dream of world rule.

Outwardly they had little in common: the Empress, personification of order and punctuality, who never drank a drop, who rose at dawn and in her 15-hour day accomplished more work than ten men; and Potemkin, who spent his days in lounging, his nights in drinking, whose gluttony was a byword and who rounded off the wildest debauches with prayers of repentance. Yet Potemkin worshiped her; he overwhelmed her with tenderness; he was past master at choosing presents valued solely for their superb frivolity. With Potemkin she became a real woman letting herself be spoiled by a man.

At first Catherine esteemed him as "the most comical and amusing character of the century," for this woman who had known so much horror yearned for gaiety and laughter. But presently she came to appreciate his real qualities . . . "Ah, what a good head the man has!" . . . Potemkin became Court Chamberlain and protector of the Tartars and other Asian peoples, important posts both. Then, suddenly, with no obvious cooling off in their passion, he left for the south, renouncing Catherine's body, but keeping her soul; he even appointed his successor to that intimate position he had relinquished. For years more her lovers were selected with his consent, or at his command. Potemkin was ready to lay at her feet anything—fortresses or flowers, provinces or paramours. (These favorites, incidentally, were expensive. They cost the country about 14 million rubles. What Potemkin himself received from Catherine's treasury must have run to nearly 50 million rubles.)

While merely Catherine's lover, Potemkin led a life of indolence, but the moment he left her embrace, his life became ruled by that "tremendous plan worthy of a Caesar" already shaped in Catherine's mind: the ruling of the Black Sea and all southeastern Europe. In 1783 she quietly annexed the Crimea, and Potemkin's business, as governor of the province, was now to turn this desert waste into a civilized country.

The task appealed to him. He embarked on a hundred projects: the building of the naval harbor at Sevastopol; vast fleets of merchant vessels and warships; importation of silkworms from China; planting of forests and vineyards; new factories and roads. He drew up plans for a magnificent new metropolis on the river Dnieper, to be named Ekaterinoslav—"Catherine's Glory." He made journeys north to inform Catherine of these new wonders. And she believed him. She believed, too, in the other miracles he reported: fields of waving corn, villages of contented, prosperous peasants—she really believed that in three years Potemkin had created the happiest, most fruitful region of her empire out of barren steppeland. She must visit the new province, see for herself these miracles.

Though Catherine was now 58 years of age, her enthusiasm had never been more abundant.

Potemkin had not made a garden out of the desert, wealth where had been squalor, but he was able to create the illusion of all this for Catherine's delight. Most of the villages, the factories existed only on paper; the steppes were still as desolate, the towns as tumbledown as always.

But Potemkin was a marvelous stage manager, and Catherine's Crimean journey was the greatest triumph of stage management ever known—an achievement worthy of being numbered among the wonders of the world.

Catherine set out on January 4 (Potemkin had gone ahead to "make arrangements") with a retinue of 40,000. Her sledge, drawn by 16 horses, was like a small house, with three windows in each wall. At every station 560 fresh horses were waiting; huge

bonfires lighted the road at night. Villagers had been ordered to repaint their houses (they painted only the walls facing the street); groups of artificial trees had been placed to screen unsightly spots; broken-down roofs had been repaired, not with tiles but with painted cardboard imitations; the populace must wear its best clothes; all the ancient and infirm must remain indoors; begging or the presenting of petitions was forbidden—all must "express their happiness by smiles and merry gestures." Years before, Catherine, traveling this road, had read misery and hunger in the emaciated, hostile faces—the truth. Now, seeing these clean streets, the well-dressed villagers, the gay merrymaking, she seemed to believe that she had really given her subjects happiness and prosperity.

"Is not my little household prettily furnished?" she asked the French ambassador as he rode beside her.

At Kiev all the guests of her retinue were provided with a furnished house, servants and carriages. After each meal the linen was given to the poor; every day the people had a new spectacle to gape at.

Catherine was a perfect hostess. Sweeping aside court etiquette, she forbade the mention of politics; though her corpulent body moved with difficulty, her brain darted swiftly over every subject—agriculture, child education, town planning, architecture. But about ten o'clock she would retire. Beside her bed was a mirror wall which slid back, revealing a second bed, that of her favorite, Mamonoff. This contrivance, one of Potemkin's little attentions, was provided throughout the journey.

As soon as the Dnieper was free of ice, the company embarked on waiting boats, and here began the dream journey through Potemkin's fairyland. Seven floating palaces followed by 80 attendant vessels carried 3000 persons. The imperial galleys were lined with costly brocade; the walls, the servants' uniforms gleamed with gold; meals were served on gold plate. Lying under her silken awning, the Empress saw towns decorated with huge triumphal arches and garlands, cattle grazing in the pastures, troops maneuvering and, at dusk, peasants dancing with carefree abandon. Even Potemkin's severest critics grew silent before these never-ending wonders, and Catherine's rapture knew no bounds.

She did not know that this fairyland vanished the moment her boat had passed, that the houses behind the triumphal arches were without roofs, doors or windows, that behind the houses were no streets, that the villages were deserted, that the cattle had been brought long distances to graze before her eyes, that the dancers were wretched serfs, taught, with pains and beatings, to perform their carefree capers.

After sunset, they were packed into carts like a traveling theatrical company and hurried to the next stand, again to provide a spectacle of holiday merrymaking.

At each of three anchorages there was a magnificent new palace with artificial waterfalls and a shady park. Potemkin could work miracles! He turned primeval jungle into formal English gardens—by transplanting trees that flourished for a few days and then slowly withered. Again, houses for Catherine's guests had been erected—jerry-built, but furnished with every conceivable luxury. And everywhere were soldiers, fine, upstanding specimens, magnificently uniformed. At Ekaterinoslav the Empress laid the foundation stone of the new cathedral. Its plans would have eclipsed St. Peter's in Rome—but the cathedral was never built. Proceeding now by carriage, the party drove through villages buzzing with industry: bricklaying, roadbuilding—everywhere activity, pulsing life, busy crowds. They could not guess that these same towns were dead and derelict, that Potemkin had snatched no less than 20 communities bodily from their homes to populate temporarily his province. Every kind of entertainment was provided. At one stop an artificial volcano spurted flame into the air all night; at Sevastopol a band of 180 musicians played at the reception dinner.

Before the windows Catherine's gaze traveled over massed regiments, down to the bay, where lay the new Black Sea fleet, built in two years. A roar of cannon broke from the decks, with shouts of "Long live the Empress!" Later followed the triumphant climax of the whole journey: At Poltava two armies met in a mock combat representing the famous victory which Peter the Great had won on the same ground.

It was effective stagecraft, and Catherine's happiness for the moment was complete. She owed it all to Potemkin. But had she discovered the hidden flaws in his methods, it might have damped her enthusiasm. Had she known that the warships were constructed of the poorest materials, that the cannon were without ammunition, that the fortress of Kherson was built of sand and, far from withstanding cannon shot, was to be severely damaged by the first thunderstorm—then she might have regarded this Crimean journey in a sober and pessimistic light. It had cost 7 million rubles and an enormous expenditure of human energy, and it had achieved nothing save the further aggrandizement of Potemkin in Catherine's eyes. That, at any rate, had been successful.

The Crimean journey and the elaborate invention of a happy, prosperous country were no more than a highly original, and very expensive, tribute paid by one of the greatest lovers of history to his mistress.

⟨∿∿⟩

PETER MINUIT was sent by the Dutch West India Company to establish a trading post in the New World. The Dutch knew that the French and the British already had established beachheads in the area. They also suspected that neither the French nor the British would be pleased at the establishment of a Dutch colony amid their new-found lands. The Dutch, being smaller but smarter, knew they did not have the strength to resist intervention by either nation. Consequently, they resolved to make their colonization as legal as possible by purchasing Manhattan Island from its occupants.

It was a noble thought, but Minuit's 60 guilders' worth of knives, axes, cloth and beads for all of Manhattan, even unimproved, has always seemed to us a monstrous swindle. And having long considered ourselves akin to underdogs, we resented the way the poor Indian was pushed around. It wasn't until we dug a little deeper into history that we discovered that another swindle was involved.

The Indians who sold Manhattan Island didn't mind. The land wasn't theirs (they were just weekenders over from Brooklyn); it belonged to the Weckquaesgeeks.

—Ralph Hancock, The Compleat Swindler (The Macmillan Company)

A CUSTOMER in a Copenhagen department store complained to the management about the attendant in the ladies' rest room, who had given her a frosty stare when she failed to leave a generous tip. "Why, we have no attendant in the ladies' room," said the manager.

A check revealed that the "attendant" was a woman who had wandered in for a rest the year before. While relaxing with her knitting, the woman had received coins from patrons who thought she was the attendant. Recognizing opportunity when it knocked, the woman had come in regularly ever since, netting while she knitted. *—Walter Kiernan*

THE DRAKE FABLE

by William T. Brannon

Would you like to invest a few dollars and receive a big slice of one of the world's great fortunes? If so, you are fair game for a 300-year-old swindle. It began in England a few years after Sir Francis Drake died aboard his ship off Portobello, Panama, on January 28, 1596; later spread to America; and has cropped up regularly in the United States ever since that time.

The story is simple: The British government confiscated Drake's estate. The famous freebooter's will was tied up in the Ecclesiastical Court and was never probated. There had been an illicit affair between Drake and Queen Elizabeth, and the government suppressed the will to keep the scandal from coming to light. A vast fortune awaits those who will help the legitimate heirs to force the British to settle.

It is an alluring story that thousands have found easy to believe. It was only a minor racket, however, until the early 20th century, when a modern version was conceived and executed by one of the most fabulous swindlers America has ever produced.

Oscar M. Hartzell was an Iowa farm boy whose parents had to struggle for a living. Oscar quit school early to help on the farm and probably would have stayed there had it not been for a suave stranger who called on his mother one day. He told her the story of the Drake estate and convinced her that she would reap a rich harvest from an investment of $10. She never saw the stranger again, nor did she hear any more of the Drake estate.

Oscar, a deputy sheriff, was impressed by the swindler's story. He went to the library in Sioux City and gathered all the information he could about the British buccaneer. He steeped himself in the lore of the Spanish Main and, specifically, Sir Francis Drake's quasi-legal plundering of Spanish ships with the blessing of Queen Elizabeth. He followed this by learning all he could about the Virgin Queen.

In the course of his travels around the farming sections near Sioux City, Hartzell talked to people who had been bilked of small sums, and it surprised him that many of the victims confidently expected to receive something for their investment. He realized that here was a big field, virtually untapped.

Hartzell saved his money and went to Chicago, where he did more research and frequented the haunts of shady gentry. Eventually, he met two kindred souls, a Mrs. Sudie B. Whitaker and Milo F. Lewis. Both were accomplished city slickers and their first impulse was to brush aside this young man who looked as if he had just come to town with a load of corn. Nonetheless, they recognized his possibilities and went in with him. Early in 1919 the three announced the formation of the Sir Francis Drake Association, whose purpose would be to wrest from the British Crown the illegally suppressed estate of the long-dead buccaneer.

The original plan was to solicit all those whose name was Drake or whose forebears had been named Drake. This in itself was an ambitious project, and Hartzell went to Iowa to start on the farmers. A big, heavyset young man, with tousled brown hair and ruddy cheeks, Hartzell could talk the farmers' language. He certainly didn't look or act like a swindler.

He told his victims that he had located Ernest Drake, then living on a farm in Missouri. This man was the sole surviving heir to the

Drake fortune, and there would be a rich reward for those who contributed to the expense of forcing a settlement. The response to this was so gratifying that Hartzell revised his plans after only a few calls. He decided to permit anybody, with or without Drake connections, to participate.

Now there was such a rush to get in that Hartzell had to make another quick change of plans. Instead of clipping the victim just once, he devised a way to bring in repeated donations. Investors could buy shares on the budget plan, just as they purchased cars and homes. Participation in the final settlement would be in proportion to the contribution. Payments could be small or large, and they could be made weekly. If this thing was handled properly, Hartzell reasoned, it could be prolonged indefinitely.

A tight organization was necessary to accomplish this. Hartzell set up local chapters, each under the direction of a collector, who would issue receipts and make regular remittances to headquarters. Hartzell promised to send the latest news of the venture to the collectors, who would relay it to the investors at "pep" lectures at the weekly meetings.

And while he was about it, Hartzell decided it was just as well to make his promises lavish. The return, he said, would be from $1000 to $5000 for every dollar invested. He was vague about the size of the final settlement, but he intimated that the sum was so large that his followers would be unable to comprehend it.

It seems likely that Hartzell himself was unable to understand fully all his claims. For example, if the estate had amounted to as little as $100 and if interest at 6 percent had been compounded quarterly, the total amount would have exceeded $26 billion.

The Iowa visit was so successful that Hartzell and his partners hired field agents to organize chapters in seven states of the Middle West. The response was so phenomenal that the operations were again extended, to four southwestern states. Hartzell's long-range plan contemplated organizing the whole of the United States and Canada, but this never materialized.

Though Lewis and Mrs. Whitaker, the city slickers, were still in

479

the Sir Francis Drake Association, Hartzell, the hayseed, became the dominant figure. From the outset, he ruled his domain with an iron hand. He divided it into 21 districts, each in charge of a field agent. The agents made regular rounds of the chapters, gathering what the collectors had taken in.

Hartzell did not demand all the money. He called his agents together and told them they could keep commissions for themselves. "I want $2500 a week," he told them. "Please see that I receive this amount."

Though the collectors gave receipts to the "donators," as Hartzell called them, and these receipts were to determine each investor's share when the settlement was made, Hartzell himself kept no records. He told the regional agents and collectors to keep their own records.

Having heard of the statutes on using the mails to defraud, Hartzell carefully refrained from writing letters. All contact with his field agents was by wire. He insisted that remittances to him be made by express.

To keep up interest in the cause, Hartzell sent regular messages, weekly or oftener, to his field agents. These were enthusiastically embellished by bulletins of progress in the estate's settlement sent to the local chapters by the agents.

The fervor of the Drake Association members surprised even Hartzell. In some cities, no meeting halls could be found large enough to accommodate all the members. An Illinois town had more than 2000 members; a small city in North Dakota claimed membership of 2500, including all the members of the Chamber of Commerce.

In one midwestern city, a minister was the collector and the stoutest advocate of Hartzell's cause. He told his followers that the British government would oppose the settlement to cover up the scandal of Queen Elizabeth's illegitimate son born of the clandestine affair with Drake. There was no question that he sincerely believed this, and in speeches as stirring as any of his sermons he convinced his listeners.

From the beginning, Hartzell warned his adherents that there would be stiff opposition from officials in both England and the United States. American money lords, he said, would side with British financial interests and would use every available weapon to prevent a settlement. He demanded that every contributor stick to a policy of "silence, secrecy and nondisturbance." No whisper of the campaign to wrest the great fortune from the British must reach the ears of the law. Hartzell threatened to "red-ink" anybody who complained or discussed his proposition with the authorities. He made it clear that anybody who talked would be summarily cut off from participation.

Nobody complained and nobody asked questions. And no hint of the swindle reached the Post Office inspectors for the first three years. Even then, their information was so vague that they had no conception of the magnitude of the scheme; nor were they in possession of any concrete evidence.

Nevertheless, Hartzell was smart enough not to tempt fate. It might look better to the investors, he reasoned, if he went to England. Mrs. Whitaker and Lewis went with him. He sent back cablegrams describing his efforts to reach the proper British officials, giving details of the intricate legal steps that must precede the settlement. This, of course, would be costly and delay was inevitable. He urged his followers to be patient and warned them again that they must maintain the utmost secrecy.

Early in 1922, Hartzell announced that he had just discovered that Lewis and Mrs. Whitaker were swindlers who had gone into the deal for what they could get out of it, and that he had forced them to withdraw from the Sir Francis Drake Association. Oddly enough, neither retaliated against Hartzell by attempting to expose the scheme.

At the same time, Hartzell denounced Ernest Drake as a fraud who wasn't the real heir he had claimed to be. Hartzell added that, through painstaking effort, he had located the sole surviving heir, who was then living in England. He had assigned full control of his claim to Hartzell.

Undoubtedly, Hartzell awaited the reaction to these announcements with some trepidation. Yet nobody asked the questions he expected: Why was there only one heir instead of thousands? Why would a man who stood to become the wealthiest person in history assign his vast claim to a stranger from America?

When nobody questioned him, Hartzell knew that his swindle could go on indefinitely. He had only one worry—the United States Post Office inspectors. If he could keep them stymied, nobody else could touch him. Hartzell thought he had the answer. Continually, almost in every message, he pounded home his edict of silence and secrecy. Every communication from Hartzell was by cable. He apparently did not know that causing others to write letters and send them by mail was a violation of the statutes.

Rumblings of the big deal reached the Post Office inspectors, however, and they began a quiet investigation. For a long time, they knew only the broad outlines of the scheme and little else. Hartzell's continuous exhortations to secrecy had had their effect. Without exception, the contributors refused to talk. But the inspectors had their own methods of gaining information, and bit by bit, through hard work, they learned who many of the principal agents in the United States were. These all could have been arrested, but the inspectors' evidence was vague at best. A charge against the principals probably would result in acquittals and this would only spur the promoters. The dossier against Hartzell and his agents was built up, but the inspectors held off until they had airtight evidence.

During the next ten years, Hartzell, unaware of the investigation, lived in luxury and ease in a pretentious apartment in Basil Street, London. He began acquiring a British accent, emulated British habits and had his suits cut by the best tailors of Savile Row. He was quickly transformed from an Iowa hayseed to a dapper man-about-town.

Hartzell continued to fan the flames of enthusiasm back home through his weekly messages. First, he warned his following that dozens of obstacles lay in his path and that the battle would be arduous. He pointed out that the estate, with its accumulated interest, was so great that the settlement might wreck the Bank of England and that it surely would rock the money structures of the world. There was no question but that it would be opposed bitterly by the international bankers and by financiers everywhere. Hartzell, however, would carry on, he assured the contributors, even though it might take years. One cable to the faithful read:

> I am going to tell you all something I have never told you before in regard to the amount of the whole affair. If you had all over and above £1 billion, which is equivalent to $5 billion, if you had all above that amount, you could buy the whole city of Des Moines and build a fence around it.

Sanguine accounts of progress followed, week by week. He had finally contacted the Prime Minister, who had reluctantly recognized the validity of the claim. But much work remained to be done. The original will of Sir Francis Drake must be dug out of the archives. Then the Herculean task of computing the interest from 1596 would begin. This would require the services of expert mathematicians and nobody could say how long the work would take. However, the great day was in sight, Hartzell announced.

This wonderful news, relayed to the chapters, kept the faithful happy for a long time. At intervals, they were fed choice morsels about the negotiations. And finally, when it appeared that the victims needed a shot in the arm, Hartzell announced that a settlement date had been set.

But the great day failed to materialize. In November 1927, Hartzell cabled his agents: "Settlement delayed for a month. Estate will be handed over with as much speed as His Majesty can conveniently allow."

This kindled the fires anew and the membership continued to dig into their pocketbooks cheerfully to feed the flames, even though Hartzell told them he was encountering other delays. This went on for six months, and in June 1928 another message arrived:

They were going to settle May 29, but one of the principal powers was ill and could not be on duty. The new Lord Chancellor who succeeded Lord Cave had to go through the papers to complete the deal. The new Lord Chancellor then discovered an error which means $1,200,000 to me. Plainly understand it does not make any difference whether it is £10 million for me or against me, it has got to be correct, according to the Lord Chancellor's decision.

This fortunate error by the Lord Chancellor served to prolong the negotiations for more than a year. Then, when it appeared that the great day was finally at hand, the stock market crash of 1929 sent the country's economics into a tailspin.

The crash was even more fortunate for Hartzell. He told his followers that word of the impending transfer had leaked out and caused the big crash. It might be months, possibly years, before the deal could be completed, but he would keep on trying.

Events that followed were made to order for Hartzell's purposes and could not have been more nearly perfect if he had designed them himself. The world depression that followed the market crash grew worse with each passing month. The downward spiral of prices, the swelling ranks of the unemployed, the growing demand for action in Washington—all these precipitated speeches by Vice President Charles G. Dawes and President Herbert Hoover. Hartzell had only to hint and the speeches were embraced by his followers as veiled opposition to the Drake settlement.

Hartzell's agents told the contributors that Huey Long was one of the main champions of the big battle. His "share-the-wealth, every-man-a-king" program really had reference to the big settlement, the agents claimed.

The postal inspectors had been fully aware of Hartzell's moves. They went into action early in 1931, and on February 28 five of Hartzell's principal agents signed a stipulation before the Solicitor of the Post Office Department. These five agreed to discontinue their activities.

This appeared to be a serious blow to Hartzell. Though the weekly remittance was still coming, the newspaper publicity resulting from the stipulation conceivably might lead the victims to take a good look at the rathole into which they were all pouring their money. Hartzell tried to forestall this with another extravagant claim:

> As you know, I have never said very much about the amount, for to be perfectly candid with you, I don't think any of the people in America capable of grasping the magnitude of the whole affair. The way they have all done and treated me, they have made a very bad enemy of me, now I am going to give you a shock about the amount. Figuring all the land in the state of Iowa at an average rate of $125 an acre, and all the bank stock, and all the bank deposits in Iowa, and railroads and cities combined, I could buy the whole lot and put a fence around the whole state and then have more money left than you all ever thought of.

He could have saved himself the trouble.

The Post Office action, surprisingly, served only to stimulate the faithful. Hartzell's former predictions of stiff opposition were recalled, and the Post Office Department's move seemed to bear them out. Cries of persecution spread through the membership.

In Iowa, which had been the first state organized and where the scheme was most firmly entrenched, Attorney General John Fletcher issued a statement calling the plan a racket and urging the people not to give any more money to it. As a result, he received thousands of letters charging that he was in the pay of the money lords who were trying to crush Hartzell and save the British financial structure.

The victims were blind to all logic. In the midst of the Depression, they squandered the family savings. They disregarded tax-delinquency notices, and thousands mortgaged their farms to buy additional shares.

The postal inspectors, alarmed at these tragedies, stepped up their investigation. On January 10, 1933, a fraud order was issued against seven agents in Minnesota, Iowa, South Dakota and Texas.

Hartzell countered with a demand that the order be resisted. He instructed his agents to send strong letters of protest to their congressmen, to the Solicitor of the Post Office and the Attorney General of the United States. He threatened to red-ink any who failed to write. Hartzell now began to think of himself as a dictator, a man with great power.

The fraud order revived the publicity about the swindle. Newspaper reporters ferreted out amazing stories of the unshakable faith of the victims which were given wide publicity. The stories were relayed to England, and the swindle was even discussed on the floor of Parliament.

The collections began to drop. Not, however, because of any loss of faith in Hartzell, but because some of the agents were out of business and those remaining had not yet arranged to take over. Hartzell fought back, and his growing power complex was evident in his next cablegram:

> I have the chain around the neck of every official on your side from the highest to the lowest that has crossed my path in this matter. Remember that the disturbance that the American people have made me has caused delay and a big loss to me. Parliament has nothing whatever to do with the date. I expect and must have $2500 each and every week until I notify you of the finish. Please make up last week's shortage immediately.

The dupes took Hartzell at his word and continued to pay—through the nose. Hartzell harangued them with all sorts of alibis for the delay in settlement. The election of Franklin D. Roosevelt in the Democratic landslide of 1932 was a serious setback, he told his followers. Roosevelt recognized the claim, he added, but was unwilling to upset the money structures of the world.

The British government, fully aware now of Hartzell's activities, was powerless to take criminal action without some evidence that he had violated a British law. A delegation of Scotland Yard detectives was sent to interview him. He refused to give the name of the "sole surviving heir," or to tell the names of the lawyers who were supposedly helping in the negotiations.

"Where is this estate now?" he was asked.

"It's all over the place," Hartzell replied, waving his arms in a vague gesture.

One of the detectives expressed doubt on that point.

"It's true, nevertheless," Hartzell asserted. "I suppose you've been listening to stories from the United States."

The detective admitted that he had seen press reports from the United States, calling the estate promotion a swindle.

"My own people have treated me very badly," Hartzell declared. "They have caused me nothing but trouble."

"One thing rather puzzles us," a detective said. "We wonder why you, an American, are so interested in this estate."

"I'm practically British," Hartzell assured him. "Someone here in the Home Office has arranged all this, and when this is ended my name will suddenly become Drake and I will then become a British subject."

After they had left Hartzell's quarters, one of the officers expressed what they all felt: "A trifle balmy, what?"

On the basis of the interview, the British were unable to place a definite charge against Hartzell. They did, however, have him declared an undesirable alien, and he was deported to the United States in January 1933, in the company of a United States vice-consul. When his ship docked in New York a delegation of postal inspectors escorted him down the gangplank. He was taken to Sioux City, in the midst of Drake Association territory, where his Iowa agents quickly arranged for his release on bail.

Almost immediately, a meeting of the victims was called, and Hartzell appeared in person to talk to them. Elegantly dressed in expensively tailored tweeds, he spoke with a pseudo-British accent.

He told his followers what they wanted to hear. All arrangements had been made for the settlement in July. Meanwhile, he was a victim of government persecution, and he needed funds to fight the absurd charges against him. Regardless of what happened, he told them, they must not lose faith in "our cause." They must not believe what they read in the newspapers. They must not believe anything except what Hartzell told them.

When Hartzell had appeared before them originally, they had trusted him because he was one of them, because he looked and acted like one of them. Now, he looked and acted like an affluent man of the world. They decided that's the way a man should be if he was to handle such a big deal. They trusted him again and, when the hat was passed, came across to the tune of $68,000. Hartzell took the money and promptly departed for New York.

Meanwhile, inspectors had gone to England to gather evidence to be presented at the trial. The manager of the American Express Company in London told them that approximately $730,000 had been transferred from New York to Hartzell between April 7, 1924, and January 30, 1933.

At Hartzell's apartment, the inspectors found his valet, W. J. Stewart, who had appropriated nearly $10,000 sent to Hartzell after he was deported. He admitted that his former employer was a swindler.

The inspectors tried to find Hartzell's private papers and any incriminating evidence they might contain, but the papers had been impounded by a firm of London solicitors, who demanded a fancy price for them. The inspectors did not have money for this purpose and did not obtain the papers.

They did, however, locate a private detective who told them something of Hartzell's private life. Hartzell had visited a clairvoyant, Miss St. John Montague, who saw great possibilities in the affluent and naïve American. She had an assistant, a buxom, dark-haired young woman who quickly caught Hartzell's eye. The clairvoyant told the girl to encourage the American to come back.

The two had hired the detective to learn all he could about

Hartzell and report to the clairvoyant. Making Hartzell's acquaintance, the private detective plied him with liquor and gained the confidential admission that the whole estate business was a swindle. The detective reported the details to Miss St. John Montague.

Hartzell was infatuated with the assistant and called as often as three times a week. The clairvoyant amazed him by telling him details of the swindle—facts he thought nobody else knew—and clipped him every time she looked into her crystal ball.

Thus the man who received money consistently from dupes in the United States was in turn swindled out of thousands of dollars by the English clairvoyant and her seductive assistant.

The inspectors found that Hartzell had philandered elsewhere. One English girl, whom he had repeatedly promised to marry, was the mother of his illegitimate son. Hartzell, after seducing her, had persuaded her father to invest $2600 in the Drake scheme. Hartzell had encouraged the girl to rent an apartment and buy furniture, for which she went into debt. He kept delaying the marriage, but sent her £3 a week after the child was born. On her father's death, he raised this to £5. He ignored the girl's pleas to pay the rent and help pay for the furniture.

The postal inspectors had amassed all the evidence they needed, and in November 1933 the trial began in Sioux City.

With the help of the British authorities, the actual will of Sir Francis Drake, written on parchment and filed in August of 1595, had been dug up in the Historical Documents Room at Somerset House. The will had been legally probated, and records of it and of the court proceedings had been photostated and certified by British officials. Because of Hartzell's frequent claim that the real skulduggery in the Drake case had occurred in the Ecclesiastical Court, a search of those ancient records had been made. The search uncovered a record of a contest between Drake's widow and his brother over disposition of some of the property in the Drake will.

One English lawyer testified that even if the will had not been probated, the estate would have been irrevocably lost now, 337

490

years after Drake's death, because the English statute of limitations on probate ran out after 30 years and no case could be reopened after that time. A British official who had converted the will from Elizabethan English into modern language confirmed the authenticity of the records of the Prerogative Court, where the will'was probated, and of the Ecclesiastical Court, where the will had been subsequently contested by Drake's widow and his brother.

Hartzell did not testify on his own behalf. But he was conscious that the courtroom was crowded with his followers, and his demeanor was calculated to impress them. His attitude was that of a slightly bored spectator who was tolerating all this because it couldn't really touch him.

He showed little emotion when he was convicted by the jury of promoting a scheme to defraud and was sentenced to ten years' imprisonment in Leavenworth. His lawyers appealed, and he was quickly released on bail. He left the courtroom wearing an air of martyrdom. This greatly cheered his indignant victims, who refused to believe the facts presented during the three-week trial and refused to accept the verdict.

The inspectors assumed that Hartzell's conviction, which had been widely publicized in the press and radio, meant an end to the fraud. They had no doubts that the higher courts would sustain the verdict and that Hartzell would soon be behind bars.

With several of his most faithful agents, Hartzell moved to Chicago, where the most astonishing phase of the entire swindle was started early in 1934. From headquarters set up in an office building near the Loop, Hartzell organized meetings of contributors throughout the Middle West. One Otto Yant was the principal speaker. He talked on international finance, the gold clique and "the deal." The meetings were usually opened with prayer, a vow of undying devotion to the flag and allegiance to the Constitution, and were closed with a plea to come across with more money.

Hartzell told his followers that his conviction was a frameup by the government, that he would be exonerated and that the day of settlement was near. Even after his last appeal had been denied and he was taken to Leavenworth early in 1935, he had each of his agents send out this message:

> I will say our deal is going fine. This last stunt of taking him away is all in the play. We have been advised all along that the outside world would think this is a fraud. If the papers came out and said the Drake estate thing was okay, we would be run to death by agents and grafters, and some of our heavy donors possibly would have trouble with kidnapers. This way no one will ever know we got the money. As to Hartzell, he is not where the papers say, even though he left Chicago with officers. We know where he is and we know the reason.

When this was sent out, together with some rather flowery additions by one of the agents, Delmar C. Short, the money began to flow again in a steady stream. And the "donators," now more hopeful than ever, kept the secret. So quietly did they conduct their business and remit their money, the Post Office inspectors were unaware that the swindle had started all over again.

It came to light when a Chicago man called at police headquarters. He said he had received a letter from his uncle in Wisconsin who wanted him to make sure that all the money that he had remitted had been properly credited to him. The nephew recalled Hartzell's conviction and his subsequent trip to prison.

Detective James Zegar was assigned to the case. Posing as the nephew of the Wisconsin contributor, he called on Otto Yant, who referred him to Delmar Short. When he inquired of Short, he was shown a file of names of the Drake club members and was assured that his uncle's money was safe.

Short told him that the settlement had already been made, that the collection offices would be closed on April 8, 1935, and that payments to the contributors would begin that August. At this time it was April 7.

The following day, Zegar and other detectives raided the offices.

They arrested Otto Yant, Delmar Short, James Kirkendall, Lester Ohmart and Joseph Hauber. The files and records of 70,000 names were confiscated, along with $7500 just received that day. In various safe-deposit boxes, the detectives found an additional $50,000.

Hauber tried a confidence game on the detectives. He said he was really a victim who had come to the Drake offices to investigate and was just on the point of going to the law. But the officers learned from others that he had been active in the swindle, attending the meetings and posing as a government official supervising the settlement, as a Scotland Yard detective or a Secret Service agent. The detectives ignored his story.

The case again came into the hands of the Post Office inspectors, who estimated that the second phase of the swindle had netted about $500,000, including the money raised for Hartzell's defense. The records seized in the raid were taken before the federal grand jury in Chicago. Hartzell and 41 other persons were indicted.

With names and addresses, the inspectors began questioning the victims. But none would admit ever having put money in the scheme to recover the Drake estate. A few said they had made some investments with Hartzell, but they reserved the right to do as they pleased with their money and they had no complaint. Balked by the victims themselves, the inspectors decided to subpoena several of them in the hope that they would not perjure themselves on the witness stand.

Most of those indicted won dismissals. The evidence presented at the first trial had to be repeated. The victims who appeared as witnesses stood their ground. Their attitude was summed up by one man who said: "I say, with all due respect to the courts, that I haven't changed my mind. There were 70,000 in the deal and they have taken only one. From what I have heard the deal is still as strong as the Rock of Gibraltar."

On January 30, 1936, the jury returned a verdict of guilty against Oscar Hartzell, his brother Canfield Hartzell, Lester Ohmart, Joseph Hauber, Otto Yant, Delmar Short and Emil Rochel. All but Oscar Hartzell were sentenced to a year and a day in Leavenworth.

Oscar Hartzell, who had continued to display signs of delusions of grandeur, was returned to Leavenworth for psychiatric examination. In December 1936 he was adjudged mentally incompetent and was sent to the Medical Center for Federal Prisoners at Springfield, Missouri. He remained a mental patient at that institution until his death on August 27, 1943.

The second trial and the imprisonment of the principal agents apparently put an end to the Drake swindle, although many Midwesterners still hoard their receipts in the secret hope that some day the treasure ship of the famous buccaneer will come in. The Post Office inspectors continued to send out periodic bulletins warning the public against investing in this and other estate schemes. The Drake swindle is dormant now, but the inspectors look for it to crop up again one of these days.

⌒⌇⌒

FOR MOST of his 33 years as a postman in Water Mill, New York, neither rain nor snow nor gloom of night deterred Lorin F. Shipper from delivering the mail in one or the other of his two vintage automobiles. In 1956 Shipper hung up his sack, locked his La Salle (vintage 1927) and Packard (vintage 1925) in his garage and doddled away the years in leisurely seclusion. In his last years as a letter carrier, however, Shipper apparently decided to lighten his bad-weather load and the reading time of his postal patrons by doing some selective editing of his mail. He left part of it undelivered—mostly junk mail.

Eight years after his retirement authorities found more than two tons of mail in Shipper's garage. Postmaster Roy G. Peterson of neighboring Southampton said about 10 percent of the letters were first class. They were delivered with the government's apologies—or at least an explanation—stamped on them. The junk mail, which included a horde of toothpaste samples, was thrown away. Shipper, aged 75 when found out, was not prosecuted; the five-year statute of limitations had run out.

"Lorin had been ill during those last few years," Peterson said, "and he used to have some trouble because he couldn't get around in those old cars of his in the winter."

One thing about the mail Shipper failed to deliver—nobody missed it. The post office said they had had no complaints.   —UPI

494

All the candidate needed for
a medical diploma was money and the
patience to wait for the mailman

EDUCATION OF A QUACK

by Stewart H. Holbrook

T he St. Louis *Star* was after big game. It had reason to believe that the National University of Arts and Sciences of St. Louis had been doing a wholesale business selling medical degrees, and that a number of professional men in the field of medicine, both in St. Louis and in Kansas City, were involved.

Early in August 1923 reporter Harry Thompson Brundige was informed by his managing editor of the existence of a diploma mill with which a well-known physician, Dr. Robert Adcox, was thought to be connected. Brundige was told to leave the *Star*, to get a job as a salesman that would permit him to circulate widely in the city, and to see what he could do about buying a degree naming him a Doctor of Medicine.

It was any ambitious reporter's dream of a perfect assignment, and young Brundige was just the man for it. He decided to operate under his first two names. As Harry Thompson he got a job as a coal salesman. Posing as a young fellow who had just come to the big city from Springfield, Missouri, he rented a room two doors west of Dr. Robert Adcox's home and moved into his new lodging house on August 13.

Next morning, sitting on the front porch, he watched the letter carrier walking up the street and saw Dr. Adcox come out to get the mail. When the postman came to the lodging house, Thompson got into conversation with him and asked if there was a doctor in the neighborhood. "I got a sore throat," he said. The postman pointed to Adcox, who was still on his porch.

Thompson went immediately to introduce himself to Adcox, who replied he had retired from practice, but with a little urging he treated the personable young stranger and suggested he come back next day. Thompson did so. This time Thompson remarked that a doctor had a pretty good life. Adcox agreed and also seemed to warm up. So did Thompson. On the following day, while Thompson's throat was being treated again, Adcox came right out and asked if the young fellow would like to be a doctor.

Thompson replied that he would, but added, with regret in his voice, that such a thing could never be—he was almost 30 years old. He could not hope to begin a medical course at his age. Furthermore, he had not even finished high school. Adcox took the bait eagerly. It was not necessary to go to school to get a medical diploma, he said. Then the doctor asked, "How much money have you saved?"

"Oh, somewhere around $1000," replied Thompson. Dr. Adcox's face seemed to light up. "If you are willing to spend your thousand to become a doctor," he said, "you are as good as a doctor right now." After only a little more resistance from Thompson, which Adcox airily dismissed, the doctor told the young man to be ready to leave with him next day for Kansas City. The bait had gone down; the hook was in.

In Kansas City, Adcox took Thompson to the Minor Building, where one Dr. Ralph A. Voight occupied a suite of nine rooms; and there, after Adcox and Voight had been closeted alone for about an hour, Thompson was called in and questioned by Voight. Thompson recalled that the interview went like this:

"So you want to be a doctor?" Voight asked me.
"That's what I came here for."

"Do you know anything about medicine?"

"Not a thing."

"Did you graduate from high school?"

"I did not."

"Well, let's see. The first thing is to get you a high-school diploma. Then we'd better get you three years' credits from a medical school and let you do your senior year at Alex's."

"What do you mean by doing the senior year at Alex's?"

"I mean that Dr. D. R. Alexander, dean of the Kansas City College of Medicine and Surgery, will enroll you for your senior year after we get the credits for you. Then, after eight months at school, you'll get your diploma and be a full-fledged doctor."

"Can't I get by without going to school?"

"Well, inasmuch as you don't know anything about medicine you ought to put in a few months of study before trying your wings. But we'll see."

Dr. Voight then began figuring on a bit of scratch paper.

"How much money have you?" he inquired.

"How much will I need?"

"Well, figuring roughly, about $1000. But I'll let you know later. However, if you want me to get busy you will have to make a deposit. Can you let me have something down?"

Thompson counted his money and asked Dr. Adcox, who had announced his intention of returning to St. Louis on the noon train, how much he would need to get back. He said it would take about $15, which sum Thompson gave him. Thompson then offered Dr. Voight a deposit of $50.

"It isn't much, but I'll take it," he said. "But you will have to send me $600 before I can start work. Can you get that much for me by Monday?"

Thompson promised to give him the money not later than Tuesday, August 21.

"Send it by certified check," Voight instructed.

497

Thompson returned to St. Louis, where he opened a checking account with a St. Louis bank, depositing $800 in currency. He then made out a check, payable to Dr. Ralph A. Voight, signed it "Harry Thompson" and had the check certified. The check was photographed in the office of the *Star*.

On Tuesday, August 21, Thompson returned to Kansas City, met Voight in his office and handed him the check. Voight protested he had asked Thompson to get a certified check. The following conversation ensued:

"Why give me this kind of check?" Voight demanded rather sharply.

"You told me to have it certified."

"I didn't mean this kind of certification—why didn't you get a cashier's check made out to bearer? Now I've got to endorse this darned thing. I don't like it."

Thompson apologized and offered to take the check back and get the kind he wanted, but Voight must have concluded that $600 in the hand was worth more than a promise for that sum, so he retained it.

Said Voight: "I've been very busy getting things lined up for you. I have taken steps to get a high-school certificate, which will arrive shortly, and I have written to a former official of the Baltimore College of Physicians and Surgeons, which is now closed, to place your name in the records as having attended classes in 1914, 1915 and 1916 and to send me a certified copy of your credits for those years. It will take about two weeks to get them. The Kansas City College of Medicine and Surgery will open two weeks from today, and I have made arrangements with Dr. Alexander, the dean, to enroll you for your senior year."

Thompson returned to St. Louis. A day or so later a cryptic letter from Dr. Voight arrived:

DEAR THOMPSON: Your letter at hand and was glad to hear from you. I have not had a reply to your letter as yet, though I expect it at any time. I have taken the liberty to make a change in the arrangements and know that you will be better satisfied with my judgment. Instead of going to the East for the stock, consisting of three shares, I have gone to the West Coast for completed stock, so you can have less trouble and be better off. I will send you a wire as soon as it arrives and you can get it here whenever you see fit to come. Unless you are at leisure at present I would not pass up your job at this time, as it is your best time, but hold on until I notify you and I am sure you will be better off.

Thompson replied at once:

DEAR DOCTOR: Received your letter and was surely pleased to note that you are going to get me a diploma instead of the three years' credits. The way you wrote about stock was very clever; but I caught on at once. I can hardly wait for that telegram telling me you have everything. Don't forget the high-school diploma. How will the diploma thing work out? Will I have to go to school or will you get me the license to practice without going to school? I am very much interested and would like to know. I bought the book you told me about and am studying it religiously. Business is good and I will stick it out here until you wire me.

Days passed. On September 4 Thompson got a wire from Voight reading: "Change in plan makes it necessary for 300 more. Wire it at once Western Union." Later that day Dr. Adcox got in touch with Thompson. He, too, had received a wire from Voight, reading: "Alex agrees to issue final paper on Pacific for honorable cause 250. Can arrange through personal friends to sit in Arkansas and complete Thompson. Wired him today 300. Had no reply. Advise him Alex building addition and needs cash ready to go at once."

Thompson asked Adcox to explain Voight's wire. Adcox did: "By Alex, he means Dr. Alexander of the Kansas City College of

Medicine and Surgery. By final paper, he means a diploma. Voight means that Dr. Alexander has agreed to give you a diploma based on the credits obtained for you from a college on the Pacific Coast. Voight will go to Arkansas with the diploma and take the state medical board examinations in your name. He also means that Dr. Alexander is getting ready to build an addition to his college and needs cash. The reference to 'honorable cause' is just one of Voight's little jokes. Don't you understand, my boy? Voight means you are about to have the degree of Doctor of Medicine conferred on you."

On September 22 a wire from Voight told Thompson to come to Kansas City; the "final document" could be had at any time now. But on arrival there next morning, Thompson found Dr. Voight stalling. The reporter recalled the discussion as follows:

"Well, doctor, I see you arrived on schedule," said Voight, "and I am looking for your diploma in every mail. It hasn't come. That bird in California certainly works slow, but he's sure, and the stuff he puts out is A-1. Dr. Alexander has promised to issue another diploma to back up the California degree, and as soon as I get them I'm going down to Arkansas to take the state board examination and get you a license. Meanwhile, I think you should go out to Dr. Alexander's college and take a few months so as to have a background for your work. You can hang out your shingle as a chiropractor or an electro-specialist and use one of my offices. You can catch enough suckers to pay your expenses while you are getting a couple of months' study. I think you ought to start in out there tomorrow."

"But," I protested, "how can I go to school until you get the diploma proving my previous medical study?"

"Dr. Alex won't care. He'll take my word for it that I'll produce your paper in the next week or two."

I told Voight that I didn't want to go to school. "It is too big a chance," I said. "The first time a professor asked me a question I'd betray my ignorance of all things pertaining to the practice of medicine."

"Why, you idiot," Voight replied, "they won't ask any questions. You'll be in the ringer class. The professors will put you on the list with the others who are there to listen and not to answer questions."

I then told Voight I would *not* go to school; that he had agreed to get me a diploma and a state license and to sell me a sucker machine, an electric apparatus manufactured by Voight and used in "treating" sick men and women.

Voight sought to calm Thompson, declaring that he really did not care whether or not Thompson went to school: it made little or no difference. But as the diploma had failed to materialize, Thompson began to put on the heat by making a persistent nuisance of himself. It worked. On October 3 Voight gave the diploma to Thompson and displayed a license to practice in the state of Tennessee, granted to Harry Thompson, M.D.

Thompson did not accept the diploma with the delight Voight might have expected. The young man gave it a long, bilious look, then pointed out that the document showed erasure marks where the name was written in. "It's a crude piece of work," he said, and passed the diploma back to Voight. Voight agreed that it was, indeed, a "rotten job." But never mind. Voight would see that he got another document and that it would be perfectly executed.

While waiting for the next medical diploma which would allow him to practice, Thompson went ahead with his plan to become a chiropractor. Adcox and Voight, between them, made all the arrangements. At first, Adcox told Thompson he would get his instruction from "a deputy sheriff assigned to duty in one of the circuit courts and who practiced chiropractic on the side." Because Thompson was afraid the deputy might recognize him as a newspaper reporter, he demurred. Adcox then phoned Dr. Florence F. Baars, a St. Louis chiropractor. "Florence," he said, "this is Doc Ad. I've got a friend here who wants to do chiropractic while he goes to school. . . . No, he don't know anything about it. But I want you and Dr. Strecker to give him a course that will enable him to get by. You know, he don't care anything about the origin of nerves or the intervertebral foramina—all he wants to know is how to give the patients their thumps. And to get the money. . . . Sure, he's all right. . . . Yes, I'll send him over this afternoon."

Doc Florence Baars told Thompson the course would take him three or four days and would cost $25. That evening Thompson was introduced to Doc Strecker, and, after he had given Doc Baars a check for $25, the first lesson got under way. It lasted one hour and five minutes. Doc Strecker, on leaving, gave him a pamphlet, *The Science of Chiropractic Explained.* Next evening Thompson got the second lesson. Time: 55 minutes. He then paid Strecker $2.50 for a booklet explaining all about adjustments. Another evening's lesson lasted only 22 minutes, and Thompson bought still another book. This one cost $12. It also completed the course in the science of chiropractic. Total expired time: two hours and 22 minutes.

Now Thompson reported back to Dr. Adcox, who congratulated him on his graduation. Thompson then wrote to Dr. Voight and said he was ready to start chiropracticing in St. Louis just as soon as he received the promised diploma in that science. Voight replied that he would advise Thompson as soon as the document came.

The good news that Thompson was ready to go into business got around quickly. Within an hour or so after Thompson talked with Voight in Kansas City, the young man got a call from Doc Strecker in St. Louis: How about an adjusting table? Strecker just happened to have one. It had been used, but it was in good condition. Thompson could have it for $22.50. Come to think of it, Thompson would need a spinal chart, and Doc Florence Baars had one she would sell for $2.50. Musing, doubtless, on the mounting expense of becoming a full-fledged master of chiropractic, Thompson purchased the table and chart.

Meanwhile, the wheels had been turning, and Thompson got a wire from Voight: The chiropractic diploma was ready. It was a

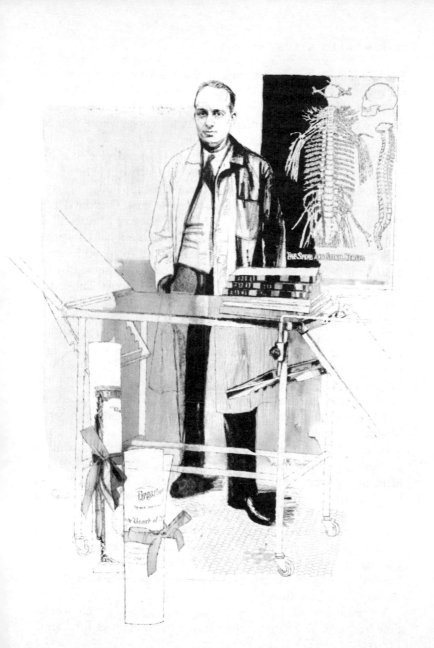

fine-looking job, too; and though it reached Thompson by way of the office of Dr. Alexander, head of the Kansas City College of Medicine and Surgery, it purported to have been issued by the Progressive College of Chiropractic, Chicago, Illinois, whose founder and president was Doc Henry Lindlahr.

Anyhow, "Doc" Harry Thompson now had a degree in chiropractic, backed by more than two hours' instruction. He had a fine adjustment table and a nice spinal chart. Cost: $64.50.

Other much desired events were coming to pass. One day Harry Thompson received his Doctor of Medicine degree as attested by a diploma from the Department of Medicine, National University of Arts and Sciences, St. Louis, Missouri. And for good measure he came into possession of a high-school certificate signed by the State Superintendent of Public Instruction of Missouri. The certificate was dated 1914, and the diploma 1916, or two years before the National University went out of business.

Harry Thompson Brundige had done his work well. On October 15, 1923, the St. Louis *Star* broke the story with the first of a series of articles. The police were busy arresting Dr. Ralph A. Voight of Kansas City; Dr. Robert Adcox of St. Louis; Dr. D. R. Alexander, dean of the Kansas City College of Medicine and Surgery; and Professor W. P. Sachs, a former examiner of Missouri schools.

In one of his articles, Brundige wrote that the total cost of his medical degree and the chiropractic degree, together with equipment and books, transportation to and from Kansas City and board and lodging, came to approximately $3000. It was a small sum to pay for the far-reaching results achieved by the exposé.

In another article of the series, Brundige recalled that Dr. Voight, once they had got chummy, proved to be quite a talker. He enjoyed relating the feats he had performed over many years to secure medical degrees and licenses to practice for persons who were in no way fit to have them.

Voight had recalled that by far the hardest job of his life was the time he "took 42 boobs to New Haven to get licenses for them."

He had paid $1500 for an advance copy of the examination ques-
tions, and then, "assisted by a couple of other smart guys who
knew their stuff," sat up all night in the Hotel Garde writing answers. It was a tough job. "We prepared 42 different sets of answers, one for each boob, and all they had to do was go into the
examination room and copy the answers in their own handwriting.
Only one failed to get his license—a dumb bird who could not copy
his paper."

There were other methods for providing a man with necessary
papers. "A cheap way," Voight went on, was "to purchase the
credentials of a recently deceased physician. If you call on the
widow before the insurance has been paid, you will find her in need
of ready cash, and on some pretense or other you can usually in-
duce her to part with the credentials of the late lamented. All you
have to do, then, is have your boob change his name, move to some
distant state and obtain a license by reciprocity in the state to which
he moves." This method sounded dangerous, but Voight assured
the reporter, "I know dozens of men who have done that little
trick and are now living in dead men's shoes."

Professor Sachs, who had issued the bogus high-school certificate, made a long confession to the St. Louis prosecuting attorney.
"My traffic in fraudulent educational credentials," he said, "began
about 11 years ago when a ring was organized. I was then superintendent of schools in Washington County, Missouri. I started by
issuing fraudulent certificates of examination and high-school diplomas from the Potosi high school. My traffic continued after I
became dean of the National University of Arts and Sciences of
St. Louis, during which time I had access to the diplomas granting
college and university degrees. I left National University to become
the examiner of schools under State Superintendent Howard A.
Cass, now deceased. I induced him to sign thousands of high-school
certificates, which are equivalent to high-school diplomas, on the
plea I needed them for immediate use.

"I attached the official seal and, throughout my tenure of office,
supplied them to other members of our ring. I took thousands of

them with me when I resigned to become dean of Walther College of St. Louis. I sold approximately 5000 of these certificates, directly or indirectly, to persons who could not have passed the examinations but later became doctors of medicine.

"I had access to the lithograph stone used to print the diplomas of the National University of Arts and Sciences, and had such diplomas printed as I needed them. I also trafficked in the papers of Walther College." Sachs added that "hundreds of county school superintendents and other officials issued high-school certificates, for a price, without giving the required examinations. The practice is almost universal. Educators generally are underpaid, and the temptation for easy money is too strong to resist."

Sachs closed his confession with a crack at the smart guy Voight. "My last transaction," Sachs said, "was in October 1923, when I supplied Dr. Voight with credentials for Harry Thompson, who, I later learned, was Brundige the reporter. Just think—it was Dr. Voight who once called me a blundering idiot, yet it was Dr. Voight who led Brundige and the police to my door."

ONE NIGHT more than 100 Washington notables attended a party in honor of Titus Oates in the Hotel Statler's South American Room. The distinguished guests were milling around, sipping cocktails and looking for the guest of honor, when each was given a slip of paper which read:

"Mr. Oates regrets he will be unable to swill with us today. If you wish to know why, we refer you to page 1111 of *Webster's Biographical Dictionary* which states: 'Oates, Titus. 1649–1705. English impostor and fabricator of the Popish Plot.' " The paper went on to say that Oates's forgery of the plot, whereby Catholics were supposedly pledged to massacre Protestants, burn London and assassinate the king, resulted in the death of about 35 persons. Sentenced to life imprisonment for perjury, he was later released by William of Orange.

The party was the idea of George Dixon, Washington newspaperman, who wanted to prove that people in Washington will attend a party for anyone. —*S/Sgt. Harold Helfer*

*Where there is an eager
market, there is an eager cheat*

30,000 MANUSCRIPTS

by Sonia Cole

T he passion for collecting autographs dates from the 19th century. One of the most ardent collectors of that time was Michel Chasles of Paris, who had acquired this hobby late in life as the result of rather curious circumstances.

Chasles, who for many years had held the chair of geometry in the Imperial Polytechnic of Paris, was admitted to the French Academy of Science in 1850 to occupy a vacancy caused by the sudden departure of a Florentine named Count Libri. This noble-man had fled to England, taking with him no less than 30,000 volumes of rare books and documents which he had abstracted from libraries in Paris.

Upon his admission to the Academy, Chasles turned his attention from mathematics to the study of the history of science. His researches among ancient documents inspired him to acquire a collection of his own. He was also anxious to obtain specimens worthy of presentation to the Academy in order to mark his gratitude for election and to replace the losses sustained by the national collections of France as a result of Count Libri's absconding.

Hearing of Chasles's collecting zeal, a Monsieur Vrain Lucas introduced himself to the elderly man one day with an intriguing story. He had for disposal, he said, a considerable quantity of manuscripts, books and autograph letters of great value. This collection had been formed by a Count Boisjourdain, who had emigrated to America in 1791 and was shipwrecked and drowned on the way. Part of his fabulous collection of manuscripts had been rescued from the waves, though some of them had been badly damaged.

Chasles could scarcely conceal his excitement when he heard this story. He was offered a letter signed by Molière for only 500 francs ($100) and two others, by Rabelais and Racine, for the modest sum of 200 francs ($40) each. He was, of course, only too delighted to buy them.

Vrain Lucas explained that he had acquired some of the Boisjourdain collection from an old man who would part with the letters only gradually when he needed money. If Chasles was interested, however, Vrain Lucas assured him he could guarantee a steady supply. Vrain Lucas declared that he was ignorant of such things himself and was incapable of understanding the value and importance of the documents in question but, having heard of Chasles's knowledge of such matters, he would offer them to him for whatever he thought they were worth. Convinced by Vrain Lucas' apparent innocence, Chasles bought everything he was offered without further question.

Ill-educated Vrain Lucas undoubtedly was. The son of a laborer, he had attended the village school at Châteaudun and then spent five years working as a clerk. During this time, he read extensively in the public library, poring over old manuscripts and books. His ambition was to work in a library, but in this he was thwarted by his lack of academic qualifications; moreover, he knew no Latin, and this was an insuperable bar.

Vrain Lucas went to Paris, where he obtained employment with a firm specializing in genealogy. The head of this business fabricated many false deeds, titles and other documents for his customers when he was unable to provide the genuine articles. A certain Marquis was anxious to establish that a famous chancellor was his ancestor, and it fell to Vrain Lucas to manufacture the necessary proof. In this he was, apparently, entirely successful, and the Marquis was well satisfied. Soon after this episode, the head of the firm retired, leaving with his pupil a collection of genuine autographs and other documents.

Starting with these, Vrain Lucas was able to build up a business of his own. By the time he introduced himself to Michel Chasles in 1862, Vrain Lucas had already been concerned in some dubious transactions. By copying the autographs in his possession, he managed to sell a number of forgeries to various collectors in Paris. He had acquired a considerable knowledge of manuscripts through his studies in public libraries and through his genealogical work. He was, moreover, a skilled psychologist; he succeeded in inspiring confidence and in flattering Chasles's vanity by making him believe that he was obtaining great bargains from an unlearned and ignorant fellow.

At first, the letters he sold were of a trivial and inconspicuous nature so that no suspicions were aroused, but gradually the manuscripts became more important. In 1865 Chasles sent to Florence a letter purporting to be in the hand of Dante for an exhibition on the occasion of the poet's sixth centenary. Unfortunately, it arrived too late to be included in the exhibition, so that it was not subjected to expert examination. The following year he offered to the Belgian Academy two letters from Charles V to Rabelais; both were published in the Proceedings of the Academy, though the chief archivists of the Academy expressed doubts as to their authenticity.

To celebrate the bicentenary of the foundation of the French Academy in 1867, Chasles read a paper entitled "A Historical Note on the Foundation of the Academy" and produced two letters: one from the poet Jean de Rotrou to Cardinal Richelieu, suggesting the formation of the Academy; the other an acknowledgment from the great statesman approving the idea. Both these documents Chasles offered to the Academy. Rotrou's letters are very rare; there are, in fact, no known originals of them. The letters were published in the Proceedings of the Academy, but with a remark expressing a certain doubt on their style.

At the next meeting of the Academy, Chasles presented two letters from Pascal to Robert Boyle dated 1652, announcing the principles of gravity before Newton's discovery had been made. These revolutionary documents were naturally received with considerable misgivings by several members of the Academy, who further pointed out that certain grammatical errors were difficult to reconcile with the author of the *Pensées*.

M. Prosper Faugère, a great authority on Pascal, vehemently denied their authenticity; the handwriting differed completely from the manuscript of *Pensées* in the Imperial Library. Furthermore, he pointed out an anachronism: a reference to coffee, but coffee was not introduced to Parisian society by the Turkish ambassador to the court of Louis XIV until 1669, seven years after Pascal's death and 17 years after this note was supposed to have been written.

Further notes from Pascal to Newton which Chasles presented to the Academy were the subject of vigorous protests from Sir David Brewster of Edinburgh, an authority on Newton. He knew of no other letters from Pascal to Newton and, from the dates on these letters, they must have been written when Newton was a mere boy of 11. It hardly seemed likely that Newton would have concerned himself with calculus, the equilibrium of fluids and the principles of gravity at that tender age. Other letters were produced from Newton's mother, thanking Pascal for his kindness to her son; she signed herself Anne Ayscough, but she had ceased to be known by this name when Newton was only four, and thereafter had always signed herself Hannah Smith.

Vrain Lucas had formed the habit of visiting his dupe on Monday evenings after the meetings of the Academy. Sometimes he waited for him in his apartment for an hour or more. Chasles would return heated from some stormy session and explain his difficulties in all innocence. For example, the dates on the letters from Pascal to Newton had been questioned—why should the

French author write to an English boy about his discoveries? Vrain Lucas said he would go at once to the "old man" and see if he could produce further documents to throw light on this dilemma. Working through the night, he would return in triumph next day with a letter from Newton's tutor explaining how he had urged his pupil to write to Pascal, under his guidance.

During the time he waited for Chasles in his apartment, it was easy, too, to slip in a new production among the documents already bought. Then when Chasles raised some point which had cropped up at the previous meeting of the Academy, Vrain Lucas would say, "But surely you already have such and such a letter which explains all this?" They would search in the files, and there it was; Chasles was old, and he was ready to believe that it had slipped his memory. His faith in Vrain Lucas was so great that he even supplied him with lists of the letters he needed; in fact, he supplied the program for the forger to follow. In 1869 Vrain Lucas was to write from prison, not without justice, "Did you not teach me yourself how Newton and Galileo wrote and what they said?"

The next matter which called for explanation was a letter from Galileo written in 1641 complaining of eyestrain. An authority pointed out that Galileo was blind from 1637 until his death in 1642 and, moreover, that he never wrote in French. Chasles insisted that Galileo's biographers must be mistaken in both these points. An astronomer of the Paris Observatory proved that the text of many of the Galileo letters produced by Chasles for the Academy was taken from a book written in 1869. He said there could be no doubt at all that the letters had been copied from the book, and not the book from these letters. Confiding his difficulties to Vrain Lucas, Chasles was soon able to produce "proof" that the author had been lent documents from Madame de Pompadour's collection from which to make notes for his biography.

One Galileo letter, written in Italian, was submitted to a special commission in Florence (it was the only letter in the whole collection not written in French). The commission concluded that the letter had been written by someone who did not know Italian: hyphens at the ends of lines, for instance, often cut words in a way in which no Italian would divide them, and the copyist had written *scuelo* instead of *scuole*, comparable to an Englishman writing "scholo" instead of "school."

At last Chasles was forced to confess his anxiety over the report from Florence, which stated categorically that the letter was a forgery. For a month, Vrain Lucas was kept under close observation. He lived with his mistress and, apart from his visits to Chasles, saw no one but her, being completely absorbed in his work. He would emerge for lunch, work all afternoon at the Imperial Library and return home in the evenings. When the Paris police searched his rooms, they found only a quantity of paper, some pens and one bottle of ink; there were no manuscripts or documents of any kind.

His custom had been to use flyleaves torn out of old books for his work; one of his weakest points was that he often used paper known to have been made later than the date of the document he forged. Some of the first manuscripts he sold were almost illegible, since they were supposed to have been damaged after the shipwreck. He dipped them in water, dirtied them, blackened them with lamp smoke and singed them (occasionally he overdid this treatment, and the documents fell to pieces when handled). Sometimes a little wax completed their appearance of antiquity. But his greatest success lay in his ability with ink.

One of Chasles's chief supports had been the chemist Antoine Jérôme Balard, who had proved that ancient ink is more difficult to remove by acids than fresh ink. Chasles's samples resisted treatment, which showed (according to Balard) that if it was a case of forgery, then the forgery had been done a very long time ago. Chasles had enjoyed a momentary triumph from the chemist's pronouncement, but one of his most consistent opponents, the astronomer Urbain Jean Joseph Leverrier, pointed out that a prime concern of a forger would be to subject his ink to special treatment and that artificial ageing might be achieved.

Two experts, the archivist Henri Bordier and the keeper of the department of manuscripts in the Bibliothèque Impériale, Emile Mabille, were called upon to make a detailed examination of the thousands of documents supplied to Chasles by Vrain Lucas. As a result of their report, Vrain Lucas was brought before the tribunal of Paris on February 16, 1870.

The accused, who was then aged 52, was described as follows:

> He looked common enough, not unlike a businessman or a schoolteacher. The heavy-lidded eyes seemed to be protected from any indiscretions his glance might convey by thick lashes; his rather vulgar nose appeared to merge into his cheeks, and his whole cast of countenance, neither gay nor sad, gave him the appearance of a countryman. His hair was dark and a little thin on top, while his mouth showed caution and discretion which were, indeed, the most striking characteristics of this very ordinary countenance.

It appeared that over a period of years, from 1860 to 1869, Chasles had been supplied with a total of nearly 30,000 autographs, attributed to 660 different persons. At the peak of his career, Vrain Lucas had produced 10,000 a year, or 25 letters a day! He did not trouble to imitate the handwriting of those whose letters he forged; with 660 authors involved, this would obviously have been impracticable. He used various scripts—italic, cursive and so on—selected according to the period he was representing.

Generally he copied passages out of books, perhaps adding some trivialities in the beginning and end to turn them into letters. Very rarely did he produce simple copies of well-known texts. His letters had to be novel, and for this it was necessary to add personal inventions. Vrain Lucas was not particularly imaginative, neither had he had the benefit of a wide education. The passages he invented in his letters were generally brief, but their brevity sometimes did not hide the platitudes they contained. Another of his methods was to add inscriptions or signatures to genuine old books which would enhance their value or interest. Sometimes he added inscriptions supposed to have been written by "Count Boisjourdain," the victim of the imaginary shipwreck, perhaps to the effect that the book had belonged to La Fontaine, or to Rabelais. Finally, Vrain Lucas spiced his sales to Chasles with a very few authentic and untouched manuscripts or books, and this was his main plea in his defense in 1870.

He told the court that he had sold Chasles enough genuine documents to justify the sum he had spent on the entire collection. Poor Chasles had parted with 140,000 francs ($28,000) all told, and the value of the authentic specimens was estimated as 500 francs ($100) at the most. Further, Vrain Lucas maintained that he had increased the sum of scientific knowledge by bringing to the notice of experts forgotten or unknown historical facts.

Although many of his productions seemed plausible enough, others were so naïve that it seems unbelievable that the same mind should have conceived them. The defending counsel pointed out at the trial that a man of Chasles's education could not possibly have accepted as genuine, documents written in French before the Christian era; there were letters signed "Platon" or "Cléopatre" and even letters from Pontius Pilate and Mary Magdalene! That Vrain Lucas should have written these, and that Chasles should have accepted them, remains one of the greatest mysteries in the whole case. Probably Chasles bought a mass of documents at a time (possibly without even looking at them all) in the hope of finding a few gems among them.

Counsel for the defendant pointed out that fraudulent transactions become criminal only when they are such that they could deceive a man of ordinary prudence. Chasles certainly did not act as a prudent man and bought everything he was offered without question. He was the victim of a mania, of an unshakable faith, which made him lose all critical faculties. Nervous and emotional himself, he was the perfect foil for the calm and painstaking Vrain Lucas.

If Chasles ever had suspicions, he seemed unwilling to admit them even to himself. After Vrain Lucas had been under arrest for four days, Chasles did inform the Academy that many of the documents were false. But he never admitted that the fabulous collection of Boisjourdain was a myth; he always believed that it existed and that he had been frustrated from possessing it by having copies palmed off on him. Eventually, he gave up insisting on its authenticity, as he was entirely without support; but he never confessed that he had been the victim of a complete fraud, nor did he relinquish his delusions about the shipwreck story which had fired his imagination for years.

Vrain Lucas was sentenced to two years' imprisonment and the paltry fine of 500 francs. After his release from jail, he found a new victim, the elderly Abbé Tochon, whom he robbed of his all (2500 francs), his watch and his few interesting books. For this he was sentenced to another three years. Again, as soon as he was let out, he turned to robbery; this time it was rare editions from a library, for which he got a further sentence of four years.

As for Chasles, he lived on for many years and continued to be held in high esteem until his death—he choked on a piece of marshmallow! Paris immortalized him by naming a road after him, and Alphonse Daudet based his novel *L'Immortel* on the story of Vrain Lucas.

⟨∾⟩

AN AUSTRALIAN infantry division stationed in England was invited to visit Manchester. They had such a wonderful time that at the end of their stay they told the mayor they wanted to make a little presentation as a gesture of thanks. Assembling at the City Hall, the Australians deluged the astonished mayor with a magnificent collection of priceless Australian curios. Overcome with emotion, he mumbled his thanks.

It was not until the next day, after the Australians had left, that the Police Department reported the burglary of the Manchester Museum—a burglary confined to the entire Australian aboriginal collection.

—*George H. Johnston, Pacific Partner*
(*Duell, Sloan and Pearce, affiliate of Meredith Press*)

*The prospects proved irresistible—a journey
to an exotic land, a beautiful senorita and money*

RESCUE OF THE SPANISH PRISONER

by Rufus Jarman

On any given day in the 1950's,
a thousand or so business and professional people in this country
would find in their mail a mysterious letter that had arrived by
air from Mexico. In 23 or more lines of typescript, it promised a
chance to participate in high adventure and romance.

It was surprising how many good, solid Americans had secret
ambitions to act like Captain Blood or Sir Lancelot and rescue
fair maidens from dark towers. Not a fortnight went by that
some good citizen who had received one of these alluring missives
from Mexico would not load himself down with cash and set off
for an unknown land—generally with ridiculous results.

The letters always promised several exciting prospects: a journey
south of the border; meetings in shadowed streets, shuttered cafés
and picturesque patios; intrigue revolving around an unfortunate
prisoner in a fortresslike stronghold; a fortune in hidden money;
and the enchanting opportunity to rescue and protect a senorita
who was always beautiful and always 18 years old.

There was only one serious weakness in this lovely dream—the
whole proposition was a fake: the prisoner, the fortune and the
beautiful senorita. It was the Spanish-Prisoner Swindle, some-

516

517

times called the Spanish-Trunk Racket or, by the Mexicans, *El Timo del Baúl*.

This ancient come-on—which had been operating for about 370 years—was so fantastic, shallow and crude that it should have been obvious to almost anybody. According to the United States Post Office Inspection Service, the old Spanish-Prisoner Swindle was just as effective in modern times as it was in the time of Philip II of Spain and Sir Francis Drake. Former Chief Post Office Inspector Clifton C. Garner said that in the 1950's United States citizens lost annually at least $600,000—and probably much more —to the mythical prisoner languishing in romantic Mexico. Today, the racket lies somewhat dormant, although postal inspectors believe it may flare up again at any moment.

Some of the victims, even while partly recognizing the racket for what it is, tried to make themselves believe in it anyway. A small-town, midwestern minister brought the Post Office inspectors in Omaha some Spanish-prisoner letters he had received. He suspected fraud, and the Post Office men assured him that that was exactly what it was, showing him case reports of a dozen other people. Through believing in letters exactly like his, they had lost their savings, and some had their lives threatened by Mexican picaroons. The minister thanked the inspectors, gathered up his letters and prepared to depart. The inspectors asked him to leave the letters with them for evidence, in case any of the swindlers were brought to trial.

"No," the preacher replied. "I think I'll take them along with me. There just might be something in it, you know."

The venerable fraud works like this: The letter writer claims to be a Mexican banker recently jailed in connection with a bankruptcy case. Before his capture he had converted all available funds into U.S. dollars and hidden them in the false bottom of a trunk which he had checked through to a customhouse in the United States. The trunk reached its destination, but the banker, accompanied by his "dear daughter," was arrested at the border. The two suitcases he carried had secret compartments containing the check stub necessary to get the trunk, the trunk key and a certified check, usually in amounts of $25,000 to $35,000 and made payable to bearer.

The police did not discover the secret compartments, so the story goes, but impounded the suitcases. The banker was sentenced to three years in prison and fined. If the fine is not paid within 45 days of his letter's date, the suitcases will be sold at auction. And so the key to the fortune concealed in the trunk will be lost. The amount of this phantom fortune is usually about $450,000. Twenty-five years ago it was only some $285,000, but the treasure has kept pace with inflation.

The banker-prisoner claims he got the name of the American who receives his letter from a friend of the American, who is his fellow prisoner—he cannot give his friend's name for fear of "disgracing his family." The banker-prisoner proposes that the American business or professional man—doctors are prime favorites—come to Mexico City and pay his fine and court costs—generally just under $10,000. (It used to be around $4000, but inflation has affected that too.) This payment will not release the prisoner, but it will free his two suitcases with the hidden check stub for the treasure trunk and the $35,000 certified check.

The American is expected to cash the check and keep the $35,000 for his trouble and expense. He is to retrieve the trunk from the U.S. customhouse, keep one third of the treasure— about $150,000—and turn the balance over to the prisoner's "dear daughter."

She, of course, is a voluptuous young woman. Her photograph is usually in a second letter, which gives the victim his travel instructions and details of the treasure. It is dispatched only after a potential victim has risen to the bait by answering the first, shorter letter that gives only general hints. In the 1950's the first letters were broadcast by the thousands—10,000 to 15,000 every two or three weeks, Post Office inspectors estimated.

Usually, every mailing from Mexico turns up several victims, from Brooklyn to Berkeley. They will send self-righteous but cautious replies stating that their humanitarian instincts have been stirred. The prospect of acquiring a large fortune is usually dismissed as quite secondary. A typical reply is this one from St. Louis:

> DEAR SIR: In regard to your letter of July 22, I would like to state that I will be happy to be of help in any way that I can to yourself and, in particular, to your unfortunate daughter. I will, beyond all doubt, center my energies in this direction, as long as these efforts are legitimate and within the law and are in line with the general promotion of humanitarian causes, in the same way that I have helped many others who were in need.

The victim is directed to communicate with no one except the contact man, "because of the delicacy of the matter." He is told to write airmail in care of a "brother-in-law" of a "prison guard who is friendly to the prisoner," telling his time of arrival. The brother-in-law is the contact man with the friendly guard, who will arrange for the suitcases, with their valuable secret, to be released to the Americans.

The victim usually flies down. He is met at the airport by the guard's brother-in-law, who escorts him to a hotel. Gradually a whole cast of mysterious Mexicans begins circulating about the American. He becomes more and more mystified, confused and, at last, frightened. There is a lot of lurking about dark street corners, whispered conferences by candlelight in dark cafés and the popping in and out of sundry sinister Mexicans.

The American is several times spirited out to the prison, a grim, stone-walled bastion at the edge of the city. There the friendly guard appears for short conferences. He confides that the plan is proving more difficult than had been anticipated, for the judge is becoming suspicious. (Of course, the guard is a member of the gang dressed in a uniform.)

Finally, the guard breaks the frightening news that the judge has discovered the plot and an order is being issued for the American's arrest as a conspirator in springing a prisoner. Fortunately, however, the guard has managed to open the suitcases and retrieve the claim-check stub and the certified check.

By now the American is horribly frightened. He is generally glad to shove the $10,000 he has brought into the eager hands of the guard's brother-in-law, who, in turn, slips the American a check stub, a key and the certified check. The victim flees across the border. He learns that the certified check is no good when he tries to cash it. The customhouse reveals that there is no trunk to match the check stub. And, of course, the "beautiful senorita" never makes an appearance. The American goes sadly home and keeps the entire humiliating experience a dark secret.

Occasionally, the recipient of a Spanish-prisoner letter will invite some friends to share. They will go down to Mexico City as a group and all get swindled together. Some years ago, after receiving a letter, an Alabama doctor borrowed $3000 on some vacant lots, and persuaded a businessman friend to come in for $6000. The pair, accompanied by the doctor's son, then lit out for old Mexico.

As there is a certain strength in numbers, the swindlers did not try to frighten them. Before parting with their $9000, this trio insisted on proof that the $30,000 bank draft was legitimate and that the trunk was really being held at Laredo. They sent telegrams, they thought, to the "National City Bank" of Galveston, on which the draft was drawn, and to the Laredo customhouse.

Within a couple of hours they had replies. A telegram purporting to be from the bank stated that the draft was indeed good. Another wire, apparently sent by the customhouse, said the trunk was right there. The trio paid their cash and took off for Galveston, where they learned there was no bank in Galveston known as the National City. There was a City National Bank, which was of no use whatever to the three Alabamans. Of course, they found no trunk at Laredo, either.

The swindlers, who had intercepted their messages before they reached the telegraph office, had facilities for simulating tele-grams. The equipment in one headquarters included a dozen electric typewriters, at which the come-on letters were batted out by a whole stenographic pool; presses to print fake newspaper stories of the banker's arrest and fake copies of his indictment; and presses for printing certified-check forms and bogus telegrams.

The Spanish-prisoner racket is believed to have developed as an aftermath of the Spanish Armada's defeat in 1588, when thousands of Spanish soldiers and sailors, captured in battle or driven ashore by shipwreck, were thrown into English prisons and held until ransomed. It was not long before some smart Spanish confidence men used their plight as a racket. They solic-ited funds from relatives, supposedly to be used for ransom, but kept the money themselves. Later on they added a yarn about hidden treasure belonging to the prisoners, which the prisoners would split with the redeemers. This was to interest persons not related to these unfortunates.

The racket continued long after the Armada prisoners were dead and gone. Fresh crops of sharpers wrote to wealthy persons in other lands, posing as prisoners in the dungeons of Spain—a land noted for dungeons—with vast fortunes they would divide with their benefactors.

As Americans became wealthy, the Spanish swindlers turned their principal attention to this country. In one two-month period in 1900, Americans turned over to postal authorities 1431 Spanish-swindle letters. In 1907 Americans are known to have lost $30,000 —probably much more—to swindlers in one Spanish province alone. They usually operated near the French border, for an easier escape. They bribed postal and telegraph employes, who tipped them off when suspicious strangers appeared in town.

In 1922 some of the swindlers moved their bases to Latin America, principally Mexico, to be more convenient to their prey. Then, the Spanish Civil War in the 1930's caused all prisoner-swindle operations to be moved across the Atlantic.

Until the 1950's, the only known prisoner racket was the

Spanish version. But it was obviously only a matter of time before somebody invented an American prisoner and set about to fleece the Latins. That distinction went to one Celedonio Sevilla, an artist of sorts, who owned the Dalla Advertising Corporation, which had headquarters in the Empire State Building. His prisoner was a certain "Nelson Lawrence Watkins," a former millionaire, in jail for defrauding his stockholders. He had a dear daughter by the name of Kathlene, who was only 15 years old. And, of course, he had concealed a trunkful of treasure.

The come-on letters were signed by a certain "Father John Miller," supposedly a prison chaplain, acting as intermediary for the prisoner. Father Miller's letters pointed out that the lucky Latin chosen to shelter the fair Kathlene and her father's fortune would have to give proof of his social acceptability and his financial stability. The letter explained that the prisoner wished a Latin American to have this responsibility because he understood "Latins are frank, loyal and trustworthy." The letters were pounded out by the hundreds in Sevilla's office and sent to businessmen in practically all the Latin American countries.

One of Sevilla's associates approached the priest in charge of a Catholic church in New York City. He explained that he was a friend of Father John Miller, a resident of South America who was then touring the States. He asked permission for Father Miller's mail to be sent in care of that church. The New York priest innocently agreed. Before long, Father Miller's letters were pouring into the church at the rate of 40 or 50 a day. They contained such answers as the following:

> With deep surprise I have read your pious message. I have resolved, after meditation, to offer my services in a cause so worthwhile as that of the unfortunate Mr. Watkins. My economic solvency and social position are such that I believe will not impede my participation.
>
> Father Miller, as mediator, I implore you to accept my help in serving Mr. Watkins. I hope you will send me the

documents, etc., in order that I may have a better understanding of the task you are undertaking.

When these answers were delivered in New York, through the unsuspecting church, Father Miller wrote back, instructing the writer to come at once to New York, prepare to put up a substantial cash guarantee and reap a treasure.

Father Miller gave some interesting details about that:

> You must have care in taking the lining from the trunk, and separate the double walls so as not to damage what is there. Among the contents are: one thousand $100 bills, eight hundred $500 bills, four thousand pounds sterling, railroad and oil shares worth many thousands of dollars. Also in the trunk are the jewels of Kathlene's mother: a pearl necklace valued at $10,000, a diamond diadem, which—that her mother may rest in peace—Kathlene must wear on her wedding day, worth $35,000. There is also the mother's wedding ring, worth $5000, a gold bracelet with the mother's name in rubies and emeralds, and some odd jewelry. There are two checkbooks on the National Bank of Argentina, with two deposits—one amounting to $16,000, the other $36,000. The little girl carries the key to the trunk on a little gold cord hanging about her neck.

In spite of all that bait, nobody got swindled in the American-prisoner racket. Sevilla had arranged with a woman who rented desk and office space in a building on West 42nd Street to accept some of Father Miller's overflow mail. She became suspicious when the person who called for it was not in clerical clothing, and told the Post Office inspectors.

Sevilla was sentenced to seven years for mail fraud, and the new American-prisoner racket died aborning. But not before several eager businessmen from South America, with adventure in their hearts, had arrived in New York, set to retrieve the hidden fortune and rescue a young girl. And this gives us the comforting assurance that not all fools are on this side of the border.

In fact, only a small fraction of Americans who receive Spanish-prisoner letters fall for them. Most people throw them away. Even some who answer them are not fooled. Among these was a Lakeland, Florida, businessman, who answered as follows:

> DEAR SENOR: Your letter of August 20 received, and I am surprised to hear that someone who knows me has spoken highly enough of me for you to trust me in this very delicate proposition. It couldn't have been anyone who knows me well. But I would like to assure you that I cannot get away at this time.
>
> I'd like to reciprocate with an amazing offer of my own to you. Naturally, I cannot give definite names and places in this letter, as it might fall into the hands of others. My proposition is this:
>
> Years ago, a certain ship was sunk with a large treasure aboard. Now, I know what ocean this happened in. If you will come to Lakeland with a large boat and two deep-sea divers with complete outfits, I will give you the name of this ocean. (It is necessary for you to keep this offer quiet.)
>
> By way of compensation for your trip, I will give you all three thirds of whatever you are able to salvage.
>
> I cannot sign my own name, for obvious reasons, but you can refer to me as Sucker. I surely hope you get out of jail soon. It must be annoying to have a suitcase full of money just around the corner and be unable to get at it.
>
> Yours very truly,
>
> SUCKER

IN SAN ANTONIO, officials noted that inmates of the Bexar County jail, who rioted for an hour, smashing windows and breaking water pipes, had first covered up their TV sets with blankets. —*Time*

The racing drivers at Indianapolis
are greenhorns compared to
the pros in getaway cars

THE FIRST FEDERAL
SAVINGS BANK GRAND PRIX

by No. 93761 as told to No. 78904

In the more hip circles here at state prison it is generally held that the two top automobile drivers of all time were Juan Fangio and Clarence Heatherton. There are probably a number of outsiders prepared to argue the point—with most of the disagreement centered on Clarence—but it's true all the same. You just have to judge by different standards, since Juan was a champion of the auto-racing world and Clarence drove getaway cars on bank heists.

Clarence was a Londoner, and he looked every bit of it. When I first met him in 1945 he was a spry little old man, done up in baggy tweeds and wearing a pair of those steel-rimmed spectacles of the sort you see only on Englishmen and characters in old Charlie Chan movies. He also sported a toothbrush mustache that gave him a half-raffish air. Clarence had driven in British races and rallies for years before he was tempted into crime by a yen for an expensive Bugatti. After his first fling, which cost him a stretch in Wormwood Scrubs, he became a full-time wheelman and never went back to proper racing. Clarence was one of the oddballs who really liked the excitement of his work, but he always insisted that he drove only for love of that elusive Bugatti—or, as time went by, perhaps a 1750-cc. Alfa Romeo or a 300 SL Mercedes.

Clarence was as efficient as a computer behind the wheel, even though he nursed a quaint set of prejudices about cars. For instance, he never got over grousing about the disappearance of the running board, a very useful feature back in the 1920's, when he started in the business. A standard technique on bank jobs in those days was to herd an assortment of cashiers and customers out to the getaway car and go tearing off with them stacked on the running boards. This show of togetherness usually kept the police from doing any careless shooting.

Another of Clarence's dislikes was the automatic transmission. I remember one time in 1960 we were parked outside a Chicago loan office, right in the middle of a job, and the old geezer decided to give me a lecture on the subject. He concluded it—after we had pulled away amidst a clanging din of alarm bells and shouts for help—with the determinedly pious observation that automatics were wicked. "An automobile," he declared, "should have a stick shift, as God intended."

In the early days of the profession when Clarence was starting out on his career, there were more makes of cars to choose from than there are today. The main considerations were size and horsepower. There was the early Locomobile, some models of which boasted up to 120 horsepower. There were the indestructible Cadillacs and the heavy, high-riding Buicks. Also popular for their speed all through the 1930's were such automobiles as the Hudson, Terraplane and Ford.

John Dillinger was a great fancier of Fords. In fact, he was so partial to them that one time while he was on the run in Illinois, with every cop in the country trying to track him down, he took time to write a letter of appreciation to Henry Ford:

HELLO OLD PAL:
Arrived here at 10 a.m. today. Would like to drop in and see you.
You have a wonderful car. Been driving it for three weeks It's a treat to drive one.

527

Your slogan should be: "Drive a Ford and watch other cars fall behind you." I can make any other car take a Ford's dust.

Bye-Bye
JOHN DILLINGER

After volunteering this testimonial, old John immediately ditched the Ford in favor of a freshly stolen Chevrolet coupé. Which proves, at least, that there is no brand loyalty among thieves.

Probably the most fondly remembered car among old wheelmen is the Cord. It was hard to come by, but much esteemed by the cognoscenti, because it was remarkably nimble and driving it demanded a certain deft touch which helped to weed out the amateurs.

By contrast, most cars on the road today make pretty crummy getaway vehicles. They are sprung and shocked for a nice spongy

ride, which is comfortable only when you don't have a cruiser on your tail. So wheelmen look for specific characteristics when selecting a car for a job. The first thing they want is a good stiff suspension that will cut down the lean on fast turns. And if they can spot a model with disk brakes and antiroll bars, all the better.

The ideal getaway car, under present-day conditions, would seem to be something like a Jaguar: fast, plenty of pickup and easy to handle in heavy traffic. A cinch to outrun anything the law might have. Unfortunately, a Jaguar is *not* the ideal getaway car. I used one a couple of years ago on a bar holdup—and if you have never tried making it through the door of a Jaguar at a dead run with a sawed-off shotgun and a sack of money clutched to your bosom, you just don't know the meaning of limited headroom.

Important as the right car is to a getaway, nothing is more important than the man at the wheel, and at this, as I say, Clarence

Heatherton was king. I liked to think that Clarence passed at least a part of his great skill on to me when he introduced me to the art of armed robbery and taught me the rudiments of git-driving. Not that I've ever had any illusions about my skill as a wheelman. The truly good drivers are specialists, and very often they are men with a proper racing background. I don't claim that race drivers are any more given to larceny than, say, jai alai players or pole-vaulters, but there is obviously a flaky fringe around the sport. When a driver does get into the rackets, he's more likely to stay behind the wheel than to take up pickpocketing.

I worked with a lot of these speedway dropouts over the years, and they are the most offbeat group of characters you could ever hope to get arrested with. Some are just flat-out kooks. There was a wheelman in Detroit, for instance, who twitched. I mean *all* the time. He had nerve spasms in his fingers, and his left eyelid fluttered like the shutter of a 16-millimeter movie camera. It didn't seem to hang him up on his driving, but he had been barred from legitimate racing when other drivers began to develop sympathetic tics.

Another specimen was a big German who still, somehow or other, finds occasional employment around Cleveland. He looked like Charles de Gaulle and once worked as a pitman for the great Fangio—for about two hours. He was a perfect driver for holdups if you could keep him away from the engine, but if he so much as tweaked a spark plug the whole motor was laid up for weeks.

A good git-man must have a knack for coaxing total perform-ance out of middling machines. He has to be careful and deliberate, and it doesn't hurt if he's a little paranoid. The best wheelman in St. Louis as a matter of fact—if he's not in jail—is a guy who quit racing when he became convinced that the rest of the drivers on the circuit were conspiring to put him through a rail. On a heist he is always certain that every stop sign, traffic light and speed limit is there just to trap him. He imagines prowl cars lurking in each alley and he has this nutty idea that all women drivers are police molls. Working with this guy is harder on the nerves than a three-month stretch in solitary—but, man, is he ever careful.

The real wheel talent shows up less in aberrations than it does in proper cornering. On city streets, approach and exit angles can be fierce, and in order not to lose speed the driver must have enough finesse to handle a power skid.

One of the oldest tricks in the profession is to let the cops get right on your tail on a gravel road, then suddenly swing the wheel hard over for a controlled, four-wheel slide, timed to dig out onto a side road. Any wheelman who can't do this with his eyes shut would be better off in a nice comfortable cell.

The variation on this—the 180-degree skid—requires pure genius. The only wheelman I ever knew who was really accomplished at it was a skinny little hillbilly named Beauregard Washburn who didn't look competent enough to drive a herd of pigs. (I never met the legendary Junior Johnson, who supposedly was unequaled at making 180-degree turns to avoid revenue agents. Johnson, alas, committed the unforgivable sin of switching to legitimate race driving.) Beauregard Washburn was all eyeballs and Adam's apple, with shaggy sideburns holding up the slack in his jaws. He'd learned to skid a car through 180 degrees—with the help of a heavy load of moonshine in the rear end—down around Nashville while playing tag with the revenue agents. The night he demonstrated the trick for me, we had a 500-pound safe in the trunk and a 3000-pound police car on our tail trying to get right in there with it. We were heading east out of Kalamazoo on a mangy little dirt road, and things looked a lot better for the cops than they did for us. But suddenly Beauregard tromped on the brakes and spun the wheel over. We must have done a quarter of a mile sideways and then backwards before Beau finally dredged up enough power to get us moving forward again. For a few minutes I was completely unglued. And so, I imagine, were the cops when they found themselves still heading east with us going west.

Occasionally a driver like Beauregard, with no background of legitimate racing, will make the grade as a top git-man, but professional criminals prefer professional drivers—since washouts are generally disasters. Some friends of mine learned this the hard way one time when they decided to make a driver out of an ex-bookie called Wimpy. They taught him everything they could and even packed him off to a school in California where they train race drivers. But Wimpy had neither the wit nor the coördination for driving. On his very first job he let a diagonal parking arrangement at a small-town supermarket job rattle him to shreds. He positioned the car in the parking slot backward to take advantage of a fast head-first start. When his pals came piling into the car with the loot, he forgot his position and laid down a quarter inch of rubber screaming out of that slot—*backward*, through the market's plate-glass window and right into a soap display.

But Wimpy wasn't the worst. On the beef that earned me my current sentence, I came bursting out of a Detroit jewelry store with guns and hot necklaces hanging out of every pocket, only to find that my idiot driver had very carefully wedged our car into a parking space. He wasn't even behind the wheel. He was, God preserve us, feeding coins into the meter.

And that's the sort of thing that is becoming more and more typical of the business. The real trouble is that there aren't enough men with racing experience coming into the profession—men like my old friend Clarence. I have a fond picture in my mind of Clarence today, a little older and with thicker lenses in his glasses, but still in tweeds and proper English to his larcenous core. He's sitting in a freshly stolen GT 350 Mustang, immediately in front of a bank in some small eastern community—one of those quiet places off the main highway with miles of country road stretching out in all directions. Clarence has one eye cocked on the town constable and the other on his confederates in the bank (common criminals, of whom he doesn't really approve), but his mind is on that fine power plant in front of him, listening to it tick over and just waiting to let it out on the only kind of race that ever really mattered to him.

That's not too unlikely a vision, but it's coming to be a very rare one. Git-driving is losing its color, I'm afraid, and is becoming less specialized. It is being taken over by clods who pull jobs on the spur of the moment and drive off willy-nilly into the back bumpers of police cars or get hung up at tollbooths with nothing smaller than a hot $20. It's enough to take the heart right out of a fellow.

Crime will probably be with us for a long time, but the Grand Prix git-driver, I fear, is as outdated as Clarence's running board.

⌇⌇⌇

EVERYONE at the neighborhood carnival seemed to be having a good time except a solemn, shabbily dressed youngster of five or six who stood alone gazing longingly at the gaudy Ferris wheel. I went over and asked, "How would you like to go for a ride with us?"

He didn't answer directly, but looked me over appraisingly and then shouted at the top of his voice: "Hey-y, fellas!"

From nowhere came at least a dozen little boys, all about the same size and buzzing with excitement.

After the ride, they disappeared as mysteriously as they had arrived, and my wife and I moved on to the next concession. As we were leaving some time later, I happened to glance back. There at his station stood the decoy, gazing hungrily up at the Ferris wheel. —W. W. Lessing

A COLLEGE football star, who had failed an examination, was disqualified just before the big game. There was great weeping and wailing and gnashing of teeth, and the distressed president of the school came to the professor who had given the fatal grade. "This is terrible!" he said, "We can't win the game without him."

"But I had to give him zero," said the teacher. "You see, he cheated."

"Cheated! Did you see him?"

"No, I didn't."

"Does he admit it?"

"No, he denies it," said the teacher. "But he—a poor student—sat next to the best student, and their answers were almost identical."

"Do you think that proves cheating?"

"In this case I do. The good student replied to the last question, 'I don't know the answer.' And the football star wrote on his paper, 'I don't know the answer either.' "

—Leonard W. Mayo, quoted by Claire MacMurray in Cleveland Plain Dealer

533

*The forger had to answer to his countrymen for
selling the old master to the Nazi general*

A MAN WHO FOOLED GÖRING

by Irving Wallace

Shortly after the defeat of Germany in World War II, the
American Seventh Army located Hermann Göring's priceless
collection of looted art in Germany's subterranean vaults. Special
Allied teams led by the U.S. Army's Monuments and Fine Arts
Division arrived to classify the plunder. The collection of 1200
paintings from all the galleries of Europe was dazzling, and to the
investigators, the oil *Christ and the Adulteress*, signed by Jan
Vermeer, the famous 17th-century Dutch artist, was just another
masterpiece.

The investigators could not know that they were uncovering the
most fantastic art scandal of the times, a crime—which started as
a practical joke—involving more than $3 million and the reputa-
tions of some of the world's leading art experts.

The springboard for the scandal was not Göring's possession
of the old master, but the fact that he had not stolen it. A zealous
Dutch expert, glancing through Göring's private papers, discovered that someone in Amsterdam had coldly sold the great painting to Göring's art procurer, Walther Hofer, in 1943, for the
equivalent of $600,000.

To the Dutch, the sale of a Vermeer to the enemy was a horrible
form of collaboration. Jan Vermeer is, like Rembrandt, a national

hero. Countless streets in Holland bear his name, and reproductions of his works are hung in even the poorest homes. His oil paintings are state treasure.

Enraged at his find, the Dutch expert scurried back to Holland with the painting. The man who had sold the picture to Göring's agent had fled, but the authorities learned that he had acquired the picture from an art dealer who had handled it on commission for a man named Reinstra. Reinstra in turn said that he had obtained the picture from Hans van Meegeren, an artist in the city of Amsterdam.

Van Meegeren was wealthy—the owner of numerous homes and two nightclubs. He had made his pile by selling his collection of six Vermeers. Five he had sold to collectors and museums in The Hague, Rotterdam and Amsterdam. The sixth was *Christ and the Adulteress*—the one Göring had obtained.

Where had Van Meegeren gotten the painting? From a collection he had bought in Italy. The authorities jumped at this. He had bought from Italian Fascists? And sold to German Nazis? He was promptly arrested.

Van Meegeren spent three weeks in jail. The Dutch police wanted him to admit he sold a sacred Vermeer to the Nazis. He refused. They hammered. Finally, Van Meegeren cracked.

"You blasted fools!" he shrieked angrily. "I sold no national treasure to the Germans! I sold a Van Meegeren, a Vermeer forged with my own hands!"

He dictated his confession. He had faked six Vermeers between 1937 and 1943. For these hoaxes he had received 8 million Dutch guldens—$3 million.

Van Meegeren had fooled art historians and scientists who had tested them, and dozens of European and American art critics who had glowingly praised the spurious Vermeers. He had proved, he boasted, that he was as good as the old masters and that the critics who had so long harassed him were asses.

If Van Meegeren's confession was true he was not a collaborationist, but a faker whose act had international implications. The leading Dutch art experts were summoned. They were anxious and indignant.

Unanimously these experts insisted that the Vermeers they had once judged authentic still were. Their reputations and livelihoods were based on the authenticity of those Vermeers.

The controversy raged in the press, the cafés, the homes of Holland. It fanned out into London, Paris and Rome; into New York and Chicago. The Netherlands authorities debated. Then one official made a suggestion. Why not let Van Meegeren paint, under police supervision, a new forgery in the manner of Vermeer? This seventh painting might prove whether he was capable of forging an old master or whether he was merely trying to save himself from collaborationist charges. In 1945 Van Meegeren began his peculiar labor of defense. The authorities permitted him to acquire all the necessary materials, and imprisoned him in a large studio.

"It is difficult," he told a friend who visited him. "I do not have the exact oils and I do not have the time to think. They rush me. And they look over my shoulder when I work. Still, I believe it will be beautiful."

Van Meegeren's oil took shape, a depiction of the Christ Child in the Temple of the Elders. Six figures on a broad canvas. All the famed Vermeer trademarks were in it—the exquisite, rich yellow and blue colorings, the refinement of technique, the *pointillé* touch.

Physically, the work was foolproof—17th-century linen used for the canvas, the paint overheated exactly as Vermeer had overheated his paints, the badger-hair brushes the same as those wielded by artists of the 1600's.

At last the job was done. The Dutch authorities appointed a jury of international art experts to study it. A special gallery in Amsterdam, displaying Van Meegeren's first six Vermeers and his fateful seventh, was the jury's headquarters.

Meanwhile, Van Meegeren brought forth other evidence to prove his guilt. The chairs in which Christ sat in two of the pic-

537

tures were drawn after Van Meegeren's fairly modern chair in his own studio.

And the hands of Christ in his paintings were not at all like those in other Vermeers; Van Meegeren had used his own hands as models for them.

During the trial the experts applied their tests to the paintings and declared the six Vermeers skillful forgeries. Van Meegeren was convicted of deliberate fraud and, in view of his poor state of health, sentenced to only one year in prison. The toll taken by the trial, however, had been too great, and Van Meegeren died on December 30, 1947, at the age of 58.

The case brought to the fore once again the question of the authenticity of many pictures in famous collections. As one Dutch critic, reviving the old art witticism, jested, "Of the 2500 paintings done by Corot in his lifetime, 7800 are to be found in America." Other critics cited evidence ranging from the two copies of Gainsborough's *Blue Boy*, which caused international consternation, to the exposure in Paris of a forgery factory turning out Picassos and Utrillos by the dozen. So expert were the latter that Utrillo had to look twice before disowning the oils forged under his name.

"The number of pictures bought, at one time or another, as Rembrandt's," Dr. Maximilian Toch, a Manhattan art detective, remarked, "is six to ten times as great as the maximum number that Rembrandt can have painted, and there is a much larger discrepancy in the case of other artists, like Van Dyck, with some 2000 attributed to him and perhaps 70 executed by him."

Supporters of Van Meegeren argue that if his phony Vermeers were passed upon and bought as originals, then he was a genius in his own right. They remind you that he did not copy a single masterpiece, but rather created brand-new masterpieces in the manner and style of the old master. They call it "creative" forgery in Holland, and they say it is not crime, but art, and that Van Meegeren was perhaps one of the greatest artists of this category in all history.

Hans van Meegeren began sketching seriously in grammar school. By the 1920's he had a minor reputation. In the early 1930's he received commissions to paint nobility in London and several American millionaires on the Riviera. About this time his bitter feud with Dutch critics and painters started. They resented his independence, his barbed wit and his financial success. When venal Dutch critics approached him with the promise of writing good reviews of his exhibits if he would pay them, Van Meegeren indignantly refused.

So they roasted him. In 1936 Van Meegeren determined to get even with his enemies, the critics.

He laid the groundwork for his hoax carefully. He weighed the old masters he might imitate and finally selected Vermeer. Why Vermeer?

"Because I had a great admiration for him," he said when found out. "Also, his style was easiest for me. And his personal life was cloaked in mystery, which would make the discovery of a new Vermeer more reasonable."

Van Meegeren's forged paintings had to be physically foolproof. The experts would test the effect of alcohol on the colors, would inject hypodermic needles to find the chemical content of the paint, would employ X rays and infrared rays to photograph the canvas, quartz lamps to penetrate the overlays. All this Van Meegeren anticipated. He dug out contemporary manuscripts and learned that Vermeer used colors like gamboge, a gum resin used as yellow pigment; lapis lazuli, a blue from powdered stones; and white zinc instead of white lead. To obtain real lapis lazuli, Van Meegeren paid as high as $2000 a tube.

"The one stumbling block I found hard to overcome," he recalled, "was the oil to be used in paint mixtures. Moderns use linseed oil. That's no good. Use it and your paint will never get hard and old. Luckily I discovered, in an old manuscript, exactly the oil Vermeer used. I used it, too, and it made my paint proof against all alcohol tests."

Van Meegeren selected for his Vermeer an inspiring portrait of

Christ breaking bread with his disciples at Emmaus. He toiled meticulously, untiringly, day after day for seven months on this painting. Not even his wife knew what he was up to. When it was done, he went over it again, point by point. Everything was there—even to the old cracks in the surface. He had learned that in the years before Vermeer the paint broke in large cracks, but the paint in Vermeer's oils broke in smaller, chainlike cracks. So Van Meegeren's imitation cracks, created by scratching them out in pattern and baking them apart in a kitchen stove, were exactly in the manner of the master.

From his knowledge of Vermeer's life, he invented the story of the "discovery." He knew Vermeer had worked side by side with Italian student painters. The Italians had done Christ at Emmaus. They had taken their products to Italy. Most likely Vermeer had done Christ at Emmaus, and most likely, in the unrecorded years of his life, he had traveled to Italy. Very well. This new Vermeer would be found in Italy. Van Meegeren would learn of it through a friend, purchase it cheaply and then resell it.

He took his handiwork to Amsterdam. Before putting it up for sale, Van Meegeren approached one of Holland's art experts, Dr. Abraham Bredius, who was then more than 80 years old. The old man, flattered that someone was consulting him again, blinked at it through dim eyes, tested it briefly and gave his written seal of authenticity.

In late 1937 the august Boymans Museum in Rotterdam tested the Vermeer with chemicals and rays and found it authentic. Van Meegeren was paid a half million guldens for his treasure. In September 1938 it starred in a showing of 450 Netherlands masterpieces gathered to celebrate Queen Wilhelmina's Jubilee. Critics from The Hague, from London, from Paris swarmed to view it. So great was their reverence that they demanded the museum floor be carpeted about the Vermeer "masterpiece" to prevent noise while they contemplated.

The museum obliged. Several critics wrote ecstatically that it was by far Jan Vermeer's best effort.

Van Meegeren was delighted. He had proved his mortal enemies idiots and made himself rich. From then on it was easy going—until that sale to Göring. "That," Van Meegeren admitted sadly, "was the beginning of the end."

⌒⌒⌒

MONTE CARLO is a worldly lady; she has seen nearly every trick in the gambler's trade and has found a way to stop them all. The latest threat, however, has been an unusually clever one, in spite of the fact that the eight wise men responsible are now in jail. For some time the bank in one of the high-stake card games had been losing steadily. There was apparently nothing to explain it, until someone finally noticed that every time the bank had a bad night there was a gentleman in dark glasses to be seen standing behind the croupier. A different gentleman each night, but the same glasses. Then the explanation came out. A gang of eight gamblers had discovered a means whereby, with the connivance of a croupier, they could mark the cards with an ink that was invisible to every eye save those looking through a certain type of dark glass. It was a simple trick thereafter to watch the cards with the croupier's help, and signal with eyebrows or nostrils to one's confederates out in front. *—The Seven Seas*

AN ATTRACTIVE girl stood in front of a department store rattling a can and crying, "Give something for the orphans." Coins tinkled into the contribution box and no one seemed to mind that it boldly proclaimed:

> GIVE! THREE-HEADED ORPHANS
> OF CLAUSTROPHOBIA
> THIS IS A FAKE

The girl was posted on that street to help find the answer to the question, "How gullible are we?" The answer seems to be, plenty. In the four different cities where the test was made, only 4 persons, out of the 264 stopped, detected the fraud. And 59 percent of those who stopped gave something. More men contributed than women, proving that men are more gullible—or more attracted to pretty canvassers. *—David Dressler in This Week Magazine*

After a life in the underworld
came the question: Why did I turn to crime?

MY STORY

by Willie Sutton as told to Quentin Reynolds

Editor's note: *On February 18, 1952, a little man with the look of a malicious leprechaun was picked up by the police in New York City. He was the famous Willie Sutton, and he was quickly tried for a bank robbery, convicted and given a sentence of 30 years to life. For reasons he himself states in this story, Willie Sutton decided to write this account of his life with the aid of author Quentin Reynolds. Bearing no brief for Sutton, a condensation of this autobiography is published for what it is, the candid memoirs of a crook. Revealing and sometimes at variance with the newspaper accounts and with the considered judgments of a jury, it is nevertheless Sutton's life story as he sees it.*

My mind goes back to 1944. I was in Eastern State Penitentiary, now the State Correctional Institution at Philadelphia, working as a secretary for the prison psychiatrist. He was a tall good-looking man with a soft voice that had a magic effect on the crazed inmates who had cracked under the strain of prison life. And he performed mental miracles.

I recall seeing, now and then, a letter from a former inmate for whom the doctor had obtained a parole. The letter would tell how the man had married, had children and gone straight. I would say, "This is one of the fellows they told you couldn't be rehabilitated." The doctor would nod and chuckle.

On one of these occasions I seized the opportunity and asked him point-blank, "What about me? I've been here ten years now. Don't you think I've learned my lesson?"

The doctor hesitated and then said, "I don't know, Willie. Apparently," he added softly, "banks present an irresistible challenge to you."

"You don't think," I asked, "that I can ever be a useful member of society?"

The doctor studied me for a moment and sighed. "Only you can answer that one, Willie."

"I'm going to prove I can, Doctor," I said, smiling. But I wasn't smiling inside. I had learned enough about psychiatry as his secretary to know that he couldn't tell me flatly what I was sure he believed: There was no chance for me to adjust myself to the environment of a free world. Just the same, I wasn't ready to accept this diagnosis.

Eight years later—on May 2, 1952—I recalled that conversation. I was standing for sentence before Judge Peter T. Farrell of the Queens County Court, in New York, who looked down at me and said, "The sentence of the court is that the prisoner be confined in a state prison for a period of not less than 30 years."

Again I thought of the doctor when I read the stories about me in the newspapers and magazines. Several writers tried to psychoanalyze me. One writer gave me a great many reasons (valid to him, I'm sure) why I had been driven into crime. I tried to follow his reasoning, but because he knew nothing about my early life he was playing a guessing game. A detective-story writer did a thoughtful series in which he held that all my life had been an attempt to escape, not only from prisons but from myself. I have no quarrel with his conclusions. Perhaps he's right—I just don't know.

I do know, however, that not even Freud could analyze a man

merely by reading newspaper stories about him. So I have decided to indulge in an experiment in self-analysis. I've been asked by many a man on a parole board, "Willie, what made you become a criminal?" And for the life of me, I've never been able to give an honest answer. Now I have plenty of time to see if I can come up with that answer. I expect to spend the rest of my days in prison. So I will set down my story. Call it a confession, if you will. But anyway, when it's down in black and white, perhaps some psychiatrist will be able to answer the question that I never could.

You could have called us Suttons the typical Brooklyn family of the early 1900's. We lived in a two-family frame house on High Street. My father, William Sutton, was a big, happy man, well satisfied with his job. He was a blacksmith. There were still plenty of horses in Brooklyn, so he had lots of work. We went to Mass every Sunday morning and had chicken every Sunday for dinner.

For us kids the whole world was bounded by Tillary Street and the East River. This was the only world we knew, and it wasn't a very pretty world. It centered on Sands Street, which was dotted with saloons catering to the sailor trade. Peaceful enough during the day, Sands Street became a battleground at night.

My first crime was minor enough. Two of us volunteered to do the shopping for our families, and the grocery clerk was delighted to let us wait on ourselves. We found it easy to slip a few groceries into our pockets or shirtfronts. From there it was a logical step to visit the same store at night. We climbed in the back window at least half a dozen times, rifling the cash register of as much as $5 a haul. We became the wealthiest kids in the neighborhood. We were never caught, never even had a narrow escape. It was my first taste of easy money—a taste I'm afraid I've never completely lost.

Just the same, I went straight for most of the next few years, even while holding down a job as messenger in a bank. But then the war came, and with it, easy-money jobs in defense plants. I got used to cash in my pockets, parties, liquor, silk shirts and girls. I volunteered for the Army, but I was 17 at the time and I was not accepted.

Despite the high life I had been living, I still had some money saved up after the war ended. But it didn't last long, and when it was gone I pulled my first big robbery. With two friends I broke into the office of a shipyard and got away with $16,000. Our flight took us, by train and car, all over northern New York State; but within two weeks we were back in Brooklyn, in jail. We all got suspended sentences.

This first actual brush with the law taught me a lesson—for a while. I read a want ad, placed by a landscape gardener. I got the job and became an avid horticulturist overnight. Anyone born in the country takes flowers, shrubs and trees for granted, but for me, every one of them was a new discovery. For about three months I commuted out to the big Long Island and Westchester estates, planted trees and shrubs all day and commuted happily home to Brooklyn. I was completely satisfied with life, and not a larcenous thought entered my mind. Then that job disappeared; people couldn't afford landscape gardening anymore. I picked up a few other jobs, but none of them lasted either. I went back to my life of crime. One of my favorite hangouts was a poolroom run by Joe Quigg. It was there that I met "Doc" Tate.

Doc was probably the greatest expert on locks in the country. A real practitioner, he always wore gloves, even in the warmest weather, to protect his sensitive fingertips. I began to learn the difference between amateurs like myself and professionals like Doc Tate. He had been caught many times. But each time he asked himself, "What did I do wrong? What precaution did I fail to take?" And he never made the same mistake twice. When I met him, he had worked out his system until it had become a fine art.

I became Doc's eager student. After a while he let me go along on jobs, in Boston, in Scranton and Wilkes-Barre, Pennsylvania. From him I learned my most valuable lessons: Use nitro and the blowtorch only when the "legitimate" ways—the punch, jimmy and other tools—fail. Do an out-of-town job, then get as far away as possible as fast as possible. Use ordinary tools, the kind that can be bought in any hardware store, and leave them behind—except the jimmy, which will get you out of many a tight, locked place. Choose your fence with the greatest of care. And plan, plan, plan. The Doc was my mentor. But I'm convinced that becoming a criminal was my fault, not his. The Doc only helped me become a successful criminal—for a while.

Shortly afterward I went into business for myself. At first I made my share of mistakes, figuring a bank safe as easier than it was and working all night for nothing, for example. But I made some good hauls too. The first time I got caught it was not because of any mistake on the job but because I had a confederate whose wife got jealous of his mistress and talked to the police. I went to Sing Sing, was transferred to Dannemora. It was September 1929 before I was a free man again. I went straight for a while, but after trying in vain to get a good job I went back to bank robbing again.

My plan of action came to me as I was walking along Broadway one afternoon and noticed an armored truck stop in front of a business house. Two of the uniformed guards approached the door, rang the bell and were admitted. In a few moments they marched from the store, climbed into their truck and drove off. The uniforms those guards wore intrigued me. I doubted very much if the clerk who admitted them to the store looked at their faces. When he saw the uniforms he waved them in. The right kind of uniform would unlock any door. I looked in the classified telephone directory and found several firms which manufactured all kinds of uniforms. That afternoon "Willie the Actor" was born.

I decided to take on my friend Jack Bassett as my partner. I told him to rent a room in the Broadway district under the name of the Waverly School of Drama. Then I had 100 letterheads and business cards printed. I typed out a letter on the imposing stationery of the Waverly School of Drama, saying that we were putting on an amateur play, and that I wanted to rent a bank messenger's uniform. I sent the letter to a dozen costume-renting outfits. Their replies were prompt. If I would send an actor in to be fitted, they were sure they could give complete satisfaction. Armed with their letter, I visited one of the theatrical costuming houses and was delighted with what I saw. They had uniforms of every description. If I wished, I could be a cop, a fireman, a Western Union messenger, an Army officer or even a knight of King Arthur's court. They asked me no questions after I handed them the letter they had sent to the Waverly School of Drama. They just assumed I was another actor. I looked over half a dozen uniforms of the type worn by messengers, and selected a neat-looking khaki outfit, inconspicuous and conservative. Wearing this getup, I felt that I could walk into the House of Morgan, if necessary, and be accepted as a bank messenger.

I had selected my bank carefully. I knew just how many employes worked there. I knew what time each arrived and when each left. I found that the first employe, a guard, arrived at eight each morning. He opened the bank and, after identifying the employes, admitted them as they arrived.

My plan began to take shape. First, however, I needed to know the name of the bank manager. A phone call to the bank secured the information. I schooled Jack Bassett very carefully as to his part in the drama. As a matter of fact, I was beginning to think of this as a drama, with myself as director and main actor. I dropped into a Western Union office and sent the Waverly School of Drama a telegram, merely to get the yellow Western Union envelope. When it arrived, I steamed it open and threw the message away. Then I typed out the name of the manager and name and address of the bank on a yellow sheet of paper. I placed this inside the envelope so that the name and address could be seen through the window of the envelope. It was a pretty good imitation of an actual telegram. I bought a small briefcase, the kind usually carried by bank messengers. Now I was ready.

Shortly after the guard entered the bank at eight o'clock, I rang the bell. The guard opened the door an inch or two, saw my uniform and swung the door back.

"I got a telegram for the boss," I mumbled. Handing him the bogus wire, a small notebook and a pencil, I asked him to sign for the telegram. He held the notebook in one hand, the pencil in the other, and began to sign. As soon as both his hands were occupied, I merely reached down and lifted his revolver out of its holster. I told him very quietly to be a good boy, to obey orders and he wouldn't be hurt. He took a few steps backward, complete bewilderment in his eyes. Then he raised his hands a little shakily. At that psychological moment Jack Bassett walked in and shut the door after him.

I knew that six employes of the bank would arrive within the next few minutes. They were all due at 8:30 and my observation had established the fact that these were very punctual workers who were never late. I told the guard that I knew how he operated each morning and that he should follow his usual custom. He looked at his gun in my hand and shrugged his shoulders hopelessly. The bell rang as the first employe arrived. The guard opened the door and the first arrival gave him a cheery hello and said, "It's a wonderful day, Fred."

"That's what you think," the guard mumbled.

The employe walked in and blinked as he saw us. The guard shut the door and Jack very politely asked the employe to sit down.

Jack had lined half a dozen chairs against the wall. The employes arrived, one by one, and took their places in the row of chairs. The last to arrive, promptly at 8:30, was the manager himself.

"All I want you to do," I told him, "is to open your vault. It would be very silly for you to refuse. If you do refuse, nothing will happen to you, but I promise you that the lives of your employes here will be jeopardized."

I could see from the calm, contemptuous look in the manager's eyes that threats to him wouldn't mean a thing. He would willingly expose himself to any danger, I felt, even death, rather than open that vault and repudiate the trust the bank had in him. But now I saw a struggle going on in his mind. Did he have the right to jeopardize the safety of his employes who sat there against the wall, plainly terrified? Doubt, indecision and then hopeless resignation showed on his face.

"I guess I have no choice," he said wearily.

"That's right," I told him, "you have no choice."

While Bassett held his gun on the six employes, I walked with the manager to the vault. It was 8:40 now. The bank opened for business at 9, and I knew that there were always several customers waiting, undoubtedly to draw out money that could be used for either petty cash or payrolls that day. I prodded the manager very gently with the guard's gun and told him to hurry. He did. The door swung open and I found two small tin boxes inside containing $48,000 in crisp new bills.

I put the money in my briefcase, told the bank manager to sit down with his employes and then gave them a little lecture. I said that my friend and I were leaving now, but that we had a third member of our group on guard outside. If anyone went through this door during the next five minutes, he would be shot. I knew, of course, that as soon as Bassett and I left, they would run for the phone to call the police. I didn't mind that. It would take the police at least ten minutes to arrive. However, I didn't want any of them running out after us, raising an alarm. I figured my little speech would keep them there at least three or four minutes. That was all the time Jack and I needed.

We slipped out the door, shut it quietly and a minute later had melted into the heavy traffic. Everything had gone like clockwork; I hadn't used a torch and there was no reason for the police ever to connect me with the job.

This, I told myself, would be my technique from now on.

During the next two months Jack and I pulled half a dozen jobs, using the same plan of action. I became well acquainted with the various theatrical costume shops on Broadway, but I never rented a uniform from the same place twice. By turns I was a Western Union messenger, postman, policeman and even, on one job, a window cleaner. Soon I was rolling in money. But I overplayed my hand and got my first big sentence: 30 years in Sing Sing. The next year was hectic; I broke out of Sing Sing and went back to robbing banks in New York. It was the same pattern repeated again and again.

I had decided that the cops were getting too hot on my trail in New York, so I moved to Philadelphia. That was a mistake. The first big job I pulled there got me sent up to Eastern State Penitentiary for 25 to 50 years. I entered Eastern on February 12, 1934, and my first four months were spent in segregation. This kind of treatment can unbalance the sanest minds, but I found refuge in books. There was a library of sorts, and I was allowed to borrow books from it. Because of my escape from Sing Sing I was, of course, a marked man. Even when the four-month period of segregation was over and I was transferred to what was known as the seventh gallery, I received very special attention from the guards. The prison officials never trusted me, but I can hardly blame them.

The warden at Eastern State Penitentiary was Herbert ("Hardboiled") Smith, a former captain of the Pennsylvania State Police. No one had ever escaped from this pen while he was in charge of it, and he was going to be sure that I didn't spoil his record. Hardboiled Smith was a gray-haired, ruddy-complexioned, heavyset man who invariably smoked cigars. He was stern, but he was respected for his intelligence. We prisoners used to feel that Smith could read our minds. Any time there was trouble in the prison Smith would invariably come up with the men who had actually caused it. He treated us fairly, and in the light of my record I couldn't blame him for the extra precautions he took guarding me.

Hard-boiled Smith was the one man I could never beat. He and his guards knew that I was "escape-minded." After I had been probably the best-behaved inmate in the pen for a while, they apparently thought that I had become reconciled to spending the next 25 years or more as their guest, so they relaxed their vigilance just a little. Then I could plan my escape.

Eastern State was built on the principle of the wheel, with the cell blocks branching out from the hub. Each cell block was visible from the hub, and guards maintained a 24-hour watch from this vantage point. After we had been locked in at night, guards patrolled the cell blocks continually and flashed their searchlights into the cells.

But one day a fellow inmate was given his parole. When he left he gave me the only thing of value he owned: a complete map of the whole sewer system of the prison. He had worked in the cellar, and over the years had learned the location and width of every sewer pipe at Eastern, and he had committed this to paper.

I noticed that late each afternoon, when our recreation period was over in the yard, a guard opened a steel door embedded in the wall close to the ground. Then he turned a wheel which lifted a solid steel door damming the flow of water from the main sewer. Usually this water would come rushing through the pipes of the prison sewer system. While the pipes were filled with water, escape through them was impossible. But I felt that if I could have a couple of hours alone in the cellar when the pipes were not flooded, I might have a chance to get to the main sewer.

There was one small barred window which ventilated the cellar. I had taken another inmate into my confidence. He only had five years to go and wasn't interested in escape himself, but he would help me all he could. During yard-out time I sat by the barred window while he stood above me, half hiding me. Within a week I'd cut through a bar. Then one day I slipped unobserved through the window into the cellar. I pushed the bar back in position. I had about one hour now to investigate. In the cellar I found a grating leading to the sewer system. I removed it and slipped down into the sewer below the cellar floor. There was just enough space for me to crawl. I crawled 200 feet. Now I came to a sewer running at right angles to my passage and slightly below it. This was filled with water and refuse. I knew that 15 feet to the right was a steel door. If I could get that door opened, the water from this section would flow through it and out into the main sewer. Once this part of the sewer system was drained, I would be able perhaps to go through that passage which led to the main sewer. But how to reach the steel door?

There was only one thing to do. I would have to swim the 15 feet, and I would have to swim mostly underwater. The air was stifling. Thousands of giant bugs were slithering through my hair and over my body. I could feel them on my neck and some of them slipped beneath my shirt. I removed all of my clothes. Lowering myself into that filthy muck was not an inviting prospect but neither was the idea of spending the rest of my life in prison. I took a deep breath, lowered myself into the water and swam toward the steel door.

I had a brick in my right hand, which made swimming more difficult. If I could raise that door up three or four inches, I could insert the brick under it and the water would then seek the lower level of the main sewer. I reached the door and felt desperately for some handle, but it was perfectly smooth. My knees scraped painfully on the rough bottom. I dropped the brick and explored the bottom of the door with both hands. The door was solid and there was no way I could raise it. I had to return. I gave myself as mighty a push as I could away from the door and swam back to where I had come from.

I could feel myself blacking out and I raised my head groggily. I had made it back. With the little strength I had left, I crawled to the relative safety of the tunnel. I was beaten, and I knew it.

I had to crawl the 200 feet back to where the grating would allow me entrance to the cellar. Somehow I made it. The air of the cellar seemed fresh and clean, and I lay there for a few moments wallowing in it. Then, still shaky, I got into my clothes, out of the cellar and by some miracle got back to my cell with 30 seconds to spare before the guards started their counting. My first attempt to escape had been a complete failure.

For 11 years I tried to beat Hard-boiled Smith. I made elaborate preparations to go over the wall, preparations that even included a painstakingly manufactured dummy of myself to fool the guards. I was discovered and spent 23 months in solitary. Later I joined a group of inmates who were laboriously digging a tunnel under the wall. It took six months, scooping our way bit by bit, but when we finally broke through on the other side, we ran right into the arms of the cops. I did my best; but Hard-boiled Smith was too smart for me. Finally I was transferred to Holmesburg County

Prison in Philadelphia. Holmesburg was supposed to be "escape-proof" too, but it proved easier than Eastern State. After 18 months five of us had laid our plans. We persuaded a friend who was leaving the prison to send a gun in to us. It came hidden in a vegetable truck. We got hacksaws from the machine shop and painstakingly sawed through our bars, leaving just enough to hold together until the time came to knock them out. On February 9, 1947, it started to snow. With a few whispered words in the yard we agreed that this was the night.

At ten minutes before midnight we broke the bars away from our doors, slunk to the end of the corridor and waited for the guards to come by on their rounds. When they did, we pulled the gun on them. We borrowed their keys and parts of their uniforms and opened the engine room to get some ladders we knew were across the yard. The snow was driving down furiously, cutting the visibility to nearly zero. We got to the wall, but just as one of the ladders touched it, the searchlight flashed on us and the machine guns on the tower swung around. We had been spotted.

One of the men was quick-witted enough to bellow, "It's all right. We're guards!" The man in the tower was confused by the snow and only able to make out the guards' caps on some of us. He held his fire. A scramble up the ladders and across the top, a long drop on the other side, and I was free again.

Guards and police were after us within 15 minutes, but we managed to slither away from them. I took a chance and bummed a ride to New York. The driver and I talked about the prison break most of the way to the city, but he never recognized me.

Now I needed a place to hide out for a while. I found it in the Farm Colony, an old people's home on Staten Island. They needed a porter. I was just their man. It was a perfect place for my purposes; no cop would think of looking for me in a $90-a-month job. For two years I worked at the Farm Colony and grew to love the kindly old men and women. They asked no questions and became my closest friends—just because I liked to sit and listen to them tell me about their past, their troubles and their treasured memo-

ries. It was a quiet, idyllic existence after my hectic life of crime, my constant nerve-grinding plotting to escape prison and my dash for freedom.

But after two years I began to feel that just to be safe I had better move on. The newspapers erupted with the story of a $1-million robbery of the Brinks Company in Boston, and some of the reporters credited me with the job. I began to have nightmares in which hundreds of people pointed their fingers at me and shouted, "You're Willie the Actor!"

I began to get nervous and restless. I took rides on the subway, got off somewhere, anywhere, and took long walks.

One day I was walking through Sunnyside, New York, a prosperous little community that is bisected by Queens Boulevard. Before I realized what I was doing, I found myself studying the layout of the Manufacturers Trust Company. Almost unconsciously my mind photographed the bank entrance, the condition of the roof, the depth of the plot, the number of people going in and out. I went into the bank, noted the position of the cages, glanced at the alarm system and computed the number of employes. When I was out on the street again I recalled what the psychiatrist had said at Eastern State: "Apparently, banks present an irresistible challenge to you."

So he was right, after all.

I went back to Sunnyside again and again and cased that bank thoroughly. Everything I saw about it convinced me that it was vulnerable. Then came a terrible battle in my mind. On the one hand was my sincere reluctance to go back to crime and my renewed faith to go straight, a faith bolstered by the kind, friendly people at the Farm Colony.

I didn't need the money; years before I had secreted a cache in a Long Island field. I had dug it up recently and found most of it still negotiable. On the other hand was the realization that I was an outlaw already anyway. Most of all, there was the challenge of the bank itself.

For weeks this internal battle raged. Finally I was able to make up my mind. I would leave the bank alone. I cannot describe how agonizing the decision was.

A few weeks later I ran into a couple of my old friends, Tommy Kling and John De Venuta. De Venuta was busily preparing a bank job. The layout sounded bad to me. I told them I wasn't interested. I also told them everything I had learned about the Sunnyside bank. Three weeks later the newspapers reported that the Sunnyside bank had been robbed and that the employes of the bank had identified me as the ringleader of the gang. No mention was made of De Venuta. I knew Kling had nothing to do with the robbery because he was so sick at that time that he could hardly get out of bed.

The flurry over the Sunnyside job was enough to make me start running again. I left Staten Island, lost myself in the crowds of New York and finally got a room in a Puerto Rican section of Brooklyn. It was two years later when, riding in a subway and hiding my face behind a newspaper, I began to feel someone's eyes on me. I don't know how you "feel" a thing like this, but I did. I folded my paper and glanced casually across the aisle. A nice-looking youngster who appeared to be about 20 was staring at me with interest. I yawned and dropped my eyes to the paper.

Had this kid made me? I didn't think so.

At my stop I arose casually and left the subway. Out of the corner of my eye I noticed him following me; but this may well have been his station too. I climbed up the stairs to the street; he was right behind me. I walked a block; he stayed with me. I crossed the street; he remained at my side. Another block and he was gone. I remembered reading in those psychiatric books at Eastern State of men who had developed a monomania about being constantly followed. I was getting like some of them, I decided.

Of course this was one time I should have paid more attention to that warning sixth sense. The boy was Arnold Schuster. He reported to the police, and within two hours I was in headquarters at Bergen Street and the fingerprint man was pointing at me:

"That's Sutton!" he cried excitedly.

"You're right," I said calmly.

The irony is that I was tried for the Sunnyside job. Although it is one of the few crimes credited to me that I did not commit, I was convicted for it.

With the conviction, I felt no resentment, no bitterness. Judge Farrell had been meticulously fair during the proceedings. I had been tried before an impartial jury. I had been brilliantly defended. Now I was on my way to where I belonged—to a life behind bars.

I was still bothered, though, by the killing of Arnold Schuster, the state's witness against me.

(**Editor's note:** *Schuster, a 24-year-old Brooklyn clothing sales-man, received quick notoriety for his part in the Sutton capture. He was praised by the police, written up in the newspapers, interviewed on television. At the same time, threatening letters and phone calls poured in, and 18 days after Sutton's capture Schuster was shot to death in the street. The police set up a huge investigation in efforts to find the murderer, but to no avail. In 1963 the Mafia criminal Joseph Valachi began "singing," and contended that Schuster was murdered on orders from underworld chief Albert Anastasia, who was later slain in a barber chair. Valachi said Anastasia became enraged when he saw Schuster on television and cried, "I can't stand squealers! Hit this guy." Despite Valachi's story, the Schuster murder is still considered an unsolved homicide by the police.*)

When the police first got me out of bed to ask me what I knew about the Schuster killing, I could hardly believe them. I recall mumbling, "This finishes me," though how much it had to do with my conviction of the Sunnyside job I don't know. By now I think most of the police believe I had nothing to do with this brutal, senseless killing. They know that this isn't the way I operate. And far from "avenging" me, Arnold Schuster's murder only made my case harder. I think it was the work of a crazed crank.

While I was waiting to be shipped off to prison, one of the guards came to my cell to tell me about something that had happened during the St. Patrick's Day parade. A bunch of kids along the route had started chanting as the cops marched by. "We want Sutton!" they yelled.

"They said that?" I was amazed.

"Yeah," the guard said in disgust. "That's what you've done, Sutton. More than one of those kids will try to be like you. I don't mind saying it made me feel a little sick."

"It makes me a little sick too," I said slowly.

I'm honest enough to admit that my conscience never bothered me much after I'd taken a bank or a jewelry shop. But this was different. If these kids only realized that at 51 I was completely through, they might not think of me as a hero. Somehow or other they had the mistaken idea that I'd gotten away with it, and that they too could get away with it. Sure, I'd pulled some big jobs, but I'd spent about half my adult life in jail paying for these crimes. I'd studied robbery the way an honest man studies law or accounting. I had made a science out of crime. And yet I'd lost.

I suppose that, all in all, I robbed society of close to $2 million. What did I have today? I was 51, penniless and facing a life of imprisonment. How in God's name could even the most impressionable youngster want to copy me?

The next morning I spoke about it to George Herz and James McArdle, the lawyers appointed by the court to defend me. Out of this conversation came the idea that I tell my whole story. I remember saying that if I could get across to these kids the truth of my wasted life, it would be well worth the effort. Whatever money the story made for me could be put into some kind of trust fund to help kids during those difficult years—the years when I made the transition from reckless youngster to criminal. Two judges and a priest, among others, were consulted and agreed that it was a good idea.

That is the main reason why I have written my story. It may or may not help a psychiatrist figure out what made an ordinary kid from an ordinary family in Brooklyn become a criminal. It may convince money-crazy kids that you can't win at crime.

As you can see, I know.

*This fast-talking salesman
and demagogue was undoubtedly the greatest
medical charlatan in history*

"GOAT-GLAND" BRINKLEY

by Harold Mehling

At 8 p.m. on April 1, 1930, the rural people of Kansas clamped headphones over their ears and tuned in the Milford station, KFKB—"Kansas First, Kansas Best." "Now, folks, friends and all who are weary and oppressed," they heard the announcer say, "Dr. John R. Brinkley will deliver his message to humanity, with love for all in his heart." Then the voice of John Romulus Brinkley came over the air.

My dear, dear friends—my patients, my supplicants. Your many letters lie here before me, touching testimonials of your pain, your grief and the wretchedness that is visited upon the innocent. I can reply now to a few—just a few. Others I shall answer by mail.

But, oh my friends, you must help me—remember that your letters asking advice must be accompanied by $2, which barely covers the cost of postage, stenographic hire and office rent. I am your friend, but not even a great baron of Wall Street could withstand the ruinous cost of helping you unless this small fee accompanies your letter.

This was John Brinkley—small, dapper, hands heavy with diamonds. He offered operations to endow older men with goat glands and thus renew their sexual vigor. Cost: $750. There is no evidence that this operation was ever effective; yet Brinkley, in 16 years, treated 5000 men from half the states in the Union. When he finally rolled up his medical degree, which had been ground out by a diploma mill, the "goat man" had earned several million dollars and the epithet of "the greatest charlatan in medical history."

Still, there have been many charlatans, and "greatest" is an abused word. What distinguished Brinkley—and sometimes made his antics humorous—was his rubbery ability to bounce back from a battery of knockout punches. Politicians, foreign officials, leaders of the American Medical Association and Herbert Hoover's Vice President stayed awake nights wondering how to cope with him. He even frightened the Democratic and Republican parties by running for governor of Kansas. Everybody who was politically anybody admitted that the reason Brinkley did not enter the statehouse was because of the way the votes were counted—or, rather, were not counted.

All in all, John Romulus Brinkley was a genuine American phenomenon, an ingenious demagogue with a master's finger on the pulse of the people.

Brinkley was born in 1885, in hilly Beta, North Carolina, a money-parched town of 200 farmers fenced off from the world by the Great Smokies and the Blue Ridge. He did not get a recognizable word past his lips until he was three, a tardiness that mortified his stern, hard-bitten mother. Candace Brinkley was determined to make the boy speak and thrashed him by the clock.

Father Brinkley was a dreamer and often told the boy why he had given him the middle name of Romulus, the legendary son of Mars. "Romulus was made a god by the Romans," the old man said, "and you will be great, too."

Tuberculosis killed Candace Brinkley before young John was six, and his father died when he was ten. The boy was left with an impoverished aunt and a head full of escapist daydreams. Slumped in Beta's one-room dilapidation of a grade school, he cast himself in messianic roles.

"I thought of John Brinkley freeing the slaves," he said later, "John Brinkley illuminating the world, John Brinkley facing an assassin's bullet for the sake of his people, John Brinkley healing the sick. . . ."

By the time he was 16, his glory-bound mind had outgrown tobacco-picking Beta. He made his way to Baltimore, where he told the dean of the Johns Hopkins Medical School that he wanted to become a doctor. The dean chatted, led the boy over a few basic educational hurdles and found him wanting. Brinkley interpreted the interview somewhat differently and claimed Johns Hopkins would not share its knowledge with him "because I didn't own a pair of shoes."

Back in the hill country after a sojourn of several years in New York, he married a Daisy Mae type of hill girl named Sally Wike. Together they went off to Chicago, where she persuaded him to enroll in an herb-medicine institution called Bennett Medical College. When he finished his studies, he was awarded a diploma, for some strange reason, from an outfit called the Eclectic Medical University of Kansas City.

With his formidable parchment, Brinkley returned to New York, where he wangled a permit to practice, and set up an herb shop. But, restless healer that he was, he became bored after only two years and turned south again to Greenville, South Carolina. He and a partner set themselves up in a rambling old house as "electro-medic specialists." But the people of South Carolina sensed that "electromedics" was either ahead of its time or timely quackery.

Brinkley soon broke with his partner and headed for Fulton, Kansas. He picked up medical licenses from Arkansas and Tennessee, in those days good enough for Kansas. Organized medicine was that disorganized.

While Brinkley was having professional ups and downs, his personal life was even more hectic. Sally Wike divorced him, taking their three small daughters with her.

That summer, while visiting in Memphis, he met a doctor's daughter and married her before the leaves fell. Minnie Telitha Jones was her name; she was a sturdy girl who, if nothing else, could stand John Brinkley. She was not even dismayed when, shortly after their marriage, he was arrested on a bad-check charge. He beat the charge, and the couple fled to Kansas together.

Fulton, small as it was, held the beginnings of big things. He and Minnie were in town less than six months when he was elected mayor. He served for a year, while tending to his patients on the side.

His clients were awed. He had begun to cultivate a goatee, and they were further impressed by the dexterousness of his oddly pale-skinned hands. A rapidly receding hairline gave him a broad forehead, and a smile played constantly over his owlish face. With his goatee and his strangely beguiling voice, he appeared more a visiting specialist from Vienna than a visiting fireman from the hills of North Carolina.

But Brinkley was not taken in by this one-horse success. He spent his evenings researching the medical facilities of other Kansas towns. By the time his mayoralty term expired, he had settled on Milford, a rut-roaded prairie town close to the Nebraska border, which had neither a doctor nor a hospital. And so Minnie and the Mayor said fond farewell to Fulton and disappeared into the setting sun. On October 7, 1917, they entered fateful Milford, where Brinkley was to become famous.

Everyone who later investigated Brinkley agrees that he opened a drugstore immediately, but the reports of how he opened his surgical career differ drastically.

According to Brinkley, he was grinding away with his mortar and pestle one afternoon when a farmer dropped in and crackerbarreled about his sad home life. The farmer led the conversation around to goat glands and finally suggested that Brinkley give him a pair. The good doctor demurred, partly because he was not sure transplantation was the road to rejuvenation, partly because he did not have a goat. The man solved that by assuming all responsibility and scaring up a goat. Brinkley operated and reported that "happy results were obtained." A year later, he announced, he delivered his patient's wife of a strapping baby boy.

The word got around and soon Brinkley was a big name in northern Kansas. In August 1918, with money from his lucrative practice, the healer established a 50-bed hospital that bore his name. It was an impressive place, with rooms for nurses and surgical assistants, dozens of trays of gleaming knives and, naturally, storage facilities for goat glands.

Milford had never seen such action. Merchants beamed as the rail station began to clog with patients. Fifty men arrived for appointments every Monday morning; 40 of these were handled by a half-dozen surgical assistants and the remainder by the great man himself.

Brinkley built neat cottages for his assistants and a dormitory for his nurses, and gave Milford a modern water-supply system.

But that old devil restlessness would not be stilled. In late 1922 he placed a call to an advertising man in Kansas City. Patent-medicine houses and pseudo-doctors were getting away with murder in their newspaper advertisements, but Brinkley wanted to go them one better. He was looking for the biggest huckster horn that money could buy.

That's what he got. The adman suggested he pioneer in the new-fangled field of radio. Thousands were buying sets just to hear Paul Whiteman, the King of Jazz. People spent entire evenings having their ears filled with sound. Why not give them the inimitable sound of John Brinkley?

And so he did. In Milford, he erected KFKB, a station so powerful it carried into Nebraska, Missouri and Oklahoma. With a license from the old Federal Radio Commission, KFKB took to the air $15\frac{1}{2}$ hours a day, acquainting the folks with the wonders and troubles of the prostate gland and supplying cornball music and yodelers for interludes. Sensing the power of repetition that is so irritatingly employed today, he drummed it into his listeners that "a man is as old as his glands."

While he knew he had a good thing, he did not realize the amazing power that radio held. Letters poured in from bedeviled people, curious about the Brinkley operations they had heard extolled. He referred them to the Brinkley Hospital; it was the least he could do.

Then he went into the business of general diagnosis and prescription by air. He rehearsed little medical homilies before his adoring Minnie, and if poor, dead Mother Brinkley could have heard him, she would have had to agree that young John sure had learned to talk:

Now here is a letter from a dear mother—a dear little mother who holds to her breast a babe of nine months. She should take No. 2 and—yes, No. 17—and she will be helped. Brinkley's 2 and 17. She should order them from the Milford Drug Company, Milford, Kansas, and they shall be sent to you, Mother—collect. May the Lord guard and protect you, Mother. The postage will be prepaid.

What did Brinkley's "2" and "17" consist of? A secret formula, perhaps? A new drug? A premature tranquilizer? No, John Brinkley's imagination was more down to earth. One was an aspirin compound and the other was castor oil, both labeled with numbers instead of names.

In the seven years that followed 1923, Brinkley's "Medical Question Box" diagnosed everything from fallen arches to cancer. On one broadcast alone, he diagnosed 44 different complaints, in each case prescribing from one to ten of his numbers-game medicinals. He gathered up lists of thousands of names, hawked his wares through the mails and hired 50 girls to open the returns. It was not unusual for 50,000 letters to arrive every day in Milford, and soon a new post office had to be built; it was bigger than all those in the surrounding area combined.

Brinkley bought a cabin plane big enough to hold a desk and secretaries, with which he flew his message of hope around the Midwest. Then he bought a $7000 Lincoln and three other cars, including a 16-cylinder red Cadillac on which the name John Brinkley was engraved in 13 places. He picked up two yachts, one a 170-footer that had belonged to movie magnate Joseph M. Schenck, and named them—what else?—the *John Brinkley I* and *II*. (When Minnie bore a son they named *him* John Brinkley III.) Brinkley's tailored suits were ordered ten at a time, his cravat held a diamond stickpin, and he became a two-fisted wearer of 12-carat diamond rings.

But life during this period was not all Cadillacs and encrusted cravats for Brinkley.

In 1924 he was called to Los Angeles by Harry Chandler, a prominent newspaper publisher, who offered him $40,000 to rejuvenate several aging employes. The California Medical Board granted him a 30-day permit, under which he performed his surgery, but no sooner did he get out of the state than a ruckus occurred. The American Medical Association offered evidence of his shoddy education and charged that he had bought his medical diploma. Brinkley, who was back in Milford, was indicted for violation of medical-practice laws and California's attorney general asked Governor Jonathan M. Davis of Kansas to return him to California for trial.

Brinkley was a popular Kansas citizen by then, however, and Governor Davis retorted, "We're going to keep John Brinkley here as long as he lives!" The Governor further indicated his confidence by reaching into a musty statute book and appointing Brinkley an admiral in Kansas' landlocked navy. Brinkley erupted in a stunning blue uniform with "scrambled eggs" and the stripes of a vice admiral.

The unorthodox practitioner also had problems with his mumbo-jumbo drugs. The potions were taking business away from the patent-medicine houses and drugstores.

So one day he received a delegation of pill-rollers who stated their economic case angrily. They might raise some legal hell, they warned. On the spot, Brinkley formed the Brinkley Pharmaceutical Association, an aggregation of druggists who would carry his privately numbered compounds. In return for the windfall, they would kick back a percentage. Soon 500 druggists were willing to do just that. In one three-month period, the kickbacks came to $27,856. So the tenor of the KFKB broadcasts changed. Now the citizens heard: "This little lady has been seeing spots before her eyes, has dizzy spells, and is constipated. Prescriptions 66 and 74, which she can procure at the Acme Drugstore in ———, at $5 and $7, will bring her relief."

That was much better for all concerned. Financial matters galloped along so well that Brinkley opened his own Bank of Milford.

This back-scratching arrangement built a powerful wall around Brinkley's operations, but it also hastened the day when he would have to face strong opposition. In 1929 the Kansas City *Star* (a Missouri paper, but influential in Kansas) started looking for a way to keelhaul Brinkley. A. B. MacDonald, a crack reporter, nosed around Milford, visited Brinkley letter-writers and patients, retraced the rejuvenator's trail to California and back, and dug deeply into his remote past. In 1930 the ink flowed, and the *Star* accused Brinkley of everything this side of murder.

It went back to his acquisition of a Kansas medical license and charged fraud. He had used his diploma-mill degree to obtain a license from the Connecticut Eclectic Board, which in turn got him licenses from Arkansas and Tennessee, which had reciprocity with Connecticut. Kansas had reciprocity with Arkansas and Tennessee, and so, the *Star* said, Brinkley had entered Kansas medicine through a rathole. Then it showed that a 1923 investigation had exposed the Connecticut Eclectic Board and revoked 167 of its licenses, including Brinkley's. Therefore, the paper asserted, he had no right to practice in Kansas under any circumstances.

Then it was revealed that Brinkley had pleaded guilty to selling alcohol during prohibition in 1920. That did not hit very hard, but another charge did. The *Star* found and interviewed Sally Wike, Brinkley's first wife, and reviewed their spattered marital life. It alleged that Sally had never left him, but had been driven out each time, and was finally deserted with her three children.

Finally, the paper came close to charging "the Brinkley industry" with outright murder. It said that a New Jersey carpenter died of tetanus after submitting to a Brinkley operation.

The cumulative effect of the exposé was devastating. As Brinkley read each day's blast, his goatee jiggled and his lips moved in excitement. He read passages to Minnie, who wept at the travail a medical pioneer had to suffer.

"John," she said on recovering her practicality, "what if people believe those lies? What will happen to your practice?"

Brinkley hustled up a lawyer and filed a libel suit against the *Star* for $5 million. Then he went down to KFKB, grasped the microphone firmly and complained to the people. He said that poor boys who try to get into exclusive clubs—such as medicine— were always persecuted. He had never been one of the clique and never would be. And anyway, the crux of the matter was that his noncommercial KFKB was luring listeners from the *Star*'s own WDAF, and was costing the station advertising revenue. That, he said, was what bothered the Kansas City *Star*.

Letters of support and encouragement poured in, and there was no noticeable letup of patients who got off the train at Milford. It was 1930, the Depression was on and bitter people were inclined to give the underdog the benefit of the doubt over any entrenched authority.

Brinkley relaxed and purchased another airplane. But in April he received an order to appear before the Kansas Board of Medical Examiners and show cause why his license to practice should not be revoked. The AMA was charging him with fraud, misrepresentation and gross immorality.

Three weeks later another blow came from Washington. The Federal Radio Commission notified him of a hearing that would determine whether his KFKB license should be renewed. The pressure had been turned on.

Brinkley conferred with attorneys and lined up hundreds of witnesses. When the medical-board hearing opened on July 15, in Topeka's Hotel Kansan, he was ready to steal the show.

His witnesses came from all walks of life—butchers, bankers, farmers, railroad men, traveling salesmen, coal miners and fellow doctors—regular and irregular.

Day after day the papers had to report what seemed to be vindicating testimony. Brinkley sat at the defense table stroking his goatee and smoking aromatic cigarettes. He said he would keep witnesses coming all summer. When the medical board shut off the deluge, he put 500 affidavits into the record.

But the "goat man" really could not win this round. The Sunday punch was delivered near the close of the hearing in mid-August, after the introduction of medical testimony that excluded any possibility of rejuvenation by goats. Suddenly Brinkley was confronted with an exhibit there was no combating. It consisted of certificates bearing the names of 42 of his patients. They were death certificates; he had had to sign them because the patients, under his care, had died.

In September his Kansas license was revoked. He said the plot against him had been engineered by the AMA. He quickly hired regularly licensed surgeons to operate for him and got ready to fight in Washington, D.C., for the retention of his radio license.

There, the hearing was no less bumptious. Brinkley took the stand and told how he had given new life to the seven Los Angeles newspapermen, when *Star* reporter MacDonald leaped to his feet and shouted, "Yes, except that one died!"

The commissioners refused to renew KFKB's license, but only by a three-to-two vote. Brinkley won the right to continue broadcasting while he appealed.

Smiling to reporters on the way to the Washington airport, he promised he would not deprive them of a good story by giving up. He and Minnie flew down to Florida to rest from their battles. There he lay in the sun and read that the Kansas Supreme Court had upheld revocation of his license and said he had organized charlatanism to prey on human weakness, ignorance and credulity. Quietly, he had his libel suit against the Kansas City *Star* dismissed and paid the court costs.

Brinkley appeared to have been knocked out, but the fact was that, up to the moment at least, he was untouched. He could still broadcast, and his hired doctors could still operate and collect for him. Furthermore, his clubbed but unbowed head was still capable of strange fertility. On the Florida sand it spawned one of the strangest sagas of modern American politics. He rose, took Minnie by the arm and flew back to Kansas to hatch it.

"John R. Brinkley will be the next governor of Kansas!" he announced on his arrival in Milford. It was late September 1930.

His secretary called the newspapers in Kansas City and Topeka. Hours later, the whole nation knew that the medicine man of Milford was running for governor of Kansas.

From the days of the Populist political uprising of the 1890's—when Kansans were urged to "Raise less corn and more hell!"—the state had been a romping ground for political mavericks, but never one like this. Reporters descended on Milford for a Roman holiday. Armed by the chuckling politicians of Topeka, they sprang a critical piece of news at Brinkley's first press conference.

"Doctor Brinkley, do you know the election laws of this state?"

"You are referring to the final dates on which candidates may file?" Brinkley asked.

Yes, they were.

"I am aware that it is too late for my name to appear on the ballots. The people of Kansas will write in the name of John R. Brinkley, and I will see you in Topeka."

For the politicians and the press, that removed any semblance of seriousness from the affair. No man could expect almost a quarter of a million people to write his name in—and that was how many he would need to win. Besides, his supporters would be crackpot illiterates. The Republicans went on campaigning for Frank Haucke, and the Democrats banged away for Harry Woodring. They only referred to Brinkley for laughs.

And they just proved once again that politicians must never overlook the holes in their own armor or underestimate the power of a demagogue.

The problem was that the regular candidates were no world-beaters to start with. When the Kansas City *Star* published their personality sketches, William Allen White, the celebrated Emporia *Gazette* editor, was moved to say that Haucke looked like a "sissy," Woodring like a "sap."

Those were the armor chinks, and to them Brinkley brought a bunker of opportunism. He was aware of the discontent the Depression had spread through the nation. In Kansas, where the drought was emasculating farmland and wheat was down to 60 cents a bushel and still sliding, the farmers were looking for a man on a white mule. Brinkley had no mule, but he had a fast airplane and a bellowing radio station.

Over station KFKB, from dawn to past dusk, in several languages, the appeal went out. He said, "Clean out, clean up, and keep Kansas clean!"—a time-tested slogan—and he told how things would change in November.

"If I am elected," he promised, "I will build a lake in every county in Kansas. The water will be evaporated and pour down as gentle rain on the fertile fields."

Brinkley offered so much over KFKB that John Gunther later called him "the first American demagogue to use radio for political purposes in a big way."

Then he flew up, down and across the state, neglecting no area, pledging old-age pensions, state-financed game preserves and, above all, lower taxes. Soon he was speaking to 10,000 people at a time, holding giant torchlight rallies, at which they learned to spell his name correctly by shouting its letters in unison: J-O-H-N R. B-R-I-N-K-L-E-Y. It was a rousing orgy of the oppressed, salaaming to their savior. The savior passed out pencils and sample ballots and sent the oppressed home to practice.

At the end of the campaign, when Brinkley was teaching spelling to 20,000 voters a rally, the politicians finally became nervous and decided to man the polling places in force. Their apprehension was well grounded, as early returns showed in the Wichita *Beacon* of November 4:

BRINKLEY SWEEPING WICHITA
Milford Candidate Is 2 to 1
Over Haucke
Woodring Runs Third

But that was premature. As election night wore on and the
politicians' faces grew longer, the order went out from Topeka to
cancel every write-in on which even an *i* had not been dotted. That
was legal, and ballots went out every window, but the next morning
Brinkley had still scared their pants off. The totals read: Woodring: 217,171; Haucke: 216,920; Brinkley: 183,278.

Brinkley claimed he had been cheated out of 56,000 votes and
had really won, but he could not get anyone in authority to listen.
Nobody wanted a recount, out of which Brinkley might well emerge
as governor. Why, the man had been credited with 30,000 more
votes than William Allen White got while *on* the ballot in 1924.
He had even received 20,000 write-ins and had won three counties
in Oklahoma!

Minnie Brinkley cried, but Brinkley was stoically philosophic.
He realized the remarkable thing he had accomplished, and it was
savor enough for the moment. After all, 1932, another election
year, was just around the corner. And didn't he have a plan up his
sleeve that would keep his voice hammering at the inner ear of his
fellow citizens?

He certainly did. In between his political gyrations, he had sized
up the radio situation down in sunny Mexico. Mexican officials
were miffed because Canada and the United States had already
taken over the best air channels on the continent. So they were not
inclined to worry about the niceties of licensing a radio station on
a channel already in use to the north.

Brinkley lined up a permit for a $350,000 border-blaster, a
100,000-watt station that was being built for him in a scratchy
hamlet just over the Rio Grande from Del Rio, Texas. In June
1931 he sold KFKB to a Wichita insurance company for $90,000

and went on the air over XER, Villa Acuña, with an engaging slogan: "Sunshine Between the Nations." And he did not have to leave Milford to do it, either. His broadcasts were recorded, at a monthly cost of $10,000. A pittance.

Now Brinkley went wild over XER. After Senor Martinez and the Dwarfie Boys finished their songs, he came on and put the needle to the orthodox medical profession: "Don't let your doctor two-dollar you to death. Come to the Brinkley Hospital." On the side, XER peddled fortune-telling, gold-mine stocks, horoscopes and oil burners. His advertising rates were $1700 an hour.

XER was easily the most powerful radio station in the world at the time. It boomed a wide swath up the Mississippi Valley to the Canadian border and was heard clearly east to Florida. In fact, Brinkley had to reduce his operating wattage when Del Rio residents picked up their telephones and got him for 15 minutes on his favorite subject, the cause and cure of prostate-gland troubles. Some people said Mexico was crazy to let him carry on like that, but Mexico took care of its own. Behind XER the government had erected giant steel towers; to hear Brinkley, Mexicans had to live in the United States.

And in the United States, Kansans received big news loud and clear; Brinkley had filed as an independent candidate for governor. On the 1932 ballot, his name would appear with those of Democratic incumbent Woodring and the Republican oilman Alfred M. Landon, who later ran for President.

Since he was recording his broadcasts, Brinkley was free to roam the state, where wheat was now down to 32 cents a bushel. He toured every county seat and hundreds of smaller communities. In Dodge City he drew bigger crowds than Democratic and Republican rallies combined, and at Liberal, Coldwater and Salina he made promises even more extravagant than he had in 1930. Speaking from a sound truck bathed in the glow of a spotlight, he used his soothsayer's monotone and pledged he would pave thousands of miles of roads, distribute schoolbooks free and reduce the minimum cost of license plates from $6.50 to $2.50.

Alf Landon retorted that such a reduction was ridiculously modest; he would bring the minimum down to 60 cents. The politicians were in a stew. When Brinkley left a huge rally at Emporia, the correspondent of the *Nation* wrote: "All signs in Kansas point to the election this year of Dr. John R. Brinkley. . . . The farmers seem to be almost solidly behind him."

Brinkley ignored the fact that a Democrat was running against him and, to its embarrassment, contributed money to the national Democratic Party.

In Emporia, the fur flew. When the folks in huge Soden's Grove burst into Brinkley's campaign song, "He's the Man!" their voices were heard down the street at the *Gazette*'s offices by the editor, William Allen White, who blew a gasket. He called seven Kansas editors and publishers together to map coördinated opposition to the Brinkley campaign.

Two weeks before election day Brinkley learned that the State Department, more out of national embarrassment than partisan pique, was pressuring the Mexican government to shut down XER. Interrupting his campaign, he flew to Washington and sat down with a fellow Kansan, Vice President Charles Curtis. He asked Curtis to assure him a fair deal and got a vague response. So he laid it on the line. If XER was closed, he would seek the Republican Presidential nomination in 1936. Curtis, sensitive to the vagaries of Kansas politics and to blackmail, hurried him over to the State Department. The pressure on the Mexicans halted.

Brinkley flew back to Kansas and wound up his campaign with a town-hopping tour of the Corn Belt. On election eve, he telephoned a victory speech down to Villa Acuña and retired, prepared to awaken as the messiah of Kansas.

It was not to be. He swept the rural vote, but he could not trump the big-city boys and their newspapers. The final vote stood: Landon: 278,581; Woodring: 272,944; Brinkley: 244,607.

Landon was reelected in 1934 and became the GOP Presidential candidate in 1936. Woodring, beaten by votes that Brinkley attracted despite the Democratic national landslide, was consoled with the Secretary of War post in the New Deal cabinet. And Brinkley said good-bye to Kansas. He closed up the Milford hospital and moved to Del Rio, where he established a new goat-gland clinic in a hotel.

Politically, the defeat was severe. But Brinkley could at least find solace in money, and XER was raking it in. He built a $200,000 marble-and-tile home on six acres and had his name installed in neon over a swimming pool and splashing fountains. He soaked in the pool on sunny afternoons and looked across the International Line to the towers of XER. And he backed up his cash assets with 7000 acres in North Carolina, an oil well, three airplanes, 12 automobiles and a cluster of south Texas citrus groves.

In Del Rio, he was warmly regarded by the leading merchants, who appreciated the business he attracted. They made him president of the Rotary Club.

Nearing 50 now, the great man felt it was time these worldly efforts were engraved for posterity. He hired a writer to listen to him by the hour and set down his exploits. Never was a paranoid's self-infatuation so faithfully recorded between hard covers. The writer amassed 75,000 usable words by employing as many rapturous adjectives as Brinkley had used scalpels. Brinkley was so grateful he peddled the book over XER.

Then he received a devastating blow. Mexico finally decided to silence his radio. In February 1934 the government announced suspension of station XER's license for breaking the laws regulating medical advertising.

Brinkley sped over to Villa Acuña and confirmed that he was regarded as a sort of north-of-the-border god in that town. The government had better not tamper with their State of Coahuila, the locals said. Faithful Minnie tried to stave off the closing by hurrying down to Mexico City with cash. But it was no go. The government sent a radio inspector to Villa Acuña to take over. When the villagers threatened to lynch him, he retreated; but early in March he returned with troops and the citizens subsided.

Brinkley stood at the edge of his estate and watched the take-over through binoculars. He knew the jig was up, and announced he was closing XER to "prevent civil war between the Mexican government and Coahuila."

That was the first blow from which he didn't bounce. The second came after an ill-advised decision to try once more for the governorship of Kansas. He filed for the Republican nomination, but Alf Landon wiped him out in the August 1934 primary.

A third deflation came two years later, when he asked the federal district court to force Kansas to reinstate his medical license. Robert E. Lewis, one of three judges who heard the case, called him "an out-and-out charlatan." So Brinkley shored up his position by establishing another hospital in Arkansas, on a country-club estate that contained a 100-acre lake and was surrounded by a 360-acre golf course. In the heart of nearby Little Rock, he opened the Romulus Drugstore, at which acid-stomach pills were mailed out at $5 for 100 and a laxative at $3 for six ounces. Orders for these items soared at one point to 2000 letters a day. Brinkley hardly had time to count the money, he was so busy commuting by plane between Little Rock and Del Rio.

But the end was clearly signaled when Dr. Morris Fishbein, editor of the AMA magazine, *Hygeia*, called him a charlatan and quack in print. Brinkley sued for libel, charging that the remarks had reduced his income from $1,100,000 in 1937 to $810,000 in 1938. But the jury was unsympathetic. It agreed with Dr. Fishbein that charlatan and quack were not libelous terms when applied to "Doctor" Brinkley.

Jarred by these various exposures, Brinkley's patients started suing and winning judgments against him. Minnie was frightened, but her audacious husband assured her that the tempest was temporary. He sold an airplane to some Britons to pay off a few verdicts, then sold a yacht to the president of Venezuela for $125,000. Then the cars were disposed of one by one, next the Little Rock hospital, and finally his last airplane, for which the U.S. Navy gave him $119,000.

Now 54, Brinkley reached in desperation for any political handhold that was convenient. He gave $5000 to William Dudley Pelley, leader of the anti-Semitic Silver Shirts, and urged him to ferret out Communists and publicity with it.

He also had his astrological chart prepared regularly, and one month in 1940 it told him gigantic things were ahead. He interpreted this to mean he should run for President of the United States, and Minnie announced he had received 500,000 letters urging him to do so. But two fellows named Roosevelt and Willkie ran instead.

In February 1941, weighed down by judgments and the countless dollars that had been paid under the table during his circuitous career, Brinkley was bankrupt. The federal court at San Antonio estimated his assets to be $221,065 and his liabilities at $1,625,565. Despite this blow, his name appeared the following June as a candidate for Texas' Democratic nomination for U.S. senator, opposing such people as Governor W. Lee, "Pappy" O'Daniel and Lyndon Johnson. William Allen White lathered up again and wrote: "He is irresistible to the moron mind, and Texas has plenty of such."

But few people cared. Brinkley was no longer an issue. In August he suffered a coronary occlusion and entered a hospital in Kansas City, where his left leg was amputated. In May 1942, at 56, "Goat-Gland" Brinkley dropped dead.

He could claim as distinction that he rifled the pockets of gullible citizens for a net of roughly $10 million, helped Alf Landon to a chance at the U.S. Presidency and almost became the first American quack to reach a political position of high standing.

IN SYDNEY, Australia, Lee Morris, 29, was arrested after a short fling at an up-to-date racket. Four times he obtained work, then telephoned anonymously to warn the employer that he had just taken on a Communist. Each firm sacked him at once with a week's pay in lieu of notice.

—United Nations World

The only way to stop
this counterfeiter was to buy him out

STAMP COLLECTOR'S
NEMESIS

by Murray Teigh Bloom

Under the letterhead of the British Philatelic Association, a 1954 news release said, in effect, that in order to curb the menace of the most dangerous stamp counterfeiter who ever lived, the BPA was buying out—blocks, stock and business—Jean de Sperati, of Aix-les-Bains, France. Unable to stop the efforts of the wily old counterfeiter, they were paying him to go and sin no more. At least one London newspaper thought it was a hoax and called Miss Eileen Evans, then public relations officer of the BPA, to verify the remarkable announcement.

Dies of stamps which had never been recognized as Sperati's work cast doubts on the authenticity of some of the rarest stamps in the world, the BPA acknowledged. Had Sperati's business been carried on, the repercussions on the value of many fine collections of genuine early issues would have tumbled badly.

Organized in 1926, the BPA has had the steadfast slogan, "For the protection and help of all interested in stamp collecting." If ever the 15 million stamp dealers and collectors of the world needed protection, it was from the incredible fakes turned out by the hatchet-jawed, 69-year-old resident of Aix-les-Bains.

The stamp-collecting fraternity was not alone in its interest in

Sperati. The U.S. Secret Service, Scotland Yard, the French Sûreté and even the International Criminal Police Organization (INTER–POL) had become aware of his operations. None, however, was able to stop him from turning out some 538 stamp varieties worth more than $5 million—if accepted as genuine. Unfortunately for collectors, an amazingly high percentage of them were so accepted and now rest in several of the world's finest collections, backed with certifications from some of philately's leading experts.

Sperati's counterfeit stamps undoubtedly were the finest ever made. They were so fine, in fact, that twice he had to demonstrate before unbelieving court-appointed experts that the stamps they passed as genuine were only genuine Speratis.

Sperati was fined, even jailed for a few weeks, and made to pay a $1400 indemnity to the Paris stamp dealers' association. Nevertheless, he still kept turning out his fakes. In December 1947 INTERPOL's secretary-general wrote the heads of European police departments that an end had been put to Sperati's activities. He could not have been more wrong. Sperati still manufactured his counterfeits—and kept selling them.

Clearly such a man was not to be stopped with ordinary legal restraints. The desperate British Philatelic Association concluded that there was only one way to stop Sperati. In the fall of 1953 a small, secret BPA committee visited Sperati in his nondescript villa overlooking beautiful Lake Bourget, in Aix-les-Bains, and began negotiations. These were not concluded until late in February 1954, shortly after I had spent some time with Sperati. For an undisclosed price—believed to be about $15,000—an aging, weary Sperati agreed to turn over to the BPA all his stock, dies and proofs, and make no more stamps.

The morning the announcement was made in London, I spoke to Miss Evans, the BPA's public relations officer. I pointed out that the announcement had called Sperati "a master printer with a profound knowledge of colour chemistry, a great photographer with peculiar skill in the manipulation of paper, combining all these talents with considerable philatelic knowledge." This had somehow overlooked the fact that he was, after all, a crook, I noted. Miss Evans was genuinely distressed.

"Oh, the man's a counterfeiter, there's no doubt of it. But we had no other way of stopping him. The BPA had to take this action, else he would have ruined stamp collecting as a business or a hobby all over the world."

Talk of stamp faking makes dealers nervous and unhappy. "It's bad for business," they say, "and if you go into too much detail on how a stamp was faked, it will only be helpful for other counterfeiters by telling them which mistakes to avoid."

But a great British stamp expert, Fred J. Melville, saw it differently: "A clever forger does not need to be told where he has failed; he prefers us to help him by not warning collectors of his errors. The no-publicity method helps the forger without affording any protection to his victims."

The first fakes, which appeared in Italy soon after the British started using postage stamps in 1840, were designed to cheat the government. These are "postal forgeries" and have a far greater value to collectors than do the real stamps they were copied from, mostly because they were good enough to fool postal officials.

In the United States, in 1895, a gang made up millions of copies of the two-cent rose-carmine stamp of 1894 and tried to sell them from Ontario in huge quantities to mail-order businesses at a discount. Many were sold to innocent buyers and used before Edward Lowry, a Chicago stamp dealer, spotted them and brought them to the attention of the U.S. Secret Service.

Today the forged two-cent 1894 stamp has a black-market value of several dollars to collectors, whereas the real two-cent stamp is considered philatelic junk. But buying one of these counterfeits for your collection is a dangerous business. According to the U.S. Code you could get a year in jail for not telling the Secret Service immediately if you heard of the existence of such a stamp. Stamp collectors have a special madness, however, and the two-cent rose-carmine counterfeit is still a much-wanted stamp, felony or no.

By 1858 there was a small industry in Verona, Milan and Naples making stamp fakes for collectors. At first, it was done with a certain amount of openness: these were not fakes; these were *facsimiles*. Not every collector could get a copy of every stamp issued. What harm was there if the collector acquired inexpensive facsimiles of valuable stamps with which to fill in the blank spots in his collection?

The great facsimile maker was François Fournier, a Swiss. He was quiet, kindly, and had a fine reputation as a stamp expert. He was even invited to serve on stamp-exposition juries. Fournier called himself an "art publisher" and insisted that his reproductions were simply "choice examples of the engraver's art."

A surprising number of dealers and collectors accepted him on his own terms. Stamp journals ran his dignified ads, and his "creations" were displayed at international exhibitions where they gathered gold medals. But, inevitably, others began marketing Fournier's facsimiles as originals. Fournier soon became a dirty word in the business, and his ads were no longer welcome. He brought out his own journal and soberly announced in it, "Only fools pay more than 10 percent of catalogue value for any stamp. Authentic facsimiles often in better state than the originals may be had from us at a few francs." His favorite cartoon showed a ragged street beggar, with the caption, "Why did this man become a beggar? No doubt because he invested all his funds in so-called genuine postage stamps."

By 1914 Fournier had his own building in Geneva and boasted of having some 25,000 customers all over the world and agents in 23 countries, including the United States. He had created 796 sets of stamps, covering more than 3671 varieties. In 1914 you could buy all 796 sets for $430: if real, the stamps would have been worth more than $10,000.

World War I wrecked the business. Alert censors seized his stamps; they were looking for secret spy messages. His foreign agents stole from him, and in a few months the business was worthless. Fournier died soon after.

Some employes tried to run it after the war, but they failed. In

1927 the Geneva Philatelic Society bought out about £800 of Fournier's forgeries to keep them from falling into the hands of the unscrupulous.

The real experts never worried too much about Fournier. He operated in the open, and his stamps could always be purchased for comparison purposes.

Long before Fournier died, every serious collector could spot one of his stamps in a few minutes.

The stamp counterfeiter the experts do worry about is the anonymous craftsman—the one who does not shout his wares from the stamp journals, does not issue collections for experts to use for comparison purposes and is enough of a stamp expert to detect the secret marks that the legitimate engravers working for the stamp-issuing countries put into the stamps.

Nor do the experts today worry about the modern mass-producers of fakes. These operators confine their efforts to stamps that are never worth more than $1 or $2—usually less. Who is going to spend hours expertizing a stamp with so low a value? How numerous and busy these operators are, is attested to by an experience that a reputable New York stamp dealer had a few years ago.

This dealer picked up a foreign-stamp packet containing 500 different stamps from a reputable store for $2. Then, spending several weekends, he expertized each of the stamps as to genuineness. He was appalled.

More than 350 of the 500 stamps were fakes.

In the 1950's, my friend Dr. Giuseppe Dosi, then chief of the Italian office of the International Criminal Police Organization and a leading expert on counterfeit money and stamps, broke up one of the major stamp-faking mobs on the Continent. In the Milan suburb where Dosi arrested the leaders, he found 225,000 stamps of more than 30 countries, together with 130 presses and ingenious cancellation machines to give the stamps the used look that satisfies the amateur, who sometimes looks upon unused stamps with a good deal of suspicion.

The gang used to turn out more than 100,000 stamps a week, distributing them through seemingly reputable wholesalers in Europe, and undoubtedly many of them found their way into inexpensive U.S. stamp packets.*

Such fakes don't worry the important collectors. They are not interested in 500 stamps for $2, items from the philatelic dime counter. They *are* interested in stamps that sell for at least $5 apiece and up—mostly up. Which means, of course, that they are concerned about only a few thousand of the 125,000 varieties of stamps that have been issued since the first in 1840.

With these valuable stamps, most experts had a certain confidence in the fact that no stamp faker had ever completely succeeded in duplicating the paper and the perforations of the original stamp. They knew, too, that color shadings and cancellations were difficult to do well. In fact, there were so many ways a stamp counterfeiter could trip himself up that the expert could feel reasonably sure of detecting a stamp forgery after about a half hour's examination.

That is, until Jean de Sperati came along.

For a man who had the impact that Sperati had on the stamp business, little is known about him. I have looked at the official police dossiers on Sperati, in Rome and in Paris, and they are remarkably uninformative.

In this vacuum, Sperati's own account of his life and times and motivations has understandably been the one that gained circulation. His story, briefly, was that as a young collector he had been stuck with a fake stamp, one which a local stamp expert had solemnly assured him was genuine.

From then on, he was determined to show up the stamp experts as frauds. In order to further this ambition, Sperati made himself an expert in printing, inks, gums, perforations and plating—all

---

* Italian stamp dealers admit sadly that most stamp fakes come from Italy. In partial extenuation, they explain that before 1861, when Austria ruled Italy, Italians considered it their patriotic duty to damage the Austrians by faking their coins and stamps. Some habits you just can't shake off.

the skills he would need to challenge and expose the experts. A good bit of this information he obtained while he and his brothers were in the picture-postcard printing business—or while he was an Italian postal official, depending on which version he used. There is more along those lines, but since it is nearly all malarkey, let's get to the real story.

About the only thing that jibes in Sperati's version and the official version is that he was born on October 14, 1884, in Pistoia, northwest of Florence, known chiefly because it was the birthplace of the pistol in 1540. His father was an Italian Army officer, Enrico de Sperati; his mother, Maria Arnalfi, was the daughter of an Italian general who won brief fame by saving Napoleon III from an assassination plot.

Giovanni—he later gallicized it to Jean—de Sperati was the youngest of three brothers. The family suffered reverses in a wholesale food business. Then one of Sperati's older brothers became involved in a stamp-faking ring in Pisa, and, before long, all the brothers and the mother were in it, too. The head of the family had died by this time.

Scanty records indicate that the family left Italy when things got hot there, but there is little to go on. In fact, in 1953 Sperati was able to win a written retraction from a Parisian newspaper which claimed that he had done time for stamp forging in Italy around 1910.

In any case, by 1910 Sperati had learned a great deal about stamp inks, printing and the other pertinent paraphernalia of stamp making—and faking. In 1911 some of his first fakes appeared quietly in Berlin. We know this today because careful philatelists have traced back some of Sperati's stamps to their first appearance at a Berlin auction.

One of the forger's earliest victims was Dr. Heinrich Koestler, a leading German dealer. Sperati kept perfecting his art discreetly, initially in Paris, then in Lyon and finally in Aix-les-Bains, the resort town in eastern France.

His *modus operandi* was not complicated. He would make a few high-priced stamps, send them off to some well-known philatelic society for expertizing, usually done for a small fee, perhaps 1 percent of the stamp's value. Then, with the expert's okay, he would offer the stamps for sale at an auction or perhaps to another dealer in another city.

A few, a very few dealers caught on—yet nothing happened. Stamp dealers are all too human. If one of them acquires a fake stamp, the honest and upright thing to do is to burn it, or mark it indelibly so that no one else can be taken in. But doing that means doing himself out of the money he has spent for the stamp. So, many a dealer said nothing, and the stamp would go through several hands until it finally landed in the hands of a collector, the ultimate gull, who accepted it as authentic.

"It's an incredible situation," Dr. Dosi told me in Rome. "If we come across a counterfeit bill, we immediately confiscate it and stamp it indelibly so that it can never be used again. But a fake stamp, when it is brought in by a customer and recognized by the dealer as a fake, is simply put back in circulation. The dealer and his customer now know it is a fake, but who else knows it? So it remains a menace to other dealers and collectors."

Nor is the law involved here, because, apart from the United States and Switzerland, few countries have truly effective legislation against making and distributing copies of stamps that are not valid for current postal use. And, of course, many of the most valuable stamps are at least 40 years old and they are no longer valid for use.

Sperati knew all this when he began. When he sent one of his products to an expert for his approval, the latter might simply return the stamp and say it was a fake; but he would not destroy it or notify the police. So Sperati would go back to his press and try to turn out a better job, or send it to a less perceptive expert for his approval.

Today, several dealers say that they knew all along what Sperati was doing and carefully avoided his products. Actually, the only dealer I could find who seemed to know what this crooked genius was up to and who made a record of it was Otto W. Friedl. I once looked at the inside cover of one of Friedl's stock albums in the office of Edward Mueller, a leading New York stamp dealer. The faded item read: "Sperati, Villa Jacques Coeur, Avenue du Lac, Aix-les-Bains. This is the most dangerous stamp forger alive today. 1922."

Unfortunately, Friedl is no longer alive so we do not know what he did with this knowledge.

In the 1920's Sperati introduced several innovations. To fool the dealers who had already caught on to his items, he deliberately made different dies of the same stamps. Wary dealers, who thought they could recognize Sperati's hand in the making of a certain valuable stamp, would be thrown off by a copy of the same stamp that seemed to have different touches.

On Sperati's homemade cancellations, for example, he could have as many as 32 varieties.

Now two other people became intermediaries. They would send off one or two of Sperati's products to a reputable dealer with a story of how they found the stamps in some old family correspondence. Often Sperati would place his products on genuine old postmarked envelopes from which the original stamps of much lesser value had been removed.

A great number of Sperati's products were sold this way. Occasionally, when the stamp would be spotted as a fake, Sperati would deliberately get in touch with the dealer to see if he was interested in buying more of the reproductions—as reproductions. Actually, this was a remarkably shrewd move.

One dealer in London explained it with a chuckle: "Sperati was appealing to the man's cupidity and really attempting to buy him off. Here he was given a chance to buy remarkably fine forgeries— the finest ever made probably—for a tenth of their real value. It was a great temptation for many dealers, and I'm afraid some of them succumbed. Once they did, of course, they would have no reason to broadcast the fact that Sperati was making the stamps. In that way, he could buy the silence of a smart dealer."

A number of stamps were mailed, through intermediaries, to dealers in the United States. Usually they would be mailed from Ireland, England or various parts of France by third parties who would get a small fee from Sperati.

The postage stamps mailed to the United States, for example, would be valuable early American issues which supposedly had been found in an old attic chest stuffed with family remembrances.

World War II presented serious problems to Sperati and his business. After the Nazi victory—Aix-les-Bains was in the unoccupied zone of the Pétain government—Sperati decided to resume operations. He knew that the mail was censored and that the government was particularly on the lookout for anyone trying to export valuables—even rare postage stamps. But he also knew that in wartime no censorship system is perfect; a great many letters slip through with cursory inspection.

The prices valuable stamps were fetching in wartime Europe made the risk worthwhile to Sperati. Arthur Lafon, editor and publisher of the now defunct *Le Timbre*, one of the leading stamp journals, has explained the stamp economics of the period:

> During the war nearly everyone collected, not just stamp enthusiasts. Many astute persons looked upon valuable stamps as the perfect means of conquering the inflation they knew would be inevitable once the war ended. Stocks and bonds were dangerous because the governments were in the habit of confiscating them. Valuable works of art were too expensive for the average man, so that left postage stamps. Philately became very popular, and some amazing prices were paid for rarities. It was an ideal time for a counterfeiter such as Sperati to operate.

Actually, Sperati did not have much choice. A small market like unoccupied France was too confining. If he tried to peddle his output only there, it would soon be obvious that an unusual number of postal rarities were turning up on the market, always a warning signal to the wary dealer. A number of Sperati's stamps got through, although many were intercepted by censors. Several stamps sent by Sperati to a New York dealer late in 1941 were intercepted by the British censors in Bermuda and forwarded to the dealer in 1946.

Finally, in 1944, the censors tripped him up. He had sent 18 stamps to a dealer in Lisbon. The letter was intercepted, the stamps appraised as being worth 300,000 francs and Sperati was arrested for trying to export capital.

Sperati was brought before an examining magistrate. Knowing it was a far lesser offense to make stamps than to export capital, Sperati insisted that the stamps were of his own making. How could they possibly be worth 300,000 francs?

The magistrate ordered the stamps given to Dr. Edmond Locard, a well-known philatelist and then director of the police laboratory at Lyon. Locard examined the stamps carefully, gave them every test and concluded that the stamps were absolutely genuine. What impressed him most, and convinced him of their authenticity, was that the paper was identical with the paper of the real stamps—not even a difference of a thousandth of a millimeter in thickness between the stamps submitted and the genuine originals.

The court fined Sperati 300,000 francs—the value of the stamps. Sperati knew the only way he could get out of his huge penalty was to show the court that he had made the stamps himself. His attorneys filed an appeal, and after a few days in his home printing shop he came up with three more sets of the 18 valuable stamps.

Thoroughly bewildered, the judge now called some other experts into the case and ordered the trial postponed. Sperati, taking no chances on having to pay the 300,000-franc fine, decided on another clincher to show up the experts and to prove that he had really made the stamps.

One day in Paris, at the café Le Cadet, a favorite hangout for many stamp dealers, three of them met over an aperitif. They examined recent acquisitions. By a rather remarkable coincidence, it soon appeared that all three had just acquired a certain valuable

Oldenburg, a rarity issued in the middle of the 19th century by this former German state. There were less than a dozen of these particular stamps known in Europe, and each was worth between $250 and $500, depending on the condition of the stamp.

The three dealers left their lunch at Le Cadet and hurried over to Léon Miro's stamp shop on the Rue Laffitte. Miro, a tall, heavyset, urbane dealer, had been president of the Paris stamp dealers' trade association for 17 years and was generally considered one of Europe's finest judges of stamps.

As the three compared notes, the story came out. They had received some stamps from a woman correspondent, who asked them to check the authenticity of the stamps. A few were fakes, but some of them seemed genuine and valuable, and they asked if they could purchase them. The woman said no, but under persistent entreaties, relented and agreed to sell each dealer the Oldenburg he had so admired. She was, it now appeared, one of Sperati's relatives.

Just to make doubly sure, Miro checked the three Oldenburgs. They were forgeries—identical forgeries—he concluded after several hours of rigid examination. When he finished he was white. He once recalled the event for me:

> I could see from tiny details on the engraving that these were not originals, details that would probably have passed nine out of ten dealers. But what I could not get over was that the paper was the same paper used on the real Oldenburgs. This was terrible news. In the past, the one thing the forger could not duplicate was the paper, the perforations, the gum. If those details did not match properly, the expert did not even have to bother to check the engraving details.
>
> Getting the proper paper has always been the hardest part of the counterfeiter's technical operations. It is *the* pitfall for those who try to make paper money or stamps. Now we were faced with the problem of a dangerous forger who appeared to have solved that problem. This was most serious.

591

I am not one of those experts who proclaim they never have been fooled. When I buy a collection for a round sum, I cannot examine every stamp individually. There could easily be some fakes that would not catch the eye when I glance over the pages. In this case of the three dealers, we were truly fortunate. They had come to me and told me all. What if they had tried to get rid of the stamps by selling them to unsuspecting collectors?

Miro promptly got his trade association into the picture by instituting an action against Sperati for 1 million francs damages to compensate the association and its members for the financial damage that Sperati's fakes had done to the dealers. They also asked for the destruction of all of Sperati's stock.

In addition, Miro and the association's counsel tried to collect proof against Sperati. This proved to be a difficult job. Dealers who had been stuck with Sperati's stamps were naturally reluctant to come forward and testify because it would show them up as gullible. Dealers who had recognized Sperati's forgeries as such and had deliberately sold them to customers as true stamps, naturally did not want to get a bad name in the trade.*

The association discovered that one of the dealers, an Amsterdam man, had dealt with Sperati as far back as 1932. Sperati had sent him some stamps for auctioning and had guaranteed them as originals. When the dealer spotted them as fakes and grew angry with Sperati, the latter casually suggested, well, perhaps they might be fakes but, after all, why couldn't they be auctioned off as facsimiles—fine ones, too.

A famous Paris dealer, Jean-Aimé Brun, whose stamp shop like

---

* Alberto Diena, one of Italy's great stamp experts, has commented on a peculiar aspect of the whole affair that bothers many collectors: "Sperati reproduced rare and expensive stamps. But it was necessary for him to have such originals to work from. How did he get them? A collector? He wouldn't be interested in having more of his rarities made! But a dealer ... well ... many dealers are awfully suspicious of one another and perhaps there is good reason. ...."

many others was in the galleries off the Palais Royal, was the official stamp expert for the Paris Court of Appeals. He told me that Sperati had even approached him and offered a collaboration: "With your fine reputation and my great talent," the forger proposed, "we could get very rich."

Like ourselves, the French love to see the cops outwitted and the experts confounded. The newspapers had a wonderful time with the story and the *Paris-Presse* gave it a banner headline on page one:

PANIC AMONG THE PHILATELISTS
FAKE STAMPS WORTH 300 MILLION FRANCS

Other papers hailed Sperati as the Machiavelli of philately. Still others editorialized that if the experts could not tell the genuine from the fake, Sperati's works of art should be just as valuable as the ones the post office issued. It was a difficult time for the experts. They were hooted unmercifully, and perhaps the judge in the case was listening.

At his first trial for fraud, Sperati received a year in jail, suspended. He was also ordered to pay 300,000 francs to the stamp dealers' association, and given a personal fine of 10,000 francs. Sperati appealed the decision, and finally, in 1952, the high court upheld the original decision and added to it, increasing his prison sentence to two years, suspended. It also raised the damages he had to pay the stamp dealers' association from 300,000 to 500,000 francs ($1400) and ordered the court's judgment inserted in ten leading stamp periodicals, the cost to come out of the 500,000 francs damages. Sperati's personal fine was raised to 120,000 francs, and he was ordered to pay court costs for all the appeals, which came to another 18,000 francs.

The best explanation I heard for Sperati's jail sentence being suspended was (a) his age and (b) he was tubercular.

In spite of this great victory over their dangerous enemy, the stamp dealers were downcast over the fact that the court refused to give them permission to have Sperati's total stock destroyed. They knew a loophole in French law had permitted Sperati to sell his facsimiles even while his trials were going on. In France, you can sell stamp reproductions as facsimiles. What's the difference? Well, if the creator of the reproductions signs them on the back, they are facsimiles and presumably there is no intent to defraud on his part.

Sperati signed his productions with a soft pencil. Could he help it if some unscrupulous dealers bought his artistic reproductions, gently erased the soft-penciled signature and sold them as originals?

Sperati took ads in some European stamp journals read mostly by dealers. Why not get a set of Sperati's "artistic productions" for "comparison purposes." You could not tell the Sperati counterfeits without a Sperati scorecard. Several dealers thought it was a good idea and paid out $1100 for a set of his copies.

As the dealers became increasingly familiar with Sperati's work, they learned how he had solved the perplexing problem of making the stamp paper, the inevitable stumbling block of most previous stamp forgers. He had found a secret method of removing the ink from less valuable stamps. Previous bleaching methods were so crude that they could be spotted immediately. Sperati had improved this greatly. Now, with the identical paper, properly watermarked, and with identical perforations, Sperati could really accomplish a great deal.

In Rome, Dr. Dosi, the INTERPOL forgery expert, showed me some of the wonderful possibilities of such an operation. He took out the leading European catalogue, *Yvert & Tellier-Champion*, for 1954, and turned to the section on Spain. That country's sixth stamp is a six-centavo black, worth $8.50 in unused condition. But No. 8, two reals in the same series, was worth $1400. By getting rid of the old color and replacing it with the red of the higher-denomination stamp, Sperati was able to increase the value enormously. He pointed to some other stamps. Here was a French stamp issued in 1863, the 40-centime orange. In used condition, it was worth only 25 cents, but unused its value shot up to $27.

Sperati often turned out stamps that were worth comparatively little. In effect, these were finger exercises on stamps for which he knew there was a steady market. In fact, some of the stamps he made were worth only a couple of dollars. The highest-value stamp he ever turned out was the Swedish three-skilling banco error of color in yellow, instead of green. The only known copy is now owned by a Canadian collector and is valued at $40,000. Sperati sold his replica for less than $100, and it was good enough to fool one of Sweden's leading philatelic experts. As usual, Sperati used the paper of a common stamp in the same series. Incidentally, his favorite countries were France, the old German states, the Italian states, Spain, Switzerland, Argentina, Colombia, the United States and Uruguay. With one exception, all of his replicas were 19th-century stamps.

As Sperati's methods and distinctive touches became known, more and more of his stamps began turning up in embarrassing places—mainly prominent collections or the stock albums of leading reputable dealers. In February 1949 Edwin Mueller, the New York dealer, wrote confidently: "The Sperati collections consist of 226 items of forgeries ... by the disclosure of his secrets in the collections of his products, he has helped greatly, probably involuntarily, in the battle against philatelic forgers and fakers, including himself. . . ."

By 1954, the known Sperati stamps were 558 and the number was rising. In Paris and London and New York, anxious dealers and collectors were frankly worried. American dealers, in particular, were in a tough spot. Because of the rigid interpretation put by the U.S. Secret Service on the law, U.S. stamp dealers are not allowed to possess copies of stamp forgeries even for comparison purposes. Leading New York dealers, such as H. R. Harmer, keep their reference collections of fakes in London vaults—or they can visit the Smithsonian Institute, in Washington, which has a huge collection of fake stamps for comparison purposes.

At a time when the secret committee of the British Philatelic Association was on the verge of concluding their negotiations with

Sperati, I spent several hours with him in Aix-les-Bains. Before I went there, I had asked some of my Paris sources for more personal information on this master counterfeiter. M. Lafon, the stamp-journal editor, warned me that Sperati was a complex personality.

"He is, *au fond*, a skilled artist with a quixotic streak in him. He is also shrewd and calculating. I remember in court at the time of his trial he wore an outsize, stained, worn gabardine coat, like a beggar. His trousers were frayed and creaseless. Did he dress that way to impress the court that he was a poor man, that he hadn't profited from his forgeries?"

In Aix-les-Bains, I discovered that this local celebrity was known by name only. A hotel clerk, who had lived in the resort town all his life, confessed that he had never seen Sperati. The local chief of police said that he had nothing against Sperati, who was quiet and kept to his own affairs.

Before my morning appointment with Sperati, I talked to a woman who had been a neighbor of the Speratis before they bought their villa, "Clair de Lune," in 1935. Neighbors understood that M. Sperati had been in the food business, in Lyon, and earlier, in Paris. They were amazed when he turned out to be the greatest stamp forger of all time.

Sperati's villa was a square, two-story, grayish stucco house on the winding, climbing Boulevard de la Roche du Roi. It was surrounded by large, somewhat outmoded hotels and discreet clinics which presumably catered to the Aix-les-Bains visitors who were not helped by the mud baths and thermal springs.

The shrubs and plantings around the villa were not well tended, and the dark, dangerous police dog I had been warned about in Paris was not to be seen. Sperati's sister-in-law answered the door and led me through a dark, musty hallway, where I nearly tripped over a child's bike. I later learned it belonged to Sperati's granddaughter, visiting him from Paris. The house was filled with a stale cooking odor.

Sperati's large study, however, was neat, well kept and had an inspiring view of Lake Bourget and Mont du Chat. The study was heated by an old-fashioned, tile-covered stove, but it was cold the day I was there. I kept my coat on.

At the entrance to the study stood two corner tables and a very neat, polished period desk. The table on the right was filled with books and illustrations of the work of Peter Paul Rubens, the great Flemish painter. I got the connection as I approached the table. Above it was a mounted quotation from a Paris journal: "Sperati is the Rubens of philately." The other corner table was covered with an eight-inch pile of copies of newspapers and magazines that had carried stories about Sperati.

The forger came in quietly. He stood about 5 feet 10 inches tall and was rather emaciated. His hatchet jaw, fiery eyes, almost white hair, bushy eyebrows and hunched-over appearance were made to order for the caricaturist. We started out in English but did not get very far. Then in French and German, both of which Sperati speaks with a heavy Italian accent, we got along.

Would I tell him what lies stamp circles in New York and London were telling about him now? Was I interested, perhaps, in being his agent for the worldwide sale of his book, published in France and called *Philately Without Experts?* (It is a clumsily written, repetitive, paper-backed volume to bolster his claim that he undertook to produce his masterful counterfeits only to show up the experts.)

How much was he going to be paid for the interview? He was a busy man, his time was valuable and all journalists paid him. "I am not a rich man," he said, waving a hand as if to dismiss all stories to the contrary. "But what great artists have had an easy life?"

When we agreed on terms, he added further conditions: He would talk only for an hour, and there were questions about his family and his work that he would not answer. Nor could I expect to inspect his laboratory on the second floor of the villa. Actually, we talked longer than an hour, both at his office and later at the hotel where I was staying.

What did he live on? Some dividends and the occasional sales of stamps. His needs were modest, he said. The climate of Aix-les-Bains was good for his delicate health.

Most of his talk repeated his prior statements about his background and his reasons for making the counterfeits. He stubbornly refused to admit he had done it for money. "Please," he insisted, gesturing elaborately, "I am an artist, not a businessman. I look upon my reproductions as works of art to be seen and admired. When I proposed an exhibition of my works by the town of Aix-les-Bains, some jealous collectors and dealers called me a brazen criminal and stopped it. Think of all those who would have come to see the beautiful works of Jean de Sperati!"

He became disturbed when I hinted that I knew the British were dickering with him for his stock and his promise to forge no more. He reluctantly admitted there were negotiations. "I am no longer young, and I have been looking for someone younger to take over the burdens of my artistic work. The British heard about it and made an offer. Perhaps if their offer is good enough, I won't have to find an assistant to perpetuate my work."

Later, the BPA journal was to write about him:

> For over 40 years, the work of Jean de Sperati, maker of high-precision reproductions of rare stamps, has given trouble to experienced philatelists. A complete record of his work has never been available and is an essential possession for every serious philatelist. Sperati, who at 71 realized he could not maintain the high standard he set for himself for accurate work, decided to dispose of his business and his stock. The latter, with all his dies and other material, has now come under the control of the British Philatelic Association. . . .

The BPA announced to leading British dealers the terms under which Sperati's stock would be distributed:

> Comprehensive reference collections of Sperati's reproductions have been prepared for the use of the BPA. . . . From the balance, examples of Sperati's work, to the value

of \$56 to \$84, will be supplied with every book sold to a BPA member. Each book will be numbered (500 in all), and all items supplied with it—indelibly marked "Sperati reproduction" on the back—will be correspondingly numbered, a record kept by the BPA. In this way, a check on the whereabouts of this otherwise dangerous material will ensure its safe custody and minimize the risk of any attempt to dispose of the material as stamps. . . . This offer is restricted to members of the British Philatelic Association and the Royal Philatelic Society, London.

The price for each volume was \$56, for a limited time only.

The agreement did not meet with unanimous approval of British dealers and collectors. Some felt it was most un-British to deal with a criminal and buy him off in this fashion. Many of the dealers protested bitterly, but would not give their reasons. As Robson Lowe editorialized in his journal, *The Philatelist*, for April 1954: "A vociferous and hysterical minority, in the main those who think that the complete exposure may handicap their own business activities, are trying to put every possible obstacle in the way. . . . These hostile vapourings can only give rise to suspicion."

One London dealer told me: "If I had a few hundred pounds' worth of Sperati's fakes on hand and carried them as genuine stamps, I'd be awfully vexed at this turn of events. Once that BPA book comes out, it's going to be extremely difficult to sell those fakes. You can't blame those dealer chaps for being damned mad."

In Paris, Guy Isnard, then Commissaire Principal of the Sûreté, and a leading student of *"L'Affaire Spérati,"* shrugged his shoulders at the news. "Perhaps it was necessary to deal with this criminal. For myself, of course, I would have nothing to do with it. But the British are more practical in these matters."

In November 1955, while passing through London, I called again on Eileen Evans of the British Philatelic Association to find out how they had fared with their Sperati venture.

"Very well," said Miss Evans. "The reaction in the philatelic world is much more favorable now. We have sponsored exhibits of Sperati stamps in Denmark, Sweden, Australia and New Zealand, and in many towns in England. Collectors all over the world have become alerted to the danger of those stamps that may still be in the hands of unscrupulous dealers who are anxious to sell them."

Five hundred sets of Sperati stamps at $56 the set comes to $28,000. If, as I was told, Sperati received only $15,000 for his total stock, the BPA came out ahead by at least $10,000, after allowing for expenses for the venture. It is probably the first time that anybody profited *honestly* from Sperati's work.

In spite of the trouble Sperati gave French dealers and collectors, French Sûreté has a small, warm spot in its police heart for the stamp counterfeiter. In 1952 Sperati did them a good turn.

He had received five 1000-franc notes from a Swiss collector who wanted some of Sperati's "artistic reproductions." Failing eyesight or not, Sperati gave the bills another look and didn't like what he found. His master's eye saw that the colors were not quite right, and he wrote the Banque de France, in Paris, that the bills were counterfeit. The Sûreté got into the act at this point and soon other bills were tracked down. The bills, worth about $2.70 each, were considered one of the most dangerous forgeries ever encountered in France. Unlike Sperati's stamps, they were confiscated. But then the Swiss collector didn't get the "artistic reproductions" either.

Sperati was upset by the experience. "These counterfeits are very dangerous. An honest businessman must have eyes in the back of his head," he said solemnly. "Perhaps," he added with a small smile, "the Banque de France could use someone with my training and background to watch out for these dangerous banknotes."

In July 1956 I asked a French friend who lives in Aix-les-Bains to inquire as to Sperati's health and psyche. He wrote back:

He is a lonely old man, without friends. Someone I know who encountered him on a walk a few months ago and spoke to him said Sperati is still embittered because the town officials refused him permission to put on an exhibition of his art work, i.e., his counterfeit stamps.

Others report that his eyes are growing weaker and that he needs extremely powerful lenses to read. When I went to see him about giving me a brief interview on your behalf, he made clear immediately that such an interview was only to be had for 10,000 francs if it were by a French newspaperman, and 30,000 by a *journaliste étranger*. However, both French and foreign newsmen who pay this large fee are assured of a free copy of his autobiography.

He is no longer any kind of a celebrity. The last item about him in a newspaper was back in 1954 and that was in the Paris *Samedi Soir:* "Le Roi des Faussaires de Timbres Prend Sa Retraite" (The King of the Stamp Forgers Retires on a Pension).

As you know, Aix-les-Bains is almost American in its publicity consciousness and is always anxious for new attractions to add to its glories as a *Station Thermale et de Tourisme*. A pity we never did undertake to promote him as one of our local attractions and to get each of France's 200,000 stamp collectors to visit Sperati and perhaps buy a sample of his art works. Of course, now that he has sold all his stock to the British, that is impossible. Perhaps that is why there is some resentment against him here. It is not just that he walks slightly stooped—like a disgruntled rheumatic who has found our thermal baths and springs of no avail—but that he did not wait, like a true patriot, for an offer from the French stamp syndicate.

A MAN brandishing a gun emptied a Chattanooga liquor store's cash register of $389.89. Then he demanded a fifth of whiskey. "That'll be $3.62," said the quick-witted woman clerk—and the bandit paid before fleeing.   —*AP*

601

He became the lion of London
by posing as a native of a land no
one knew anything about

GEORGE PSALMANAZAR: THE INCREDIBLE IMPOSTOR

by John P. Long

In London, in 1703, an extraordinary young man was introduced to Bishop Compton, the Anglican bishop of the metropolis of London—the city of Defoe, Swift, Addison and Steele. The young man's name was George Psalmanazar, whose antecedents remain a mystery to this day and whose *Historical and Geographical Description of Formosa*—published a year after his introduction to the Bishop—is perhaps the most amazing literary imposture in history.

This remarkable volume contained the complete history of Formosa, an island more remote to Englishmen of that day than the planet Mars is becoming to us. Its customs, religion, geography, climate and the history of its people were narrated by the author with great care and considerable skill. An alphabet, a map of the island and plates representing the divinities of the country were attached to the volume—details which seemed to establish its authenticity.

Its erudition staggered the learned world of the time, and at 24 young Psalmanazar found himself the literary lion of the day. The fact that he announced himself a native Formosan, and was suspected with a kind of horrible fascination of being a cannibal

to boot, seemed in no way to interfere with society's esteem. Unhappily, the book was a complete fabrication from beginning to end and the author one of the world's greatest impostors.

George Psalmanazar was probably a Frenchman, born in southern France about 1679, though on more than one occasion he claimed Ireland as his native land. In his memoirs he states that his father came from a poor but ancient family. He was educated first at a French school, under Franciscan monks, where his remarkable talent for languages was at once obvious. Later he studied at a Jesuit college, apparently as a seminarian, but he soon left school and attempted teaching. After tutoring two small boys for only a brief time, however, he literally took to the road as a vagabond. On the way to Avignon he stole a pilgrim's staff and a cloak from a church and forged or obtained in some way a certificate showing him to be a theology student of Irish descent on a pilgrimage to Rome. Begging his way from inn to inn, speaking fluent Latin, he was a successful mendicant. His career as an impostor had begun.

Psalmanazar did not travel long as a pilgrim. In his 16th year he found himself in Germany, tiring somewhat of the unsafe role of an Irish theologian. He had heard the Jesuits speak of China and Japan, and he determined to pass as a Japanese, a recent convert to Christianity and a native of the island of Formosa. His knowledge of the Orient was extremely vague, but most of the world in which he lived and traveled had never even heard of Formosa.

He began immediately to invent an entirely new language, an alphabet and a calendar with the year divided into 20 months. The writing was from right to left in the Oriental manner. He decided upon what he believed a suitable religion for the country of his adoption, forged a certificate of his new character to the seal of his Avignon credentials and turned his steps to the Netherlands.

He was no simple pilgrim. His remarkable story, his wide reading and knowledge, his fluency in Latin, aroused considerable attention. At Liège he entered the Dutch service as a soldier. He was transferred with his regiment to Sluys, Holland, where he again changed his status, to an unconverted native of Formosa. He became acquainted with Alexander Innes, chaplain of a Scots regiment stationed at Sluys, became a ready convert and was baptized. He obtained his discharge and proceeded with remarkable promptness to London with the Reverend Mr. Innes, apparently according to a preconceived plan. Chaplain Innes had written to Bishop Compton about his convert, and the stage was set for this attractive and unusually talented young Formosan to appear in the literary and social world of London. It is not certain whether Chaplain Innes was duped by young Psalmanazar, but it does appear that the Bishop was completely deceived by the young pilgrim and soldier.

Psalmanazar's first task from his new patron was to translate the church catechism into the Formosan language, a diversion to which he was quite agreeable. He was paid liberally, the work was pleasant and no one could know whether the completed volume was technically correct, an ideal arrangement for the author. To simplify things further, the book could be put to no use whatsoever, because missionaries were barred from Japan and all its islands. Thus the catechism could embark upon completely uncharted seas. The famous *Historical and Geographical Description of Formosa* soon followed, being the story of "an island subject to the Emperor of Japan, giving an account of the religion, customs, manners, etc., of the inhabitants; together with a relation of what happened to the author on his travels, particularly his conferences with the Jesuits and others in several parts of Europe. Also, the history and reasons of his conversion to Christianity, with his objections against it in defense of paganism, and their answers, etc. By George Psalmanazar, a native of the said island, now in London. Illustrated with several cuts."

The promises implied in this formidable and delightful title were more than justified in the history itself. "His island of Formosa," Isaac Disraeli remarks in his *Curiosities of Literature*, "was an illusion eminently bold, and maintained with as much felicity as erudition; and great must have been that erudition which could form a pretended language and its grammar, and fertile the genius which could invent the history of an unknown people." If Mr. Disraeli's language is florid, his analysis is, nevertheless, accurate. We find the Formosan history an amazing account of a country and its people, skillfully narrated and powerfully imaginative.

The early history of the island seems borrowed almost directly from the story of the capture of Troy. The throne of Japan was occupied by the Emperor Merryaandanoo, a fugitive Chinese. His expedition to Formosa, under the pretense of seeking aid from the Formosan gods to cure his sickness, was made in a large convoy of flatboats, or *arkha-kasseos*, bearing 300 *norimmonnos*, or huge litters, each filled with gaping sheep, oxen and calves for sacrifice to the gods. If the foreign gods were appeased and the Emperor cured, he had promised the Formosans their strange deities would be established throughout Japan. The great fleet, with 200 oars flashing on each side of the boats, made landing.

The litters were borne on the backs of elephants, two of the beasts carrying one between them, and the sacred procession began to the capital city of Xternetsa. A large retinue of Japanese officers followed the caravan. As the ceremonies were about to begin, 9000 Japanese soldiers climbed down the backs of the elephants, ready for action. Thirty soldiers had been hidden in each of the *norimmonnos*, with the sheep, oxen and calves, the animals peering out through curtained windows left open for ventilation, but the soldiers nowhere in sight. The king of Formosa capitulated at once, and the country was won.

The religion of the Formosans was polytheism, with a yearly sacrifice of 18,000 boys' hearts (a detail which proved an awkward stumbling block when critics pointed out that such a figure would soon deplete the island). Transmigration of the soul was an accepted belief, as well as worship of demons or evil spirits. Life's finale was an elaborate cremation with "appropriate ceremonies."

The natives were quite handsome in appearance, the history narrated, and the women of particular beauty, among the fairest in the world. Polygamy was permitted, but "if one takes more wives than his means will maintain, he is to be beheaded," certainly a considerable restraint to the practice.

The criminal laws were harsh. Murderers were hanged upside down and shot to death with arrows. A slanderer had his tongue bored through with a hot iron, and one who bore false witness had his tongue cut out. Disobedient sons and daughters (those who struck their fathers or mothers) were dealt with summarily, their legs and arms cut off and the bodies flung into the sea.

Cannibalism was not common, but the natives ate the bodies of prisoners of war and of criminals legally executed. The flesh of the latter was considered a dainty treat. It is no wonder Psalmanazar was looked upon with great curiosity, as it might well be that he had devoured some of these choice morsels upon more than one occasion! Snake for breakfast, the poison removed, was highly recommended—particularly in the early morning with a pipe of tobacco and a cup of tea.

"In my humble opinion," the author wrote, "the most wholesome breakfast a man can make."

Following publication of the history, Psalmanazar was sent to Oxford. There followed a brief period of quiet scholarship, but with the appearance of a second edition, a growing amount of criticism and doubt as to the truth of the manuscript was put forth by many. Doubts grew to certainty, and finally—the pronounced absurdities in the book self-evident—the imposture was denounced by its critics.

Psalmanazar disappeared from public view and began a career of idleness and extravagance. At the age of 32, however, he entered a long and honorable life of painstaking scholarship, spending many years upon a voluminous *Universal History*, now forgotten. He became, too, a sincerely religious man. Dr. Samuel Johnson revered him, stating, "His piety, penitence and virtue exceeded almost what we read as wonderful even in the lives of the saints."

Psalmanazar lived to be 84 and died at his lodgings in Ironmonger Row, Old Street, London, on May 3, 1763. In his last will and testament he wrote in the fullness of his heart:

But the principal manuscript I felt myself bound to leave behind is a faithful narrative of my education and the sallies of my wretched youthful years, and the various ways in which I was in some measure unavoidably led into the base and shameful imposture of passing upon the world for a native of Formosa and a convert to Christianity, and backing it with a fictitious account of that Island and of my travels, conversion, etc.; all, or most of it, hatched in my own brain, without regard to truth or honesty.

If the obscurity I have lived in during such a series of years should make it needless to revive a thing in all likelihood so long since forgot, I cannot but wish that so much of it was published in some weekly paper, as might inform the world, especially those who have still by them the fabulous account of the island of Formosa, etc.; that I have long since owned both in conversation and in print, that it was no other than a mere forgery of my own devising, a scandalous imposition on the public, and such as I think myself bound to beg God and the world's pardon for writing, and have been long since, as I am to this day, and shall be as long as I live, heartily sorry for and ashamed of.

◦◦◦

SOME YEARS ago a man hired the opera house in a small Pennsylvania town for one night, but engaged no ushers or other staff. About a month before the date for which he had rented the hall, he put a large sign on the most prominent billboard in town, stating in huge letters: "He Is Coming!"

A week before the fateful night, this was replaced by: "He Will Be at the Opera House on October 31!" The day before the event there was the simple legend: "He Is Here!" The following morning: "He Will Be at the Opera House Tonight at 8:30!"

That night the man himself sat in the box office and sold tickets at $1 a head to a capacity audience. When the lights went up inside, however, all the crowd could see was a huge sign reading: "He Is Gone!"

—*Walter Winchell, quoting S. J. Kaufman*

To some they were scalawags, but to
themselves and many others they were patriots spiriting
back to Scotland its great national symbol

NO STONE UNTURNED

by Ian R. Hamilton

One night in December 1950, with three other young Scottish patriots, I broke into Westminster Abbey and removed the Coronation Stone—Scotland's own Stone of Destiny. It was a spectacular deed that fired the imagination of men everywhere. By recovering the Stone for Scotland we righted an ancient wrong and struck a symbolic blow at the very heart of Englishry. Yet the exploit hurt no one. And this, too, was symbolic; for violence and destruction are anathema to the Scots, whom I consider the most civilized people in the world.

It is almost forgotten that Scotland is the oldest nation in Europe. Our political institutions have been entirely absorbed by the English Crown and are administered by a Parliament which is only 10 percent Scottish. Yet, in spite of this, we have preserved our church, our own courts of justice and our own separate and distinct legal system.

Above all we have preserved our character as Scotsmen. For two and a half centuries Scotland's pride has been a shrunken thing. But World War II helped revitalize our sense of "community," and when my generation returned from the armed forces we found a spirited, growing Nationalist movement working for a measure of self-government. The aim was not separation from England but a more honorable union, "in all loyalty to the Crown and within the framework of the United Kingdom." Yet, in spite of overwhelming popular support for the Scottish Nationalists, the government refused to accede to even their most moderate demands.

In Glasgow University in those days there were many of us who sat and talked about many things, but always the talk came back to Scotland. And gradually as the months rolled on and the politicians in London continued to neglect Scotland, the talk got bitter. As a 25-year-old law student who dabbled in politics, I did not consider myself a man of action. But now my political discontent became a burning passion that would not let me rest. And it grew plain to me that I was to be thrust into action.

It was no sudden flash of inspiration which turned us to the Stone of Destiny. This Stone has always been associated with the right of government. The Coronation Throne of a long line of Celtic kings, it was wrenched in 1296 from the Abbey of Scone with sword and arson by Edward I, King of England, who took it from the Scotsmen as the symbol of their liberty. The memory is one not easily erased from Scottish minds. When Robert Bruce had carried Scotland to final victory, one of the terms of the peace was that the Stone of Destiny be returned. But this covenant was never honored, and the Stone remained in Westminster Abbey.

By early November 1950, I had definitely admitted to myself that I was going after the Stone. I enlisted the aid of a young man whom I shall call Keith, and we settled down to plan our campaign. We hoped to do something which might earn a place in the history books and would almost certainly earn ourselves a dark English jailroom.

Toward the middle of November I went to Glasgow's Mitchell Library and withdrew all the books I could find which dealt with Westminster Abbey and the Stone of Destiny. (In the end the library slips with my name on them were the only concrete evidence the police had against me.) I waded through pages of description and history, studied photographs, drew maps, made some calculations.

Armed with the figures, maps and plans, I approached a Glasgow businessman for £50 (then worth about $140) to finance the enterprise (the total expenditure was to be less than £70). When he saw that I was in deadly earnest, this ardent Nationalist was keen to help. He in turn introduced me to a member of the Glasgow Town Council. Both the businessman and the councilor had in previous years been associated with abortive plots for recovery of the Stone. As our advisers they were able to act like a House of Lords with an impetuous Lower Chamber, and, throughout, they gave us invaluable assistance.

One night I went to London to reconnoiter. As my train crossed the border, I was seized with shaking excitement. I thought of how my forefathers from Clydesdale had many times passed this way, in defense of Scotland's honor or bent on hearty plunder. But though I was traveling south with only the recovery of a block of stone as my aim, I did not think, considering the times, that my forefathers would be ashamed of me.

In London the next morning, this excitement was redoubled. It was a fine sensation to be at the heart of England not as a tourist but as a spy. I joined the handful of sightseers in Westminster Abbey and for a considerable time moved about in the calm duskiness of the sanctuary. I already had a considerable knowledge of the building, but I particularly wanted to learn all I could about locks and doors.

The Stone was contained in a boxlike aperture under the seat of the Coronation Chair, in Edward the Confessor's Chapel. I examined it carefully. It is a block of roughhewn sandstone about 17 inches broad by 27 inches long, and 11 inches deep. It weighs more than 400 pounds. On either end, a few links of chain terminating in an iron ring provide handles for carrying it. A small lath along the front of the old oak chair held the Stone in place, and I saw that this could easily be removed without damage to the ancient workmanship.

Before I left I engaged one of the guides in conversation. How did they keep the place so clean—surely an army of cleaners came in every night when the Abbey closed. No? I made a mental note. A few other leading questions and another prowl around showed me where the night watchman's office was situated. I left the Abbey with all the information I required for successful burglary. Most of that night I wandered around back streets in the vicinity, studying the approaches to the building and observing all signs of police activity. On the train for Glasgow next morning, I was tired but full of burning contentment. I now knew beyond all shadow of doubt that what we planned was possible. The difficulty was there, but that was a challenge.

Keith and I evolved the following plan: One of us would conceal himself in the Abbey toward closing time, hiding in a chapel which was then under repair. I claimed this honor for myself, for the conception had been mine. After being locked in, I would lie quietly in hiding until 2 a.m., or as soon thereafter as the night watchman had completed his rounds. I would then screw the lock off an outer door and admit an accomplice. We would remove the Stone from the Chair, lash it to an iron bar and carry it outside, where a small inconspicuous car would be waiting. On a quiet side street the Stone would be transferred to a larger and faster car, which would head straight for Dartmoor, where the Stone would be hidden temporarily. Meanwhile, the small car would race toward Wales: if it had been seen at the Abbey, it would lead the police on a false scent.

This was a good plan. But in practice it had to be sorely amended under stress of unforeseeable circumstances.

Christmas seemed to me the only possible time for the enterprise, for the English celebrate very thoroughly then, and I maintained we should come down on them while they were lying in drink with their minds unbuttoned. Keith had inescapable engagements for every day over the holidays and argued that the plan would keep. But I was stubborn. Secrets of this nature do not mature like good wine. Moreover, I had screwed my resolution

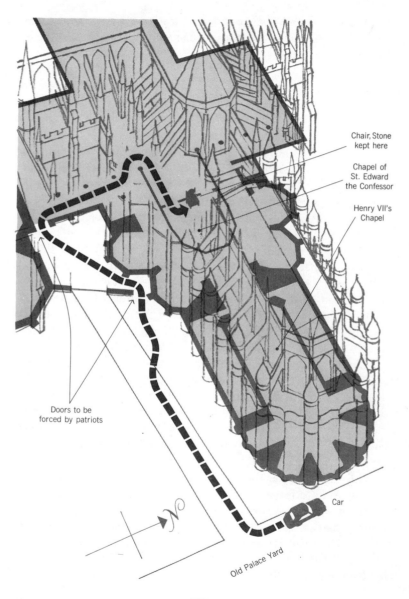

Chair, Stone
kept here

Chapel of
St. Edward
the Confessor

Henry VII's
Chapel

Doors to be
forced by patriots

Car

N

Old Palace Yard

613

to the last turn and I was not sure that it would not suddenly unwind if I was denied the prospect of immediate action. "I'll go myself," I told him.

Then one evening I attended a university dance with Ann, a young teacher of domestic science whose political views were almost identical with mine. Small and dark and large-eyed, Ann was a Highlander, and she spoke with the quiet tongue that knows English only as a second language. I was moody and depressed, thinking of who among the people I knew would willingly throw over their prospects and come to London. Suddenly I knew without any doubt. Ann was an idealist who would not be greatly concerned about her own welfare if she could do something to serve the movement. A pretty woman is never suspect, and a brave woman could fire the imagination of the world.

I put down my drink and spoke to her for the first time in ten minutes. "What are you doing at Christmas, Ann?"

"I'm going home," she said.

"I'm going to London to bring back the Stone of Destiny."

She laughed. "I mean it," I said, and I did. "Would you like to help?"

"No," she said, but she meant yes. "What can I do?"

Things happened rapidly thereafter. As our No. 3 man we acquired Roland, a 24-year-old engineering student who had the Scotsman's delight in high and risky enterprise. He was quite short of stature, but of considerable physical strength, and his mad recklessness got him into many scrapes that no dour Scot was designed for. As driver-in-chief, he immediately went to hire a car—a 12-year-old Ford.

With three people, our team was now complete, and we were almost ready to leave. We met and went over our maps and diagrams as often as we had a spare moment to foregather. Meanwhile, I had collected a burglar's tool kit, including an immense 24-inch jimmy of which I was inordinately proud. With loving care, I had made myself a shoulder sling which left the jimmy hanging from armpit to trouser pocket. The files, wire, hacksaw, wrench and other tools of my new profession I carefully stowed about my person. Thus equipped, I would put on my coat, go down to a little café in Gibson Street and talk to my friends, with the delicious cold steel against me and a smile of sheer joy on my lips.

At the last minute we recruited a fourth man, Malcolm, who could bring an Anglia car. He was a tall young fellow, with a frank, boyish face and a crop of golden hair. He was only 20 and looked younger. Which was the more reliable, Malcolm or his Anglia car, I do not know. But I do know that I would go around the world with either of them, and there would be laughter and confidence all the way.

At last, on the evening of Friday, December 22, we piled into the two cars and drove out of Glasgow on the road south.

It was afternoon of the next day when we reached London and shot along Whitehall, past Scotland Yard and the Houses of Parliament to the Abbey. Together we reconnoitered the historic shrine.

Although we had had no sleep the previous night, we were all keen to have a go at it that same evening. So after an early dinner and a final council of war, we split into two parties, and Malcolm and Ann drove off to make themselves familiar with the route west to Dartmoor. If things went wrong I would not see them again until I had passed through prison.

Sitting in the old Ford, I raked in my grip, produced the burglar's tools and stowed them about me. When I had my coat on, all was hidden, except for a slight stoutness, which, since Roland ascribed it to my inherent motherliness, kept us laughing all the way as we drove to the Abbey and parked the car. I was approaching the supreme adventure of my life. Excitement seized me again, but I kept it down until it was only a pressure along my ribs, which occasionally unwound itself in an involuntary twitch.

Big Ben struck 5:15 as I walked casually into the Abbey out of the shining, noisy darkness of a London evening. Inside, the light was soft, yet it seemed to illuminate me and probe me out as a persistent and sinister visitor to the Abbey. I pulled my heavy coat about me and hated the damning jimmy at my side.

Followed by Roland, I walked slowly up the north transept, pausing only to gaze at an occasional Latin inscription. The venerable guide was in conversation with a woman and he paid no attention to me. I walked on and into the shadows of the north transept. I hoped to hide at the extreme end of it, under a cleaner's trolley. Down in the aisle Roland walked slowly past. No one else was in sight. He nodded to me briefly, absentmindedly. I crawled in under the trolley and, having covered my face with my coat, lay perfectly still.

Steam from my breath condensed on my face. The hard stone of the Abbey floor under me was less real than my heart, which thudded and pounded and threatened to stick in my gullet. This I had always reckoned would be the most dangerous part. To be caught with my pockets stuffed with housebreaking tools before I had a chance even to touch the Stone of Scone would be ignominy of the basest sort, and I was young enough to fear derision more than anything else.

Gradually I relaxed. My leg ceased to twitch. Quarter to six struck and then the hour. Roland would now be out of the building, for it closed at six. When quarter past six struck I looked up. God be praised! The lights were out. I could now move in safety to St. Paul's Chapel, where I was certain I could hide safely.

Hearing nothing but the vague murmur of traffic in the world outside, I crept stiffly from my hiding place. I had gone three paces when I suddenly heard the jangling of keys. Even as I listened, a light swept around the corner of the transept and shone in my face. White and shocked with fear, I looked up at a tall, bearded watchman.

"What the devil are you doing here?"

"I've been shut in," I said, hanging my head on my chest and making myself smaller.

"Why didn't you shout, then?" he asked. His voice was clear and authoritative, but not unkind.

"I thought I'd get a row," I said, and my voice quivered on the edge of tears.

"Well," he said, "you're lucky I didn't hit you on the head. We're patrolling about here all night, you know."

For the first time a wild hope flamed up that perhaps he would not hand me over to the police, who would be bound to search me. Then, as I moved, the jimmy slipped from its sling, and was held only by my arm pressed tight against my side. I broke out in a white sweat and, opening my eyes wide, said to myself: "I mustn't be sick. I mustn't be sick." Then suddenly we were moving toward the door. Thinking I was sheltering in the Abbey because I had nowhere else to go, the watchman asked if I had any money. When I told him that I did, he led me down the steps and, with a kindly word and a "Merry Christmas," let me out into the concourse of men with nothing on their consciences.

I had bungled a fine plot and let down as good a team of robbers as ever came out of Scotland. I could have wept with impotence and shame.

By uncanny good fortune I found Roland quickly, and we went over to Trafalgar Square, where he had arranged to meet Ann and Malcolm. We all felt pretty sick. We considered trying the same plan again the following night, but gave it up as too dangerous. Another coarse and blundering attempt could only end in failure and bring disrepute down on our country and on our movement. But it was unthinkable that we should go home yet.

"We might break in from the outside," said Malcolm, who had not shown the slightest dismay in our initial failure. "Bruce watched his spider try seven times. We've only tried once. Let's go along to the Abbey and look for spiders."

We made several more excursions that night, prowling around the Abbey grounds to glean what information we could. It must have been well on into morning when we parked our two cars on a side street and tried, in spite of the bitter cold, to get a few snatches of sleep. It was not only that hotel rooms would have depleted our meager funds but in the cars we lived as a sort of military community, preserving our fragment of Scotland and our integrity of purpose, which we might have lost had we sought warmth and soft beds.

We spent the next day in and around the Abbey, which was filled with Christmas worshipers, ever on the lookout for the scrap of information which would give us a clue to a successful raid. Dusk fell on a raw, cheerless night, and soon a thin, freezing mist began to fall.

Ann had been feeling ill all day, and now she was white-faced and shivering with the flu. This seemed inevitably to mean the end of our expedition, but she would not hear of it. After exacting from me the most solemn promise that if there was to be any excitement whatsoever we would get her, she went to a cheap little hotel for a few hours of sleep.

Roland, Malcolm and I then returned to the Abbey and the problem of breaking into it. We marshaled the facts that we knew. First, the Poets' Corner door, the most secluded door to the Abbey, was of pine and could possibly be forced from the outside. Second, we had learned that a new watchman came on at 11 o'clock. If he patrolled all night he could be expected to hear us forcing the door. However, none of us believed that an unsupervised watchman would pad about the dim corridors of the Abbey more often than, say, once every two hours. Then, too, all around us were signs of the wildest conviviality; there was always the chance that the new watchman would have blunted his perceptions by spending his evening in a pub.

A lane led from Old Palace Yard to the door we intended to force. The door itself was partly hidden from the road by a flying buttress, but access to it was barred by a locked and brightly lit gate, which was in full view. We felt we could bypass this gate, however, by forcing our way through a masons' repair yard which was fenced off only by a wooden hoarding in which there was a padlocked door.

We were delighted to see that insobriety was abroad in the streets. That would keep the police busy. We left the cars and walked aimlessly about, calling out "Merry Christmas" to everyone we passed. As time melted away, we became more and more strung up. Conditions were ideal.

When Big Ben struck two o'clock we knew that our time had come. A few people still sang through the streets, but they were a camouflage rather than a danger. With our jimmy we quickly forced our way through the masons' yard and reached the Poets' Corner door. But we would not assail this until we had got Ann from her hotel. I drove over with Malcolm in the old Ford and pulled up outside Ann's hotel while Roland waited around the corner with the Anglia. I hammered on the door. At length a voice asked, "What do you want?"

"I want Miss Duncan," I said.

"All right, all right," complained the voice. "I'll tell her."

While I waited out in the car beside Malcolm, a man presently came up to the hotel door, knocked and was immediately admitted. We wondered what business could bring him to the hotel at this late hour. As we laughed and joked rather uneasily, the stranger came back out of the hotel and walked straight toward us. The hotel manager, suspicious of our call at 3 a.m., had telephoned the police!

The official flashed a Metropolitan Police warrant card under my nose. "I'm a detective," he said. "Can I see your driving license?"

I fished it out and gave it to him. He took down my name and address. My palms sweated, and the jimmy buttoned up under my jacket seemed as large as a tree trunk.

"What's the trouble?" I asked.

"Several hundred cars have already been stolen tonight. What is the license number of your car?"

Like a fool, I had forgotten to memorize it. "I don't know," I said. "I hired the car."

His questions got more and more difficult, for I could remember neither the name nor the address of the garage it came from. That had been Roland's work, and although he sat just around the corner I did not want to refer the detective to him, lest he take Roland's name and the number of the Anglia also. Finally the detective blew a short blast on his whistle, and a large police car appeared from nowhere and drew up. I turned on the righteous indignation. "I've read all the law books," I said. "Not one of them says that the citizen must know the number of the car that he is driving."

Ann now came out of the hotel, joined us and began confirming everything I said. But our arguments merely exasperated the detective. At all costs, we wanted to avoid being run in on suspicion of car stealing, even if we would prove our innocence and be released in the morning. "Look," I said. "There is a man sitting around the corner in an Anglia car who can prove everything I'm saying. He's got the car-hire receipt."

The detective went off to check it, taking Malcolm with him as surety. A moment later he returned, conversing affably with Roland and comparing the car-hire receipt with the number of the car, which he had carefully written down in his little black book.

"I hope you're satisfied, Constable," I said sententiously. "You nearly made a terrible blunder."

He apologized again and again. There were, it seemed, many dishonest people about, and one had to do one's duty. As we drove away we suddenly relaxed. To my astonishment, I discovered that I had enjoyed every minute of the excitement. This was something nearer to honorable fight than the ignoble brush with the watchman, when I had lied like a petty criminal held by the ear.

We were certain that the hotel proprietor and the detective would later connect us with the disappearance of the Stone. Yet neither of them did so. Looking back on it, I like to think that the Almighty sent the detective to try us before vouchsafing us the miracle of success.

Ann, feeling better after her rest, was ready for anything. We were all flushed with excitement and avid at the prospect of more. We had bid our hands to the limit: It only remained to see if all our finesses came off.

Four o'clock rang out from Big Ben. If our calculations were correct, the watchman should have finished his rounds. I parked the old Ford in a parking space not far from the Abbey, locked it and put the keys in my overcoat pocket, and rejoined the others in the Anglia. Old Palace Yard was deserted, so Malcolm swung straight into the lane. The engine reverberated terrifyingly off the Abbey walls. Halfway up the lane he switched out the lights. At the top, we got out and Ann slipped into the driver's seat. Malcolm, Roland and I crossed a patch of light and stood against the Poets' Corner door, crucified by the rays of a gas lamp. At least we should not work in darkness. Roland put his shoulder against the door. "The jimmy!" he hissed.

At first we made little impression on the door. We were desperately afraid of noise, and each creak sounded like a hammer blow. But finally we deadened our ears to noise; the three of us put our weight on the end of the jimmy, and the door flew open with a crash that Ann, waiting in the car, heard and shuddered at the noise.

But our way was now open. We swept into the Abbey, pulling the door closed behind us. A light glowed dimly at the west end of the nave, but the rest was in black darkness. We went down the transept in silent hurry and crept up a flight of steps into the Confessor's Chapel. In the darkness of the chapel my torch shone wanly on the green marble tomb of Edward I. The Stone was before us, breast high, under the seat of the Coronation Chair, which stood on a kind of trestle. We prized gently at the bar of wood which ran along the front of the chair but, dry with age, it cracked and splintered. The three of us worked in a sweating fever to get the Stone out. With one man holding the torch, one prizing at the sides with the jimmy and one pushing at the back, we moved it. It slid forward. The English Chair would hold it no longer.

One last heave. "Now!" said Roland. I pushed from the back. It slid forward, and they had it between them. But it was too heavy to carry, so I laid my overcoat on the ground; we would drag the Stone on that. I seized one of the iron rings and pulled strongly. It came easily—too easily for its weight. "Stop!" I said and shone my torch.

I shall not forget what the faint light revealed: I had pulled away a section of the Stone, and it lay in terrifying separation from the main part. Everything was now turned bad. "We've broken Scotland's luck," came Malcolm's awful whisper.

Suddenly I saw that most of the broken area was very dark. The Stone had been cracked for years and they had not told us. "No, we haven't!" I said. "They did it. They've cheated us by keeping the news from us."

"Get moving!" said Roland.

I picked up the small part. It weighed 90 pounds, but in my excitement I picked it up like a football, plunged out the door and through the darkness of the masons' yard. Ann had seen me coming and had the car halfway down the lane. She opened the door, and I rolled the piece of Stone into the back.

"It's broken," I said. "Get back into cover." By the time I was in the Abbey the car was again at the top of the lane.

Except for our gasps for breath and an occasional grunt of effort, Malcolm, Roland and I made little noise. Between us we slung the weighted overcoat down the chapel steps one by one, then dragged it across the nave. Sweat blinded us. Suddenly and miraculously we were at the door, all at the end of our strength. "One more pull," said Malcolm. "We're not going to be beaten now." I opened the door, and as I did so I heard the car start up. Far too early, Ann was moving it forward into the lane, whence it was clearly visible from the road. "The fool!" I said, and dashed out.

"Get the car back into cover!" I spat. "We're not ready yet."

Ann looked at me coolly. "A policeman has seen me," she said. "He's coming across the road."

I got into the car beside her and silently closed the door, then switched on the lights. I fought breath into myself, and wiped the dust of the Abbey off my hands onto Ann's coat. I put one hand over the back of the seat, groped for Malcolm's spare coat and carefully draped it over the fragment of the Stone. Then I took

623

Ann in my arms. She was as calm as though we were on our way home from a dance. It was our third night virtually without sleep, and we were both so drugged with tiredness that our minds were cold as ice. Fear or panic played no part.

The policeman loomed up in front of us. "What's going on here?" he thundered. Ann and I did not fall apart until he had had plenty of opportunity to observe for himself.

"It's Christmas Eve, you know, Officer," I explained.

"Christmas Eve!" he answered. "It's five o'clock Christmas morning, and you're sitting on private property here. Why did you move forward when you saw me coming?"

"I knew we shouldn't be here," I said humbly. "We put on the lights to show you that we were quite willing to move on."

"But where can we go?" asked Ann, vamping him. "The streets are far too busy."

"You should be off home," he told her severely. But then he began to warm to us. To my horror, he took off his helmet and laid it on the roof of the car. He lit a cigarette and showed every sign of staying till he had smoked it. "There's a dark car-park just along the road," he said.

"Och, well," said Ann, thrusting her head into the lion's mouth, "we can always get you to run us in and give us comfortable cells."

"No, no," said the constable knowingly. "There's not a police-man in London would arrest you tonight."

"A good night for crime!" I said, and we all laughed.

All this time I had been conscious of a scraping sound going on behind the wooden fence. Ann heard the noise, too, and we engaged the constable in loud conversation. Surely Malcolm and Roland would hear us and be warned. But out of the corner of my eye I saw the door in the fence slowly open. Roland's head and shoulders appeared. Suddenly he froze. He had seen the policeman. His lips formed an amazed oath. Inch by inch he edged back, and the door closed behind him.

The policeman finished his cigarette and put on his helmet. "You'd better be going now," he said.

"We had indeed!" I said, wiping the sweat out of my eyes.

Ann started the engine. Never has a clutch been let in so jerkily; never has a car veered from side to side so crazily. I looked back: As Ann intended, the constable was following us down the lane— too amazed at the crazy driving to pay attention to anything else. But once we reached the road, Ann put her toe down hard on the accelerator.

Now the fat was properly in the fire. We still had a chance, but it was a slim one. Somehow we must get back and collect the greater part of the Stone, which still lay with our two friends in the masons' yard, and get it into hiding. Meanwhile, the Anglia was a dangerous car—the policeman must have taken the license number. We decided that Ann should set off westward, in the hope that she would be outside the area of greatest police activity before morning came.

At the parking space, I transferred the piece of Stone from the back seat to the trunk, and took Malcolm's old overcoat to wear myself. Then I felt in my pockets for the keys to the other car— to my horror I remembered they were in my overcoat, with the boys in the Abbey. Without another backward glance we drove off. I got out at a traffic light, wished Ann luck and for the benefit of a passerby kissed her good-night. "It's been a lovely party, darling," I said. Her eyes flashed appreciation of the irony, and she drove off.

I went back toward the Abbey at a jog trot. When I passed a policeman, I kept my head well down lest it was our friend and he should recognize me. No one was in sight as I swung into the lane and passed through the door into the masons' yard. There the Stone lay, but of Malcolm and Roland there was no sign.

"Malcolm! Roland!" I called in a whisper, but the whole night had gone silent. Fear ran a feather over my hair. I eased open the broken door of the Abbey and went in. The light still glowed at the far end of the nave. I risked a breathless whistle. There was no response. My two friends had been swallowed up by the night, and my overcoat with them.

Perhaps they would be waiting for me at the parking space. I went back there and found the Ford, but no human being was in sight. I sat on the car fender and lit a cigarette. We had got the Stone to the edge of freedom, and our luck had turned against us. Success had been ours and we had failed to grasp it. We would go to jail. I drew smoke and it tasted like sand.

Suddenly a new thought struck me. I threw away my cigarette and broke into a run back to the Abbey. Presumably, Malcolm and Roland had looked for the car keys in my overcoat pocket and had not found them, so perhaps they had fallen out in the Abbey as we dragged the Stone. The chance was slim, but it was the last frail hope.

I ran to the Abbey, and went in for the third time that night. I had left my torch with Ann, so on hands and knees in the darkness I groped along the route we had taken to the chapel. Then I lit matches and retraced my steps by their flickering light. Suddenly, near the door, I put my foot on something uneven—the keys. The ring had been flattened by the passage of a heavy weight, but the keys were undamaged. I am not easily moved by thoughts of heaven and hell, but I believe that a more than canny force was around us that night.

I ran back all the way to the car and got it started. As I drove along Old Palace Yard I noticed two policemen on duty, but I had no time to wait and see them out of sight. Already there were pedestrians abroad. I looked to see the time, and it was only then I remembered that my watch had fallen from my wrist when we lifted the Stone from the Chair.

Subterfuge was now useless. I backed straight up the lane with the car lights on. I had no clear idea of what I would do, except that I was going to get the Stone into the car. It was three times as heavy as I was, and I have since seen strong men strain to move it, but success was mine if only I could muster the strength.

I caught hold of the Stone and dragged it to the car without the slightest difficulty. I raised one end up into the car; then, lifting the whole weight, I got it in end over end. I think it went quite easily. I do not remember straining. Let the cynics laugh and archbishops howl "Sacrilege!" but the hands of God were over mine when I lifted that Stone.

As I drove from the lane the night watchman was telephoning the police to report his loss. I did not know that then, but it would have made no difference. I had stared into the cold eyes of defeat and seen them warm to victory. In my elation, I shouted and sang. The evil luck which had dogged Scotland for six centuries was shattered, and she could enter on glorious rebirth. Let them take me now, and all Scotland was at my back. I was filled with a wild exultation and something which was very near to divine glory.

I reckoned that I had at most an hour and a half before the police could get their forces marshaled. I must find open ground and hide the Stone. The trouble was that I did not know the road. Stupid from lack of sleep, I lost my way and wandered around in a maze of side streets. A cold, gray dawn was beginning to creep in from the east, and, almost in tears, I was driving desperately down a back street when the last of the miracles happened which brought us success. There, plodding away from me, were the familiar figures of Roland and Malcolm. I pulled up with a squeal of brakes, calling, "I've got it, I've got it. Look! It's in there!"

I could take only one of them with me, for with all the weight I was fearful of the car's springs. Malcolm fell inside. We agreed to meet Roland at Reading Station that afternoon at four o'clock. Then I let in the clutch, and Malcolm and I raced south with the Stone, exhausted and lightheaded with victory.

A hundred times I recited all that had happened to me since I had left him in the Abbey. Then it was Malcolm's turn to talk. When he and Roland heard us drive away from the Abbey, they had crept down the lane, almost on the heels of the policeman. They reached the parking space just as Ann and I were driving away in the Anglia. Not finding the keys for the other car in my overcoat, they assumed that I had them with me. Then a police car passed them, and, thinking the game was up, they started to walk aimlessly until, by the grace of God, I found them.

627

"What happened to my overcoat?" I asked.

Malcolm looked around anxiously. "Didn't you get it?" he asked. "We left it just behind the car."

That was a blow, for my name was on it. We had got the Stone away, but we had left behind us a complete case for the prosecution, handing the police the evidence on a tray.

Malcolm and I drove southeast toward Rochester. Out in the open country we followed a little cart track off the main road. Then we dragged the Stone out of the car and left it lying in a hollow, half hidden by a few sprays of bramble. It was a precarious hiding place, but at the moment we had no alternative.

We felt sure the police had circulated the number of our car. Moreover, since my duel with the detective outside Ann's hotel, I was too dangerous to be allowed near the Stone. It seemed best then for Malcolm alone to meet Roland at Reading at the appointed hour of four. Together they could hire another car and transport the Stone to Dartmoor, while I acted as a decoy by making for Wales in the Ford.

First, however, we drove back to London, for we wanted to recover that incriminating overcoat if we possibly could. I do not know how we got back into town, for we had only a vague idea of the road. But eventually we approached the Abbey again. At the parking space there was no one in sight, but the overcoat, now worn and torn beyond repair, was still lying there where Malcolm and Roland had left it!

Malcolm and I drove to Reading, arriving about ten o'clock. I left him in the Station Square, and after we had wished each other luck, I set off for Wales.

I had assumed that the police would connect our being questioned outside Ann's hotel with the disappearance of the Stone. But presently I began to feel that I was perhaps being overcautious in laying down a false trail. None of the police cars I passed showed the slightest interest in me, so I decided to return to Reading and help Malcolm and Roland retrieve the Stone. It was a wise decision. Had I continued to give the police credit for the intelligence

I thought they possessed, I would have arrived hopelessly in Wales, and Malcolm would have had the whole responsibility for moving the Stone, for Roland never arrived in Reading.

I met Malcolm there, and he was glad to see me. Together we waited and met each train from London, our hopes dwindling as we saw no sign of Roland. At half past four we gave up, pressed the starter and headed back for the Stone.

On the way, we stopped at a telephone box, and I called Keith. He was jubilant. "Never mind talking riddles," he said when I started to use the cumbersome code we had invented. "I'll take the risk. You've been on the radio and you're in all the papers. The border roads are closed for the first time in 400 years, and the whole of Scotland is mad with excitement. There are two descriptions out; they're good but not 100 percent accurate. How are you standing up to it?"

"Fine!" I said. I could have listened to him all night.

"Well, lie low," he said. "And good luck!"

We climbed back into the car and went on, still worried about Roland's absence, which seemed inexplicable. (Later we learned that in a London restaurant Roland had noticed a man regarding him with suspicion. When he left, the man followed, shadowing him persistently. By the time he had shaken off the pursuer it was too late for our rendezvous in Reading, so he took a train back to Glasgow.)

As Malcolm and I drove back toward the Stone I fell silent, thinking of the reaction to what we had done. In Scotland we had revived something of the spirit which had kept us the oldest unconquered nation in Europe; more remarkable, our action had had almost as great an effect in England. While the Abbey hounds snarled, and the planners polished their pince-nez, and the resources of law and order fluttered, ordinary men who love to see the pompous deflated received the news with great amusement and felt we had done something they could applaud. We were desperately tired, but responsibility weighed on us. What we had done was now a public affair, and nothing must be permitted to turn our faces north until we had put the Stone where it could never be found. It was a duty which laughed at rest.

We retrieved the Stone from where we had left it, and that night wandered over half the county of Kent, hunting for a proper hiding place. About midnight, near Rochester, we found an ideal place. Some ten yards off the road there was an easily identifiable line of trees and a steep embankment littered with straw and scraps of paper. Halfway down the slope I hollowed a recess in the soft earth; we slid the Stone into it and covered it with earth and litter. It was a good job.

Our duties ended, I stumbled into the back seat, and Malcolm put his toe down for Scotland. I slept like a dead man. It was almost 90 hours since we had been in bed and we were very tired, but the homing instinct, strong within us, made us reject the idea of going to a hotel. So we spelled each other at driving several times during the night and continued homeward; at times we parked by the side of the road and both slept.

Next morning, delirious with tiredness, we shouted and sang triumphantly in the cold brisk air. We had raided the very heart of Englishry and were returning unscathed, while all around us the authorities gnashed their teeth and held committee meetings. So now we careered up England, roaring and singing, to the amazement of the stolid English pedestrians, who must have thought us drunk.

It was the middle of the afternoon before we were stopped. I was sleeping in the back seat when Malcolm said quietly: "It's the police, Ian."

I was awake immediately. A police car had pulled alongside and signaled us to stop, and now two constables came around to Malcolm's window, notebooks at the ready. They asked for his driving license and noted the name and address. "Where have you been?" they asked. "London," replied Malcolm promptly.

"Where are you going?"

"Home," he said, simply.

"What's the trouble?" I asked.

"It's this here Coronation Stone," said one of the constables. "You haven't seen it, have you?"

I could have laughed at the folly of the question. "No!" I cried. "But I've heard about it. It's a good show. Should have been done years ago."

The constable looked at me sourly. "We live on the one island and some think we should be all one people," he said.

"Aye, maybe," I said. "But the Scottish people don't think that, and they're the ones who have the edge on you today."

Without a word the constable handed Malcolm back his license and waved us on. We could not believe our luck. We crossed the border about ten o'clock with a marvelous feeling of relief. The very trees and hedges seemed more friendly, and we knew that if we were ever hard pressed we would only have to knock on a door and a friend would open it. All Scotland was our fireside, and every Scotsman was our kin.

Glasgow was like a pleasant dream. I had expected to return to my melancholy little room with its unmade bed, so I was grateful when Malcolm insisted I spend the night at his home. His family welcomed me in, and the warmth of their happiness was wrapped like a blanket around us. Sitting by a crackling fire, Malcolm and I told our story in all its fantastic detail. We tripped over each other to prompt our memories, and always we would be interrupted and a newspaper would be thrust into our hands so that we might read what the world was saying. The room was light; the fire leaped and blazed; these were our own people. We could hardly believe it.

To our intense delight we learned that Ann had been there only a few hours previously, before going on north to her home, and now we heard her story.

After she left me Ann stopped at another traffic light and as she moved off heard a great crash behind her. She pulled over to the side and, to her dismay, saw her portion of the Stone lying on the road ten yards behind her. In my excitement I had forgotten to close the trunk properly and it had swung open. Ann was a small girl, and that bit of the Stone weighs 90 pounds. Without a thought she picked it up, staggered to the trunk and put it in, this time making sure the lid was tight. Ann left the car with unsuspecting friends in Birmingham and came home by train. (A fortnight later I was to go there and drive home the Anglia with the piece of Stone. I hope these good English people have forgiven us all for our deception.)

When we had heard Ann's story, Malcolm and I felt quite happy. A meal was waiting for us, but we were too tired to eat. Common decency howled for a bath, but common decency went unheard. Stiff and weary, we undressed and fell into bed.

Now, above all, we had to get into our usual haunts and act in a normal fashion, for our absence might have been noted. We decided to be social buffoons, objects of contempt rather than suspicion. We would talk and speculate about the Stone until we became Stone bores. In our cups we would boast that we had taken it, or that we had been ready to take it if someone had not forestalled us. We would talk like young Nationalist extremists. It was the safest thing we could do, since the Glasgow police were too intelligent ever to bother with any of the avowed extremists.

To my surprise the University Union, which should have been deserted, since it was Christmas vacation, was filled with all the familiar figures, and there was endless conjecture about the Stone. Solemnly we discussed who might have done the deed. This man was accounted for; that man might have done it but he drank too much to keep a secret; another had been talking about doing it for years but was a vainglorious lout with no ability. "Well, I'm beaten," I said. "I reckoned I knew every Nationalist in Scotland and I still can't put my finger on who did it."

Our double bluff worked, and, all things considered, there was remarkably little suspicion of us. Three months later, when Scotland Yard's chief superintendent roped us all in for questioning, I overheard one student say: "What! Ian Hamilton have anything to do with the Stone? Nonsense! The only person who would ever suspect Ian Hamilton is Ian Hamilton."

There was one more matter to be settled. As yet no one knew whether the Stone had been taken by anarchists, Communists or souvenir hunters. In addition, His Majesty was distressed, and we felt that we had to clarify our position. We therefore prepared a petition to the King, reaffirming our loyalty to His Majesty and stating our reasons for removing the Stone.

There was much discussion as to where to post this petition. I wanted to send it out from Edinburgh, for I thought we might bluff the police into concentrating their inquiries there. The others wanted it sent out from Glasgow. The police, they contended, would expect us to leave such a document as far as possible from our own doorstep; if we left it in Edinburgh, they would suspect Glasgow, and vice versa. They overestimated the intelligence of the forces against us. In actual fact, we left the petition in a Glasgow newspaper office and it was on Glasgow that the police immediately concentrated their inquiries. The stupidity of Scotland Yard was our most constant danger.

Over the New Year's weekend we drove south to recover the Stone. A second expedition was perhaps foolhardy at that time, with the police hunt at its height. They had been stopping all cars on the border for the last five days, but they could not go on doing that indefinitely, and I assumed the border would be open again in two days. In my mind lurked the threat of impending arrest; I wanted to see the Stone recovered before that happened.

Our advisers insisted that those of us who had been in London at Christmas should not go back again, with the police looking for us, but I was not going to be shouldered out now. Malcolm came, too, since it was his father's Armstrong-Siddeley car we meant to use. Our new teammates were Keith and a friend, Peter. In high spirits, we set off at night, over ice-coated roads.

En route, the question of the best place in the car to put the Stone was on my mind. If the police stopped us I wanted at least a chance to bluff it out. I checked over the car and discovered that the front passenger seat could be lifted completely out and be replaced by the Stone. True, the passenger would be uncomfortable. But with a traveling rug over the Stone and a coat over the passenger's knees, nothing would be visible so long as we kept the near side door locked.

It was eight o'clock the next evening when we drove out of London toward Rochester. The road was almost deserted. One after another, Malcolm and I picked out our landmarks in the gray night. There was the little cart track beside which we had first hidden the Stone; a few miles farther on, a familiar line of bushes. Then we swept past the line of trees. Before them, two dancing fires cast shadows on a gypsy caravan.

The chances were a million to one against it; such a thing was unbelievable, but there was no doubt about it. The gypsies were camping directly on top of the Stone. We had traveled 450 miles in vain. The Stone was guarded as surely as if it were back in Westminster Abbey.

Two hundred yards up the road we stopped the car and walked down toward the fire. There were two caravans. We drew near the first, where an ancient gypsy couple sprawled against the fence, their boots outstretched to the blaze. The man could have put his hand through the fence and touched the Stone.

"Can we have a heat at your fire?" Keith asked. The woman invited us in with a smile. We sat silent for a long time in the firelight, and then Keith started to talk. He talked about the gypsies, the free life they lived and how they were harried by the authorities. He told them about our little country in the north which, like the gypsies, was striving to preserve its liberty and be itself. Then he talked about liberty itself and how in the end it is the only precious thing. Freedom could be preserved only in men's hearts, and as soon as they stopped valuing it, it disappeared. "We're not like that," he ended. "And to keep our freedom we need something out of that wood. We are doing right, but we will go to jail if we are caught."

The man, who had as yet scarcely spoken, answered him. "You can't get it just now," he said without moving. "There's a local man at the next fire; you can't trust him."

For a long time we continued staring into the glowing fire as though it contained all wisdom and all knowledge. At last a man came from the direction of the other fire, mounted his bike and rode off down the road. Now it was safe. My excitement uncoiled like a spring and I vaulted the fence. The Stone was exactly as we had left it, untouched. The four of us, with the aid of two gypsy men, manhandled it up the slope and into the car.

I fumbled in my pocket and finally produced £3, which I offered to one of the gypsies. "No!" he said, "No!" Feeling like a commoner among kings, I thanked them for their hospitality, and we left the warmth of their fire. I do not know if the gypsies realized whom they helped that night. I like to think that they did.

We turned homeward, cruising gently into London and pulling quietly in and out of the Saturday-night crowds at Trafalgar Square and Marble Arch. The newsboys were still shouting the headlines, "STONE: ARREST EXPECTED SOON," while the Stone passed by half a yard away. But we journeyed through London without challenge and continued north.

It began to snow, making the driving a nightmare. We kept to the secondary trunk roads, which were not so busy as to be carefully watched but which were busy enough not to be blocked by the snow. We stared into the white hell, skidded and edged around corners, thinking of the bloody mush the Stone would make of us if we overturned. But gradually we forgot our fears. As each mile came up on the clock, it meant we had brought the Stone yet a mile closer to Scotland. Even if we were finished now, every mile had made history.

Sunday morning was clear and fresh. We stopped to purchase some newspapers, and, as we went on, Keith read out tidbits. The papers bulged with what we had done. Everyone of position in England was very huffy indeed. While the common Englishman laughed and wondered why Scotland had not had self-government long ago, his rulers called us thieves and fanatics. I did not feel like a fanatic. I felt like a wee boy who had pressed a fire alarm and who now watches the fire engines roar past.

"Look at this," said Keith, and he held out a newspaper with the headline: "STONE: £1000 REWARD." I had a great feeling of pride. I had never been worth so much money before. Yet I felt a twinge of uneasiness—£1000 might be enough to make the most honest man sell a stranger.

We made it back to Scotland without incident, however, and at half past two we slipped across the border. A few miles inside Scotland we stopped. The symbol of her liberty had come back to Scotland, and some sort of rude ceremony was needed to mark the return. We drew back its covering and exposed the Stone to the air of Scotland for the first time in 600 years. From our provision basket we produced a gill of whisky we had kept for just this occasion. We each poured a little of the fine spirit on the Stone and proposed a toast. Thus, quietly, with little fuss, with no army, with no burning of abbeys or slaying of people, we brought back the Stone of Destiny.

That same night we delivered the Stone to a factory outside of Glasgow, where it was put away in a packing case. Now our job was done, and others were to take up where we had left off.

The months that followed were a period of inactivity on our part, and we were all tense. As the Stone was passed from hand to hand, many people became involved in the secret. Despite the rich rewards offered, not one of them gave us away. Several journalists stumbled on information which the police might have valued, and they, too, conveniently forgot about it. But we knew the net was drawing closer.

From the beginning we had accepted the fact that the police would inevitably catch up with us. We had always been led to believe that Scotland Yard, though perhaps slow, inexorably sifts every clue until it gets its man. It was rather disturbing to a law-abiding citizen like myself to discover that this was not the case. We had sprinkled the Abbey with clues, yet Scotland Yard was clueless. Far from using deduction and all the scientific methods of criminal investigation, Scotland Yard conferred with a clair-voyant, who held his head in silence, and with a water diviner, who led them at public expense to the River Trent. Most stretches of water in Greater London were dragged in search of the Stone, and all up and down the country water diviners could be seen twitching twigs.

Fortunately for the reputation of the British constabulary, things were different in Glasgow. The police there must have hated their job; but they had their duty to do, and they did it efficiently. It took them three months to find us.

The blow fell toward the middle of March. Two detectives from London went north to Plockton, where Ann had recently taken up a teaching appointment. They questioned her for five and a half hours, but the girl would not break down and confess. Two days later they came for Roland, Malcolm and myself. They questioned us on our movements and tasked us with our guilt. They had a heavy chain of circumstantial evidence woven around us, yet I felt that it was more honorable to lie than to surrender. Much to our surprise, we were all set free.

Yet we were not quite at peace. We had never intended to remove the Stone completely from all ken and we had now to weigh the advantages of bringing it again to light. There were many considerations, but our main reason for action was that the Stone was valueless to us hidden in a factory cellar. All along we ourselves had set the pace. We would end by putting the ball at the feet of authority. If they left the Stone in Scotland we had won our point, but if they snatched it away they would outrage Scottish feeling.

We arranged to have the Stone repaired by the best mason in Scotland. It would be given to the Church of Scotland at the ruined Abbey of Arbroath, where, in 1320, with the sound of the North Sea in their ears and the smell of their burnt homes still in their nostrils, the Estates of Scotland had met to reaffirm their freedom. On the morning of April 11, 1951, Keith and I left Glasgow with the Stone of Destiny. At midday we carried it down the grass-floored nave of Arbroath Abbey to the high altar.

I never saw the Stone again. The authorities swooped upon it and bundled it back across the border by night, while Commons,

Lords and clergy raised their voices in protest. But I still remember that moment at the altar where we left the Stone and where I heard the voice of Scotland speak as clearly as it did in 1320: "We fight not for glory nor for wealth nor for honor, but only and alone for freedom, which no good man surrenders but with his life."

Editor's note: *The Coronation Stone was returned to Westminster Abbey. However, the authorities decided that "the public interest did not require" that the four young Scottish conspirators should be prosecuted.*

<hr />

WHEN A moneylender complained to Baron Rothschild that he had lent 10,000 francs to a person who had gone off to Constantinople without leaving any acknowledgment of the debt, the Baron said:

"Well, write to him and ask him to send you the 50,000 francs he owes you."

"But he owes me only ten," said the moneylender.

"Precisely," rejoined the Baron, "and he will write and tell you so, and thus you will get the acknowledgment of it."   —*T. B. Reid, Modern Eloquence*

HANGING some paintings in his London house, Horace De Vere Cole, the celebrated British practical joker, ran out of twine. He walked to the nearest shop for another ball. On his way home he saw an elegant stranger approaching. The man was so stiffish, so splendidly dressed, that Cole could not pass him by. "I say," he said, "I'm in a bit of a spot. We're surveying this area in order to realign the curb, and my assistant has vanished. I wonder if I could prevail upon your time for just a few moments?"

"To be sure," said the stranger, ever the proper Englishman.

"If," said Cole, "you'd be so kind as to hold the end of this string. Just stand where you are and keep a tight hold on it for a few moments."

The splendid gentleman took hold of the end of the string and Cole began backing away from him, unwinding the ball. He continued all the way to the corner, turned the corner and disappeared. Halfway up the block, the string gave out. He was about to tie it to a doorknob when Providence sent him a second gentleman, fully as elegant as the first. Cole stopped him. Cole handed him the string and asked him to hold it. Then Cole hastened through an alleyway to the shop for another ball of twine and returned home. How long the two men stood there holding the string he never knew.

— *H. Allen Smith, The Compleat Practical Joker (Doubleday & Co., Inc.)*

ILLUSTRATIONS BY

JOHN BALLANTINE • ISA BARNETT

FRITZ BUSSE • WILLIAM HOFMANN

JOE KRUSH • OSCAR LIEBMAN

ANTHONY SARIS

ACKNOWLEDGMENTS

PIED PIPER OF BOSTON, by Alan Hynd, as "The Pied Piper of Boston," in *True, The Man's Magazine*, © 1956 and pub. by Fawcett Publications, Inc. THE GREAT IMPOSTOR, by Robert Crichton, cond. in *Coronet* from the book, © 1959, Robert Crichton; pub. by Random House, Inc. SAWING-OFF OF MANHATTAN ISLAND, by Herbert Asbury, as "The Sawing-Off of Manhattan Island," in *All Around the Town*, © 1934 and pub. by Alfred A. Knopf, Inc.; © 1962, Herbert Asbury. MRS. CHADWICK SHOWS HER METTLE, by Willis Thornton, as "The Fabulous Fraud From Eastwood," in *Maclean's Magazine*, © 1949 and pub. by Maclean-Hunter Pub. Co., Ltd. HOW TO BLAST A BANK, by Evan McLeod Wylie, cond. from *True, The Man's Magazine*, © 1961 and pub. by Fawcett Publications, Inc. POINT OF HONOR, by Milton Esterow, as "The Unimaginable," is reprinted with permission of The Macmillan Company from *The Art Stealers* by Milton Esterow; copyright © 1966 by Milton Esterow. BRITAIN'S GREAT TRAIN ROBBERY, by Pete Hamill, cond. from *The Saturday Evening Post*, © 1964 and pub. by The Curtis Pub. Co. OPERATION U.S. MINT, by William S. Fairfield, as "The Thief and the $80,000 Bricks," in *Argosy*, © 1956 and pub. by Popular Publications, Inc. KING OF THE SPOOK WORKERS, by William Lindsay Gresham, from *Argosy*, © 1957 and pub. by Popular Publications, Inc.; reprinted by per-

mission of Brandt & Brandt. A CASE OF SALTED GEMS, by Harold Mehling, as "A Case of Salted Diamonds," in *The Scandalous Scamps*, © 1956, 1958, 1959, Harold Mehling; pub. by Holt, Rinehart & Winston, Inc., in Canada by George McLeod, Ltd. HE STOLE A BILLION, by Allen Churchill, as "The Man Who Stole a Billion Dollars," in *Pageant*, © 1951 and pub. by Hillman Periodicals, Inc. HOW I MADE A CRIME WAVE, by Lincoln Steffens, cond. from *The Autobiography of Lincoln Steffens*, © 1931 and pub. by Harcourt, Brace & World, Inc; © 1959, Peter Steffens. RISE AND FALL OF A SOVIET AGENT, by Edward R. F. Sheehan, cond. from *The Saturday Evening Post*, © 1964 and pub. by The Curtis Pub. Co. FABULOUS BARON OF ARIZONA, by Clarence Budington Kelland, cond. from *The Saturday Evening Post*, © 1947 and pub. by The Curtis Pub. Co. THE TWO FACES OF RICHARD WHITNEY, by Harold Mehling, from *The Scandalous Scamps*, © 1956, 1958, 1959, Harold Mehling; pub. by Holt, Rinehart & Winston, Inc., in Canada by George McLeod, Ltd. GRAND CENTRAL'S $100,000 DEAL, by Alan Hynd, as "Grand Central's 100 Grand Swindle," in *True, The Man's Magazine*, © 1964 and pub. by Fawcett Publications, Inc. MASTER OF THE DOUBLE CROSS, by William C. White, cond. from *The North American Review*, © 1934, North American Review Corp. A CROOK EVERYONE LIKED,

639

by Beverly Smith, Jr., as "The Crook Everyone Liked," in *The Saturday Evening Post,* © 1959 and pub. by The Curtis Pub. Co. CARDIFF GIANT, by Andrew D. White, from *The Autobiography of Andrew D. White,* © 1904, 1905 and pub. by The Century Co. THE BARON AND HIS URANIUM KILLING, by Toni Howard, cond. from *The Saturday Evening Post,* © 1953 and pub. by The Curtis Pub. Co. THOSE TERRIBLE WILLIAMSONS, by John Kobler, cond. from *The Saturday Evening Post,* © 1956 and pub. by The Curtis Pub. Co. A RENAISSANCE MAN, by Myron Brenton, as "A Forger With Dreams," in *Coronet,* © 1961 and pub. by Esquire, Inc. MAN WITH GREEN MAGIC, by Harold Mehling, as "The Man With the Green Magic," in *Coronet,* © 1956 and pub. by Esquire, Inc. HORSE PLAY, by Eugene B. Block, from *The Great Stagecoach Robbers of the West,* © 1962, Eugene B. Block; pub. by Doubleday & Co., Inc. VOYAGE OF THE INNOCENT PIRATES, by Evan McLeod Wylie, as "Innocent Landlubbers in a Piratical Fiasco," © 1959 and pub. by Time Inc. A VERY, VERY LATE BANK ROBBERY, by Ted Hall, as "The Great but Very, Very Late Bank Robbery," © 1962 and pub. by Time Inc. THE UNREAL WORLD OF DR. DROWN, by Walter Wagner, as "The Quacks," in *The Golden Fleecers,* © 1966, Walter Wagner; pub. by Doubleday & Co., Inc. UNMASKING OF THE PILTDOWN MAN, by Alden P. Armagnac, cond. from *Popular Science Monthly,* © 1956 and pub. by Popular Science Publishing Co., Inc. HOT PROSPECT, as "The Job," in *Time,* © 1963 and pub. by Time Inc. FRITZ KREISLER'S "DISCOVERIES," by Louis Biancolli, as "The Great Fritz Kreisler Hoax," in *Etude,* © 1951, Theodore Presser Co. THE GREAT FALSE FRONT, by Craig Thompson, as "America's Boldest Swindle," in *The Saturday Evening Post,* © 1953 and pub. by The Curtis Pub. Co.; reprinted by permission of Brandt & Brandt. CATHERINE IN WONDERLAND, by Gina Kaus, cond. from *Catherine, the Portrait of an Empress,* © 1935 and pub. by The Viking Press, Inc. THE DRAKE FABLE, by William T. Brannon, as "The Fabulous Drake Swindle," in *Mercury Book Magazine,* © 1955, Mercury Press, Inc. EDUCATION OF A QUACK, by Stewart H. Holbrook, as "The St. Louis and Kansas City Scandals," is reprinted with permission of The Macmillan Company from *The Golden Age of Quackery* by Stewart H. Holbrook; copyright © 1959 by Stewart H. Holbrook. 30,000 MANUSCRIPTS, by Sonia Cole, from *Counterfeit, Counterfeit,* pub. in U.S., 1956, by Abelard-Schuman Ltd. RESCUE OF THE SPANISH PRISONER, by Rufus Jarman, as "How the Spanish-Prisoner Swindle Works," in *The Saturday Evening Post,* © 1952 and pub. by The Curtis Pub. Co. THE FIRST FEDERAL SAVINGS BANK GRAND PRIX, by No. 93761 as told to No. 78904, from *Sports Illustrated,* February 21, 1966, © 1966 and pub. by Time Inc. A MAN WHO FOOLED GÖRING, by Irving Wallace, cond. from *The Saturday Evening Post,* © 1947 and pub. by The Curtis Pub. Co. MY STORY, by Willie Sutton as told to Quentin Reynolds, as "Confessions of an Archthief," © 1953 and pub. by Time Inc. "GOAT-GLAND" BRINKLEY, by Harold Mehling, from *The Scandalous Scamps,* © 1956, 1958, 1959, Harold Mehling; pub. by Holt, Rinehart & Winston, Inc., in Canada by George McLeod, Ltd. STAMP COLLECTOR'S NEMESIS, by Murray Teigh Bloom, as "Sperati," in *Money of Their Own,* © 1957, Murray Teigh Bloom; pub. by Charles Scribner's Sons. GEORGE PSALMANAZAR: THE INCREDIBLE IMPOSTOR, by John P. Long. from *Catholic World,* © 1949 and pub. by the Missionary Society of St. Paul the Apostle (The Paulist Fathers). NO STONE UNTURNED, by Ian R. Hamilton, cond. from the book, © 1952, Ian R. Hamilton; pub. by Funk & Wagnalls.

PHOTO CREDITS *(for section following page 320)*